D0861224

Troubleshooting SharePoint

The Complete Guide to Tools, Best Practices, PowerShell One-Liners, and Scripts

Stacy Simpkins

Apress®

Troubleshooting SharePoint

Stacy Simpkins
Brandon, Florida, USA

ISBN-13 (pbk): 978-1-4842-3137-1   ISBN-13 (electronic): 978-1-4842-3138-8
https://doi.org/10.1007/978-1-4842-3138-8

Library of Congress Control Number: 2017960834

Cover image designed by Freepik

Managing Director: Welmoed Spahr
Editorial Director: Todd Green
Acquisitions Editor: Joan Murray
Development Editor: Laura Berendson
Technical Reviewer: Samarjeet Singh Tomar
Coordinating Editor: Jill Balzano
Copy Editor: Kim Burton-Weisman
Compositor: SPi Global
Indexer: SPi Global
Artist: SPi Global

Distributed to the book trade worldwide by Springer Science+Business Media New York, 233 Spring Street, 6th Floor, New York, NY 10013. Phone 1-800-SPRINGER, fax (201) 348-4505, e-mail orders-ny@springer-sbm.com, or visit www.springeronline.com. Apress Media, LLC is a California LLC and the sole member (owner) is Springer Science + Business Media Finance Inc (SSBM Finance Inc). SSBM Finance Inc is a **Delaware** corporation.

For information on translations, please e-mail rights@apress.com, or visit http://www.apress.com/rights-permissions.

Apress titles may be purchased in bulk for academic, corporate, or promotional use. eBook versions and licenses are also available for most titles. For more information, reference our Print and eBook Bulk Sales web page at http://www.apress.com/bulk-sales.

Any source code or other supplementary material referenced by the author in this book is available to readers on GitHub via the book's product page, located at www.apress.com/9781484231371. For more detailed information, please visit http://www.apress.com/source-code.

Printed on acid-free paper

This book is dedicated to Saanvi, Owen, Willow, Oaklyn, and Weston.

Contents

About the Author

Stacy Simpkins is a SharePoint engineer with Rackspace, the number-one managed cloud company. He is passionate about SharePoint and loves helping customers understand and get the most out of SharePoint. Prior to Rackspace, Stacy worked with the federal government as an IT specialist and across multiple industries (food, legal, manufacturing, health insurance, and professional services) architecting and developing small, medium, and large SharePoint environments as a consultant. As a consultant, he served as a solutions architect for Magenium Solutions and as a senior consultant for Sogeti LLC. Stacy holds numerous Microsoft Certifications. During his limited free time, he enjoys blogging about SharePoint and other Microsoft products, speaking at user group meetings, and leading the Tampa Bay SharePoint user group.

About the Technical Reviewer

 **Samarjeet Singh Tomar** is a SharePoint Engineer for the Blue Cross Blue Shield Association (BCBSA), a national federation of 36 independent, community-based and locally operated Blue Cross and Blue Shield companies. He is passionate about SharePoint and .Net Core, Tableau, Angular, D3, Power-BI and helping customers and business in automate and visualization. Prior to BCBSA, Samar worked with various industry domains and service area. He is passionate about learning and implementing different technology and build scalable solution using proven practices. During his limited free time, he enjoys blogging about SharePoint and other technologies, he loves travelling and playing computer games.

Acknowledgments

I'd like to thank my fellow Rackspace SharePoint engineers for their contributions: Scott Fawley, J. T. Shoupe, Stephen Swinney, Danny Pugh, Mike Ross, Mike Clarke, Jarod Oliver, Daocheng Li (Richard), Mark Watts, Ryan Holderread, Brad Slagle, and Tray Harrison. Originally, I had planned to provide a short bio of everyone on this list; however, we weren't able to pull them all together before printing. To everyone on this list, I sincerely thank you for your fanatical support and the awesome SharePoint knowledge, and the wisdom you've shared with me over the last year.

Introduction

This introduction covers, at a high level, the topics that this book discusses. The book assumes that you already have a development SharePoint environment that you can use to perform the exercises. If you don't have a development farm and are not sure about the steps needed to create one, you should get a copy of my book *Building a SharePoint 2016 Home Lab: A How-To Reference on Simulating a Realistic SharePoint Testing Environment* (Apress, 2016). Although it is possible to read each chapter independently, there are parts of chapters that build off previous chapters and/or assume some requisite SharePoint knowledge. The following is the 40,000-foot view.

Chapter 1. Least-Privileged SharePoint Builds

This chapter thoroughly discusses building a SharePoint farm using least privileging. It starts to peel away the troubleshooting onion, layer by layer, and explains why a least-privileged build is important for troubleshooting.

Chapter 2. Key Settings of a Good Build

This chapter is the first of two parts that cover the key settings of a good build. You'll learn about SQL aliases, MSDTC, to IIS WAMREG and DCOM, Network Service, and the local security needs of a farm account.

Chapter 3. More Key Settings of a Good Build

This chapter finishes the discussion on key settings in the file system as they relate to App Fabric and Distributed Cache, User Profile Synchronization, publishing infrastructure, account management, logging locations and levels, and path-based vs. host headers, also known as host named site collections.

Chapter 4. Files, Virtual Mappings, and IIS Settings

This chapter explores the changes that SharePoint makes to a Windows server file system and discusses how this relates to IIS. It looks at IIS logging and opens the discussion that surrounds the connection between IIS logs, SharePoint logs, and Windows logs.

Chapter 5. Database and Security Operations

This chapter opens SQL Server Management Studio and looks at the SQL Server settings, database settings, server roles, database mappings, SQL logging, and various PowerShell and/or command-line operations as they relate to SharePoint database security operations from within SSMS and/or SQL Server configuration.

Chapter 6. SQL Backup and Restore, and Useful CLI

This chapter covers a few more SQL-related topics, such SQL database backup and restore options, unattached restores, SQL file restores, and PowerShell site collection backup and restore. We look at some Windows OS commands that yield helpful troubleshooting information, including systeminfo, ncpa.cpl, msinfo32, SC, and others as I talk about finding answers to troubleshooting questions.

Chapter 7. Search Configuration and Troubleshooting

This chapter peels back a deeper layer of the troubleshooting onion as it relates to issues with search, search configuration with PowerShell, and the search service application. We look at some cool scripts and take a fairly good dive into search.

Chapter 8. Troubleshooting Services

This chapter looks at troubleshooting User Profile Synchronization Connections, Excel Services, Office Web app connections, and patching Office Web apps. We look at managed metadata term stores and discuss the connection to the User Profile Service. I'll discuss web.config modifications and using PowerShell to determine if the web.config is modified. Along with looking at web.config, PowerShell interrogates timer jobs, log levels, and databases. Finally, PowerShell is used to unprovision and provision services.

Chapter 9. Tools: ULS, merge-splogfile, and Other PowerShell cmdlets

This chapter's primary focus centers on ULS logs, ULS viewer, merge-splogfile, and other PowerShell cmdlets that pertain to Windows logs. It discusses the numerous settings of ULS viewer and some various scenarios and methods. The chapter explains the connection between SharePoint and Windows event logs and helps the reader understand how to decipher what the logs are saying and how to use the logging system and configure it.

Chapter 10. Tools: Network Packet Tools and Page Performance

This chapter discusses the use of ProcMon, WireShark, Fiddler, NetMon, developer dashboard, and more! It also covers a few more tools used to look at network packets, IIS logs, and page load performance.

Chapter 11. Tools: SharePoint Health Analyzer Demystified

This chapter discusses the SharePoint Health Analyzer report, the Performance Analysis of Logs (PAL) tool for SharePoint, the SharePoint Manager tool, the SharePoint feature admin tool, and finally, a summation of the three chapters on troubleshooting tools.

Commonly Used Shortcuts

In this book, we use keyboard shortcuts, the run bar, and commands quite a bit. Table-A lists some of the commands with a brief description.

Table-A. Keyboard Shortcuts and Commands Used in This Book

Command\Keyboard Shortcut	Description of Run Command
Windows key + R	Opens the run bar
Cmd	Opens the Command window
Comexp	Opens the Component Services manager
Compmgmt.msc	Opens the Computer Management console
ipconfig	Opens the ipconfig information
nslookup	Opens a command-line interface to DNS
Ncpa.cpl	Opens the network connections
Regedit	Opens the registry editor
Control netconnections	Opens the network connections
Msinfo32	Opens the system information
Sysdm.cpl	Opens the system properties
Services.msc	Opens the Services console
Dsa.msc	Opens the Active Directory users and computers
Dnsmgmt.msc	Opens the Domain Name System manager
Gpmc.msc	Opens the Group Policy Manager
Control Panel	Open the control panel
Lusrmgr.msc	Open the Local Users and Groups administration console
Notepad	Opens Notepad
Adsiedit.msc	Opens the Active Directory Service Interface editor

Summary

The goal of this book is to provide you with a much broader troubleshooting arsenal for SharePoint and perhaps a deeper understanding of how the file system relates to the databases. We do not delve into unsupported activities, such as table modifications, as that would not be in best practice; however, there are a couple points in the book where we come close, as we look into certain tables inside the SharePoint SQL Server database tables. No animals were hurt during the making of this book and all of the tools you see used in this book are available free of charge and are downloadable on the Internet.

CHAPTER 1

■ ■ ■

Least-Privileged SharePoint Builds

Why Least Privilege

In this chapter, you're introduced to least-privileged SharePoint builds. It is important to understand the components of a least-privileged build because it aids in troubleshooting the odd behaviors that can arise when builds that were once least privileged have been modified. Least-privileged SharePoint builds follow the best practice recommendations of Microsoft, and as a result, offer better performance.

As you read through Chapter 1 (and the entire book), you don't need to have a SharePoint environment to follow along; but it would definitely be a plus and you'll get more out each chapter and the chapter exercises, if you have a farm. If you don't have a farm and do not know how to build one, you should purchase a copy of my book *Building a SharePoint 2016 Home Lab: A How-To Reference on Simulating a Realistic SharePoint Testing Environment* (Apress, 2016). This book moves along at a little slower pace than the book in your hands. With that said, let's get going.

An Ounce of Prevention Is Worth a Pound of Cure

Knowing if a farm is least privileged is often half the battle in troubleshooting various issues with SharePoint. When SharePoint is installed using an administrative account, a common mistake is to use the same account for all services. This happens when the same account that is used to install or set up SharePoint is also used to access or connect to the databases that are stored on SQL Server. The account used to access the SQL databases is known as the *farm account*, which should not be a local administrator.

■ **Note**   The only time the farm account is a local administrator is during a User Profile service setup and configuration.

It's really easy to make the mistake of using the install account for the farm account. The post setup Configuration Wizard (psconfiggui.exe) prompts for the farm account. This is where that "ounce of planning is worth a pound of cure," because even though there are blogs and TechNet forums posts that advise on methods of how this account can be modified after the fact, it is always cleaner, and in your best interest, to plan a farm account separate from the install account—before installing SharePoint.

Once the setup account has been erroneously given as the farm account, and the databases are created, the cat is out of the bag. The best way to correct this is too start with a fresh build. There are a couple of methods that you can use to determine if the farm you're working with is over-privileged. Method number one is the Windows operating system's Services console.

© Stacy Simpkins 2017

S. Simpkins, *Troubleshooting SharePoint*, https://doi.org/10.1007/978-1-4842-3138-8_1

For example, if you open the services console (services.msc) and notice that all the SharePoint services are running under an account that looks like the farm account (say, something like 2013Farm), it's probably a safe bet that you're not working with a least-privileged farm. Figure 1-1 shows a farm that was installed in an over-privileged fashion.

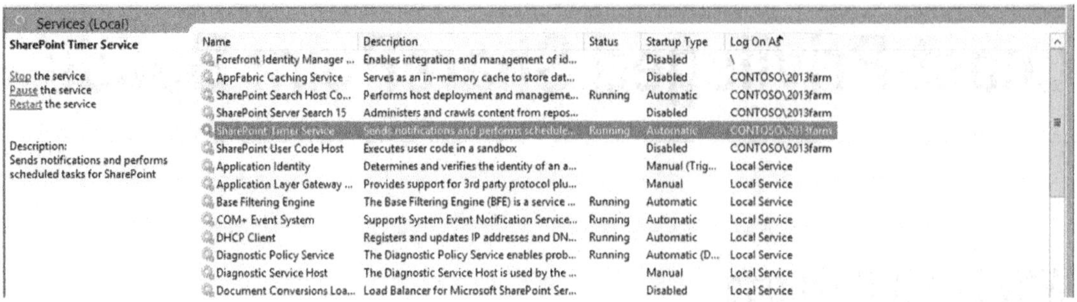

Figure 1-1. *Farm account used as the identity for all services*

The only Windows operating system service related to SharePoint that the farm account should run is the SharePoint timer service (SPTimerV4). The farm account should not be used to run the SharePoint administration service (SPAdminV4) since this service performs automated changes that require local administrator permission on the server.

The farm account would never be used to run the search services, as this would be worse than using the search service administration account as the crawler account. In both cases, SharePoint search results would include unpublished versions and would show these versions in search queries to users who shouldn't be able to read them until they were published. This is why we always use a search service account for the SharePoint Search Host Controller service (SPSearchHostController) and for the SharePoint Server Search 15 Service (OSearch15). A separate SharePoint service account is then used as the default content account, otherwise known as the *crawler*, or *crawl account*.

If you've never least privileged a SharePoint environment, you're probably starting to see that it is not as easy as just inserting the binaries and running the Configuration Wizard to completion, and possibly the farm Configuration Wizard, all with the same login account. As I mentioned earlier, this is a common occurrence, and one that is easily rectified by a farm rebuild using PowerShell scripts to build the farm and provide the least-privileged access.

So what do to if you're seeing an account listed for most of the services, you can make sure that this is the case by running the following PowerShell:

```
(Get-SPFarm).DefaultServiceAccount.Name
```

This one-liner returns the farm account. If the two match up, then it's up to you to determine how to go about least privileging the farm.

Figure 1-2 shows the results of running the PowerShell one-liner.

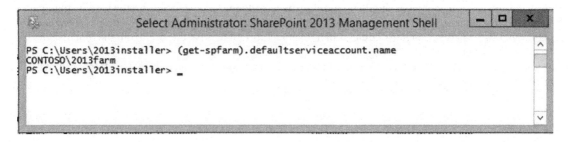

Figure 1-2. *defaultServiceAccount is the farm account*

You might be dealing with a farm that has many solutions deployed. These solutions might not like having to live in an environment where they cannot run in some form of "over privilege." Before completely throwing out the seemingly over-privileged build, you should dig a little deeper and open IIS Manager (inetmgr.exe). Once you have Internet Information Services (IIS) Manager open, the identities that the application pool accounts are using will give another indication of whether the environment is somewhat least privileged, or if it is possibly over-privileged to some extent. In other words, the Windows operating system Services console and the PowerShell one-liner are not the end-all/be-all decision makers deciding whether the farm is too bad off from a least-privileged standpoint.

If you open the IIS Manager and see something similar to Figure 1-3, there was an attempt to least privilege the farm, and it may be salvageable. You might be able to adjust the various service identities using Central Administration and/or PowerShell, and be completely fine.

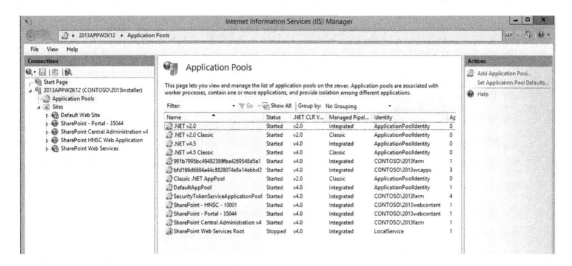

Figure 1-3. *IIS Manager shows signs of least privilege*

I say "maybe" because if the same account used to install SharePoint was used for the farm account, my experience has shown me that it is best to rebuild this type of farm. If you know for certain that that was not the case, then you should proceed with looking at the rest of the least-privileged settings—before making your determination. If you're not sure, there's another troubleshooting step to possibly yield the desired results; these are to determine what has happened to the farm that is exhibiting some form of over-privilege. Hopefully, it is not due to the setup account erroneously used as the install and the farm account.

The account that was used to run the Configuration Wizard is the owner of both the Central Administration and the configuration databases in SQL. This account should not be the farm account. The farm account is the account that should be running the SharePoint Timer Service and the identity that the Central Administration web site is running with when looking at the application pools within IIS Manager. I know that I've said that a couple of times, but it is very important to drive this point into the root of your SharePoint least privileging knowledge.

Figures 1-4 and 1-5 show that an account other than 2013Farm was used to create the farm's Central Administration and configuration databases.

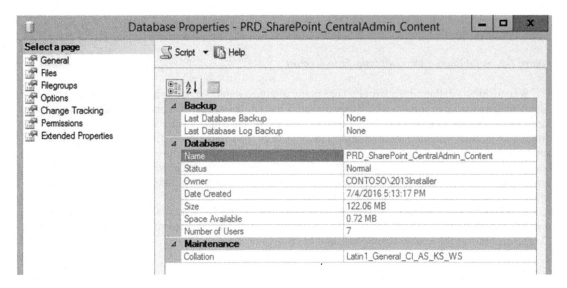

***Figure 1-4.** Central admin content database is owned by the installer, as are all databases*

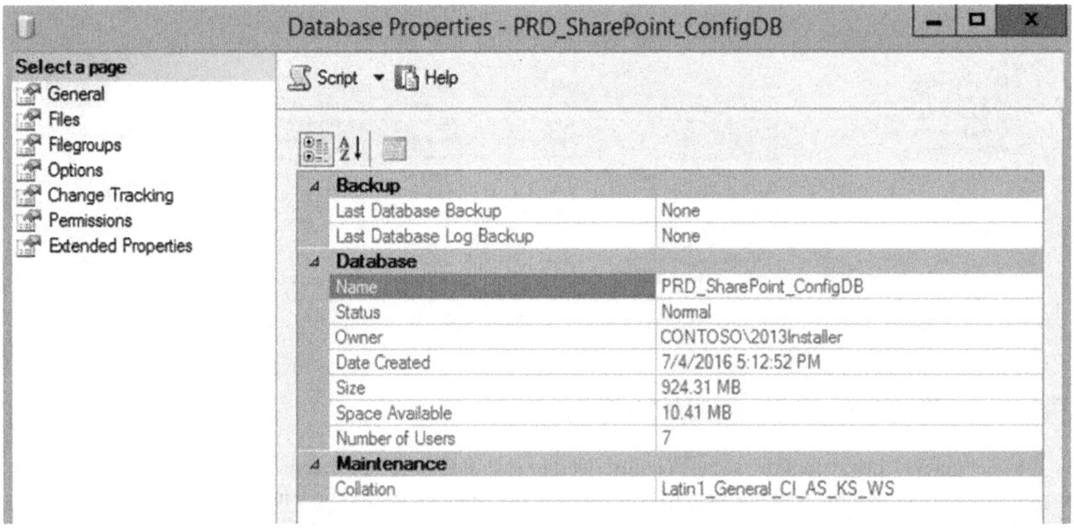

***Figure 1-5.** The configuration database is owned by the account used to install or set up SharePoint*

This means that the farm account that runs the Central Administration site in Figure 1-3 was not used as the setup account.

From looking at the accounts used to run the SharePoint services in Figure 1-1, there is more work to be done to get this farm to a least-privileged state; and we still have not decided if the farm is going to need a rebuild, as we haven't looked at the SQL database logins, SQL settings, registry permissions, or any of the file system permissions. One thing is certain, though: we have determined that the farm was not installed with the farm account. A setup or install account was used, and so far we know that various Windows SharePoint Services are running over-privileged.

The identities used by the various application pools in IIS look legit. That is, they look as if they are least privileged. We noticed that the application pool that hosts most of the SharePoint service applications is running under a different account than the application pool that serves the content to the web application that hosts the host named site collections. This is because the method that installed this farm utilized PowerShell to create the application pool that hosts the SharePoint service applications. A little later in this chapter, we'll look more deeply at IIS Manager, the identities used to run the various application pools, and some of the various file locations that SharePoint reaches into from within IIS.

Local Group Membership

The only IT service account that should be a member of the local administrators group on any server in the farm is not a SharePoint service account at all; it is the SharePoint install or setup account. It is often thought of as a service account because it is used to perform administrative functions in SharePoint, such as installing the farm and performing the initial configuration. This setup account is needed to set up the farm up in a least-privileged fashion.

Earlier, I mentioned the farm account needing local administrator membership for the configuration of the User Profile service and I forgot to mention that after the User Profile service application is configured and the User Profile synchronization service is synchronizing, that the farm account should be removed from the local administrators group on all servers in the farm. It is OK to leave the setup account in the local administrators group to log in administratively and to set up new service applications and perform other administrative duties.

Speaking of local groups, SharePoint creates three of them during installation and the farm account is added to all three of these groups. When providing a consultant with farm account-esque access to your farm, remember that the consultant's account does not and should not be added to the WSS_RESTRICTED_WPG_V4 local group, as this group should only contain the farm account. If you're looking at a farm for least privilege and you notice accounts other than the farm account have membership in the WSS_RESTRICTED_WPG_V4 local group, chances are good that there is some over-privileged code running somewhere in this farm. If the code is properly written, it should not be necessary to modify this group.

When a SharePoint farm is created, the account that is entered into the Configuration Wizard (psconfiggui.exe), as the farm account, is automatically added to each of the following groups:

- WSS_ADMIN_WPG

- WSS_RESTRICTED_WPG_V4

- WSS_WPG

This automatic group population actually happens during setup; and then each time that a server is joined to the farm, via the Configuration Wizard, or via the command-line psconfig.exe or PowerShell. The setup user account is automatically added to

- WSS_ADMIN_WPG

- IIS_WPG

It also has elevated privileges in SQL Server, as does the farm account, but with a slight twist that I'll discuss in just a minute. If you ever notice a disparity in the accounts in these groups, there are really only three ways that this can happen. The first is that the server has gremlins in it. The second is that someone manually modified the membership. Finally, the third is via code or solution deployment. I like the first way because it is the most common explanation.

Ask the Domain Controllers

If you ever encounter a farm with disparity between the three Windows SharePoint Services worker process groups, you should start asking questions. If you see a user that does not belong in the group, you should ask is when the user was added. You can open the domain controller and look at the security logs for event ID 47—a member was added to a security-enabled local group. You can do this manually using the event viewer (eventvwr.msc), or you can use a totally awesome piece of PowerShell that a good friend of mine, Mr. J. T. Shoupe, a fellow SharePoint engineer at the world's number-one managed cloud company, Rackspace, introduced to me.

```
$spservers=Get-SPServer | where {$_.Role -ne "Invalid"}
 foreach($spserver in $spservers)

{

$filename=$spserver.name
write-host ----------------------- $filename -----------------------
get-winevent -FilterHashtable @{Logname='System';ID=5138} -MaxEvents 3 | select TimeCreated,
ID, Message

}
```

In this example, J. T. was looking for instances where the IIS web server was unable to communicate with the Windows Process Activation Service (WAS). Because application pools depend on WAS to function properly, you may have to restart the application pool on a schedule if you see a lot of 5138 event IDs. The real point I'm trying to make here is that the part of the script that reads ID=5138 could easily be changed to 4732, and the part that reads Logname='System' could be replaced with Logname='Security' if you wanted to scour the security log for event ID 4732. You can always look for more than three events by changing –MaxEvents 3 to –MaxEvents 4, or a number higher than 3.

The way to use this PowerShell is to open a SharePoint Management Shell and paste it in after you've adjusted it for your logname, ID, and MaxEvents. Don't worry if you don't understand all the PowerShell at the moment; in an upcoming chapter, we'll dig into PowerShell a little bit further and look at how it has some really awesome troubleshooting capabilities. Let's keep talking about "the who" part of this query.

Another question that can be answered by the domain controllers logs is *when the local security group was changed*, searching for event ID 4735. It might even tell you who made the change. Chances are good that the change was made by a service account, which narrows the "who-done-it" to those people who have or had access to the passwords. Hopefully, that was or is a small list.

Solutions could be written in such a way that they modify the membership of local groups. You can use a list of deployed solutions to find yourself a good starting point for the search in the domain controllers to determine if any group memberships were changed at the same time or right around the time of a solution deployment. To get such a list, manually click through each deployed solution to look at the last time it was deployed, or use this PowerShell:

```
Get-SPsolution | sort lastoperationendtime | ft name, lastoperationendtime
```

The use of the sort-object cmdlet is purposefully left at the default of ascending so that the most recently deployed solutions are at the bottom of the list that is generated. This gives you a timeline of when solutions were deployed. Then you can use J. T.'s script to determine if any local group memberships changed around the same time.

It is a good idea to have all the solutions in your farm documented with what they do and what changes they make to the file system, registry, IIS, and so forth. Most governance documents specify that each solution should be thoroughly documented in such a way that the "hit by a bus" theory is protected. Not that I'd wish any developer to get run over by a bus, or hit by one, or backed over by one, because that would not be good. It would also "not be good" to have an undocumented solution make unwanted changes to security groups, service identities, and or application pool identities.

Database Permissions for Farm Account Vs Install Account

In SQL Server, there's a login known as *sysadmin* or SA, which is, for the most part, the god of SQL. Then, there are accounts that have the fixed server role of sysadmin; not to be confused with SQL login SA. And finally, there are accounts that have both db_creator and securityadmin. When an account has db_creator and securityadmin, it essentially is the same as having a public login and sysadmin. The farm account that is used to connect to the databases is given db_creator and security admin during the initial farm configuration; and for the farm to function, these fixed server roles should remain after the farm is created. The farm account is not a member of the local administrators group on SQL Server.

The install account is a member of the local administrators group on every application, web front end, distributed cache, search, and SQL Server in the farm. The install account also has db_creator and securityadmin fixed server roles. Both accounts have db_owner of the server farm configuration database and of the server farm Central Administration content database. The install or setup account needs to be able to log in to the computer running SQL Server in order for the install configuration wizards or PowerShell cmdlets to succeed.

After the farm is created, the farm account has db_owner on every SharePoint database. With SharePoint 2013, a manual change is required for the Performance Point database, wherein the db_owner has to be manually added.

The final difference between the farm account and the install account is that the farm account has membership in the WSS_CONTENT_APPLICATION_POOLS role for the configuration database and for the Central Administration content database. Membership in this role gives the farm account elevate permissions to a subset of stored procedures.

File System Permissions for Members of the WSS_Admin_WPG Local Group

This section discusses a few file system paths that the WSS_Admin_WPG local group has, for the most part, full control over. Oddly enough, a file system path that this group does not have full control over, but instead can only modify, is the infamous root folder of the hive, which is located at %COMMONPROGRAMFILES%Microsoft Shared\Web Server Extensions\15, with the path %COMMONPROGRAMFILES% = c:\program files\common files. This is the directory for the core SharePoint 2013 files. In SharePoint 2010, the path is %COMMONPROGRAMFILES%Microsoft Shared\Web Server Extensions\14.

If the *access control list* (ACL) is modified for this folder in any way, all sorts of things start to go haywire; for example, solution deployments do not function properly or a feature activation fails or does not activate correctly. Figure 1-6 shows the contents at the root of the hive. I've always found it strikingly odd that the members of WSS_Admin_WPG can only modify at this folder level when the group has full control over a plethora of other Windows system folders and only a few of the hive's subfolders. As you read on, pay special

7

attention to which folders inherit their permissions from the 15 hive, so that if you ever need to determine if manual changes were made to the file system permissions, you'll have a good starting point.

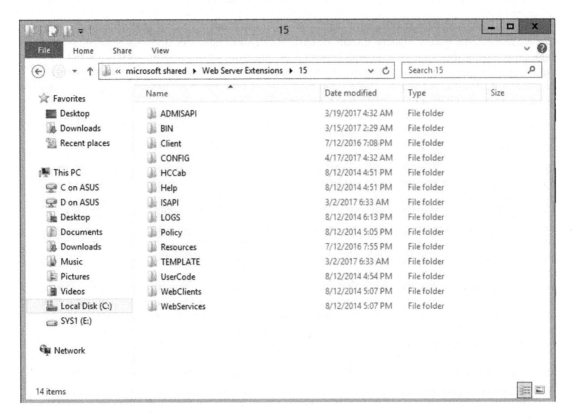

Figure 1-6. *The 15 hive folders*

The directories directly beneath the hive that inherit and only allow the farm account to modify these directories and all the subfolders and files are as follows: BIN, client, HCCab, Help, ISAPI, Policy, Resources, Template, UserCode, WebClients, and WebServices.

Of the folders that inherit permissions directly from the root of the hive, the BIN folder is one of the most heavily accessed folders because it contains the OWSTIMER, PSCONFIG, SPMETAL, WSStracing, and WSSAdmin files. There are a lot of other .dll and .exe files in this folder that are responsible for supporting SharePoint. The local service on each server has read\execute on this directory. If this directory is modified, parts of SharePoint will start to fail; and if it is removed, SharePoint will break.

The local service also has read rights to the key in registry that contains the document conversion service.

The Client folder contains files for the support of Microsoft Online; whereas, the HCCab folder contains .cab files that are broken down in such a way as to represent the various languages installed in the system; they are also used in the help system. Speaking of the help system, the Help folder holds a compiled HTML file that serves the SharePoint Help system.

When looking at IIS, you'll notice that some of the folders have a shortcut icon but other folders do not have the icon. The folders with the shortcut icon are virtual folders that map to various locations within the global assembly cache (GAC). GAC is a term used to describe areas on the file system that hold key SharePoint files. The ISAPI folder is part of this GAC that contains numerous web service (.asmx) files known as *web service discovery pages* (.aspx) files. The ISAPI folder also is home to dynamic link library (.dll) files that support the operations for SharePoint that are handled through web services. The ISAPI folder has a shortcut icon in IIS because it is a virtually mapped folder; that is, its files do not reside under the default %SystemDrive%\inetpub\wwwroot\wss\VirtualDirectories location; but instead, they live inside C:\Program Files\Common Files\Microsoft Shared\Web Server Extensions\15\isapi and are mapped in IIS to the virtual folder named _vti_bin.

The Policy folder also inherits from the root and it contains files that redirect assemblies. Different versions of SharePoint support different levels of redirection; for example, SharePoint 2013 supports the redirection of SharePoint 2010 and 2007 assemblies.

The Resources folder contains .resx files that are used to localize SharePoint. In other words, these files are used to represent different languages. The default install of SharePoint has the base set of files that do not have a language identifier, and then, for the most part, a corresponding file that has the language identifier. For example, core.resx, which contains descriptions for web parts, is accompanied by core.en-US.resx. I said "for the most part" because some files do not have language agnostic files. These resource files are copied by language packs as you add them. The default install of SharePoint is in English. It is a really good idea to never modify these files manually. The same is true with most IIS settings and changes made in the Windows Services console. We need to allow SharePoint to handle these changes as much as possible. Sometimes, we'll need to take things into our own hands, but hopefully, this is not very often.

The TEMPLATE folder is where you'll find the most development taking place. I'd wager this folder and its subfolders, FEATURES and IMAGES, are the three that are most heavily targeted by developers. The TEMPLATE folder has folders inside it that support customizations made to the farm. The TEMPLATE folder also has a plethora of folders that contain out-of-the-box SharePoint features and core files for SharePoint sites. Modifications to ACLs on this folder cause odd behavior within SharePoint. The ADMIN subfolder contains the master pages and templates for the Central Administration web site, along with other core features for Search, Secure Store Service, Business Connectivity Services, and content deployment. The LAYOUTS subfolder contains a plethora of files that are used for all sorts of administrative actions within SharePoint sites. Whenever you've navigated to site settings or site content, you have accessed files inside of the LAYOUTS subfolder. The virtual directory, which is exposed inside IIS, is named _layouts.

The TEMPLATE folder is also home to the CONTROLTEMPLATES subfolder, which contains files that are used in list item forms. These templates control the layout of the list item forms. Along the same line of thought, there is a subfolder under the TEMPLATE folder named DocumentTemplates, which houses a file named wkpstd.aspx. The wkpstd.aspx file is used to create document libraries; so, if you're having trouble creating document libraries, check that the ACL of the DocumentTemplates folder has not been changed and that the date of the wkpstd.aspx is not recent. A recent date on this file could indicate a modification that should not have been made.

When you create copies of sites in the form of site templates, the SiteTemplates folder is used. It contains the base files used in the process of creating a site template for blogs, team sites, wiki sites, meeting workspaces, Tenant Administration, and Central Administration. Table 1-1 summarizes the site templates that are available in different versions of SharePoint On-Premises and SharePoint Online.

Table 1-1. Available Site Templates

Category	Site Type	Site Collection	Site 365 for small business	Office 365 for small business	Office 365 for medium or large business	SharePoint Server Foundation 2013	SharePoint Server 2013 or SharePoint Server 2016	SharePoint Online
Collaboration	Team	Yes	Yes	Yes	Yes	Yes	Yes	Yes
Collaboration	Blog	Yes	Yes	Yes	Yes	Yes	Yes	Yes
Collaboration	Project	Yes	Yes	Yes	Yes	No	Yes	Yes
Collaboration	Community	Yes	Yes	No	Yes	No	Yes	Yes
Enterprise	Document Center	Yes	Yes	No	Yes	No	Yes	Yes
Enterprise	Records Center	Yes	Yes	No	Yes	No	Yes	Yes

The TEMPLATE folder's IMAGES subfolder contains shared files that are shared by all the SharePoint web applications on the server. These files are image files and they are accessible by the _layouts/images virtual directory. There is a subfolder of the TEMPLATE folder named SQL that contains stored procedures for SQL Server. There is a subfolder named THEMES under the TEMPLATE folder that provides the files used in SharePoint themes. Knowing this is important when troubleshooting issues with any of these.

The WorkflowActivities subfolder contains only one .dll file; so, if there are workflow issues, you can easily rule out the file system as the issue by checking the subfolder for a file named Microsoft.SharePoint. WorkflowServices.Activities.dll, which has the same date on all of the servers in your farm.

The XML subfolder contains XML files that provide support for the files used to render some of the SharePoint field and schema definition, which helps with the look and feel by mapping the JavaScript files used by the different actions in SharePoint. This folder gets enhancements and the addition of field types and definitions, which are added by SP, CU, and/or platform additions; for example, Project Web app (PWA) and SQL Server Reporting Services (SSRS) integration adds more XML files to this folder.

By no means does this do justice to the awesome power of the files that I just mentioned. There is a reason that all the directories inherit—with the exception of the ADMISAPI, CONFIG, and Logs directories. One of the reasons is that it makes it hard for code to perform any sort of action that would alter ACLs, which is intentional because changes to ACLs in the SharePoint hive can have detrimental impacts.

The UserCode folder under the root of the hive inherits its permissions, giving the farm account only modify, as it contains files used in support of sandboxed solutions. The WebClients Folder has numerous subfolders that contain .config files for client settings for various service applications and services within SharePoint. If one of them is different from the next, this might result in inconsistent behavior in a service application. There may be modifications to one of the servers in a load balanced farm. The WebServices folder contains web.config files for the application root in a subfolder named root. It has web.config files for quite a few of the key service applications. In an upcoming exercise, you'll see that the WebServices folder houses web.configs for Secure Store Service, Topology Services, PowerPoint Conversion, BCS, Subscription Settings, and Security Token.

Now that we've covered the directories that inherit from the hive, let's talk about one of the directories that does not inherit its permission from the hive: the ADMISAPI directory. This directory contains files related to SOAP services for the Central Administration site. The members of the WSS_ADMIN_WPG group have full control over this folder, its subfolders, and files. If your farm is exhibiting issues with remote site creation, or if it is experiencing weird behavior, such as things sometimes working and sometimes not working, take a look at the directories access control list and look for any changes. Later, in one of the exercises, you'll notice that this folder is mapped in IIS to the _vti_adm virtual folder within IIS. The default permissions on the file system folder are shown in Figure 1-7. Notice how some are inherited and some are explicitly given.

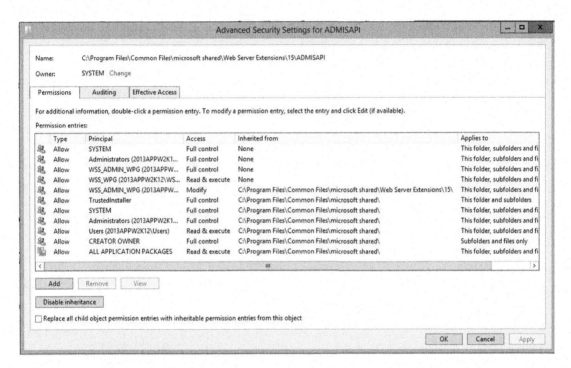

Figure 1-7. *ADMISAPI default permissions*

The CONFIG directory also affects IIS and how web applications behave (as far as provisioning is concerned. The CONFIG folder has files that are needed for a lot of different SharePoint operations, including upgrade mapping operations where objects are mapped from one version of SharePoint to the next—with 2010 to 2013 and 2013 to 2016. If the ACL shown in Figure 1-8 is altered, the problems with web application provisioning will arise. The same is true if the contents of this directory are modified.

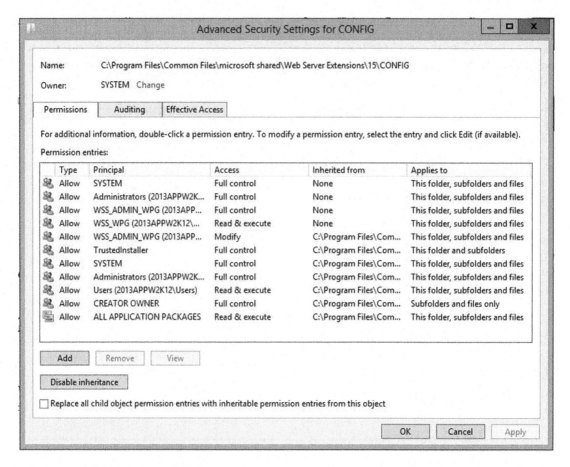

Figure 1-8. *CONFIG directory default permissions*

As you'll notice in the exercises that wrap up this chapter, membership in the local administrators group grossly changes the number of privileges an account or service that runs under that account possesses. This is why the farm account is removed from the local administrators group after a User Profile service is configured in SharePoint 2010 or 2013; it is not even required in the local admins group in SharePoint 2016 due to the changes in the FIM (forefront identity manager) service.

Logging File Paths

The default directory for the SharePoint Unified Logging System is located in %COMMONPROGRAMFILES%\ Microsoft Shared\Web Server Extensions\15\LOGS, or, in other words, C:\Program Files\Common Files\ microsoft shared\Web Server Extensions\15\LOGS. Just change the 15 for a 14 if working with SharePoint 2010, or to a 12 if working with SharePoint 2007. It seems as if Microsoft doesn't like the number 13, or maybe the SharePoint team didn't since they skipped right over it when going from SharePoint 2007's hive to SharePoint 2010.

It's a best practice to move as much logging and writing off the OS drive as possible. This logging directory is able to be relocated after a build is completed; whereas, some of the SharePoint directories cannot be relocated once the farm is up and online. Only at install, can you move the parent directory, located at %ProgramFiles%\Microsoft Office Servers\15.0, by opting to change the drive location during the install. Figure 1-9 shows the SharePoint 2010 install. All you need to change is the C:\ drive to a D:\ or E:\ drive. This is a one-time event, and if you exercise this option, all future servers need to have the requisite D:\ or E:\ drive. If you move one, you might as well move both: to move the search index location and in case you decide to expand your search topology in the future.

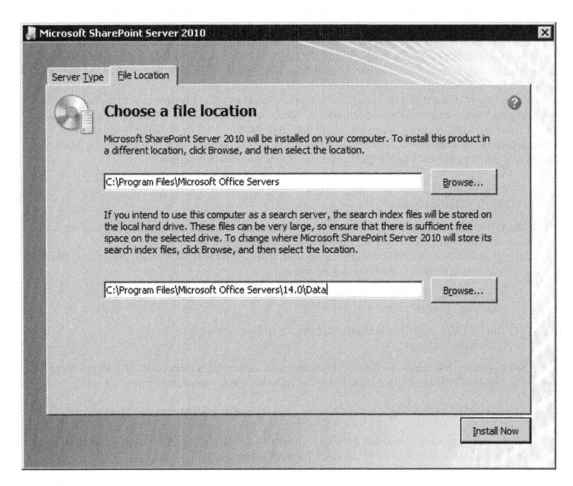

Figure 1-9. *Default file paths one-time only move option*

I do not want to confuse the files that are located underneath %ProgramFiles%\Microsoft Office Servers\15.0 or %ProgramFiles%\Microsoft Office Servers\15.0\Logs with the location of the ULS logs. As I stated earlier, the ULS logging default location is under the Hive\Logs folder. Since this is defaulted to the OS drive, it's a best practice to move ULS logging to D:\ or E:\. This can be done via PowerShell, which we'll look at later on in some exercises in an upcoming chapter.

%ProgramFiles%\Microsoft Office Servers\15.0\Logs is where runtime diagnostic logs are generated (not stored). If you're having trouble with logging, check that the ACL has not been modified and that the WSS_ADMIN_WPG local group has explicitly applied full control over this folder and its subfolders and files. Not to confuse things, but the same is true about the permissions for wherever the ULS logs are writing; that is, the WSS_ADMIN_WPG has full control over that location as well.

The files and folders underneath %ProgramFiles%\Microsoft Office Servers\15.0 include a directory named WebServices. If you're having trouble with services such as search or Excel, you should check this directory for any "tomfoolery"—err, modifications. The Data directory (located at %ProgramFiles%\Microsoft Office Servers\15.0\Data) is the root of all search functionality, so if you're having search troubles, make sure that this folder's ACL has not been modified.

The WSS_ADMIN_WPG group has full control over the default location for IIS web sites in SharePoint. This is located at C:\Inetpub\wwwroot\wss. If you're having trouble with administrative functions that enumerate or make changes to sites and subsites, make sure that this directory has not been altered. Speaking of site resolution locations, the WSS_ADMIN_WPG local group has read/write capability at the location of the Windows operating system's HOSTS file. Since the dawn of time, this location has always been located at %windir%\System32\drivers\etc\HOSTS.

Finally, the WSS_ADMIN_WPG can provide access to and has full control over the SharePoint cache, including the Cache config, which is a subfolder of %AllUsersProfile%\ Microsoft\SharePoint. The config folder in use is a GUID named folder underneath %AllUsersProfile%\ Microsoft\SharePoint\config; inconsistencies can arise here that may cause timer jobs to fail. Clearing this cache location may also solve issues with psconfig.exe and psconfiggui.exe when either of them receives errors.

Registry Permissions

The WSS_ADMIN_WPG local group provides elevated access to various locations in registry that perform and house critical settings. These are not to be altered, as issues will arise.

If you're having trouble with document conversions, check that the WSS_ADMIN_WPG group has only read and write permissions over the following locations:

- `HKEY_LOCAL_MACHINE\Software\Microsoft\Office Server\15.0\ LoadBalancerSettings`

- `HKEY_LOCAL_MACHINE\Software\Microsoft\Office Server\15.0\ LauncherSettings`

The local system has to have read permissions on the LauncherSettings for document conversions to work. The Local SYSTEM also has full control over the following registry location for machines to join the farm:

`HKEY_LOCAL_MACHINE\Software\Microsoft\Shared Tools\Web Server Extensions\15.0\Secure`

If you're having trouble provisioning services, check that this key has not been altered and make sure that LOCAL SYSTEM and WSS_RESTRICETED_WPG have full control:

`HKEY_LOCAL_MACHINE\Software\Microsoft\Shared Tools\Web Server Extensions\15.0\Secure\FarmAdmin`

If you're having trouble with joining a server to the farm or with general SharePoint functions, check that the WSS_ADMIN_WPG group has full control over the following locations:

- `HKEY_LOCAL_MACHINE\Software\Microsoft\Shared Tools\Web Server Extensions\15.0\Secure`

- `HKEY_LOCAL_MACHINE\SOFTWARE\Microsoft\Office Server\15.0`

If you're having trouble with search, check the WSS_ADMIN_WPG group for full control over these locations:

- `HKEY_LOCAL_MACHINE\Software\Microsoft\Office Server\15.0\Search`

- `HKEY_LOCAL_MACHINE\Software\Microsoft\Shared Tools\Web Server Extensions\15.0\Search`

If SharePoint is behaving oddly, check that the WSS_ADMIN_WPG has read permissions at this location:

```
HKEY_LOCAL_MACHINE\SOFTWARE\Microsoft\Office Server
```

If you're having trouble opening Central Administration or with odd logging behavior in your farm account, check this location for congruency on all of your servers:

```
HKEY_LOCAL_MACHINE\Software\Microsoft\Shared Tools\Web Server Extensions\15.0\WSS
```

Application Pool Accounts

Application pool accounts in IIS are automatically added to the WSS_WPG local group by SharePoint when application pools are created using the GUI or via PowerShell. The WSS_WPG group has read and execute access on the following directories:

- `C:\Inetpub\wwwroot\wss`

- `%ProgramFiles%\Microsoft Office Servers\15.0`

Members of the group have the ability to modify the contents of web.configs and to make changes to sites that do not involve permissions; members also have access to the server-side SharePoint binaries that are not located in the hive.

The application pool accounts have read access on the following location:

```
%AllUsersProfile%\ Microsoft\SharePoint
```

The following gives application pools the ability to interact with the files in the configuration cache, among other files that are located under this directory:

```
%ProgramFiles%\Microsoft Office Servers\15.0\WebServices
```

If you are experiencing issues with services such as search or Excel, it is important to check the WebServices directory to make sure that the WSS_WPG group has read access.

The application pool accounts have read access on the following hive locations, including all subfolders and files:

- `%COMMONPROGRAMFILES%\Microsoft Shared\Web Server Extensions\15\ADMISAPI`

- `%COMMONPROGRAMFILES%\Microsoft Shared\Web Server Extensions\15\CONFIG`

And if you're having the type of troubles that I explained in the WSS_ADMIN_WPG section, you need to keep these two directories in mind for the WSS_WPG group with read access.

Finally, the WSS_WPG group has modify permissions on the ULS logging location. If logging is not happening, make sure that this group has the proper permissions on the following location (when using the default logging location):

```
%COMMONPROGRAMFILES%\Microsoft Shared\Web Server Extensions\15\LOGS
```

WSS_WPG Registry Access

The application pool accounts that are members of the WSS_WPG group have read access on the following registry locations:

- `HKEY_LOCAL_MACHINE\SOFTWARE\Microsoft\Office Server\15.0`

- `HKEY_LOCAL_MACHINE\Software\Microsoft\Shared Tools\Web Server Extensions\15.0\Secure`

- `HKEY_LOCAL_MACHINE\Software\Microsoft\Shared Tools\Web Server Extensions\15.0\WSS`

If the 15.0\Secure is modified, you might find it very difficult to add a machine to the farm, or to run SharePoint. If the 15.0\WSS is altered, diagnostic logging will probably fail and there might be issues with adding servers to the farm or running the Configuration Wizard and/or its command-line equivalent.

The application pool accounts have both read and write access at the following locations:

- `HKEY_LOCAL_MACHINE\Software\Microsoft\Office Server\15.0\Diagnostics`

- `HKEY_LOCAL_MACHINE\Software\Microsoft\Office Server\15.0\LoadBalancerSettings`

- `HKEY_LOCAL_MACHINE\Software\Microsoft\Office Server\15.0\LauncherSettings`

The same is true for these locations, as was true for the WSS_ADMIN_WPG group, with respect to the difference in each group's permissions, as far as what can happen if modified or altered (e.g., problems with diagnostic logging and/or issues with the load-balancer-handling document conversion).

Application Pool Accounts in IIS

Least-privilege SharePoint service applications app pool accounts are not local administrators on the box; they should not need to be farm admins or to have WSS_Admin_WPG membership. If SharePoint service applications app pool accounts need membership in any of the these, then the code only works if it has greater than least privileging, as you saw with what the WSS_Admin_WPG group can do to the file system. When a content web application is created to store site collections, a managed account is used to run the application pool. Using the regular domain user account that does not have membership in any elevated group gives the content web application least privileging, because this account is not used to run Windows services as service applications; they only run the application pool that serves the web applications that houses site collections, sites, subsites, and content.

Speaking of service applications and SharePoint, it is a best practice to break out the Search Service application into its own application pool and then to run the other SharePoint service applications under a Shared Hosted Services application pool. In a truly least-privileged farm, the Secure Store Service application has its own service application pool; it is not hosted inside the same application pool as the other service applications. The Shared Hosted Services application pool houses all of the various service applications in SharePoint and it runs under a managed account named something along the lines of 2013svcapps, or SP_SA_AP for SharePoint service applications application pool account. When a service application is created, the account used to run the service application is automatically added to the WSS_WPG local group. It is given different permissions within SQL, depending on the service applications that uses it.

When the Shared Hosted Services application pool is created, the account used to run it is automatically assigned the SP_DATA_ACCESS role for any existing content databases. It is assigned the WSS_CONTENT_APPLICATION_POOLS role associated with the farm configuration database and with the Central Administration content database.

When it comes to SharePoint 2013, the IIS application pool that houses the search service application uses a regular domain user that is not a member of domain admins, local admins, WSS_Admin_WPG, or any elevated group. When the search service application is created in SharePoint 2013, part of that process should create a separate application pool in IIS that uses a special service account for search, usually named something like SP_search. Please note that this is not the default content access account. The default access account is also called the crawl account, which is used to access content in all the sites by being manually assigned full read permissions on the web applications that host the sites.

The Excel services unattended account is a regular domain user that is used in conjunction with the secure store service to create the unattended service account and allow Excel services in SharePoint 2013 to contact external content from data sources that require a user name and password. This account must be a domain user account and must not be a member of the local administrators group.

The My Sites application pool account is another regular domain user account that has no administrative privileges on the local server other than membership in WSS_ADMIN_WPG. It is automatically added to the WSS_ADMIN_WPG and WSS_WPG local groups when the service application that the My Sites web application utilizes is provisioned. The My Sites web application has the "allow self-service site creation" enabled as one of its requirements, without which My Sites would not be able to provision for each user. The account is assigned to the WSS_CONTENT_APPLICATION_POOLS role that is associated with the farm configuration database and with the Central Administration content database. It gets SP_DATA_ACCESS to all of the content databases.

The WSS_CONTENT_APPLICATION_POOLS database role is associated with the farms configuration database and the Central Administration site content database. The role makes it possible for its members to query and update the site map and have read-only access to parts of the configuration database.

TechNet says, "The secure WSS_SHELL_ACCESS database role on the configuration database replaces the need to add an administration account as a db_owner on the configuration database." (https://technet.microsoft.com/en-us/library/cc678863.aspx).

When you use the add-spshelladmin PowerShell cmdlet to add a user name, you're only adding that user to the configuration database's WSS_SHELL_ACCESS role. J. T. has a handy one-liner that adds an admin user to all the content databases by using the following:

```
Get-SPContentDatabase | Add-SPShellAdmin -UserName Domain\UserName -verbose
```

After running this command, the user that you specified in the user parameter value is added to the WSS_SHELL_ACCESS role on all content databases. By adding a user to the role, you are giving them execute access to all the stored procedures for the database, as well as the ability to read and write on all the database tables.

Because the SP_DATA_ACCESS role replaces the db_owner role in SharePoint 2013 to some degree, it is the role that should be used to grant object model level access to databases during upgrades and new deployments. It provides the following permissions:

- Grants EXECUTE or SELECT on all SharePoint stored procedures and functions

- Grants SELECT on all SharePoint tables

- Grants EXECUTE on user-defined types where the schema is dbo

- Grants INSERT on the AllUserDataJunctions table

- Grants UPDATE on the Sites view

- Grants UPDATE on the UserData view

- Grants UPDATE on the AllUserData table

- Grants INSERT and DELETE on the NameValuePair tables

- Grants CREATE table permission

Central Administration's application pool runs under the same account that runs the timer service: the farm account. This is why the farm account should not be a local administrator, as that would give this site more privilege than it needs to operate. The farm account is also used to run the Security Token Service application pool that is responsible for web service calls related to authentication. The farm account runs the Topology Services application pool, as well, which is the pool responsible for overall control of what runs where and on which servers via IIS. We'll dive a little deeper into this in Chapters 2 and 3.

PowerShell to Reset Local Permissions and Files

So what do you do if you think something has been changed in your farm in one of the file systems, folders, or registry settings? PowerShell to the rescue—and/or the post-setup configuration wizard.

If you think that something has been changed with respect to an ACL, you can use Initialize-SPResourceSecurity on each of your farm's servers to enforce security on the local server in all the files, folders, and registry keys. You could also run psconfig.exe –cmd secureresources, which is the command-line equivalent of the PowerShell cmdlet.

Unfortunately, this does not handle database permissions for the members of the WSS_WPG group.

The Install-SPFeature cmdlet is used during a new install and after joining a farm. It also scans the system for any missing features and then reinstalls them in the farm. This works great for finding any missing features that may have been erroneously removed by undocumented development.

Inspecting for Least Privilege

In this section, you'll perform some exercises on the identities that are running SharePoint. You'll look at local group memberships, the identities that are running IIS application pools and where they are changed in SharePoint. You'll create a farm admin account, inspect IIS and the file system, and restore the file system–level security.

In this first exercise, let's look at the accounts that are running Windows SharePoint Services.

WINDOWS SHAREPOINT SERVICES

This exercise looks at Windows SharePoint Services and SharePoint Central Administration to determine which accounts are utilized to run Windows SharePoint Services at the operation system level. Next, you learn how to modify the account that each service is using so that SharePoint is aware of the changes.

Verify Identity Using services.msc

1. Open the Services management console by typing **services.msc** on the run bar and clicking OK.

2. In the name column, scroll down the alphabetically sorted list to the services starting with SharePoint*. Take a look at the identity that is used to run the SharePoint Timer Service. The following screenshot shows the SPTimerV4 service is running under the farm account as expected.

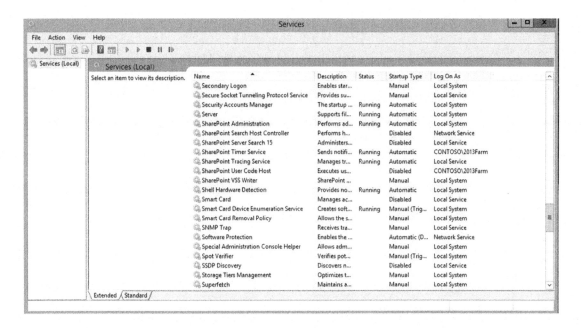

This screenshot in was taken during a farm install when search had not been provisioned. After search was provisioned, the account used to run the SharePoint Search Host Controller and SharePoint Server Search 15 changed to 2013SearchSvc, as shown in the following screenshot.

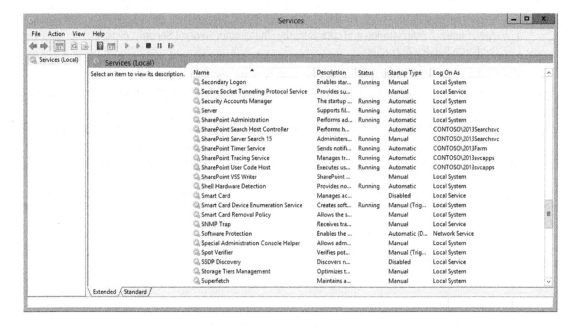

Note fter the least-privileged farm is fully created, the SharePoint user code host runs under a least-privileged account; the same is true for other services, such as the search services.

Verify Identity using PowerShell

1. Open a command line administratively by right-clicking the Windows logo and clicking Command Prompt (Admin).

2. Once the command line opens, type **PowerShell**, and click Enter.

3. After the prompt returns, type the following code (also shown in the following screenshot) and then press Enter.

```
gwmi win32_Service -filter "name='sptimerv4'" | ft name, startname
```

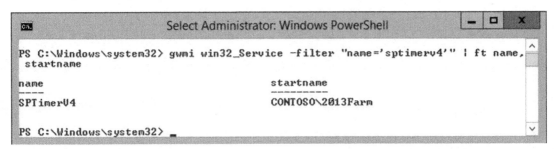

You can see that the SharePoint timer service is set to start using the account named 2013Farm.

Verifying the Farm Account Identity in Central Admin

1. Open Central Administration and click Security. Then, under General Security, click Configure Service Accounts.

2. Click the drop-down menu and select the farm account. You should see the same account that you saw in the Windows OS–level Services console (services.msc).

If you ever run into a situation where this account does not match what is in Windows, your best bet is to rebuild the farm, if at all possible. If a rebuild it not feasible, then this is where you make changes to any of the accounts in use by Windows SharePoint Services, and you follow any changes with an IIS reset in every server in your farm. You should avoid making the changes directly in the Windows operating system console, or in the IIS Management console; since SharePoint is not aware of this, it will most likely cause issues.

In the next exercise, you'll look at how to invoke the local group management console from the command line and check group membership, as well as a quick way to verify group membership using the net command.

LOCAL GROUP MEMBERSHIP

Open the Local Group Management Console

In this exercise, you open the local users and group management console administratively to look at group membership.

1. Open an administrative command line. Type **Lusrmgr.msc** and press Enter. The local users and groups management console opens.

2. Click **groups** and then open the administrators group. Make a mental note of the members that you see in this group, thinking about what I discussed in earlier. Note that the farm account is (hopefully) not a member of the administrators group.

3. Open the WSS_WPG group at the very bottom of the list of groups. Note how the various service accounts that run service and content application pools in IIS are all members of this group, along with NT Authority\LOCAL SERVICE, NT Authority\ NETWORK SERVICE, and NT AUTHORITY\SYSTEM, as shown in the following screenshot.

4. Open the WSS_ADMIN_WPG group. You should expect to see the installer account, the farm account, and the BUILTIN\Administrators as members of this group, as shown in the following screenshot.

5. Open the WSS_Restricted_WPG _V4 group. Note how the farm account is the only identity allowed to be a member of this group.

■ **Note** The WSS_Restricted_WPG_V4 group should never allow any identities other than the farm account, as this would surely over-privilege the farm.

---

6. Open the IIS_IUSRS group, as shown in the following screenshot, and note that the identities used in IIS are members of this group. Read the description of this group.

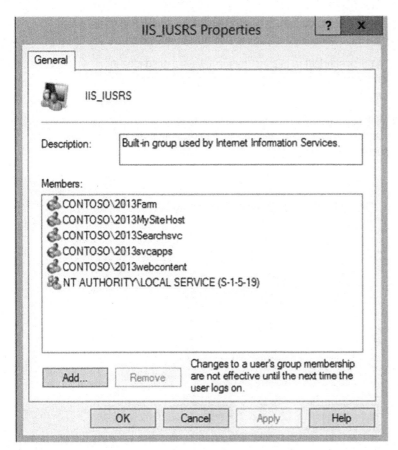

Check Group Membership Using the Command Line

1. At the command line, type **net localgroup administrators** and press Enter.

2. At the command line, type **net localgroup WSS_ADMIN_WPG** and press Enter.

3. At the command line, type **net localgroup WSS_WPG** and press Enter.

4. At the command line, type **net localgroup WSS_Restricted_WPG_V4** and press Enter.

5. At the command line, type **net localgroup IIS_IUSRS** and press Enter.

The command-line method of the check local group membership is much faster, as long as you know the group names.

Now let's take a look at the user accounts that the Internet Information Services (IIS) Manager is using. We already know that we should see different accounts in use by various application pools. Let's take a look!

IIS IDENTITIES AND HOW THEY MAP TO SHAREPOINT

This exercise compares the service accounts that are in use by SharePoint application pools. It also looks at the Service Accounts Credential Management page in Central Administration.

1.   Open the IIS Manager. A quick shortcut to this program is always a good idea in any SharePoint farm. You can open it by opening a run bar, typing **inetmgr**, and pressing Enter or clicking OK.

2.   Once the IIS Manager opens, expand the server node and click Application Pools. Once the application pools are visible, adjust the column widths so that the values are clearly visible, as shown in the following screenshot.

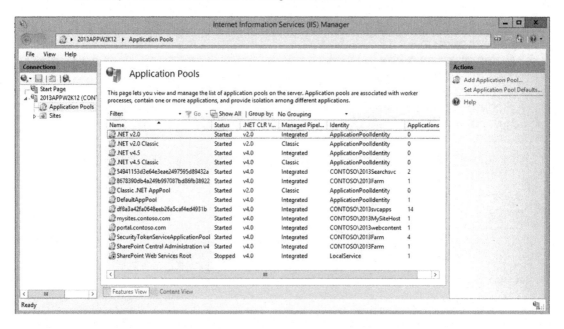

3.   Navigate back to the Service Account Management page in Central Administration by opening Central Administration and clicking Security. Then, under General Security, click Configure Service Accounts.

4.   Hopefully, you'll find that the identity shown in Farm Account on the Service Accounts page in Central Administration matches what is shown in IIS. In the following screenshot, you can see that the Central Administration application pool is running under the farm account.

■ **Note**   Earlier in this chapter, we identified the farm account via PowerShell by running the following cmdlet, which should agree with what you discovered in this exercise:

(Get-SPFarm).DefaultServiceAccount.

Service Accounts ⓘ

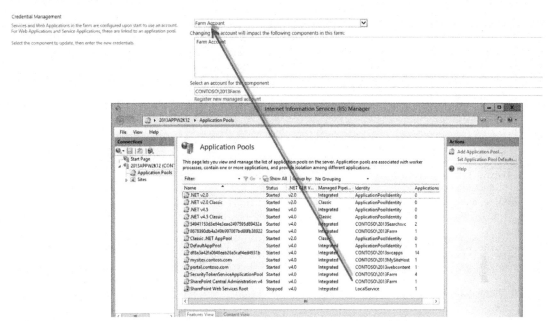

5. Click the drop-down menu on the Service Accounts page and select Service Application Pool - SharePoint Hosted Services. Note how this account matches up with the application pool named df8a3a42-fa06-48ee-b26a-5caf4ed4931b. The fact that this application pool in IIS uses the same identity is all well and good, but other than exploring the application pool to view the applications, how can we be certain that this is the SharePoint application pool?

6. Open an administrative SharePoint Management Shell and type the following:

```
Get-SPServiceApplicationPool
Get-SPServiceApplicationPool | ft Name, ProcessAccountName, ID, -auto
Get-SPServiceApplicationPool | ft Name, ID, -auto
```

PowerShell returns the name of the SharePoint Service application pools along with the associated GUID, as shown in the following screenshot.

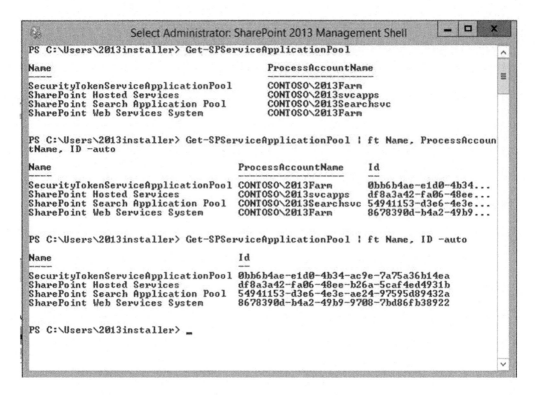

7. Another method to identify which IIS application pool is the pool used by a SharePoint service application is to have the Service Accounts page open and the service application pool selected (similar to what's shown in the following screenshot), and then open IIS Manager.

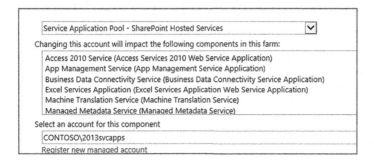

8. Right-click the service application pool that serves 14 applications, and then click View Applications, as shown in the following screenshot.

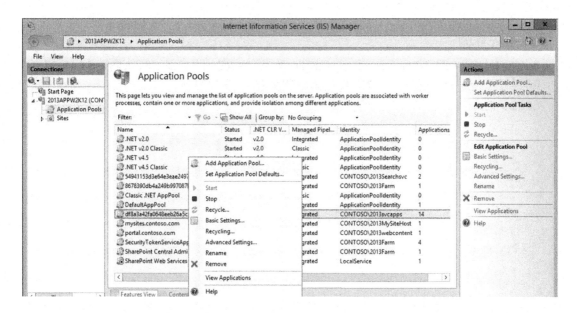

9. Once the window changes, adjust the physical path so that you can see the mappings, as shown in the following screenshot.

The following farm was installed in such a way that some of the files were not stored on the operating system drive, but instead were stored on the D:\ drive.

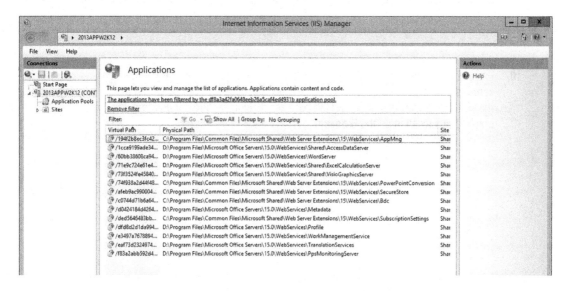

Now that we've definitely identified which application pool in IIS is serving up the bulk of the service applications in this farm, let's make sense of those virtual paths in the first column.

In order to do this, we need to open the sites node and then drive to the SharePoint Web Services, as shown in the following screenshot. Don't worry if your farm does not have physical paths to a different drive, because the different drive does not affect least privilege. The only reason that these different paths would exist is if the option to store binaries on a different drive was chosen during the SharePoint install.

If you're having trouble joining a server to an existing farm, check the physical paths in IIS and then adjust your install of SharePoint accordingly if you see paths other than C:\.

OK, let's discuss the virtual path a little.

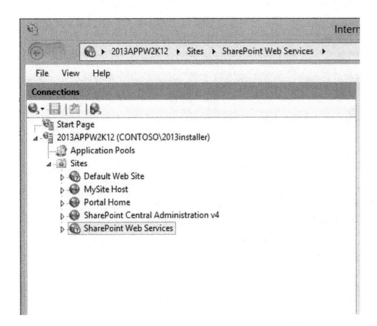

10. Expand the SharePoint Web Services node under Sites and choose one of the web services to explore. In the following screenshot, I choose the web service with the name that started with 1cca9199ade. After clicking Explore, I found that it is mapped to a location on the D drive of the server.

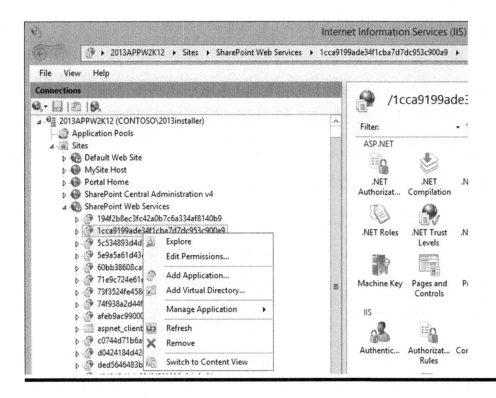

After having looked at all this, I can't help but recall that proverbial question: If a tree falls in the forest and no is there to hear it, does it make a sound? Quite obviously, the tree makes a sound when it falls; no one hears the sound, but the sound is there nonetheless.

When it comes to SharePoint, you could ask this question: If a SharePoint farm is least privileged for safety reasons, but 35 people know the farm account ID and password, is it really safe? I've seen this before, and I'd argue that the farm is least privileged but in need of a governance document. Anyways, I wanted to bring that up because you might encounter a situation where you need to give a user farm admin privileges without giving away the farm account. The next exercise discusses how this is accomplished.

MAKING A FARM ADMIN

There might come a day when your company hires consultants to come into your environment and perform a review of SharePoint. The consultant will definitely ask for access to your farm with farm admin privileges. Personally, I'd want to hover over the consultant and watch them work; but since that might be viewed as highly offensive, we instead need to create a farm admin account.

■ **Note** The farm admin account that we are creating is similar to the setup user, not "the farm account." This account should be able to perform everything the setup user account is capable of performing.

1. Log in to every server in the farm and add the user's account to the Local Administrators group.

2. Add the user's account to the Farm Admin SharePoint Group.

3. Add the user's account to SQL Server with sysad and db_creator fixed server roles.

4. Add the user's account to the Shell_Admin_Access role of every content database.

5. Add the user's account to the Shell_Admin_Access role of the configuration database and the Central Administration content database.

6. Verify that the account was added to the WSS_ADMIN_WPG and WSS_WPG groups.

INSPECTING IIS AND THE FILE SYSTEM AND RESTORING ORDER

In this exercise, you look at the ACLs on a couple of the hive folders. On a couple of registry keys, you look at virtual mappings in IIS that map to various locations in the hive. Then, you learn about PowerShell and command-line commands to reset these permissions.

■ **Note**   At no time do we change any of the permissions.

File System and IIS Mappings

1. Log on to the server in your farm that runs Central Administration. Open the IIS Manager (inetmgr.msc).

2. Open Windows Explorer and navigate to the root of the SharePoint hive. This example uses a SharePoint 2013 farm, so navigate to C:\Program Files\Common Files\microsoft shared\Web Server Extensions\15.

3. Right-click the ADMISAPI folder and then click Properties. Click the Security tab and then the Advanced button. Note in the following screenshot that the folder is owned by SYSTEM and that there are some permissions that are explicitly granted to the WSS_ADMIN_WPG and WSS_WPG groups. There are also inherited permissions.

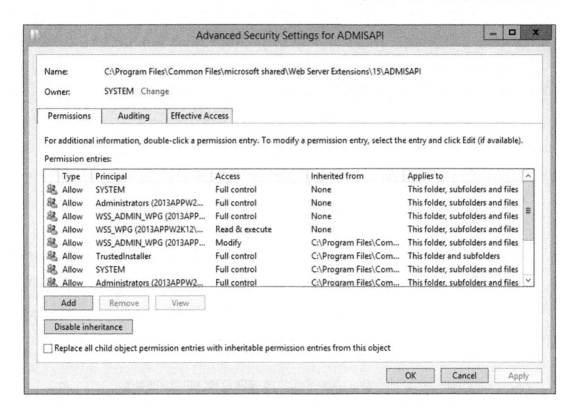

4. Close the permissions windows by cancelling or using the red X. Close Windows Explorer so that you are looking at IIS Manager.

5. Open the Central Administration site, as shown in the following screenshot.

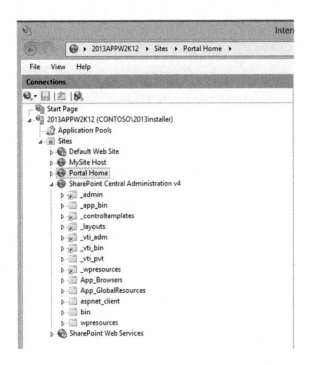

6.   Click Explore (see the following screenshot) to navigate to the virtual directory
     named _vti_adm. Note where it maps.

7.   Note that the directory maps to C:\Program Files\Common Files\Microsoft Shared\
     Web Server Extensions\15\admisapi.

8. Since Windows Explorer is open to the hive, let's look at one of the folders that inherits its permissions from the SharePoint Hive's root folder. This example uses a SharePoint 2013 farm, so navigate back to the 15 hive. Remove the \admisapi portion from C:\Program Files\Common Files\Microsoft Shared\Web Server Extensions\15\admisapi in Windows Explorer so that you're at the root, as shown in the following screenshot.

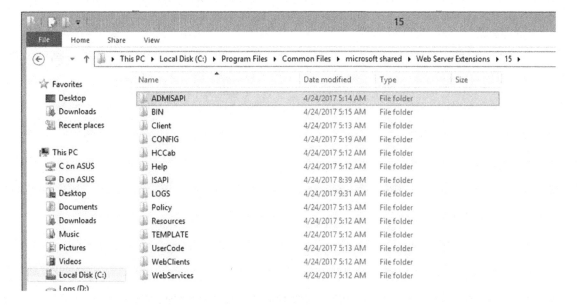

9. Right-click the folder named BIN, and then click Properties. Click the Security tab and then the Advanced button. Note in the following screenshot that all the permissions are inherited. There are zero explicitly given permissions and the WSS_WPG group does not have permission to this folder.

■ **Tip** Knowing how SharePoint permissions are supposed to be set, where they inherit and do not inherit, and what this affects, helps troubleshoot issues. It might not solve them, but it helps you rule out possible culprits.

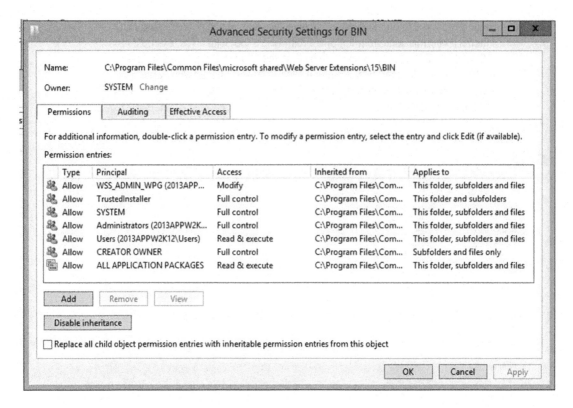

10. Take a few minutes to look at the virtual folders inside your SharePoint sites and the non-virtual folders.

The folders that have shortcut icons like the _vti_adm (shown in the previous screenshot) do not map to a location within the IIS web root. The folders that do not have a shortcut icon contain SharePoint-related files within the default IIS root for SharePoint, which is usually located at %SystemDrive%\inetpub\wwwroot\wss\VirtualDirectories.

Each web application gets a unique folder under this location and then each site has mappings to these various locations. Table 1-2 provides a high-level analysis of the IIS to file system mappings.

Table 1-2. *IIS Mapped Folders*

Folder Name	Virtual	Central Admin Only	Mapped Folder Path
_admin	Yes	Yes	%CommonProgramFiles%\Microsoft Shared\Web Server Extensions\15\template\admin
_app_bin	No	No	C:\inetpub\wwwroot\wss\VirtualDirectories\<SITEF OLDER>_app_bin
_controltemplates	Yes	No	%CommonProgramFiles%\Microsoft Shared\Web Server Extensions\14\template\controltemplates
_layouts	Yes	No	%CommonProgramFiles%\Microsoft Shared\Web Server Extensions\14\template\layouts
_login	Yes	--**	%CommonProgramFiles%\Microsoft Shared\Web Server Extensions\15\template\identitymodel\login
_vti_adm	Yes	Yes	%CommonProgramFiles%\Microsoft Shared\Web Server Extensions\15\admisapi
_vti_bin	Yes	No	%CommonProgramFiles%\Microsoft Shared\Web Server Extensions\15\isapi
_vti_pvt	No	No	C:\inetpub\wwwroot\wss\VirtualDirectories\<SITEF OLDER>_vti_pvt
_windows	Yes	--**	%CommonProgramFiles%\Microsoft Shared\Web Server Extensions\15\template\identitymodel\windows
_wpresources	Yes	No	%CommonProgramFiles%\Microsoft Shared\Web Server Extensions\wpresources
App_Browsers	No	No	C:\inetpub\wwwroot\wss\VirtualDirectories\ <SITEFOLDER>\App_Browsers
App_GlobalResources	No	No	C:\inetpub\wwwroot\wss\VirtualDirectories\ <SITEFOLDER>\App_GlobalResources
Aspnet_client	No	No	C:\inetpub\wwwroot\wss\ VirtualDirectories\<SITEFOLDER>\aspnet_client
bin	No	No	C:\inetpub\wwwroot\wss\ VirtualDirectories\<SITEFOLDER>\bin
wpresources	No	No	C:\inetpub\wwwroot\wss\ VirtualDirectories\<SITEFOLDER>\wpresources

*** Does not exist in Central Administration site mappings*

Registry Locations

In this part of the exercise, we'll open the registry editor and take a look at the permissions on the root SharePoint key.

1. Open the registry editor and navigate to HKEY_LOCAL_MACHINE\SOFTWARE\ Microsoft\Office Server\15.0, as shown in the following screenshot.

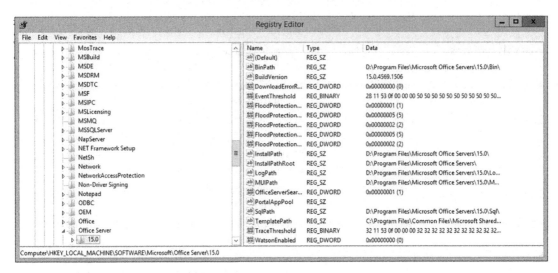

2. Right-click the 15.0 key and then click Permissions ä Advanced. Note that both WSS_ADMIN_WPG and WSS_WPG have explicitly assigned permissions.

Resetting Permissions

If you ever need to reset the file, folder, or registry permissions back to their original permissions, you can perform the following tasks.

3. To reset the permissions using PowerShell, open the SharePoint management console administratively. Type **Initialize-SPResourceSecurity** (as shown in the following screenshot) and press Enter.

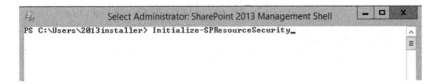

4. To reset the permissions using the command line, navigate to the BIN directory and type **Psconfig –cmd secureresources** (as shown in the following screenshot), and then press Enter.

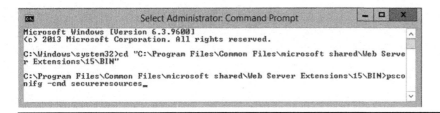

Next Steps

This chapter looked at the security settings of a least-privileged build and discussed some of the issues that can occur when changes are made or when least privilege is not in place. Next, you'll look at some of the key settings in a SharePoint build that alleviate troubles.

CHAPTER 2

Key Settings of a Good Build

In this chapter, we continue building out our base troubleshooting knowledge by learning about key settings of a good build. For the same reasons that a solid understanding of a least-privileged build helps you understand where to look at permissions when certain things are going wrong, a firm foundation on how the farm is constructed and being able to standardize that process helps you troubleshoot and remove inconsistencies. By standardizing the build process, we are setting the farm up for expected conditions and this makes it easier to identify unexpected behaviors and helps in troubleshooting those behaviors by being able to insure least privileging and key settings. This way, we can be certain that if something isn't the way it is supposed to be, that it wasn't due to an improper build.

Before we dive too deep into the PowerShell scripts used to standardize a farm build, we'll do a cursory review of some PowerShell concepts, at a high level. And, we'll see how PowerShell in and of itself can be a troubleshooting tool. When we start to discuss the PowerShell scripts, we'll try to point out the deficiencies of that vs. the more automated AutoSPInstaller method.

As we already mentioned, a good build starts with least privilege. You've learned about how important it is to know what the standard permission levels are in SharePoint and how least privilege plays into these permissions for the file system, in Chapter 1. So, you know that it is important to standardize and that deviations from the standards lead to unexpected behaviors. Along with least privileging, a good build includes key settings that help improve performance and reduce extraneous entries in the logs. Any time we can reduce events in the logging system, it is a good day; since that means there is less work for SharePoint to perform. A good build is rolled-out in such a manner as to become repeatable. The best ways to standardize builds is through PowerShell scripting and automation.

Let's chat a bit about using PowerShell to automate and standardize your builds in a least-privileged fashion. Then after we have that fairly nailed down, let's talk about an awesome scripting solution available on Codeplex's website named AutoSPInstaller. Codeplex is in the process of shutting down, with a target shutdown date of December 15, 2017. The AutoSPInstaller website is located at `https://autospinstaller.com` and this site has download links, as well.

Let's get our arms around some basic PowerShell concepts, look at the PowerShell Object model, and finish up our PowerShell discussion by analyzing a couple of scripts used to build Central Administration and the Service Applications. Then we'll do fairly high-level review of some of the things to be aware of when it comes to using the AutoSPInstaller vs. when using PowerShell. We'll talk about the timesaver of installing the prerequisites in offline-mode.

Finally, let's talk about key settings that neither the AutoSPInstaller nor the PowerShell scripting samples address.

© Stacy Simpkins 2017
S. Simpkins, *Troubleshooting SharePoint*, https://doi.org/10.1007/978-1-4842-3138-8_2

PowerShell Aliases

Aliases in PowerShell are used to save time and to make it easier to perform actions. In a lot of cases, the Aliases shorten the learning curve by allowing administrators to use commands that they already know in place of learning new PowerShell cmdlets, (pronounced "command litz"). Aliases sometimes begin with a dollar sign and sometimes they are native to PowerShell. Any alias that is native to PowerShell is not preceded by a dollar sign ($); for example, the alias for the Add-PSSnapin cmdlet is asnp, which is easy to remember if you think of "Add snap." The PowerShell one-liner that turns a regular PowerShell session into a SharePoint Management Shell is as easy as asnp *SharePoint*—provided that the PowerShell session was open administratively.

Aliases that are not native to PowerShell have a dollar sign preceding them. For example, $devdash, $webApp, and $ssa are all manually created aliases and only persistent in the current session; whereas native aliases are part of PowerShell and they persist from session to session. When creating an alias to be used only in the session or in scripts, I try to keep the aliases as short as possible and as descriptive as possible, with descriptiveness being most important; but not the ruler of all things. Following this logic, a good alias for SharePoint Search Service application is $ssa.

To create an alias all you need to do is type something like this:

```
$x = 1
$x = a
$x = a1
```

After you typed each of these lines with $x and then pressed Enter, you would've seen that the alias changes. You may already know all of this and it is old hat to you; but to someone who has not had much exposure to PowerShell, this is hopefully good stuff. This leads me to my next point: you may already know that you can put PowerShell cmdlets in variables. When you start analyzing SharePoint scripts and writing your own scripts, you'll put PowerShell cmdlets in variables.

Verb-Noun

PowerShell cmdlets are always in verb-noun format. When IT pros talk about PowerShell cmdlets, they usually do not pronounce they hyphen. So if a SharePoint professional was asking you to run Clear-SPLoglevel to reset the logging level across the entire farm back to the default settings, she would probably say, "Run clear sploglevel," and you would type Clear-SpLoglevel. This action would set the trace severity property back to its default values.

You would need to return logging to normal after you had previously set it to "VerboseEx" using Set-SPLogLevel –traceseverity VerboseEx. VerboseEx is used in troubleshooting issues within SharePoint and it turns the logging up as high as it will possibly go. This causes the ULS logs to grow, exponentially in size, so you don't want to leave your farm at this level.

All PowerShell cmdlets Are Objects

An object is something that has methods and properties. The methods allow you to administer the object and the properties tell you things about the object. Sometimes you can set the properties and other times you cannot set the properties; but rather can only read or get the property. No matter what, you can query information from the objects using PowerShell that isn't readily available or apparent using the GUI.

Some PowerShell objects have more properties than others do. Often, the properties in one object easily relate to the properties in other cmdlets. The main thing is to understand that PowerShell objects have information inside them in the form of properties and these objects have methods that can be used to update these properties.

Running Administratively and the SharePoint Management Console

When working with the SharePoint management console on a SharePoint server, you should always make sure that you're in a console that is open administratively. That is, if you look at the title of the window, it says: Administrator: SharePoint 2013 Management Shell and not SharePoint 2013 Management Shell. The reason you want to be open administratively is so that you never run into any blocking issues, err things that keep your code from running, due to not being open administratively, after all, you're using this SharePoint Management Shell to administer SharePoint.

In order to ensure that the PowerShell is open administratively, take a look at its advanced properties and double check the shortcut opens administratively. If it doesn't, then check the box to run as an administrator. In Figure 2-1, the SharePoint admin has already right-clicked on the shortcut and changed the advanced properties to "Run as administrator".

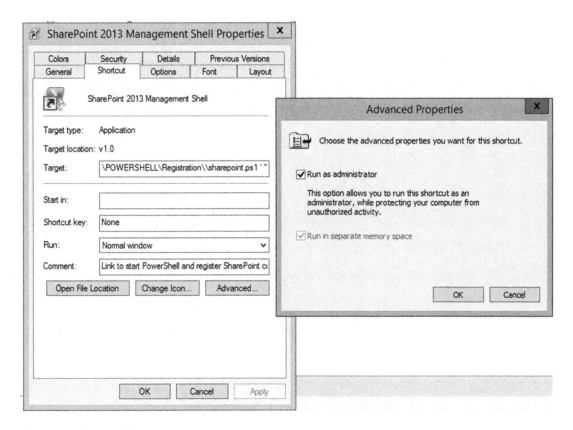

Figure 2-1. *Run as administrator*

Variable Instantiation

When you begin administrating SharePoint using PowerShell, you have to get objects into variables so that you can manipulate the property, or possibly add a property. Publishing Infrastructure is one of those areas where you must create a value inside the property of the web application named properties. This is required in whichever web application where you'll be enabling publishing. The Properties property is a hashtable type of property, so it can hold more than one value. When you use the AutoSPInstaller to install SharePoint, it automatically set's the super user and super reader accounts that are used by the publishing infrastructure. Before the days of AutoSPInstaller, this used to be done using the stsadm command and it is still possible to use that command; but it is easier to set the properties using PowerShell. It is also a lot easier to verify the properties of the web app have been set using PowerShell.

The manual code used to set the super user and super reader accounts is as follows:

```
$wa = Get-SPWebApplication -Identity "<WebApplication>"
$wa.Properties["portalsuperuseraccount"] = "<SuperUser>"
$wa.Properties["portalsuperreaderaccount"] = "<SuperReader>"
$wa.Update()
```

You can query the web application by first instantiating the web application object, with all of its properties into a variable named $wa, by running get-spwebapplication to get the URL of one of the web apps to query and instantiate. Figure 2-2 shows the web application being instantiated into a variable named $wa, and then we used a thing called *dot sourcing* to drive into the properties of the web application.

Figure 2-2. *Properties exist because they are returned*

When we ran the dot source $wa.Properties.portalsuperuseraccount it returned the value that we had replaced <SuperUser> with in the preceding code example. If we hadn't used the AutoSPInstaller to install our SharePoint farm and create a web application, this process would need to be performed manually. And, if you build a farm with AutoSPInstaller and then create additional web applications, you'll need to create the portalsuperuseraccount and portalsuperreaderaccount in order for the publishing cache to perform correctly.

In Figure 2-2, we asked PowerShell to show us the Members of the Properties property, which is one of the places that we noticed that what is returned is a hashtable. We can see that in the .NET typename of System.Collection.Hashtable. In Figure 2-3, we used dot sourcing to expand the members of the Properties hashtable by typing:

```
$wa.Properties
```

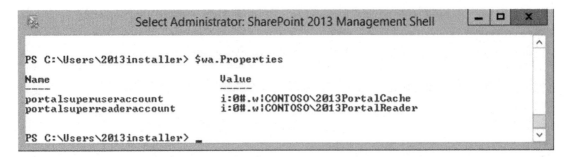

Figure 2-3. *Dot sourcing the properties parameter*

The web application object returned by Get-SPWebApplication is instantiated into the variable $wa. Then once we have the web application instantiated into the variable, we can query the properties. This would be the same as running (Get-SPWebApplication `http://portal.contoso.com`).Properties, as shown in Figure 2-4.

```
PS C:\Users\2013installer> (Get-SPWebApplication http://portal.contoso.com).Prop
erties

Name                            Value
----                            -----
portalsuperuseraccount          i:0#.w|CONTOSO\2013PortalCache
portalsuperreaderaccount        i:0#.w|CONTOSO\2013PortalReader

PS C:\Users\2013installer> _
```

Figure 2-4. *Values of the web application properties*

Once, we have the property portalsuperuseraccount and portalsuperreaderaccount returning the values that we need, we have to burn them in. We have to update the property. This is where the methods of the PowerShell object come into play. Since we are updating the object itself, we'll use the method named Update. We determined that this method existed by instantiating the web application to a variable and then we piped (|) that to Get-Member using the alias for Get-Member, which is gm. This is the code:

```
$wa | gm
```

Figure 2-5 shows partial output of running that code. You can see the update method second from the bottom in the partial screenshot of Figure 2-5.

```
Select Administrator: SharePoint 2013 Management Shell       _ □ X

PS C:\Users\2013installer> $wa | gm


   TypeName: Microsoft.SharePoint.Administration.SPWebApplication

Name                                          MemberType      Definition
----                                          ----------      ----------
AddBackupObjects                              Method          void Add...
AddMigrateUserToClaimsPolicy                  Method          void Add...
Clone                                         Method          System.O...
CurrentUserIgnoreThrottle                     Method          bool Cur...
Delete                                        Method          void Del...
EnsureDefaultJobs                             Method          void Ens...
Equals                                        Method          bool Equ...
GetChild                                      Method          T GetChi...
GetDeletedSites                               Method          Microsof...
GetHashCode                                   Method          int GetH...
GetIisSettingsWithFallback                    Method          Microsof...
GetListItemLastModifiedDates                  Method          Microsof...
GetMappedPage                                 Method          string G...
GetObjectData                                 Method          void Get...
GetResponseUri                                Method          uri GetR...
GetSecurityTokenServiceEndPointAddress        Method          uri GetS...
GetSelfServiceCreationPageUrl                 Method          string G...
GetType                                       Method          type Get...
GrantAccessToProcessIdentity                  Method          void Gra...
Invalidate                                    Method          void Inv...
IsUnthrottledPrivilegedOperationsAllowed      Method          bool IsU...
IsUserLicensedForEntity                       Method          bool IsU...
Migrate                                       Method          void Mig...
MigrateUsers                                  Method          void Mig...
MigrateUsersToClaims                          Method          bool Mig...
OnAbort                                       Method          bool OnA...
OnBackup                                      Method          bool OnB...
OnBackupComplete                              Method          bool OnB...
OnPostRestore                                 Method          bool OnP...
OnPrepareBackup                               Method          bool OnP...
OnPreRestore                                  Method          bool OnP...
OnRestore                                     Method          bool OnR...
Provision                                     Method          void Pro...
ProvisionGlobally                             Method          void Pro...
QueryFeatures                                 Method          Microsof...
RenameApplicationPool                         Method          void Ren...
RequireDynamicCanary                          Method          bool Req...
SelfServiceCreate                             Method          Microsof...
SetDailyUnthrottledPrivilegedOperationWindow  Method          void Set...
SetRequireDynamicCanary                       Method          void Set...
ToString                                      Method          string T...
Uncache                                       Method          void Unc...
Unprovision                                   Method          void Unp...
UnprovisionGlobally                           Method          void Unp...
Update                                        Method          void Upd...
UpdateCredentials                             Method          void Upd...
```

Figure 2-5. Get-SPWebApplication http://portal.contoso.com | gm

Objects as a Form of Troubleshooting

When you're experiencing issues in SharePoint, PowerShell is your friend. Modifying the file system directly without the use of a wsp file is your enemy. There are numerous things that you can do with PowerShell that you cannot do within the GUI, in the newer versions of SharePoint. For example, starting with SharePoint 2013, you can only change your search topology via PowerShell. In an upcoming chapter, we'll look at how this is done.

PowerShell is a troubleshooting tool that is often overlooked. It is through PowerShell that most of the higher-level administration tasks are performed; so, it is through PowerShell that the admin troubleshoots whether these changes were made or where certain settings are configured. For Example,

Search Performance levels are set using PowerShell in SharePoint 2013 and 2016 and you use Get-SPEnterpriseSearchService to find the PerformanceLevel. By default, the performance level is set at Reduced, as you can see in Figure 2-6.

Figure 2-6. *Using PowerShell to query search settings*

When looking at the properties and methods of PowerShell objects in the SharePoint Management Shell, the point that I'm trying to make is that they can tell you things at a glance that you may have to open several different GUI-based windows to see, assuming that all the information could be seen in the GUI. For example, in the case of the Enterprise Search Service cmdlet that we just ran, it showed us information that we would need to open Central Administration outgoing mail settings, services on server, and the Windows operating system services console. With PowerShell, we could see the email alias shows that it is sending mail aliased as SharePoint@contoso.com. The Windows service named SharePoint Server Search 15 (OSearch15) is running under Contoso\2013SearchSvc, the service is online, so there is no need to open the services console (services.msc) or the services on server page in Central Administration. We also see that the service is showing online.

Now, this might be old hat for you, and maybe the next part of this is just the same. But what if you're wondering about the timer jobs that are associated with search and were wondering when they last run, how would you go about getting them? Well, one way is to run a cool Get-SPTimerJob cmdlet that looks for the word search maybe. But would you get them all? The answer is "it depends." It depends on how you structured that get-sptimerjob one-liner. Here's a one-liner that will give you all the timer jobs associated with search and when they last ran.

```
(Get-SPEnterpriseSearchService).jobdefinitions | ft name, lastruntime
```

As you can see in Figure 2-7, for some reason the Software Quality Metrics reporting for Search has not yet ran. This might be because it might be disabled, or perhaps there is something else at play. It also looks like the Spelling Customizations Upgrade for.... hasn't run in a while. Using the get-member command, we can pipe (Get-SPEnterpriseSearchService).jobdefinitions to Get-Member like this:

```
(Get-SPEnterpriseSearchService).jobdefinitions |Get-Member
```

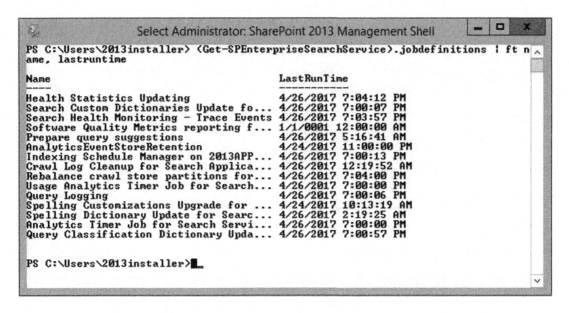

Figure 2-7. Last run time of 01/01/0001 midnight means never

This returns all the methods and properties for each job. This causes your screen to scroll and you can stop that scrolling by pressing Ctrl+C at the same time, so control key and C key together. We then notice that one of the properties is IsDisabled. Running this PowerShell, we can see the results:

```
(Get-SPEnterpriseSearchService).jobdefinitions | ft name, isdisabled
```

In Figure 2-8, it's obvious that the Spelling Customizations Upgrade for Search Application<GUID> is disabled and there must be another reason that the other job named Software Quality something or other has not ran. Perhaps it is weekly or monthly, as this is a new farm and a brand-new search service application. Are you starting to see the way that PowerShell can help you troubleshoot? I hope you said yes, or at least a half-hearted "sorta."

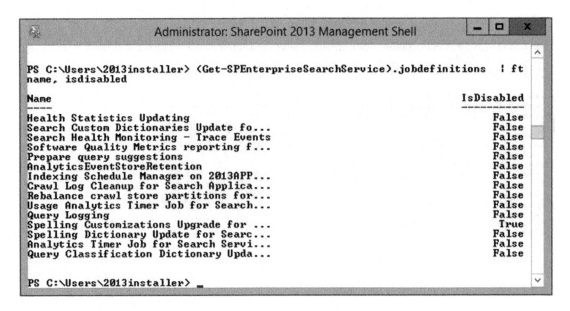

Figure 2-8. *Spelling customization is disabled but why hasn't software...ran*

There are operators in PowerShell that let us sort and query streams of objects in the pipeline. When we run a cmdlet like (Get-SPEnterpriseSearchService).jobdefinitions, it returns a stream of objects in the pipeline. We can use the where-object cmdlet which is aliased with a ? mark, to query the name field, as follows:

```
(Get-SPEnterpriseSearchService).jobdefinitions | ? {$_.Name -like "Software quality metrics*"}
```

In Figure 2-9, we see this code in action and that the reason the date shows as if the job never ran is because the job is weekly and isn't set to run until Saturday. So, with this farm being just built, a "never ran" date makes sense. Whenever you see 1/1/0001 12:00:00 AM, this means the job has not ran.

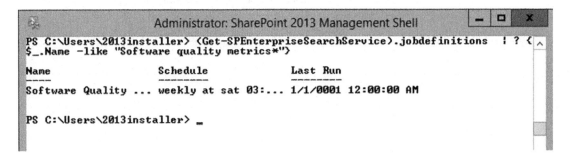

Figure 2-9. *Weekly job yet to run*

The key takeaway here is that PowerShell is a really great troubleshooting tool and to understand that we didn't cover everything there is to learn about PowerShell. There are some really good resources online and some great books on PowerShell. Don Jones's PowerShell in a month of lunches is a great series of YouTube videos that you can watch in order. Granted, while they do not cover anything within the SharePoint arena, they do cover a lot of things that we didn't go over.

Another key takeaway here, is that there are usually a lot more properties that are waiting for you inside of any given object. Take the Get- SPEnterpriseSearchService cmdlet; for example, it has way more than six properties. If you piped it to get-member, you already know that there are more than the default six properties.

In fact, Get-member is your best friend, when it comes to using PowerShell as a troubleshooting tool. You can take any cmdlet and pipe it to the Get-Member cmdlet to find out all sorts of things. Make sure to include any required parameters, unless you would like to be prompted for them, the way I was prompted in Figure 2-10.

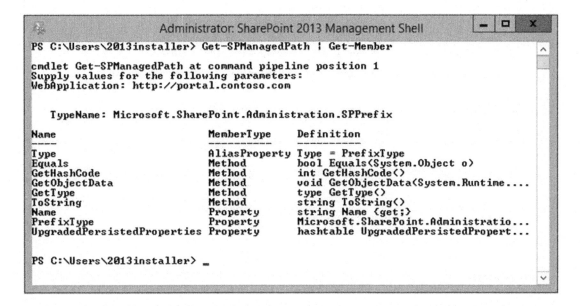

Figure 2-10. *Sometimes parameters are required*

Often, cmdlets have required parameters. Lucky for us, PowerShell has a built in help system. And just like the Get-Member cmdlet, the Get-Help cmdlet works with any cmdlet. The only difference is that you do not pipe the cmdlet you're seeking help for to the Get-Help cmdlet. Instead, you just run the get-help cmdlet with whichever cmdlet you want. For example, if you wanted to get help on the cmdlet Get-SPWebApplication, you would only need to type:

```
Get-Help Get-SPWebApplication
```

What happens next is that PowerShell kicks out the basic help information for Get-SPWebApplication. Figure 2-11 shows the outcome of the Get-Help Get-SPWebApplication one-liner.

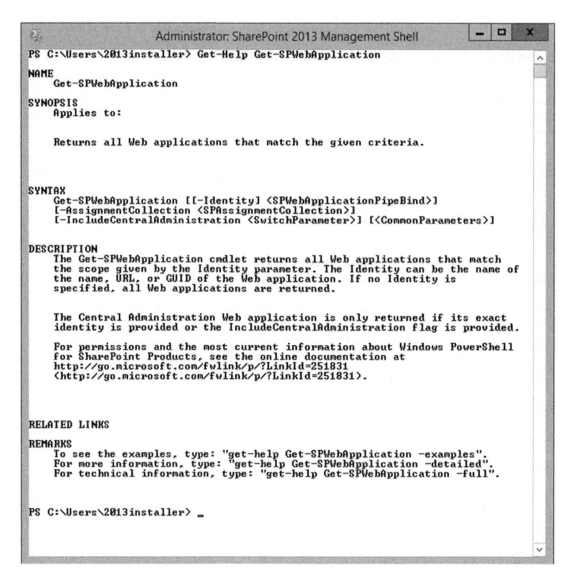

Figure 2-11. Getting help on a cmdlet

Looking at the syntax, we can tell right away that the data required for the –Identity parameter is not required and that even the –Identity parameter itself is not required. We can also see that the rest of the parameters are not required but are optional. We can also tell that if either of the optional parameters are used that they have a mandatory value that must follow. For example, notice that the –Identity parameter has brackets surrounding it, like this: [-Identity]. That means that this parameter is optional, the next set of brackets around the datatype and the parameter name tells us that the value of the datatype is also optional. The value for the type of data that the Identity parameter takes is called SPWebApplicationPipeBind. This tells you that you can pass this value into other cmdlets via the pipe method.

At the bottom of Figure 2-11, we can use some of the common parameters, such as –examples, –detailed, and –full. When we ran Get-Help Get-SPWebApplication –full, we opted to leave out any of the parameters and just go with one of the common parameters of Get-Help command, -full. The resulting screen revealed a lot more information.

Avoiding Scrolling Truncation

Scrolling truncation is not the formal term for loosing information that scrolled into the SharePoint Management Shell. Sometimes, the results of a PowerShell one-liner generate more than the default 300 lines that the Management Shell window allows in its buffer. This is why it is a good idea to modify that value. In Figure 2-12, you can see that we've right-clicked the title bar of the PowerShell window, scrolled down to defaults, and navigated to the Console Window Properties' Layout tab. The buffer is defaulted to 300 lines.

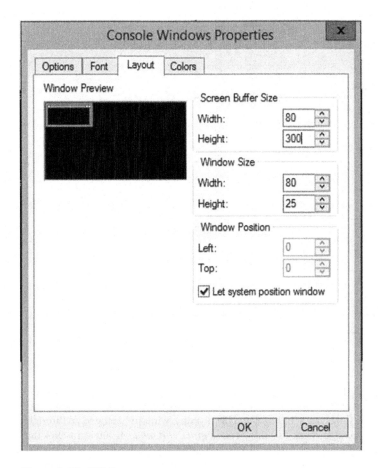

Figure 2-12. *300 lines*

After we modify the buffer to a higher number—let's say 3000 to 5000 lines, the problem with not being able to avoid scrolling truncation should mostly disappear. I say "mostly" because even with 5000 lines, there are still many PowerShell one-liners that scroll outside of this buffer range. For example, if you ran Get-ChildItem –recurse from the root of your C:\ drive, this would still be subject to the buffer limit. In Figure 2-13, we can see the modification for the increase in buffer size.

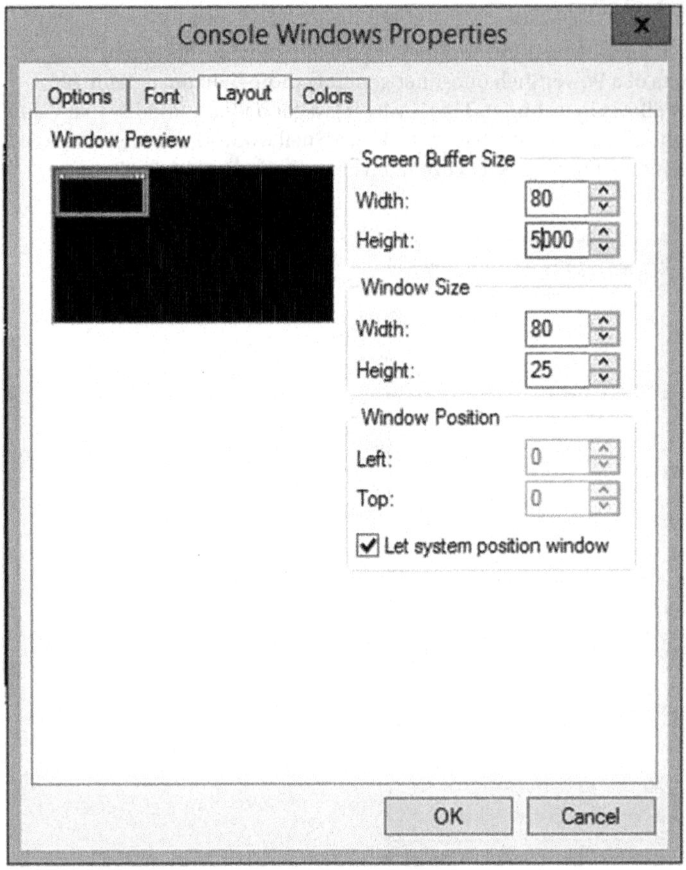

Figure 2-13. *5000 lines*

Now that we've pretty much stopped the issue of cmdlet output scrolling off the screen, let's make it easy to copy and paste information out of our command line. Have you ever wondered why on some servers you can just click down, drag across, and select the sections you'd like to copy, without having to go through the menu system? The reason that was possible is due to a thing called *quick edit mode*. If you right-click the title bar again, select the default; you can then check the Quick Edit box. After you've done it for the Default setting or the Properties setting, do it for the other setting. Just right-click the title bar, click Defaults, then in the Options tab, click Quick Edit, as shown in Figure 2-14.

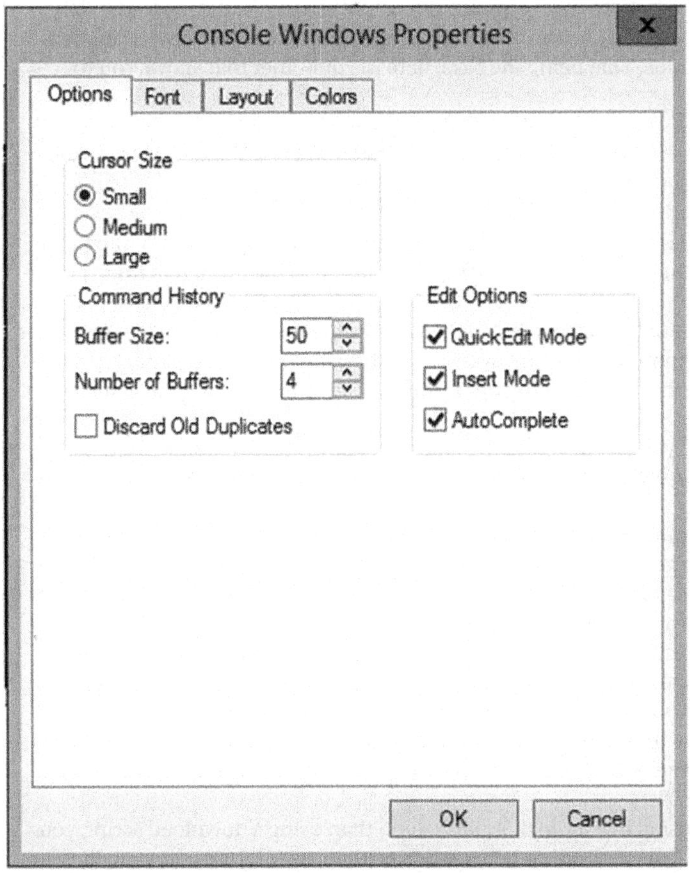

Figure 2-14. *Quick Edit Mode*

With quick edit mode enabled and the buffer at 5000 lines, you should be good to go for most tasks. There may be situations where 5000 lines are not enough. I wouldn't recommend increasing it too much higher because this buffer exists in memory, unless you have all sorts of memory available. Instead what you could do is push the output to a file, using the out-file cmdlet.

Enumerating Sites

There will be times when you are auditing a new environment, or maybe your boss asks you how many sites there are in your SharePoint farm. This is where you'll more than likely be glad that you increased the buffer and you'll appreciate the ability to easily copy the results. It might be a great candidate for the out-file cmdlet, too.

You can use PowerShell to get all the sites and subsites from all of the various site collections in all of the web applications in your farm. If you notice, I said that backwards, on purpose. As your boss, probably doesn't know the difference between his page and a site collection. Another way to think of this is that a site collection and a subsite or subweb are probably synonymous in your bosses mind, and no different from a web application. Nothing could be further from the truth. When troubleshooting SharePoint, it is important to understand the stacking order of site topologies.

Web applications house numerous databases. Site collections can only span one database and they are housed inside of databases. Databases can house numerous site collections. Site collections can have hundreds of thousands of sites and subsites. That being the case, here is a one-liner that allows you to enumerate all the sites in your farm:

```
Get-SPWebApplication | Get-SPSite -Limit All | Get-SPWeb -Limit All | FT URL -auto -wrap |
Out-File c:\TroubleShooting\AllSites.txt
```

The reason for the –auto and –wrap is to tell PowerShell not to truncate anything and just wrap to the next line if need be. The reason for the Out-File cmdlet is to take a precaution in the event that there are more than 5000 lines of site URL's.

We've cruised through some PowerShell concepts and looked at how to utilize PowerShell to query the object model and interrogate it for information that is not available in the GUI. Let's take a gander at some scripting to build a farm, as well as a method for speeding up the build time by eliminating the need to download the binaries on each server.

If you use an offline install method, you can decrease the amount of time that is required for the prerequisite installer. You can either manually download the prerequisite files to a network share or use a PowerShell script to download the files.

Craig Lussier has written an awesome set of scripts that make performing an offline install of the 2013 prerequisites much easier. You can get a copy of the SharePoint 2013 offline prerequisite install script at https://gallery.technet.microsoft.com/DownloadInstall-SharePoint-e6df9eb8. There are instructions on how to use Craig's script at that site. Essentially the process boils down to running three different scripts. One of the scripts performs the step of getting the Windows features on the server and another script downloads the prerequisites to the folder you specify. Finally, there is a script that kicks off the prerequisiteinstaller.exe. These scripts assume you're working with a server running Windows Server 2012 R2. The key is to make sure you give the scripts the correct locations. Make sure to give the prerequisites download script the location shown in Figure 2-16 and make sure to give the installer script the location shown in Figure 2-15.

If you want to perform the offline install in a more manual fashion than using a download script, you can download each of the prerequisites from the Internet on a machine that has Internet connectivity. The 2013 prerequisites are available for download at the following locations:

Microsoft SQL Server 2008 R2 SP1 Native Client: http://download.microsoft.com/download/9/1/3/9138773A-505D-43E2-AC08-9A77E1E0490B/1033/x64/sqlncli.msi

Microsoft Sync Framework Runtime v1.0 SP1 (x64): http://download.microsoft.com/download/E/0/0/E0060D8F-2354-4871-9596-DC78538799CC/Synchronization.msi

Windows Server App Fabric: http://download.microsoft.com/download/A/6/7/A678AB47-496B-4907-B3D4-0A2D280A13C0/WindowsServerAppFabricSetup_x64.exe

Cumulative Update Package 1 for Microsoft AppFabric 1.1 for Windows Server (KB2671763): http://download.microsoft.com/download/7/B/5/7B51D8D1-20FD-4BF0-87C7-4714F5A1C313/AppFabric1.1-RTM-KB2671763-x64-ENU.exe

Windows Identity Foundation (KB974405): http://download.microsoft.com/download/D/7/2/D72FD747-69B6-40B7-875B-C2B40A6B2BDD/Windows6.1-KB974405-x64.msu

Microsoft Identity Extensions: http://download.microsoft.com/download/0/1/D/01D06854-CA0C-46F1-ADBA-EBF86010DCC6/rtm/MicrosoftIdentityExtensions-64.msi

Microsoft Information Protection and Control Client: http://download.microsoft.com/download/9/1/D/91DA8796-BE1D-46AF-8489-663AB7811517/setup_msipc_x64.msi

Microsoft WCF Data Services 5.0: http://download.microsoft.com/download/8/F/9/8F93DBBD-896B-4760-AC81-646F61363A6D/WcfDataServices.exe

Microsoft WCF Data Services 5.6 (rename this download to WcfDataServices56.exe): http://download.microsoft.com/download/1/C/A/1CAA41C7-88B9-42D6-9E11-3C655656DAB1/WcfDataServices.exe

If you're not using Craig Lussier's scripts, then after you've downloaded all of the prerequisites, you can use the SharePoint media and these steps to install them on SharePoint 2013:

Step 1

First, make sure the Windows Server Media is in the location specified by the -Source parameter and that the source location parameter is pointing to the correct folder on your system, else update this parameter in your script for the location relative to your environment. For example, on my server, the Windows CD was mounted to the E:\ drive, so this meant that the side-by-side folder was located inside the sources folder at E:\sources\sxs.

Then, once you're good to go with the path for step 1, execute the following two lines of code:

```
Import-Module ServerManager
Add-WindowsFeature Net-Framework-Features,Web-Server,Web-WebServer,Web-Common-
Http,Web-Static-Content,Web-Default-Doc,Web-Dir-Browsing,Web-Http-Errors,Web-App-
Dev,Web-Asp-Net,Web-Net-Ext,Web-ISAPI-Ext,Web-ISAPI-Filter,Web-Health,Web-Http-
Logging,Web-Log-Libraries,Web-Request-Monitor,Web-Http-Tracing,Web-Security,Web-
Basic-Auth,Web-Windows-Auth,Web-Filtering,Web-Digest-Auth,Web-Performance,Web-Stat-
Compression,Web-Dyn-Compression,Web-Mgmt-Tools,Web-Mgmt-Console,Web-Mgmt-Compat,Web-
Metabase,Application-Server,AS-Web-Support,AS-TCP-Port-Sharing,AS-WAS-Support,
AS-HTTP-Activation,AS-TCP-Activation,AS-Named-Pipes,AS-Net-Framework,WAS,WAS-Process-
Model,WAS-NET-Environment,WAS-Config-APIs,Web-Lgcy-Scripting,Windows-Identity-
Foundation,Server-Media-Foundation,Xps-Viewer -Source E:\sources\sxs
```

Depending on the state of your server before your ran step 1, you may or may not be prompted to restart. Please restart even if you are not prompted to restart. After your server comes back online, repeat step 1 on any of the remaining servers in your farm not including your SQL server.

Step 2

Make sure that the $SharePoint2013Path variable points to the correct location on your server. The location is shown in Figure 2-15.

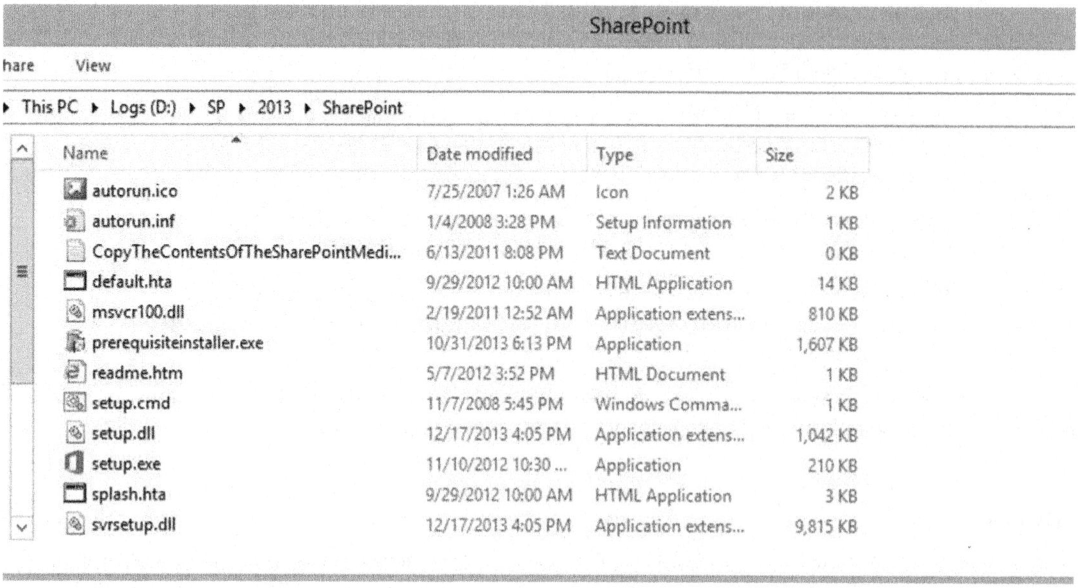

SharePoint

hare   View

▸ This PC ▸ Logs (D:) ▸ SP ▸ 2013 ▸ SharePoint

Name	Date modified	Type	Size
autorun.ico	7/25/2007 1:26 AM	Icon	2 KB
autorun.inf	1/4/2008 3:28 PM	Setup Information	1 KB
CopyTheContentsOfTheSharePointMedi...	6/13/2011 8:08 PM	Text Document	0 KB
default.hta	9/29/2012 10:00 AM	HTML Application	14 KB
msvcr100.dll	2/19/2011 12:52 AM	Application extens...	810 KB
prerequisiteinstaller.exe	10/31/2013 6:13 PM	Application	1,607 KB
readme.htm	5/7/2012 3:52 PM	HTML Document	1 KB
setup.cmd	11/7/2008 5:45 PM	Windows Comma...	1 KB
setup.dll	12/17/2013 4:05 PM	Application extens...	1,042 KB
setup.exe	11/10/2012 10:30 ...	Application	210 KB
splash.hta	9/29/2012 10:00 AM	HTML Application	3 KB
svrsetup.dll	12/17/2013 4:05 PM	Application extens...	9,815 KB

Figure 2-15. *Location of SharePoint binaries*

Before running step 2, make sure all the prerequisites are downloaded saved in the PrerequisiteInstallerFiles folder that is located inside of the folder that hold the SharePoint binaries. Figure 2-16 shows the location within the file system in which to store the prerequisites.

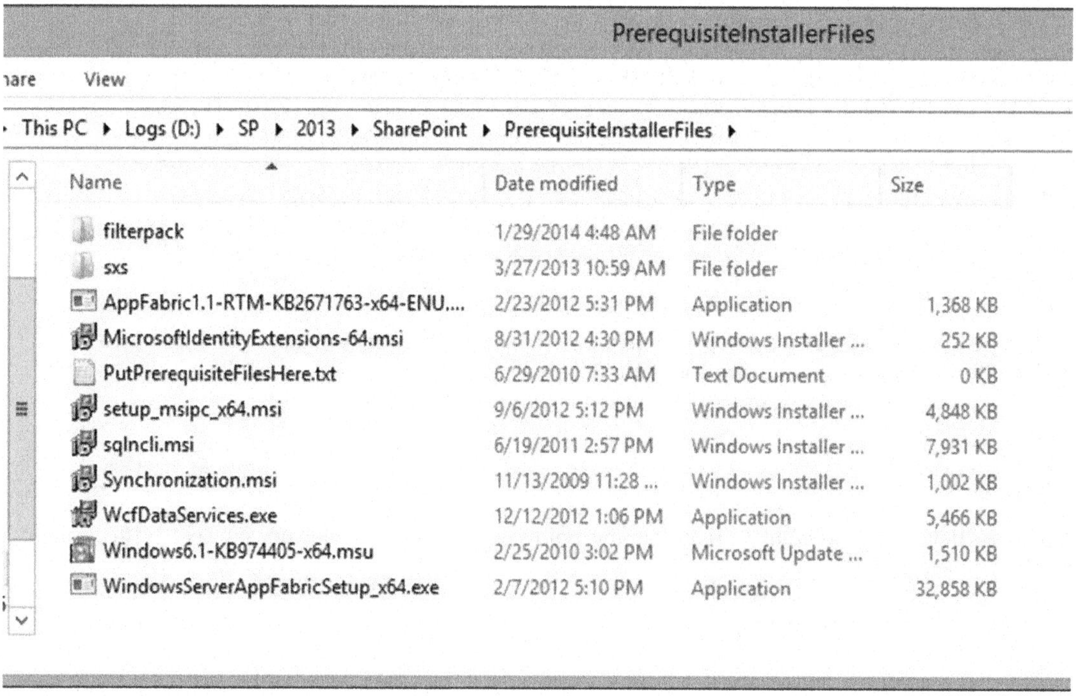

PrerequisiteInstallerFiles

ıare   View

▸ This PC ▸ Logs (D:) ▸ SP ▸ 2013 ▸ SharePoint ▸ PrerequisiteInstallerFiles ▸

Name	Date modified	Type	Size
filterpack	1/29/2014 4:48 AM	File folder	
sxs	3/27/2013 10:59 AM	File folder	
AppFabric1.1-RTM-KB2671763-x64-ENU....	2/23/2012 5:31 PM	Application	1,368 KB
MicrosoftIdentityExtensions-64.msi	8/31/2012 4:30 PM	Windows Installer ...	252 KB
PutPrerequisiteFilesHere.txt	6/29/2010 7:33 AM	Text Document	0 KB
setup_msipc_x64.msi	9/6/2012 5:12 PM	Windows Installer ...	4,848 KB
sqlncli.msi	6/19/2011 2:57 PM	Windows Installer ...	7,931 KB
Synchronization.msi	11/13/2009 11:28 ...	Windows Installer ...	1,002 KB
WcfDataServices.exe	12/12/2012 1:06 PM	Application	5,466 KB
Windows6.1-KB974405-x64.msu	2/25/2010 3:02 PM	Microsoft Update ...	1,510 KB
WindowsServerAppFabricSetup_x64.exe	2/7/2012 5:10 PM	Application	32,858 KB

Figure 2-16. *SharePoint prerequisites have their own folder*

After you've verified that you're pointing to the directory that holds your SharePoint binaries; and, that the prerequisites folder has all of the prerequisite installer files stored inside, you are ready to run step 2. To run step 2, just copy and paste the following two lines of code into a SharePoint Management Shell.

```
$SharePoint2013Path = "C:\AutoSPInstaller\SP\2013\SharePoint"

Start-Process "$SharePoint2013Path\PrerequisiteInstaller.exe" –ArgumentList
"/SQLNCli:$SharePoint2013Path\PrerequisiteInstallerFiles\sqlncli.msi
/IDFX:$SharePoint2013Path\PrerequisiteInstallerFiles\Windows6.1-KB974405-x64.msu
/IDFX11:$SharePoint2013Path\PrerequisiteInstallerFiles\MicrosoftIdentityExtensions-64.msi /
Sync:$SharePoint2013Path\PrerequisiteInstallerFiles\Synchronization.msi
/AppFabric:$SharePoint2013Path\PrerequisiteInstallerFiles\WindowsServerAppFabricSetup_x64.exe
/KB2671763:$SharePoint2013Path\PrerequisiteInstallerFiles\AppFabric1.1-RTM-KB2671763-x64-
ENU.exe /MSIPCClient:$SharePoint2013Path\PrerequisiteInstallerFiles\setup_msipc_x64.msi
/WCFDataServices:$SharePoint2013Path\PrerequisiteInstallerFiles\WcfDataServices.exe
/WCFDataServices56:$SharePoint2013Path\PrerequisiteInstallerFiles\WcfDataServices56.exe"
```

After you have completed step 2, the prerequisites are installed, and you're ready to run the setup.exe file, if you're building a farm with PowerShell. If you're using AutoSPInstaller, you are ready to run the setup.exe file on each server, just to save time. AutoSPInstaller runs setup automatically if you forget one of the servers.

Running setup is as simple as right-clicking the file, clicking Run As Administrator, and then supplying the SharePoint license key, when prompted along with a few more selections, such as the type of farm your building and file locations. You can see why an automated process such as AutoSPInstaller provides a more standardized build and gives a firmer foundation with less room for manual deviations from the standard build.

PowerShell Script to Create Central Administration

The lines used to create the configuration database and the database to house the Central Administration site and its content are fairly straightforward. Read through each line of code and then after you're done, we'll talk about what's happening in each section. The code you see here would be put into a ps1 file and run from the SharePoint Management Shell, as follows.

```
Set-ExecutionPolicy Unrestricted
Add-PSSnapin microsoft.sharepoint.powershell -ErrorAction SilentlyContinue
Write-Host "When prompted for credentials, give SharePoint the farm account, not the install
account that you are signed in with, then provide the passphrase, note: you will not be
prompted for passPhrase if it is baked into the script" -ForegroundColor green
New-SPConfigurationDatabase -DatabaseName 2013_SharePoint_Config -DatabaseServer
SharePointAlias -Passphrase (ConvertTo-SecureString "1Qaz2Wsx3Edc4Rfv"
-AsPlainText -Force) -FarmCredentials (Get-Credential) -AdministrationContentDatabaseName
2013_SharePoint_CentralAdmin_Content -SkipRegisterAsDistributedCacheHost
$CAPort = 5000
$CAAuth = "NTLM"
Install-SPHelpCollection -All
Initialize-SPResourceSecurity
Install-SPService
Install-SPFeature -AllExistingFeatures
New-SPCentralAdministration -Port $CAPort -WindowsAuthProvider $CAAuth
Install-SPApplicationContent
```

```
New-ItemProperty HKLM:\System\CurrentControlSet\Control\Lsa -Name "DisableLoopbackCheck"
-value "1" -PropertyType dword
## Note you might not have an SCP in your domain, so you may want to exclude the next two lines ##
$ServiceConnectionPoint = get-SPTopologyServiceApplication | select URI
Set-SPFarmConfig -ServiceConnectionPointBindingInformation $ServiceConnectionPoint -Confirm: $False
Write-Host "Make sure to register the managed accounts for Service Apps and for Web Content
before continuing with the 2013Install script" –ForegroundColor Green -BackgroundColor Yellow
```

This code sample, created a 2013 farm using an alias of SharePoint SQL; and if the alias was not in place, the code failed with all sorts of red lines. If you were creating a SharePoint 2010 farm, you would just need to remove the –SkipRegisterAsDistributedCacheHost parameter.

One of the key settings in a good build is the SQL Alias. The reason for this best practice is very simple. It is so that the entire farm is portable. For example, if the SQL server had a "virtual heart attack" and became a "smoking hole in the ground," creating the farm using an alias would allow you to transfer the SQL database logins to a new SQL server, move the database files to the new SQL server, and begin SharePoint operations. Whereas, if you hadn't used a SQL Alias, you would only be able to reattach the content databases and a few of the SharePoint Service applications. In other words, without an alias, you'd be staring down the barrel of the proverbial "Time to Rebuild" Shotgun.

There are a basically two different ways to create the SQL Alias. When you create a farm using the AutoSPInstaller, the script creates the SQL alias for you automatically via PowerShell. If you are going to create a farm using manual PowerShell scripts, you'll have to create this alias before running the scripts that create the configuration database and Central Administration. Or, you have to include scripting to create the alias within your scripts before the databases get created. The only data you need to create the Alias is the Alias name, the name of the Database server, and if using a named instance, then the name of the named instance and any non-standard port.

You can add this bit of PowerShell to create the SQL Alias, or you can create it manually. We'll look at creating the alias manually in one of the exercises at the end of the chapter. This script creates a 64-bit and a 32-bit SQL Alias on the server. Run this script on all servers in your SharePoint farm before running the psconfig to create the configuration database or create the Alias manually with the clicong.exe utility.

```
$SQLAlias = "SQLALIASNAME"
 $sqlserver = "SQLservername\instancename,1433"

Write-Host "Creating x64 SQL Alias"
New-Item -path HKLM:SOFTWARE\Microsoft\MSSQLServer\Client\ConnectTo
 New-ItemProperty HKLM:SOFTWARE\Microsoft\MSSQLServer\Client\ConnectTo -name $SQLAlias
-propertytype String -value "DBMSSOCN,$sqlserver"

Write-Host "Creating 32bit SQL Alias"
New-Item -path HKLM:SOFTWARE\Wow6432Node\Microsoft\MSSQLServer\Client\ConnectTo
 Write-Host "Configured SQL Alias on the Server"
 New-ItemProperty HKLM:SOFTWARE\Wow6432Node\Microsoft\MSSQLServer\Client\ConnectTo -name
$SQLAlias -propertytype String -value "DBMSSOCN,$sqlserver"
```

The script to create the SQL alias, in its raw form, assumes you're using a named instance on a specific port. The example code assumes the default SQL port 1433 is being utilized. You can update this, as required for your environment, by changing the port number, if using a static custom port, or removing the named instance. If you are using a dynamic custom port, remove the comma and port number - ,1433. If using the default instance than leave off the instance name and only include the SQLServerName.

When you run the script, you may get a little "red puke" in the output, if the registry location already exists on your server, and you can safely ignore that message. The message looks similar to the following:

```
New-Item : A key at this path already exists
At line:1 char:9
+ New-Item <<<< -path HKLM:SOFTWARE\Microsoft\MSSQLServer\Client\ConnectTo
  + CategoryInfo      : ResourceExists: (Microsoft.Power...RegistryWrapper:RegistryWrapper)
[New-Item], IOException  + FullyQualifiedErrorId : System.IO.IOException,Microsoft.
PowerShell.Commands.NewItemCommand
```

This is due to the script does not have any try catch logic built into it and since this isn't a book on PowerShell scripting, but rather a book on troubleshooting, we won't talk about developing the try catch logic. The error message is just PowerShell's way of saying, "I didn't create the registry location because it already existed." When using PowerShell to troubleshoot, it is important to learn to understand what it is trying to say when it pukes in red.

OK, so now that we've got the SQL aliases in place, let's briefly talk about what we see this Central Administration script doing to the system. The idea behind this discussion is to further your knowledge of PowerShell and of creating a farm with PowerShell. This knowledge aids in troubleshooting; since you have something to compare against when things go wrong and because your build is standardized, it's even easier to see where things have deviated. The hard part is determining why they've deviated.

If you're already a master or mistress at creating farms using PowerShell, and/or AutoSPInstaller, then you should skip ahead to the section entitled Component Services.

The first line tells PowerShell set the execution policy on the server to unrestricted. This is required due to this script not being signed with a trusted certificate. You can always set the execution policy back to remote signed when you have finished, if you need too. This is a pain, though, since you might find yourself having to set the policy unrestricted to run other scripts too.

```
Set-ExecutionPolicy Unrestricted
```

The next line brings the SharePoint binaries into the game by converting the plain administrative PowerShell session into an administrative SharePoint Management Shell Session.

```
Add-PSSnapin microsoft.sharepoint.powershell -ErrorAction SilentlyContinue
```

When you run this command, you do so by putting all of the code into a text file and then renaming the text file with a ps1 extension. Then you call the code by navigating to the directory that you stored it inside and calling the ps1 file. For example you might type something like this to navigate to the directory:

```
Cd "C:\directory\"
```

Then to run the command you'd just call the PowerShell file. Assuming you named it, centralAdmin. ps1, you would call it like this:

```
C:\directory\>  .\centralAdmin.ps1
```

The purpose of the next line is simply to give some feedback text in the SharePoint Management Shell window and to give that feedback using green text with the normal window background color.

Write-Host "When prompted for credentials, give SharePoint the farm account, not the install account that you are signed in with, then provide the passphrase, note: you will not be prompted for passPhrase if it is baked into the script" -ForegroundColor green

The New-SPConfigurationDatabase creates a new configuration database for a new farm with a specific name. It sets the farm passphrase to 1Qaz2Wsx3Edc4Rfv and then it prompts the admin to enter in the credentials for the farm account, so this method is not as automated as the AutoSPInstaller. The AutoSPInstaller will not prompt you for the farm account password, as you've already input the pw into the XML file that the AutoSPInstaller utilizes. When the parameter for the Administration Content Database Name is specified, this cmdlet causes the Central Administration content database to generate.

```
New-SPConfigurationDatabase -DatabaseName 2013_SharePoint_Config -DatabaseServer
SharePointAlias -Passphrase (ConvertTo-SecureString "1Qaz2Wsx3Edc4Rfv"
-AsPlainText -Force) -FarmCredentials (Get-Credential) -AdministrationContentDatabaseName
2013_SharePoint_CentralAdmin_Content –SkipRegisterAsDistributedCacheHost
```

In the next two lines, we're setting the port number that the Central Administration site runs under and we are setting the authentication provider.

```
$CAPort = 5000
$CAAuth = "NTLM"
```

Like all PowerShell cmdlets, the get-help cmdlet reveals detailed information about each of the following lines. The Install-SPHelpCollection cmdlet installs the Help site collection files in your farm.

```
Install-SPHelpCollection -All
```

We already know that the next line enforces security for all resources, including files, folders, and registry keys

```
Initialize-SPResourceSecurity
```

The get-help cmdlet had this to say about the next line: "The Install-SPService cmdlet installs and optionally provisions service on a farm. This cmdlet installs all services, service instances, and service proxies specified in the registry on the local server computer. Use this cmdlet in a script that you build to install and deploy a SharePoint farm or to install a custom developed service." – PowerShell get-help Install-SPService

```
Install-SPService
```

The Install-SPFeature –AllExistingFeatures tells the SharePoint farm to install all the features that are present on the file system for the 14, 15, or 16 Hive, depending on which version of SharePoint you are installing. You should definitely run get-help Install-SPFeature if you are a developer, so that you can learn about the developmental power of this cmdlet. During the initial build, this line installs all the features that are present.

```
Install-SPFeature –AllExistingFeatures
```

The new Central Administration cmdlet creates the Central Administration Web application and it knows to store it in the previously created Central Administration content database, because the configuration database knows where the web application should store its site. This cmdlet runs the Central Administration site on the port we chose and uses NTLM as the authentication protocol.

```
New-SPCentralAdministration -Port $CAPort -WindowsAuthProvider $CAAuth
```

This next line copies shared application data into the web application folders.

```
Install-SPApplicationContent
```

The following line attempts to create the DisableLoopbackCheck registry value. I'll talk more about this later. If you're running the script a second time, this line generates a "red line," or what I like to call "red puke," because it doesn't check to see if the registry item exists; if the item does exist, the red puke just says that the property could not be created as it existed, or something to that affect.

```
New-ItemProperty HKLM:\System\CurrentControlSet\Control\Lsa -Name "DisableLoopbackCheck"
-value "1" -PropertyType dword
```

The following line is just a PowerShell comment that is not really needed.

```
## Note you might not have an SCP in your domain, so you may want to exclude the next two
lines ##
```

These next two lines attempt to set the Service Connection Point data if you have created a SCP for SharePoint. If you have not created a SCP the line tells you that it couldn't be created.

```
$ServiceConnectionPoint = get-SPTopologyServiceApplication | select URI
Set-SPFarmConfig -ServiceConnectionPointBindingInformation $ServiceConnectionPoint -Confirm:
$False
```

This final line reminds the admin performing the semi-automated install that she needs to register the managed accounts for the SharePoint Service Application App pool and for the service account that is used for the content application app pool, before running the script to install.

Write-Host "Make sure to register the managed accounts for Service Apps and for Web Content before continuing with the 2013Install script" –ForegroundColor Green -BackgroundColor Yellow The above PowerShell is used to display a message about creating managed accounts.

If you had opted to use AutoSPInstaller, there is far less room for non-standardization. That is, when you run the installs with these semi-manual PowerShell scripts that require some configuration, it is not as easy to standardize as it is when you use the AutoSPInstaller. You'll really see what I mean, as we discuss the PowerShell to install all the various SharePoint Service application inside the Shared Hosted Services app pool.

PowerShell Script to Create Service Applications

The PowerShell script that is used to create the SharePoint Service applications is the base of our least privileging. It creates an application pool in IIS to house the non-search service applications and it creates an application pool for search. Each application pool runs under a non-administrative user account that is not a member of any local administrative groups. The process of creating the service applications adds these accounts to the IIS_IUSRS, Performance Monitor Users, and WSS_WPG local security groups.

The script used to create the service applications is much longer than the script used for creating the configuration database and the Central Administration content database. Since the configuration database controls all sorts of things in SharePoint and is the very first database in any SharePoint farm on the planet, it's no wonder that this script to create the service applications will not work if the configuration database and the Central Administration site are not provisioned and online.

Read through each line of this script that is used in SharePoint 2010 and don't worry if some of it doesn't make sense, or if you're not sure what each part is doing, as we'll discuss each section in further detail, next.

```
#####################################################
# This script replicates most of the functionality found in the SharePoint
Products Configuration Wizard with the EXCEPTION of the USER PROFILE
SERVICE#####################################################
Add-PSSnapin Microsoft.SharePoint.PowerShell -erroraction SilentlyContinue
## Settings you may want to change ##
$databaseServerName = "SharePointSQL" #assumes you're using a SQL Alias configured with
cliconfg.exe
$searchServerName = "2010APP" #Front end Server that will run central admin, the server
you're on right now
$saAppPoolName = "SharePoint Hosted Services"
$appPoolUserName = "Contoso\2010svcapps" #This is the service application pool account it is
not the farm admin account for Timer and Central admin, sometimes calle#d the farm account,
it is not the setup account, or install account
$ssaAppPoolName = "SharePoint Search Service Application Pool"
$SearchappPoolUserName = "Contoso\2010Search"
## Service Application Service Names ##
$accesssSAName = "Access Services"
$bcsSAName = "Business Data Connectivity Service"
$excelSAName = "Excel Services Application"
$metadataSAName = "Managed Metadata Web Service"
$performancePointSAName = "PerformancePoint Service"
$searchSAName = "SharePoint Server Search"
$stateSAName = "State Service"
$secureStoreSAName = "Secure Store Service"
$usageSAName = "Usage and Health Data Collection Service"
$visioSAName = "Visio Graphics Service"
$WebAnalyticsSAName = "Web Analytics Service"
$WordAutomationSAName = "Word Automation Services"

$saAppPool = Get-SPServiceApplicationPool -Identity $saAppPoolName -EA 0
if($saAppPool -eq $null)
{
Write-Host "Creating Service Application Pool..."

$appPoolAccount = Get-SPManagedAccount -Identity $appPoolUserName -EA 0
if($appPoolAccount -eq $null)
{
Write-Host "Please supply the password for the Service Account..."
$appPoolCred = Get-Credential $appPoolUserName
$appPoolAccount = New-SPManagedAccount -Credential $appPoolCred -EA 0
}

$appPoolAccount = Get-SPManagedAccount -Identity $appPoolUserName -EA 0

if($appPoolAccount -eq $null)
{
```

```
Write-Host "Cannot create or find the managed account $appPoolUserName, please ensure the
account exists."
Exit -1
}
New-SPServiceApplicationPool -Name $saAppPoolName -Account $appPoolAccount -EA 0 > $null
}

Write-Host "Creating Usage Service and Proxy..."
$serviceInstance = Get-SPUsageService
New-SPUsageApplication -Name $usageSAName -DatabaseServer $databaseServerName -DatabaseName
"Usage" -UsageService $serviceInstance > $null

Write-Host "Creating Access Services and Proxy..."
New-SPAccessServiceApplication -Name $accesssSAName -ApplicationPool $saAppPoolName > $null
Get-SPServiceInstance | where-object {$_.TypeName -eq "Access Database Service"} | Start-
SPServiceInstance > $null

Write-Host "Creating BCS Service and Proxy..."
New-SPBusinessDataCatalogServiceApplication -Name $bcsSAName -ApplicationPool $saAppPoolName
-DatabaseServer $databaseServerName -DatabaseName "BusinessDataCatalog" > $null

Get-SPServiceInstance | where-object {$_.TypeName -eq "Business Data Connectivity Service"}
| Start-SPServiceInstance > $null

Write-Host "Creating Excel Service..."
New-SPExcelServiceApplication -name $excelSAName –ApplicationPool $saAppPoolName > $null
Set-SPExcelFileLocation -Identity "http://" -ExcelServiceApplication $excelSAName -
ExternalDataAllowed 2 -WorkbookSizeMax 10 -WarnOnDataRefresh:$true
Get-SPServiceInstance | where-object {$_.TypeName -eq "Excel Calculation Services"} | Start-
SPServiceInstance > $null

Write-Host "Creating Metadata Service and Proxy..."
New-SPMetadataServiceApplication -Name $metadataSAName -ApplicationPool $saAppPoolName
-DatabaseServer $databaseServerName -DatabaseName "Metadata" > $null
New-SPMetadataServiceApplicationProxy -Name "$metadataSAName Proxy" -DefaultProxyGroup
-ServiceApplication $metadataSAName > $null
Get-SPServiceInstance | where-object {$_.TypeName -eq "Managed Metadata Web Service"} |
Start-SPServiceInstance > $null

Write-Host "Creating Performance Point Service and Proxy..."
New-SPPerformancePointServiceApplication -Name $performancePointSAName -ApplicationPool
$saAppPoolName -DatabaseServer $databaseServerName -DatabaseName "PerformancePoint" > $null
New-SPPerformancePointServiceApplicationProxy -Default -Name "$performancePointSAName Proxy"
-ServiceApplication $performancePointSAName > $null
Get-SPServiceInstance | where-object {$_.TypeName -eq "PerformancePoint Service"} | Start-
SPServiceInstance > $null

##START SEARCH

$ssaAppPool = Get-SPServiceApplicationPool -Identity $ssaAppPoolName -EA 0
if($ssaAppPool -eq $null)
```

```
{
Write-Host "Creating Search Service Application Pool..."

$SearchappPoolAccount = Get-SPManagedAccount -Identity $SearchappPoolUserName -EA 0
if($SearchappPoolAccount -eq $null)
{
Write-Host "Please supply the password for the Service Account..."
$ssappPoolCred = Get-Credential $SearchappPoolUserName
$SearchappPoolAccount = New-SPManagedAccount -Credential $ssappPoolCred -EA 0
}

$SearchappPoolAccount = Get-SPManagedAccount -Identity $SearchappPoolUserName -EA 0

if($appPoolAccount -eq $null)
{
Write-Host "Cannot create or find the managed account $SearchappPoolUserName, please ensure
the account exists."
Exit -1
}

New-SPServiceApplicationPool -Name $ssaAppPoolName -Account $SearchappPoolAccount -EA 0 > $null

}

## Search Specifics, we are single server farm ##

$searchServerName = (Get-ChildItem env:computername).value
$serviceAppName = "Enterprise Search Services"
$searchDBName = "Search"

Write-Host "Creating Search Service and Proxy..."
Write-Host " Starting Services..."
Start-SPEnterpriseSearchServiceInstance $searchServerName
Start-SPEnterpriseSearchQueryAndSiteSettingsServiceInstance $searchServerName

Write-Host " Creating Search Application..."
$searchApp = New-SPEnterpriseSearchServiceApplication -Name $searchSAName -ApplicationPool
$ssaAppPoolName -DatabaseServer $databaseServerName -DatabaseName $searchDBName
$searchInstance = Get-SPEnterpriseSearchServiceInstance $searchServerName
 Write-Host " Creating Administration Component..."
$searchApp | Get-SPEnterpriseSearchAdministrationComponent | Set-SPEnterpriseSearchAdministr
ationComponent -SearchServiceInstance $searchInstance
 #Crawl
Write-Host " Creating Crawl Component..."
$InitialCrawlTopology = $searchApp | Get-SPEnterpriseSearchCrawlTopology -Active
$CrawlTopology = $searchApp | New-SPEnterpriseSearchCrawlTopology
$CrawlDatabase = ([array]($searchApp | Get-SPEnterpriseSearchCrawlDatabase))[0]
$CrawlComponent = New-SPEnterpriseSearchCrawlComponent -CrawlTopology $CrawlTopology
-CrawlDatabase $CrawlDatabase -SearchServiceInstance $searchInstance
$CrawlTopology | Set-SPEnterpriseSearchCrawlTopology -Active
 Write-Host -ForegroundColor white " Waiting for the old crawl topology to become inactive" -NoNewline
```

```
do {write-host -NoNewline .;Start-Sleep 6;} while ($InitialCrawlTopology.State -ne "Inactive")
$InitialCrawlTopology | Remove-SPEnterpriseSearchCrawlTopology -Confirm:$false
Write-Host
 #Query
Write-Host " Creating Query Component..."
$InitialQueryTopology = $searchApp | Get-SPEnterpriseSearchQueryTopology -Active
$QueryTopology = $searchApp | New-SPEnterpriseSearchQueryTopology -Partitions 1
$IndexPartition= (Get-SPEnterpriseSearchIndexPartition -QueryTopology $QueryTopology)
$QueryComponent = New-SPEnterpriseSearchQuerycomponent -QueryTopology $QueryTopology
-IndexPartition $IndexPartition -SearchServiceInstance $searchInstance
$PropertyDatabase = ([array]($searchApp | Get-SPEnterpriseSearchPropertyDatabase))[0]
$IndexPartition | Set-SPEnterpriseSearchIndexPartition -PropertyDatabase $PropertyDatabase
$QueryTopology | Set-SPEnterpriseSearchQueryTopology -Active

Write-Host " Creating Proxy..."
$searchAppProxy = New-SPEnterpriseSearchServiceApplicationProxy -Name "$searchSAName Proxy"
-SearchApplication $searchSAName > $null
#####END SEARCH

Write-Host "Creating State Service and Proxy..."
New-SPStateServiceDatabase -Name "StateService" -DatabaseServer $databaseServerName | New-
SPStateServiceApplication -Name $stateSAName | New-SPStateServiceApplicationProxy -Name
"$stateSAName Proxy" -DefaultProxyGroup > $null

Write-Host "Creating Secure Store Service and Proxy..."
New-SPSecureStoreServiceapplication -Name $secureStoreSAName -Sharing:$false -DatabaseServer
$databaseServerName -DatabaseName "SecureStoreServiceApp" -ApplicationPool $saAppPoolName
-auditingEnabled:$true -auditlogmaxsize 30 | New-SPSecureStoreServiceApplicationProxy -name
"$secureStoreSAName Proxy" -DefaultProxygroup > $null

Get-SPServiceInstance | where-object {$_.TypeName -eq "Secure Store Service"} | Start-
SPServiceInstance > $null
Write-Host "Creating Visio Graphics Service and Proxy..."
New-SPVisioServiceApplication -Name $visioSAName -ApplicationPool $saAppPoolName > $null
New-SPVisioServiceApplicationProxy -Name "$visioSAName Proxy" -ServiceApplication
$visioSAName > $null
Get-SPServiceInstance | where-object {$_.TypeName -eq "Visio Graphics Service"} | Start-
SPServiceInstance > $null
Write-Host "Creating Web Analytics Service and Proxy..."
$stagerSubscription = ""
$reportingSubscription = ""
New-SPWebAnalyticsServiceApplication -Name $WebAnalyticsSAName -ApplicationPool
$saAppPoolName -ReportingDataRetention 20 -SamplingRate 100 -ListOfReportingDatabases
$reportingSubscription -ListOfStagingDatabases $stagerSubscription > $null
New-SPWebAnalyticsServiceApplicationProxy -Name "$WebAnalyticsSAName Proxy" -
ServiceApplication $WebAnalyticsSAName > $null
Get-SPServiceInstance | where-object {$_.TypeName -eq "Web Analytics Web Service"} | Start-
SPServiceInstance > $null
Get-SPServiceInstance | where-object {$_.TypeName -eq "Web Analytics Data Processing
Service"} | Start-SPServiceInstance > $null
```

```
Write-Host "Creating Word Conversion Service and Proxy..."
New-SPWordConversionServiceApplication -Name $WordAutomationSAName -ApplicationPool $saAppPoolName
-DatabaseServer $databaseServerName -DatabaseName "WordAutomation" -Default > $null
Get-SPServiceInstance | where-object {$_.TypeName -eq "Word Automation Services"} | Start-
SPServiceInstance > $null
######################################### End Script
#Now proceed to manually configuring your service applications (e.g. the Secure Store
Service for Excel Services, Visio graphics, and performance point. The managed metadata
service #for a content type hub)
```

I hope you're starting to see why using AutoSPInstaller is the way to go with rolling out and standardizing a build. The troubleshooting reason for standardizing a build is so that you know that the farm should be set to your configuration each time it is built. And, this standardization gives you a comparison point for the current status of anything in your farm, provided that the initial configuration is documented.

Let's look at this script's initial variables with the understanding that any lines in the script that start with a pound sign (#) are just comments or notes. The first actual line in the script, that isn't a comment, makes it so you could run this script from a regular administrative PowerShell session, as it converts any administrative PowerShell session to a SharePoint Management Shell session.

```
####################################################
# This script replicates most of the functionality found in the SharePoint
Products Configuration Wizard with the EXCEPTION of the USER PROFILE
SERVICE####################################################
Add-PSSnapin Microsoft.SharePoint.PowerShell -erroraction SilentlyContinue
```

The next 20 lines list most of the script's variables. You will want to modify these for your environment and then after you create a farm, you should keep a copy of the scripts somewhere to use a reference point, should the need arise. In the case of the AutoSPInstaller, you only have one XML file that you need to keep.

I hope you're finding that these lines are fairly self-explanatory in that they ask for the name of the SQL alias not the actual name of the database server. Then the application pool names and user accounts used in least privilege are gathered, followed by the names for each of the SharePoint Service Applications. If you're asking the question, "why didn't he make variables for the database names?" after noticing that they are hard-coded in the script, then you're already ahead of the game. And, you've already started troubleshooting this SharePoint script.

```
## Settings you may want to change ##
$databaseServerName = "SharePointSQL" #assumes you're using a SQL Alias configured with
cliconfg.exe
$searchServerName = "2010APP" #Front end Server that will run central admin, the server
you're on right now
$saAppPoolName = "SharePoint Hosted Services"
$appPoolUserName = "Contoso\2010svcapps" #This is the service application pool account it is
not the farm admin account for Timer and Central admin, sometimes called the farm account,
it is not the setup account, or install account
$ssaAppPoolName = "SharePoint Search Service Application Pool"
$SearchappPoolUserName = "Contoso\2010Search"
## Service Application Service Names ##
$accesssSAName = "Access Services"
$bcsSAName = "Business Data Connectivity Service"
$excelSAName = "Excel Services Application"
$metadataSAName = "Managed Metadata Web Service"
```

```
$performancePointSAName = "PerformancePoint Service"
$searchSAName = "SharePoint Server Search"
$stateSAName = "State Service"
$secureStoreSAName = "Secure Store Service"
$usageSAName = "Usage and Health Data Collection Service"
$visioSAName = "Visio Graphics Service"
$WebAnalyticsSAName = "Web Analytics Service"
$WordAutomationSAName = "Word Automation Services"
```

Starting with the line that begins, $saAppPool=Get-SpServiceApplicationPool... and continuing down through the line that starts with New-SPServiceApplicationPool and ends with > $null, is a section of code that has if then else logic that gathers the managed account to be used for the Service application pool, unless the managed account already exists. It also looks to see if the app pool is created before it even checks for the existence of that managed account, then if it finds the app pool it proceeds to the line that creates the usage service. If it can find the app pool or the managed account, it prompts, "Please supply the password for the service account," and the account field of the credential window that pops up already contains whichever account you used for this application pool, based on the value that you assigned to $appPoolUserName. If it does not find the app pool and finds the managed account that was supplied in the $appPoolUserName variable, it creates the app pool and writes to the screen that it is Creating Service Application Pool....

```
$saAppPool = Get-SPServiceApplicationPool -Identity $saAppPoolName -EA 0
if($saAppPool -eq $null)
{
Write-Host "Creating Service Application Pool..."

$appPoolAccount = Get-SPManagedAccount -Identity $appPoolUserName -EA 0
if($appPoolAccount -eq $null)
{
Write-Host "Please supply the password for the Service Account..."
$appPoolCred = Get-Credential $appPoolUserName
$appPoolAccount = New-SPManagedAccount -Credential $appPoolCred -EA 0
}

$appPoolAccount = Get-SPManagedAccount -Identity $appPoolUserName -EA 0

if($appPoolAccount -eq $null)
{
Write-Host "Cannot create or find the managed account $appPoolUserName, please ensure the
account exists."
Exit -1
}
New-SPServiceApplicationPool -Name $saAppPoolName -Account $appPoolAccount -EA 0 > $null
}
```

The next three lines create the Usage Application and its database named Usage. This is one of those spots in the script where it might have been better form to use a variable vs. hard coding. The reason is for portability between environments. In other words, if we wanted to use this script for other farms and we wanted our other farm to have different database names, we would have to comb through the script looking for –DatabaseName parameters.

Had the script used variables for the databases, there would be an even longer variables section at the top of the script; but that would allow for one place to change instead of having to look through the full script.

After the script writes to the screen that it is "Creating Usage Service and Proxy..." it creates a new service application with whichever value was assigned to $usageSAName and it creates a database on the database server that is represented by the SQLAlias.

```
Write-Host "Creating Usage Service and Proxy..."
$serviceInstance = Get-SPUsageService
New-SPUsageApplication -Name $usageSAName -DatabaseServer $databaseServerName -DatabaseName
"Usage" -UsageService $serviceInstance > $null
```

Next, the script creates the Access Service application, then it starts the Access Database Service. The Access Database Service typename property should not be changed because it is a system name and is hardcoded for that reason, so as that it would not be changed from build to build or ever. I won't keep saying that the script writes to the screen, but it does write to the screen each time you see a write-host line.

```
Write-Host "Creating Access Services and Proxy..."
New-SPAccessServiceApplication -Name $accesssSAName -ApplicationPool $saAppPoolName > $null
Get-SPServiceInstance | where-object {$_.TypeName -eq "Access Database Service"} | Start-
SPServiceInstance > $null
```

After the Access Service application is created, the Business Connectivity Service (BCS) application and its database is created and then the BCS service is started. Each time you see the Get-SPServiceInstance piped into a where-object cmdlet in this script you'll notice that the exact system name of the service is used to identify which service to pipe to the start-spserviceinstance. The >$ null that follow each line tell the script to wait until the service is started.

```
Write-Host "Creating BCS Service and Proxy..."
New-SPBusinessDataCatalogServiceApplication -Name $bcsSAName -ApplicationPool $saAppPoolName
-DatabaseServer $databaseServerName -DatabaseName "BusinessDataCatalog" > $null

Get-SPServiceInstance | where-object {$_.TypeName -eq "Business Data Connectivity Service"}
| Start-SPServiceInstance > $null
```

After the BCS is online, the script creates the Excel Service application and starts it. So why is this important in troubleshooting? Well, if you come into work Monday, and find that your Excel service is not working and then proceed to look into the issue only to find that the there is no Excel service application in your farm any longer; but now there is one called Xcel service application services. With the standardized build and the scripts documented, you know that someone has created a new service application and possibly removed or orphaned your original service application.

```
Write-Host "Creating Excel Service..."
New-SPExcelServiceApplication -name $excelSAName –ApplicationPool $saAppPoolName > $null
Set-SPExcelFileLocation -Identity "http://" -ExcelServiceApplication $excelSAName
-ExternalDataAllowed 2 -WorkbookSizeMax 10 -WarnOnDataRefresh:$true
Get-SPServiceInstance | where-object {$_.TypeName -eq "Excel Calculation Services"} | Start-
SPServiceInstance > $null
```

After Excel Services is online and hosted inside the SharePoint Hosted services application pool in IIS, the script creates the Managed MetaData Service application. And unlike the Excel Services application, which does not have a database, the Managed MetaData Service application cmdlet that creates the service application also creates the database.

Then after the service application is created, the cmdlet to create a proxy for the service application is used to create the connection to the endpoint that lives in IIS inside the Shared Hosted Services application pool. The proxy cmdlet also connects the proxy to the default proxy group using the –DefaultProxyGroup parameter. This makes it so that SharePoint automatically connects any new web applications to be able to see the managed metadata service application.

```
Write-Host "Creating Metadata Service and Proxy..."
New-SPMetadataServiceApplication -Name $metadataSAName -ApplicationPool $saAppPoolName -
DatabaseServer $databaseServerName -DatabaseName "Metadata" > $null
New-SPMetadataServiceApplicationProxy -Name "$metadataSAName Proxy" -DefaultProxyGroup -
ServiceApplication $metadataSAName > $null
Get-SPServiceInstance | where-object {$_.TypeName -eq "Managed Metadata Web Service"} |
Start-SPServiceInstance > $null
```

If I said, "Please see the managed metadata explanation and replace with performance point to save trees," would that be OK? These lines are the same as the lines used for ManagedMetadata, except that they call performance point cmdlets.

```
Write-Host "Creating Performance Point Service and Proxy..."
New-SPPerformancePointServiceApplication -Name $performancePointSAName -ApplicationPool
$saAppPoolName -DatabaseServer $databaseServerName -DatabaseName "PerformancePoint" > $null
New-SPPerformancePointServiceApplicationProxy -Default -Name "$performancePointSAName Proxy" -
ServiceApplication $performancePointSAName > $null
Get-SPServiceInstance | where-object {$_.TypeName -eq "PerformancePoint Service"} | Start-
SPServiceInstance > $null
```

The next 22 lines create the search service application app pool using a separate service account that the one used for the Shared Hosted Service Application app pool.

```
##START SEARCH

$ssaAppPool = Get-SPServiceApplicationPool -Identity $ssaAppPoolName -EA 0
if($ssaAppPool -eq $null)
{
Write-Host "Creating Search Service Application Pool..."

$SearchappPoolAccount = Get-SPManagedAccount -Identity $SearchappPoolUserName -EA 0
if($SearchappPoolAccount -eq $null)
{
Write-Host "Please supply the password for the Service Account..."
$ssappPoolCred = Get-Credential $SearchappPoolUserName
$SearchappPoolAccount = New-SPManagedAccount -Credential $ssappPoolCred -EA 0
}

$SearchappPoolAccount = Get-SPManagedAccount -Identity $SearchappPoolUserName -EA 0
```

```
if($appPoolAccount -eq $null)
{
Write-Host "Cannot create or find the managed account $SearchappPoolUserName, please ensure
the account exists."
Exit -1
}

New-SPServiceApplicationPool -Name $ssaAppPoolName -Account $SearchappPoolAccount -EA 0 > $null


}
```

The next three lines gather the variables used in creating the Search Service application, then the Enterprise search service instance is started along with the service responsible for managing search. After the script has finished starting the services is writes to the screen that it is creating the search service application.

The New-SPEnterpriseSearchServiceApplication is called and this creates the Search database. Then after the Search Admin database which is named Search, in this example, by the $searchDBName variable has come online, the script creates the admin components.

After the admin component is online, the process creates the remaining search databases, starts the service application proxy, and brings search online.

```
## Search Specifics, we are single server farm ##

$searchServerName = (Get-ChildItem env:computername).value
$serviceAppName = "Enterprise Search Services"
$searchDBName = "Search"

Write-Host "Creating Search Service and Proxy..."
Write-Host " Starting Services..."
Start-SPEnterpriseSearchServiceInstance $searchServerName
Start-SPEnterpriseSearchQueryAndSiteSettingsServiceInstance $searchServerName

Write-Host " Creating Search Application..."
$searchApp = New-SPEnterpriseSearchServiceApplication -Name $searchSAName -ApplicationPool
$ssaAppPoolName -DatabaseServer $databaseServerName -DatabaseName $searchDBName
$searchInstance = Get-SPEnterpriseSearchServiceInstance $searchServerName
 Write-Host " Creating Administration Component..."
$searchApp | Get-SPEnterpriseSearchAdministrationComponent | Set-SPEnterpriseSearchAdministr
ationComponent -SearchServiceInstance $searchInstance
 #Crawl
Write-Host " Creating Crawl Component..."
$InitialCrawlTopology = $searchApp | Get-SPEnterpriseSearchCrawlTopology -Active
$CrawlTopology = $searchApp | New-SPEnterpriseSearchCrawlTopology
$CrawlDatabase = ([array]($searchApp | Get-SPEnterpriseSearchCrawlDatabase))[0]
$CrawlComponent = New-SPEnterpriseSearchCrawlComponent -CrawlTopology $CrawlTopology
-CrawlDatabase $CrawlDatabase -SearchServiceInstance $searchInstance
$CrawlTopology | Set-SPEnterpriseSearchCrawlTopology -Active
 Write-Host -ForegroundColor white " Waiting for the old crawl topology to become inactive"
-NoNewline
do {write-host -NoNewline .;Start-Sleep 6;} while ($InitialCrawlTopology.State -ne "Inactive")
$InitialCrawlTopology | Remove-SPEnterpriseSearchCrawlTopology -Confirm:$false
Write-Host
```

```
#Query
Write-Host " Creating Query Component..."
$InitialQueryTopology = $searchApp | Get-SPEnterpriseSearchQueryTopology -Active
$QueryTopology = $searchApp | New-SPEnterpriseSearchQueryTopology -Partitions 1
$IndexPartition= (Get-SPEnterpriseSearchIndexPartition -QueryTopology $QueryTopology)
$QueryComponent = New-SPEnterpriseSearchQuerycomponent -QueryTopology $QueryTopology -
IndexPartition $IndexPartition -SearchServiceInstance $searchInstance
$PropertyDatabase = ([array]($searchApp | Get-SPEnterpriseSearchPropertyDatabase))[0]
$IndexPartition | Set-SPEnterpriseSearchIndexPartition -PropertyDatabase $PropertyDatabase
$QueryTopology | Set-SPEnterpriseSearchQueryTopology -Active

Write-Host " Creating Proxy..."
$searchAppProxy = New-SPEnterpriseSearchServiceApplicationProxy -Name "$searchSAName Proxy"
-SearchApplication $searchSAName > $null
#####END SEARCH
```

After the search service application is created the state service is provisioned and like so many of its fellow SharePoint service applications is given membership in the default proxy group.

```
Write-Host "Creating State Service and Proxy..."
New-SPStateServiceDatabase -Name "StateService" -DatabaseServer $databaseServerName | New-
SPStateServiceApplication -Name $stateSAName | New-SPStateServiceApplicationProxy -Name
"$stateSAName Proxy" -DefaultProxyGroup > $null
```

The Secure Store Service application holds credentials and in a truly least-privileged environment, Microsoft says it should have its own application pool. And, in businesses where security is paramount, like the credit card processing industry and healthcare, this seems like it would be a business requirement. In order to save resources on the server, most builds run the Secure Store Service application inside Shared Hosted Services, as we have done in this build.

```
Write-Host "Creating Secure Store Service and Proxy..."
New-SPSecureStoreServiceapplication -Name $secureStoreSAName -Sharing:$false -DatabaseServer
$databaseServerName -DatabaseName "SecureStoreServiceApp" -ApplicationPool $saAppPoolName
-auditingEnabled:$true -auditlogmaxsize 30 | New-SPSecureStoreServiceApplicationProxy -name
"$secureStoreSAName Proxy" -DefaultProxygroup > $null
Get-SPServiceInstance | where-object {$_.TypeName -eq "Secure Store Service"} | Start-
SPServiceInstance > $null
```

Visio graphics is created. No database is needed. Service is started using the system name for the service.

```
Write-Host "Creating Visio Graphics Service and Proxy..."
New-SPVisioServiceApplication -Name $visioSAName -ApplicationPool $saAppPoolName > $null
New-SPVisioServiceApplicationProxy -Name "$visioSAName Proxy" -ServiceApplication
$visioSAName > $null
Get-SPServiceInstance | where-object {$_.TypeName -eq "Visio Graphics Service"} | Start-
SPServiceInstance > $null
```

The web analytics service that is deprecated in SharePoint 2013 and 2016 because it is built into the new search component analytics, is not deprecated in SharePoint 2010 and is brought on line like all the other service applications.

```
Write-Host "Creating Web Analytics Service and Proxy..."
$stagerSubscription = ""
$reportingSubscription = ""
New-SPWebAnalyticsServiceApplication -Name $WebAnalyticsSAName -ApplicationPool
$saAppPoolName -ReportingDataRetention 20 -SamplingRate 100 -ListOfReportingDatabases
$reportingSubscription -ListOfStagingDatabases $stagerSubscription > $null
New-SPWebAnalyticsServiceApplicationProxy -Name "$WebAnalyticsSAName Proxy"
-ServiceApplication $WebAnalyticsSAName > $null
Get-SPServiceInstance | where-object {$_.TypeName -eq "Web Analytics Web Service"} | Start-
SPServiceInstance > $null
Get-SPServiceInstance | where-object {$_.TypeName -eq "Web Analytics Data Processing
Service"} | Start-SPServiceInstance > $null
```

Finally, the Word Conversion Service application is created and brought online. At this point in the review, you already noticed that it has a database on the SQL server.

```
Write-Host "Creating Word Conversion Service and Proxy..."
New-SPWordConversionServiceApplication -Name $WordAutomationSAName -ApplicationPool
$saAppPoolName -DatabaseServer $databaseServerName -DatabaseName "WordAutomation" -Default >
$null
Get-SPServiceInstance | where-object {$_.TypeName -eq "Word Automation Services"} | Start-
SPServiceInstance > $null
############################################## End Script
#Now proceed to manually configuring your service applications (e.g. the Secure Store
Service for Excel Services, Visio graphics, and performance point. The managed metadata
service #for a content type hub)
```

The last line that begins "#Now proceed to manually..." seems like an afterthought; it is only visible when editing the script and does not emit to the screen is just more evidence of why AutoSPInstaller is the way to go with standardized builds.

I hope you enjoyed reading about the PowerShell to stand up a SharePoint farm. If you were to use the above service apps script for 2013 you would want to comment out or remove the lines for Search and web analytics and replace them with the SharePoint 2013 cmdlets. This post on my blog has the full script (not listed here to save paper): https://anothersharepointblog.com/provisioning-a-sharepoint-2013-farm-sharepoint-service-applications.

Building a Farm with AutoSPInstaller

In order to run the AutoSPInstaller, you need to have all of your service accounts created in Active Directory and know the passwords to said accounts, and have completed the online form. When completing the online form, you need to know the names of the databases and any prefix that may be required by your requirements. After you have this information, it is time to fill out the form on the AutoSPInstaller.com website that creates the XML file that is used in the installation.

Once the form is created, a great way to save time is to run the prerequisite installer on all of your servers. Then run setup.exe up to, and not including the post-setup Configuration Wizard. After that, you're ready to execute the AutoSPInstaller; you will not have to wait for restarts since the prerequisite installation is already completed.

■ **Tip** The prerequisite installation and setup install up to the point of the post-setup Configuration Wizard is done to save time; it is not a requirement because the AutoSPInstaller is capable of handling the install without the prerequisites being run.

Table 2-1. *Accounts Used in Least Privileging, Recap*

Account Name	Description
SP_Farm	Farm Account
SP_CacheSuperUser	Object Caching Account
SP_CacheSuperReader	Object Caching Account
SP_Services	Service Application Account
SP_PortalAppPool	Portal Application Pool Account
SP_ProfilesAppPool	MySites Application Pool Account
SP_SearchService	Search Service Application Pool Account
SP_SearchContent	Search Content Access Account
SP_ProfileSync	User Profile Sync Account
SP_ExcelUser	Excel Unattended ID
SP_VisioUser	Visio Unattended ID
SP_PerfPointUser	Performance Point Unattended ID
SP_Install	Setup Account

The main reason to use AutoSPInstaller to build your farm is for the standardization of the build. There are key settings that the current AutoSPInstaller does not address, such as DCOM settings, MSDTC settings, and Component Services security for the computer running User Profile services. I'll go over those settings after discussing AutoSPInstaller. The use of AutoSPInstaller—along with an offline install of the prerequisites—is arguably the best method for installing SharePoint. The offline install of the prerequisites speeds up the installation process since there isn't any need to download them.

Using AutoSPInstaller is as easy as filling out a form and making sure that the files are in the correct locations on the servers. Then after you've got everything where you need it, and your account is a member of the domain administrators group, you're ready to begin.

To use AutoSPInstaller or PowerShell to install SharePoint, you need a license key, of which any will do, even an MSDN copy, depending on how you're using SharePoint. For example, you wouldn't use an MSDN copy in a development farm, unless every user who accessed the development farm had a MSDN license. You could use an MSDN copy in your home lab, however. Then after you have the non-MSDN license, you'll need to download the AutoSPInstaller files from GitHub, and then download the SharePoint binaries and copy them to the a location inside the AutoSPInstaller file structure. You determine the location on your server where the AutoSPInstaller files are stored. Inside the AutoSPInstaller directory, there are folders for your binaries. You'll place the binaries in the correct folder. For example, the SharePoint 2013 binaries go in the SharePoint folder inside of the folder named 2013. Figure 2-15 displays the folder structure location of where the SharePoint 2013 Binaries are loaded into the AutoSPInstaller directories.

Once the form at www.autospinstaller.com is filled out, and the XML file is downloaded, just copy it to the AutoSPInstaller folder. Then when you are ready to start your build, drag and drop the XML file on to the file named AutoSPInstaller.bat, and watch the build go to town. Figure 2-17 shows that the XML file is named 2013Install.xml.

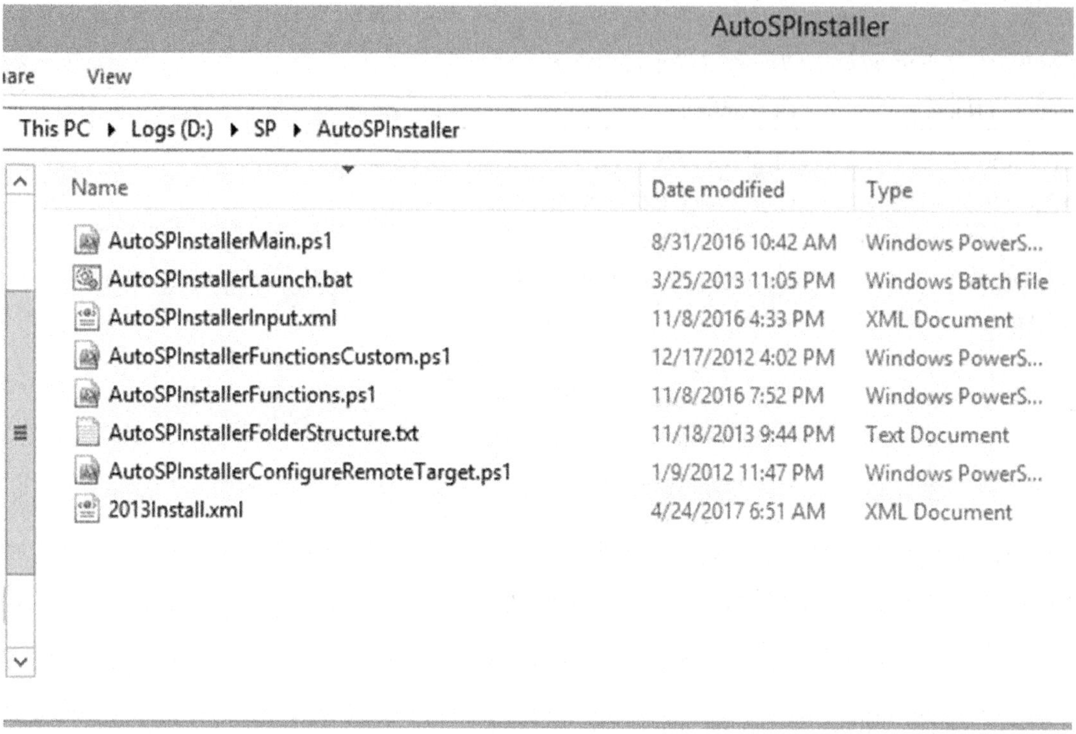

Figure 2-17. *XML file for AutoSPInstaller*

After you drag the XML file onto the bat file, the AutoSPInstaller will get underway. It really is an awesome program. Figure 2-18 shows the Cumulative Update (CU) for the App Fabric; but I hadn't put them in the update files location.

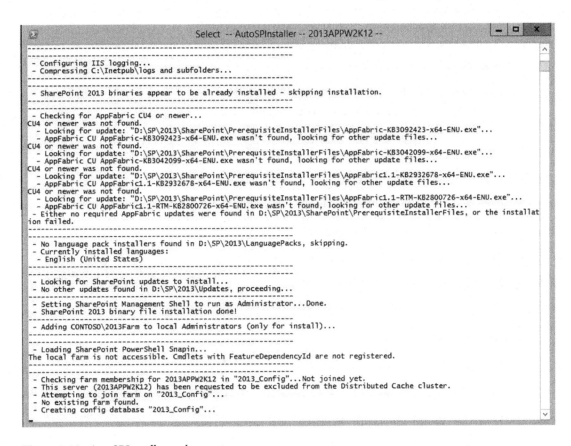

Figure 2-18. AutoSPInstaller underway

This file has all of the default build settings and should be stored away for safe keeping in the event that the farm is blown away, corrupted, or starts behaving improperly this file can be used as a reference and if needed, as a rebuild. When the build finishes there are still some key build settings that you'll need to address.

MSDTC and DCOM Settings

One of the things that neither the PowerShell nor AutoSPInstaller addresses are settings that need to be made to the Microsoft distributed transaction coordinator (MDTC). The settings changes are made to allow SharePoint to function more fluidly and to reduce MDTC related errors in the Application and System logs of the Windows event viewer.

Since SharePoint servers communicate with each other in such a way that it is difficult for the MDTC transaction manager to determine if an incoming connection request is from a remote machine. Therefore, for security reasons, the MDTC transaction manager treats this connection request as a remote connection request. And if the Network Clients security option is not enabled, this can cause the MDTC TM to reject this connection attempt.

In order to prevent issues like the one we just explained and numerous others, we make the following changes to the MDTC service security settings:

- Enable Network DTC Access

- Allow Inbound Transaction Manager Communication

- Allow Outbound Transaction Manager Communication

- Do not require Authentication for MDTC TM communication

- Enable XA Transactions

- Enable SNA LU 6.2 Transactions

The steps taken in configuring the MDTC TM are all completed within the Component Services console, which is available under Administrative Tools or by calling comexp.exe from an administrative command line. Figure 2-19 shows the Component Services console opened from the command line.

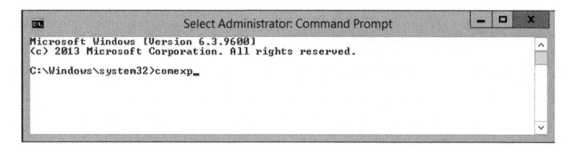

Figure 2-19. *One way to open Component Services*

Once the Component Services manager is open, navigate to Component Services ➤ My Computer ➤ Distributed Transaction Coordinator, and select Local DTC. Right-click and select Properties (see Figure 2-20).

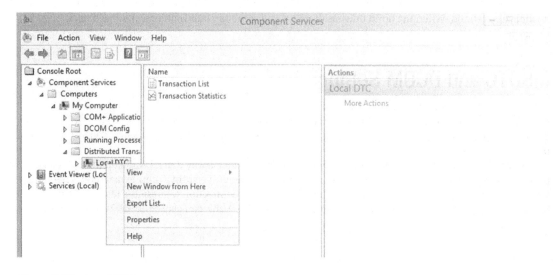

Figure 2-20. *Local DTC*

After the properties open, a quick look at the security tab shows why the various events listed on TechNet at `https://technet.microsoft.com/en-us/library/dd337715(v=ws.10).aspx` can sometimes fill the logs in your SharePoint Server and cause endpoints to become unreachable. Figure 2-21 shows the MDTC TM settings before the settings changes. You can see that Network DTC Access is not allowed, which can lead to falsely based rejections to SharePoint Service Application endpoints.

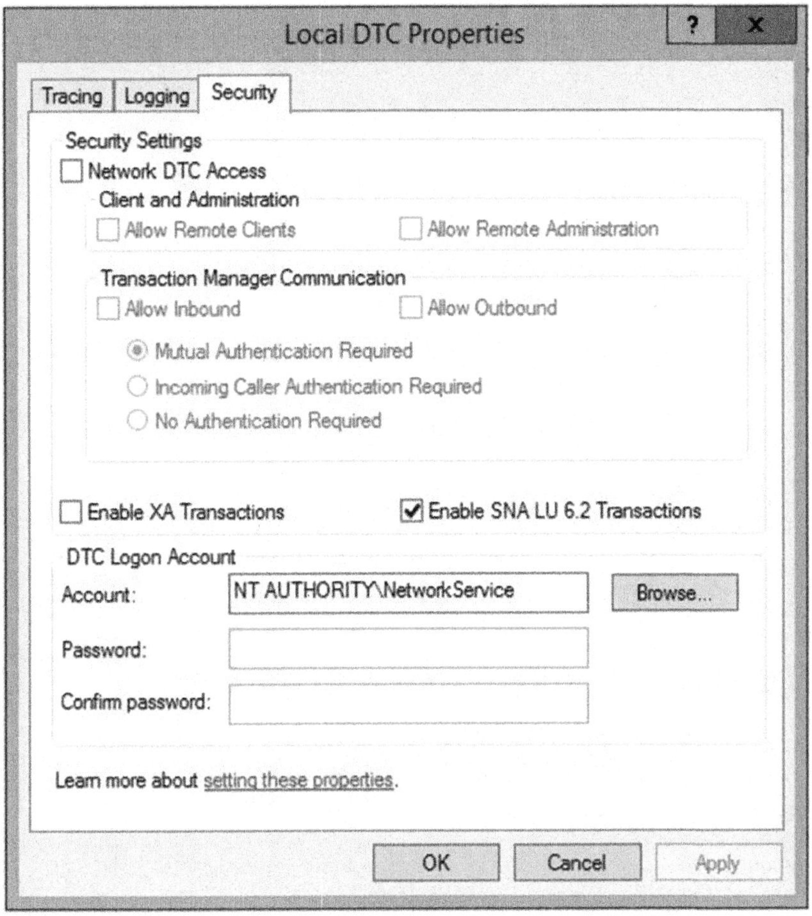

Figure 2-21. MDTC improperly configured

The only tab with settings that needs to adjustment is the security tab. After the settings adjustments are in place, the Security tab should look like Figure 2-22.

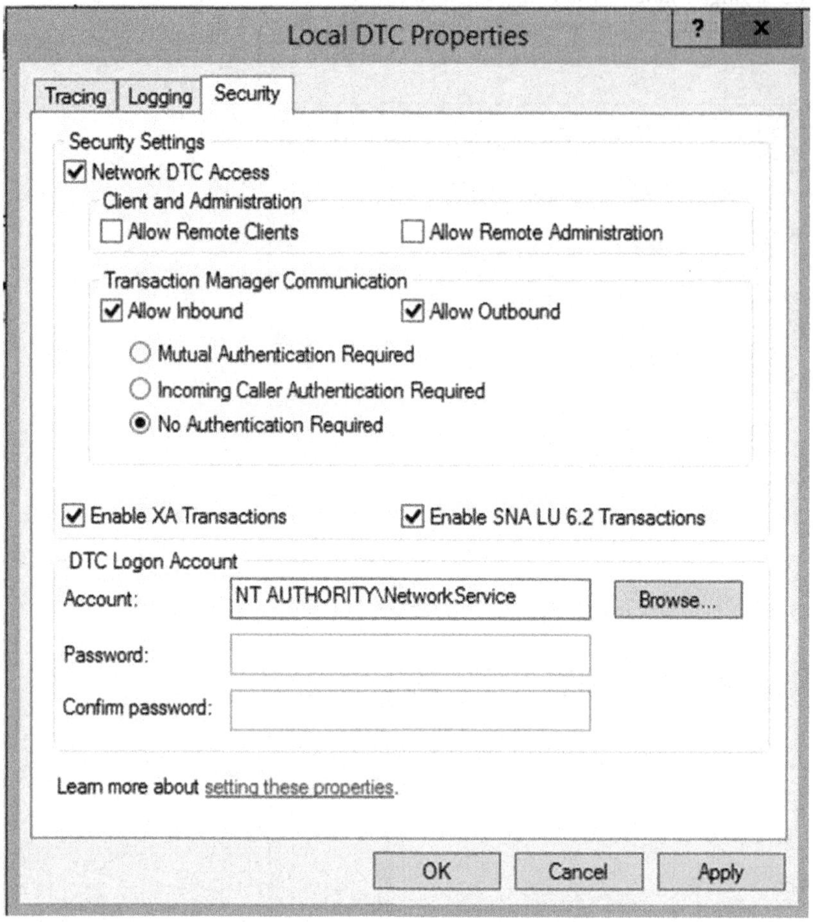

Figure 2-22. *MDTC properly configured*

When you make this change, the server automatically asks you to stop and start the MSDTC service, as shown in Figure 2-23.

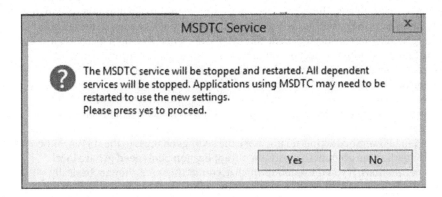

Figure 2-23. *Do you want to restart?*

Go ahead and say Yes to the prompt in Figure 2-23; you should be presented with the message that the MSDTC service has been restarted, as shown in Figure 2-24

Figure 2-24. *MSDTC restarted*

Perform the MSDTC TM settings changes on all of the SharePoint servers in the farm and on the SQL servers. This key setting of a good build is the first place to look when messages about endpoints not listening start showing up in the logs. Having said that, this is not the end all endpoint related fix; but it fixes a lot of situations where the transaction manager may have erroneously terminated the communication.

Now that you've made that settings change using the Component Services management console to the Local DTC, it's time to make another settings change to a couple more components. This time we'll be making a few changes that have caused event ID 10016 and 10017 and Event 1015 to appear in Windows logs, since WSS 2.0 and 3.0.

Making these changes used to be as easy as just using the Component Services management console, as spelled out in the Microsoft Support article at http://support.microsoft.com/kb/920783. However, with the new operating systems, even a domain administrator cannot make the needed changes. Let's talk about the changes (why and where they are needed) before we talk about how to implement them.

SharePoint is heavily dependent on the numerous DLLs that it has in its file system. The accounts that run the various application pools in a least-privileged build need to have the processes that run inside these application pools allowed to locally activate and launch calls to the dll files and to IIS without having the log files fill up with errors each time that happens. The accounts already have access through the file system to run the files; but they don't have the access they need via the Component Object Model. As a result, these errors can make our troubleshooting harder from the need to wade through more events as we hunt for root causes.

These errors that come from this setting are just unwanted noise. Nothing is getting fixed here, other than the logs not having extra entries. There is a component called the IIS WAMREG admin service that is responsible for IIS web application manager (WAM) functionality. The WAM component is used by IIS in access and interact, with processes that it doesn't specifically host itself but with which it needs to interact (or even start). WAM is a Component Object Model application package that works with a file named DLLHOST.exe to host out-of-process ISAPI extensions and ASP files, of which SharePoint has plenty of both.

The AutoSPInstaller and the PowerShell scripts do not make the settings changes to the IIS WAMREG admin service. As I alluded to earlier, the account that runs the IIS application pools need to have local activation and local launch permissions. If you think about which accounts these are, they are basically all of the accounts that are members of the WSS_WPG group and you could add the group vs. adding each account; but I like to add the accounts directly as that rules out the possibility of any issue occurring that would prevent group members from not inheriting permissions correctly. Not that I've seen that before; but it is better to be safe than sorry, when it comes to stopping extra errors that have no bearing on anything.

The process to change these errors is that we need to access the components that are related to event ID 10016. There are actually two components that lead to event ID 10016: the IIS WAMREG admin service and the MSIServer DCOM Component. In Server 2008 and earlier you could modify the permissions in the Component Services management console and call it a day; but with the newer server operating systems starting with Server 2008 R2 and Server 2012, this setting is locked down and you have to take ownership of a couple of registry keys before you can modify the setting.

This is the IIS WAMREG admin service DCOM component registry key:

```
HKEY_CLASSES_ROOT\AppID\{61738644-F196-11D0-9953-00C04FD919C1}
```

This is the MSIServer DCOM component registry key:

```
HKEY_CLASSES_ROOT\AppID\{000C101C-0000-0000-C000-000000000046}
```

After you've taken ownership of the key, you can access the Launch and Activation Permissions since the customize button will not be grayed out, as it is in Figure 2-25.

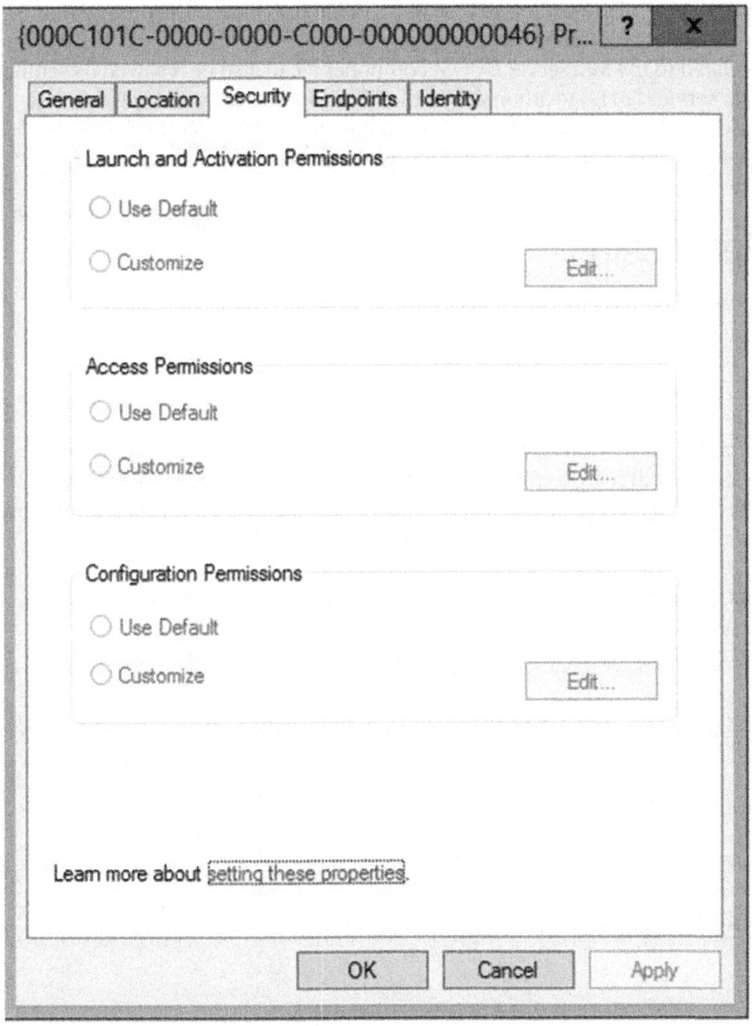

Figure 2-25. MSIServer DCOM Ccmponent grayed out

You need to close and reopen the Component Services management console (comexp.exe), after you've taken ownership away from the trusted installer by using registry, if you have it open. Once you've edited the launch and activation permissions for each of these two DCOM components, and then restarted the Windows server named DCOM server process launcher, the event IDs for 10016, 10017, and 1015 should be few and far between.

When you research these errors online, you might see mention of changing registry permissions for the WSS_WPG group or worse yet adding the farm account to the local admins group on the SharePoint servers. Do not do this; while it would fix these errors, it violates least privilege and is strongly discouraged. Instead, just modify the Launch and Activation permissions on the two DCOM components to allow the identities that run application pools and are members of the WSS_WPG group so that they have local activation and local launch. If you're getting a message that reads something like, "Event ID 6616 Critical Requested registry access is not allowed" you should avoid modifying registry manually and instead, run Initialize-SPresourceSecurity or psconfig –cmd secureresources. Altering any of the key registry locations or file system permissions mentioned in Chapter 1 could result in unexpected behaviors and violate least privilege.

Event ID 1015, while mostly related to the MSIServer DCOM component, can also be resolved by setting the Background Intelligent Transfer service (BITs) to automatic in the Windows Services console (services. msc). There is an exercise at the end of the chapter with a step-by-step how-to on the process related to taking ownership of the registry keys and modifying the DCOM settings is handled.

Network Service Permissions

Another key setting that is often overlooked is the permissions for the network service on the following registry key:

```
HKEY_LOCAL_MACHINE\Software\Microsoft\Office Server\15.0\Search\Setup
```

It is important for search to work correctly. You shouldn't have to manually set the permissions on that registry key, it should already be set with read permissions but you should check that the permissions are correct. The following is another registry key related to search and volume shadow copy that is important to check:

```
HKEY_LOCAL_MACHINE\SYSTEM\CurrentControlSet\Services\VSS\VssAccessControl
```

At this location, you should have a Reg_Dword key for each of the accounts, as shown in Figure 2-26.

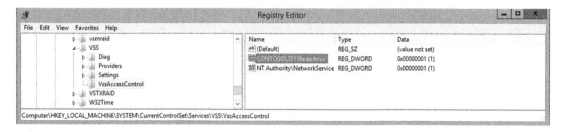

Figure 2-26. *VSS access control*

By creating an entry so that the Network Service account and the account used for search have a value of 1, you'll decrease event ID 8193.

Local Security for the Farm Account

I've already gone into a lot of detail about the local farm account security needs. The only time it is ever elevated is during the initial build and whenever provisioning the user profile synchronization service. Other than that, the local farm account should **never** be a local admin. It should be members of the following local security groups:

- IIS_IUSRS

- Performance Log Users

- Performance Monitors

- WSS_Admin_WPG

- WSS_RESTRICTED_WPG_V4

- WSS_WPG

Due to the very sensitive access that WSS_RESTRICTED_WPG_V4 group has on the SharePoint server, the farm account should be the only member of this group.

In this chapter, we've taken what we learned about least-privileged builds and looked at how they come to be a reality by looking at either a PowerShell scripting option or through the use of the AutoSPInstaller, which installs SharePoint using a SharePoint Hosted Service application pool running under a non-administrative account. This application pool houses all of the service applications that are not search related because a separate app pool is created for the search applications.

Let's look at a few exercises to put a nice wrap on this chapter.

SET MSDTC SETTINGS

In this exercise, we'll set the Microsoft Distributed Transaction Coordinator Transaction Manager security settings to allow network client access to create a more fluid and better-performing SharePoint farm.

1. Open an administrative command line. Type **comexp** and press Enter.

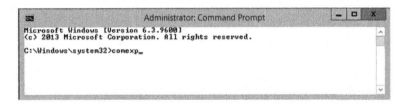

2. When the Component Services management console opens, navigate to the local DTC settings by clicking Component Services ➤ Computers ➤ My Computer ➤ Distributed Transaction Coordinator.

3. Right-click Local DTC and select Properties. Then click the Security tab and make the selections, as shown in the following screenshot.

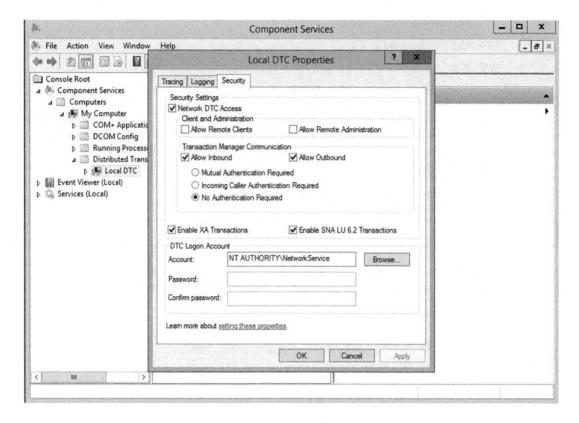

4. Click Apply and then Yes at the prompt to restart the service. Click OK when Windows lets you know that it has restarted.

5. Go to each server in your farm, including the SQL servers, and repeat these steps.

SET IIS WAMREG ADMIN SERVICE AND MSISERVER DCOM COMPONENTS

In this exercise, we'll set the DCOM components for the IIS WAMREG admin service and MSIServer DCOM component so that the proper accounts have local activation and local launch.

1.   Open the registry editor. You can use the same command prompt that you used in the previous session, only this time, type **regedit**, as shown in the following screenshot.

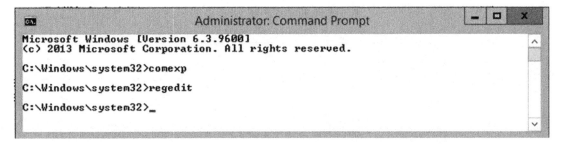

2.   When the registry editor opens, navigate to the following registry location:

HKEY_CLASSES_ROOT\AppID\{61738644-F196-11D0-9953-00C04FD919C1}

A quick way to find this location is to search for 6173, as shown in the following screenshot. Start at the computer node. Press F3 and type **6173**. Then click Find Next.

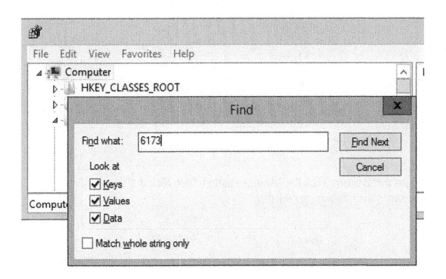

Once you've found the registry location, you need to take ownership of the key by using the install account. Hopefully, this is the account you are logged in to the server as. Editing registry is like doing brain surgery on your computer: one false move and the server could cease to function; so make sure that you've found the key as displayed in the following screenshot.

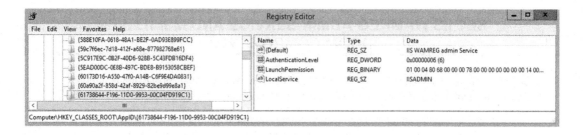

3. Right-click {61738644-F196-11D0-9953-00C04FD919C1} and then click Permissions, as shown in the following screenshot.

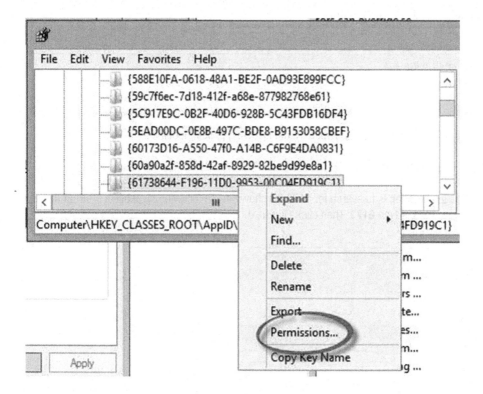

4. After the Permissions menu opens, click the Advanced button. Then click the Change link, as shown in the following screenshot.

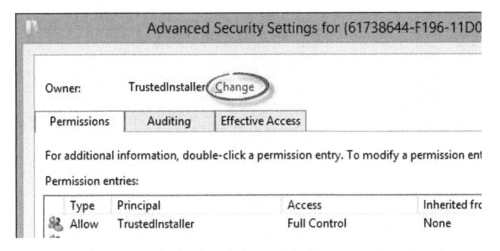

5. Enter your account name in the "Enter the object name to select" box and then click OK. Check the "Replace owner on subcontainers and object" check box. Click the Apply button and then the OK button. In the following screenshot, I entered contoso\2013installer because I logged in with the setup account.

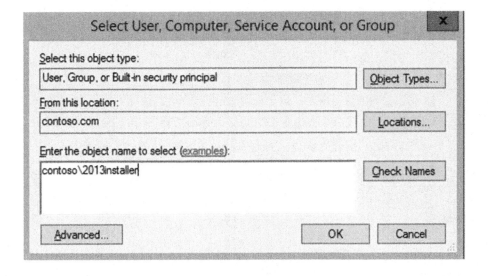

6. Now that you are back at the Permissions screen, add the setup account you're using to the access control list (ACL) using the Add button. Give it full control by checking the Full Control box. Then click Apply and OK.

7. Navigate to the following registry location: HKEY_CLASSES_ROOT\AppID\{000C101C-0000-0000-C000-000000000046}. Repeat the same steps as for the MSIServer registry key. The registry key for the MSIServer is shown in the following screenshot.

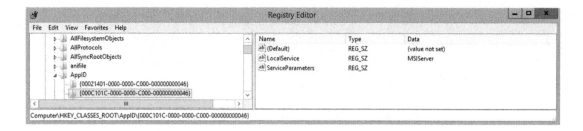

8. After you've added the setup account that you are logged in with to both registry keys, and you've made the changes, open the Component Services management console (comexp.exe).

9. Navigate to the DCOM Config section of Component Services. Scroll to IIS WAMREG Admin Service, right-click, and then click Properties. When IIS WAMREG admin Service Properties opens, the Edit button for Launch and Activation Permissions should be clickable and not grayed out, as shown in the following screenshot.

10. It is time to click Edit and add the domain accounts of the members of the WSS_WPG group to Launch and Activation Permissions. If you do not have these user names handy, you can obtain them from local users and groups (lusrmgr.msc) or from the WSS_WPG command-line net localgroup. Click the Edit button under Launch and Activation permissions on the Security tab, if you haven't already, and enter the accounts in the ACL, as shown in the following screenshot. Give them local launch and local activation. Once all the accounts are entered click OK, click Apply, and then OK.

11. Repeat this for the MSIServer DCOM object by scrolling down to it, but this time click the Customize Radio button under Launch and Activation Permissions to make the Edit button illuminate. Then click Edit. Make the same changes that you made to the ACL of the IIS WAMREG Admin service.

12. Now that both DCOM components are updated, stop and start the DCOM server process launcher by restarting your server.

MANUALLY SET SQL ALIAS

In this exercise, you'll learn how to use the GUI to set the SQL alias.

1. Open a run bar. Type **cliconfg**, and then press Enter or click OK.

2. When the SQL Client Utility opens, click the Alias tab, as shown in the following screenshot. Note how there is already a SQL alias configured. This alias could hold all the databases in the farm, or maybe it just holds the service application databases and the Central Administration and configuration databases. Or maybe it just holds the configuration and the Central Administration databases. It isn't possible to spin up the configuration and Central Administration content databases on separate instances.

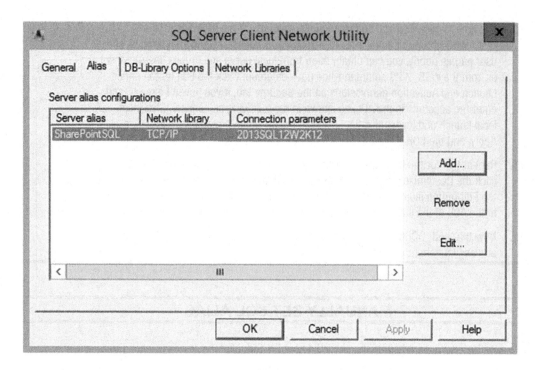

To create a new alias, click the Add button, and then click the TCP/IP radio button under the Network Libraries. Add the information for the Name of the Server Alias and the server name or servername\ named instance in the appropriate boxes. You can leave the "Dynamically determine port" selected or you can uncheck it and add a new port—something other than the default 1433, as shown in the following screenshot, we're using the default port.

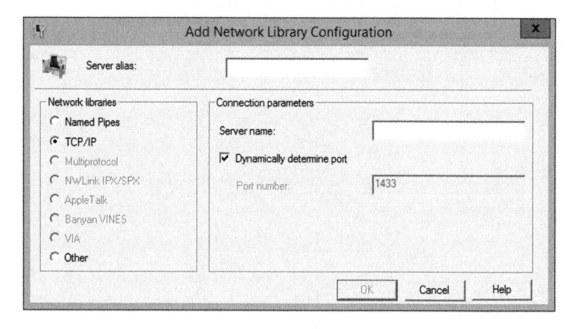

3. After you make your new alias, you can click OK, Apply, and OK.

And that is all there is to creating a SQL server alias manually for the x64-bit applications. To create the SQL alias for the x86-bit application, you need to navigate to C:\Windows\SYSWOW64\cliconfg.exe and perform the same steps, or use PowerShell.

Before we end this chapter, let's think about how we could use PowerShell to troubleshoot or query the SharePoint object model to determine what databases were held in the SQL Alias named SharePointSQL. Well we know that there might be a command to get all the SharePoint databases (or at least we hope there is) so that we can run get-command –noun *database –verb get and see that there definitely commands that get database information. There is one command that appears to get all the database commands, as shown in Figure 2-27, since it is more general in nature. That cmdlet is Get-SPDatabase.

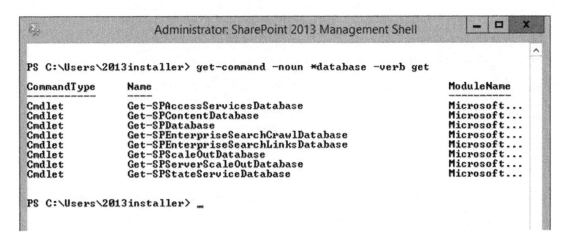

Figure 2-27. *Get-command –noun *database –verb get*

So, taking what we already know about getting information about cmdlets, we would then pipe this command to get-member or its alias gm with this command:

```
Get-SPDatabase | gm
```

After the screen stops scrolling, notice that Get-SPDatabase has a property called Server and one called Name, so we decide to run Get-SPDatabase and pipe it to format-table for the name and the server properties using this command:

```
Get-SPDatabase | ft Name, Server
```

And, the results are shown in Figure 2-28. We can see that, in this case, all the databases are held in the SharePointSQL alias.

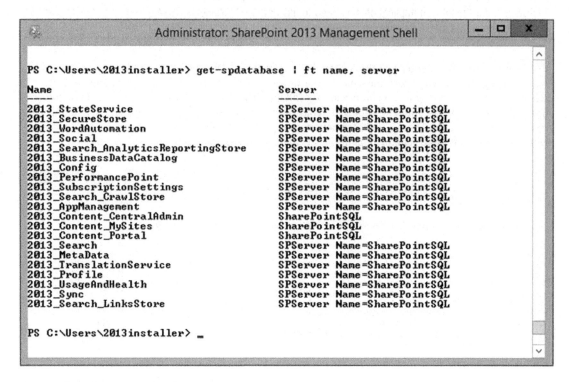

Figure 2-28. *The server is the alias*

Next Steps

I hope you enjoyed this chapter as you learned about PowerShell and how to use it to query the object model. You also learned about offline prerequisite installation. I talked about some key settings to a good build that affect interfarm communications. In Chapter 3, I'll talk about more key settings and look at the SharePoint 2013 and 2016 Distributed Cache, and discuss how to fix it when it's broken. You'll use PowerShell to determine what is configured, and then further configure it.

■ ■ ■

## CHAPTER 3

More Key Settings to a Good Build

In this chapter, we're going to pick up with the Component Services console for a key setting related to user profile synchronization in SharePoint 2010 and 2013 and we'll discuss the importance of this setting. Then, we'll switch gears by looking at the Windows operating system's App Fabric 1.1 for Windows Server, and learn how to troubleshoot and configure SharePoint 2013 and 2016's Distributed Cache service. We'll look at some PowerShell used with configuring Distributed Cache in a farm that is using the minimum role technology.

After we've discussed Distributed Cache configuration and troubleshooting, we'll switch back over to configuring and troubleshooting User Profile Synchronization in SharePoint 2010 and 2013. Since the Forefront identity bits have been removed from SharePoint 2016, there isn't anything to discuss there in regards to the SharePoint User Profile synchronization service. We're not going to discuss the Microsoft Identity Manager server, which is the 2016 on-premises answer for synching metadata from Active Directory.

Once we have User Profile Synchronization thoroughly beaten into the ground, we'll discuss minimal download strategy and compare it with publishing infrastructure. We'll discuss issues that can arise with the publishing infrastructure and resolutions to said issues. After we've looked at what publishing infrastructure introduces to a site collection and its sites and how to configure it, we will discuss rolling out host-named site collections and the steps that are part of that process.

The PowerShell to create host-named site collections will be broken down and dissected. Host-named site collections are the same thing as host header site collections and I only make a point to mention it because Microsoft has decided to abandon the HNSC naming convention and go with HHSC, so from this point forward in the book, when we talk about host-named site collections, we'll try to refer to them as *host header site collections* or HHSCs. We will talk about how to roll out the HHSCs, why you might want to use them as opposed to *path-based site collections* (PBSCs), and key settings that are required to bring HHSCs online.

Finally, we'll wrap up the chapter with a short discussion around account management, governance, logging locations, and logging levels. In this discussion, we'll discuss changing passwords for accounts in a section on Account management. We will look at the various logs available for troubleshooting and discuss some key things you can look for in some of the logs.

COM+ Security for User Profile Sync

On the server that runs user profile synchronization, the COM + Security settings should allow the farm account to remotely launch and remotely activate files. This is not the case by default and is one that you can easily modify. This key setting to a good build allows the farm account the local launch, remote activation, and remote launch permissions on the computer object's COM security. This will help with issues when the User Profile Synchronization service is stuck on starting. It's not a panacea, but it is a preventative measure in avoiding that ugly situation of the user profile sync not starting. It will also help communication.

To set this setting, open the Component Services console and right-click the My Computer object that is located inside of the computers folder inside the Component Services node within the Component Services

Console. Once you've found it and right-clicked it, click properties and then select the COM security tab. Inside of the Launch and Activation Permissions limits, you can add the farm account to the ACL and then give the account Local Launch, Remote Launch, and Remote Activation.

App Fabric and Distributed Cache

If you're experiencing issues with your 2013 or 2016 farm and you've already double-checked the permissions, and the least privileging settings are all properly in place, then one of the first places to look is the Distributed Cache—especially, if the problems are related to any of the following:

- Page Load Performance Apples

- Authentication

- Newsfeeds

- OneNote Client Access

- Security Trimming

For example, if users are complaining that it is taking forever for pages to load and you are not seeing anything in performance monitor that would indicate that memory is exhausted, look at the health of the Distributed Cache by running Use-CacheCluster followed by Get-CacheClusterHealth. Hopefully, you'll have scores in the healthy column that are 8 or higher and all zeros in the rest of the categories, as shown in Figure 3-1.

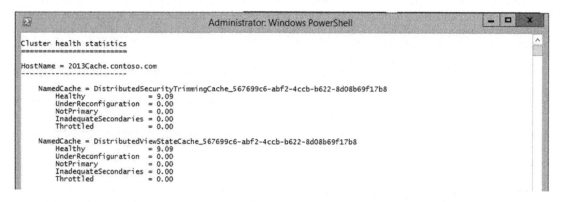

Figure 3-1. *Distributed Cache is healthy*

When you perform any sort of action with Distributed Cache, you always start out with the use-cachecluster command. If you're having trouble with users being allowed into sites one minute, and then getting access denied or other weird behavior relating to permissions the next, it might have to do with the Distributed Cache not being large enough and having flushed information about authentication. If that happens, you need to change the size of the cache and possibly the number of servers that are running the Distributed Cache service. You'll also want to make sure there aren't any competing services on the server and we'll talk more about that in just a few.

Since Distributed Cache is a memory hungry beast, it is a good idea to give it what you can afford, given your system and considering Microsoft's best practice recommendations. Microsoft recommends using a dedicated Distributed Cache server, when possible, and definitely adjusting the size of the Distributed Cache if you ever add or remove memory from a server, since the cache does not automatically adjust.

When you first install SharePoint 2013 or SharePoint 2016 on a server, the Distributed Cache will appear to have configured itself at 5% of the installed memory if you look at the cache host config by running the Get-cachehostconfig command. The Distributed Cache service has actually taken 10% of the total memory though. When the cache is first configured, it uses 5% of the memory for data storage and 5% for memory management overhead. As the cached data grows, the Distributed Cache service uses the entire 10% of the allocated memory, which is why you should be cognizant of this service and now how to change the cache size and know the limits.

Speaking of limits, if your server has more than 320GB of RAM, the Distributed Cache will only be allowed 16GB of memory, automatically. And, because it is not a good idea to allocate more than 16GB of memory to Distributed Cache, you should never allocate more than that, even for servers with 34GB or more RAM. The reason that servers that have 320GB or more RAM are automatically capped at 16GB is that when the cache gets bigger than that, it becomes unstable. I've never had a server that big; so, I'm just going to take Microsoft's word for it when they say that the server could stop responding, unexpectedly, for more than 10 seconds, if the Distributed Cache memory allocation is allocated more than 16GB.

When you are deciding how big to set a Distributed Cache make sure to reserve at least 2GB of memory for the other processes and services that are running on the server and then to divide the remaining memory by half to arrive at the Distributed Cache size. For example, if you had a server with 32GB of RAM, Microsoft's guidance says to save 2GB for processes and services on the host, which would leave 30GB remaining. If you divided that in half, the Microsoft guidance would have Distributed Cache set at 15GB. This is only 1GB shy of the maximum size of 16GB.

One thing to keep in mind with Distributed Cache is that you really get the most bang out of it when you actually have more than one Distributed Cache host. Whatever you do, do not run a SharePoint 2013 or 2016 farm without a Distributed Cache host, even if it has to share the host with Excel Services, Search Services, Project Server Web application, and/or SQL services. In cases where you only have one server in your farm, as is usually the case in development, just cap the Distributed Cache out at a lower value and allocate more than the 2GB for the other services. Run search at the reduced performance level in this case.

Considering available memory, it is a best practice recommendation to keep the cache host memory resources below 95% utilization to avoid throttling. When the cache host server memory resources get up around 95%, the Distributed Cache will start throttling requests, meaning it will cause operations and things to wait. When this happens, those five areas mentioned earlier could start to exhibit issues. That's not to say that they would not show issues until throttling begins. And, once throttling begins, it will not stop until the memory utilization drops below 70%. It is for this reason that you should not run competing services that are memory hounds like search services on the same server as Distributed Cache. This is recommended to achieve maximum performance. Microsoft also recommends not running Excel services, Project Server, or SQL server on the Distributed Cache host, as they are all memory intensive services, too.

If you're already running Distributed Cache on a server where Excel Services, Search Services, Project Server service, and SQL service are not running and you're experiencing issues, you should take a look at the health of the cluster and possibly changing the amount of memory allocated to Distributed Cache and/or consider adding another host to the cluster. My experience has shown that the Distributed Cache cluster is happiest when it has three or more servers and when it is properly sized.

Speaking of sizing, we already talked about how to determine the maximum size and what to avoid in terms of the maximum; but we didn't talk about the minimum size. The minimum size for a Distributed Cache is based on Microsoft's recommended minimum physical memory requirement of 8GB for a server that is running Distributed Cache. This means that if you were determining the size of the cache using the Microsoft formula that the minimum cache size is 3GB (Minimum recommended physical memory 8GB – 2GB for other processes and services = 6GB / 2 = 3GB).

So now that we have an idea of what size our cache should be, taking into account other things running on the server and that the cache should be at least 3GB, how do we set the cache? How do we determine how big the cache currently is? And how do we least privilege the cache?

When setting the size of your Distributed Cache memory size, you need to consider how many cache hosts are present in the cache cluster. Unlike patching Distributed Cache, when you set memory you need to shut down the Distributed Cache service on all cache hosts in the cluster; because if you fail to shut down the service on all hosts, the entire cache will become unstable and you'll have a hard time getting all the cache hosts online. When you're applying an App Fabric CU to a farm with one Distributed Cache host, you will shut down the Distributed Cache service on the server. The same is true when you have more than one cache host in your farm. The difference with patching is that your farm will still have the benefit of the other server or servers that are running Distributed Cache service while you patch the one of the nodes in your cluster.

For example, let's assume you have a farm with three servers that run the Distributed Cache service and let's also assume that CU8 for the App Fabric 1.1 for Windows Server service was just released. Currently, the most recent cumulative update for the Windows Service App Fabric 1.1 for Windows Server is CU7. What is this App Fabric 1.1 for Windows Server service, you might be asking? Why is he talking about app fabric, I thought we were talking about patching Distributed Cache. Well, the answer is we are talking about patching Distributed Cache. The App Fabric service is the Windows OS service and the SharePoint service named Distributed cache are really one in the same. In fact, you don't patch Distributed Cache when SharePoint is patched.

Back to our example, the farm with three Distributed Cache servers and how to patch it. At a really high level, you shut down the Distributed Cache on one machine, patch it, make any post patch configurations, and then start the Distributed Cache service. After that is completed on one machine, you move onto the next. This differs from increasing the size of the memory for the cache; since when increasing the size of the cache memory allocation, which has to be the same on all machines, the first order of business is to shut down the cache-cluster, then change the size, and then start the cluster. And, actually, the act of running the PowerShell to update the cache size will cause the cluster to come online if it is completely healthy.

The PowerShell used to patch this farm with a new CU is performed in an administrative PowerShell session on one machine:

```
Asnp *SharePoint*
Stop-SPDistributedCacheServiceInstance –Graceful
```

Next, you should wait a minute or two for the operations to transfer to the other hosts. After a few minutes have passed would have already downloaded the update file and would execute it and next through to finish. Then after the cumulative update is applied, you might configure garbage collection, or there might be another configuration. If you've never updated the Distributed Cache in a SharePoint 2013 farm, you'll need to configure garbage collection, because it wasn't introduced until CU3 for the App Fabric 1.1 for Windows Server service.

There are PowerShell scripts out there that you can run to configure the garbage collection, or you can do it manually without the use of scripts. In order to manually configure the garbage collection, navigate to C:\Program Files\AppFabric 1.1 for Windows Server folder, as shown in Figure 3-2.

Once in the folder you would edit a file named DistributedCacheService.exe.config

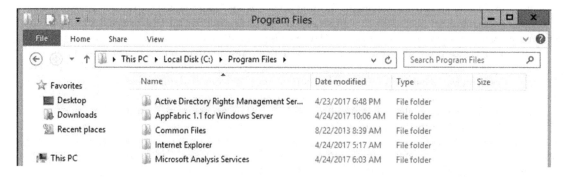

Figure 3-2. *App Fabric 1.1 folder*

by right-clicking it and opening it with Notepad, as shown in Figure 3-3.

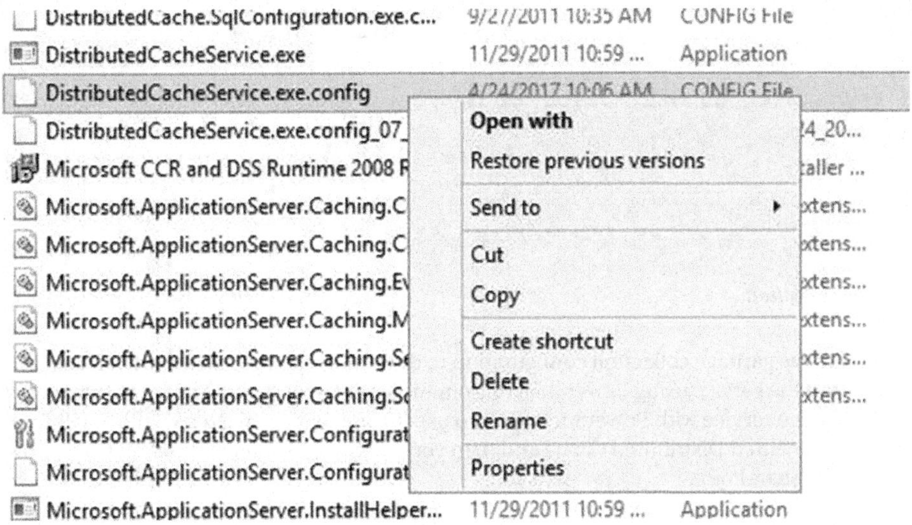

	DistributedCache.SqlConfiguration.exe.c...	9/27/2011 10:35 AM	CONFIG File
DistributedCacheService.exe	11/29/2011 10:59 ...	Application
DistributedCacheService.exe.config	4/24/2017 10:06 AM	CONFIG File
DistributedCacheService.exe.config_07_		

```
                                  Open with                          |4_20...
                                  Restore previous versions          :aller ...
                                  Send to                        ►   xtens...
                                  Cut                                xtens...
                                  Copy                               xtens...
                                  Create shortcut                    xtens...
                                  Delete                             xtens...
                                  Rename
                                  Properties
```

Microsoft.ApplicationServer.InstallHelper... 11/29/2011 10:59 ... Application

Figure 3-3. *Right-click and open with*

Once you have the file open in Notepad, you'll notice the section named <configuration> and that this section spans the entire file. At the very end of the file, you'll find the end of the <configuration> section and it will look like this: </configuration>. It is right in front of this ending tag that you'll place the following lines of code to configure the garbage collection before restarting the Distributed Cache service.

```
<appSettings>
  <add key="backgroundGC" value="true"/>
</appSettings>
```

Figure 3-4 shows what the DistributedCacheService.exe.config looks like before it is configured for garbage collection.

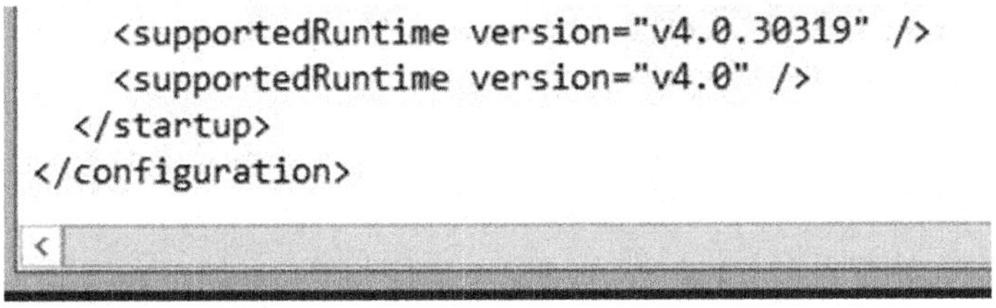

```
    <supportedRuntime version="v4.0.30319" />
    <supportedRuntime version="v4.0" />
  </startup>
</configuration>
```

Figure 3-4. *No garbage collection*

After the file is configured for garbage collection, the last few lines look like the image in Figure 3-5.

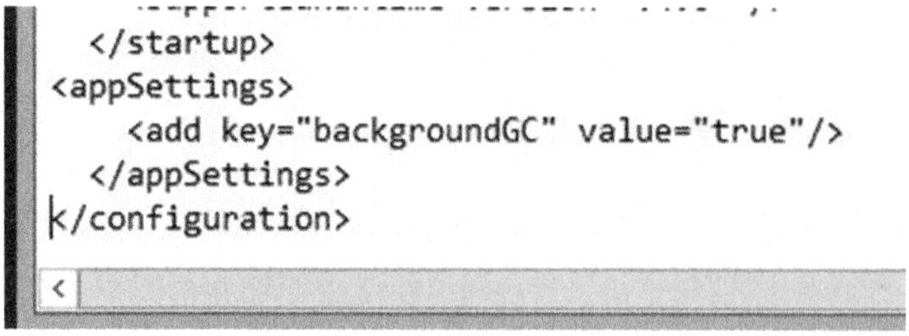

```
--rrr-- ---------------- ------------  - ---  , -
  </startup>
<appSettings>
    <add key="backgroundGC" value="true"/>
  </appSettings>
</configuration>
<
```

Figure 3-5. *Garbage collection*

After having added the garbage collection configuration to the config file, you can save it and start the service. You can start the service using PowerShell or from the services on server page in Central Administration. To start the service with PowerShell you can use the following two lines. In the first line, you grab the service instance named Distributed Cache and then you call the provision method that is part of every service instance in SharePoint.

```
$ServiceOnServer = Get-SPServiceInstance | ? {$_.TypeName -eq "Distributed Cache" -and
$_.Server.Name -eq $env:computername}
$ ServiceOnServer.Provision()
```

If you recall the get-member cmdlet from chapter 2, you could pipe get-spserviceinstance to get-member and after the screen stopped scrolling, you could scroll up a little and see the various methods, with provision being one of them. Provision is to start as unprovision is to stop when it comes to services on the server in SharePoint.

After you have the service started, you would complete this procedure on the other two servers in your cluster and then reset IIS and test for any of the issues you had previously been experiencing in your farm. There's a good chance that you may have solved the issue by upgrading the cluster to the most recent tested CU and by configuring garbage collection.

If your cache memory size is too small, the cache may be constricted, and it has to flush more frequently. In order to increase the size of the cache, you need to stop the Distributed Cache service on all the hosts. You could open PowerShell on each host and use the Stop-SPDistributedCacheServiceInstance –Graceful or you could log in to Central Administration, navigate to the services on the server page, and stop all the instances that you see running. After you have stopped the Distributed Cache service, you could run the following PowerShell to verify that it is no longer provisioned:

```
$ServiceOnServer = Get-SPServiceInstance | ? {$_.TypeName -eq "Distributed Cache} | ft
typename, status, server –auto -wrap
```

Once the service is no longer provisioned or started on any server in the farm, you can update the size of the cache to your desired size. Before you can update the cache size, you should use a command to get the cache host configuration into your shell and see what size the cache is currently. There are numerous ways to do this but the easiest is to just run the following command:

```
Use-CacheCluster
Get-AFCacheHostConfiguration -ComputerName ComputerName -CachePort "22233"
```

You would need to substitute your computer name for ComputerName; for example, your command would look like the following if your server was named 2013Cache:

```
Use-CacheCluster
Get-AFCacheHostConfiguration -ComputerName 2013Cache -CachePort "22233"
```

Once you run the preceding command, and feel that you are ready to change the size of the memory in use by the cache, you run the update-spdistributedcachesize cmdlet. To do this, you have to convert from GB to MB since the command used to increase the size of the cache is as follows:

```
Update-SPDistributedCacheSize -CacheSizeInMB CacheSize
```

This command only has to be run on one machine in the cluster. After you run this command, it will update the cache size on all your hosts. If you were changing the cache size to 6GB, the command would read:

```
Update-SPDistributedCacheSize -CacheSizeInMB 6144
```

After you ran that, the host would start up with the new memory size and then the other hosts would start up and the cache size would increase on those hosts, as well. One very important aspect of all of this to consider is that the actual physical memory on these machines should be the same size. Another key takeaway from all of this is to never stop and start the App Fabric 1.1 for Windows Server service from within the Services console (services.msc).

Up until this point, we have looked at configuring the size of the Distributed Cache memory allocation on each cache host, garbage collection, and patching the service; but we have not looked at least privileging the AppFabric Service. This is one of those situations where PowerShell is the only way to least privilege without breaking the service or corrupting the cache. When you're going to change the identity that runs the AppFabric 1.1 for Windows Server to something other than the farm account, you must use PowerShell. As you can see from the service accounts page does not have an option for the AppFabric Service, as shown in Figure 3-6.

```
Select one...
Farm Account
Windows Service - Claims to Windows Token Service
Windows Service - Distributed Cache
Windows Service - Document Conversions Launcher Service
Windows Service - Document Conversions Load Balancer Service
Windows Service - Microsoft SharePoint Foundation Sandboxed Code Service
Windows Service - Search Host Controller Service
Windows Service - SharePoint Server Search
Windows Service - User Profile Synchronization Service
Web Application Pool - mysites.contoso.com
Web Application Pool - portal.contoso.com
Service Application Pool - SecurityTokenServiceApplicationPool
Service Application Pool - SharePoint Hosted Services
Service Application Pool - SharePoint Search Application Pool
Service Application Pool - SharePoint Web Services System
```

Figure 3-6. No options in GUI use PowerShell

You should least privilege the Distributed cache preferably before configuring the memory size and before or after patching, but not during either of those events.

The reason that I like to least privilege first is that part of the process involves removing and adding the Distributed Cache service instance from all but one Distributed Cache host in your cluster. For example, if you have three Distributed Cache hosts, before you change the identity that runs the App Fabric 1.1. For Windows Server service, you should remove the other cache hosts from the distributed cache cluster. Before you remove a cache host, make sure to stop the Distributed cache service and remove the Distributed Cache service instance from the server.

```
Stop-SPDistributedCacheServiceInstance –Graceful
```

Wait a couple of minutes after stopping the instance before you remove it completely. Then do the same thing on the next node, leaving only one node remaining. These are the commands used to remove the Distributed Cache Service Instance.

```
Remove-SPDistributedCacheServiceInstance
Add-SPDistributedCacheServiceInstance
```

Once the cluster has only one host running the Distributed Cache service, you can commence with changing the alias. *Do not change the alias with the Distributed Cache service stopped.* The following lines of code are the one way to change the Distributed Cache service instance with PowerShell. Whatever you do, **do not change the identity with the Services console (services.msc)**. You'll notice in the lines of code that follow only one required change is needed and that is the change to the domain\user_account value in the first line.

```
$acct = Get-SPManagedAccount "domain\user_account"
$farm = Get-SPFarm
$svc = $farm.Services | ? {$_.TypeName -eq "Distributed Cache"}
$svc.ProcessIdentity.CurrentIdentityType = "SpecificUser"
$svc.ProcessIdentity.ManagedAccount = $acct
$svc.ProcessIdentity.Update()
$svc.ProcessIdentity.Deploy()
```

After you run this command, it should take *at least 8 minutes for the change to take effect,* and if it doesn't, then something is wrong. You'll know something is wrong when you go to start the cache and it quickly cycles to stopped, or hangs in an unknown status. When this happens, the best thing you can do is to set things back to square one. Clear the slate, so to speak, and get back to ground zero.

If it takes at least 8 minutes, then go ahead and add the other Distributed Cache hosts back into the farm and then update the size of the cache and configure garbage collection if not already configured.

If there is still a problem, the following paragraphs will help.

A senior SharePoint engineer named Scott Fawley shared this series of scripts with me. Scott spent over a decade with Microsoft SharePoint support before joining Rackspace. Trust me. This is the way to *get your server back to ground zero* in regards to Distributed Cache, if it is acting up.

If you were having trouble with multiple servers in the farm, you would need to do this on all of them. As we go over these lines, I'll share another gem that will let you gather all the servers in your farm that have been in, or have the Distributed Cache service instance and then remove it.

You can tell you're back at a clean slate when you've ran these commands and the App Fabric 1.1 for Windows Server service shows as disabled in the Windows Services Console (services.msc). Use this script to get back to ground zero and remove the Distributed Cache cluster:

```
Remove-SPDistributedCacheServiceInstance

$SPFarm = Get-SPFarm
$cacheClusterName = "SPDistributedCacheCluster_" + $SPFarm.Id.ToString()
$cacheClusterManager = [Microsoft.SharePoint.DistributedCaching.Utilities.SPDistributedCache
ClusterInfoManager]::Local
$cacheClusterInfo = $cacheClusterManager.GetSPDistributedCacheClusterInfo($cacheClusterName);
$instanceName ="SPDistributedCacheService Name=AppFabricCachingService"
$serviceInstance = Get-SPServiceInstance | ? {($_.Service.Tostring()) -eq $instanceName -and
($_.Server.Name) -eq $env:computername}
if([System.String]::IsNullOrEmpty($cacheClusterInfo.CacheHostsInfoCollection))
{
$serviceInstance.Delete()
}
```

Don't worry about any red vomit from this command. It will sometimes have some, but that is OK, it probably means that you've already partially uninstalled the instance. After running the preceding code, you want to make sure that Distributed Cache is not installed anywhere else in the farm, unless your farm is a single server farm. Here's the script to verify if Distributed Cache is installed on any of the other vm's in your farm, and a line to delete them:

```
$svc = Get-SPServiceInstance | Where {$_.TypeName -eq "Distributed Cache"}
$svc.Delete()
```

This command should be run **after** the command that gets the cache cluster and removes it. Make sure that all the hosts that were previously in the cluster show the app fabric 1.1 for Windows Server with a disabled state. The previous command will remove the Distributed Cache service instance off any servers in your farm.

After all servers are back to ground zero, *run the following lines on the one server* on which you would like to begin your cluster:

```
$SPFarm = Get-SPFarm
$cacheClusterName = "SPDistributedCacheCluster_" + $SPFarm.Id.ToString()
$cacheClusterManager = [Microsoft.SharePoint.DistributedCaching.Utilities.SPDistributedCache
ClusterInfoManager]::Local
$cacheClusterInfo = $cacheClusterManager.GetSPDistributedCacheClusterInfo($cacheClusterName);
$instanceName ="SPDistributedCacheService Name=AppFabricCachingService"
$serviceInstance = Get-SPServiceInstance | ? {($_.Service.Tostring()) -eq $instanceName -and
($_.Server.Name) -eq $env:computername}
if([System.String]::IsNullOrEmpty($cacheClusterInfo.CacheHostsInfoCollection))

Add-SPDistributedCacheServiceInstance
$cacheClusterInfo.CacheHostsInfoCollection
```

After you run these lines, close your PowerShell session, and then open a new administrative session and run the following:

```
Use-Cachecluster
Get-CacheHost
```

You should be presented with the status of the cluster and *it should only show one host* with an UP status. Go ahead and change the identity that the service runs under using this code, which is the same as from earlier in the chapter:

```
$acct = Get-SPManagedAccount "domain\user_account"
$farm = Get-SPFarm
$svc = $farm.Services | ?{$_.TypeName -eq "Distributed Cache"}
$svc.ProcessIdentity.CurrentIdentityType = "SpecificUser"
$svc.ProcessIdentity.ManagedAccount = $acct
$svc.ProcessIdentity.Update()
$svc.ProcessIdentity.Deploy()
```

After 8 minutes passes, you can check the status of the cluster again by running Get-CacheHost, and if things are looking good, then add the other hosts to the cluster. Finally, update the cluster size by shutting them all off, changing the size on the first host that was in the cluster, and then running the command to update the cluster, as shown here:

```
Update-SPDistributedCacheSize -CacheSizeInMB 6144
```

Ok, so that is all well and good, but what do you do if you're still getting some sort of crazy message about no cache host info or an error reading cache info? Where is this info located? In this case you look at the C:\Program Files\AppFabric 1.1 for Windows Server\DistributedCacheService.exe.config and verify if the file has the same information in the cluster config node and then you check in registry to see that the information is present. But if it ever gets to this point, you're honestly better at ripping out the cache cluster from the farm using the previous steps. Then after the cluster is removed, you could compare the info in the config file among the different members in the farm. Every server in the farm, even the ones that are not members of the Distributed Cache cluster should all be at the same CU level and have the same information in the config file. Figure 3-7 shows a partial view of the clusterconfig line, it shows the provider and the connection string.

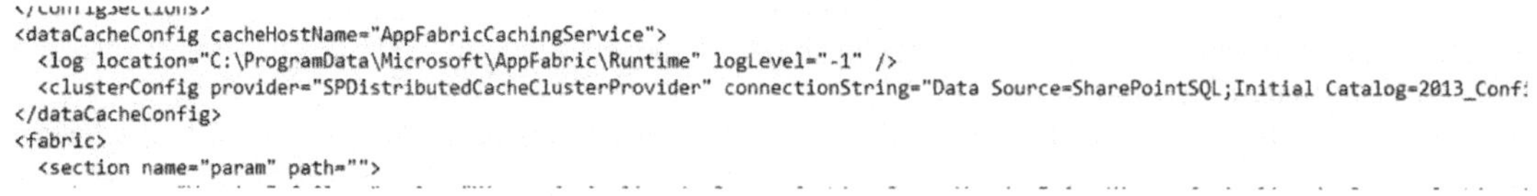

```
</configSections>
<dataCacheConfig cacheHostName="AppFabricCachingService">
  <log location="C:\ProgramData\Microsoft\AppFabric\Runtime" logLevel="-1" />
  <clusterConfig provider="SPDistributedCacheClusterProvider" connectionString="Data Source=SharePointSQL;Initial Catalog=2013_Conf:
</dataCacheConfig>
<fabric>
  <section name="param" path="">
```

Figure 3-7. *CacheCluster config*

After you've copied this info, you can look in registry and compare the values for the provider and connection string in the config file with what is shown for those same values at this registry location HKLM\SOFTWARE\Microsoft\AppFabric\V1.0\Configuration. Figure 3-8 shows a farm that is either having trouble or is shows a server where the Distributed Cache service instance has not been installed and started. In this case, the server had not had Distributed Cache service instance installed.

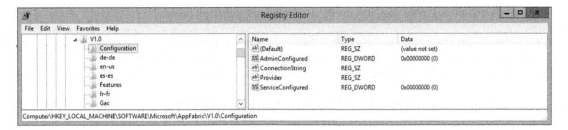

Figure 3-8. *Distributed cache not installed*

Once the Distributed Cache services installed and started, the registry will hold data for the connection String and Provider as the config file, as shown in Figure 3-9.

```
<clusterConfig provider="SPDistributedCacheClusterProvider" connectionString="Data Source=SharePointSQL;Initial Catalog=2013_Cc
</dataCacheConfig>
```

Figure 3-9. *Distributed Cache installed*

Notice how you can see the correlation between the config file and registry. If you're ever in a situation where they disagree, your best bet is to remove all the Distributed Cache hosts and clear out the cluster. After doing that, you'll want to make sure all the hosts are at the same CU level, even if they are not going to run the Distributed Cache instance.

There have been seven CUs for the App Fabric 1.1 for Windows Server service released since its inception. Garbage collection is possible starting with CU3. Table 3-1 lists the CU levels and their associated version information.

Table 3-1. *App Fabric for Windows Server Cumulative Update Versions*

CU Level	Product Version
CU1	1.0.4639.0
CU2	1.0.4644.0
CU3	1.0.4652.2
CU4	1.0.4653.2
CU5	1.0.4655.2
CU6	1.0.4656.2
CU 7	1.0.4657.2

You can use this one-liner to return the product version of your App Fabric.

```
(Get-ItemProperty "C:\Program Files\AppFabric 1.1 for Windows Server\PowershellModules\
DistributedCacheConfiguration\Microsoft.ApplicationServer.Caching.Configuration.dll" -Name
VersionInfo).VersionInfo.ProductVersion
```

The output of this script, which I did not devise, is shown in Figure 3-10.

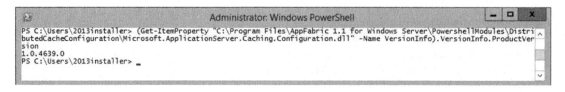

Figure 3-10. *App Fabric is patched to version 1.0.4639.0, CU1*

When it comes to SharePoint 2016, servers that are using the minimum role technology of Search, Application, front end, or Application with Search do not have the Distributed Cache service instance. If you want a 2016 Server to run the Distributed Cache service instance, you need to make sure that that 2016 server is running the Front-end with Distributed Cache, Custom, Single Server, or Distributed Cache minimum role.

- WebFrontEnd (Front-end server role) Page Load Performance Apples

- Application (Application server role)

- DistributedCache (Distributed Cache server role)

- Search (Search server role)

- Custom (Custom server role)

- SingleServerFarm (single-server farm server role)

- WebFrontEndWithDistributedCache (front-end with Distributed Cache) <- - only possible if have Nov2016 CU or higher

- ApplicationWithSearch (application with search) - Nov16CU required

When working with 2016 and performing any of the actions that I outlined, you should change the role to web front end if you want to remove the Distributed Cache service from the server to remove it from the cluster. You can change the role of a server directly from Central Administration in SharePoint 2016, or via PowerShell. Then after you have only one server with one of the roles that instantiate the Distributed Cache service, you could change the identity for the App Fabric 1.1 for Windows Server service. If you were looking to change the size of the cluster, the same rules apply as far as stopping all the hosts in the cluster before updating the size. You can use these lines to stop the 2016 Distributed Cache service instance.

```
$instanceName ="SPDistributedCacheService Name=AppFabricCachingService"
$serviceInstance = Get-SPServiceInstance | ? {($_.service.tostring()) -eq
$instanceName -and ($_.server.name) -eq $env:computername}
$serviceInstance.Unprovision()
```

Run that on each server in your farm and then proceed with updating the size using the Update-SPDistributedCacheSize cmdlet. The same rules apply for sizing as did in 2013 and the same rules apply for configuring garbage collection. What's weird is SharePoint 2016 installs with the App Fabric 1.1 for Windows Server service with CU7 applied; but the garbage collection is not automatically configured. That just seems odd to me.

In closing this Distributed Cache discussion, I have to mention that Microsoft has a really awesome resource named Plan and use Distributed Cache that is available for download in .pdf or .visio format from https://www.microsoft.com/en-us/download/details.aspx?id=35557. I would highly recommend getting a copy of this to use a reference tool.

User Profile Synchronization

User profile synchronization is one of the most commonly misunderstood services. One of the common misunderstandings is that it has everything to do with site access and security. Another common misunderstanding is that it has nothing to do with site access and security. Both of those misunderstandings are founded in a phrase you hear thrown around a lot when people talk about SharePoint, "it depends." In reality, User Profile synchronization only has a little bit to do with site access. User profile service is mostly used for user metadata that can be surfaced in people search.

The part of the User Profile service that has to do with permissions relates to how access is provided to your SharePoint sites, and their content relates to Active Directory groups that are synched. If you provide access directly to users and do not use Active Directory groups for access to your sites, then the User Profile service application does not have anything to do with site access. However, if you use Active Directory groups as the only means of providing site access, or you use a combination of domain groups inside SharePoint groups along with users directly added to your sites, then the user profile service has something to do with site access. Because if one of the four key settings of the user profile for a user is out of sync with the user profile info synchronized within the group information, then that could cause SharePoint to deny access to sites.

The built-in User Profile service application in SharePoint imports the following four key user attributes, which is why this service is a key setting in the farm to have correctly configured:

- The Windows Security Identifier (SID)

- The Active Directory Domain Services (AD DS) user principal name (UPN)

- The Simple Mail Transfer Protocol (SMTP) address

- The Session Initiation Protocol (SIP) address

When first provisioning the user profile service, you should make sure you are patched to at least the May 2015 CU for SharePoint 2010 and 2013, with November 2016 being the preferred CU level to spin up your farm with. Once the farm is created, you should remember an important order of operations for getting the User Profile Service created and synchronizing. There are couple of different ways to think of this process, so I'll say them a both ways. Here goes.

The first one is don't try to provision the service application if you haven't already started the User Profile service and never use the farm account interactively for this provisioning. That is, do not log in with the farm account. The second rule is don't try to start the sync service until you have created and started the User Profile service application. The third rule is create a dedicated web application for mysites and make sure that the managed path exists and that self-service site creation is on in that web app, before you create the site collection in that web application. You could also create the MySite host site collection at the root of the web application. You should perform these steps with the install account. The install account should be a local admin. The farm account should be a local admin during this provisioning; it can be removed after the sync has started and the connection to Active Directory is established.

Another way to think of this madness, is once you have the web application created and the managed path is created as a wildcard path, make sure that self-service site creation is allowed on the web application. Create a MySite host site collection at the root of the web application and then make sure the user Profile service instance is started on services on server page in central admin. After those two things are done, create the service application in manage service applications and then start the sync service on the services on server page. After the sync service starts, make sure the account that is going to create the connection to Active Directory has the correct permissions, and then create the sync connection. Perform all of this with the install account, and make sure that it and the farm account are local admins. Then establish the connection with Active Directory for the account used in the connection settings. After the sync has started, the connection is in place, and a sync has ran, remove the farm account from the local administrators.

When configuring the User Profile service application in SharePoint 2010 and 2013, you should never manually touch the related Windows services. The related Windows services are the Forefront Identity Management Service and the Forefront Identity Management Synchronization Service. The only time you'd ever touch either of these is if you had a farm that was June 2011 CU or newer and the Forefront Identity Management Service was running but the Forefront Identity Management Synchronization Service was not, in this case you would start the Forefront Identity Management Synchronization Service.

There are few things you can troubleshoot when the service will not start, one of them is to make sure the farm account has the local security policy, user rights assignment, of allow logon locally, and is a member of the Local administrators. Then log in with the farm account and then log the farm account off and log back in with the setup account to continue with getting the user profile service started. This logging in of the farm account and then logging off, helps to burn in all the farm account's Windows settings. That is as far as you should go with the farm account. Make sure the install account is a domain admin and member of local administrators on all the machines in the farm, before trying to start the User Profile Synchronization service.

If the service still fails to start after those actions then stop the synchronization service using PowerShell, since there probably isn't a stop action on the services on server page as the service is stuck on starting. This PowerShell will stop the sync service:

```
$UPS = Get-SPServiceInstance -EA "SilentlyContinue" | Where {$_.TypeName -eq "User Profile
Synchronization Service" -and $_.Server -match $server}
$UPS.Unprovision()
```

Then after the sync service stops, you'll want to delete any timer jobs that might be hanging out and trying to sync some user profiles. These next two lines are only going to return something in a situation where the sync service is truly stuck on starting.

```
$timerjob = Get-SPTimerJob -EA "SilentlyContinue" | where {$_.Name -eq
"ProfileSynchronizationSetupJob"}
$timerjob.Delete()
```

When you run these lines, you might get some red puke that says, "You cannot call a method on a null-valued expression." And do not worry about that because it is PowerShell and SharePoint's way of telling you that the timer job didn't exist.

After that, you need to remove the certificates that the ForeFront Identity service creates when it is trying to start the sync. You can remove them with PowerShell, but don't try to sync just yet. To remove these manually, you open the certificate manager and look through each store for any certificates that have the words Forefront Identity Manager in their subjects. To remove these with PowerShell, make sure you have a PowerShell session open administratively and then just paste these lines of code into your window and after pasting Enter a couple of times until your prompt returns.

```
$allCertStores = Get-ChildItem -Path cert:\LocalMachine | %{$_.name}
  foreach ($certstore in $allCertStores)
 {
    $store = New-Object System.Security.Cryptography.x509Certificates.x509Store($certstore,
    "LocalMachine")
    $store.Open("ReadWrite")
     $certs = $store.Certificates | ? {$_.subject -like "*ForefrontIdentityManager*"}
    ForEach ($cert in $certs)
    {
     if($cert){$store.Remove($cert)}
    }
  $store.Close()
  }
```

After you're done, you should clear the SharePoint Configuration cache by stopping the timer service, navigating to the cache location, deleting out the XML files, setting the cache.ini file value back to 1, and repeating this on every server in the farm, then start the timer service and watch that all the XML files are re-created. There are many blog posts about clearing the config cache on the interwebs. I have one that is a re-blogurtation of an awesome script I didn't write at https://anothersharepointblog.com/clearing-the-config-cache-with-powershell.

At this point, if you're still having trouble, you can try to reset the UPS back to square one with the advice from Spencer Harbar, using the following PowerShell.

```
Add-PSSnapin Microsoft.SharePoint.Powershell
# These will only work if there is one DB and one SA on the box.
# If more than one, then use Get-SPDatabase and Get-SPServiceApplication
# to grab the GUID and pass that in instead of the pipebind

$syncDBType = "Microsoft.Office.Server.Administration.SynchronizationDatabase"
$upaSAType = "User Profile Service Application"
$syncDB = Get-SPDatabase | where-object {$_.Type -eq $syncDBType}
$upa = Get-SPServiceApplication | where-object {$_.TypeName -eq $upaSAType}

$syncDB.Unprovision()
$syncDB.Status = "Offline"
$upa.ResetSynchronizationMachine()
$upa.ResetSynchronizationDatabase()
$syncDB.Provision()

# We MUST restart the timer service for the state to be reflected in
# Services on Server and Manage UPA
Restart-service SPTimerV4

# At this stage we MUST add the Farm account to the SyncDB (the above
# steps remove the user) remember the default schema must be 'dbo'.
# If we don't do this, UPS provisioning will fail.
```

Please pay close attention to the advice that Spencer gives, where he annotates in the script that this script is for a farm with only one User Profile service application and that after running the script that you should set the farm account privileges on the Sync db. Setting the account privileges is explained in the next paragraphs.

If things are still not working, another thing to check is that the farm account and the install account both have access to the User Profile service application databases. For example, if you've opened the ULSViewer, a tool we'll talk about in depth in a later chapter, you might see the following entry occurring when the profile sync is trying to start:

```
05/07/2017 08:22:22.00 OWSTIMER.EXE (0x0950) 0x1880 SharePoint Portal Server User
Profiles    9i1w  Medium  ILM Configuration: Error 'ERR_CONFIG_DB'. de5aef9d-212f-807b-
4ebf-317f8875cab4
```

If you're seeing this, it means that your account does not have sufficient privileges on the sync database.

Log in to your SQL server and open the SQL Server management Studio (SSMS). Once you have SSMS open, take a look at the user mappings for each of these accounts. Make sure that the accounts have db_owner role on the Profile, Social, and Sync databases. After you've made any changes, you should try to start the synch once more.

At this point, you've tried many things to get this service going and you definitely have patched your farm to the May 2015 CU or higher level successfully. If that is the case, you should start the User Profile Service on the Services on Server page, and then try to start the sync once more.

As a last-ditch effort and before re-creating the User Profile service application, you might try to log in with the farm account and start the sync. This really should be avoided, however, as the farm account should never be used interactively. Use the install account to install the User Profile service. You could however; be logged in with the install account and open PowerShell as the farm account and then run your scripts to install the User Profile service, as the farm account. Spencer Harbar has a really good blog post that describes it at http://www.harbar.net/archive/2010/10/30/avoiding-the-default-schema-issue-when-creating-the-user-profile.aspx.

Another action that will sometimes get the sync to start working is to "jiggle the bits" by running the post-setup Configuration Wizard (psconfiggui.exe). When running the psconfig wizard, make sure to keep the server in the farm and keep the Central Administration site on the server. After the psconfig wizard has ran successfully, take a look at the servers in the farm page and ensure that all the SharePoint servers have a "no action required," and if any of them are anything but that, run the psconfig wizard on the server that does not have "no action required". If the psconfig wizard does not complete successfully, open the log file and search for "ERR" with case sensitivity turned on. Look at the error and try to decipher what it is saying. The text from these logs and other logs is the best way to google or Bing search for any error you encounter in SharePoint.

Once, you've run psconfig, try to start the sync. And at this point, you'll want to have the ULSViewer open and tracking the process. You can get a copy of the ULSViewer from the official download location at https://www.microsoft.com/en-us/download/details.aspx?id=44020. After you download the executable to your SharePoint server and double click it, you should open from ULS and filter on Profile. Chapter 9 has more detailed steps on how to do this, in case you're unfamiliar with ULSViewer.

If the sync is still not starting, Bjorn Roalkvam has written an awesome script that has yet to let me down when trying to get the user profile service started. If this script can't start the sync and you've verified that database permissions are correct, then you'll definitely need to rebuild the User Profile Service Application.

You can download a copy of the script from Bjorn's blog at https://sharepointbjorn.com/2014/06/25/user-profile-synchronization-autofixer/. Bjorn's blog also has a really straightforward explanation of how to use the script; so, I'll let you go there and read about it. Basically, you need to run it with the correct account and know the farm password and that's it, it does all the rest. And as I already mentioned, but will mention one more time for emphasis, if this script cannot start your user profile sync, then you need to make sure your farm is at the proper patch level and re-create the User Profile service application.

Considering all of these steps, it is best to recap all the troubleshooting steps to get the User Profile Synch Started before rebuilding. Verify the following:

- The farm account is a local admin and has logged in once and then logged off

- The install account is being used to start the sync

- The farm account has the allow logon locally user rights assignment in local security policy

- The previous Forefront Identity Manager (FIM) certs have been deleted from the local cert store

- The Timer job for profile sync setup named ProfileSynchronizationSetupJob has been deleted, if it existed

- The SharePoint Config Cache has been cleared

- The SharePoint farm is patched to at least the May 2015 CU or higher

- Verified that the install and farm accounts have db_owner role on the profile, social, and most importantly the sync database

- Set the UPS back to square one

- Stopped the User Profile Service, restarted it, then tried to sync

- Ran PSConfigGUI.exe

- Ran the script by Bjorn Roalkvam

If the farm is new, this is the first series of attempts, and you have performed all the steps, and the user profile sync still will not start, you should rebuild the User Profile service application. *If the farm is not a new build, you do not want to hastily rebuild the User Profile service application since there might be a lot of custom User and Organization Properties and custom Organizational Profiles and Sub-types that a rebuild would eradicate.* So, before you rebuild on an existing farm make sure to document and customizations that have been made in the User Profile service application.

If you've decided to remove the User Profile service application, you can do so via Central Administration ➤ Manage Service Application page by selecting the User Profile service application and then clicking the Delete icon in the operations group on the ribbon. If you opt to use this method, as opposed to PowerShell, then remember to select the "Delete Data associated with the Service Application" box, as shown in Figure 3-11.

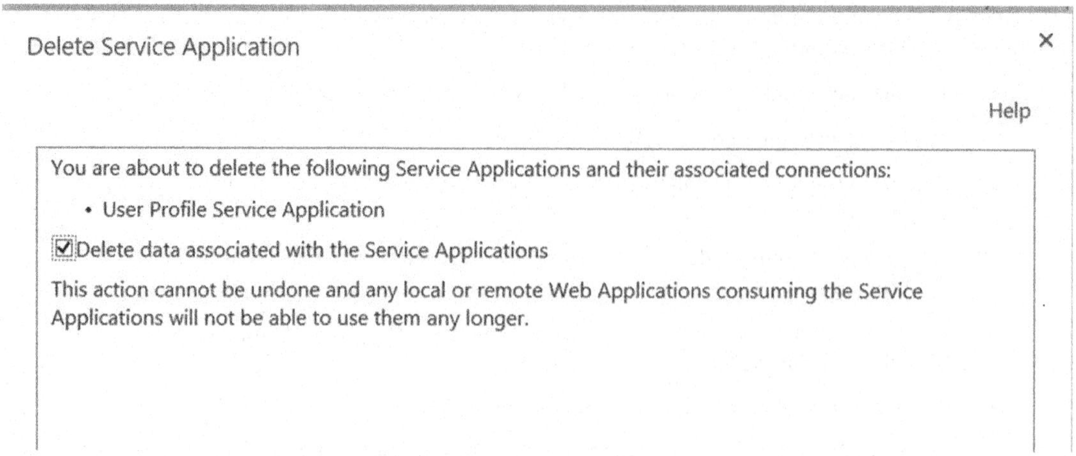

Figure 3-11. *Deleting the User Profile service application via the GUI*

If you would like to remove the User Profile service application and all of its data using PowerShell, you can run these commands:

```
Get-SPServiceApplication | ? {$_.typename -like "user*"} | Remove-SPServiceApplication -
RemoveData -confirm:$false
Get-SPServiceApplicationProxy | ? {$_.typename -like "user*"} | Remove-
SPServiceApplicationProxy -RemoveData -confirm:$false
```

Re-creating the User Profile service application is a straightforward action that can involve the GUI or PowerShell. If you're creating the User Profile service application with PowerShell, you have to be cognizant of the User Account Control Settings on the server, as they can cause the schema of the databases to provision incorrectly, which will cause issues.

After you get the sync started, you can create the connection in the User Profile service application to sync with Active Directory. If you encounter any errors with creating the connection, make sure that the account being used to connect to Active Directory has Replicate directory changes in Active Directory and if you're dealing with a server running Windows Server 2008, the account should also have Replicate Directory Changes All. We'll look at this again when we get to the chapter on logs.

Patching

Since patching the farm is a very important part of a good build, let's talk about troubleshooting issues with patching and some methods and things to keep in mind when applying patches. The first part about patching to understand is that there isn't any magical order of servers to patch. A lot of the interwebs will say you should patch the application server that runs Central Administration first and then follow it with the remaining servers in the farm. It's just a preference.

When applying a patch, you can do so manually or you can use a script like the one Russ Maxwell wrote and that I have re-blogged at https://anothersharepointblog.com/applying-cus-to-sharepoint-2013-servers-with-powershell. It works great because it stops the Search service, IIS Admin service and SharePoint Timer service; which increases the rate at which patches burn-in. Then after the patch is applied to the server, the script will restart the services, provided you do not accidentally allow a patch to restart the server beforehand. So, when using the script, as I highly recommend, make sure to answer no to any prompts that want to restart the server after the patch is applied. Then, after the script restarts the search services, the IIS admin service, and the SharePoint timer service, you can restart and all will be well with the world.

After the restart happens and the server comes back online, you should run the post-setup Configuration Wizard (psconfiggui.exe) from either the GUI or using PowerShell. If you opt to use PowerShell, this is the cmdlet:

```
PSConfig.exe -cmd upgrade -inplace b2b -force -cmd applicationcontent -install -cmd
installfeatures
```

Sometimes the psconfig will report failures on databases where SharePoint features have not been properly removed from the database. This usually happens on content databases. You can get around this sometimes by running the upgrade-spcontentdatabase command on a database by database basis using the –skipintegritychecks parameter. If you take this approach, make sure that the database is not set to read-only, since a read-only database will not upgrade. You can check this in SQL by looking at the options page in the database properties, as shown in Figure 3-12.

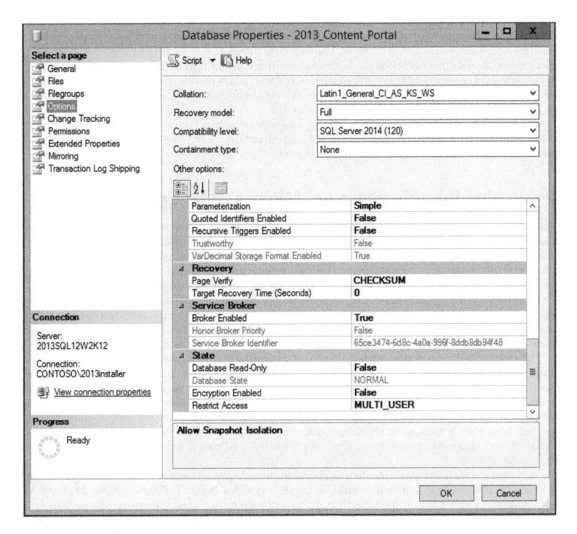

Figure 3-12. *Database is not read only*

As long as the read-only is false, you're good to go; but if it is true, you should change it to false, and then try to upgrade the database. The cmdlet to upgrade the database is

```
Upgrade-SPContentDatabase <DatabaseName> -skipintegritychecks
```

The skipintegritychecks parameter sounds bad and ugly, as if we are not doing something important, but all we are doing is telling SharePoint to forget about those missing features and missing setup files it was reporting in the previous attempt where psconfig failed. Missing features and missing setup files are what result when a solution is deployed to a site collection, activated inside the sites, then retracted and removed without first being deactivated in the sites. This doesn't mean that the database is corrupt, necessarily, but it is lacking in integrity, since it will have references in it for features and setup files that are no longer present in the farm. When this happens, the psconfig will usually fail and say that it found all these features and they are not present in the farm; but they are in the database.

After you've ran the upgrade-spcontentdatabase, run the psconfig once more via the command line or via the GUI and you should get a successful run.

Whenever psconfig fails, it is best to troubleshoot the log it provides on the first failure. Usually the log will indicate if SharePoint couldn't access a database or if there were issues with missing features or setup files and the database that has references to the features. This is a huge help if you're dealing with a farm with hundreds of content databases, as maybe it is only a few that have issues. Once you've determined the database and have checked the database and it is not read-only, make sure that the install account has db_owner and that the farm account has db_owner as well.

Finally, in closing out this section on patching, remember that there is absolutely no shame in running the psconfiggui.exe vs. the psconfig.exe. Actually, I prefer to run the wizard via the GUI first and resort to PowerShell when I need to pull out "the big guns," so to speak.

Publishing Infrastructure vs. Minimal Download Strategy

The publishing infrastructure brings a new feature called design manager, which allows developers to create SharePoint master pages based on html designs that they've created. The problem is that the master pages that get generated by design manager are not minimal download strategy aware. The minimal download strategy (MDS) master pages have this control called AjaxDelta that helps with the speed of the page load by controlling what parts of the page should be loaded on a refresh and what parts should be cached.

If you want to use a page created with the publishing infrastructure, or if you would like to take advantage of the publishing infrastructure for use in sites that use variations, you should deactivate the MDS feature. If you don't, there is a chance that you'll encounter two page loads, first for the start.aspx page that the MDS uses and then the full path to the publishing page behind the start.aspx.

When troubleshooting issues with page loads you should always look at how publishing is playing into the load times. If your servers have some decent RAM, let's say 24GB or more, you can turn off MDS and use a master page that was optimized for publishing and get some really awesome page loads. On the other hand, if you don't have a lot of RAM, MDS can give you some pretty awesome performance by only re-loading parts of the page that are wrapped by the AjaxDelta. So, if you're experiencing a flash like where the page starts to load and then it loads really quick again, you should look at either de-activating the MDS and using publishing, using publishing pages that have master pages that address the AjaxDelta, or just using master pages that were made for MDS.

In Chapter 2, we talked about how to turn publishing on using PowerShell at the object model level and at the web application level; but we didn't discuss the settings within the site collection that need to be set to get publishing in full force. After the SuperUser and SuperReader are set, open site settings and navigate to the top site if you're not already there. In other words, open site settings on the site collection and then once there make sure that you do not see a "go to top level site" link.

Publishing activation has to be performed in a specific order. It is not possible to activate publishing on a sub-site of a site collection if the feature is not activated at the site collection level.

Click Manage Site Features under Site Actions, and de-activate the Minimal Download Strategy. Then go back to the top level, Site Collection Settings page, and click Site Collection Features under Site Collection Administration. After you have deactivated MDS, activate the publishing feature, from the Site Collection Features page. Then click Manage Site Features under the Site actions and activate publishing at the web level. Don't worry. If you do this out of order, SharePoint prompts to ease your troubleshooting pain, telling you about the dependencies that publishing infrastructures require.

Click Site Collection Output Cache, and when it opens, enable the output cache so that your master pages can begin to cache in your server's memory. Choose a profile for anonymous users and/or for authenticated users based on your usage requirements. Pick between sites that will be used primarily for collaborative purposes or for mostly information consumption, in the case of an extranet where things are just published. Then check the boxes related to how you would like to allow your designers to harness the page output cache, and click OK. You'll be back at the Site collection settings page and have just one more setting to make to put publishing fully in force and that is the site output cache. The site output cache is to SPWeb what the site collection output cache is to SPSite. Once you've clicked Site Output Cache, make the settings to all sites and subsites, and then apply them to all the subsites. It's a good idea to inherit whenever possible, so all you really need to do here is check the "Apply these setting to all sub-sites" box, and then click OK.

Once the publishing infrastructure is activated, it creates one list and five libraries named Pages, Workflow Tasks, Images, Site Collection Images, and Site Collection Documents. Sometimes users get a little crazy with SharePoint Designer or with third party tools and they delete and then try and re-create the library Pages. This happens to other libraries too, but I mention pages since it seems to happen there more than anywhere else. You can easily determine if the library was re-created manually and not by the publishing infrastructure by hovering over the ellipsis next to the app icon for the given library and you'll see this message "This system library was created by the Publishing feature to store pages that are created in this site." If you're looking at the pages library on a library created manually, chances are good that it will not have the system wording on hover.

Account Management

When you think about account management, what comes to mind? I think about my bank account and how much money is in there. And then I quickly get depressed, and so on, and so forth. When it comes to SharePoint, I think of the service accounts that are used in least privileging. Of all the accounts, the farm account is the most important, followed by the accounts that run the various service application pools and the account that is used to run the application pool for web applications that house content inside site collections. The install account, while an all-powerful administrative account, would be last on this list since it does not run any services, or at least it shouldn't.

When it comes to changing the passwords on these accounts, I've heard horror stories about administrators talking about thinking that to do that a new farm would be required and nothing could be further from the truth. The passwords for these accounts can be changed in Active Directory and as long as the passwords have never been manually entered into IIS, SharePoint will handle the rest. Where administrators run into problems with account management is when changes are made directly in IIS or directly inside the Windows Services console. The reason that this poses a problem is that SharePoint is not aware of these types of changes to identities. So, avoid manually changing identities in IIS and use the service accounts page in Central Administration if you want to change the account that a given Windows Service or SharePoint application pool runs underneath.

Then when the time comes to change the passwords, you can do so using Active Directory. Or you can use the command line using the net user command. We'll have an exercise at the end of the chapter that covers changing the password via the command line.

Logging Locations and Levels

When it comes to logging in SharePoint, there are a few different logs that you'll use when you're troubleshooting. Here's a list of the various logs:

- Windows Event Logs, Application, System, Security, Resource Exhaustion, etc.

- IIS website logs and failed requests logs

- IIS Error logs and SMTP logs

- SharePoint ULS logs

The Windows event logs are located at the following directory by default %SystemRoot%\System32\ Winevt\Logs\. The %systemroot% path variable is C:\windows in all Windows operating systems. If you ever wonder where a variable resolves to, you can look it up on the interwebs or type it in a run bar and click OK and let Windows Explorer show you the path.

The IIS website logs are located at C:\inetpub\logs\LogFiles and the failed request logs are located at C:\inetpub\logs\FailedReqLogFiles. Both of these logs are in UTC time by default, so that is something to keep in mind when troubleshooting so as to make sure you're not looking forwards or backwards in time, since the server time, if not in the UTC time zone, will be different from the IIS Logs. Another thing to help make some sense of these logs is how to determine, which log is for which site and the answer to that is as follows: Open IIS Management Console (inetmgr.exe) and then click Sites, as shown in Figure 3-13.

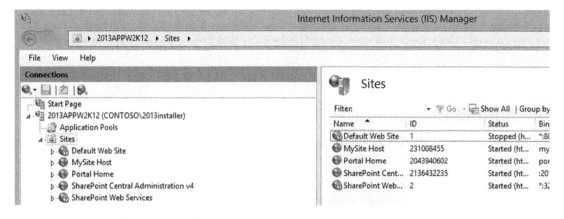

Figure 3-13. *Site IDs*

Notice how each site has an ID. Now if you navigate to C:\inetpub\logs\LogFiles, you can see that each site has its own folder. For example, the Portal Home site has logs inside of the folder named C:\inetpub\ logs\LogFiles\W3SVC**2043940602**. When reading the IIS logs, you'll notice four values at the end that are really helpful. Consider this diagram and then the bulleted list of explanations.

```
sc-status sc-substatus  sc-win32status time-taken
=======================================================
503     19       0        218
```

- sc-status - is the major part of the HTTP status code

- sc-substatus - is the sub status e.g. for a 503.19 HTTP status the sub-status would be the 19 part

- sc-win32status - is a Windows system error code

- time-taken - is the time taken to send the response in milliseconds

If you look through your IIS logs and see a bunch of 200s, you should have your favorite refreshing, ice-cold beverage of choice, because 200s mean, "OK. The client request has succeeded." The TechNet article at https://support.microsoft.com/en-us/help/943891/the-http-status-code-in-iis-7.0,-iis-7.5,-and-iis-8.0 has a detailed listing of what the various sc-status codes are trying to say. This is a good page to have saved as a favorite, copied into an OneNote, and possibly even saved into a Word document or an Excel file. The only reason I didn't copy it into this book is because I have grandkids and I want their grandkids to be able to climb trees.

If you look through your IIS logs and see something like this, you'll notice that there was an access denied situation followed by a really long page load:

```
2017-05-07 21:01:19 127.0.0.1 GET /PublishingImages/Forms/Thumbnails.aspx - 80 - 127.0.0.1
Mozilla/4.0+(compatible;+MSIE+7.0;+Windows+NT+6.3;+WOW64;+Trident/7.0;+.NET4.0E;+.NET4.0C;+.
NET+CLR+3.5.30729;+.NET+CLR+2.0.50727;+.NET+CLR+3.0.30729) http://portal.contoso.com/_
layouts/15/viewlsts.aspx 401 1 2148074254 15
2017-05-07 21:03:03 127.0.0.1 GET /PublishingImages/Forms/Thumbnails.aspx - 80
0#.w|contoso\2013installer 127.0.0.1 Mozilla/4.0+(compatible;+MSIE+7.0;+Windows+NT+6.
3;+WOW64;+Trident/7.0;+.NET4.0E;+.NET4.0C;+.NET+CLR+3.5.30729;+.NET+CLR+2.0.50727;+.
NET+CLR+3.0.30729) http://portal.contoso.com/_layouts/15/viewlsts.aspx 200 0 0 103684
```

When you have a sc-win32status, you can sometimes use net helpmsg <sc-win32status number>, to find out more information. But this does not work every time. Sometimes the number shown is not a valid status. A list describing all the various win32status numbers for codes 0–400 is at https://msdn.microsoft.com/en-us/library/ms681382.aspx. The error codes go from 0–15999, so the 21408074254 is definitely not an error code that relates to a win32status.

The IIS error logs are located at C:\Windows\System32\LogFiles\HTTPERR. These logs are also UTC and they report any errors that might be happening in your SharePoint. If there is nothing to report, you'll just see a hyphen, which is hopefully the case.

The IIS SMTP logs are located at C:\Windows\System32\LogFiles\smtpsvc1 by default. These logs give you troubleshooting information about mail operations within SharePoint.

The SharePoint logs come in two flavors: *diagnostic logs* and *usage logs*. Both of these logs are located at the default location C:\Program Files\Common Files\microsoft shared\Web Server Extensions\15\LOGS. It is possible and a best practice to move logging off the operating system drive over to a separate drive—in which case the logs could be anywhere.

It is not anarchy though. You can determine where the logs are located by looking at the monitoring settings within Central Administration and running a quick PowerShell, or by opening the ULSViewer and choosing to open from ULS. The ULSViewer program can detect where ULS is logging.

The way to find the logs in Central Administration is as follows: Click Monitoring ➤ Configure Diagnostic logging and scroll down. The logging location is listed under the Trace Log section in the Path box. To determine where usage data collection is taking place, click Monitoring ➤ Configure usage and health data collection and scroll down to the Usage Data collection settings and take a gander at the Log file Location box.

To find the log file locations using PowerShell, you would type (Get-SPDiagnosticConfig).LogLocation to find the tracing logs location, and you would type (Get-SPUsageService).usagelogdir to find the usage and health logs location. They do not have to be in the same directories; it is an administrative preference. From a standpoint of writing scripts to look through ULS logs, it is a lot less burdensome on the scripter if the usage and health logs are in the same directory as the trace logs.

The default logging levels are set so that the logs do not get too large yet still contain medium and higher level information about events. In any troubleshooting scenario, it is not uncommon to turn up the logging level to VerboseEx, which offers the most information you can get from the logs. When you turn this up using PowerShell, don't forget to turn it back to normal. Clear-SPLogLevel is the quick and easy way to set the logging level back to normal. Set-SPLogLevel –TraceSeverity VerboseEx is the command used to set the logging level all the way up across the entire farm.

Path-based vs. Host-named Site collections

When SharePoint originally came out, path based site collections were really the primary focus; however, when SharePoint 2010 hit the scene, Microsoft started talking about the all glamourous Host named site collection. When 2013 made its debut, Microsoft advised that HNSCs were the recommended best practice in terms of performance to roll out site collections. That's not to say that path based are bad, because they're not, they just do not scale very well.

Microsoft has tested path based site collections and determined that the supported limit per web application is 20 site collections. Since a farm has supported limit of only 20 web applications per farm, this means that if you opted to go with path based site collections, the max site collections with different URL's for your farm would be 400 (20×20). A farm of this magnitude would have a pretty decent memory footprint, as all those application pools in IIS would require additional horespower.

When it comes to Host named site collections (HNSC), which are also known as host header site collections (HHSC), the maximum limit that is supported is 750,000, of which 500,000 would be MySite site collections and 250,000 would be related to other types of sites. The HHSC is only created using PowerShell and all the HHSCs are created inside of the same web application. Far fewer resources are required to run HHSCs and you can get a lot more site collections for far less actual resources.

The nice thing about HHSCs is how they are presented to the user. In IIS, they all live inside the same site and have their own unique bindings. To the user, you could have the accounting.contoso.com inside the same IIS web that the insurance.contoso.com and the litigation.contoso.com are served from. You could use a wildcard certificate like *.contoso.com or if you wanted to use separate singularly named certs, you could do that too, by using the server name identification feature in IIS.

When HHSCs get created the get spun up inside of a web application. While it is possible to house path based site collections inside a web application that house HHSCs, I would not advise this practice; but instead would advise having a single web application for all of your HHSCs and then have however many you need for your path based site collections.

When accessing Path based or host header site collections from the server, you need to account for the loopback security feature in Internet Explorer by either creating a dword named DisableLoopbackCheck or by using Multistring value named BackConnectionHostNames. There isn't a need for both, as either will work. The nice thing about DisableLoopbackCheck is that it covers all current and future site collections, whereas the BackConnectionHostNames needs to be updated each time a site collection is created. The site collections must be able to be opened on the server where search crawls occur; so one of the first things to troubleshoot if search is not getting results is to see if the search account can open the site collection from the server it uses to crawl.

Let's do some exercises related to account management, logging levels, gathering logs, and creating host-named site collections.

MANAGING ACCOUNT PASSWORDS

In this exercise, we'll see how to change the account password for the farm account using Active Directory and via the command line.

Using the Active Directory Users and Computers GUI

Log in to your domain controller with the setup user account or another account that is a domain admin.

1. Right-click the domain and find the farm account, as shown in the following screenshot, by clicking Find and then typing the name of the farm account.

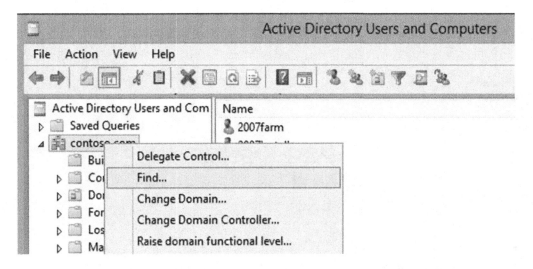

2. After you type the name of the farm account, click Find Now, and then right-click the account. Be very careful to click Reset Password..., as shown in the following screenshot.

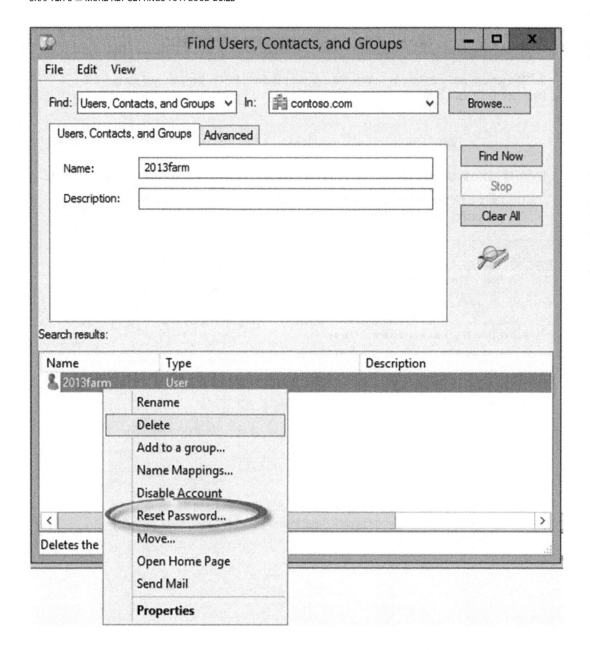

3. After you type the password in both times and click OK, nothing should skip a beat, unless someone has manually entered a password outside of SharePoint. For example, if someone manually entered the farm account password in IIS or in the Services Console, things might hang, services might stop, app pools might cease to function, it might be a bad day. Do not fret though, there is a good chance the Sun will rise tomorrow.

After you have finished changing the password, you could open Notepad as a different user and use the password to see that the change took affect. Since you're on the Central Administration server, you could just open the ULS Viewer and see that logging is happening. If you close and open central admin, and it fails to open, then someone has modified IIS. If this were to happen, you would run psconfig –cmd secureresources or initialize-SPResourceSecurity.

Using the Command Line

1. Open a command prompt administratively on your web front end or app server while logged in with the install account. Do not attempt to perform while logged in with the farm account, because you should never be logged in with the farm account.

2. Type the following command to change the password of the farm account, and then press Enter:

Net user 2013farm MyP@ssword0 /domain, as shown in the following screenshot.

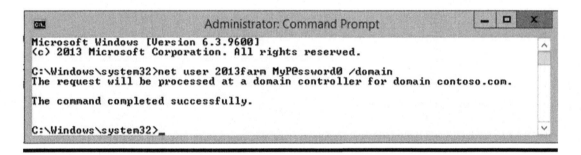

After the command completes successfully you can test it by opening Notepad as a different user and using the new password, MyP@ssword0.

The exercise on managing account passwords demonstrated that we can change the farm password at any time. One thing that can cause an app pool to shut down, and a farm to lock, is if the wrong password is manually entered into a login window for the farm account. If this ever happens to you, you can bet that you will be modifying the logging level.

LOGGING LEVELS

In this exercise, we'll take a look at the logging levels in your farm, set them to default and look at them again and then we'll raise them to VerboseEx and verify that they are raised; before, we set them back to the default levels.

1. Open a SharePoint Management Shell administratively.

2. Type **Get-SPLogLevel a**nd press Enter.

3. Type **Clear-SPLogLevel** and press Enter.

4. Notice how the Trace Severity is set at Medium.

5. Type **Set-SPLogLevel –TraceSeverity VerboseEx** and press Enter.

6. After step 5 completes, run Get-SPLogLevel, and notice how the Trace Severity is now VerboseEx.

7. Type **Clear-SPLogLevel** and press Enter. After it completes, verify that the logging level is set to Medium once more by running Get-SPLogLevel.

The exercise on logging levels demonstrated how we can verify our logging levels using PowerShell, but it didn't talk about the GUI. This is because it is not possible to set the trace severity any higher than verbose in the GUI, as you can see in Figure 3-14.

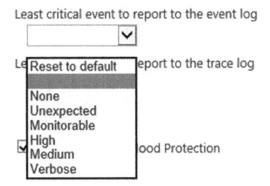

Figure 3-14. *No VerboseEx setting possible via GUI*

VerboseEx is the absolute most information that you can gather from SharePoint's Unified Logging System. In fact, if you know the steps to an error that you've received, you should first create new log files, using New-SPLogFile (another action that is not possible via the GUI) and New-SPUsageLogFile, and then turn up the logging level to VerboseEx before reproducing the error. Then after the error has been produced, wait about 15 to 30 seconds and then clear the logging level back to default.

Knowing how to increase the logging level across the farm helps a lot. Using ULSViewer to look at events preceding the error helps in troubleshooting and being able to consolidate all the events based on a time of day from all the servers in the farm is even more helpful. You can even gather logs based on the correlation ID and the time of day from all servers. In this next exercise we'll look at how this is possible using PowerShell.

MERGE-SPLOGFILE

In this exercise, we'll get SharePoint to give us a correlation ID that we can use in our exercise on gathering logs. When we gather the logs from all the servers, we more than likely will only see the one server due to the topology of the farm used in this exercise and how we generated the correlation ID. In a real world example that you will encounter if you support SharePoint, administer SharePoint, or develop with SharePoint, there is a good chance that you will see more than one machine in your merged log.

1. Open an Internet Explorer and type the URL to your SharePoint site.

2. Change the name of the page in the URL from "default.aspx" to "troubleshootingSharePoint.aspx" and press Enter.

3. SharePoint will direct you to the Page Not Found Aspx page if your site has the page not found aspx page.

4. Open site settings and click site permissions, under the users and permissions section.

The URL of the page you're on should end in _layouts/15/user.aspx if you're using SharePoint 2013, _layouts/user.aspx if you're using SharePoint 2010, or _layouts/16/user.aspx, if using SharePoint 2016.

5. Change the page name from user.aspx to users.aspx and press Enter. This time you will not be redirected to a page not found error screen and instead you'll receive a correlation ID, similar to the following screenshot.

Sorry, something went wrong

An unexpected error has occurred.

TECHNICAL DETAILS

Troubleshoot issues with Microsoft SharePoint Foundation.

Correlation ID: 2eacef9d-110b-807b-4ebf-3d40be1bfe57

Date and Time: 5/8/2017 8:03:19 AM

GO BACK TO SITE

6. Open a SharePoint Management Shell administratively.

7. Type **Merge-SPLogFile,** followed by the –Correlation parameter and the GUID from the error found in step 5, followed by the –Path parameter and a path to a file on your system where you can save files, similar to what's done in the following screenshot.

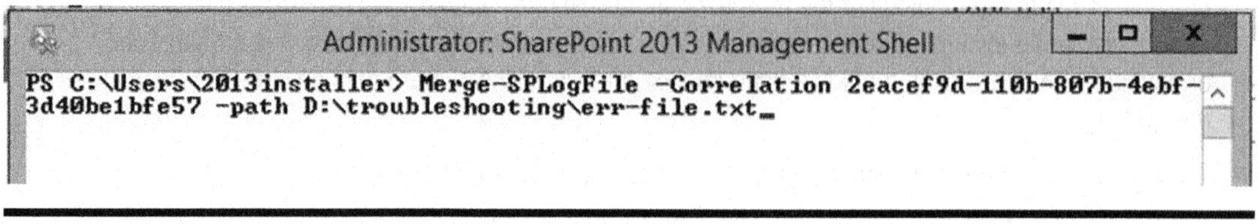

After you've entered something like Merge-SPLogFile -Correlation 2eacef9d-110b-807b-4ebf-3d40be1bfe57 -path D:\troubleshooting\err-file.txt and pressed Enter, SharePoint tells you that it is merging the diagnostic logs and that this could take a little time. After this finishes, what we've just done is merged through all the logs in all the servers in the farm, for a specific correlation ID. And because the error occurred on the one server, only one server is returned in the results. For example, if you look at Figure 3-15, you can see that the only server returned is 2013APPW2K12, and sorry about the eye chart, hopefully you are following along on a development farm or home lab farm.

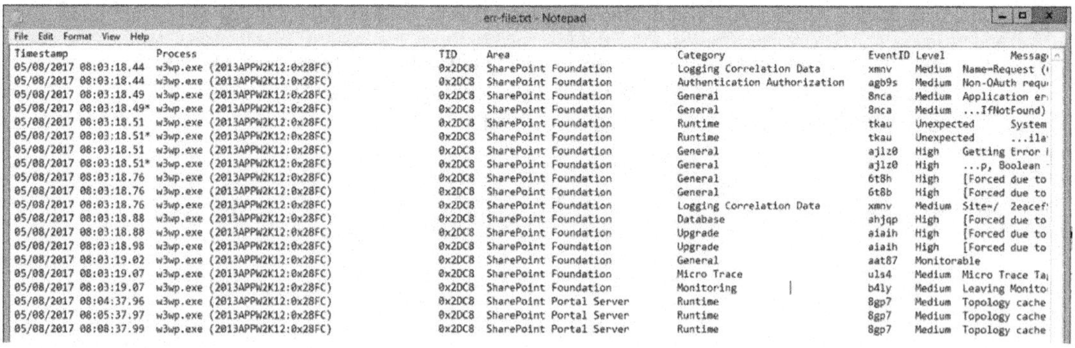

Figure 3-15. *Unexpected*

If you'll notice about five lines down in this merged log file, there is an unexpected event. It has an unexpected level. If we look for unexpected events and then look at what transpired in the farm before the unexpected event, we can often find information that may solve the issue, or give us really good google fodder (search terms for queries). In this case, we see that the system couldn't find the file named users.aspx because it doesn't exist, as shown in Figure 3-16. The log says "The file '/_layouts/15/users.aspx' does not exist."

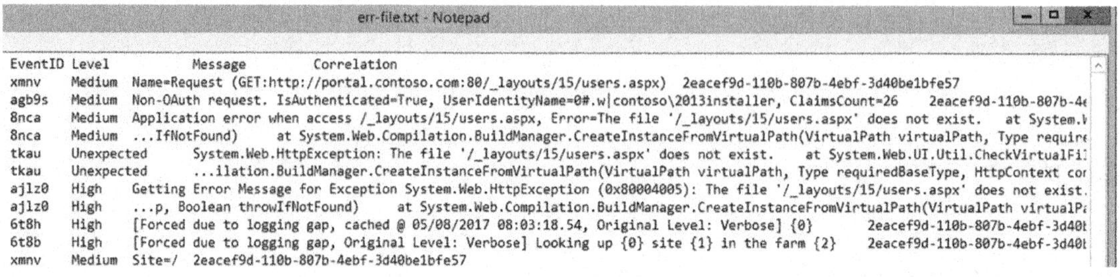

Figure 3-16. *Application error on line 4*

This is all good that we were able to zero in on the error we created on the server we created it on; but what if we didn't know all of that info, and all we had was a date and time range to go on? We'll in that case we would run a command like that shown in Figure 3-17.

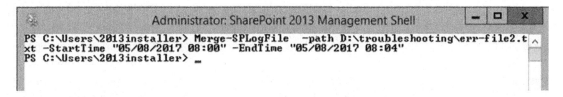

Figure 3-17. *What happened during this time?*

When typing the starting time and ending time, it is always the date and time, not the time and date. I have no idea why the PowerShell team made it this way, since time and date are easier to remember. Well, just remember that it is date and time of the accident. The syntax is

```
Merge-SPLogFile –Path <PathToFile> -StartTime "mm/dd/yyyy hh:mm" –EndTime "mm/dd/yyyy hh:mm"
```

The hours and minutes are based on a 24-hour clock. So midnight is 00:00 and noon is 12:00.

If you wanted to gather logs based on the time of day and a correlation ID, you would just need to add the –Correlation parameter.

HNSC or HHSC

The creation of the host-named site collection is done using PowerShell. You can create the web application that will host the host-named site collection using the GUI if you want, or you can create it using PowerShell. Since I'm fairly sure you already know how to create a web application via the GUI, and in the interest of great-great-grandchildren, tree-climbing expeditions, and the environment, I've opted to save the paper and explain how to create the web app with PowerShell.

Before we can begin the exercise, we need to get some variables planned out according to Table 3-2.

Table 3-2. *Host Header Site Collection Variables*

Variable name	Variable Value	Variable Purpose
$applicationPool	"HNSC01ApplicationPool"	The name of the application pool
$ServiceAcct	"Contoso\2013WebContent"	The service account that runs the app pool
$WebApp	"SharePoint - 10001 - HNSC"	The name of the Web application in IIS
$webAppURL	"http://hnsc.Contoso.com"	The URL to the web app
$contentDB	"2013_WSS_Content_HNSC01"	The content DB for the top site that is never used

(continued)

Table 3-2. (*continued*)

Variable name	Variable Value	Variable Purpose
$primarySiteCollectionOwnerAcct	"Contoso\SamarT"	The name of the top site primary SCA
$PrimarySCOwnerEmail	"samar.tomar@Contoso.com"	The primary SCA's Email
$webAppOURL	"http://hnsc.Contoso.com:10001"	The full url to the web app for the new site cmdlet
$HNSC3DB	"2013_WSS_Content_ GetintoContoso"	The name of the content db for the first HHSC
$primarySiteCollectionOwnerAcct	"Contoso\StacyS"	The name of the primary SCA for this HHSC
$PrimarySCOwnerEmail	"stacy.simpkins@Contoso.com"	The HHSC primary SCA's email
$HNSC3Name	"Get Into contoso Test Site"	The name of the new site collection
$HNSC3URL	"http://GetInto.Contoso.com"	The URL for the new site collection

HOST-NAMED OR HOST HEADER SITE COLLECTIONS

In this final exercise of the chapter, we cover one way to create Host-Named Site Collections. Microsoft has started calling them Host Header Site Collections on exams, but I'm having a hard time wrapping my mind around that name change since I've been calling them HNSCs for a few years.

1. Gather your values for the variables so that you can substitute as needed and make substitutions to the code in this exercise.

2. Open your hosts file and make an entry that points the local host 127.0.0.1 to hnsc. contoso.com, adjust where needed for your environment. The host file is located at C:\windows\system32\drivers\etc and can be modified using Notepad.

3. Make another entry in the host file for 127.0.0.1 getinto.contoso.com.

4. Open a SharePoint Management Shell administratively.

5. Copy and paste the following variables into your management shell after you've updated them for your environment, as shown in the following screenshot.

```
$applicationPool = "HNSC01ApplicationPool"
$ServiceAcct = "Contoso\2013WebContent"
$WebApp = "SharePoint - 10001 - HNSC"
$webAppURL = "https://hnsc.Contoso.com"
$contentDB = "2013_WSS_Content_HNSC01"
```

```
                Administrator: SharePoint 2013 Management Shell        _  □  x
PS C:\Users\2013installer> $applicationPool = "HNSC01ApplicationPool"
PS C:\Users\2013installer> $ServiceAcct = "Contoso\2013WebContent"
PS C:\Users\2013installer> $WebApp = "SharePoint - 10001 - HNSC"
PS C:\Users\2013installer>
PS C:\Users\2013installer> $webAppURL = "http://hnsc.Contoso.com"
PS C:\Users\2013installer> $contentDB = "2013_WSS_Content_HNSC01"
PS C:\Users\2013installer> _
```

6. If you're working with SharePoint 2010, copy this one-liner. Skip to step 7 if you're
    working with SharePoint 2013 or 2016. After you copy it, press Enter a couple of
    times to make sure that it's started its magic.

    ```
    #2010
    New-SPWebApplication -ApplicationPool $applicationPool -ApplicationPoolAccount
    $serviceAcct -Name $WebApp -URL $webAppURL -Port 10001 -databaseName $contentDB
    ```

7. If you're working with SharePoint 2013, copy this one-liner, and press Enter a
    couple of times.

    ```
    #2013
    New-SPWebApplication -ApplicationPool $applicationPool -ApplicationPoolAccount
    $serviceAcct -Name $WebApp -URL $webAppURL -Port 10001 –AuthenticationProvider
    (New-SPAuthenticationProvider) -databaseName $contentDB
    ```

■ **Note**   We are running the web application up on port 10001 simply to show that the top site is not
used. We could have used port 443 and the –securesocketslayer parameter if we had the proper certificates
on the server.

After the web application is created, we need to create the top site, but not before we set some bindings in IIS.

8. Navigate into IIS Manager (inetmgr.exe) and create a couple of new bindings on the
    new web application by opening sites and modifying the binding for the high port
    and setting one on port 80 and then another for the first HHSC, as shown in the
    following screenshot.

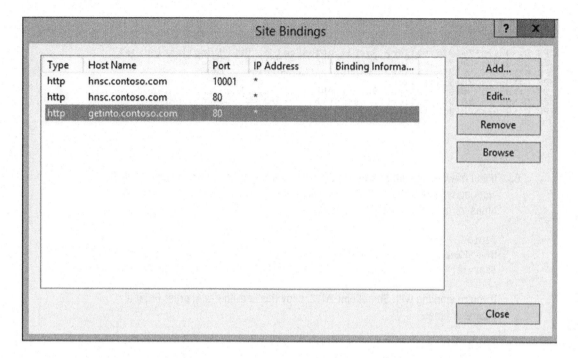

9. Paste the following lines of code into your management shell after you've modified them to meet your environmental requirements, and press Enter a couple times.

```
$primarySiteCollectionOwnerAcct = "Contoso\SamarT"
$PrimarySCOwnerEmail = "samar.tomar@Contoso.com"

$webAppOURL = "http://hnsc.Contoso.com:10001"

New-SPSITE -URL $webAppOURL -owneralias $primarySiteCollectionOwnerAcct
-owneremail $PrimarySCOwnerEmail -Template STS#1
```

After the site is created, as shown in the following screenshot, go ahead and continue to step 10.

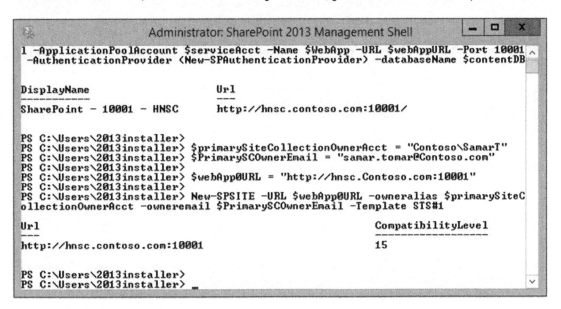

10. After you've updated the code for your environment, paste the following lines of code into your management shell and press Enter a couple of times.

```
$HNSC3DB = "2013_WSS_Content_GetintoContoso"
$webApp0URL = "http://hnsc.Contoso.com:10001"
 New-SPContentDatabase $HNSC3DB -WebApplication $webApp0URL
```

After the database is created, as shown in the following screenshot, you can proceed to step 11.

```
Administrator: SharePoint 2013 Management Shell                    _  □  X

PS C:\Users\2013installer> $HNSC3DB = "2013_WSS_Content_GetintoContoso"
PS C:\Users\2013installer> $webApp0URL = "http://hnsc.Contoso.com:10001"
PS C:\Users\2013installer>
PS C:\Users\2013installer> New-SPContentDatabase $HNSC3DB -WebApplication $webAp
p0URL


Id                 : 0d297ea1-dff3-4f99-b8bd-683735cc49c7
Name               : 2013_WSS_Content_GetintoContoso
WebApplication     : SPWebApplication Name=SharePoint - 10001 - HNSC
Server             : SharePointSQL
CurrentSiteCount   : 0


PS C:\Users\2013installer> _
```

11. After you've updated the code for your environment, paste the following lines of code into your management shell and press Enter a couple of times.

```
$primarySiteCollectionOwnerAcct = "Contoso\StacyS"
$PrimarySCOwnerEmail = "stacy.simpkins@Contoso.com"
$HNSC3Name = "Get Into Contoso Test Site"
$HNSC3URL = "http://GetInto.Contoso.com"
$HNSC3DB = "2013_WSS_Content_GetintoContoso"
$webAppoURL = "http://hnsc.Contoso.com:10001"

New-SPSite -url $HNSC3URL -Name $HNSC3Name -hostheaderwebapplication $WebAppoURL
-ownerAlias $PrimarySiteCollectionOwnerAcct -owneremail $PrimarySCOwnerEmail
-contentDatabase $HNSC3DB -Template STS#0Discuss parts of the scripts
```

Don't be alarmed by the warning about the "port specified…" message, this is just SharePoint's way of reminding you to create the bindings in IIS and make sure you have resolution through DNS or via a local hosts entry or both, as shown in Figure 3-18.

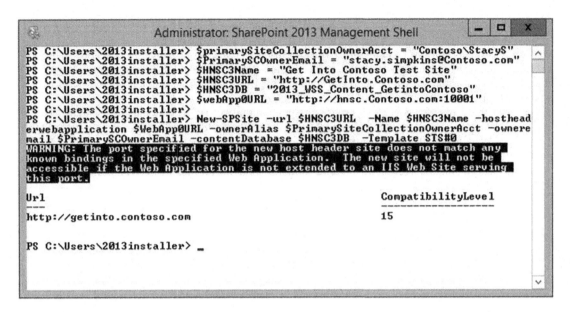

Figure 3-18. First host-named site collection is created

Navigate to your new site using a browser session that is running as StacyS, or your equivalent account and enter the credentials when prompted. The reason you're being prompted is due to the site not being in trusted sites on the server, and/or the server might not have the DisableLoopbackCheck set. You can check the DisableLoopbackCheck dword for its existence and value of 1 by navigating to HKLM\SYSTEM\CurrentControlSet\Control\Lsa, as shown in Figure 3-19.

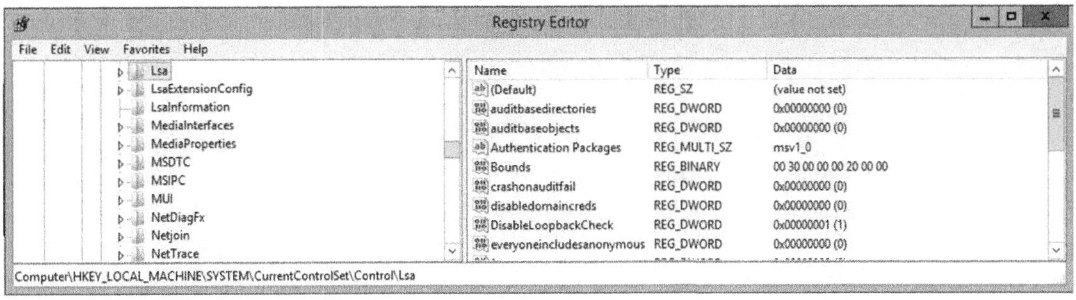

Figure 3-19. DisableLoopbackCheck is disabled

If you add the getinto.contoso.com site to the local intranet sites in the security settings of your browser on the server, you will not be prompted for credentials when accessing the site on the server, assuming the DisableLoopbackCheck is set to 1.

Next Steps

Well, we've certainly gone over a lot in this chapter: Distributed Cache, User Profile services and synch, applying cumulative updates to SharePoint, publishing infrastructure and minimal download strategy, changing the farm password, various logs and changing the ULS logging level, and path-based vs. host header or host-named site collections.

The one thing we didn't cover is Desired State Configuration, or DSC. DSC is still too new to this author and as such, unfortunately, I do not have enough expertise to discuss it in detail. It does require PowerShell 4.0. As Mark Watts, one of the SharePoint technical leads at Rackspace, recently proclaimed, "DSC is definitely the way the future of scripted SharePoint builds are headed." I totally agree with him.

In the next chapter, we'll revisit IIS mappings and talk about the file system and troubleshooting issues with site resolution.

CHAPTER 4

■ ■ ■

Files, Virtual Mappings, and IIS Settings

To know what has changed in your SharePoint, a great place to start, is from knowing what the base looked like, or should look like. To do that, you have to know the how the build comes together and the key settings to the good build. It doesn't hurt to know how to troubleshoot the service applications and know the CU level of your farm. We'll talk more about this in this chapter and use PowerShell to look at the service applications and their connections within IIS and the file system.

In Chapter 1, I spoke about the permissions that surround various locations within the Windows Server as it relates to changes that SharePoint makes to the file system, registry, and IIS. I spoke about how SharePoint adds identities to the various local groups that are used in a least privileged SharePoint environment. We looked at IIS folders within SharePoint sites and talked about the difference between virtual mapped folders and non-virtual folder mappings.

Then in Chapters 2 and 3, I spoke about key SharePoint settings that are part of automated builds and some that are outside of any automation. We also spoke about a couple of key service applications, Distributed cache and user profile service. We touched on logging and PowerShell; but we didn't put too much context around the use of the logs and PowerShell in troubleshooting.

In this chapter, we are going to talk, in further depth, about the changes that SharePoint Server makes to a Windows Server in the following locations:

- File System

- IIS

- Logs

- Registry

- PowerShell

We're going to look at changes to the file system, IIS, registry, and logs from a troubleshooting perspective and from a preventative troubleshooting perspective and talk about what is OK, what is not OK, and what to look for when troubleshooting. In other words, we're going to talk about how to troubleshoot IIS, registry, and the file system both manually and by looking at the logs. When I say manually, I'm talking about identifying changes to files, registry, and IIS by knowing where files were and what has changed in them in contrast to where they were from perspective of the build level of any given farm.

You'll use IIS Manager a lot when working with SharePoint. Mostly for troubleshooting if anything was manually changed that should not have been manually changed. You'll also use IIS Manager 6.0 to configure and troubleshoot mail resolution. You can access IIS Manager from the command line or from the run bar by

© Stacy Simpkins 2017

S. Simpkins, *Troubleshooting SharePoint*, https://doi.org/10.1007/978-1-4842-3138-8_4

typing **inetmgr**. You can access the IIS Manager 6.0 that controls SMTP settings, by typing **inetmgr6**. You'll access these consoles when configuring the settings that are OK to manually configure:

- SSL

- Bindings

- SMTP settings

Both of the IIS Manager consoles allow for modification of the IIS default logging location. It's more of a personal preference when it comes to IIS logs as to whether you move them off to a different drive. I opt to leave them in the default locations. The same is true for the Windows OS system logs. Just leave them in the default location. There really isn't any performance gain to move them off the OS partition.

Troubleshooting for what has changed is a manual process. Looking at the logs is a manual process too. I see pouring through logs as its own animal when compared to perusing the file system for changes.

We'll use PowerShell to dive a bit deeper into the object model and the information that it holds.

We're not going to talk about development best practices or how to develop in SharePoint. The only thing we'll say about development is that for the most part and in very basic terms, manual changes to the file system, IIS, and registry should be avoided for the most part. That's not to say that development shouldn't make any manual changes because sometimes it is the only way. In any case, where manual changes are required, a very hard look should be taken to determine if that is true, as manual changes often lead to trouble in SharePoint.

WSPs should be used to make these changes and manual changes to files should only be made when there no other way, when making a manual change is unavoidable. We'll demonstrate how the SharePoint object model can be used to make changes that SharePoint is aware of.

The point I'd like to stress, is that good developers know when to make changes and how to make them with SharePoint solution packages or with .NET Code that SharePoint solution packages are aware of thereby potentially making SharePoint aware.

I talked about some of the directories that we touched on in Chapter 1. We'll dive in deeper into some of the non-virtual directories that SharePoint adds to a SharePoint site within IIS. We'll take the same type of dive with the virtual directories.

If you recall from earlier chapters, the difference between the two types of folders was that virtually mapped folders reach into a location outside of the IISroot and they are easily identifiable by the shortcut icon with the arrow. In other words, the targets of the virtually mapped folders do not live inside of the default IIS directory, %SystemDrive%\inetpub\wwwroot\wss\VirtualDirectories, which is the default directory inside which SharePoint creates directories for new IIS sites.

The non-virtual folders do not have the shortcut icon and they are housed in the default location, %SystemDrive%\inetpub\wwwroot\wss\VirtualDirectories of the server's file system. Figure 4-1 displays both virtual and non-virtual folders. You'll also notice that there are virtual folders that point to the root of the 2013 SharePoint hive, the 15 folder or directory. SharePoint expects the permissions on these directories to only be modified with WSPs, if at all, and never manually modified.

Figure 4-1. *Virtual and non-virtual folders*

■ **Note** Avoid manually changing SharePoint files and sites outside of SharePoint PowerShell cmdlets, or through the use of WSP packages.

SharePoint uses the default web site in IIS as its model site from which to create new sites. This is a jolly good reason to leave this site powered off and to avoid modifying it in any way. When settings in IIS or files in the file system are changed manually, meaning they are not done via the Central Administration GUI, with a SharePoint Management Shell PowerShell command, or with the use of a Windows SharePoint services solution package (.wsp) file, issues will almost certainly arise. One of those issues is failed replication of site content between web front ends, or worse yet, the inability to join a new server to the farm.

As mentioned earlier, the only settings in IIS that should be manually modified are server certificates and site bindings. The reason for this is simple. SharePoint thinks that it is in control of IIS, it does not suspect any changes to be made within IIS Manager outside of those two locations. This includes most of the non-virtual and virtually mapped files in the file system. SharePoint only respects changes made to the file system and OS that are done via .wsp files or via the GUI. It is OK to manually adjust the SMTP and other settings within the IIS Management 6.0 console.

In terms of manual changes, please be careful with the SharePoint Management Shell. For example, if you used the SharePoint Management Shell and a non-SharePoint PowerShell cmdlet to change an *access control list* (ACL) of a file or directory, this would be bad because SharePoint would not know about the change. Remember, just because you can does not mean you should. If you want to experiment, the get-acl and set-acl cmdlets are where to start googling; but remember don't do that to your SharePoint directories, as these are not SharePoint cmdlets. SharePoint is aware of cmdlets with nouns that start with SP.

Got Weird Stuff?

If you're troubleshooting issues with site creation, replication, blob cache issues, differences in web.configs, or servers not joining the farm, look at file timestamps based on the patch level of your farm and check IIS for any indication of any manual modifications.

■ **Note** These IIS settings should only be looked at and should not need to be modified, without a WSP.

If you have Visual Studio (VS) installed on the server, which you should never do to a production or UAT\staging farm, you might notice some strangeness. For example, some of the mime types might require changes and you may see weird things happen if this farm has multiple web-front ends, as VS will make modifications unbeknownst to SharePoint. This causes issues. Visual Studio should really only be installed on a development farm. Modifying the mime types is one of those manual changes that are OK.

Essentially, SharePoint just does not like it when people, or PowerShell scripts, adjust files, permissions, or other settings, that it thinks it is in control of, without it knowing about these changes. If you find yourself looking to make manual modifications to web.configs, make sure that SharePoint will be OK with them. Manual changes that are OK are usually well documented on TechNet or in blogs written by MVPs or Microsoft Certified folks.

When manual changes have been made outside of Central Administration, SharePoint PowerShell cmdlets, or a WSP, you'll eventually notice it, because things will begin to stop working as they're supposed to work and there will be some sort of strange behavior, events in the logs, and/or unexpected errors. One thing that is for sure, though, is that if you open up IIS and see sites that are not represented inside SharePoint, there is a good chance that those sites were manually modified at some point. Either they were modified with a setting inside IIS Manager, which caused them to fail to gracefully retract after they were deleted from SharePoint; or, possibly, and worse yet, they are not SharePoint sites at all. The only time this is OK, to have a non-SharePoint site on a SharePoint server, is if said site is used to perform IIS redirections.

Speaking of redirections, one of the worst places to create them is inside of the default IIS site. In fact and as I'd mentioned earlier but I'll say it again, the default IIS site should be turned off and should never be modified; since it provides the base image for all future SharePoint sites. This practice of not modifying the default IIS site ensures stability in your farm. We'll have an exercise at the end of this book that creates a site for redirects.

Unfortunately, there isn't a cookbook that spells out every single issue and root cause, which is not what this book is intended to be; this book helps explain troubleshooting SharePoint.

Application sites or web sites that are non-SharePoint sites should be housed on application servers and not within SharePoint IIS. Then through the use of the new app model, those applications can be integrated. All sites and site bindings in the SharePoint server's IIS Manager should be traceable back to Central Administration, as an extended site, *host header site collection* (HHSC), or *alternate access mapping* (AAM) for a *path-based site collection* (PBSC).

When talking AAMs, normally, PBSCs are extended with an AAM to support a different authentication method to access the same data; and then, this is done under a different URL or Port. When sites are extended, a new site in IIS is created by SharePoint and there'll be a binding for the new URL. You'll need to verify that that binding exists; or, manually create the binding in some cases. Either way, if you're accessing the site with a different URL than the original web application, you'll have these additional bindings and possibly AAMs, depending on what type of site collection you're dealing with, path-based or host-named. I say that to make note that host header site collections, also called host-named site collections, do not have AAMs; but they do require bindings. Also, depending on your governance policy, you'll use BackConnectionHostNames or DisableLoopback within registry of your HHSCs in order for search to crawl the sites.

When sites are just surfaced under a different URL, there may or may not be an AAM. As previously mentioned, in the case of HHSCs, there will not be an AAM; but there will be a binding for traffic to succeed. In the case of path-based site collections (PBSCs), a binding is needed in order for the traffic to be successful, if the traffic is coming in on a different URL to the site collection than what was originally created when the web application's top site was created. This is important to know when trying to determine why a site is not opening. It is also important to understand DNS and the local hosts file on Windows servers, and how all that jazz plays together.

When you're troubleshooting site resolution, you need to check IIS for bindings, for the site being online, for the site URL responding to pings, for the application pool that services the site being online, and for the correct AAM settings, taking into account whether the site is a host header site collection or a path-based site collection. You might also use a host file entry when testing directly from the server to avoid having the server contact its DNS server. Host file entries are also used on crawl servers to avoid crawling across the WAN in some environments and depending on the network setup. It is important to know which type of site you're dealing with when troubleshooting resolution and whether any of the virtual and non-virtual folders have been modified in any way. You need to know this so that you know whether the site has a binding, should have its own site in IIS, and so forth.

You can easily determine if a site is a path-based site collection, or a host-named site collection, by looking at the view all site collections page in Central Administration. With a HNSC, the only site collection with a slash (/) in its URL is the top site. The remaining host-named site collections do not have a / in front of their URL on this page. In Figure 4-2, you can see that the root site of the site collection that holds the host-named site collections has the / and that the host-named site collection, getinto.contoso.com, does not have the slash.

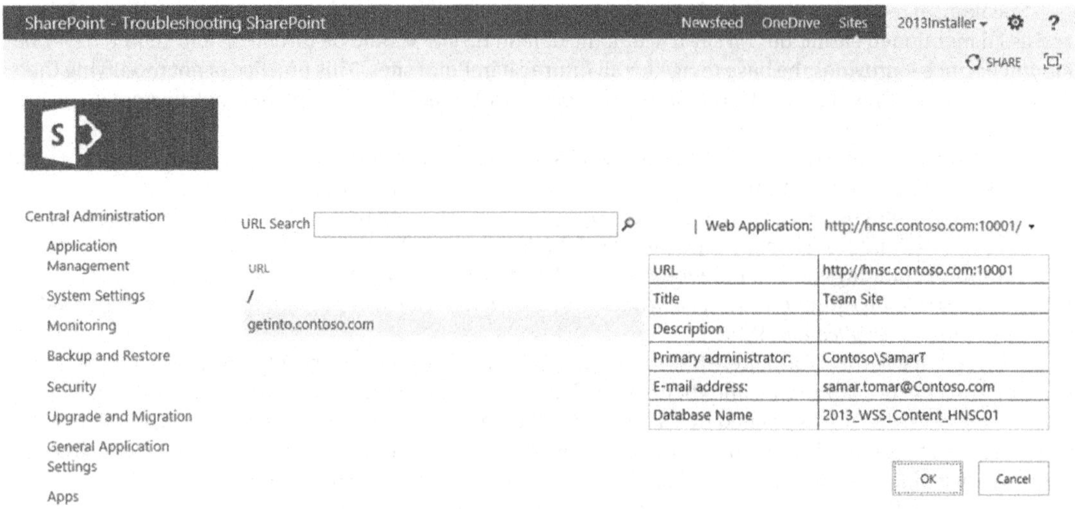

Figure 4-2. *Host-named site collection*

Self Service sites are always path-based because it is not possible to create self-service site collections as HHSCs. You can mix your drinks' but you shouldn't mix HHSCs within a web application that houses a PBSCs, or you might want to drink. Sorry, that was a poor attempt at humor. Let's reiterate that though the web application that houses HHSCs should not be used for PBSCs sites, even at the root site collection of the web app. The HHSC web application should never house Self-service site collections, or have as a MySite host at its root, because the root site or top site of a web application; housing host-named site collections, is not supposed to be used for anything, according to Microsoft. In fact, you could opt to never create that top site and search would still crawl all through the HHSCs in the web application.

Path-based site collections are easily identifiable by the slash that they have in front of the URL on the view all site collections page in Central Administration. Figure 4-3 displays the MySite web application in the test farm. As you already, know MySites are always path-based because HHSCs do not support self-service site creation. Notice in Figure 4-3 that both the root and the site collections have the "/".

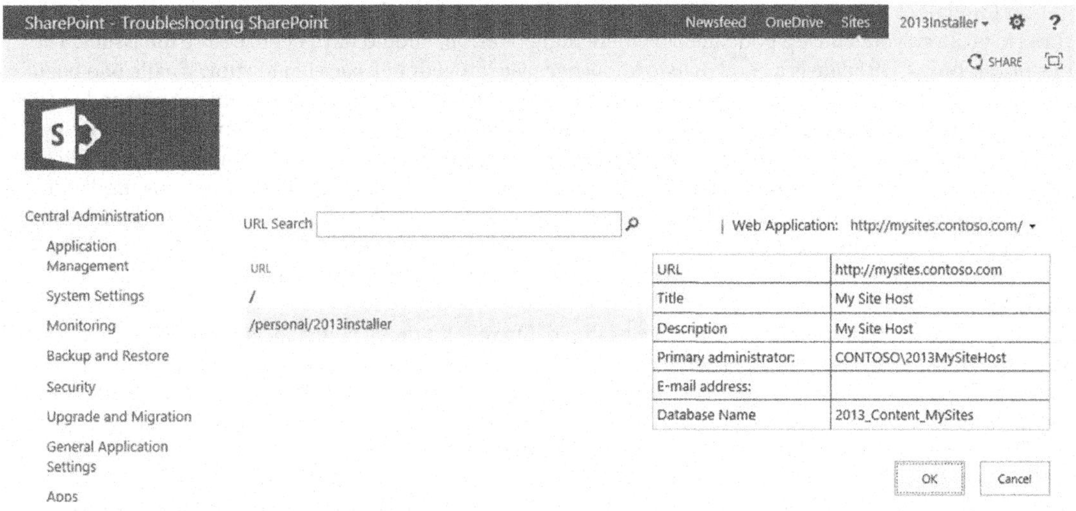

Figure 4-3. *Path-based site collections*

You can also use PowerShell to determine if a site is a host header site collection or a path-based site collection. All you do is instantiate the site into a variable and then look at its property named HostHeaderIsSiteName. This is the code:

```
(Get-SPSite <URL>).HostHeaderIsSiteName
```

After you run that code, you'll get either True or False. True indicates that you're dealing with a site that thinks that it's a host-named site collection. Figure 4-4 shows a path-based site collection and a host-named site collection being queried with PowerShell.

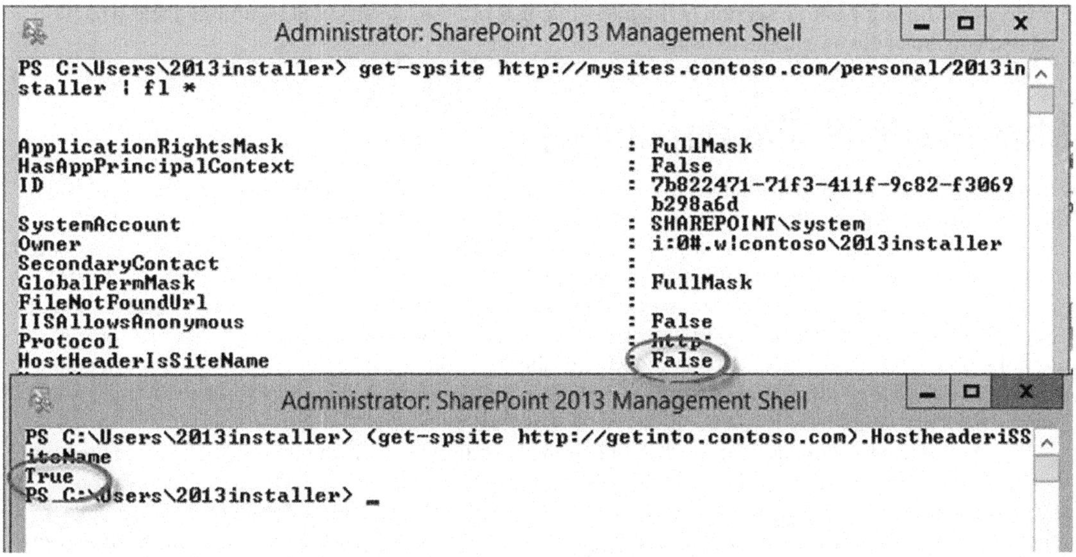

Figure 4-4. *A host header site collection*

At the start of this chapter, I made a reference to knowing where things should be, so that when stuff starts to go awry, you'll have a good idea of where things were, or should have been, before the issues. The out-of-the-box (OOB) date is a good date to know because it is your tell-tale sign to know if a file had been modified. Then once you know if the date for the suspected file is not in agreement with the patched or OOB date, the developer interrogation meetings can begin. Just kidding. SharePoint developers are your friends; they are not the devil (sometimes their code can seem a little demonic, though, depending on how well or poorly it is written). Knowing these dates will give you a better view into what might have transpired and can help understand if patches have been applied. Knowing your developers can really let you know what has happened, assuming you have a good relationship. Remember working with your developers or admins is not about a finger-pointing contest; but rather, is about working as a team to make the best SharePoint possible!

The out of the box date depends on the version of SharePoint that you install. For example, if your install started with SharePoint Server 2013 Service Pack 1, then a lot of the SharePoint related files will be dated somewhere between 1/21/2014 and 1/24/2014, with the predominance of them being 1/23/2014. If you look up the technical details of service pack 1 at `https://support.microsoft.com/en-us/help/2817458`, you'll notice that the last revision date on the article was January 22, 2014.

If you followed that SP1 install with the CU for November 2016, you would start to notice files with 10/11/2016. And, if you have mad calendar skills like I do, your brain would start kicking in and saying something like, "hey, November should be an 11 not a 10. What's the deal?" This is where your knowledge of the cumulative update would kick in and say something like "Maybe, those dates relate to the October CU that is also part of the November CU, all things being cumulative and what not?" Then when you navigated over to Todd Klindt's site, navigated into the SharePoint 2013 Builds, and looked at the October 2016 CU, the 10/11/2016 date would become very clear. This is the date of the October 2016 CU. Since the November CU is cumulative, the server that was formerly SP1 now has quite a few files with 10/11/2016 as their time stamp.

You'll see these dates whether you are looking at the files in the SharePoint Hive, the SharePoint binary location, or the non-virtually mapped IIS folders in the IISroot. Hopefully, any dates you find in the hive, IISroot, or in your SharePoint binaries at C:\program files\microsoft office servers, or a custom location if you opted for that when you installed SharePoint, will be traceable back to a date of a CU and will not have some untraceable date. If you're ever unsure, you should have a SharePoint lab that you can use as your very own SharePoint compass. A place where you can create a farm that is at the same patch level as the environment you're troubleshooting. The CU pages on support.microsoft.com usually have a link to a csv file, in the file information section of the page, that lists out the files that will be updated and what the updated version of the file should look like.

SharePoint IIS Site Directories

Within IIS there exists, a non-virtually mapped folder named _app_bin that leads back to a directory inside the IISroot. Inside this directory are files that are sometimes used in development of navigational type changes. One file in particular that is targeted is the file named layouts.sitemap. This file's date changes when the site it resides under is created, or when the psconfig wizard is run. The system keeps two backups and gives them a date time stamp in their name with the following syntax: layouts.YYYY_M_D_HH_MM.sitemap. This syntax lets you know when the last two prior changes were made, that may have involved running of psconfig. When it comes to psconfig, this site will not show an updated date until the psconfig is run on the server where this file resides. In other words, it's possible for the farm two have different dates of the layouts. sitemap file if psconfig was only run in one server in a two server farm.

Developers make changes to cross-site collection navigation through changes to XML files in the hive that connect back to the layouts.sitemap file. This change will cause the file date to change on just the web server where the WSP that made the changes to the XML files was deployed. Earlier in this chapter, I mentioned we would talk about manual changes that are sometimes unavoidable. This is one of those times where manual changes are required on the other servers. Keep good notes and a good governance policy around these types of changes.

A governance document for your farm is not a troubleshooting tool; but it can help to control the so-called "wild west of changes," if it is well written and includes the principles on who has access to service accounts and environments. This is really important in ensuring stability through controlled change. In a later chapter, we'll look at some PowerShell that you can use to audit who accessed what sites and servers.

■ **Note**   A good governance practice for code deployment is one where developers create the WSPs and deployment steps in dev, and then write installation guides for the admin to follow when she performs the steps to deploy the code into UAT\Staging and then production.

The next non-virtually mapped folder is named _vti_pvt, which has three files inside of it by default. One of those files is named buildversion.cnf. If you take a copy of buildversion.cnf to your client workstation and open it, you'll see that it contains the build version of farm. Don't make any manual changes to files in your file system on the SharePoint server.

The date on the buildversion.cnf file and the other two files represent when the farm was built, or when it was patched to its current level. Vermeer Technologies Inc. is the company that created FrontPage before Microsoft bought VTI, which is where the vti part of the folder name comes from. I have no idea about the pvt and really both are insignificant for the most part. But it's good to know that the dates of buildversion.cnf, service.cnf, and services.cnf have some significance as far as when psconfig was last run.

App_Browsers will have three files, compat.browser, compat.crawler.browser, compat.moss.browser, and their dates are all 1/23/2014 if you're working with a SharePoint 2013 farm that is SP1 or higher. When SharePoint 2016 came out, the date on these files was 2/9/2016. These files are responsible for browser interaction. If the browser is showing weird behavior and you've ruled out distributed cache, and the resources look OK on your server, you could look at this directory and its files and rule out any manual changes to the file system.

App_GlobalResources contains .resx files that pertain to services and service applications in SharePoint. The files in this folder, in each of the SharePoint sites, are resource files that are prime targets of cumulative updates, as they touch many of SharePoint's services. There is no reason to update these files manually. It is possible for .NET code to touch all of the files I've mentioned, including these files. The dates on the files will reflect the OOB date of 1/23/2014 and some will have dates for the latest patch that had changes.

The aspnet_client folder contains a system_web folder, which houses a folder named 4_0_30319 that is empty by default. This folder and its folder system might be used at a later date by the operation system or Microsoft could target it in the future for SharePoint, so you might as well leave it alone. It's basically a sleeping dog, so we'll just let it lay there all alone.

The bin folder is empty by default; but dynamic link library files are sometimes deployed here by solutions. There is a BIN folder in the Global Assembly Cache (GAC) too. The local folder is empty by default. If there is content in this folder, how did it get there in the local IISroot bin folder? Figure 4-5 shows the local, non-virtual folder being empty. The BIN folder in the GAC is not empty.

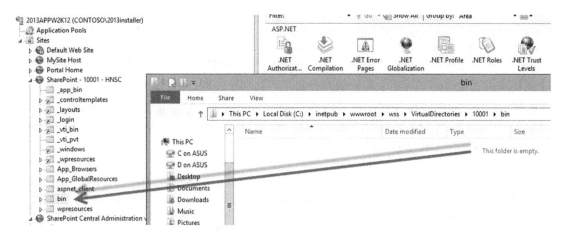

Figure 4-5. *Local non-virtual bin folder*

If you noticed, there are two web part resources folders. One is the local, non-virtually mapped, folder. This local web part resources folder holds the web.config for the web parts with local settings. The Virtually mapped folder holds the web.config that is deployed into the Global Assembly Cache (GAC) and it does not contain the local settings. The dates on these two files are the OOB dates depending on the version of SharePoint first installed and before CU updates.

You can instantly tell if a site is a SharePoint site by taking a quick look in the various non-virtual folders, specifically App_GlobalResources. That's my favorite one to pop open. But as you've probably already noticed, the virtually mapped folders scream, "This is a SharePoint site!" without even opening them. For example, _layouts, this folder is the way that IIS calls into the GAC for many SharePoint files.

Virtually Mapped Folders

The _controltemplates maps into the controltemplates folder that is a subfolder of the templates folder and holds files that are responsible for layouts of the forms of SharePoint lists. There is never any reason that the permissions for this folder or any of the previously mentioned folders or the folders that follow would ever need to be modified, either within IIS or within the file system. Doing so, making that sort of change, will surely confuse SharePoint. The dates of these files range right around the date of the initially installed version. With 2013 the range is from 1/21/2014-1/23/2014 and with 2016 the files are all 2/9/2016. Knowing this folder has hooks into almost everything in your farm that uses a form and that the dates, are what they are, will give you a good place to look for any modification, should you notice something odd with regards to a specific form.

Backward compatibility is handled by the various virtually mapped folders in IIS. These backward compatibility providers offer mappings into the previous versions hive location for whichever folder. For example, the _controltemplates folder maps to the C:\Program Files\Common Files\Microsoft Shared\Web Server Extensions\14\template\controltemplates and the 15 folder inside the _controltemplates folder maps to the 15 hive location in a SharePoint 2013 farm, e.g. it maps to C:\Program Files\Common Files\Microsoft Shared\Web Server Extensions\15\template\controltemplates.

All of the various system pages in SharePoint are located under the _layouts virtually mapped folder that maps into Layouts folder under the template folder underneath the hive. The backward compatibility can really be seen in action when looking at the folder structure in IIS in Figure 4-6, where you'll notice that the top level _layouts maps to the 14 hive location, and then there is a 15 folder that maps to the 15 hive.

Figure 4-6. *Backward compatibility*

It is a good idea to know if the file date is correct and to know how to troubleshoot this by having a lab farm that you can use as a guide. You should explore the other virtually mapped folders, if you haven't already. These virtual folders map into the SharePoint servers file system. This file system is what is referred to when talking about the global assembly cache. That is files outside of the IISroot and in the server file system.

The _login virtually mapped folder that is part of every SharePoint site, with the exception, of Central Administration, houses the default.aspx and web.config that are used by claims based authentication. Both files have the OOB date and neither are affected by the November 2016 CU.

The _vti_adm virtual directory maps into the admisapi folder in the GAC. It houses SharePoint Central Administration web site–specific web services, web service discovery pages, and the web.config for Central Administration.

The _vti_bin virtual directory maps into the ISAPI folder in the GAC. The ISAPI folder is located at C:\Program Files\Common Files\Microsoft Shared\Web Server Extensions\15\isapi and it contains 270 files and 11 folders on a server that has SharePoint 2013 SP1 with the November 2016 CU. These files consist of web service (.asmx) files, web service discovery pages (.aspx), and dynamic link library (.dll) files that are used to support SharePoint web services.

CUs hit this directory quite often. For example, there is a dynamic link library in this location that will give you a good idea of the currently applied CU level on the file system of the server. I say good idea because the only way to be certain is to check all the files that a given CU changes and then correlate this to the schema in place on the databases, if the CU changes the schema. And finally, to correlate the version with what is reported in the Manage Patch Status page that gets its information from the ServerVersionInformation table found in the config database.

The product version on the Microsoft.SharePoint.dll file is located on the Details tab of this file. You can right-click the file, click properties, and then click the Details tab to see this info, or you can modify your Windows Explorer so that it has the product version for each file displayed. This is what I recommend, it saves you some time is determining the product version.

If a farm's databases are at a previous version than the files on the SharePoint servers, there might be a higher product version on this .dll file than what is reported in Central Administration's configuration database version on the server on the Farm page. The same will be true of the file system versions being higher for the files affected by a CU than the build version that is reported by (get-spfarm).buildversion cmdlet. In fact, you shouldn't trust either the database version reported on the Manage Server in Farm page (_admin/FarmServers.aspx) or the version retrieved by (Get-SPFarm).buildversion cmdlet. The reason not to trust those two to identify the farm's CU version is because not all CUs update this information. Look at the OWSSVR.dll file's product version for validating an update.

The Microsoft.SharePoint.dll, The Manage Server in Farm page, Get-SPFarm, all give you a good idea of where the farm is patched; but they are not as definitive a source, as the Central Administration Manage Patch Status page. The Manage patch status page gives the best idea of where the farm is currently patched to since this info on the Manage Patch Status page comes from the ServerVersionInformation table in config database. It is a little-known fact that this table is updated whenever binaries are run on a SharePoint server and **before** psconfig is run. So, if you see a difference between the .dll file version and the (get-spfarm).buildversion, the Manage Patch Status page will probably agree with both the .dll file and the (get-spfarm).buildversion at various line items. But, again, compare the product version of the OWSSVR.dll file to what build version is reported on the support.microsoft.com KB for the given update.

As previously mentioned, applying the binaries in for a CU does a lot of things, one of which is the process updates the ServerVersionInformation table in the config database. Then when the psconfig is run, the build version and the information on the Manage Servers in Farm page changes, if there is a schema change, and the DLL product version will be more in line with the results of the (get-spfarm).buildversion and the configuration database build version displayed on the Manage servers in farm page.

The _windows virtually mapped folder that is part of every SharePoint site, with the exception of Central Administration, houses the default.aspx and web.config that are used by NTLM based authentication. Both files have the OOB date and neither is affected by the November 2016 CU.

We already spoke about the virtually mapped directory named _wpresources mapping into the global assembly cache and not holding local configuration; but rather holding settings for web parts that are globally deployed. It maps to C:\Program Files\Common Files\Microsoft Shared\Web Server Extensions\wpresources in the GAC and holds one file, the global resource web.config, which has the OOB date in a farm that has SP1 and November 2016 CU.

What we've just discussed barely skims the surface on all the various files that are involved with SharePoint Sites and the Central Administration Site. Microsoft has a great TechNet page at https://technet.microsoft.com/en-us/library/cc721634.aspx that lists out the key folders that SharePoint puts on the server. This page lists the description of each folder and explains the files inside of the folder and each file's purpose. Granted, this link is for SharePoint 2010, but it still pertains to current versions.

SharePoint Web Services

Each time a SharePoint Service Application is created there is an application created under the SharePoint Web Services site. Each of these applications is GUID named by SharePoint and they contain a virtual path that maps the service application's files in the GAC. You can find the mapped folder in the GAC by first identifying the service application's GUID with PowerShell, then right-clicking the GUID in IIS, and clicking Explore.

We did part of this in Chapter 1. If you recall, we performed an exercise where we used PowerShell to determine which IIS Application Pool held which SharePoint Service Applications. We identified that the SharePoint Hosted Services application pool was represented by a GUID when looking at the app pools in IIS. The cmdlet we used to find that was Get-SPServiceApplicationPool. Figure 4-7 shows the results of that cmdlet.

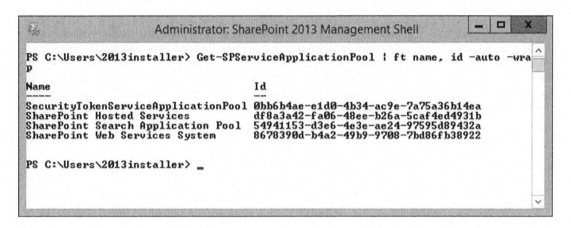

Figure 4-7. *Get-SPServiceApplicationPool*

The ID of the SharePoint hosted services is df8a3a42-fa06-48ee-b26a-5caf4ed4931b. When looking at IIS we can see that this Application Pool holds 14 SharePoint Service Applications. If we ask SharePoint to show us the SharePoint Service applications and sort them by ID, the resulting list corresponds with the applications that are listed underneath the SharePoint Web Services site. Figure 4-8 shows the Service Applications sorted by ID.

```
Administrator: SharePoint 2013 Management Shell                    [ _ ][ □ ][ X ]

PS C:\Users\2013installer> Get-SPServiceApplication | sort ID

DisplayName              TypeName                 Id
_____              _____                 __

App Management Se...     App Management Se...     194f2b8e-c3fc-42a0-b7c6-a334af8140b9
Access 2010 Service      Access Services 2...     1cca9199-ade3-4f1c-ba7d-7dc953c900a9
State Service            State Service            35249d51-602a-4a9a-b906-b8c0361f2462
Search Service Ap...     Search Service Ap...     5c534893-d4d2-49ec-ae33-eae058621174
Search Administra...     Search Administra...     5e9a5a61-d43c-47de-ad41-a6236151c4b5
Word Automation S...     Word Automation S...     60bb3860-8ca9-44d4-8a53-6f66da72f953
Excel Services Ap...     Excel Services Ap...     71e9c724-e61e-4526-8972-dbbb3455bd84
Visio Graphics Se...     Visio Graphics Se...     73f3524f-e458-40fb-bba2-5d29fd2e7a61
PowerPoint Conver...     PowerPoint Conver...     74f938a2-d44f-4854-9dde-fb7b8f85e47c
User Profile Service     User Profile Serv...     84169c29-4052-4f4a-a6e6-7fe90b56c621
Application Disco...     Application Disco...     877a2047-7c40-445b-aba8-7226b4329da7
Security Token Se...     Security Token Se...     8a61163d-0d31-4135-89fa-64e55378bdd9
Secure Store Service     Secure Store Serv...     afeb9ac9-9000-4af7-ac2d-96f483697781
Business Data Con...     Business Data Con...     c0744d71-b6a6-40d8-a57d-122b8ee3639e
Managed Metadata ...     Managed Metadata ...     d0424184-d426-42c0-b952-505ba3e644ff
Subscription Sett...     Microsoft SharePo...     ded56464-83bb-4f9f-ac08-1412dbfb5b50
Work Management S...     Work Management S...     e3497a76-7889-4489-9e8c-490c70c1e832
Machine Translati...     Machine Translati...     eaf73d23-2497-4176-8f8d-f2da9db96c82
PerformancePoint ...     PerformancePoint ...     f83a2abb-592d-4493-8cb6-2695ffdeeb55
Usage and Health ...     Usage and Health ...     fb36203a-03fa-4f82-9d8b-d58e797e9b19


PS C:\Users\2013installer> _
```

Figure 4-8. *SharePoint service applications correlate with Applications in IIS*

Now if you were interested in where the files were stored on the file system for the User Profile service application, you would open IIS, open the SharePoint Web Services site, right-click the application for the User Profile service application, click Manage Application, and then click Advanced Settings. In my case, the User Profile service application has an ID of 84169c29-4052-4f4a-a6e6-7fe90b56c621 and therefore it has an application in the SharePoint web services named 84169c29-4052-4f4a-a6e6-7fe90b56c621. After you open the advanced settings, you'll see something similar to Figure 4-9.

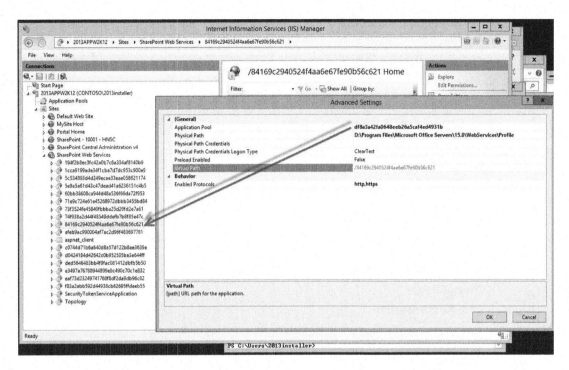

Figure 4-9. *Advanced Settings of an IIS application for a SharePoint Service application*

Once you've used get-spserviceapplication to identify the GUID for the SharePoint service application that you're troubleshooting, you can see if it is properly connected to the correct service application within IIS and you can verify that its application under the SharePoint web services is pointing to the correct location.

In the example in Figure 4-9, we can see that the User Profile Service Files located in the GAC have been moved off the C drive. If you recall, this is only possible during the initial install of the farm. In this case they are located at D:\Program Files\Microsoft Office Servers\15.0\WebServices\Profile because all we did was change the C:\ to a D:\ when the binaries were installed. Sometimes, you might come across builds where the files are stored in D:\SharePointBinaries, D:\SharePointFiles, or something to that affect. If the physical folder is actually a mapped directory that is not local to the server it needs to behave at the same speeds as a drive that is local to the server.

The applications under the SharePoint Web Services site all point to files that are stored in the GAC. All of these web services files had OOB dates in my lab server with SP1 and November 2016 CU, with the exception of Excel Web Services, which had a modified date of when the last time I had run the psconfig wizard.

To troubleshoot the file system, registry, and IIS, not only do you need to understand where files are located and be able to determine if the files or their ACLs have been modified; but you also need to know where to look at logs and what the logs are saying, and how to parse the logs.

It doesn't cost much from a disk perspective to turn IIS logging up for the simple mail transport protocol; so one setting that you should make is to enable all of the logging choices inside IIS Manager 6.0 (inetmgr6). IIS Manager 6.0 is where you configure settings for SharePoint incoming and outgoing mail.

145

To get detailed logs, before you are called to troubleshoot an issue with mail or alerts, you should configure SMTP to log all possible events. As I mentioned in Chapter 3, the default location for IIS logs is C:\Windows\System32\LogFiles. If that directory had been changed for the SMTP location the logging properties, as shown in Figure 4-10, would let you know where the directory was relocated toward; however, in our case, the default location is in use.

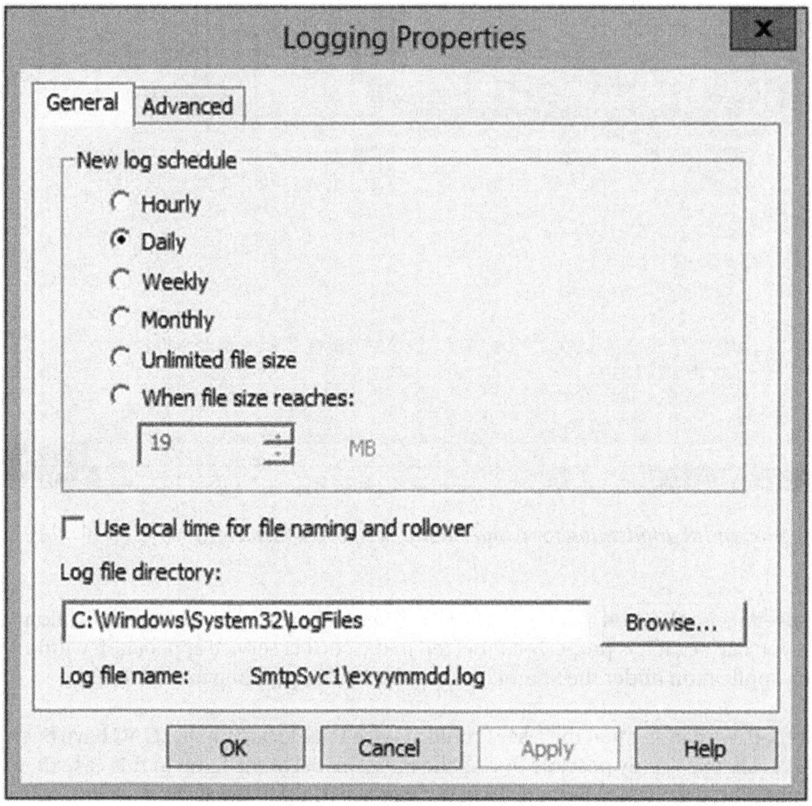

Figure 4-10. *Logging location*

To make sure you gathering all the details you can about SMTP, you should click the Advanced tab of the logging properties and select all of the boxes, as shown in Figure 4-11.

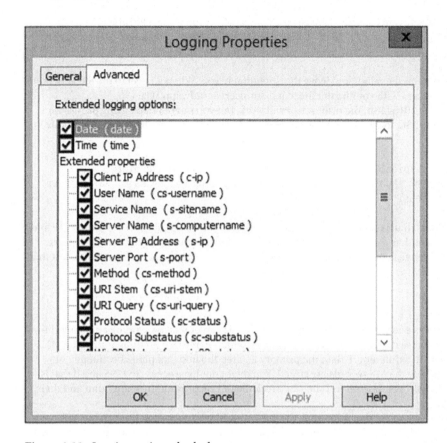

Figure 4-11. Logging options checked

To get the logging properties opened, you would need to execute inetmgr6.exe, then once it opens you would right-click SMTP virtual server, click Properties, select the Enable Logging check box (if not already checked), click Properties, and then the click the Advanced tab and select all of the options, click Apply, and then click OK.

In Chapter 3, we covered where to find the IIS logs for the actual web sites and how to determine which logs were for which sites. When you are troubleshooting SharePoint using the IIS logs you can search for your site URL and see if the logs are giving you 200s or something else that is trying to tell you what is happening. When it comes email search for the alias that is having trouble getting mail. The IIS SMTP and error logs are not the only place to check for issues with email. The event viewer and ULS logs will also provide information about email. Another location to look at in regards to mail is the mail queues, which are located at C:\inetpub\mailroot. When mail is sent by SharePoint it will appear in the queue momentarily and then it will leave the queue as it sends to its destination. Incoming mail will appear in the C:\inetpub\mailroot\drop folder if the default settings are not changed in inetmgr.

You can troubleshoot the server's ability to receive mail by enabling email on a list or library and then sending that list or library a mail. You can test the server's ability to send mail by using the following:

```
Send-MailMessage -to "recipient@anothersharepointblog.com" -from "SharePoint@
anothersharepointblog.com" -Subject "Test" -body "Test for Send-MailMessage" -SmtpServer
<Hostname>
```

You can modify the parameter values, but leave the quotation marks. When you get to the SMTPServer parameter, replace <Hostname> with your hostname (e.g., –smtpserver mdwapp01).

If you have a SharePoint 2016 farm, the prior script will work, but you might not be using port 25 for mail and you might be using SSL, in which case you could use the following PowerShell after you modify it for your environment.

```
Send-MailMessage -to "recipient@anothersharepointblog.com" -from "SharePoint@
anothersharepointblog.com" -Subject "Test" -body "Test for Send-MailMessage" -SmtpServer
mdwapp01.contoso.com -UseSsl -Port 587
```

After you've verified that mail is sending, you should also verify that it is sending on the primary IP and not some other IP, if the server has more than one IP. This is needed to ensure that alerts make it to their intended recipients, as exchange is probably set to relay for the primary IP. Here is a command-line test that you can run.

```
Ping <hostname> -4
```

If the ping comes back as another IP and not the primary IP, the server may be sending email out the wrong NIC. Using the "-4" forces it to respond with IPv4. If the domain name that is configured in the MX record wants an A record with a different IP than the primary IP, then the info that ping <hostname> -4 might be correct. DNS is where the MX records are stored. You might not have access to DNS and if that is your situation ask your domain administrator if she can check the MX records for the SharePoint and their corresponding A records.

If the server sends mail on one IP that is internal, the network address translation (NAT) table will translate that IP into a public IP. That public IP needs to have an A record that is referenced by a MX record for mail coming into your domain. For example, if your domain is anothersharepointblog.com then you would need an MX record that points anothersharepointblog.com to an A record name that in turn points the mail to the public IP. Table 4-1 demonstrates the relationship between the different records. If you're SharePoint server is internal then the record value for the A record would be the public interface of the NAT device.

Table 4-1. Mail resolution records

Record FQDN	Record Type	Record Value	MX Pref
mailServer.AnotherSharePointBlog.com	A	47.196.125.11	
AnotherSharePointBlog.com	MX	mailServer.AnotherSharePointBlog.com	10

Sometimes incoming mail settings on lists and libraries get confused by manual changes to the initial name that was configured on the list or library. When this happens you will sometimes see mail stacking up in the drop folder. If you have thousands of sites and even more lists and libraries, it could seem like a daunting task to identify the lists that have mail enabled and the aliases that those lists or libraries are using for mail. Fortunately, this PowerShell comes to the rescue:

```
$SPWebApp = Get-SPWebApplication http://URLtoYourWebApplication
#creates a text file named Email-enabled-lists.txt
"E-Mail,List,Site" > "EMail-Enabled.txt" #Write the Headers in to a text file
foreach ($SPsite in $SPwebApp.Sites)  # get the collection of site collections
{
        foreach($SPweb in $SPsite.AllWebs)  # get the collection of sub sites
        {
        foreach ($SPList in $SPweb.Lists) # get the lists in each sub site
                {
                if ( ($splist.CanReceiveEmail) -and ($SPlist.EmailAlias) )
                {
# Give some feedback to admin
 WRITE-HOST "E-Mail -" $SPList.EmailAlias "is configured for the list "$SPlist.Title "in
"$SPweb.Url
#Append the data to the txt file
$SPList.EmailAlias + "," + $SPlist.Title +"," + $SPweb.Url >> EMail-Enabled-lists.
txt                }
        }
}
}
```

After you've obtained the list of all the email-enabled lists, take a look at your drop folder under C:\inetpub\mailroot\drop or the custom location, if a custom location was specified inside of inetmgr6. Once you've identified the drop folder and opened it, it will become clearly evident if it is not moving messages. Assuming you've verified that you have incoming email configured correctly in the farm and DNS, you can open each .eml file in the drop folder and see the to: location. Then you can use the list you generated when enumerating your sites to determine which list the incoming email belongs, by matching up the alias, list name, and site.

Once you match up the list, you may need to go into settings, into email settings for the list, and then remove the alias, apply that change, then put the alias back and apply the alias, by clicking OK.

If your list is a custom list, you'll need to get the list ID and append this to _layouts/15/emailsettings. aspx?List=<Insert List ID Here>.

All site collections in SharePoint contain at least one web site, the top web; any subsites are additional webs. So the hierarchy is web applications contain site collections, which are referred to as Sites in the object model and the Sites contain subsites, which are referred to as webs in the object model. You can obtain the list ID with a little PowerShell:

```
$site = get-spsite http://portal.contoso.com
$site.allwebs.lists | ft title, id
```

The only issue with this approach is that it uses the site collection object and the allwebs property, which includes the top site and all the subsites. Theoretically, this peels back a layer and exposes potentially thousands of lists and libraries and their titles and IDs. Figure 4-12 displays part of the output for the preceding commands for the site collection.

```
                  Administrator: SharePoint 2013 Management Shell        [─][□][X]

PS C:\Users\2013installer> $site = get-spsite http://portal.contoso.com
PS C:\Users\2013installer> $site.allwebs.lists | ft title, id

Title                                   ID
─────                                   ──

appdata                                 0233ee45-a5ee-4d33-bafb-cd976502f299
Cache Profiles                          4eb744e1-8529-4c85-b4a5-fbfe4e4c3050
Composed Looks                          e73e118f-8f21-4c21-974d-ea668dcd9a70
Contacts                                c035a24f-19dc-4257-961d-e8efcf14e900
Content and Structure Reports           54512b82-5a1d-4780-becf-89da5ef5ab75
Content type publishing error log       b9361549-5ad0-4d64-908d-a2ae1ac6e680
Converted Forms                         bd100aca-9725-4686-89df-b1fff45f9715
Device Channels                         db25e17b-1cf5-48cd-859f-c9628acc9dd5
Documents                               80108dd6-9ab6-4594-be64-8296afae35d1
Events                                  5cd2c773-64f1-44af-b729-57ce3e58b419
Form Templates                          52a7025f-5b88-49b3-80e9-2b589d11943f
Images                                  2e5e8f78-f951-417a-9ee3-1389efbd0c06
Links                                   3d192092-d8aa-4135-b06f-cbeb3cc89219
List Template Gallery                   14f5ee10-7933-4a8a-a5e5-d30771486c44
Long Running Operation Status           75087499-e2c7-40ea-b5b0-19ef980803fa
Master Page Gallery                     4a39bb3c-d60c-4c5e-9e68-3971452938d3
Notification List                       a35b8536-6f7f-4165-9033-6fcb8ca51a6c
Pages                                   dbbcd057-068a-4a83-9ac3-cf8dff496f74
Project Policy Item List                34591b5e-e9e7-4262-a69e-b091c61b902c
Quick Deploy Items                      466cb3fd-6e2a-4223-99c3-b635386d2289
Relationships List                      d4b16149-f8a8-48be-b9ff-59b21d4f491f
Reusable Content                        5608573f-c961-4fde-b2f6-12a9e7738dbe
Site Collection Documents               5a6735fb-8758-416f-b1e4-3a5964716bc8
Site Collection Images                  e034dbe2-230b-48d1-977d-26ceca935f14
```

Figure 4-12. *Lists in a site collection*

Appending an Out-File cmdlet to the last line would generate a text file that you could search through for the name of the list and then identify the ID. Here's an example of an out-file cmdlet appended to the end of the last line:

```
$site.allwebs.lists | ft title, id | out-file c:\myfile.txt
```

The reason you need the ID is that in a custom list that has email enabled, the GUI will not have a link for you to reach the email settings page. So you'll need to access it by appending a string to your site or web URL. The string that is appended is as follows:

```
_layouts/15/EmailSettings.aspx?List={ListGUID}
```

Make sure you convert your list ID from

```
_layouts/15/EmailSettings.aspx?List={69163F9C-0BA4-4981-A3F3-FF0F48948A69}
```

to

```
_layouts/15/EmailSettings.aspx?List=%7B69163F9C%2D0BA4%2D4981%2DA3F3%2DFF0F48948A69%7D. In
order to make the conversion you'll replace "{"with"%7B", "}" with "%7D", and "-"with"%2D"
```

If you wanted to return only the lists for a given subsite, you can use get-SPWeb and the lists property, as shown in Figure 4-13.

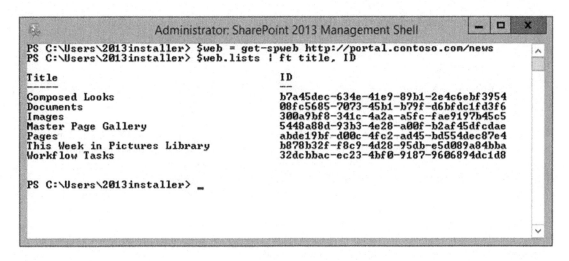

Figure 4-13. *Lists in a subsite*

This seems like a good place to look at the get-member cmdlet as a troubleshooting tool. And to recognize what is wrong with something, you have to know what that something should look like when everything is OK. This is where the get-member cmdlet is so awesome. Did you know that you can use the get-member against itself? Yes, you can get-member against the get-member. And, why would you want to do that? The answer is so that you can get the results to wrap and display more information about the various methods and properties.

For example, the lists property of the web object that Get-SPWeb returns is a collection. The actual .NET name is Microsoft.SharePoint.SPListCollection Lists. That's really not that important, but the fact that it is a collection is good to know because that means it more than likely has its own sublayer of properties. And as you saw in Figure 4-13, The Lists property had at least two child properties, Title and ID. In reality it has a lot more than two sub properties.

If you use get-member to interrogate SharePoint about lists, SharePoint will tell you that there are three main types of lists:

- Microsoft.SharePoint.SPList

- Microsoft.SharePoint.SPDocumentLibrary

- Microsoft.SharePoint.SPPictureLibrary

All of these types of lists have similar methods, with the one exception being that the Microsoft. SharePoint.SPList does not have the GetItemsInFolder method, which makes sense, as regular lists do not have folders; whereas document libraries and picture libraries have folders.

When it comes to properties the regular SharePoint list does not have the property named CheckedOutFiles; whereas the Microsoft.SharePoint.SPDocumentLibrary and SPPictureLibrary both have the ability to let files get checkout and as such they need a way to add a file to an array or collection of checked out files that can be obtained. The properties for a SPDcoumentLibrary and a SPPictureLibrary are the same. The SPList is lacking the following properties:

- CheckedOutFiles

- DocumentTemplateUrl

- EmailInsertsFolder

- IsCatalog

- ServerRelativeDocumentTemplateUrl

- ThumbnailsEnabled

- ThumbnailSize

- WebImageHeight

- WebImageWidth

So now the next time someone asks you what the difference between a library and list is, you can tell them that there really isn't too much difference and that the list has one less method and nine fewer properties than a library. You could also mention that the libraries have properties related to images and thumbnails and that they have the ability to identify all of the checked out files.

Some properties only allow the admin to get information and others allow the admin to not only get info but to set info. Whenever you want to change a property, you should look for an update method and then call that method after you have instantiated the property into a variable. For example, if you wanted to change the title of a list you could first find the list ID, then instantiate that list into a variable, test that you have the list by dot sourcing its title, and then modify the title and update it.

```
$web = get-SPWeb http://portal.contoso.com/news
$Imagelist = $web.lists | ? {$_.id -eq "300a9bf8-341c-4a2a-a5fc-fae9197b45c5"}
$Imagelist.title
#Returns the list title Images
$Imagelist.title = "Cool Images"
$Imagelist.title
#Returns the list title Cool Images
$Imagelist.update()
```

This example is about as close as this text will come to any sort of development. It utilized a SP PowerShell cmdlet to make the change to the images list. Granted this could've been completed through the GUI; but the point here is because it was a SharePoint cmdlet, SharePoint was aware of the change.

Sometimes changes are made to files in places where they shouldn't be made. And sometimes these changes are so detrimental that they corrupt the site to a point where it will not open and instead give a message like the one shown in Figure 4-14.

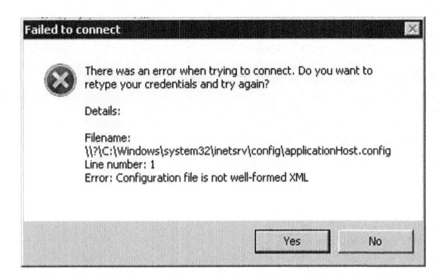

Figure 4-14. *site has really been jacked with*

Sometimes when this message appears, you can get the site working again by restoring the applicationhost.config backup, if this issue is due to the file 'applicationhost.config' being corrupted. To restore from the backup, make a copy of the current applicationhost.config file located at C:\Windows\ system32\inetsrv\config\, then delete the potentially corrupted file, and finally copy the applicationhost. config from the backup directory located at C:\inetpub\history\. After you have done this in every server in the farm, restart IIS; the problem should be fixed.

I have a blog post about resetting the IIS across an entire farm at https://anothersharepointblog.com/ reset-iis-on-all-servers-in-a-farm. I didn't create the script; but it works great in SharePoint farms that are not using the Minimum Role Technology; so, non-SharePoint 2016 farms. The script is as follows:

```
###########################################################################
# This Script allows you to do an IIS RESET to all the servers in a SharePoint Farm
# required parameters: N/A
###########################################################################
If ((Get-PSSnapIn -Name Microsoft.SharePoint.PowerShell -ErrorAction SilentlyContinue) -eq
$null )
{Add-PSSnapIn -Name Microsoft.SharePoint.PowerShell}
 $host.Runspace.ThreadOptions = "ReuseThread"
#Definition of the function that performs the IIS RESET in all the servers
function Do-IISreset
{
    try
    {
        #Getting the servers where the IISReset is going to be done
        $spServers= Get-SPServer | ? {$_.Role -eq "Application"}
        foreach ($spServer in $spServers)
        {
```

```
            Write-Host "Doing IIS Reset in server $spServer" -f blue
            Iisreset $spServer /noforce "\\"$_.Address
            iisreset $spServer /status "\\"$_.Address
        }
        Write-Host "IIS Reset completed successfully!!" -f blue
    }
    catch [System.Exception]
    {
        write-host -f red $_.Exception.ToString()
    }
}
Start-SPAssignment –Global
#Calling the function
Do-IISReset
Stop-SPAssignment –Global
 Remove-PSSnapin Microsoft.SharePoint.PowerShell
```

If you are running this on a SharePoint 2016 farm, you'll want to remove the | ? {$_.Role -eq "Application"} or it will only reset IIS on the app server. You remove this from the line that reads:

```
    $spServers= Get-SPServer | ? {$_.Role -eq "Application"}
```

Essentially, if you're able to open the site from the server with or without a hosts entry, you know the site is working and there isn't any issue within IIS to be concerned with. If you are unable to open the site from the server, and you have already determined that a binding exists, you might try running a nslookup command to determine if DNS has a record for your site. If you're able to open the site with a host entry, then the issue might be within DNS if the site is not opening without the hosts entry.

The hosts file is located at C:\windows\system32\etc\drivers. You can quickly get to this location by typing **drivers** on the run bar, and clicking OK. The hosts file may or may not contain references to the sites on the web server using the web server IP. It is completely OK to modify the hosts file to include references to sites on SharePoint servers that have the Microsoft SharePoint Foundation Web Application Service instantiated and running on the services on server page or by running get-spserviceinstance instance to determine what services are running, so that these servers resolve site names to their own IP address.

The following PowerShell can be used to determine which servers are running the service that causes IIS to spin up the SharePoint sites:

```
Get-SPServiceInstance | ? {$_.typename -like "Microsoft SharePoint foundation web*"} | ft
typename, status, server –wrap
```

Figure 4-15 shows this PowerShell in action. Notice how the service is spun up on both servers in the farm.

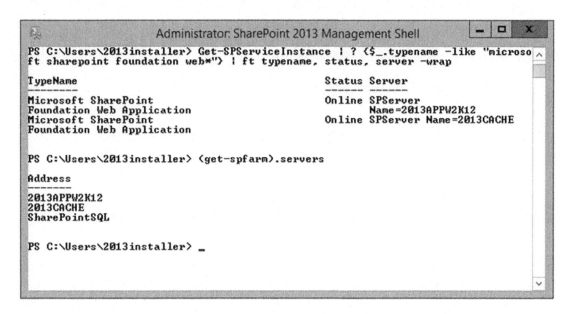

Figure 4-15. *The servers property of the get-spfarm, services on server*

By default, the system logs are located at %SystemRoot%\System32\Winevt\Logs\ which should translate into C:\Windows\System32\Winevt\Logs\. These event viewer logs are stored in files with .evt extensions. None of these files is set to archive; but rather they are configured to overwrite after a maximum log size of 20480KB or 20MB is reached. If you find that your logs are getting quite full and not holding a long enough history, you can increase this setting either through group policy or manually.

To manually increase the size of the log file, you can open computer management, click System tools, Event viewer, and Windows logs, right-click the log that you would like to increase, and then click Properties. From the General tab, you can increase the maximum log size. Figure 4-16 shows the default settings for the application log.

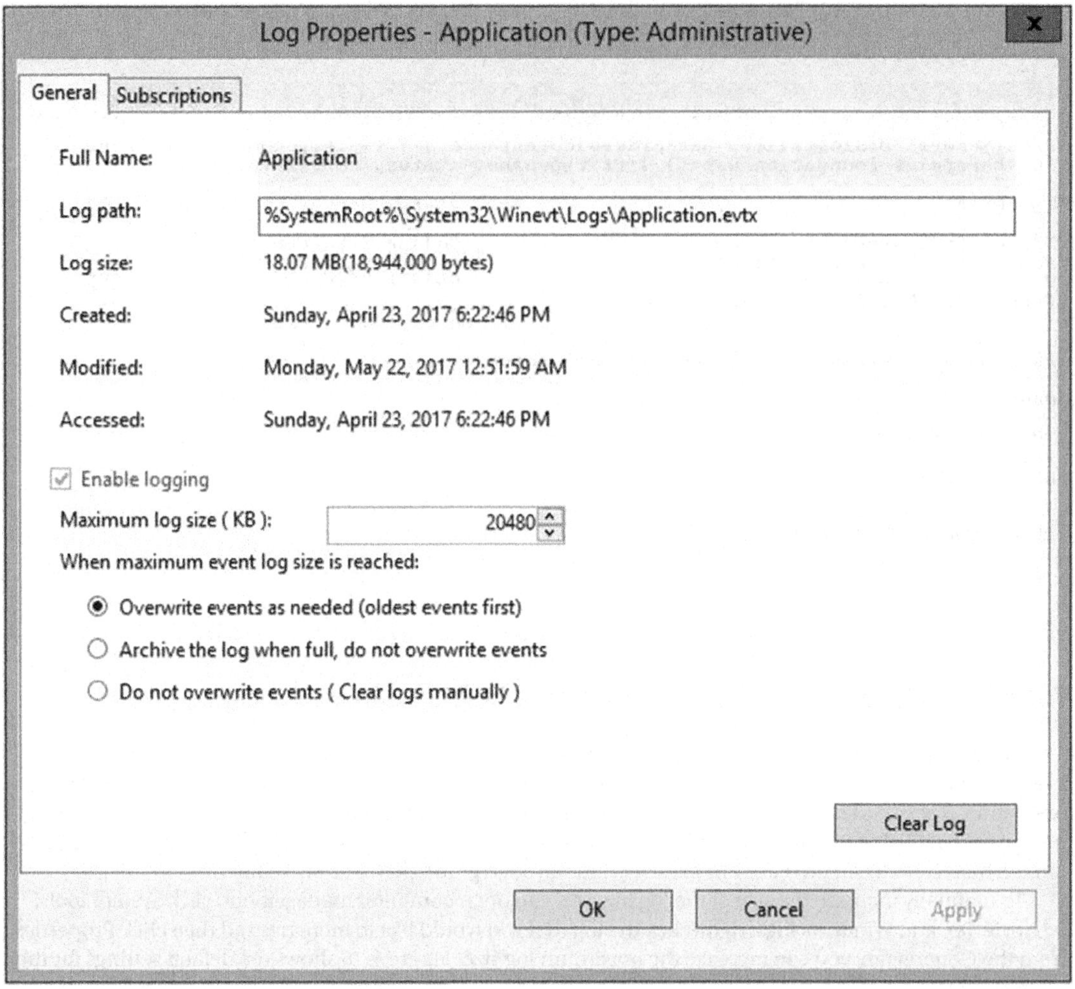

Figure 4-16. *Overwrite vs. do not overwrite*

I would not recommend clearing the logs manually, since the server may shut down when it cannot log. You could opt to archive the logs when they reach the designated size, in which case you would need to manually monitor drive usage by the logs. The group policy that sets the maximum log size is located under computer configuration, administrative templates: Policy definitions (ADMX files) retrieved from the local computer, Windows components, Event Log Service, and then choosing the appropriate log. Figure 4-17 shows the setting for the application log and in this domain it is not being controlled by group policy.

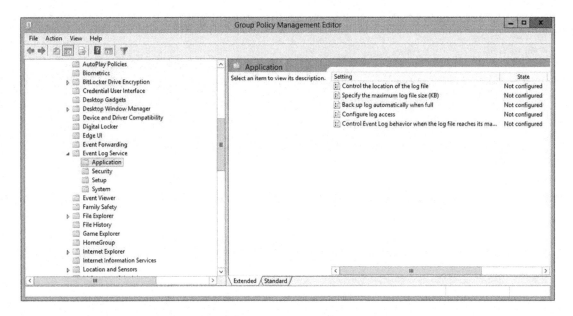

Figure 4-17. *Specify the maximum log file size not configured*

When searching through the Windows event logs it's a good idea to first filter the log by to only display reds and yellows. In other words, you remove the whites. The whites are the informational messages which you'll look at after you identify the red (critical or error) or yellow (warning) messages that may or may not be related to the issue you're troubleshooting.

To filter the log, open computer management (compmgmt.msc) and navigate to the event viewer (eventvwr.msc) or just open the event viewer directly from the run bar by typing **eventvwr.msc**. You can also open the computer management by going to administrative tools. Once you have the event viewer open, you can see how many events fall into the red and yellow categories. In Figure 4-18, only nine critical events, six error events, and two warning events have occurred in the last 24 hours. This farm was built using least privilege and the AutoSPInstaller.

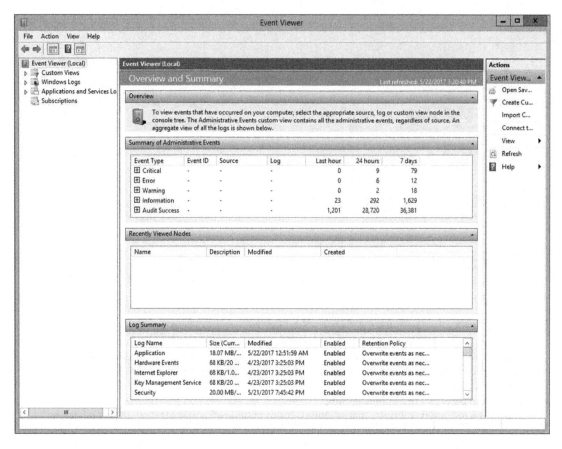

Figure 4-18. *Not too shabby*

To filter the log file before you look at it, just expand the Windows Logs and then click the log you want to filter to select it, then right-click it and click Filter current log. Once the filter current log window opens, click the Critical, Warning, and Error Event levels. This will give you a red, yellow, and red, respectively. It is here that you can also just filter on a particular event ID. Figure 4-19 shows the Application Log about to be filtered on Critical, Warning, and Error Events.

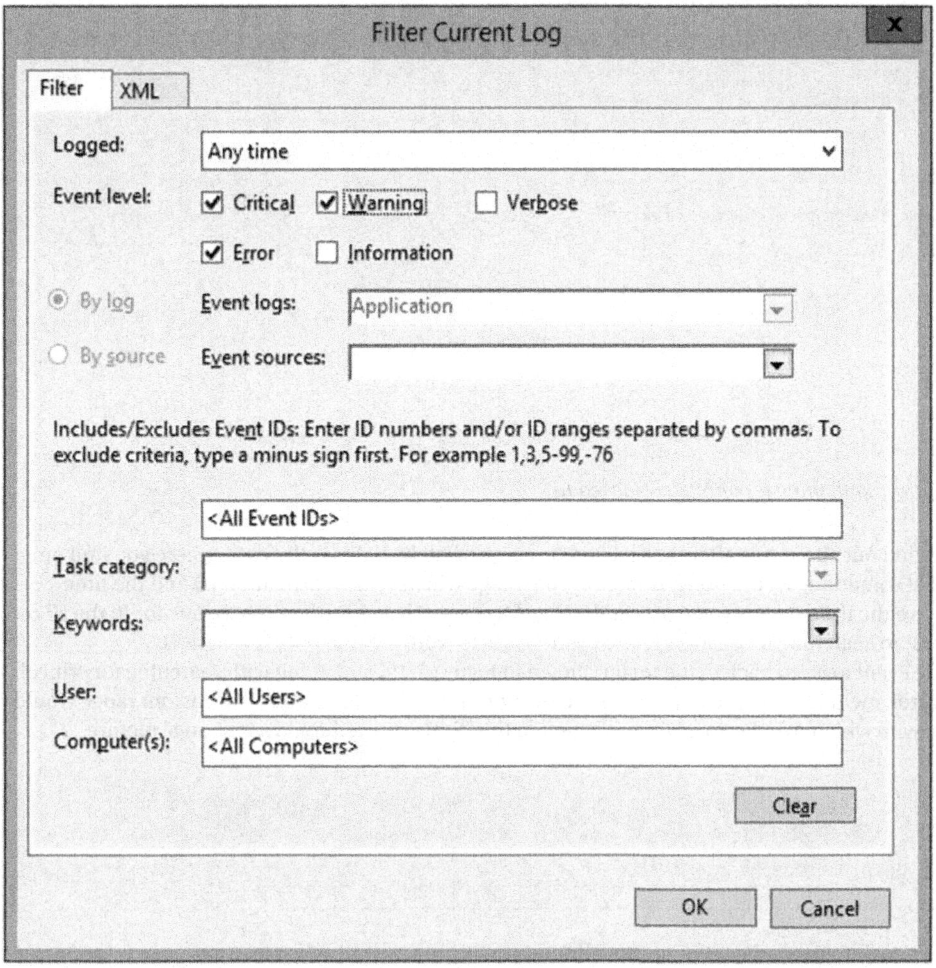

Figure 4-19. *Red, yellow, and red*

Sometimes, your users will give you a correlation ID to use for searching in the ULS logs and along with that correlation ID they'll include a time that the error occurred. Usually, this will come in the form of a picture, like the one in Figure 4-20.

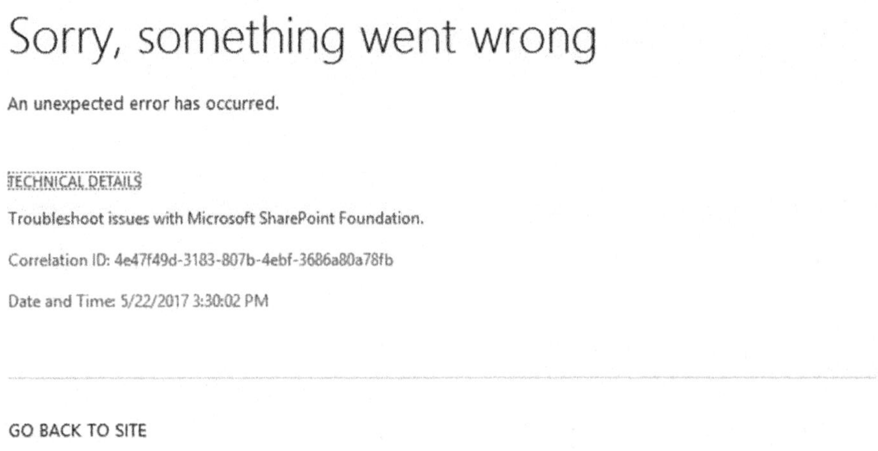

Sorry, something went wrong

An unexpected error has occurred.

TECHNICAL DETAILS

Troubleshoot issues with Microsoft SharePoint Foundation.

Correlation ID: 4e47f49d-3183-807b-4ebf-3686a80a78fb

Date and Time: 5/22/2017 3:30:02 PM

GO BACK TO SITE

Figure 4-20. *Sorry, something is completely jacked up*

You might find out about this after the fact and not immediately. If this is the case, where you find out after the fact that something went wrong, hopefully the image will have the correlation ID and the time stamp. If you have the time stamp, you can sort the Windows event logs for event IDs to look for in the ULS logs, when you start searching those logs. These event IDs also work great in google searches.

To filter the event logs, go back to the image shown in Figure 4-19, and along with searching for critical, warning, and error, include a custom date range like the one shown in Figure 4-21. The custom range would be more in line with whichever date and time is listed on the "Sorry, something went wrong" picture.

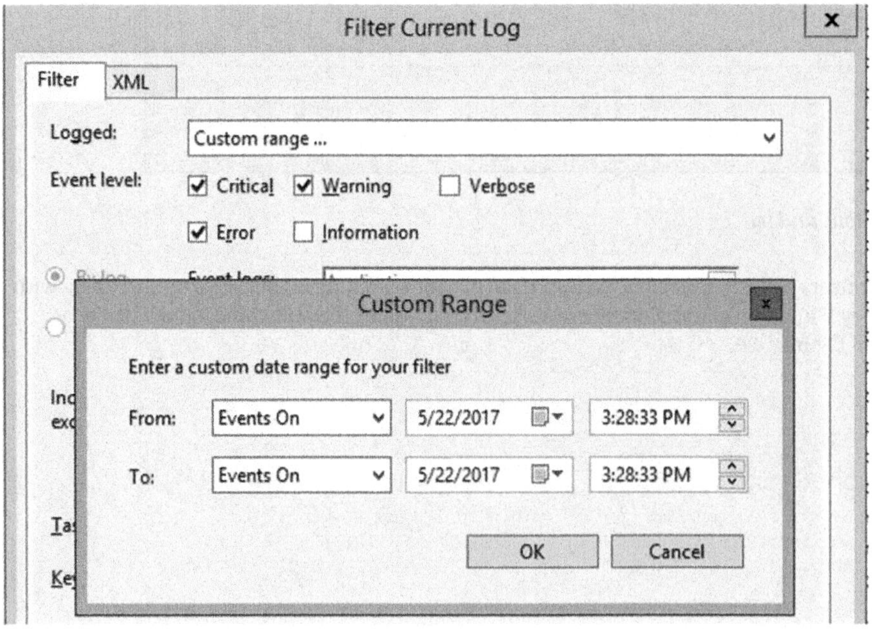

Figure 4-21. *Customized date searching*

After you have that red and yellow event IDs you're ready to open the ULS logs. The ULS logs are by default located at C:\Program Files\Common Files\microsoft shared\Web Server Extensions\15\LOGS unless you have moved them to a non-operating system drive; which is a best practice due to the amount of writing that happens on these logs. By default the trace logs record any event with a trace severity of medium or higher, as a result, it is a good idea to move the logging. We already covered the PowerShell that is used to move logging. You can move logging via the Central Administration GUI, just make sure the logging directory exists before you change the logging location. The logging location is located on the "configure diagnostic logging (<central admin URL:Port>/_admin/metrics.aspx) page" and on the "Configure usage and health data collection (<central admin URL:Port>/_admin/LogUsage.aspx) page".

Once you have the ULS logging location, you can open the logs with Notepad, or better yet, ULSViewer. A future chapter goes into much more detail on the ULSViewer, so I won't go into it very far here other than to say that filtering by the correlation ID and any Windows event IDs is a great way to drill into the section of the logs that contain information with the key terms used to search for resolutions. The Windows event logs allow you to copy the information out as text, and we will go into that in a later chapter; since you'll use that text and text found in the ULS to perform your queries in Bing or Google.

Keep in mind that not everything has been documented in the interwebs. For example, I've always found it odd that SharePoint doesn't add the account used for service application pools in IIS to the WSS_Admin_WPG group. The reason for this is that instead SharePoint gives the WSS_WPG group full control to various file system locations. This is not documented in the any of the TechNet articles named "Account permissions and security settings in SharePoint..." The SharePoint 2013 version of this article is located https://technet.microsoft.com/en-us/library/cc678863 (v=office.15).aspx. If you look at the ACL of the index and compare that to what is listed in that article, you'll see that the WSS_WPG group having full control to the search index location is not documented in the interwebs; but in fact, it is the case in your farm. Figure 4-22 shows the location of the index in the test lab farm and the ACL for the folder that holds the index.

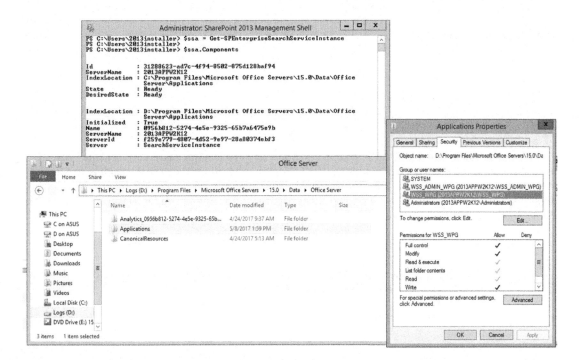

Figure 4-22. *Index location and ACL*

You can determine the index location using PowerShell. The index in Figure 4-22 has issues, from a standpoint of where it is instantiated, and we'll get into that in Chapters 7 and 8. To determine the index location, use this script that a fellow Rackspace SharePoint engineer and friend of mine, Scott Fawley, contributed:

```
$ssa = Get-SPServiceApplication –Name "<Search Service Application>"
$active = Get-SPEnterpriseSearchTopology -SearchApplication $ssa -Active
Get-SPEnterpriseSearchComponent -SearchTopology $active
```

You need to get the name or know the name of the SharePoint Search service application so that you can replace <Search Service Application> if needed. In the test farm used in the writing of this book, the search service application was named Search Service Application

All you need to run it is the name of the Search Service application. To determine the name, you can run the following:

```
Get-SPServiceApplication | ? {$_.typename -like "Search*"}
```

The results will be similar to that shown in Figure 4-23.

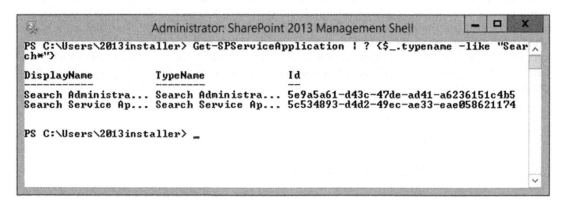

Figure 4-23. *Search service application*

From here you'll want to use the Search Service App... and to make sure of the correct name to use in the Scott's script, you'll just need to modify the Get-SPServiceApplication cmdlet so that it pipes to a format table cmdlet which will reveal the full, non-truncated, displayname; or, you could find the search service application name in the manage service applications page in Central Administration. If you opt to go the PowerShell route, here is the one-liner:

```
Get-SPServiceApplication | ? {$_.typename -like "Search*"} | ft displayname
```

Scott also shared a script where you do not need the name of the search service application. This script easily gets the index location of the search service application and it's on many blogs:

```
$ssa = Get-SPEnterpriseSearchServiceInstance

$ssa.Components
```

After you run it, it will display the following, if you created your farm with the binaries over on the D drive. Notice how in Figure 4-24, the C drive still has references on the C drive for the search index while the D drive gets part of it, as well.

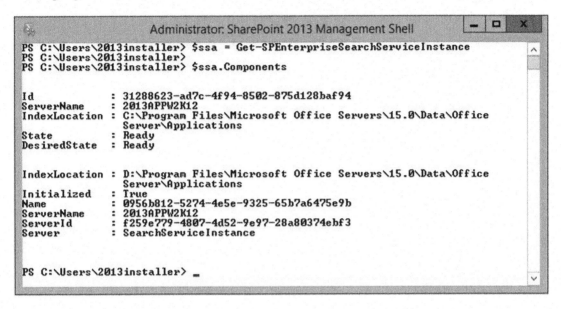

Figure 4-24. *The search index is split*

We'll talk more about search in Chapter 7 and Chapter 8, when I discuss manipulating search topology and troubleshooting search. The account used for the SharePoint Hosted Services application pool in a least privileged farm is not a member of the local administrators and I've always found it odd that SharePoint doesn't add the account used for service application pools in IIS to the WSS_Admin_WPG group. The reason for this is that SharePoint gives the WSS_WPG group full control to various file system locations. This is not documented in the any of the TechNet articles named "Account permissions and security settings in SharePoint…" The SharePoint 2013 version of this article is located https://technet.microsoft.com/en-us/library/cc678863 (v=office.15).aspx and if you read that article, you will not see any mention of WSS_WPG having full control over the applications directory. However, WSS_WPG members definitely have full control over the index, as we saw in Figure 4-22 and in Figure 4-25. Notice how the WSS_WPG group has full control over the applications directory so that it can index.

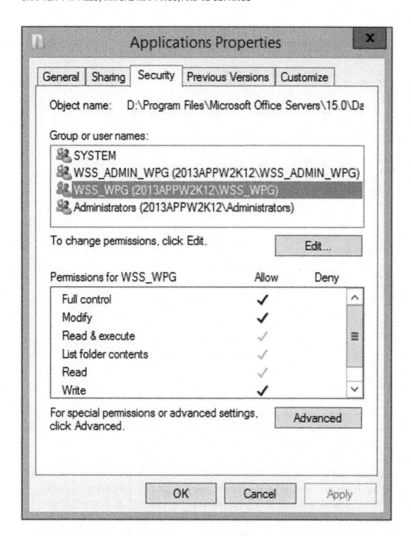

Figure 4-25. *SharePoint gave WSS_WPG full control*

Things like this are why you can't believe everything on the Internet about SharePoint. However, when it comes to searching for resolutions to errors in SharePoint, the Internet is one of the best places to look; you just need to be careful that you understand what the blog post is advising before you take action on any advice. This is why it is best to have a farm where you can reproduce the issue in some cases.

If you search the Windows OS logs for event IDs that you find in the ULS logs and search the ULS logs for critical, error, and warning events that you find in the Windows event viewer logs, you'll find the best search terms for your queries. In a future chapter, we'll demonstrate this and add some pictures along with a really cool script that will let you search through logs on your server. At this point we just wanted to make mention of that relationship between the logs. The same sort of relationship exists between the IIS logs and the ULS logs, which we'll look at in Chapter 9.

What About Registry?

Up until this point, we haven't really touched on registry too much. There was the brief moment where I mentioned the use of BackConnectionHostNames vs. DisableLoopbackCheck when it comes to being able to crawl content on the application server or navigate to SharePoint sites from the server that they have IIS bindings.

The DisableLoopbackCheck is the less secure option and as usual is the easiest to manage. All you need to do is create a DWORD named DisableLoopbackCheck, and then set its value to 1. The location for this registry entry is HKLM\SYSTEM\CurrentControlSet\Control\Lsa. BackConnectionHostNames accomplishes the same thing that DisableLoopbackCheck accomplishes, only it does so without reducing the security of the server. The BackConnectionHostNames entry is a Multi String reg key and is located at HKLM\SYSTEM\CurrentControlSet\Control\Lsa\MSV1_0. It requires more work because each time a HHSC or PBSC is created the site collection needs to be added to the list of site collections within the multistring. Neither DisableLoopbackCheck nor BackConnectionHostNames exist by default; only one is needed. It does not provide any additional security to use both.

If, for whatever reason, you need to retrieve the MS Office product key from your SharePoint servers; in other words, the key that was used to install SharePoint. You can use the following script that J. T. wrote:

```
function Search-RegistryKeyValues {
param(
[string]$path,
[string]$valueName
)
Get-ChildItem $path -recurse -ea SilentlyContinue |
% {
if ((Get-ItemProperty -Path $_.PsPath -ea SilentlyContinue) -match $valueName)
{
$_.PsPath
}
}
}
# find registry key that has value "digitalproductid"
# 32-bit versions
$key = Search-RegistryKeyValues "hklm:\software\microsoft\office" "digitalproductid"
if ($key -eq $null) {
# 64-bit versions
$key = Search-RegistryKeyValues "hklm:\software\Wow6432Node\microsoft\office"
"digitalproductid"
if ($key -eq $null) {Write-Host "MS Office is not installed.";break}
}
$valueData = (Get-ItemProperty $key).digitalproductid[52..66]
# decrypt base24 encoded binary data
$productKey = ""
$chars = "BCDFGHJKMPQRTVWXY2346789"
for ($i = 24; $i -ge 0; $i--) {
$r = 0
for ($j = 14; $j -ge 0; $j--) {
$r = ($r * 256) -bxor $valueData[$j]
$valueData[$j] = [math]::Truncate($r / 24)
$r = $r % 24
}
```

```
$productKey = $chars[$r] + $productKey
if (($i % 5) -eq 0 -and $i -ne 0) {
$productKey = "-" + $productKey
}
}
Write-Host "MS Office Product Key:" $productKey
```

Just save that into a ps1 file, and call the ps1 or paste all of it into your Management Shell and enter a few times. This could come in really handy if you're troubleshooting your SharePoint records and can't find the info about an enterprise key that you once had.

The Hive exists in the file system at C:\Program Files\Common Files\microsoft shared\Web Server Extensions and it exists in registry at HKLM\SOFTWARE\Microsoft\Shared Tools\Web Server Extensions. Under this location there is a key named 15 that represents the Hive. Under that key are all sorts of keys that hold data about the farm. The permissions for these and other registry settings should never need to be modified for any code. In fact, the WSS_Admin_WPG and WSS_WPG groups do not have access on the ACL of the 15 hive's key in registry. If those two group had permission on the 15 key, then the farm would not be least privileged.

The local administrators group has full control on the 15 key, and this full control is inherited from the Microsoft key, HKLM\SOFTWARE\Microsoft. The ability to check a pristine lab or to create a lab to use as a reference is important for troubleshooting permissions in a farm's registry.

Under the 15 key, there are numerous keys, as displayed in Figure 4-26.

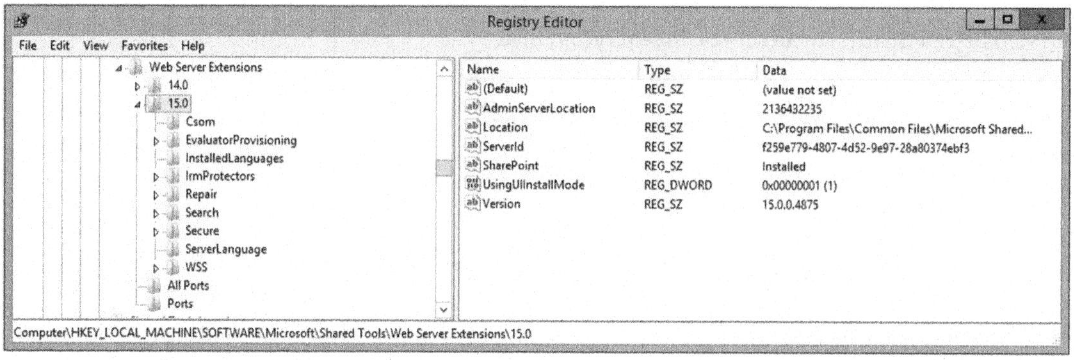

Figure 4-26. *WSS key*

The WSS_Admin_WPG and WSS_WPG group have explicitly granted permissions on the Search key, the Secure key, and the WSS key. They have zero permissions on the 15 key or any of the other keys shown in Figure 4-26. Notice that the 15 key lets the server know where the hive is located in the location REG_SZ value and that the server shows SharePoint as installed.

WSS originates from Windows SharePoint Services and inside this key are all sorts of settings. Here you can find things like the location of the logs, the maximum log sizes, and the maximum size on disk to be used by the logging, whether the SharePoint binaries were installed on the C or the D drive, and the URL for the Central Administration website. There are other keys under the WSS key that have info as well; for example, the InstalledProducts key contains GUIDS for the products that might be installed. Table 4-2 is a breakdown of what you might find under this key.

Table 4-2. *SharePoint Products and SKU Numbers*

Product SKU	Product
BEED1F75-C398-4447-AEF1-E66E1F0DF91E	SharePoint Foundation 2010
1328E89E-7EC8-4F7E-809E-7E945796E511	Search Server Express 2010
B2C0B444-3914-4ACB-A0B8-7CF50A8F7AA0	SharePoint Server 2010 Standard Trial
3FDFBCC8-B3E4-4482-91FA-122C6432805C	SharePoint Server 2010 Standard
88BED06D-8C6B-4E62-AB01-546D6005FE97	SharePoint Server 2010 Enterprise Trial
D5595F62-449B-4061-B0B2-0CBAD410BB51	SharePoint Server 2010 Enterprise
BC4C1C97-9013-4033-A0DD-9DC9E6D6C887	Search Server 2010 Trial
08460AA2-A176-442C-BDCA-26928704D80B	Search Server 2010
84902853-59F6-4B20-BC7C-DE4F419FEFAD	Project Server 2010 Trial
ED21638F-97FF-4A65-AD9B-6889B93065E2	Project Server 2010
926E4E17-087B-47D1-8BD7-91A394BC6196	Office Web Companions 2010
35466B1A-B17B-4DFB-A703-F74E2A1F5F5E	Project Server 2013
BC7BAF08-4D97-462C-8411-341052402E71	Project Server 2013 Preview
C5D855EE-F32B-4A1C-97A8-F0A28CE02F9C	SharePoint Server 2013
CBF97833-C73A-4BAF-9ED3-D47B3CFF51BE	SharePoint Server 2013 Preview
B7D84C2B-0754-49E4-B7BE-7EE321DCE0A9	SharePoint Server 2013 Enterprise
298A586A-E3C1-42F0-AFE0-4BCFDC2E7CD0	SharePoint Server 2013 Enterprise Preview
D6B57A0D-AE69-4A3E-B031-1F993EE52EDC	Microsoft Office Web Apps Server 2013
9FF54EBC-8C12-47D7-854F-3865D4BE8118	SharePoint Foundation 2013
716578D2-2029-4FF2-8053-637391A7E683	SharePoint 2016 Enterprise
4F593424-7178-467A-B612-D02D85C56940	SharePoint 2016 Standard
435d4d60-f4cf-421d-abc8-129e4b57f7a6	SharePoint 2016 Trail
5DB351B8-C548-4C3C-BFD1-82308C9A519B	SharePoint 2016 Trail

Here's a PowerShell that you can run to find the SKUs that are installed on your SharePoint server, not to be confused with the install key. This code is adapted from posts in the interwebs that utilize a function written by Ed Wilson.

```
Function Get-RegistryKeyPropertiesAndValues
{
  <#
  .Synopsis
  This function accepts a registry path and returns all reg key properties and values
  .Description
  This function returns registry key properties and values.
  .Example
  Get-RegistryKeyPropertiesAndValues -path 'HKCU:\Volatile Environment'
  Returns all of the registry property values under the \volatile environment key
  .Parameter path
```

```
    The path to the registry key
   .Notes
    NAME:  Get-RegistryKeyPropertiesAndValues
    AUTHOR: Ed Wilson, msft
    LASTEDIT: 05/09/2012 15:18:41
    KEYWORDS: Operating System, Registry, Scripting Techniques, Getting Started
    HSG: 5-11-12
   .Link
     Http://www.ScriptingGuys.com/blog
#Requires -Version 2.0
#>

Param(
 [Parameter(Mandatory=$true)]
 [string]$path)
Push-Location
Set-Location -Path $path
Get-Item . |
Select-Object -ExpandProperty property |
ForEach-Object {
New-Object psobject -Property @{"property"=$_;
   "Value" = (Get-ItemProperty -Path . -Name $_).$_}}
Pop-Location
}
$products = @{
    "BEED1F75-C398-4447-AEF1-E66E1F0DF91E" = "SharePoint Foundation 2010";
    "1328E89E-7EC8-4F7E-809E-7E945796E511" = "Search Server Express 2010";
    "B2C0B444-3914-4ACB-A0B8-7CF50A8F7AA0" = "SharePoint Server 2010 Standard Trial";
    "3FDFBCC8-B3E4-4482-91FA-122C6432805C" = "SharePoint Server 2010 Standard";
    "88BED06D-8C6B-4E62-AB01-546D6005FE97" = "SharePoint Server 2010 Enterprise Trial";
    "D5595F62-449B-4061-B0B2-0CBAD410BB51" = "SharePoint Server 2010 Enterprise";
    "BC4C1C97-9013-4033-A0DD-9DC9E6D6C887" = "Search Server 2010 Trial";
    "08460AA2-A176-442C-BDCA-26928704D80B" = "Search Server 2010";
    "84902853-59F6-4B20-BC7C-DE4F419FEFAD" = "Project Server 2010 Trial";
    "ED21638F-97FF-4A65-AD9B-6889B93065E2" = "Project Server 2010";
    "926E4E17-087B-47D1-8BD7-91A394BC6196" = "Office Web Apps 2010";
    "35466B1A-B17B-4DFB-A703-F74E2A1F5F5E" = "Project Server 2013";
    "BC7BAF08-4D97-462C-8411-341052402E71" = "Project Server 2013 Preview";
    "C5D855EE-F32B-4A1C-97A8-F0A28CE02F9C" = "SharePoint Server 2013";
    "CBF97833-C73A-4BAF-9ED3-D47B3CFF51BE" = "SharePoint Server 2013 Preview";
    "B7D84C2B-0754-49E4-B7BE-7EE321DCE0A9" = "SharePoint Server 2013 Enterprise";
    "298A586A-E3C1-42F0-AFE0-4BCFDC2E7CD0" = "SharePoint Server 2013 Enterprise Preview";
    "D6B57A0D-AE69-4A3E-B031-1F993EE52EDC" = "Microsoft Office Online";
    "9FF54EBC-8C12-47D7-854F-3865D4BE8118" = "SharePoint Foundation 2013";
    "716578D2-2029-4FF2-8053-637391A7E683" = "SharePoint 2016 Enterprise";
    "4F593424-7178-467A-B612-D02D85C56940" = "SharePoint 2016 Standard";
    "435d4d60-f4cf-421d-abc8-129e4b57f7a6" = "SharePoint 2016 Trail";
    "5DB351B8-C548-4C3C-BFD1-82308C9A519B" = "SharePoint 2016 Trail"
 }
$registryPath = "HKLM:software\Microsoft\Shared Tools\Web Server Extensions\$((Get-SPFarm).
BuildVersion.Major).0\WSS\InstalledProducts"
```

```
Get-RegistryKeyPropertiesAndValues -path $registryPath |
    ForEach-Object { Write-Host "Installed product: $($products.Get_Item($_.value)) (SKU ID:
$($_.value))" }
Write-Host "Installed version: $((Get-SPFarm).BuildVersion)"
```

After you run that code, it courses through your registry and pulls out the build version of your farm and the installed SKUs, as shown in Figure 4-27.

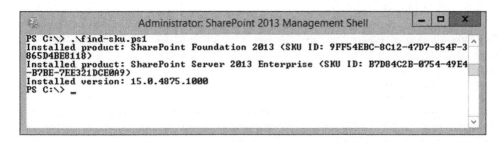

Figure 4-27. *The version of SharePoint running*

When you use SSL for Central Administration, the CentralAdministrationURL REG_SZ key sometimes resets itself after psconfig is run, causing issues with Central Administration opening. You can get to the location as shown in Figure 4-28.

Figure 4-28. *Central Administration URL*

You can look at the datapath REG_SZ key to determine if the SharePoint binaries were installed on an alternate location other than the default. Don't change the datapath after SharePoint is installed. In fact, don't change anything here except the CentralAdministrationURL, and only change that if you're using a vanity URL for SharePoint or SSL and are having issues after running psconfig.

Here is a PowerShell that you can run to ask registry what the value is of CentralAdministrationURL

```
Get-ItemProperty -Path "HKLM:HKEY_LOCAL_MACHINE\SOFTWARE\Microsoft\Shared Tools\Web Server
Extensions\15.0\WSS\" -Name CentralAdministrationURL | select CentralAdministrationURL
```

Here is a PowerShell that would allow you to change the Central Administration URL in registry, to your URL:

```
$CentralAdminURL = "http://your-URL:5000/default.aspx"
Set-ItemProperty -Path "HKLM:HKEY_LOCAL_MACHINE\SOFTWARE\Microsoft\Shared Tools\Web Server
Extensions\15.0\WSS\" -Name CentralAdministrationURL -Value $CentralAdminURL
```

169

Registry should be the last place to go when making manual edits. For example, you might notice that under the Secure key under HKEY_LOCAL_MACHINE\SOFTWARE\Microsoft\Shared Tools\Web Server Extensions\15.0\Secure that there is a Connection string for the configuration database. This is the key that SharePoint uses to locate its configuration database. Instead of modifying the key directly in registry, use the SQL client configuration tool.

When you look at the root key of the SharePoint registry settings for a SharePoint 2013 farm, you'll be looking at HKLM\SOFTWARE\Microsoft\Office Server\15.0. Here you can find the build version of the farm, the initial install path that was chosen during the binary installation, among other information about the farm when it was initially deployed.

Whenever you're looking at registry, you should do just that and look. If you decide to make a change, you should first make a backup of registry. You can do that by exporting the registry for the entire computer. This is accomplished by right-clicking the top node, the computer node, choosing Export, and giving the .reg file a name. In regards to SharePoint, you're always better off to have the export of the key that was changed followed by an export of registry in its entirety.

This was by no means a comprehensive cover of SharePoint's registry changes; but hopefully, it took you a little deeper. You can refer back to Chapter 2 and traverse the registry to each location to learn more. We will be getting into registry in different parts of this book as we look at troubleshooting service applications, SQL Server, or wherever the registry fits best.

Before we end this chapter, we should have at least one exercise. After all what chapter would be complete without an exercise?

CREATE A REDIRECT SITE

In this exercise, we'll create a site that will redirect all traffic coming in on port 80 over to port 443. Before you create this rule, make sure that you have a site running on SSL in your SharePoint. If you don't know how to do that, you should pick up a copy of Building a SharePoint 2016 Home lab, there is a really good write up in that book on how to run a site with SSL. OK, enough shameless self-promotion, let's do this!

Install URL rewrite. You can download the installer from `http://go.microsoft.com/?linkid=9722532` and then copy it into the Azure VM.

1. Create a new site in IIS called REDIRECT.

    a. Enter **REDIRECT** for the site name. The following screenshot shows an empty **Site name** field.

    b. Enter **C:\inetpub\wwwroot\Redirect** for the physical path.

    c. Leave the host header blank so all traffic on port 80 is redirected regardless of URL.

    d. Click **OK**.

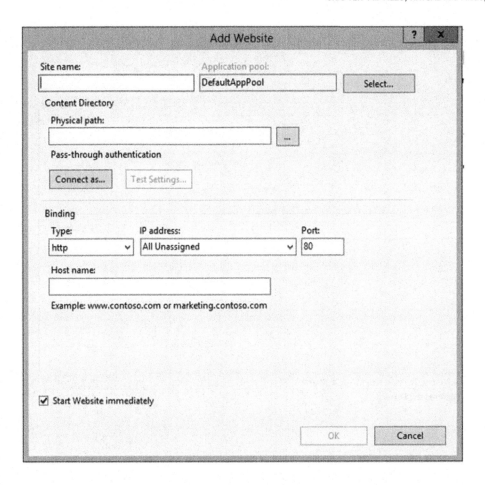

2. Create a redirect rule for HTTP to HTTPS, as shown in the following screenshot.

    a. Click **URL Rewrite module** under the Redirect site.

    b. Click **Add Rule(s)**.

    c. Select blank rule under the Inbound Rule.

    d. Requested URL: **Matches the Pattern**.

    e. Using: **Regular Expressions**

    f. Pattern: **(.*)**

    g. Conditions, Local grouping: **Match All**

Edit Inbound Rule

3. Click the **Add** button in the Conditions section and then type **{HTTPS}** in the Input field.

   a. Type **off** in the Pattern field. Make sure that **Ignore case** is selected, and then click **OK**.

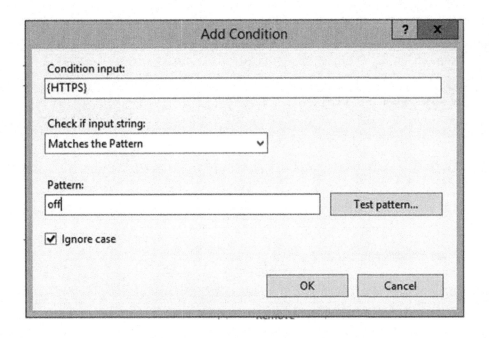

4. Under the Action section, the Action type should be **Redirect**.

    a. The redirect URL should be **https://{HTTP HOST}.**

    b. The **Append query string** box should be selected and the Redirect type is **Permanent (301)**.

I'd like to point out a couple of things that this rule does that is really awesome.

- It removes the need to modify the default site or have the default site turned on.

- It doesn't modify any SharePoint site to create the redirect and it doesn't affect SharePoint.

In closing, one of the worst things that can ever happen to a SharePoint farm is for there to be modifications made to IIS outside of those that occur naturally with settings made in Central Administration, or using SharePoint PowerShell cmdlets, or SharePoint solution packages. As I mentioned earlier, but it is important to stress, the reason to avoid editing IIS settings directly in the IIS Management console (inetmgr. exe) is that it can lead to synchronization issues and orphaned sites, passwords not updating for service identities, and other issues. The only edits that are OK to perform in IIS Manager directly are changes related to configuring Kerberos, adding SSL certificates, setting up of bindings, and creating a redirect site.

In the next chapter, we'll talk more about the changes made to registry and we'll take a good look at how SQL server plays into this madness and some good settings to be aware of for SQL. In reality, the SQL chapter that follows could've been part of the one of the chapters on key settings; but it is so important that it merits its own chapter.

CHAPTER 5

SQL

SQL is the backbone of SharePoint. And, when SQL is properly configured, SharePoint will perform at its best, assuming the servers are properly sized. We'll talk about overall sizing recommendations for a farm toward the end of this chapter, taking the SQL server and the SharePoint servers into account.

In the previous four chapters, I spoke about the base build for a basic, least-privileged, SharePoint farm and we looked at the settings that need to, at the very least accompany; or better yet, be incorporated into, an automated build. As part of this, we looked at a build with PowerShell and with the AutoSPInstaller code that is available at http://autospinstaller.com and talked about key settings that should be made to the farm. We also looked at how PowerShell is useful in finding out information and troubleshooting settings. We'll utilize PowerShell with SQL in this chapter.

In Chapters 1–3, we looked at the process of getting a least-privileged build established and we discussed things to consider when facing issues in a farm. Since there isn't a one-size-fits-all solution to all SharePoint problems, we focused on a "know what should be" approach, so that we can use that as a comparison to "what is" when the issues arise.

In Chapter 4, we looked more closely at the file system both in the GAC and in the IISroot. We also looked at registry a little bit in Chapter 4. In this chapter, we'll check out more registry keys, and will look at some SQL queries that can help troubleshoot issues.

I spoke about some of the changes that are needed to make sites resolve when using host header site collections, or when names change for path-based site collections. During that discussion, I mentioned that there are settings that were OK to modify outside of SharePoint and many that should only be modified via the SharePoint GUI, using SharePoint PowerShell cmdlets, or via the SharePoint Object Model with .wsp files.

One theme that has hopefully permeated these chapters is that SharePoint does not like it when it does not know about changes. In fact, it freaks the hell out. Maybe not immediately, but eventually it will have issues in some form or fashion. I described a few of these changes and then mentioned that manual changes to ACLs, files, folders, IIS settings, and IIS permissions should be avoided. In this chapter, that theme continues, only it continues with SQL.

Some changes are good and some are bad. In fact, there is one manual change, in particular, that is needed in order for SharePoint to install. Without this change, we get nowhere. I've mentioned this setting in previous chapters and we'll discuss it a little more, because to have a SQL chapter without it, would be like talking about fishing and forgetting to discuss hooks. There are other SQL settings that are made to achieve better performance, which we'll get into in this chapter.

The actions that you may have to perform during disaster recovery in regards to SQL server are also part of this chapter. Sometimes, you perform these actions via the SQL Server Management Studio (SSMS) and sometimes you use SSMS and the SQL Server Configuration Manager. The command line can determine which port SQL is listening on; so, we'll check that out and compare that to SQL Configuration Manager.

© Stacy Simpkins 2017
S. Simpkins, *Troubleshooting SharePoint*, https://doi.org/10.1007/978-1-4842-3138-8_5

PowerShell is sometimes used to administer SQL and we'll peer into the SQL PowerShell Module. Speaking of PowerShell, we'll see how taking a backup of a site collection using the backup-spsite cmdlet differs from creating a backup with SQL and things to keep in mind. We'll confront an issue that can sometimes present itself during .bak restores and we'll restore SQL .bak files that were created in SQL.

This chapter has some pretty cool SQL queries that enumerate email lists, find database sizes, determine drive latency, list out files in use by SQL, show what queries are eating CPU, get I/O utilization by database, and determine the logical vs. physical name of databases in your farm. Along with these explicitly mentioned SQL queries, there are more T-SQL scripts in this chapter that troubleshoot and find information.

We also talk about SQL security and SQL logins in this chapter. Regarding things that SharePoint thinks it has control over, you should really avoid modifying any of the default settings for the various logins or any of their permissions, as this will surely upset SharePoint. Todd Klindt said it best when it comes to keeping things standardized when he said, "SharePoint is unpredictable enough on its own without SQL Server pitching in."

We'll finish this chapter with an exercise that covers installing SQL Server Reporting Services (SSRS) for SharePoint 2013 on a SQL server running SQL 2012 or SQL 2014.

Before we get started, I'd like to point out that I am not a scripting expert; but all of these scripts have been vetted and there isn't anything proprietary about any of them. Most of them were found on the Internet, or they soon will be after someone pirates this book. It is bad to pirate books, music, and movies and it is something you shouldn't do. Along that theme, there are things you shouldn't do when it comes to SQL with SharePoint.

I really shouldn't make a joke about it because if you ever run into this predicament, it will not be funny. What I am talking about is the things that are not supported by SharePoint. The following is a list of unsupported changes, taken verbatim from this Microsoft TechNet support article at `https://support.microsoft.com/en-us/help/841057/`.

Examples of unsupported database changes include, but are not limited to, the following:

- Adding database triggers

- Adding new indexes or changing existing indexes within tables

- Adding, changing, or deleting any primary or foreign key relationships

- Changing or deleting existing stored procedures

- Calling existing stored procedures directly, except as described in the SharePoint Protocols documentation: `https://msdn.microsoft.com/en-us/library/cc339475.aspx`

- Adding new stored procedures

- Adding, changing, or deleting any data in any table of any of the databases for the products that are listed in the "Applies to" section

- Adding, changing, or deleting any columns in any table of any of the databases for the products that are listed in the "Applies to" section

- Making any modification to the database schema

- Adding tables to any of the databases for the products that are listed in the "Applies to" section

- Changing the database collation

- Running DBCC_CHECKDB WITH REPAIR_ALLOW_DATA_LOSS (However, running DBCC_CHECKDB WITH REPAIR_FAST and REPAIR_REBUILD is supported, as these commands only update the indexes of the associated database.)

- Enabling SQL Server change data capture (CDC)

- Enabling SQL Server transactional replication

- Enabling SQL Server merge replication

■ **Note**   this list is not all encompassing and is just an example of things that should not be done and if an unsupported database modification is discovered during a support call, the customer will need to restore the last known good backup that existed before the change, or, roll back all the database modifications.

So what happens if there isn't a good copy that the customer can roll back to? What if the customer cannot roll back the database modifications? In either of those cases, it is manual recovery time since Microsoft SharePoint Support can only operate within their boundaries.

At the bottom of the article, there is an "Applies to" section that contains the following versions of SharePoint:

- Microsoft SharePoint Server 2016

- Microsoft SharePoint Foundation 2013

- Microsoft SharePoint Server 2013

- Microsoft SharePoint Foundation 2010

- Microsoft SharePoint Server 2010

- Microsoft Office SharePoint Server 2007

- Microsoft Office Forms Server 2007

- Microsoft Office SharePoint Portal Server 2003

- Microsoft Content Management Server 2001 Enterprise Edition

- Microsoft Windows SharePoint Services 3.0

- Microsoft Windows SharePoint Services 2.0

That's all of them folks! That's right this article applies to all versions of SharePoint. It goes on to say that all versions "were tested by using a database structure as designed by the SharePoint Development Team and were approved for release based on that structure." This means that Microsoft SharePoint databases should not be modified, period!

This is because "Microsoft cannot reliably predict the effect to the operation of these products when parties other than the Microsoft SharePoint Development Team or Microsoft SharePoint Support agents make changes to the database schema, modify its data, or execute ad hoc queries against the SharePoint databases." Like every rule, there are exceptions to the rule and these "Exceptions are described in the "Supported Database Modifications" section" toward the middle of the article.

For example, sometimes during a support call, the Microsoft Support staff may give customers scripts that modify databases. And, even the Microsoft Support agents need to get approval from the SharePoint Product team in each case, where this happens, before the script that modifies the database, can be run without violating the clause "execute ad hoc queries against the SharePoint databases." That being said, there are ad hoc queries in this book and they read from SharePoint; however, and this is a very big however, they do not write to SharePoint.

Does that mean that it's cool if you only read from SharePoint databases? Well, technically and according to this article, no. But, in my experience, the occasional query that reads from SharePoint never hurt it. I have seen where for whatever reason someone set up queries that ran on a schedule. Since SharePoint was not aware of this manually created job that ran queries, it was unable to avoid "unexpected locking." The fix was easy: delete that stupid job and its manual queries.

Speaking of unsupported "read operations," the Microsoft TechNet, Read Operations Addendum has this to say: "Reading from the SharePoint databases programmatically, or manually, can cause unexpected locking within Microsoft SQL Server which can adversely affect performance. Any read operations against the SharePoint databases that originate from queries, scripts, .dll files (and so on) that are not provided by the Microsoft SharePoint Development Team or by Microsoft SharePoint Support will be considered unsupported if they are identified as a barrier to the resolution of a Microsoft support engagement."

Basically, it boils down to this: SharePoint does not like it when it does not know about the changes being made to its databases, file system, registry, and IIS. SharePoint wants to be in control and it will have a hard time if it figures out anything is not the way it thinks it should be. This is why any software that is installed in a farm or near a farm that makes modifications to databases will make the entire farm unsupported. According to the official text, "Microsoft strictly prohibits all third-party modifications to SharePoint databases. As such, installing or using any third-party tool that modified data stored in SharePoint databases will result in that entire SharePoint farm becoming unsupported."

Does this mean that you cannot check database integrity, shrink a database, reorganize an index, clean up the history, or update the statistics? Absolutely not! All of those things are perfectly fine to do. The support documentation "Support for changes to the databases that are used by Office server products and by Windows SharePoint Services" at https://support.microsoft.com/en-us/help/932744, lists the tasks that are safe to perform using the maintenance plan wizard. That being said, it is still better to perform these tasks manually, during a planned maintenance window.

Keeping your databases in tip-top condition, free of white space, and as small as possible, will help keep performance high and support calls low. That's not to say that you can't run ginormous databases, because you can if you give SQL the horsepower in CPU and RAM that it will need to run those big girls. The same is true for making sure that SharePoint is aware of changes and modifications. Now, there are some things that SharePoint is not necessarily aware of that you can do to your SQL that will allow SharePoint to function and give better performance for SharePoint.

Before we get into the configurations of SQL that will give better performance to SharePoint, let's backup a second and talk a little bit about the SQL Install. If you recall in the least-privileged install of SharePoint there was an install account that we had made a domain admin and then removed from the domain admins. We can use that account to install SQL on the SQL server, as long as it is not a domain admin and is a local admin on the SQL server. This is done to avoid issues with SQL Server creating its own service principal names in Active Directory. And, just like in the case of SharePoint, that install account will not run any of the SQL services, just as it doesn't run any of the SharePoint services.

An even better method is to create two least-privileged accounts. Create a SQLdata account (svc_sqldata) and a SQL install account (svc_sqlinstaller). Then give the SQLInstaller service account local administrator on the SQL server so that it can install SQL. Make sure it is not a domain admin, so that SPNs are not being created, as this will cause an issue for you when you start to enable Kerberos for authentication in SharePoint. Now that you have these two accounts, you should go about installing SQL using the SQLInstaller service account. When you come to the screen that asks you for the accounts used to run the SQL Server Agent and the SQL Server Database Agent, use the least-privileged approach by giving it the SQLdata service account that you created. Using the SQLdata service account to run the services creates a least-privileged SQL install because this account is not a local administrator and is just a regular domain user with no elevated rights. This way if someone comes along and attempts to inject some garbage code, that code will be limited in what it can do. In the screenshot taken from the Tailspin Toys install, shown in Figure 5-1, you can see that we created a service account named Tailspintoys\svc_sqldata to run the SQL Server Agent and the SQL Server Database Agent.

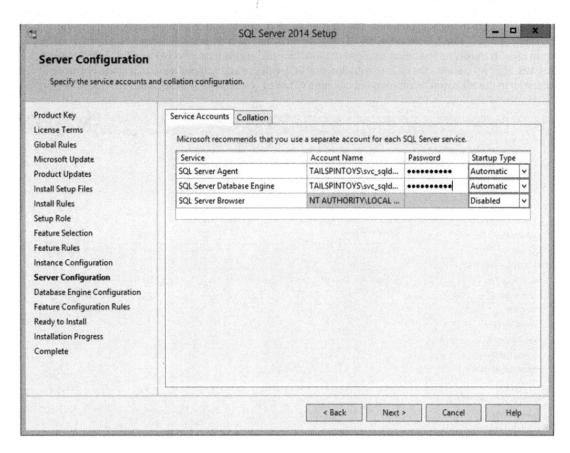

Figure 5-1. *Least-privileged service account to run SQL*

When it comes to the SQL collation used for SharePoint, there are posts out there on the interwebs from consultants and other folks out there who will tell you that you should not modify the default collation, which is contrary to Microsoft's advice. Microsoft recommends in this post `https://technet.microsoft.com/en-us/library/cc288970.aspx#section1`, that "The SQL Server collation must be configured for case-insensitive." They go on to say, "The SQL Server database collation must be configured for case-insensitive, accent-sensitive, Kana-sensitive, and width-sensitive" to ensure that file name uniqueness is consistent with the Windows operating system.

Don't worry though, if you've already created your SQL server and spun up SharePoint using the default collation of **SQL_Latin1_General_CP1_CI_AS**, as your farm will still function just as well as a farm that is spun up with the default collation changed to the Microsoft recommendation of **Latin1_General_CI_AS_ KS_WS**. Figure 5-2 shows the default collation that SQL will use and you can leave that alone or you can change it to the Microsoft recommended collation of Latin1_General_CI_AS_KS_WS.

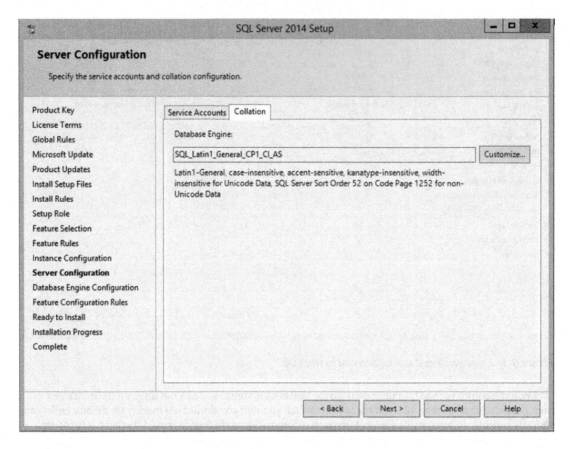

Figure 5-2. *Default SQL collation change it to Latin1_General_CI_AS_KS_WS*

SharePoint will create all of its databases using Latin1_General_CI_AS_KS_WS, no matter what the default collation is set to. That being said, Microsoft support recommends changing the value in Figure 5-2 to the value shown in Figure 5-3. Figure 5-3 gives a view of the properties for the configuration database for a Contoso farm and it uses the Latin1_General_CI_AS_KS_WS collation.

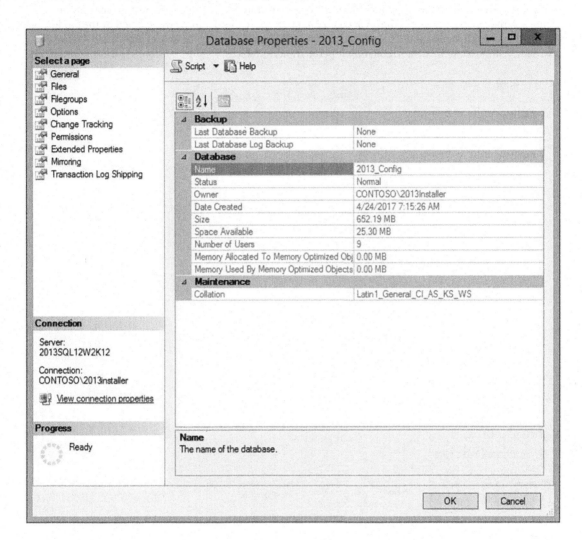

Figure 5-3. Latin1_General_CI_AS_KS_WS collation created by SharePoint

The support article that recommends using Latin1_General_CI_AS_KS_WS as the instance default is located at http://support.microsoft.com/kb/2008668. There isn't anything wrong with a farm that uses the default SQL collation; but that does not mean that you should ever change the collation values other than at install. Don't change them for SharePoint databases or after you have installed SQL. This is where those governance documents and runbooks that document your builds come in handy. Notice how in Figure 5-4, the database owner is the SA account, that is because this database was created by the SA during the creation of the instance and the database in Figure 5-3 was created by the SharePoint install. Figure 5-4 also demonstrates that the default collation is perfectly acceptable.

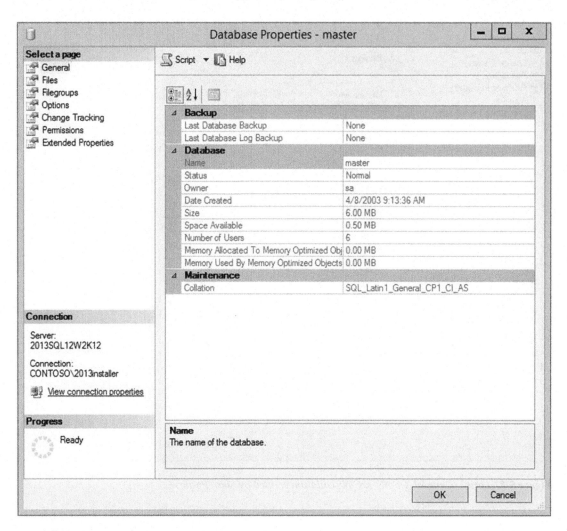

Figure 5-4. SQL_Latin1_General_CP1_CI_AS collation created by default install of SQL

Another thing to keep in mind is to always use Windows authentication mode when installing SQL for SharePoint, as shown in Figure 5-5.

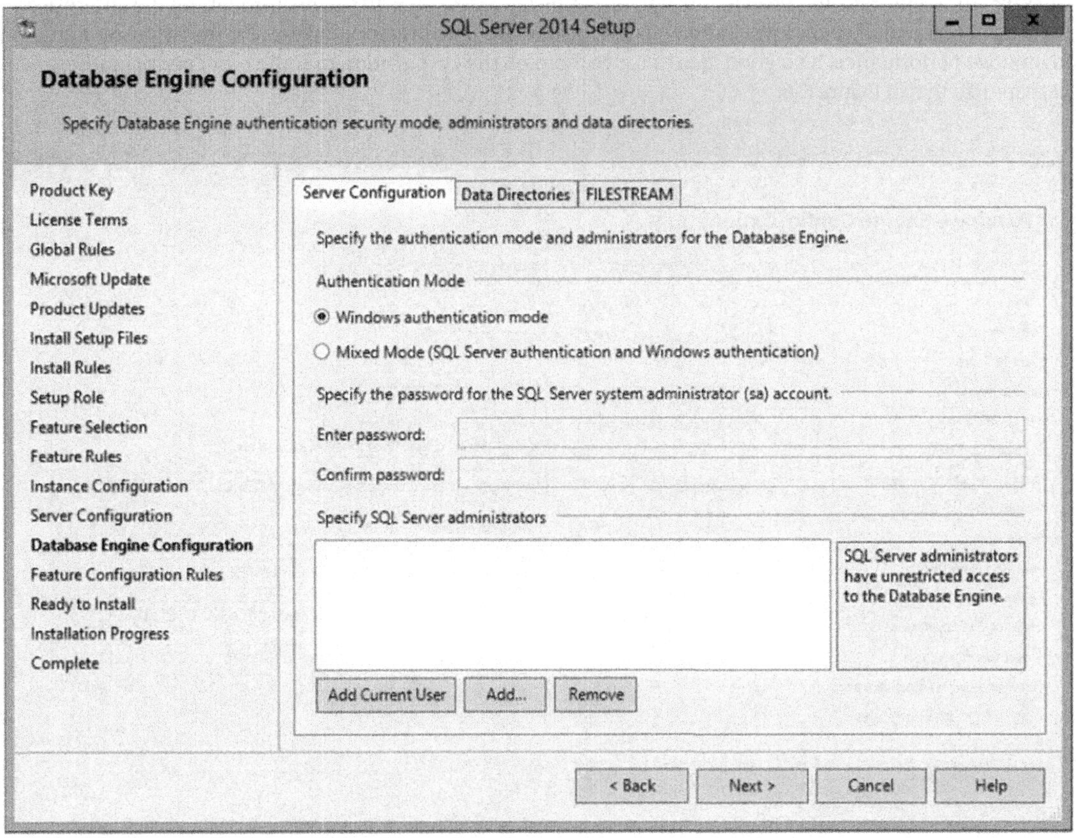

Figure 5-5. *Windows authentication mode*

The screen in Figure 5-5 shows where you set your SA account for SQL. For security purposes and least privileging, do not use the SQLdata account or the SQLInstaller account; but rather use a separate account. I've seen companies create a separate domain user account for each SQL server SA account, which is far safer than the same account used for all SQL server instances on all SQL servers throughout the enterprise. It's also on this screen, shown in Figure 5-5, that the default data directories are set for the instance. And, to improve performance, it's a good idea to move them off the OS partition to some other configuration, perhaps like that of Figure 5-6.

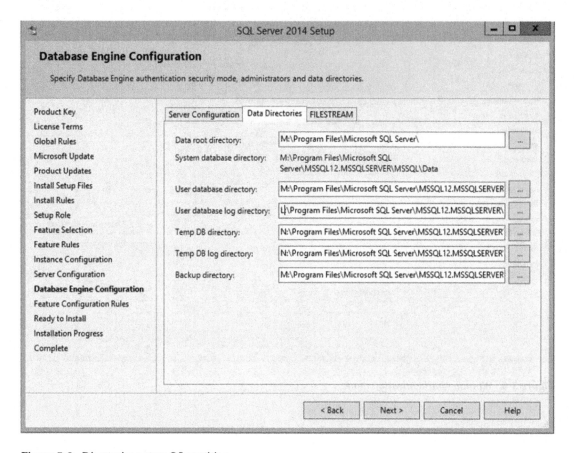

Figure 5-6. *Directories not on OS partition*

One other thing that needs mentioning is that for best performance, SharePoint should be installed on a dedicated SQL server. And this SQL server should only run the one instance for SharePoint if it is to be used in production. In situations where it is desired to use named instances, and then break out the service application databases from the content databases, the SQL server should still be dedicated to the one farm.

___

■ **Tip**　when you install SharePoint the install account needs the server roles of db_creator, public, and securityadmin. It is OK to use db_creator, public, and sysadmin, but it is not fully least-privileged.

___

OK, now that SQL is installed in a least-privileged fashion, we can log in with the svc_sqlinstaller account and make a critical change that needs to be made before SharePoint is installed on the application and web front-end servers. That change is the *maximum degree of parallelism* (MAXDOP) to 1. Figure 5-7 shows the MAXDOP setting.

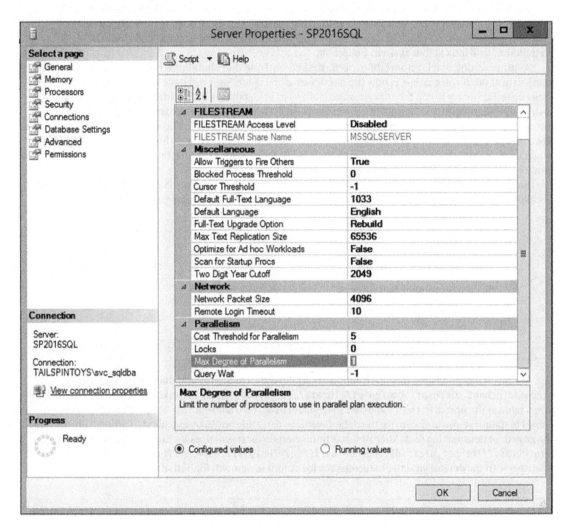

Figure 5-7. *MAXDOP must be at 1, period, end of story, get over it!*

The main reason for this requirement is that SharePoint was not written in such a way that it can handle parallelism. Set that MAXDOP to 1 and get over it. If your database admins ask you why this is, just reiterate what we've already said and add to it that SharePoint has stored procedures that were not written to work with parallelism. They'll hear you say that and then most of them will agree. For the ones that don't agree, you'll need to work that out; but understand that SharePoint 2013 forward will not install correctly with the default MAXDOP of 0 and it will have issues if the MAXDOP is later changed back to 0 after being changed to 1 to "accommodate the install." Trust me! SharePoint must have MAXDOP at 1 for its lifetime, not just for install. Yes, 2010 and earlier installed without this setting, but 2013 going forward are re-architected and require MAXDOP of 1.

Another thing that you absolutely, do not, repeat do not, want to mess with is the default roles within the SQL server and what they are permitted to do in the SQL server. I've seen DBAs in very secure environments try to "lock down" the environment by changing these permissions. Don't do this. SharePoint doesn't know about this and it will break in very abnormal and hard to discern ways. You'll be sorry you did, if you do. Another point, and along the same line, about permissions, is just let SharePoint handle them and don't modify them, with one exception. The farm account will need to have db_owner on the PerformancePoint database in a SharePoint 2013 farm and you'll have to manually handle this for SharePoint. We'll look at that again in Chapter 8.

Another setting that is important to performance, and one that SharePoint does not know about and won't care about if you change, is how the databases grow. SharePoint will have kittens (slang term for get really upset) if you try to cap the maximum size of any of its databases from within SQL. So don't do that, instead use SharePoint quotas on site collections coupled with setting the MaximumSiteCount property of the content database, to the appropriate number of site collections, so as to account for a size and number of site collections in each content database that would keep the database below the recommended size limit. When it comes to service application databases, it is OK to set them to their estimated future size, but is not a requirement for better performance.

Before we look at controlling the growth factors, I need to mention that whenever you're dealing with troubleshooting the size of a database, you should take into account the following characteristics:

- Location Requirements

- Size information and growth factors

- Read \ Write characteristics

- Scaling recommendations

- Associated health tasks

- Supported backup tools

- Default Recovery model

Microsoft has published this information about the different SharePoint databases, at this post: https://technet.microsoft.com/en-us/library/cc678868.aspx and I've taken that post and reformatted into a table at the post at https://anothersharepointblog.com/sharepoint-2013-databases. When it comes to database size and growth, the default settings can and should be modified to proactively manage the growth of data and log files. Microsoft has published the best practices for SQL Server in a SharePoint farm https://technet.microsoft.com/en-us/library/hh292622.aspx. In Figure 5-8 shows the model database with the default growth characteristics for automatic growth for both data and logs.

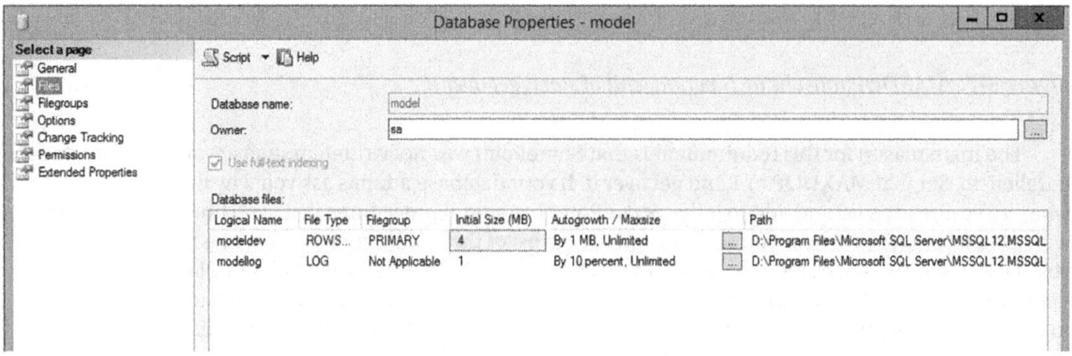

Figure 5-8. Model database with default growth settings

The main problem with the growth setting is that database growth is not a one size fits all. This is why the guidance from Microsoft says that "when possible, increase all data files and log files to their expected final size, or periodically increase these at set periods, for example, every month or every six months, or before the rollout of a new storage intensive site". This is also why it is a good idea to have some knowledge of what the final size of any given database will be. Table 5-1 lists the five size groupings for SharePoint databases.

Table 5-1. *Database Sizes*

Descriptor	Size range
Very Small	Up to 100MB
Small	1GB or less
Medium	Up to 100GB
Large	Up to 1TB
Extra-large	More than 1TB

When considering setting final sizes, you should definitely take into account the guidance from Microsoft previously mentioned and available at https://technet.microsoft.com/en-us/library/cc678868.aspx. And remember, do not set a limit on the database size *within SQL*.

In Figure 5-8, the default database size is 4MB and then it is set to grow in 1MB increments; whereas, the logs are set to grow by 10% of the database size. Using a percentage for log growth is a bad idea. This would mean that a 100GB database would auto grow its logs by 1GB each time the log needed to grow. A better approach is to use a megabyte value that makes sense with the size of the database.

The reason that Microsoft recommends changing the growth increment to a MB value is so that you're less likely to run out of storage and less likely to have log files that are full of white space. The MB growth value should take into account the size of the database and use the rule of thumb that the larger the database, the larger the increment for log growth. Since this is different for each database, you should come in after SharePoint creates the databases and set the growth increment, and if you can afford it, you could set the sizes for each database their targeted final growth size, if you have the storage space. Again, you're not putting a cap on the DB here, you're just increasing the size of the database so that it does not have to grow. In Figure 5-9 we can see that the config database growth factors have been set so that the database will grow in 100MB increments and the logs will grow by 10MB.

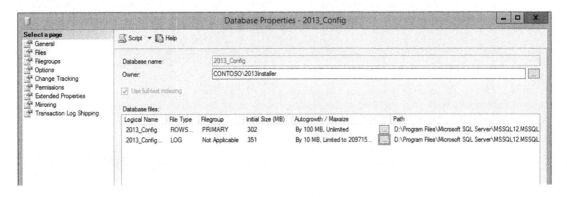

Figure 5-9. *Database auto growth settings*

As I'm sure you already know; but for the folks reading this book who don't know, there are essentially three types of SharePoint databases:

- Configuration

- Content

- Service Application

Configuration database consist of the config database and the Central Administration content database. And as Microsoft TechNet says at `https://technet.microsoft.com/en-us/library/ff945791.aspx`, "They contain data about farm settings such as the databases that are used, Internet Information Services (IIS) web sites or web applications, solutions, Web Part packages, site templates, default quota, and blocked file types. A farm can only have one set of configuration databases."

Content databases store the site content. This content includes all the site documents, web part properties, list data, and User Names and Permissions for the site. A content database can contain numerous site collections; but a site collection cannot contain numerous content databases. A web application can contain numerous content databases, but a content database cannot contain numerous web applications. It's a best practice to try to maintain content databases below 200GB in SharePoint for performance reasons. More guidance can be found at the TechNet post at `https://technet.microsoft.com/en-us/library/cc262787(v=office.15).aspx#ContentDB`.

Service applications store the data for the service applications. For the most part the default recovery model that SharePoint gives to new service applications is the Full Recovery model.

Back in the days before always on availability groups (AAG), there was advisement out there about setting the model database to a simple recovery model but this really has no bearing on SharePoint because SharePoint set's its own recovery models on the various service application databases based on what the service application's role is in the farm. For example, SharePoint gives the configuration, the Central Administration content, the Secure Store service, the business data connectivity, and the app management databases a full recovery model; whereas, SharePoint gives the search administration database, search crawl store, search analytics reporting store, and search link store databases a simple recovery model. What this means is that in order for you to add the search databases into an always-on availability group, you will need to change the recovery model to full and take a full backup of the databases.

The same is true for the SharePoint logging database and the three User Profile services databases, social, profile, and sync. Before you can add them into an always-on availability group, you need to change them to a full recovery model. And in the case of the logging database, it is recommended that you leave that beast out of the AAG due to the high level of writes that it takes and the excessive load it could put on the AAG.

I've spoken about using a SQL Alias when installing SharePoint and we need to cover that once more just from a standpoint of why it is a good idea. However, before we do, let's talk about the new database Roles that SharePoint 2013 brings to SQL. In Table 5-2, we see the four roles.

Table 5-2. *Roles Created in SQL by SharePoint*

Role Name	Role Description
WSS_CONTENT_ APPLICATION_POOLS	Applies to application pool account for each web application that is registered with the SharePoint farm. Members that have this role are able to run stored procedures. This role is applied to the config db and the Central Administration db. Some of the other databases use this role as well; for example, the state database.
WSS_SHELL_ACCESS	Replaces the need to add an admin account to the db_owner role on the SharePoint Configuration database. Members of this role have read and write permissions on all databases. By default when a user is added to this role it only adds them with read and write to the config database.
SP_READ_ONLY	This role replaces the sp_dboption role, which was removed in SQL 2012 and it is used for setting a database to read-only mode. This role gives its members read-only capabilities on all stored procedures within a database and execute capabilities on user-defined types where the user has the schema of dbo.
SP_DATA_ACCESS	This is the default role for database access that SharePoint gives to application pool accounts during creation or upgrade. This role essentially replaces db_owner, but it hasn't been fully implemented so there will be times when you'll need to have db_owner ; this role will not provide that level. This role has truly replaced the db_owner on the config db, app, state service, usage, and the SharePoint Central Administration content database.

The SQL Alias is best implemented by using the client side utility (cliconfg.exe). There are some schools of thought out there that think that the client side utility will eventually go away, and that might be true; but so far, including the Windows Server 2016 operating system, cliconfg.exe is still a viable means to set the Alias. This is the fish hook I was referring too in that early comment about discussing Fishing without discussing hooks.

We went over how create the SQL Alias in Chapter 2, prior to installing SharePoint; however we didn't talk about the various other reasons that it is a good idea to utilize SQL Aliases. Table 5-3 lists some of the additional reasons that SQL Aliases are a good idea to use.

Table 5-3. *Why It's a Good Idea to Use Aliases*

Event	Reason
Product upgrades	Allows you to move databases between different SQL servers without rebuilding the farm
Decommissioning old hardware	SharePoint is oblivious to moving to the new SQL Server
Migration to new hardware and VMs	Allows you to move databases between different SQL servers without rebuilding the farm
Environment failures	Allows you to restore to last known good backup
Host renaming environments	Allows you to move the database to the newly named SQL server

The process of moving SharePoint databases from one SQL server to another is fairly straightforward and it involves moving the logins used by the SharePoint. There are two schools of thought out there about this process, as well. One school of thought is to shut down the key services that are used by SharePoint in an attempt to cease communication of the front-end server and the database server. The other school of thought, and the best method, is to shut down the SharePoint servers before moving the databases.

Before moving the databases, make sure to run the SQL query that creates the stored procedure named sp_help_revlogin and then execute the sp_help_revlogin so you can get the query that you'll need to run on the destination SQL server.

Open a SQL query window and paste in the following script, which is available at https://support. microsoft.com/en-us/help/918992/how-to-transfer-logins-and-passwords-between-instances-of-sql-server.

```
USE master
GO
IF OBJECT_ID ('sp_hexadecimal') IS NOT NULL
  DROP PROCEDURE sp_hexadecimal
GO
CREATE PROCEDURE sp_hexadecimal
    @binvalue varbinary(256),
    @hexvalue varchar (514) OUTPUT
AS
DECLARE @charvalue varchar (514)
DECLARE @i int
DECLARE @length int
DECLARE @hexstring char(16)
SELECT @charvalue = '0x'
SELECT @i = 1
SELECT @length = DATALENGTH (@binvalue)
SELECT @hexstring = '0123456789ABCDEF'
WHILE (@i <= @length)
BEGIN
  DECLARE @tempint int
  DECLARE @firstint int
  DECLARE @secondint int
  SELECT @tempint = CONVERT(int, SUBSTRING(@binvalue,@i,1))
  SELECT @firstint = FLOOR(@tempint/16)
  SELECT @secondint = @tempint - (@firstint*16)
  SELECT @charvalue = @charvalue +
    SUBSTRING(@hexstring, @firstint+1, 1) +
    SUBSTRING(@hexstring, @secondint+1, 1)
  SELECT @i = @i + 1
END
SELECT @hexvalue = @charvalue
GO


IF OBJECT_ID ('sp_help_revlogin') IS NOT NULL
  DROP PROCEDURE sp_help_revlogin
GO
CREATE PROCEDURE sp_help_revlogin @login_name sysname = NULL AS
DECLARE @name sysname
DECLARE @type varchar (1)
DECLARE @hasaccess int
DECLARE @denylogin int
DECLARE @is_disabled int
DECLARE @PWD_varbinary  varbinary (256)
DECLARE @PWD_string  varchar (514)
```

```
DECLARE @SID_varbinary varbinary (85)
DECLARE @SID_string varchar (514)
DECLARE @tmpstr  varchar (1024)
DECLARE @is_policy_checked varchar (3)
DECLARE @is_expiration_checked varchar (3)
DECLARE @defaultdb sysname

IF (@login_name IS NULL)
  DECLARE login_curs CURSOR FOR
SELECT p.sid, p.name, p.type, p.is_disabled, p.default_database_name, l.hasaccess,
l.denylogin FROM
sys.server_principals p LEFT JOIN sys.syslogins l
    ON ( l.name = p.name ) WHERE p.type IN ( 'S', 'G', 'U' ) AND p.name <> 'sa'
ELSE
  DECLARE login_curs CURSOR FOR
SELECT p.sid, p.name, p.type, p.is_disabled, p.default_database_name, l.hasaccess,
l.denylogin FROM
sys.server_principals p LEFT JOIN sys.syslogins l
    ON ( l.name = p.name ) WHERE p.type IN ( 'S', 'G', 'U' ) AND p.name = @login_name
OPEN login_curs
FETCH NEXT FROM login_curs INTO @SID_varbinary, @name, @type, @is_disabled, @defaultdb,
@hasaccess, @denylogin
IF (@@fetch_status = -1)
BEGIN
  PRINT 'No login(s) found.'
  CLOSE login_curs
  DEALLOCATE login_curs
  RETURN -1
END
SET @tmpstr = '/* sp_help_revlogin script '
PRINT @tmpstr
SET @tmpstr = '** Generated ' + CONVERT (varchar, GETDATE()) + ' on ' + @@SERVERNAME + ' */'
PRINT @tmpstr
PRINT ''
WHILE (@@fetch_status <> -1)
BEGIN
  IF (@@fetch_status <> -2)
  BEGIN
    PRINT ''
    SET @tmpstr = '-- Login: ' + @name
    PRINT @tmpstr
    IF (@type IN ( 'G', 'U'))
    BEGIN -- NT authenticated account/group
SET @tmpstr = 'CREATE LOGIN ' + QUOTENAME( @name ) + ' FROM WINDOWS WITH DEFAULT_DATABASE =
[' + @defaultdb + ']'
    END
    ELSE BEGIN -- SQL Server authentication
        -- obtain password and sid
            SET @PWD_varbinary = CAST( LOGINPROPERTY( @name, 'PasswordHash' ) AS varbinary (256) )
        EXEC sp_hexadecimal @PWD_varbinary, @PWD_string OUT
        EXEC sp_hexadecimal @SID_varbinary,@SID_string OUT
```

```
        -- obtain password policy state
        SELECT @is_policy_checked = CASE is_policy_checked WHEN 1 THEN 'ON' WHEN 0 THEN
        'OFF' ELSE NULL END FROM sys.sql_logins WHERE name = @name
        SELECT @is_expiration_checked = CASE is_expiration_checked WHEN 1 THEN 'ON' WHEN 0
        THEN 'OFF' ELSE NULL END FROM sys.sql_logins WHERE name = @name

            SET @tmpstr = 'CREATE LOGIN ' + QUOTENAME( @name ) + ' WITH PASSWORD = ' +
            @PWD_string + ' HASHED, SID = ' + @SID_string + ', DEFAULT_DATABASE = [' +
            @defaultdb + ']'
IF ( @is_policy_checked IS NOT NULL )
        BEGIN
          SET @tmpstr = @tmpstr + ', CHECK_POLICY = ' + @is_policy_checked
        END
        IF ( @is_expiration_checked IS NOT NULL )
        BEGIN
          SET @tmpstr = @tmpstr + ', CHECK_EXPIRATION = ' + @is_expiration_checked
        END
    END
    IF (@denylogin = 1)
    BEGIN -- login is denied access
      SET @tmpstr = @tmpstr + '; DENY CONNECT SQL TO ' + QUOTENAME( @name )
    END
    ELSE IF (@hasaccess = 0)
    BEGIN -- login exists but does not have access
      SET @tmpstr = @tmpstr + '; REVOKE CONNECT SQL TO ' + QUOTENAME( @name )
    END
    IF (@is_disabled = 1)
    BEGIN -- login is disabled
      SET @tmpstr = @tmpstr + '; ALTER LOGIN ' + QUOTENAME( @name ) + ' DISABLE'
    END
    PRINT @tmpstr
  END
FETCH NEXT FROM login_curs INTO @SID_varbinary, @name, @type, @is_disabled, @defaultdb,
@hasaccess, @denylogin
    END
CLOSE login_curs
DEALLOCATE login_curs
RETURN 0
GO
```

After this completes, go ahead and run the stored procedure that it creates named sp_help_revlogin. Both of these two steps are performed on the source SQL server. After you run sp_help_revlogin, it creates a script to run on the target SQL server. Copy the output of the sp_help_revlogin into a query window on the target SQL server's SSMS console and execute the script on the target server, only.

All of the SharePoint servers need to be able to talk to your SQL server. SQL traffic happens across port 1433 or 1434 by default, unless SQL has been hardened prior to SharePoint being installed, in which case traffic could be traversing a different port. When hardening SQL server, it is a best practice to do this before installing SharePoint. Determining which port the SQL Server is listening on can be accomplished by looking at SQL Configuration Manager, querying for the network statistics using the command line, and by testing the connectivity from the SharePoint servers. Testing the connectivity is more of a hit and miss method and really doesn't tell you what port SQL is listening on; so much as, whether or not communication is able to take place.

To determine which port SQL is configured to listen, you need to know the SQL server IP address or addresses, the instance name, and how to open SQL Configuration Manager. SQL Configuration Manager is easily opened from the desktop or from one of the following locations in the file system, depending on the version of SQL that you have installed. Table 5-4 lists the SQL version and the file system location of SQL Configuration Manager.

Table 5-4. *SQL Configuration Manger Locations*

SQL Version	File System Location
SQL Server 2016	C:\Windows\SysWOW64\SQLServerManager13.msc
SQL Server 2014	C:\Windows\SysWOW64\SQLServerManager12.msc
SQL Server 2012	C:\Windows\SysWOW64\SQLServerManager11.msc
SQL Server 2008	C:\Windows\SysWOW64\SQLServerManager10.msc

The Configuration Manager is available from the server Start menu, after SQL is installed. Let's find out what port it is set to listen on, assuming there is an instance installed.

Open Configuration Manager and click SQL Server Services to verify that there is an instance and that it is running. You should see an instance similar to that shown in Figure 5-10. Don't worry if your SQL Server does not have the SQL Full-text Filter Daemon Launcher running.

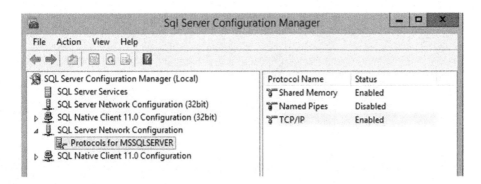

Figure 5-10. *Default instance*

If you have a named instance, you would see something like SQL Server (SharePoint) and if you are using the default instance, you'll see SQL Server (MSSQLSERVER). Make sure that the SQL Server (MSSQLSERVER) and SQL Server Agent (MSSQLSERVER) are running, and then click SQL Server Network Configuration, followed by Protocols for MSSQLSERVER, as shown in Figure 5-11.

Figure 5-11. *SQL Server Network Configuration*

At this point, you need to know the IP address of your server. You may have more than one nic, and if that is the case, you need to know the one that SQL is listening on; more than likely it will be the preferred IP. If you don't have the IP, open a command line and type **ipconfig /all**, as shown in Figure 5-12.

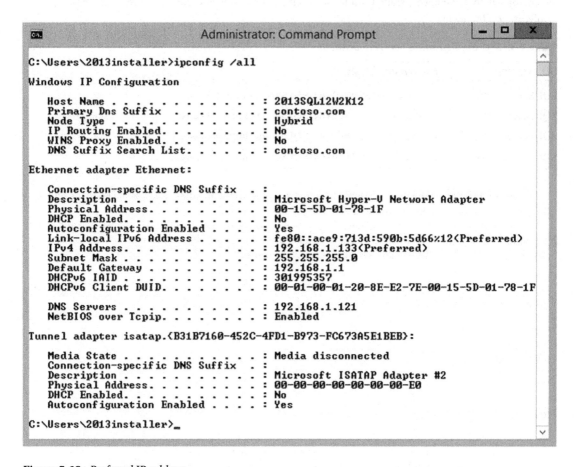

Figure 5-12. Preferred IP address

Back in the SQL Configuration Manager, double-click the TCP/IP protocol name on the right side of the protocols for MSSQLSERVER. After it opens, click the IP Addresses tab. Look for any IP address that is active, and then take note of the port. As you can see in Figure 5-13, this instance is listening on the preferred IP of 192.168.1.133 on port 1433.

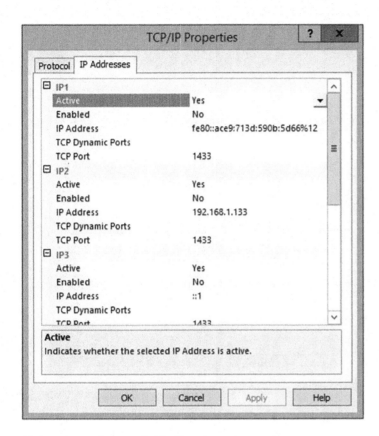

Figure 5-13. What port is SQL listening on?

If you scroll down in Figure 5-13, you can see that the server is also listening on IPv6 on port 1433. Figure 5-14 shows the server listening on IPv6 and Figure 5-13 shows the IPv4 address and port 1433.

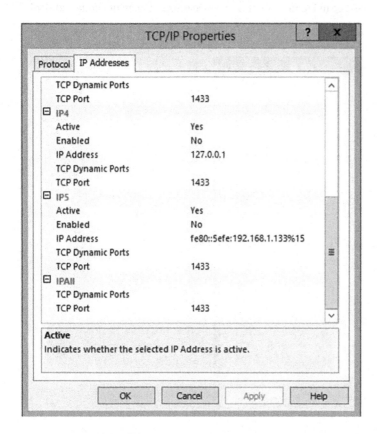

Figure 5-14. *ipv6 and port 1433*

Earlier I mentioned that we could also determine the port that SQL is listening on using the command line. I forgot to say that to determine that port, we need the process ID that the SQL Server instance is running under. If you look at Figure 5-10, you can see that the PID for the SQL Server default instance is 1220. You can also get the PID for SQL from Task Manager by looking at the Details tab on the Task Manager and finding the sqlservr.exe. Using the Task Manager method is best used when you already know that only one instance is being served off the SQL server. In a case where more than one instance is running, you'll have more than one instance of the executable showing up as running in the Details tab on the Task Manager.

OK, so now that you have this PID, open an administrative command line and type **netstat -ano | find /i "1220"** or if your PID was 1243, you would type **netstat -ano | find /i "1243"**. After you type the netstat command, you'll notice that the server is listening for port 1433 and 1434 in regards to that process ID. You may even have some ephemeral ports connected to it, as shown in Figure 5-15.

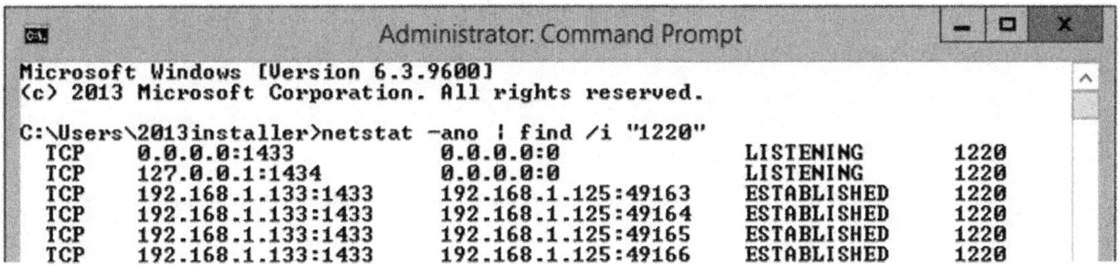

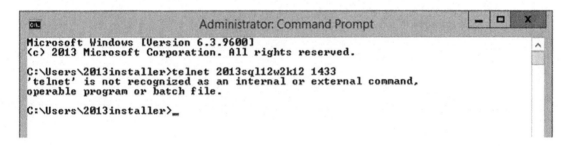

Figure 5-15. Listening on port 1433

As far as testing is concerned, it is way easier if you know for certain which port SQL is listening on and if you are certain that the firewall is allowing traffic on that port. To test basic connectivity to the SQL server, the telnet utility is your best bet. If you want to test connectivity to a SQL instance, then you'll need to make sure the basic connectivity is established and use an .udl file to test connectivity to the actual SQL server.

On your SharePoint server, open a command prompt and type, **telnet <servername> port**, where telnet is telnet, <servername> is the name of your server, and port equals the port that the SQL server is listening on. You can just try 1433 for the port if you are not sure and didn't try out any of the earlier things we talked about in checking for the port that SQL is using in your environment. Figure 5-16 shows the command prompt on a server where telnet is not installed.

Figure 5-16. No telnet

To install telnet type **pkgmgr /iu:"TelnetClient"** and press Enter, and then close and reopen your command-line interface. After your command window opens, and you type in the telnet servername port and press Enter, you'll be presented with an empty command window or you'll receive a message that indicates that telnet was not successful. If this happens, you'll need to make sure the firewall has an inbound rule to allow SQL server to communicate. You can run this command to create the inbound rule for domain-based traffic:

```
netsh advfirewall firewall add rule name = SQLPort dir = in protocol = tcp action = allow
localport = 1433 remoteip = localsubnet profile = DOMAIN
```

Or, you can open wf.msc and create a rule that allows inbound traffic on port 1433.

Finally, after the network connection is definitely working to the SQL server from the SharePoint server, and after you have installed a SharePoint instance, you can test the connectivity to the databases by creating an .udl file on the desktop of the SharePoint server. Here are the steps.

1. Create a text document named test.txt.

2. Rename the text document from test.txt to test.udl.

3. Double click the test.udl file.

4. Enter in the name of the alias that you're using for SQL.

5. Choose Use Windows NT Integrated Security.

6. Click the drop-down menu and select the database that you'd like to test connectivity.

7. Click Test connection.

After you complete the preceding steps, you should get a "Test Connection Succeeded" message similar to what's shown in Figure 5-17.

Figure 5-17.

The telnet and the .udl are two excellent troubleshooting tools to have in your arsenal. If, for whatever reason, you're worried that the telnet program has issues, you can always uninstall it with **pkgmgr / uu:"TelnetClient"** and then reinstall it with **pkgmgr /iu:"TelnetClient"**. And then you can test basic connections on the network interchange card on the server by testing the localhost 127.0.0.1 address and whichever port you know allows inbound traffic.

Sometimes when you try telnet to the SQL server on port 1433 or 1434 it will not connect, even though SharePoint is installed and is working. If this happens, you can bet that your SQL is either, clustered and listening on a different port other than port 1433, or your SQL has been "hardened." When SQL has been hardened, the preceding steps will yield different port numbers. And if you look inside SQL Configuration Manager, you'll probably notice that there is an Alias set there and that this alias has the hardened port number listed. The steps to harden the SQL should be done before installing SharePoint and not afterward. Microsoft has a great post on this subject at https://technet.microsoft.com/en-us/library/ff607733.aspx#proc4.

Now that you have determined that you can connect to the SQL server and have validated whether you can connect to SQL databases or not, you are steps closer to solving any sort of connectivity issues. Unfortunately, establishing connectivity to the server and to the databases is just the beginning. You might have to log in to the SQL Server Management Studio (SSMS) to troubleshoot issues with SQL.

To open the SSMS, open a run bar, type **ssms**, and then click OK. Once the SSMS opens, you'll need to enter the server name and click Connect. You shouldn't have to change the server type to Database Engine, unless it is at something other than that; and you should be OK with Windows Authentication, provided you are logged in to the SQLInstaller account.

If you're not sure if your SQL is clustered, you can easily find out by running a very simple T-SQL statement, **SELECT SERVERPROPERTY('IsClustered')**. If the statement returns a 1, you're dealing with a SQL cluster and if it returns a 0, you have a single SQL server instance. To run the query, just click New Query, paste the statement **SELECT SERVERPROPERTY('IsClustered')**, and then click Execute.

From the Query window, you can ask SQL anything and you can do a lot of damage from here, including making your farm unsupported. The SSMS can be a great troubleshooting tool, but if used incorrectly it can break your SharePoint. Basically, any query that reads from your databases runs the risk of locking your databases, which is why you should make sure it uses the **WITH (NOLOCK)** statement. If it doesn't, then it runs the risk of locking tables in your database.

Usually, ad hoc queries that do not modify and only read will not leave your farm in an unsupported state, as all they do is read. You can use ad hoc queries to troubleshoot database sizes, memory utilization by database name, buffer cache hit ratio, and page life expectancy, among other tasks. Don't worry, you won't be out of support by running the occasional ad hoc query to troubleshoot your environment.

As the SharePoint admin, you sometimes become the SQL DBA for the SharePoint environment, when you have to troubleshoot how things are going. You can give these scripts to your SQL DBA if you are lucky enough to have a dedicated DBA and you two can work together to make your SharePoint's SQL absolutely pristine!

When it comes to white space, you can look at the properties of each database; but nowhere in the properties will you see the white space that is present in your log files or in your data files. The only way to determine this is to look at the available free space in the shrink file utility. When log growth is a percentage value, the white space in the logs can grow quite quickly. T-SQL ad hoc queries to the rescue!

A veritable SharePoint god at Rackspace, Stephen Swinney, shared this fantastic script with us that is totally awesome! All you need to do to identify all the white space in your databases is to copy and paste this into a new query and execute that query.

```
Create Table ##temp
(
    DatabaseName sysname,
    Name sysname,
    physical_name nvarchar(500),
    size decimal (18,2),
    FreeSpace decimal (18,2)
)
```

```
Exec sp_msforeachdb '
Use [?];
Insert Into ##temp (DatabaseName, Name, physical_name, Size, FreeSpace)
    Select DB_NAME() AS [DatabaseName], Name,  physical_name,
    Cast(Cast(Round(cast(size as decimal) * 8.0/1024.0,2) as decimal(18,2)) as nvarchar) Size,
    Cast(Cast(Round(cast(size as decimal) * 8.0/1024.0,2) as decimal(18,2)) -
        Cast(FILEPROPERTY(name, ''SpaceUsed'') * 8.0/1024.0 as decimal(18,2)) as nvarchar)
        As FreeSpace
    From sys.database_files
'
Select * From ##temp
```

The output from this T-SQL will look like Figure 5-18.

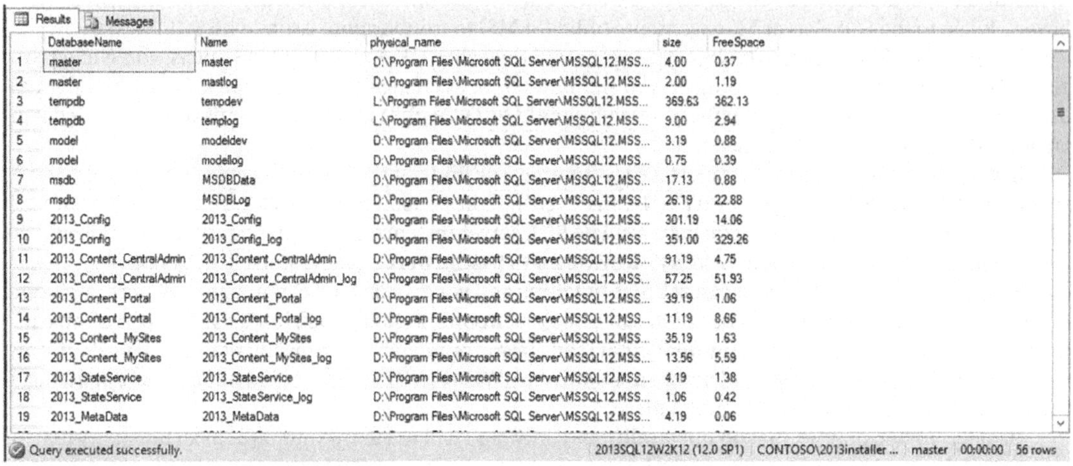

	DatabaseName	Name	physical_name	size	FreeSpace
1	master	master	D:\Program Files\Microsoft SQL Server\MSSQL12.MSS...	4.00	0.37
2	master	mastlog	D:\Program Files\Microsoft SQL Server\MSSQL12.MSS...	2.00	1.19
3	tempdb	tempdev	L:\Program Files\Microsoft SQL Server\MSSQL12.MSS...	369.63	362.13
4	tempdb	templog	L:\Program Files\Microsoft SQL Server\MSSQL12.MSS...	9.00	2.94
5	model	modeldev	D:\Program Files\Microsoft SQL Server\MSSQL12.MSS...	3.19	0.88
6	model	modellog	D:\Program Files\Microsoft SQL Server\MSSQL12.MSS...	0.75	0.39
7	msdb	MSDBData	D:\Program Files\Microsoft SQL Server\MSSQL12.MSS...	17.13	0.88
8	msdb	MSDBLog	D:\Program Files\Microsoft SQL Server\MSSQL12.MSS...	26.19	22.88
9	2013_Config	2013_Config	D:\Program Files\Microsoft SQL Server\MSSQL12.MSS...	301.19	14.06
10	2013_Config	2013_Config_log	D:\Program Files\Microsoft SQL Server\MSSQL12.MSS...	351.00	329.26
11	2013_Content_CentralAdmin	2013_Content_CentralAdmin	D:\Program Files\Microsoft SQL Server\MSSQL12.MSS...	91.19	4.75
12	2013_Content_CentralAdmin	2013_Content_CentralAdmin_log	D:\Program Files\Microsoft SQL Server\MSSQL12.MSS...	57.25	51.93
13	2013_Content_Portal	2013_Content_Portal	D:\Program Files\Microsoft SQL Server\MSSQL12.MSS...	39.19	1.06
14	2013_Content_Portal	2013_Content_Portal_log	D:\Program Files\Microsoft SQL Server\MSSQL12.MSS...	11.19	8.66
15	2013_Content_MySites	2013_Content_MySites	D:\Program Files\Microsoft SQL Server\MSSQL12.MSS...	35.19	1.63
16	2013_Content_MySites	2013_Content_MySites_log	D:\Program Files\Microsoft SQL Server\MSSQL12.MSS...	13.56	5.59
17	2013_StateService	2013_StateService	D:\Program Files\Microsoft SQL Server\MSSQL12.MSS...	4.19	1.38
18	2013_StateService	2013_StateService_log	D:\Program Files\Microsoft SQL Server\MSSQL12.MSS...	1.06	0.42
19	2013_MetaData	2013_MetaData	D:\Program Files\Microsoft SQL Server\MSSQL12.MSS...	4.19	0.06

***Figure 5-18.** Grid view has many options*

Once you've identified the databases with a lot of white space, you may want to decrease their growth factors. You might have to make sure that their logs are not growing based on a percentage. Then, after you've finished working with the output of the previous script, make sure to get rid of the evidence by running the following T-SQL:

```
drop table ##temp
```

If you want to find out everything about your SQL version, including what KB it is patched to and its SQL build version, you can run **select @@version**. If you're only concerned with if finding out if you have Enterprise, for example, you can run **select serverproperty('Edition')**. If you want to find the Product Version, Product Level, and Edition, this T-SQL query will get it for you:

```
SELECT SERVERPROPERTY('productversion'), SERVERPROPERTY ('productlevel'), SERVERPROPERTY
('edition')
```

The version, level, and edition are really important when you are looking to install SSRS on the SharePoint front-end servers, as you need to correctly match the add-on to have success.

If you want to know how much memory your SQL server is using, you can go to the Details tab of the Task Manager, find the process named sqlserver.exe, and find the memory consumption in KB, or you can run the following T-SQL statement:

```
SELECT
(physical_memory_in_use_kb/1024) AS Memory_usedby_Sqlserver_MB,    (locked_page_allocations_
kb/1024) AS Locked_pages_used_Sqlserver_MB,    (total_virtual_address_space_kb/1024) AS
Total_VAS_in_MB,
process_physical_memory_low,    process_virtual_memory_low
FROM sys.dm_os_process_memory;
```

Figure 5-19 displays both approaches to determining the memory being consumed by your SQL server instance. This is important to be able to find when you are troubleshooting issues with SQL performance.

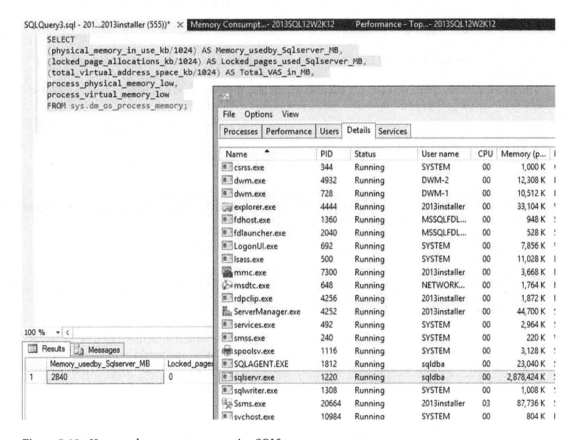

Figure 5-19. *How much memory are you using SQL?*

Now that you know how much memory is in use by SQL, let's see how much input/output is has been used and which databases, have over time, used the most I/O. Run this T-SQL to see which databases are the most read/write intensive:

```
WITH Aggregate_IO_Statistics
AS
(SELECT DB_NAME(database_id) AS [Database Name],
CAST(SUM(num_of_bytes_read + num_of_bytes_written)/1048576 AS DECIMAL(12, 2)) AS
io_in_mb
FROM sys.dm_io_virtual_file_stats(NULL, NULL) AS [DM_IO_STATS]
GROUP BY database_id)
SELECT ROW_NUMBER() OVER(ORDER BY io_in_mb DESC) AS [I/O Rank], [Database Name],
io_in_mb AS [Total I/O (MB)],
        CAST(io_in_mb/ SUM(io_in_mb) OVER() * 100.0 AS DECIMAL(5,2)) AS [I/O Percent]
FROM Aggregate_IO_Statistics
ORDER BY [I/O Rank] OPTION (RECOMPILE);
```

The output of this ad-hoc query lets you quickly see which databases have had the most input and output over time.

If you wanted to extract a list of all the databases from SQL that you could compare with a list obtained from SharePoint using the Get-SPdatabase cmdlet, you could run this T-SQL:

```
SELECT name
FROM master.dbo.sysdatabases
WHERE name NOT IN ('master','model','msdb','tempdb')
```

If SQL server has enough memory it won't have to read pages or write pages to disk to often and the Page reads/second and page writes/second will stay below 90. If there is a memory issue, these counters will be higher than 90. This is an ad-hoc query to obtain these values:

```
SELECT object_name, counter_name, cntr_value
FROM sys.dm_os_performance_counters
WHERE [object_name] LIKE '%Buffer Manager%'
AND [counter_name] = 'Page reads/sec'
OR [counter_name] = 'Page writes/sec'
```

When SQL server has to page a lot, and disk activity is high, this is indicative of insufficient memory. In a perfect world, SQL would never have to read any pages directly from disk and would be able to get what it needed from the buffer cache that resides in memory. If that were the case, the Buffer Cache Hit Ratio would be 100. Basically, anything higher than 90 is acceptable. The ad-hoc query to look at the Buffer Cache hit ratio is shown here:

```
SELECT object_name, counter_name, cntr_value
FROM sys.dm_os_performance_counters
WHERE [object_name] LIKE '%Buffer Manager%'
AND [counter_name] = 'Buffer cache hit ratio'
```

Another way to see if the server has sufficient memory for its load is to look at the page life expectancy. If pages are staying in memory for longer than 300 seconds or 5 minutes than things are probably pretty good. You don't want to see big fluctuations with the page life expectancy and should monitor it over time. If you're noticing frequent, quick, drops, there might be memory issues that need looking into. Here's the ad hoc query:

```
SELECT object_name, counter_name, cntr_value
FROM sys.dm_os_performance_counters
WHERE [object_name] LIKE '%Buffer Manager%'
AND [counter_name] = 'Page life expectancy'
```

What if you don't like running queries and you would rather just look at a cool report? Well, there are plenty of built-in reports ready to give you information about your SQL server, as you can see in Figure 5-20.

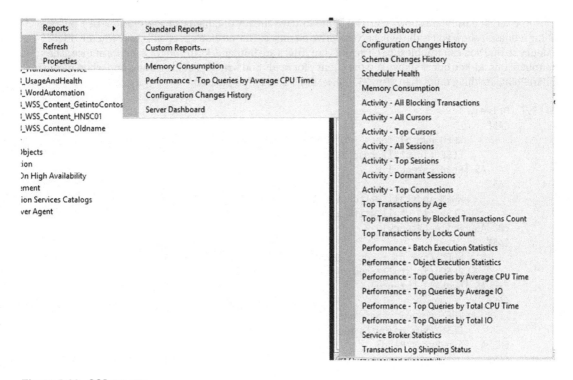

Figure 5-20. *SQL reports*

To look at any of the standard reports, right-click the instance, click Reports ➤ Standard Reports, and then select the standard report that you wish to view. The Memory Consumption report will give you the page life expectancy. If you would like a report of the files in use by SQL, you'll need to either create a custom reporter run the following ad hoc query:

```
SELECT
'DB_NAME' = db.name,
'FILE_NAME' = mf.name,
'FILE_TYPE' = mf.type_desc,
'FILE_PATH' = mf.physical_name
FROM
sys.databases db
INNER JOIN sys.master_files mf
ON db.database_id = mf.database_id
```

The server dashboard shows you a lot of the stuff we already obtained using ad-hoc queries, but one thing it doesn't show you is the SQL Server's drive latencies. This ad-hoc query will show you the drive latency so that you can troubleshoot if any of your drives are bottlenecks in your SQL performance. The output of this ad-hoc query shows you the latency for reads and writes in milliseconds, and when it comes to SharePoint, anything more than 20 to 25 milliseconds is usually a problem.

```
SELECT [Drive],
       CASE
               WHEN num_of_reads = 0 THEN 0
               ELSE (io_stall_read_ms/num_of_reads)
       END AS [Read Latency],
       CASE
               WHEN io_stall_write_ms = 0 THEN 0
               ELSE (io_stall_write_ms/num_of_writes)
       END AS [Write Latency],
       CASE
               WHEN (num_of_reads = 0 AND num_of_writes = 0) THEN 0
               ELSE (io_stall/(num_of_reads + num_of_writes))
       END AS [Overall Latency],
       CASE
               WHEN num_of_reads = 0 THEN 0
               ELSE (num_of_bytes_read/num_of_reads)
       END AS [Avg Bytes/Read],
       CASE
               WHEN io_stall_write_ms = 0 THEN 0
               ELSE (num_of_bytes_written/num_of_writes)
       END AS [Avg Bytes/Write],
       CASE
               WHEN (num_of_reads = 0 AND num_of_writes = 0) THEN 0
               ELSE ((num_of_bytes_read + num_of_bytes_written)/(num_of_reads + num_of_writes))
       END AS [Avg Bytes/Transfer]
```

```
FROM (SELECT LEFT(mf.physical_name, 2) AS Drive, SUM(num_of_reads) AS num_of_reads,
               SUM(io_stall_read_ms) AS io_stall_read_ms, SUM(num_of_writes) AS num_of_writes,
               SUM(io_stall_write_ms) AS io_stall_write_ms, SUM(num_of_bytes_read) AS
               num_of_bytes_read,
               SUM(num_of_bytes_written) AS num_of_bytes_written, SUM(io_stall) AS io_stall
     FROM sys.dm_io_virtual_file_stats(NULL, NULL) AS vfs
     INNER JOIN sys.master_files AS mf WITH (NOLOCK)
     ON vfs.database_id = mf.database_id AND vfs.file_id = mf.file_id
     GROUP BY LEFT(mf.physical_name, 2)) AS tab
ORDER BY [Overall Latency] OPTION (RECOMPILE);
```

This next ad hoc query allows you to identify any orphaned sites present in your farm's config database. Once you've obtained the orphaned sites ID, you can use stsadm to delete the site. The first time you run this ad hoc, you'll get a message that the orphanlist database does not exist, and therefore cannot be dropped. Just execute it once more and you'll be presented with any orphaned sites. Before you can run the query, you need to update the line that reads: select @configdb = 'YOUR_CONFIG_DB_NAME'.

This query is safe to run; all it does is return results that you can pump into stsadm commands.

```
Use TEMPDB
        Drop table orphanlist

        CREATE TABLE [dbo].[orphanlist](
        [farm] [varchar](250) COLLATE SQL_Latin1_General_CP1_CI_AS NULL,
        [databasename] [varchar](250) COLLATE SQL_Latin1_General_CP1_CI_AS NULL,
        [SiteID] [uniqueidentifier] NULL,
        [sitepath] [varchar](250) COLLATE SQL_Latin1_General_CP1_CI_AS NULL,
        [type] [varchar](250) COLLATE SQL_Latin1_General_CP1_CI_AS NULL
        )

        drop table orphan_hopper
        declare
        @dbname as varchar(250),
        @cmdstr as varchar(2000),
        @dbid as varchar(250),
        @configdb as varchar(250)

        select @configdb = 'YOUR_config_db_HERE'

        select @cmdstr =
        'select distinct b.name as ''databasename'', b.id as ''dbid'' into orphan_hopper
        from
          [' + @configdb + '].dbo.sitemap as a inner join
          [' + @configdb + '].dbo.objects as b on a.databaseid=b.id inner join
          [' + @configdb + '].dbo.objects as c on c.id=a.applicationid inner join
          [' + @configdb + '].dbo.objects as d on b.parentid=d.id inner join
          [' + @configdb + '].dbo.objects as e on d.parentid=e.id  '
        exec (@cmdstr)
```

```
    DECLARE DBCursor CURSOR For
      Select databasename, dbid
      From orphan_hopper

    OPEN DBCursor
    FETCH NEXT FROM DBCursor into @DBName, @dbid

    WHILE @@FETCH_STATUS =0
    BEGIN
     INSERT INTO orphanlist([Type], farm, databasename,[sitepath], SiteID)
     EXEC
      ('
select ''Potential ConfigDB orphan:'' + '''+@dbname+'''   as [Type], '''+@
configdb+''' as [farm], '''+@dbname+''' as [databasename],path as [sitepath],
id as [SiteID] from ['+@configdb+'].dbo.sitemap where id not in (select id from
['+@dbname+'].dbo.sites) and databaseid = '''+@dbid+'''
union
select ''Potential ConfigDB orphan:'' + '''+@dbname+'''   as [Type], '''+@
configdb+''' as [farm], '''+@dbname+''' as [databasename],path as [sitepath],
id as [SiteID] from ['+@configdb+'].dbo.sitemap where id not in (select siteid from
['+@dbname+'].dbo.webs where parentwebid is null) and databaseid = '''+@dbid+'''
union
select ''Potential ContentDB orphans:'' + '''+@dbname+''' as [Type], '''+@
configdb+''' as [farm], '''+@dbname+''' as [databasename],fullurl as [sitepath],
siteid as [SiteID] from ['+@dbname+'].dbo.webs where parentwebid is null and siteid
not in (select id from ['+@configdb+'].dbo.sitemap where databaseid = '''+@dbid+''')
union
select ''Potential ContentDB orphan:'' + '''+@dbname+'''   as [Type], '''+@
configdb+''' as [farm], '''+@dbname+''' as [databasename],fullurl as [sitepath],
siteid as [SiteID] from ['+@dbname+'].dbo.webs where parentwebid is null and siteid
not in (select id from ['+@dbname+'].dbo.sites)
')
     FETCH NEXT FROM DBCursor into @DBName, @dbid
    END
    CLOSE DBCursor
    DEALLOCATE DBCursor

select * from orphanlist
```

After executing the query a couple of times, you'll get output like that shown in Figure 5-21, if there are no orphaned sites in the config database. Look at the bottom of the image, nothing is returned.

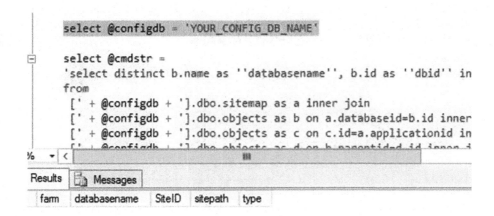

Figure 5-21. *No orphans*

Before we discuss ways to get information from SQL using PowerShell and SSRS installs in SharePoint 2013 on SQL 2012 or 2014, I had to share this really cool one-liner that gives the log sizes and the % of the file that is actually used by logging. This means that the SharePoint databases toward the top of this list could stand to have their logs shrunk.

```
dbcc sqlperf(logspace)
```

After you run that ad hoc query, the output will look like that in Figure 5-22. Notice how the configuration database says only 5.51784% is actually used by logs.

	Database Name	Log Size (MB)	Log Space Used (%)	Status
1	master	1.992188	52.15686	0
2	tempdb	8.992188	24.23979	0
3	model	0.7421875	48.94737	0
4	msdb	26.17969	12.9066	0
5	2013_Config	350.9922	5.51784	0
6	2013_Content_CentralAdmin	57.24219	10.42036	0
7	2013_Content_Portal	11.17969	50.41929	0
8	2013_Content_MySites	13.55469	55.73487	0
9	2013_StateService	1.054688	60.37037	0
10	2013_MetaData	1.054688	60.37037	0

Figure 5-22. *Log size vs. percent used by logs*

The more contiguous the databases are, the better they work. You can see that the numbers found in Figure 5-22 are telling the truth if you take a couple minutes to look at the actual files. You can troubleshoot the non-contiguous, white space, in the files by right-clicking a database, clicking Tasks, Shrink, Files, and then selecting the log file, as shown in Figure 5-23. This is the same database that Figure 5-22 showed as only using part of the database for logging—5% or so. While the numbers are not exact, they are close enough and give you a good idea of things you can tune.

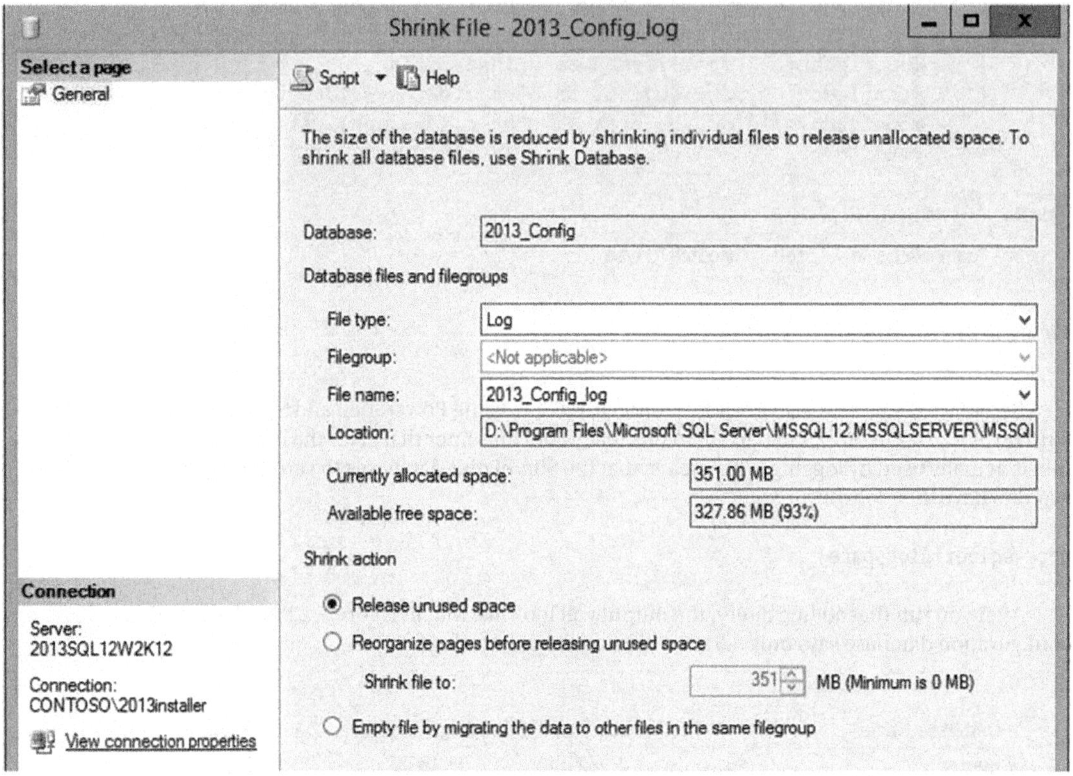

Figure 5-23. Database with white space—look at that free space!

PowerShell

When you're getting ready to determine which of your databases are ready to be added to an always-on availability group, you will need to quickly see which databases have the full recovery model and which ones have the simple recovery model. You can use the PowerShell drive for SQL server to test this out. To get the PowerShell drive available, you can run

```
import-module sqlps –disableNameChecking
```

After you run that one-liner, your PowerShell drive might automatically change to the SQLSERVER PowerShell drive, as shown in Figure 5-24. If it doesn't change to the SQL Server drive you can always run Get-PSDrive to determine the name of it and then run Set-Location SQLSERVER:.

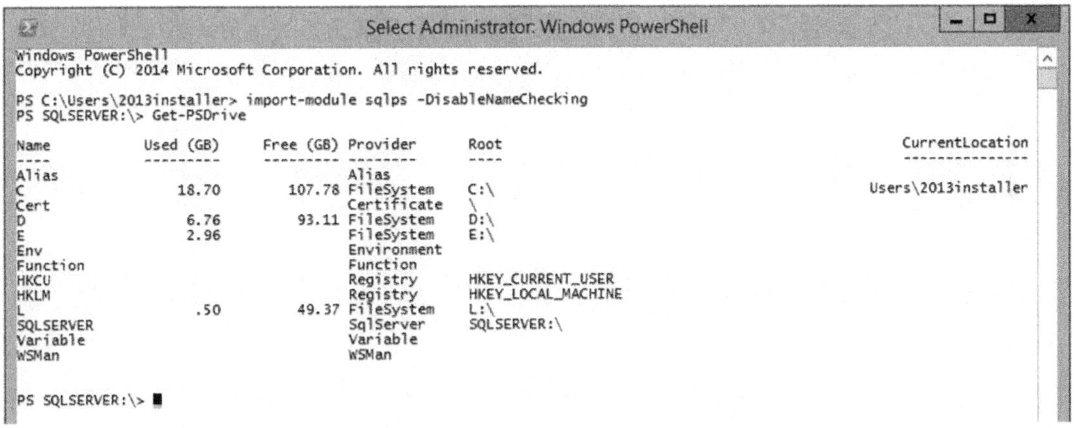

Figure 5-24. *CD location SQLSERVER: is same as Set-Location SQLSERVER:*

After you have the SQL Server drive up, you can use the get-childitem command's alias of dir to find the subdirectories and the Set-Location's alias of CD to change the directory to the SQL instance. From here, you can find out information about your databases. In Figure 5-25, you can see this in action, where we imported the SQL PowerShell drive, then used dir and cd to interrogate the module.

```
                                          Administrator: Windows PowerShell
PS C:\Users\2013installer> import-module sqlps -DisableNameChecking
PS SQLSERVER:\> dir

Name                Root                         Description
----                ----                         -----------
DAC                 SQLSERVER:\DAC               SQL Server Data-Tier Application
                                                 Component
DataCollection      SQLSERVER:\DataCollection    SQL Server Data Collection
SQLPolicy           SQLSERVER:\SQLPolicy         SQL Server Policy Management
Utility             SQLSERVER:\Utility           SQL Server Utility
SQLRegistration     SQLSERVER:\SQLRegistration   SQL Server Registrations
SQL                 SQLSERVER:\SQL               SQL Server Database Engine
SSIS                SQLSERVER:\SSIS              SQL Server Integration Services
XEvent              SQLSERVER:\XEvent            SQL Server Extended Events
DatabaseXEvent      SQLSERVER:\DatabaseXEvent    SQL Server Extended Events
SQLAS               SQLSERVER:\SQLAS             SQL Server Analysis Services


PS SQLSERVER:\> cd SQL
PS SQLSERVER:\SQL> dir

MachineName
-----------
2013SQL12W2K12


PS SQLSERVER:\SQL> CD 2013SQL12W2K12
PS SQLSERVER:\SQL\2013SQL12W2K12> dir

Instance Name
-------------
DEFAULT


PS SQLSERVER:\SQL\2013SQL12W2K12> cd Default
PS SQLSERVER:\SQL\2013SQL12W2K12\Default> dir
Audits
AvailabilityGroups
BackupDevices
Credentials
CryptographicProviders
Databases
Endpoints
JobServer
Languages
LinkedServers
Logins
Mail
ResourceGovernor
Roles
ServerAuditSpecifications
SystemDataTypes
SystemMessages
Triggers
UserDefinedMessages
PS SQLSERVER:\SQL\2013SQL12W2K12\Default> _
```

Figure 5-25. *Navigate to default instance*

Once you've navigated to the default instance, you can easily get a list of logins and when they were created, which shows if they are a SQL login or a Windows User login, by running dir logins as shown in Figure 5-26.

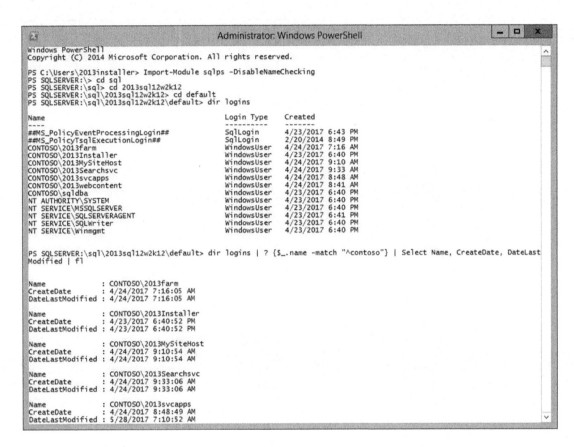

Figure 5-26. *Got logins*

If you want to know when the logins were last changed, you can run:

```
dir logins | ? {$_.name -match "^contoso"} | Select Name, CreateDate, DateLastModified | fl
```

Figure 5-26 previously demonstrated some of the output of this awesome one-liner. Don't be alarmed if you just made a change to one of your logins and you don't see the time correctly displayed, it will display properly after SQL server runs its internal job that updates statistics.

Back to that list of databases with info, here is the one-liner that shows the recovery model:

```
dir databases | sort size | select Name, createdate, status, recoverymodel, size, owner |
out-gridview
```

The cool thing about this single line of PowerShell is in its output cmdlet. It sends the information that would've gone to the screen, to a grid view that allows you to sort. As you can see in Figure 5-27, the output has columns. If you click one—for example, size, it would sort the databases in descending order by size.

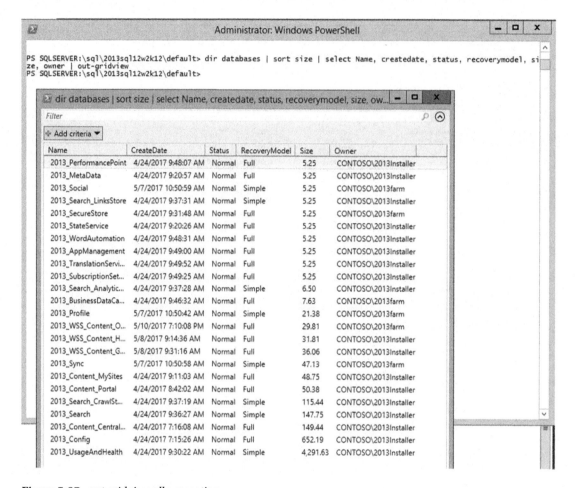

Figure 5-27. *out-gridview allows sorting*

You can also filter the results, by using the Add Criteria button and then setting criteria, as shown in Figure 5-28.

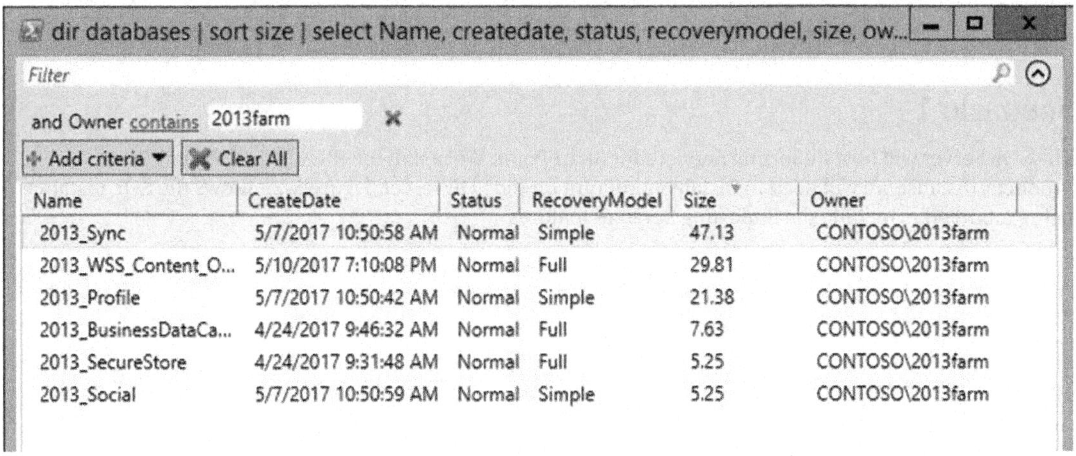
dir databases | sort size | select Name, createdate, status, recoverymodel, size, ow...
Filter
and Owner contains 2013farm
Add criteria
Clear All
Name CreateDate Status RecoveryModel Size Owner
2013_Sync 5/7/2017 10:50:58 AM Normal Simple 47.13 CONTOSO\2013farm
2013_WSS_Content_O... 5/10/2017 7:10:08 PM Normal Full 29.81 CONTOSO\2013farm
2013_Profile 5/7/2017 10:50:42 AM Normal Simple 21.38 CONTOSO\2013farm
2013_BusinessDataCa... 4/24/2017 9:46:32 AM Normal Full 7.63 CONTOSO\2013farm
2013_SecureStore 4/24/2017 9:31:48 AM Normal Full 5.25 CONTOSO\2013farm
2013_Social 5/7/2017 10:50:59 AM Normal Simple 5.25 CONTOSO\2013farm

Figure 5-28. *Filter based on criteria*

We're going to cover SQL backup and restore operations in Chapter 6, along with a couple more really cool SQL ad-hoc queries.

Configuring SharePoint-Integrated Reporting with SQL Server 2012/2014

This section on Installing Reporting Services SharePoint Mode for SharePoint 2013 was adapted from the MSDN post at `https://msdn.microsoft.com/en-us/library/jj219068.aspx`. The purpose of this section is to explain how to configure SharePoint-integrated Reporting Services when using Microsoft SQL Server 2012 or 2014.

There are two different approaches that you can take depending on your desired topology scenario. The following are the high-level steps:

Scenario 1:

- SharePoint 2010 or SharePoint 2013
- MS SQL Server 2012 SP1 Standard or higher running the Reporting Services - SharePoint shared feature
- SharePoint 2010 or SharePoint 2013 installed on the SQL Server
- Reporting Services Add-in for SharePoint Products installed on each server running SharePoint

Scenario 2:

- SharePoint 2010 or SharePoint 2013
- MS SQL Server 2012 SP1 Standard or higher *not* running Reporting Services - SharePoint shared feature
- MS SQL 2012 Reporting Services - SharePoint shared feature installed on a SharePoint server
- Reporting Services Add-in for SharePoint Products installed on each server running SharePoint

■ **Important**   The shared feature 'Reporting Services – SharePoint' must be installed on a server running SharePoint, however if this feature is not installed on the SQL server, then it requires a separate SQL license.

Scenario 1

The SQL Server will host Reporting Services for SharePoint. We install the RS Add-in for SharePoint Products, because we will need to install SharePoint on the SQL server. Figure 5-29 shows the SQL instance being modified to include the Reporting Services features.

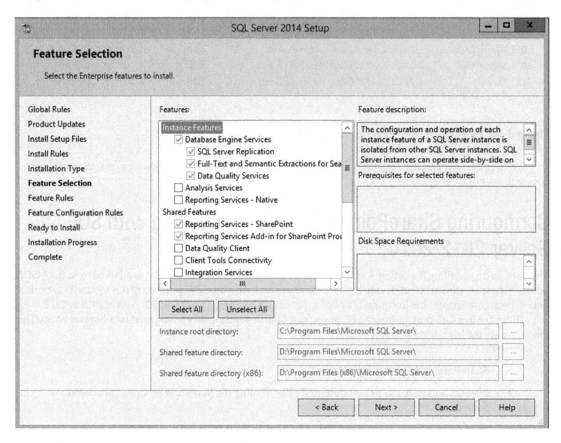

Figure 5-29. *Selecting the Reporting Services features*

You need to install the Reporting Services Add-In for SharePoint Products on every server in the farm. The version needs to match the edition of the MS SQL database engine. For example, if you patch SQL Server to SQL 2012 to Service Pack 2 + Cumulative Update 5, then you need to install the Microsoft SQL Server 2012 SP2 Reporting Services Add-in for Microsoft SharePoint on every server on the farm, and then patch it with Cumulative update 5 for SQL Server 2012 SP2. This requirement is the same as option 1 and the same applies to any version of SQL.

If you were working with SQL 2014 on your database server then you would be installing the SQL Server 2014 Reporting Services Add-in for Microsoft SharePoint on every server on the farm, and then patch it with whichever level it should be at to match the level of your database server.

Scenario 2

The SQL server will **NOT** be hosting Reporting Services for SharePoint. We will install the Reporting Services – SharePoint and Reporting Services Add-in for SharePoint Products shared features on a SharePoint server. When SQL Server is not hosting the Reporting Services there is no change needed to the SQL instance as there was in Scenario 1.

■ **Note** You will not see SQL Reporting Services in services.msc. SSRS now runs as a service application in SharePoint.

You need to install the Reporting Services Add-In for SharePoint Products on every server in the farm. The version needs to match the edition of the MS SQL database engine. For example, if you patch SQL 2012 to Service Pack 2 + Cumulative Update 5, then you need to install the Microsoft SQL Server 2012 SP2 Reporting Services Add-in for Microsoft SharePoint on every server on the farm, and then patch it with Cumulative update 5 for SQL Server 2012 SP2.

If you were working with SQL 2014 on your database server then you would be installing the SQL Server 2014 Reporting Services Add-in for Microsoft SharePoint on every server on the farm, and then patch it with whichever level it should be at to match the level of your database server.

We really should make a point to emphasize how extremely important it is to make sure you have the exact same level of RS Add-in for Microsoft SharePoint, as this is the key to success in this. If you get a lower version or a higher version the service will not start, and you'll get an error starting as shown in Figure 5-30.

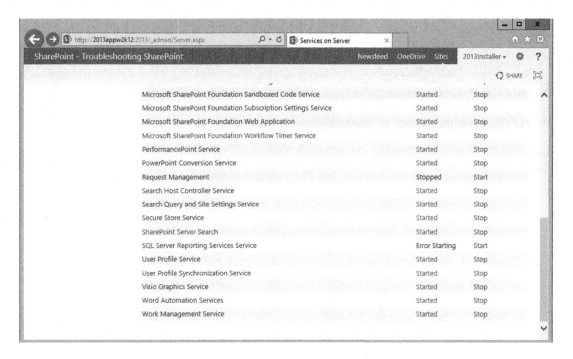

Figure 5-30. Error starting

Install and configure SSRS Service Application (Both Scenarios):

On the SharePoint server that you installed Reporting Services – SharePoint on, run the following PowerShell commands, as shown in Figure 5-30:

- Install-SPRSService

- Install-SPRSServiceProxy

After the SQL server reporting services service application is installed, you can run the following PowerShell command to start the SSRS service: **Get-SPserviceinstance -all |where {$_.TypeName -like "SQL Server Reporting*"} | Start-SPServiceInstance**, as shown in Figure 5-31.

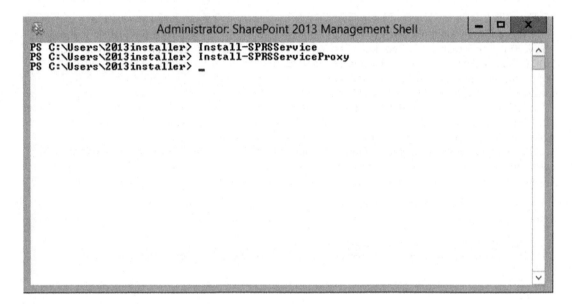

Figure 5-31. *Install the SSRS service application*

If you get a status anything other than provisioning or online, there is something wrong. For example, *if you get a status of disabled*, as shown in Figure 5-32, you need to *make sure that you have installed the Reporting Service, the correct version of the add on, and the correct update for SQL server.*

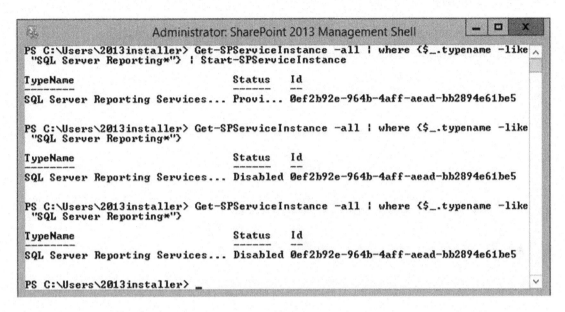

Figure 5-32. *Problems with getting SSRS installed*

If you haven't installed Reporting services on the server and the update for SQL, or if you installed the wrong version (let's say 2012 when you have a 2014 backend), and then you'll need to install the correct version. Or when you try to start the service instance from services on the server, you'll get something like Figure 5-33.

Sorry, something went wrong

Installation Error: Could not find SOFTWARE\Microsoft\Microsoft SQL Server\120 registry key.

TECHNICAL DETAILS

Troubleshoot issues with Microsoft SharePoint Foundation.

Correlation ID: 15dbf79d-1194-807b-4ebf-3138942921fd

Date and Time: 6/2/2017 6:14:31 PM

GO BACK TO SITE

Figure 5-33. *SQL CU not installed on SharePoint Server*

After the service instance has started and it shows as online, as shown in Figure 5-34, you can proceed to create the SSRS Service application from the Manage Service Applications under application management. Don't try to do this if you haven't started the service and if get-spserviceinstance yields disabled or provisioning.

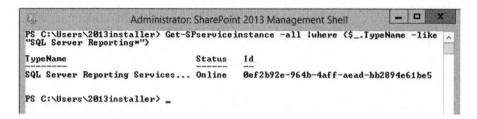

Figure 5-34. *Make sure that you have started the service on the services on server page*

In Central Administration, you will now see SQL Server Reporting Services Service Application in the list of available service applications, as shown in Figure 5-35. Click it.

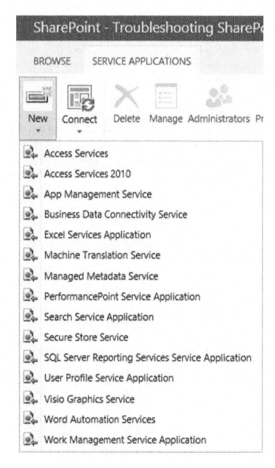

Figure 5-35. *SSRS service application*

Fill in the appropriate details.

The application pool must be the one that uses the shared service application app pool. This application pool is called SharePoint Hosted Services, if you used the PowerShell from earlier in the text. See Figure 5-36, where we named the service application and chose the existing service application.

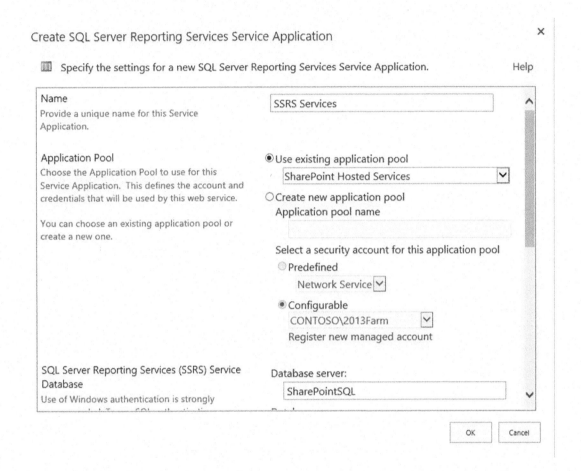

Figure 5-36. *Name the service application and choose the service app*

Make the database name something clean and don't forget to associate the service application with the web application(s), as shown in Figure 5-37.

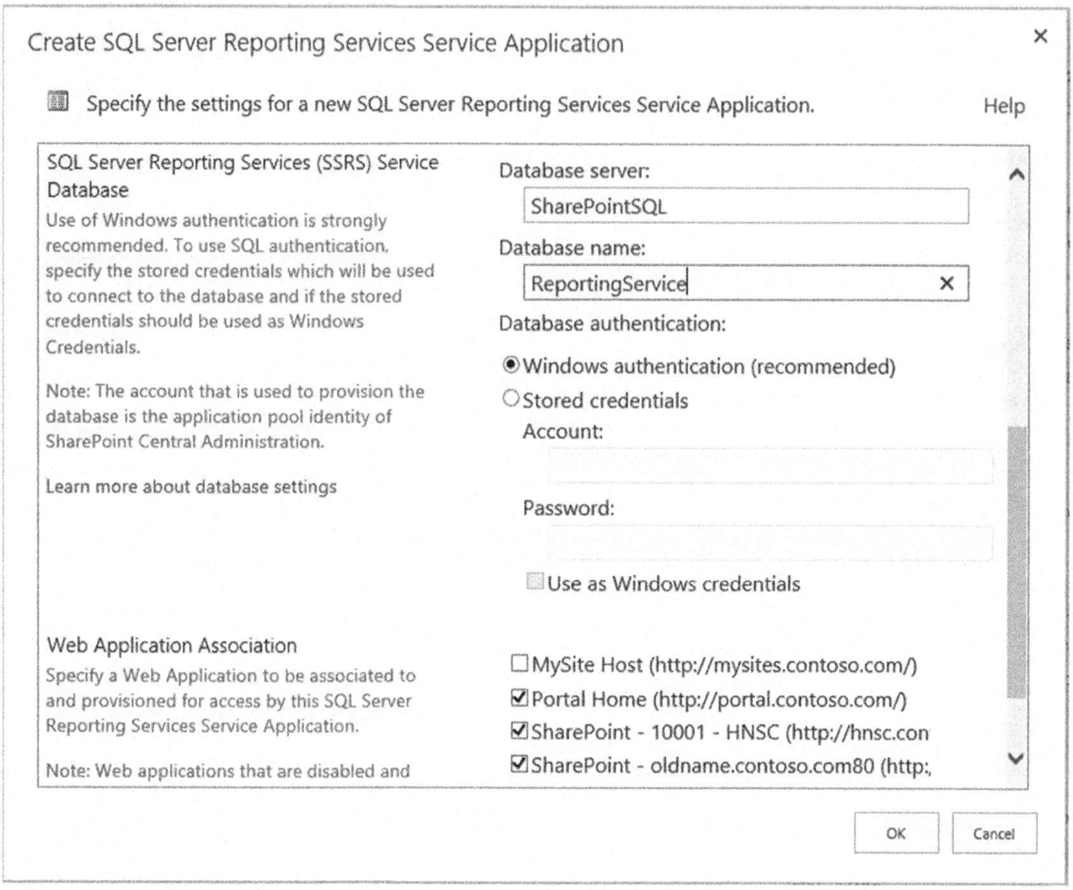

Figure 5-37. Give the database a name and associate the service application

Click OK, and SharePoint will start creating the service app for SSRS, as shown in Figure 5-38.

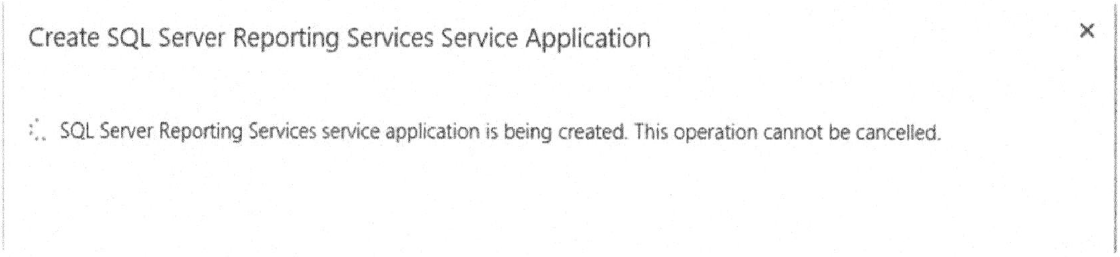

Figure 5-38. Creation of SSRS service application

After the SSRS service app is created, you will be presented with the following screen as shown in Figure 5-39. Click Provision Subscriptions and Alerts.

Create SQL Server Reporting Services Service Application   ✕

  ▦   Create SQL Server Reporting Services Service Application   Help

The SQL Server Reporting Services service application has been successfully created.
The SQL Server Reporting Services service application has been successfully created.
Reporting Services subscriptions, schedules, and data alerts require SQL Server Agent. You may need to provision Reporting Services to allow access to SQL Server Agent. Click on the following link: Provision Subscriptions and Alerts

OK

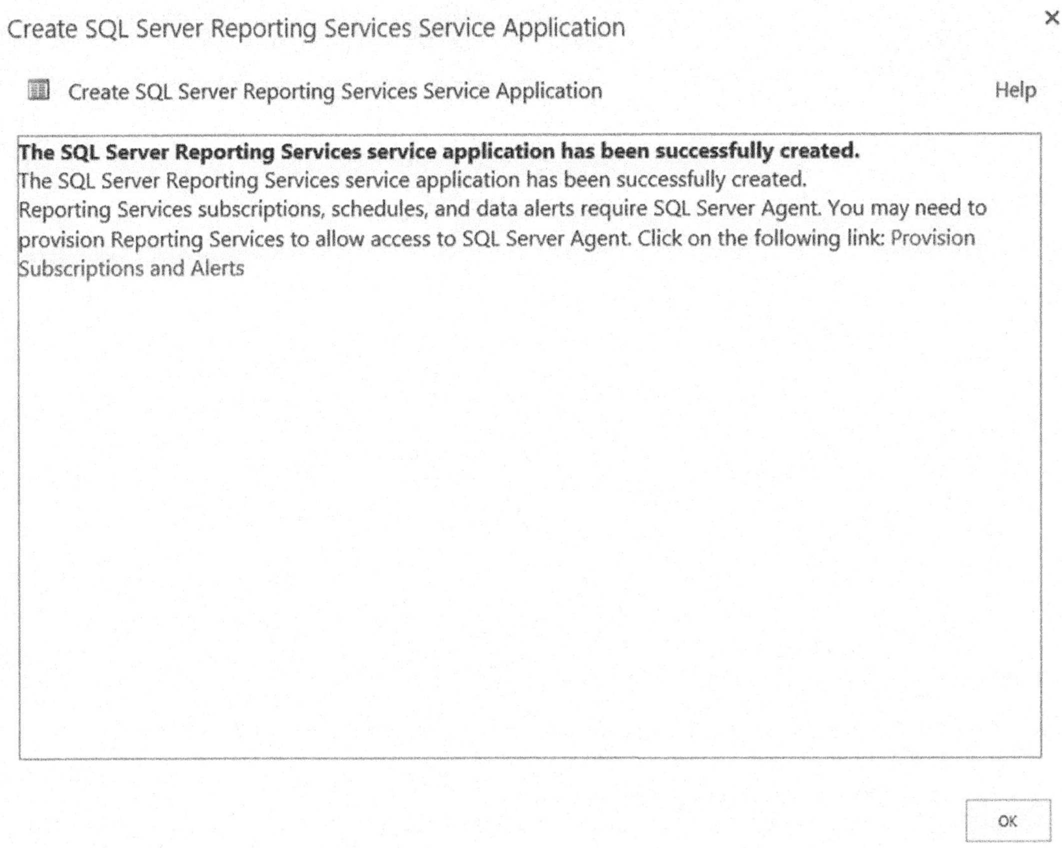

Figure 5-39. Provision subscriptions and alerts

Ensure that the SQL Server Agent service is running on the SQL server, as shown in Figure 5-40.

In the Allow Reporting Services to use SQL Server Agent section, enter the <DOMAIN>\SP_Admin account information, and click Use as Windows credentials. Click OK.

Click the Download Script button and save the <ssrs service app>-GrantRights.sql file. Copy the file to the SQL server, or open it and copy/paste the contents into a query window in SQL. Execute the script and it will create the RSExec role. Ensure that the script executes successfully before proceeding.

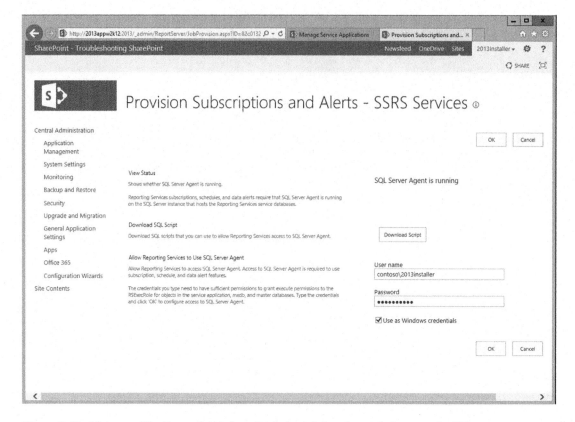

Figure 5-40. *Make sure it's all completed, downloaded, copied and pasted, then run the SQL query*

SSRS for SharePoint is now installed and configured.

Now that we have SSRS for SharePoint installed and configured, let's test it out in an exercise to round out the chapter. Let's create a report and verify SQL reporting Services using the AdventureWorks database.

VERIFY SQL REPORTING SERVICES

The purpose of this exercise is to create a report and verify SQL Reporting Services using the AdventureWorks2014 database.

1. Download the AdventureWorks2014 database and restore it in your SQL report server (`http://msftdbprodsamples.codeplex.com/releases/view/93587`).

■ **Note** I recommend grabbing a copy of all the AdventureWorks databases that you think you're going to want to use in the next two to three years if you think you'll be using any version of SQL earlier than SQL 2016. The CodePlex site plans to archive on December 15, 2017, according to the post at `https://blogs.msdn.microsoft.com/bharry/2017/03/31/shutting-down-codeplex/`. Although the post says that the archive contains all the files, it is still a good idea to grab your copies while you can grab them.

---

2. In one of your SharePoint sites, create a **Report Library** by selecting **Site Actions** ➤ **More Options**, and then select **Library** ➤ **Report Library** (SharePoint 2010) or click **Add lists, libraries or other apps** ➤ **Report Library** (SharePoint 2013), as shown in the following screenshot.

Report Library
App Details

3. Give the library a name; for example, **SSRS Reports**.

4. Once created, click **Library Settings** so that we can change the content types.

5. Click **Add from existing site content types**, as shown in the following screenshot.

Content Types

This document library is configured to allow multiple content

Content Type

Report

Web Part Page with Status List

▫ Add from existing site content types

▫ Change new button order and default content type

6. From the list of content type groups, select the **SQL Server Reporting Services Content Types** group.

7. Add **Report Builder Model**, **Report Builder Report**, and **Report Data Source** to the list on the right, as displayed in the following screenshot.

Select site content types from:

| SQL Server Reporting Services Content Types ∨ |

Available Site Content Types: Content types to add:

	Add >		Report Builder Model Report Builder Report Report Data Source
	< Remove		

Description:
Create a new report data source.

Group: SQL Server Reporting Services Content Types

8. I removed the **Report and Web Part Page with Status List** content types to tidy things up, as shown in the following screenshot. This left only the three SSRS content types.

Content Types

This document library is configured to allow multiple

Content Type

| Report |
| Web Part Page with Status List |

Report Builder Model

Report Builder Report

Report Data Source

9. Navigate to your lists and then click **Files ➤ New Document ➤ Report Data Source**, as shown in the following screenshot.

10. Grant the svc account that runs the application pool that you used when you created the SSRS service application. You can determine this account from troubleshooting IIS and looking that application pool that the SSRS service application is a part of. The following screenshot shows that the login does not exist for the account until you give it a dbo login.

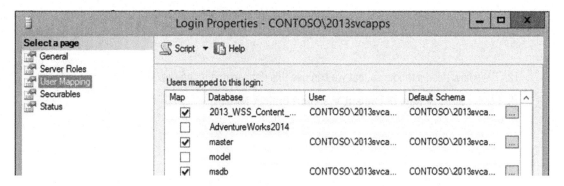

11. Enter the appropriate connection string and user account that has access to the AdventureWorks2014 database (you granted the user access in SQL in the previous step), and click OK, as shown in the following screenshot.

Use this page to edit a data source that can be shared by reports, models, or shared datasets.

	OK	Cancel

Data Source Type: Microsoft SQL Server ▼

Connection string
Enter a connection string for accessing the report data source.

Data Source=SharePointSQL; Initial Catalog=AdventureWorks2014

Credentials
Enter the credentials used by the report server to access the report data source.

○ Windows authentication (integrated) or SharePoint user
○ Prompt for credentials
  Provide instructions or example:
  Type or enter a user name and password to access the d
  ☐ Use as Windows credentials
● Stored credentials
  User Name:
  Contoso\2013svcapps
  Password:
  ••••••••
  ☑ Use as Windows credentials
  ☐ Set execution context to this account
○ Credentials are not required

Test Connection
Connection created successfully.

Availability
☑ Enable this data source

	OK	Cancel

12. We now need a model so that we can use this data source in the Report Builder.

13. Click **Files** ➤ **New Document** ➤ **Report Builder Model**.

14. Give the **Model** a name, as shown in the following screenshot.

Generate Model

Use this page to create a Report Builder model. Click the OK button to generate a model. Generating a model may take several minutes.

	OK	Cancel

Name *

AdventureWorks2014Model ✕ .smdl

Data Source Link *
Select the shared data source (.rsds) file to use for this model.

...

	OK	Cancel

15. The data source link has a picker that will display all the data sources in the site whether in the same site or in the current site collection, as shown in the following screenshot.

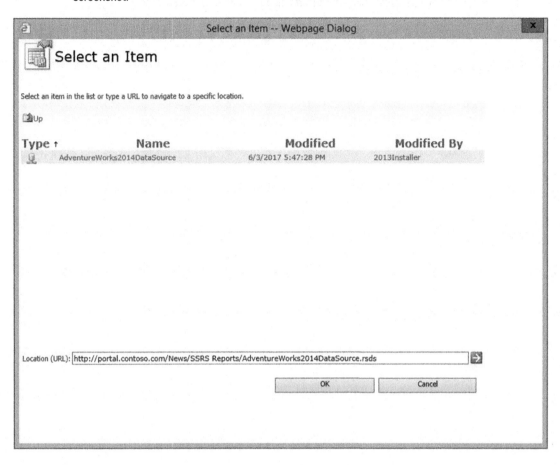

16. Select the data source and click OK, and then OK again, as shown in the following screenshot.

Use this page to create a Report Builder model. Click the OK button to generate a model. Generating a model may take several minutes.

	OK	Cancel

Name *

AdventureWorks2014Model .smdl

Data Source Link *
Select the shared data source (.rsds) file to use for this model.

http://portal.contoso.com/News/SSRS Reports/Adventur ...

	OK	Cancel

17. Now we have all the components we need to create a report.

18. Click **Files ➤ New Document ➤ Report Builder Report**. When prompted to run the Report Builder application, click **Run** when the following screen appears.

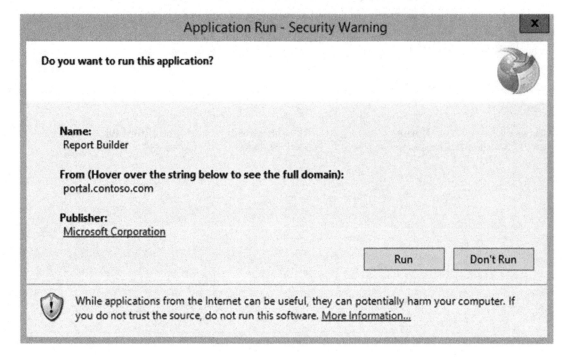

19. At the **Getting Started** screen, click **Table or Matrix Wizard**, as shown in the following screenshot.

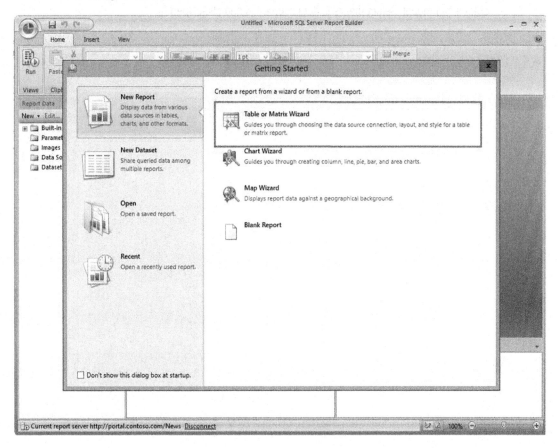

20. On the next screen, click **Create a dataset** and click **Next**.

21. On the next screen (see the following screenshot), we need to choose a data
     source. Click **Browse** and navigate to the Report Library where you saved the data
     source and model. Select the .rsds data source file and click **Open**.

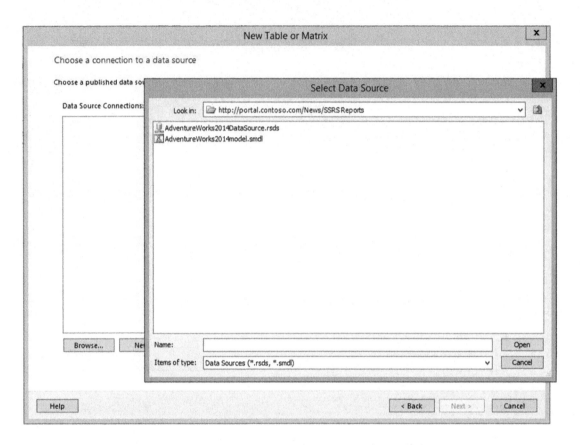

22. Click **Next** on the **Table or Matrix Wizard**. You may be prompted for the data source password. Enter the password and check **Save password with connection.**

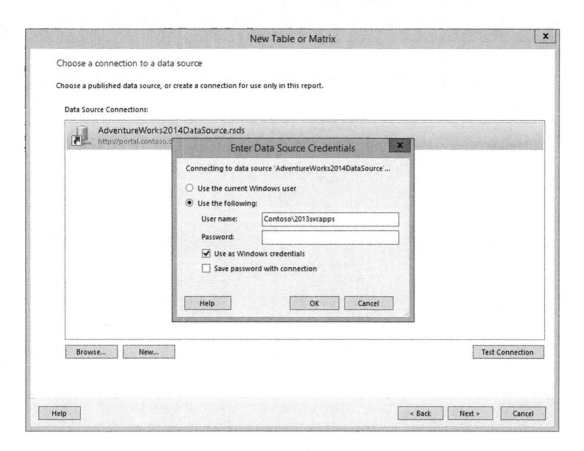

If you get a problem with connecting to the data source, make sure that you've set the cliconfg at C:\windows\system32 and at C:\windows\syswow64.

23. Click **OK**. You are taken to the following screen.

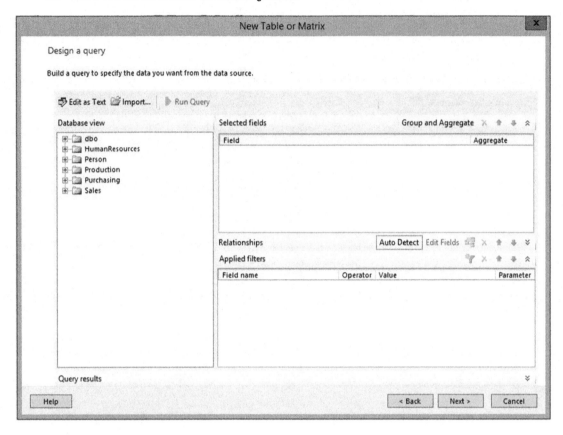

24. Expand **Purchasing** ➤ Views and select **vVendorWithAddresses**, as shown in the following screenshot.

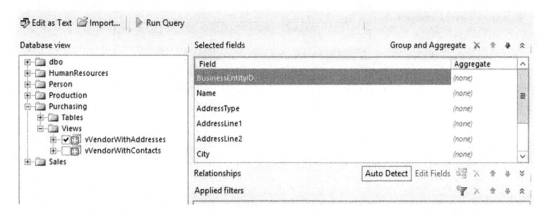

25. Click **Next** and drag-and-drop the fields into the columns that you wish to use, as shown in the following screenshot.

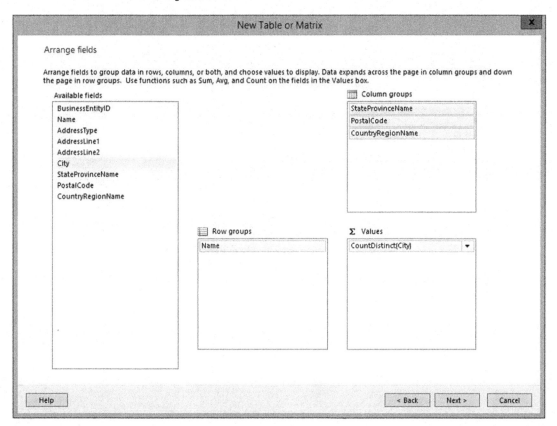

26. Click **Next** and choose the layout you want, as shown in the following screenshot.

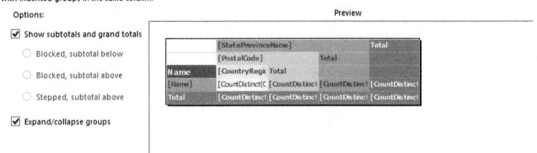

27. Click **Next,** choose your style, and click **Finish**.

28. Click **Run** on the next screen to test the data connection, as shown in the following screenshot.

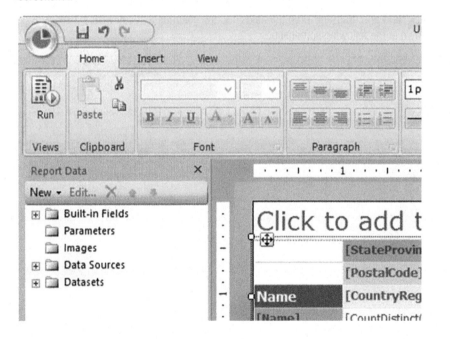

29. If you get results like those in the following screenshot, then SSRS works!

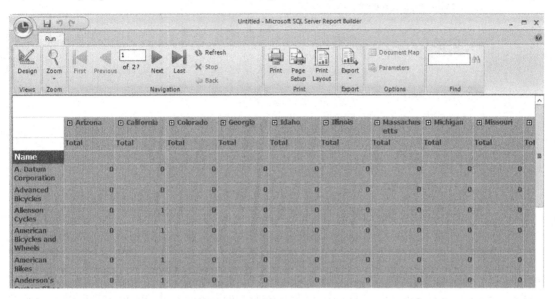

30. Click **Save**, as shown in the following screenshot, to save the report back to the **Report Library** we created earlier, give it a name (e.g., testReport.rdl). Make sure to get in the right library directory.

31. If you browse to the **Report Library**, you will see all the files we created, as shown in the following screenshot.

SSRS Reports

⊕ new document or drag files here

All reports and dashboards   Find a file   🔎

✓	🗋	Name		Modified	Modified By
	🗎	TestReport ✻	•••	A few seconds ago	☐ 2013Installer
	🗺	AdventureWorks2014model ✻	•••	22 minutes ago	☐ 2013Installer
	🔱	AdventureWorks2014DataSource ✻	•••	34 minutes ago	☐ 2013Installer

We just covered a lot of different areas in SQL, mostly related to connectivity and performance. None of the ad hoc queries that were in this chapter would qualify in the type of ad hoc queries that would violate the support agreement, even the one that interrogates the config database for orphaned sites. The GitHub for this book will have all of the various code samples from each chapter.

Chapter 6 covers additional SQL topics, uses some command-line one-liners, fires up a PowerShell one-liner or two, and investigates the Windows OS and its logs a little more. You'll see the right way and the wrong way to search for help on Bing.

CHAPTER 6

■ ■ ■

SQL Backup and Restore and Useful CLI Commands

In the previous chapters, we considered knowing what should be in place on a base build as the main reference point for troubleshooting what had changed. This knowledge is based on changes that SharePoint makes to the Windows operating system's file system and registry before any solutions or customizations are made to the farm or any of its web applications, site collections, and web sites. We went into some detail about the backend SQL Server and looked at both, supported and unsupported, changes to SQL. We also reviewed some of the changes that are needed on SQL to get SharePoint working and to keep SQL performance optimized; but I forgot to mention setting the maximum memory that the SQL server will utilize. So, we will definitely cover that in this chapter.

This chapter covers a few more important SQL-related topics, such as SQL database backup and restore options, unattached restores, and SQL file restores. The section on backup and restore will briefly discuss PowerShell site collection backup and restores, as well as web site exports and imports.

During the additional SQL coverage, we'll look at a couple more ad hoc queries, some PowerShell one-liners, and some database-related errors that can sometimes surface in the Windows event logs. We'll go through the steps to resolve the event ID 5586 as it relates to the size of the usage logging database. In addition, we will go over the process of finding orphaned features within a database and deleting those pesky, little psconfig false-message-giving buggers.

Since I'm discussing event IDs, this seems like a good point to mention that it is nearly impossible to have a SharePoint server that has completely error and warning free event logs. It is not impossible to keep errors and warnings to a minimum, although, and that is one of the goals we are hoping to accomplish with this book.

We're going to start the chapter out by looking at some Windows operating system commands that you can run from the run bar, or in some cases, only from the command line console (cmd.exe). We'll talk about how they can be useful in troubleshooting. Then after we look at the Windows event log, we'll hit all that SQL stuff.

Sometime in your career working with SharePoint, you might encounter a solution that erroneously overloads a site's application pool causing the app pool to shut down. You'll need to quickly get into IIS and start the app pool. Other things can cause an app pool to fail to start, such as manual changes to the settings of an app pool or its identity. It's never a good idea to manually change app pool settings including the password for the account or identity that runs the app pool. You should handle all of that through the Central Administration site. You can enter **inetmgr** or **inetmgr.exe** on the command line or on the run bar and this will open the Internet Information Services (IIS) Manager.

Once you have IIS open you can open the server node, then the application pools node, and you'll quickly be able to see any application pools that are in a stopped state. It's normal for the SharePoint Web Services Root to be in a stopped state. If you attempt to start an app pool and it promptly stops, you might want to open SharePoint and make sure you've entered the correct password for the app pool. The best way to test the password is to try to open Notepad with that user. Right-click the Notepad app on the Start menu. Hold down the Shift key when you right-click so that you can open as another user.

© Stacy Simpkins 2017
S. Simpkins, *Troubleshooting SharePoint*, https://doi.org/10.1007/978-1-4842-3138-8_6

If the password you tried doesn't work, make sure to check in Active Directory Users and Computers (ADUC), either from a domain controller or from this computer. Sometimes, the Windows image that your IT department rolls out will have the Remote Server Administration Tools (RSAT) installed. In which case, you can type **dsa.msc** on the run bar or in a command line interface and you'll get the ADUC. Once ADUC opens, quickly click the View menu and make sure Advanced Features is selected. If it does not have a check next to it, then select it.

After Advanced Features is enabled, additional tabs will become visible in object properties. One of them is the Object tab. This tab tells you where the object is located within the directory. Before you can see where an object is located, you need to perform a quick search. Either you can use the Action menu to perform your search for the user, or you can right-click the domain and click Find. Once you have the user, right-click the user, click Properties, and then click the Account tab. From the account tab, a domain administrator can accomplish many things; but the only thing we are concerned with here, is the ability to unlock an account. Locked accounts in Active Directory will show the "Unlock Account: Account is locked out" message vs. the standard Unlock Account. That is, an Unlocked Accounts tab just says, Unlock Account.

The dsa.msc command is a handy one to remember since it allows you to open Active Directory users and computers with just eight keystrokes, including the enter keystroke, on servers that have the RSAT installed or from the domain controller. In some really locked down environments, you'll need to get the domain admin to do various troubleshooting for you or get the domain admin to make you a domain admin, in which case you can get things done a lot more efficiently.

After you unlock the account, assuming it was locked, try the test with Notepad once more, and if Notepad doesn't open on the first time, you'll need to verify that you used the correct password (and this almost goes without saying). Since this is a service account, and since you're a domain administrator, you can reset the password via the ADUC GUI or via an administrative command line.

To reset the password via an administrative command line interface, you'll use the following command. And before we discuss the command, I'd like to mention that in an effort to save trees, going forward we'll not include the .exe on commands that end in .exe. We will include the .msc for any Microsoft Saved Console (msc) commands. From the cli (cmd), type the following, where the user name is just the username not including the domain you're a member of and the password is the password for that account that you would like to reset:

```
Net user USERNAME PASSWORD /DOMAIN
```

For example, Net user dev-SP_Connect ?7!kx1*Z9w$A /DOMAIN would reset the password for an account named MyDomain\dev-SP_Connect with a password of ?7!kx1*Z9w$A. This is very handy if you want to reset all your SharePoint accounts to new passwords. As long as, no one has manually made any changes to any of the account and passwords inside of the IIS console or the Windows operating system's services console (services.msc), then running the net command with the user parameter and the /domain switch will quickly become your best friend.

Since we've been talking about checking IIS, it seems like a logical place to mention the IIS Manager 6.0 that is installed in your SharePoint servers to handle incoming mail. We're not going to spend much time on this other than to say it's easy to remember the command for IIS 6.0 since it is similar to the command for IIS, just add a 6: **inetmgr6**. Once you've typed inetmgr6 on the run bar or on a command line, IIS Manager 6.0 will open, and from here, you can troubleshoot issues with incoming mail, which we'll cover in Chapter 8. You can close IIS 6.0 if you're reading this book and looking at your server at the same time. I'd also like to point out, that if you're reading a pirated copy, all you're doing is inviting bad karma to make a visit to your life.

When it comes to the various services running on the server, the Windows Services console (services. msc) is where you can go to see the status of those services and you can sort the view by status to see if it's running or stopped. You can sort by the log on as column to quickly see the services that use local system, local service, or a custom identity. All the fields are sortable, but none of them quickly tells you whether the service has any dependencies. You'd have to open the service and look at its dependencies tab.

You can quickly get the service information from the command line or from PowerShell. To gather it from the command line, you use the *service controller command* (SC), as follows:

```
sc query type= service state= all > c:\myDirectory\allserviceslist.txt
sc query type= service state= inactive > c:\myDirectory\Stoppedserviceslist.txt
sc query type= service > c:\myDirectory\Runningserviceslist.txt
```

The SC command is very powerful and it can do a lot more than read information about services and output that to a file in some directory. If you type **SC /Help**, and then at the bottom type **y** when it asks if you would like help with query and queryx commands, you'll be presented with more information; but it will not be as helpful as the information in PowerShell. For example, open a PowerShell session and type **get-help get-spservice** and notice these remarks at the bottom of the output:

```
REMARKS
    To see the examples, type: "get-help Get-Service -examples".
    For more information, type: "get-help Get-Service -detailed".
    For technical information, type: "get-help Get-Service -full".
    For online help, type: "get-help Get-Service -online"
```

If you run the example parameter, you'll see that it helps to know the names of the services with using the get-spservice cmdlet. Why is this important to a SharePoint engineer? Because you need to know about the underlying operating system, be able to determine this quickly, and be familiar with PowerShell. As you saw in the earlier chapters, the get-member cmdlet will yield information about any PowerShell cmdlet. Get-service is no different.

One of my favorite things to do with any output from a PowerShell command is sort it. Another cool thing that PowerShell does, that the command line does not do, as easily, is get information about remote machines. Example 8's get-help get-service –examples is an excellent case on how to sort. Example 9 shows a really cool way to check the status of a service in all the servers in your farm from one server, as you can see in Figure 6-1.

```
┌──────────────────────────────────────────────────────────────────────────┐
│ ⚙       Administrator: SharePoint 2013 Management Shell    ─ □ X           │
├──────────────────────────────────────────────────────────────────────────┤
│ ──────────────────────────── EXAMPLE 8 ────────────────────────           │
│                                                                           │
│ PS C:\>get-service s* | sort-object status                                │
│                                                                           │
│ Status    Name              DisplayName                                   │
│ ──────    ────              ───────────                                   │
│ Stopped   stisvc            Windows Image Acquisition (WIA)               │
│ Stopped   SwPrv             MS Software Shadow Copy Provider              │
│ Stopped   SysmonLog         Performance Logs and Alerts                   │
│ Running   Spooler           Print Spooler                                 │
│ Running   srservice         System Restore Service                       │
│ Running   SSDPSRV           SSDP Discovery Service                        │
│ Running   ShellHWDetection  Shell Hardware Detection                      │
│ Running   Schedule          Task Scheduler                                │
│ Running   SCardSvr          Smart Card                                    │
│ Running   SamSs             Security Accounts Manager                     │
│ Running   SharedAccess      Windows Firewall/Internet Connectio...        │
│ Running   SENS              System Event Notification                     │
│ Running   seclogon          Secondary Logon                               │
│                                                                           │
│ PS C:\>get-service s* | sort-object status -descending                    │
│                                                                           │
│ Status    Name              DisplayName                                   │
│ ──────    ────              ───────────                                   │
│ Running   ShellHWDetection  Shell Hardware Detection                      │
│ Running   SharedAccess      Windows Firewall/Internet Connectio...        │
│ Running   Spooler           Print Spooler                                 │
│ Running   SSDPSRV           SSDP Discovery Service                        │
│ Running   srservice         System Restore Service                       │
│ Running   SCardSvr          Smart Card                                    │
│ Running   SamSs             Security Accounts Manager                     │
│ Running   Schedule          Task Scheduler                                │
│ Running   SENS              System Event Notification                     │
│ Running   seclogon          Secondary Logon                               │
│ Stopped   SysmonLog         Performance Logs and Alerts                   │
│ Stopped   SwPrv             MS Software Shadow Copy Provider              │
│ Stopped   stisvc            Windows Image Acquisition (WIA)               │
│                                                                           │
│ This command shows that when you sort services in ascending order by the  │
│ value of their Status property, stopped services appear before running    │
│ services. This happens because the value of Status is an enumeration, in  │
│ which "Stopped" has a value of "1", and "Running" has a value of 4.       │
│                                                                           │
│ To list running services first, use the Descending parameter of the       │
│ Sort-Object cmdlet.                                                        │
│                                                                           │
│                                                                           │
│ ──────────────────────────── EXAMPLE 9 ────────────────────────           │
│                                                                           │
│ PS C:\>get-service -name winrm -computername localhost, Server01, Server02 │
│ | format-table -property MachineName, Status, Name, DisplayName -auto     │
│                                                                           │
│ MachineName   Status   Name   DisplayName                                 │
│ ───────────   ──────   ────   ───────────                                 │
│ localhost     Running WinRM Windows Remote Management (WS-Management)      │
│ Server01      Running WinRM Windows Remote Management (WS-Management)      │
│ Server02      Running WinRM Windows Remote Management (WS-Management)      │
│                                                                           │
│ This command uses the Get-Service cmdlet to run a "Get-Service Winrm"      │
│ command on two remote computers and the local computer ("localhost").     │
│                                                                           │
│ The Get-Service command runs on the remote computers, and the results are │
│ returned to the local computer. A pipeline operator (|) sends the results │
│ to the Format-Table cmdlet, which formats the services as a table. The    │
│ Format-Table command uses the Property parameter to specify the properties│
│ displayed in the table, including the MachineName property.               │
│                                                                           │
│                                                                           │
│ ──────────────────────────── EXAMPLE 10 ───────────────────────           │
│                                                                           │
│ PS C:\>get-service winrm -requiredServices                                │
│                                                                           │
│ This command gets the services that the WinRM service requires.           │
└──────────────────────────────────────────────────────────────────────────┘
```

Figure 6-1. *Example 8 and Example 9*

So when considering the PowerShell vs. the command line, PowerShell wins hands down!! You can even get a report from all servers in your farm using this PowerShell:

```
$spservers=Get-SPServer | where {$_.Role -ne "Invalid"}
Foreach ($spserver in $spservers)
{
$filename=$spserver.name
Get-EventLog -LogName "System" | where-object {$_.EventID -eq 6005} | select
MachineName,  TimeGenerated, Source, Message
}
```

While the command line's, SC query command gives you information about whether a service has dependencies or is dependent; it doesn't tell you which of those two is in fact dependent, it only tells you if the service is its own service, in which case it is has a type of "10 WIN32_OWN_PROCESS". If it has dependencies or is dependent on another service, it will be of type "20 WIN32_SHARE_PROCESS". This is helpful to know when troubleshooting why a service like IISADMIN or W3SVC is having trouble starting. Some of the possible issues that could contribute to this are that there might have been manual changes made to a password of the identity that these services are running on, one of their dependent services might be stopped for some reason, or worse yet an ACL in registry for these services might have been erroneously modified. That's not a comprehensive list, but it is worth ruling out after trying to manually start the service that is not restarting on its own.

When you open Windows Task Manager (**taskmgr**) from either the run bar or the command line and look at the processes tab, you can expand some of the processes and others, like the IIS worker process, are not expandable. Notice, in Figure 6-2, we were able to expand the SharePoint Timer service and it's now mystery that the underlying Windows service is the SharePoint timer service; but what about that IIS worker process at the top of the processes, sorted by memory? How do we tell what application pool that that IIS worker process is related to?

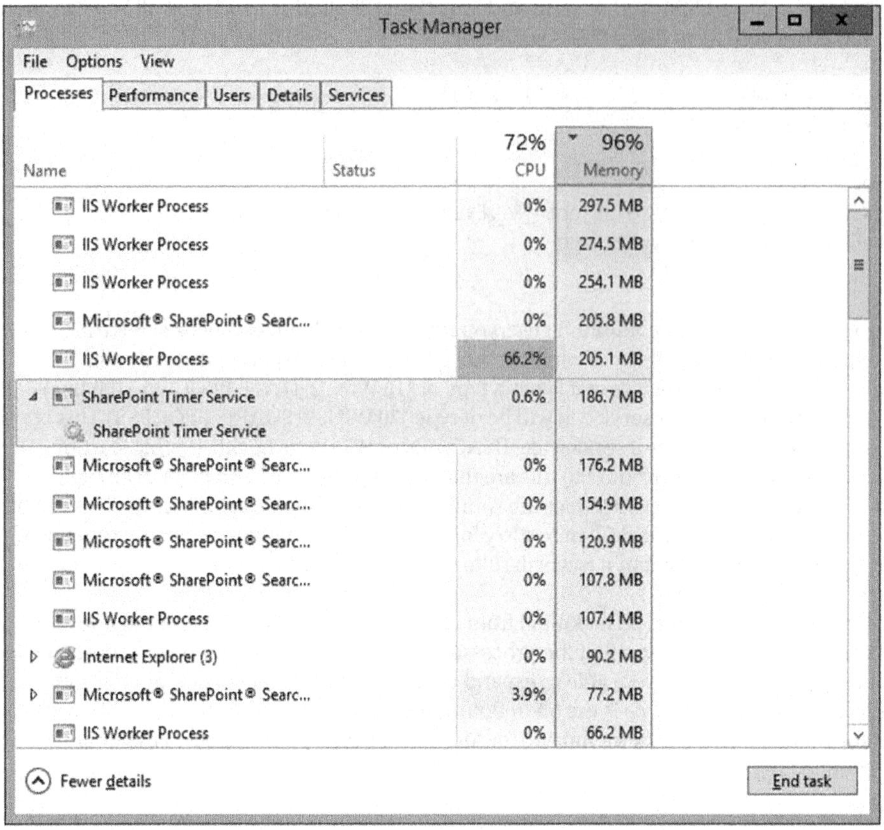

Figure 6-2. *Processes sorted by memory*

To determine the application pool that is consuming around 297.6MB of memory, or to find the pool that is consuming 66.2% of the memory, we'll need to find the process ID(PID). We could use PowerShell and run get-process, sorting the virtual memory in descending order.

```
Get-process | sort virtualmemorysize –Descending
```

This command will give us the output shown in the image in Figure 6-3. Here we can see that there is a process named noderunner and a World Wide Web service process (w3wp) that are consuming most of the memory. If we switch the Task Manager to the details view and sort it by memory, in server 2012 R2, this gives us the information we need to almost determine which application pool is using the memory. It gives the user name, the PID, and the memory in use.

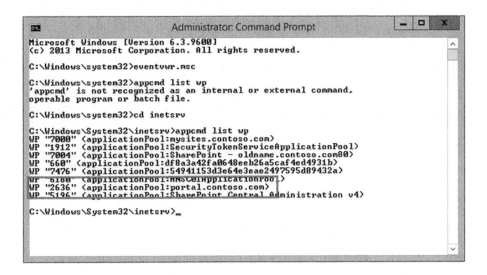

Figure 6-3. Task Manager details view sorted by memory

Now if you open an administrative command-line (cmd) and type the appcmd to list out the various worker processes, it will return a nice list that includes the PID. You can now use inetmgr to recycle the application pool associated with that worker process, assuming that it is impacting the other sites on the server. This is much less invasive than a server restart.

Figure 6-4 shows that when I ran the **appcmd list wp** command, it first returned an error because I did not have a path specified for the appcmd in my system variables. Not to worry, though: just change the directory to the correct location and run the command once more.

```
Administrator: Command Prompt
Microsoft Windows [Version 6.3.9600]
(c) 2013 Microsoft Corporation. All rights reserved.

C:\Windows\system32>eventvwr.msc

C:\Windows\system32>appcmd list wp
'appcmd' is not recognized as an internal or external command,
operable program or batch file.

C:\Windows\system32>cd inetsrv

C:\Windows\System32\inetsrv>appcmd list wp
WP "7000" (applicationPool:mysites.contoso.com)
WP "1912" (applicationPool:SecurityTokenServiceApplicationPool)
WP "7004" (applicationPool:SharePoint - oldname.contoso.com80)
WP "660" (applicationPool:df8a3a42fa0648eeb26a5caf4ed4931b)
WP "7476" (applicationPool:54941153d3e64e3eae2497595d89432a)
WP "6180" (applicationPool:HNSCoIApplicationPool)
WP "2636" (applicationPool:portal.contoso.com)
WP "5196" (applicationPool:SharePoint Central Administration v4)

C:\Windows\System32\inetsrv>_
```

Figure 6-4. Found ya!

You can also find this same information by opening inetmgr, clicking the server node, and then clicking worker processes. Often, a restart quickly fixes issues like the worker process that was chewing up resources; but this is contrary to the best approach. It is like pulling the rug out from under SharePoint's feet. Obviously, that is just an analogy, as SharePoint does not have feet. Restarting the server could cause timer jobs to hang or fail.

You can tell when a server restarted by many different methods. One quick method is to look at the Performance tab in the Task Manager, as shown in Figure 6-5.

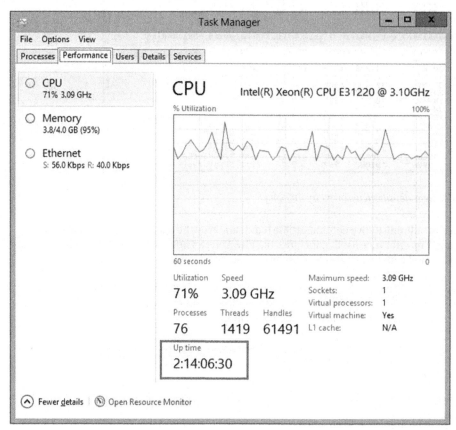

Figure 6-5. *Server has been up for two days plus*

As you can see in that performance tab, this server is under resourced and has been up for 2 days, 14 hours, 7 minutes, and 50 seconds at the time of that screenshot. That's really cool to see, but what if you're not a Harvard math whiz? When did the server restart, on what day, and so forth? OK, what time is it? Let me subtract 48 hours from that time. No wait, 62 hours, 7 minutes, and 50 seconds. You see what I'm getting at. That's why the systeminfo command is much more useful.

To find the last time the system was booted, use this command:

```
Systeminfo | find "System Boot Time:"
```

The output is shown in Figure 6-6. It's much easier and quicker than doing the math from the Task Manager Performance tab. That's not to belittle the Task Manager because if your server is sluggish and behaving oddly, taskmgr is the first place to look and if it hasn't been restarted in 30 days, a restart of the farm should be scheduled.

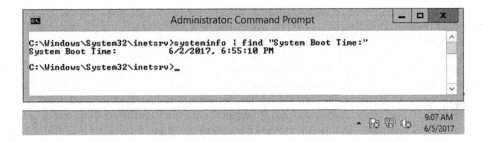

Figure 6-6. *Find System Boot Time*

Again, PowerShell to the rescue! If you want to know when a machine was shut down, query the event log for event ID 6006, which states when the logging of events stopped, and then pipe that to a formatted table using this command:

```
Get-EventLog -LogName "System" | where-object {$_.EventID -eq 6006} | select MachineName, TimeGenerated, Message -First 2 | FT MachineName, TimeGenerated, Message -wrap
```

Follow that one-liner with the same query only for event ID 6005, using this command:

```
Get-EventLog -LogName "System" | where-object {$_.EventID -eq 6005} | select MachineName, TimeGenerated, Message -First 2 | FT MachineName, TimeGenerated, Message -wrap
```

The results will look something like Figure 6-7. If you want to get more than the last two times the server was restarted, change the –first parameter on the select-object part of the pipe.

```
PS C:\Users\2013installer> Get-EventLog -LogName "System" | where-object {$_.Eve
ntID -eq 6006} | select MachineName, TimeGenerated, Message -first 2 | ft machin
ename, timegenerated, message -wrap

MachineName                TimeGenerated              Message
-----------                -------------              -------
2013appw2k12.contoso.com   6/5/2017 9:17:46 AM        The Event log service
                                                      was stopped.
2013appw2k12.contoso.com   6/2/2017 6:47:38 PM        The Event log service
                                                      was stopped.


PS C:\Users\2013installer> Get-EventLog -LogName "System" | where-object {$_.Eve
ntID -eq 6005} | select MachineName, TimeGenerated, Message -first 2 | ft machin
ename, timegenerated, message -wrap

MachineName                TimeGenerated              Message
-----------                -------------              -------
2013appw2k12.contoso.com   6/5/2017 9:21:56 AM        The Event log service
                                                      was started.
2013appw2k12.contoso.com   6/2/2017 6:50:19 PM        The Event log service
                                                      was started.


PS C:\Users\2013installer> _
```

Figure 6-7. *Server was down for 4 minutes and 10 seconds on 6/5/2017*

Finding the restart information for all your servers in your farm, including the SQL servers will help you resolve issues that you're noticing in the Event Viewer (**eventvwr.msc**) and it will explain unexpected events in the ULS logs. Restarts of the SQL server will show up as lost connection with database and database unavailable in the application log and ULS logs, even when the SQL is clustered if the timer job is aware of the node that it is connected or if the failover does not happen quick enough.

The systeminfo command has a lot more than just the last time the system was restarted. You can get the information about the total physical memory, available physical memory, virtual memory maximum size, available virtual memory, and virtual memory in use, among other metrics. You can get these same metrics from MSINFO32, executed from the run bar or from a command line. And, using either MSINFO32 or systeminfo, you can obtain information from a remote computer. Figure 6-8 shows the use of the /S switch to extract the virtual memory information for a remote system; as you can see, the hostname of the server this command is run from is not the /S server.

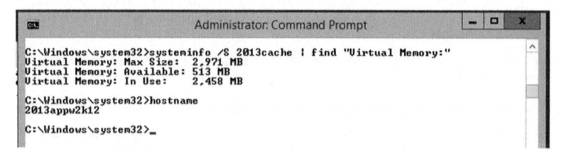

Figure 6-8. *systeminfo for 2013cache obtained on 2013appw2k12*

To obtain remote system information using the msinfo32 GUI, go to the View menu and connect to a remote computer. After the System Information GUI refreshes, you'll see the remote computer provided you have administrative permissions on the remote computer. Speaking of administrative permissions, you can easily check them by opening the local users and groups console and taking a look at the members of each group. Just type **lusrmgr.msc** from the command line or from a run bar and the console will open. You can also use the net localgroup <name of the local group> to see the members of a particular group. This method was demonstrated in an exercise in Chapter 2.

When troubleshooting SharePoint you may need to take a look at the network settings, one quick way to get there is to type **control netconnections** or **ncpa.cpl** on the run bar or from a command line. From here, you can open the correct network connection for your SharePoint server and verify that it has the correct information for the domain controller and that it has a static IP address. If you're dealing with a server in Azure or AWS, do not set the IP to static, as this will break the trust that the VM has with the Azure or AWS platform. Let Azure and AWS handle the server IP.

You can see the server's IP by looking at network connections or by running ipconfig—all from a command line. Ipconfig /all will not prove very fruitful if run from the run bar. It will run, but you will not see the output.

There are numerous ports that need to be open for SharePoint to run correctly in the firewall if you have servers in the farm that are in different networks. If the servers are in the same subnet, then the ports should be OK. If you need to create a rule, wf.msc will open the Windows firewall. Table 6-1 lists out the ports used for SharePoint and gives a brief explanation of why they are needed.

Table 6-1. *Ports Needed for a SharePoint Farm*

Protocol	Port	Usage	Comment
TCP	80	http	Client to SharePoint web server traffic (SharePoint–Office Web Apps Communication).
TCP	443	https	Encrypted client to SharePoint web server traffic. (Encrypted SharePoint–Office Web Apps communication.)
TCP	1433	SQL Server	Default SQL Server communication port, may be configured to use custom port for increased security.
TCP	1434	SQL Server	Default SQL Server port used to establish communication, may be configured to use custom port for increased security.
TCP	445	SQL Server	When SQL Server is configured to listen for incoming client connections by using named pipes over a NetBIOS session, SQL Server communicates over TCP port 445.
TCP	25	SMTP	Cannot be configured if port is used by simple mail transport protocol for email integration.
TCP	16500-16519	Search	Ports used by the search index component Intra-farm only. An Inbound rule is added to Windows firewall by SharePoint.
TCP	22233-22236	App Fabric Distributed Cache	These are the ports used by the Distributed Cache.
TCP	808	WCF	Windows communication foundation communication.
TCP	32843	Service Applications	Default http port used for communication between app and web servers for service applications.
TCP	32844	Service Applications	Default HTTPS port used for communication between app and web servers for service applications.
TCP	32845	Custom Service Applications	net.tcp binding: TCP 32845 (only if a third party has implemented this option for a service application. An inbound rule is added to Windows firewall by SharePoint.
TCP	5725	User Profile Synchronization Service(FIM)	Synchronizing between SharePoint and Active Directory
TCP & UDP	389	User Profile Synchronization Service(FIM)	LDAP Service
TCP & UDP	88	User Profile Synchronization Service(FIM)	Kerberos
TCP & UDP	53	User Profile Synchronization Service(FIM)	DNS
UDP	464	User Profile Service (FIM)	Kerberos change password
TCP	809	Office Web apps	Intra-farm Office Web Apps communication

You can test communication on all ports using *telnet*. You can also check that the servers can find each other by pinging the various servers in your farm with ping.

When it comes to sites working in SharePoint, the following must be in place:

- Correct records in DNS

- Bindings in the SharePoint farm

- Site exists within SharePoint

- Certificates are not expired if site is running securely

- Application pool is running

- Site is running

- Identities are not locked out

That last point of identities not being locked out really should go without saying, since if they were locked out then the application pool and the site would be stopped. And if you tried to start the site, it would not be successful. If you ever run into this, correct Active Directory, then set the managed account in SharePoint to the correct password. You may have to delete the managed account and re-create it. If that happens, you can create it via the GUI or with New-SPManagedAccount cmdlet.

We already covered the component services console in some depth in Chapter 2, but I need to mention that the console is available from the command line and from administrative tools. You may have noticed that the services console (services.msc) and the Event Viewer (eventvwr.msc) are both baked into the component services (comexp) and I wanted to mention it in case you hadn't noticed. You used the component services console to check that the app pool accounts have the proper permissions for the distributed component object model launch and activation. This insures that the various SharePoint Dynamic Link Libraries and other files can communicate and that the app pools will function better.

Before we move onto the SQL continuation from the previous chapter, I want to mention that the computer management console (compmgmt.msc) contains all of the service consoles discussed until this point, with the exception of the component services. Computer management also contains a node for disk management (diskmgmt.msc), a node for the Task Scheduler (taskschd.msc), a node for performance monitor (perfmon.msc or perfomon), a node for device manager (devmgmt.msc), a node for WMI Control (wmimgmt.msc), and a node for Windows Server Backup.

The computer management console on a SQL server contains a node for the SQL Server Configuration Manager. In Chapter 5, Table 5-4 listed all of the locations on the file system where you could find the executable. If you open registry editor by typing **regedit** on the run bar or command line, you can navigate into HKLM\SOFTWARE\Microsoft\Microsoft SQL Server to find out all the information about your SQL install. Don't change anything in registry without first making a backup of that key. You should be 100% certain of the outcome that your changes will have on the environment.

You can get more information about your SQL server by running this ad hoc query:

```
SELECT
        SERVERPROPERTY('ProductLevel') AS ProductLevel,
        SERVERPROPERTY('ProductUpdateLevel') AS ProductUpdateLevel,
        SERVERPROPERTY('ProductBuildType') AS ProductBuildType,
        SERVERPROPERTY('ProductUpdateReference') AS ProductUpdateReference,
        SERVERPROPERTY('ProductVersion') AS ProductVersion,
        SERVERPROPERTY('ProductMajorVersion') AS ProductMajorVersion,
        SERVERPROPERTY('ProductMinorVersion') AS ProductMinorVersion,
        SERVERPROPERTY('ProductBuild') AS ProductBuild
```

The results will let you know if the SQL is a base install, meaning it hasn't had a cumulative updated applied, since it will have a NULL value for the ProductUpdateLevel. Another cool thing that this ad hoc gives is the ProductUpdateReference, which is a KB number. You can take that number and immediately find the Microsoft support post for your most recent SQL update at `https://support.microsoft.com/KB/<KBNumber>`. For example, consider the output of the command for the test farm used to make parts of this book, shown in Figure 6-9. It has a KB number of 3194720, which would make the URL for the support article `https://support.microsoft.com/KB/3194720`.

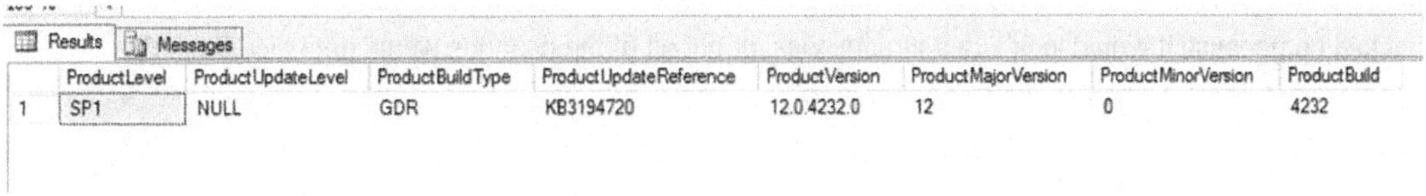

	ProductLevel	ProductUpdateLevel	ProductBuildType	ProductUpdateReference	ProductVersion	ProductMajorVersion	ProductMinorVersion	ProductBuild
1	SP1	NULL	GDR	KB3194720	12.0.4232.0	12	0	4232

Figure 6-9. *SQL 2014 SP1*

This KB number is helpful when it comes to installing SSRS, as you have already seen in Chapter 5, because it gives you the SQL Server version. The SQL version is important when it comes to restores, too. When you try to restore from a higher version of SQL to a lower version, the restore operation will fail. This is a simple thing to fix. Simply get the right version to restore from or to.

To restore a SQL .bak file on your server, follow these steps.

1. Right-click the databases node and then choose **Restore Files and Filegroups**...

2. **Type the name** that your database should have in the To Database: field.

3. Select the **From device:** radio button.

4. **Navigate** to the location on disk where you've saved the .bak file that you are looking to restore.

5. The ellipsis button allows you to navigate the file system and **add** the file.

6. After you've found the file, **click OK**.

7. Select the **Name of the File check box**, and then click OK.

8. After the database is restored, make sure to **give the farm account dbo** on the database.

To restore a SharePoint .bak file on your server, open the SharePoint Management Shell and run a version of the following:

```
Restore-SPSite <URL> -Path <Path to .bak file>
```

Or,

```
Restore-SPSite <URL> -Path <Path to .bak file>  -force
```

The only requirements for this to succeed are a SharePoint backup that was created with Backup-SPSite, not a SQL backup and knowing if a site collection already exists. If a site collection already exists, make sure to use the –force parameter. The restore-spite will throw errors if you try to restore the site collection to a web application that contains databases that have already reached their maximum site count. In that case, either you can increase the site count in one of the databases or you can add a new content database.

When you move databases between SQL servers, you're either going to perform detach and attach or you're going to take a SQL backup (.bak). Detach and attach is used when migrating to a new version of SharePoint and the .bak is used when truing up a dev or staging environment.

■ **Note** When you make the SQL backup file remember to set the copy-only so as not to upset the differential base. If you fail to set the copy-only backup, SQL Server will mark all the delta's as having been backed up and the next time whichever backup appliance runs the backup for your SQL, this database will not be properly backed up because it would look like it already was, or not all of the changes would get backed up. Use copy-only when truing up between environments.

This database backup file cannot be used to restore just one site collection, the way a SharePoint .bak file is utilized. The SQL .bak file could contain more than one site collection. What follows are the steps to create a .bak file that you can use, in SQL, to restore the database to another SQL server.

1. Right-click your database and select or hover over tasks.

2. Click Back Up.

3. Click **Copy-Only** backup check box VERY IMPORTANT.

4. Click Remove to Remove the default destination and choose a new destination.

5. Click Add, click the ellipsis to navigate into a location on disk, and give the file a name.

6. Make sure the filename ends with a .bak extension.

7. Click OK three times.

8. After the backup completes, click OK once more.

If you wanted to restore that .bak file created in SQL, you could copy it to another SQL server and restore it using the previous steps for a SQL .bak file. If the .bak file was created with the Backup-SPSite, it will only be able to be restored in SharePoint, as mentioned earlier. The Backup-SPSite requires the URL of the site and a path to create the backup.

```
Backup-SPSite <URL> -Path <Path to .bak file including .bak file name>
```

For example

```
Backup-SPSite https://www.saanvirocks.com –path c:\backups\saanvi.bak
```

The Backup-SPSite can only be run on site collections and it requires a site collection URL or ID and a path to a directory that has enough free space. There used to be a limit of 15GB; but this limit was with MOSS 2007 and has since been lifted to 100GB with SharePoint 2010; but the limitation on the manifest file not getting bigger than 2GB still exists in most drives. The manifest size is based on the sheer number of objects inside the site collection. So, it's a good idea to know how big the site collection is. The following is the PowerShell to find the size in megabytes on your site collection.

```
$sc = Get-SPSite https://www.saanvirocks.com
$sc | select url, @{label="Size in MB";Expression={$_.usage.storage}}
```

If you run into this where the backup is failing, you might be able to go with the SQL .bak route, and restore the database to your farm and then perform an unattached restore to get the SharePoint .bak file. Then after you have the SharePoint .bak file you can restore using restore-spsite.

If you have the wrong kind of .bak file and try to restore it inside of SharePoint, you'll receive a message similar to this one:

Your backup is from a different version of Windows SharePoint Services and cannot be restored to a server running the current version. The backup file should be restored to a server with version '1262884508.196508.17294360.0.'

If that happens to you, just make sure you're using the correct type of .bak and not one that was generated with STSADM -o export or via SQL when restoring via Restore-SPSite.

To perform an unattached backup and restore, you first need to get the SQL .bak file restored to your SharePoint farm as a database or have the database attached to SQL, just not attached to a SharePoint web application. And you need to make sure the farm account can log in to the database. I've found that dbo works best for the log in to give to the farm account for the unattached database.

After the database is restored and attached inside SQL, navigate to Backup and Restore inside Central Administration, and then click "Recover data from an unattached content database". On the Unattached Content Database Data Recovery screen, enter the name of the database after you've verified that you're on the correct instance. Sometimes, a SharePoint farm might have one instance for service application databases and one instance for content databases; so, make sure you know where the databases were restored, to what instance.

Enter the database name and select backup site collection if you're looking to create a .bak file that contains the site collection. If you're after a list or a subsite, you can choose "Export site or list" and then you'll get a .cmp file. The compressed migration package (.cmp) will be able to be restored using the import-spweb. After you click Next, you'll need to navigate to the site collection, site, or list that you're looking to backup and then provide a path for the export file, and a name for the file. If you are exporting a list or a site, use .cmp for the file name, and if you're backing up a site collection, use .bak.

Whenever you are moving databases between versions of SharePoint, make sure that the web applications that they were attached to before the move use the same authentication methods. For example, if you have a 2010 SharePoint web application, there is a good chance that it is using classic non-claims, authentication. In this case, you should convert the web application to claims in SharePoint 2010 before you move the database.

There are essentially five main parts of converting the 2010 web application and the data to claims when the web application and the data are still on the 2010 server.

1. Make sure that you have administrative rights on the server and that the account you're using is db_owner and securityadmin on the database in SQL.

2. Run the PowerShell to set your account as the administrator for the site.

3. Configure the site to allow your account full access.

4. Run the PowerShell to migrate the users.

5. Run the PowerShell to perform the conversion.

The command to set your account as the administrator of the site is as follows:

```
$WebAppName = "http://<yourWebAppUrl>"
$wa = get-SPWebApplication $WebAppName
$wa.UseClaimsAuthentication = $true
$wa.Update()
```

The following are the commands to enable the user policy so that your account has full control:

```
$account = "yourDomain\yourUser"
$account = (New-SPClaimsPrincipal -identity $account -identitytype 1).ToEncodedString()
$wa = get-SPWebApplication $WebAppName
$zp = $wa.ZonePolicies("Default")
$p = $zp.Add($account,"PSPolicy")
$fc=$wa.PolicyRoles.GetSpecialRole("FullControl")
$p.PolicyRoleBindings.Add($fc)
$wa.Update()
```

The command to perform the migration from classic to claims is as follows:

```
$wa.MigrateUsers($true)
```

Finally, the command to provision the web application to use the claims based identities, is as follows:

```
$wa.ProvisionGlobally()
```

If alerts stop working after the migration, you should re-create the alerts. If the users receive a "you do not have permission to access" message after the conversion, make sure that the super user and super reader accounts are configured to use the claims based account name. If you're unsure what that name is, you can go to Central Admin and look at the user policy for the web application under the application management, manage web applications.

Now that the web application is migrated to claims, you can easily detach the database and copy the .mdf, .ldf, and any .ndf files to the new SQL server. To detach the database follow these steps.

1. Open SSMS.

2. Right-click the database and choose Tasks.

3. From the Tasks menu, choose Detach.

4. Select the Drop Connections check box and leave Update Statistics unchecked.

5. Click OK.

Now you can copy the database data file (.mdf) and its associated log file (.ldf) to the new server. Once on the new server, you'll want to attach this file. Just right-click the databases node in SSMS and choose "Attach..." Once the Attach database window opens, navigate to where you copied the .mdf and .ldf files. After you select the .mdf file, the Attach databases show the database details. Make sure that the current file path is correct; otherwise, the database attach will not be successful.

After the database is attached and you've migrated the logins or added the permissions for at least the farm account, you can run mount-spcontentdatabase to mount it to the web application of your choosing. The web application must already exist and sites with the same site ID should not be present anywhere else in the farm. Do not attempt to mount a database with site IDs for sites that are already in your farm; otherwise, you run the risk of orphaning site collections. And, as I already mentioned, the logins need to be established for the database to successfully add to the farm.

SQL Server is a memory-hungry beast. When it is installed, the default maximum memory is 2,147,483,647MB, which equals 2,048TB (terabytes), or way more memory than most servers have installed. Just as a general rule, it is a good idea to set the memory setting to about 2GB to 4GB less than what is physically installed on the server. You can configure this by right-clicking the SQL Server node in SSMS, and then clicking Properties. Once the Server Properties window opens, click Memory, and configure away. Figure 6-10 shows the server properties for a server that is undersized to run SQL; but it was very good for the home lab.

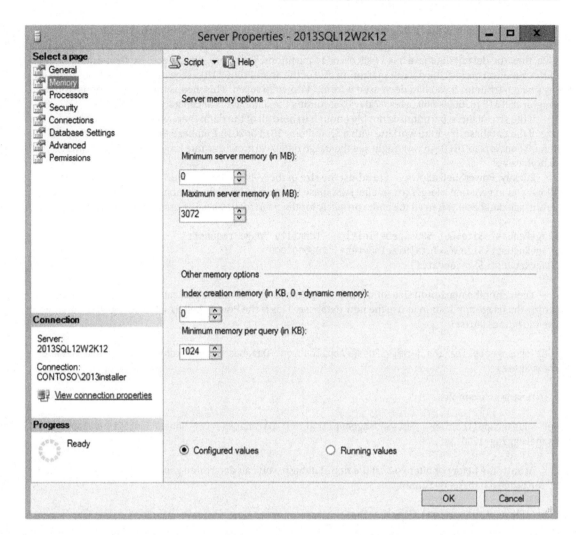

Figure 6-10. Memory should be about 2GB to 4GB less than the total physical memory

Event ID 5586

The only SharePoint SQL database that it is OK to query directly is the usage application's database—or the database used for usage logging. Sometimes the usage logging database default maximum size of 6GB is not big enough for the number of bytes worth of data that a SharePoint 2010 farm requires. When this happens, the application log starts to generate event ID 5586 and the ULS logs display a message that says that the partition has exceeded the maximum bytes. The error will look something like this:

```
05/12/2017 09:30:04.78    OWSTIMER.EXE (0x1E24)    0x2C98    SharePoint
Foundation    Health    i0m6    High    Table RequestUsage_Partition12 has 444858368 bytes
that has exceeded the max bytes 444858368
```

What this means is that the database needs to be increased or the retention period needs to be decreased. The usage database is split up into partitions. If you think of it like a pizza, and each partition is a slice, then the default database has 14 slices, or 14 partitions. Therefore, if you decrease the number of days in the retention period, the default maximum size of the SharePoint 2010 usage db is still 6GB, but there are say seven partitions, if you had decreased it from 14 down to seven. This means that the partitions would be roughly 850 MB (6200000000 bytes / 7 days), assuming the database is at capacity.

If the size of these partitions is not big enough to hold all of the data; then, you will need to increase the size of the database. If you're working with a SharePoint 2013 or 2016 Database the MaxTotalSizeInBytes by default converts to 10TB, so you might see the usage database growing quite large. PowerShell to the rescue in both cases!

Luckily, PowerShell allows you to adjust the size of the MaxTotalSizeinBytes property. This property allows you to generate a larger (or smaller) database upon creation of the database. Before you create the new usage database, you need to set the property for the page requests using the following PowerShell:

```
$PageRequestsSize=Get-SPUsageDefinition -Identity "page requests"
$PageRequestsSize.MaxTotalSizeInBytes= 12000000000
$PageRequestsSize.update()
```

Then after the maximum size for the page requests usage definition, you can create a new database by setting the usage application to use the new database. This is the PowerShell to set the usage definition to use the new database:

```
 Get-spusageapplication | Set-SPUsageApplication –DatabaseServer <dbServer> –DatabaseName
<newDBname>
```

Here is an example:

```
Get-spusageapplication | Set-SPUsageApplication –DatabaseServer SharePointSQL –DatabaseName
UsageLogging_12GB
```

At any time before or after you set the new database, you can determine which database is being used by the usage database, by running:

```
(Get-SPUsageApplication).UsageDatabase
```

Another way to test whether the setting has taken is by running this ad hoc query.

```
SELECT * FROM [UsageLogging_12GB].[dbo].[Configuration] WITH (nolock) WHERE ConfigName LIKE
'Max Total Bytes - RequestUsage'
```

After you've increased the size of the database, or in the analogy, the size of the pizza, then you can have more partitions and they'll be bigger than the partitions, or slices, given the same number of slices or partitions. Essentially, increasing the page requests definition is like magically making that small pizza an extra large.

Sometimes when you try to upgrade a database with upgrade-spcontentdatabase or when you run the post-setup configuration wizard via the GUI or via the cli using psconfig, you might encounter messages in the logs about missing features in the farm. When this happens, the upgrade or psconfig usually gives a failure message, even though, for the most part, the action was successful. You can identify and then remove these annoying, orphans with the following PowerShell.

To identify the orphans, just run *Get-SPFeature | ? { $_.Scope -eq $null }*. This finds features in your farm that missing from one of the scopes: farm, site, or web. At this point, if you try to use uninstall-SPFeature along with the ID for one of the features, you will receive an error message

```
Uninstall-SPFeature : Cannot find a Feature object with Path or Id: f6fa69a1-f5d2-479e-99b6-
f5244a304918 in scope Local farm. At line:1 char:1 + Uninstall-SPFeature f6fa69a1-f5d2-479e-
99b6-f5244a304918 + ~~~~~~~~~~~~~~~~~~~~~~~~~~~~~~~~~~~~~~~~~~~~~~~~~~~~~~~~~~~~~~~ + CategoryInfo
: InvalidData: (Microsoft.Share...ninstallFeature:SPCmdletUninstallFeature) [Uninstall-
SPF eature], SPCmdletPipeBindException + FullyQualifiedErrorId : Microsoft.SharePoint.
PowerShell.SPCmdletUninstallFeature
```

The output that you receive when you run Get-SPFeature | ? { $_.Scope -eq $null } includes a column titled DisplayName. You could use the values in the display name on a case-by-case basis to delete the individual orphaned features by running the following:

```
$Orphanfeature = Get-SPFeature | ? { $_.DisplayName -eq "My_Orphaned_Feature_DisplayName" }
$Orphanfeature.Delete()
```

In that example, you would replace My_Orphaned_Feature_DisplayName with the actual display name of your orphaned feature.

If you do not want to delete them on a case-by-case basis, you could run this:

```
Get-SPFeature | ? { !$_.Scope } | % { $_.Delete() }
```

Or

```
Get-SPFeature | ? { $_.Scope -eq $null } | % { $_.Delete() }
```

After you have ran identified the orphaned features and cleaned them out of your farm, you should be able to run the upgrade-spcontentdatabase or psconfig.exe without the failure about the missing features that were due to the orphans.

Now that we have learned, a few command line commands used in troubleshooting different issues within the farm, let's learn how to work with the usage database.

WORKING THE USAGE LOGGING DATABASE

The purpose of this exercise is to find the usage database, change the retention period, and then change the size of the database by creating a new database that uses a larger page request definition. This assumes that you are seeing event ID 5586 and messages in your ULS logs similar to the following:

05/12/2017 09:30:04.78 OWSTIMER.EXE (0x1E24) 0x2C98 SharePoint Foundation Health i0m6 High Table RequestUsage_Partition12 has 444858368 bytes that has exceeded the maximum bytes 444858368

The first thing we need to do is identify the database being used by the usage application.

1. Open a SharePoint Management Shell and run the one-liner to find the database.

```
(Get-SPUsageApplication).UsageDatabase
```

After you have identified the database, you might want to determine its size.

2. Use the get member cmdlet to determine which property to dot source against the previous cmdlet.

```
(Get-SPUsageApplication).UsageDatabase | get-member
(Get-SPUsageApplication).UsageDatabase.disksizerequired
```

■ **Note** There is a cool thing you can do in PowerShell where you can convert data on the fly using this format: @{label="Some Name for your column"; expression = {$_.disksizerequired/1024/1024}}

---

3. Now, let us use this cool new feature to get the usage database, and then pipe it into a format table object that does that math conversion, converting bytes to megabytes.

```
(Get-SPUsageApplication).UsageDatabase | ft Name, @{Label="Size in MB";
Expression={$_.disksizerequired/1024/1024}}
```

The output will look similar to the following screenshot.

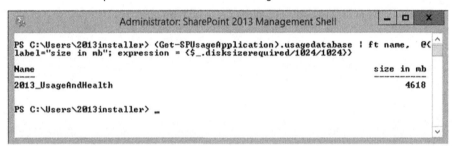

In SharePoint 2013 and 2016, the default maximum size that the usage database can grow to in bytes is 10TB. The following screenshot shows the default size of a SharePoint 2013 usage logging db.

```
Administrator: SharePoint 2013 Management Shell                    ▬ ▢ ✕

PS C:\Users\2013installer> $p = Get-SPUsageDefinition -Identity "page requests"
PS C:\Users\2013installer> $p.MaxTotalSizeInBytes
10000000000000
PS C:\Users\2013installer> _
```

Let us go ahead and decrease the size of the database that the usage application uses, by creating a new database after we set the page request definition to 12GB.

4. Open a management shell and type the commands needed to update the page
    requests definition and then set the usage application to use this new database.

```
$PageRequestsSize=Get-SPUsageDefinition -Identity "page requests"
$PageRequestsSize.MaxTotalSizeInBytes= 12000000000
$PageRequestsSize.update()

Get-spusageapplication | Set-SPUsageApplication -DatabaseServer
SharePointSQL -DatabaseName 2013_UsageLogging_12GB
```

5. After you have set usage application to use the new database, go ahead once more,
    verify that it is using the correct database, and then check the size.

```
(Get-SPUsageApplication).UsageDatabase
(Get-SPUsageApplication).UsageDatabase.disksizerequired
```

The following screenshot demonstrates the preceding steps. Notice that after the database has
decreased in size, it will not immediately be at its maximum size. Hopefully, the new maximum size
will be bigger than what is required of the farm for usage logging and will prevent event ID 5586 from
reoccurring.

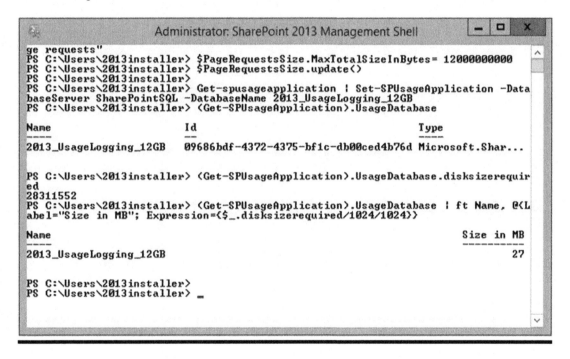

This chapter covered some useful cli commands that can be used to troubleshoot issues within the
operating system as they relate to services and accounts. We also visited some additional SQL topics.
    In Chapter 7, we're going to be getting into search using PowerShell and the GUI.

CHAPTER 7

■ ■ ■

Search Configuration and Troubleshooting

OK, before we go any further, I want to let you know that a better name for this chapter may have been, "What Scott Fawley, Brian Pendergrass, Jon Waite, and other former and current Microsoft guys once said," "Best of the Best Search Posts on the Internet," or "What they said and the way I see it," as this content is based on conversations, Internet posts, and videos that I've come across over the years, and some of my own findings. I'm just another SharePoint search dude with a message and I hope you enjoy the message and get something useful out of it.

At this point, we've hammered home the point that SharePoint expects things to be in certain places. I've mentioned avoiding manual changes. We discussed a few of the changes to the file system, IIS, some registry settings, and some of the SQL settings that SharePoint brings, and some that it needs you to make.

We emphasized knowing what the foundation of a good farm should look like. We talked about the use of least privileging and in a few places why this is best practice. We addressed the concept of avoiding any changes outside of the SharePoint GUI, via a SharePoint cmdlet, or via a wsp. Search is no different from any of those perspectives. There are numerous settings that SharePoint expects with regards to search.

Of all the services in SharePoint, Search is one of my greatest gray hair producers; maybe, as much as user profile sync service and distributed cache, but it's really a hard one to call. That being what it is, Search is an awesome SharePoint Service and, arguably, one of the most powerful!

When you boil search troubleshooting down, there are really two sides to the troubleshooting of search, the crawling side and the querying side. And, I'll explain what I've learned about that next.

In this example, crawling is everything from the crawler finding content, sending that document to the content processing component, which processes it and then sends it to the indexer and some of the information to the analytics component. After the Indexer gets the data from the content processor, the indexer inserts references to the content in its index on the file share and lets the crawl store database know where the data is located in the index, before telling the content processor to let the crawler know that the document is fully crawled.

The query side of search, in this example, is everything from when a user submits a query, to when the results of that query are returned. What happens is the web server, who knows not a thing about where the data is stored, gets the query from one of its search Web Parts. The web server knows about the search web service, searchservice.svc, and it sends a Windows Communication Foundation (WCF) request to the Query Processing component. In SharePoint 2010, the Search Query and Site Settings service did the lifting; but with the advent of SharePoint 2013, it is the Query Processing component that sends the request to the Index. The index lets the Query Processing component know what information to return to the user.

In this chapter, we're going to examine that process in greater detail. We'll check out some PowerShell to use in troubleshooting search and like previous chapters, we'll look at how search in configured OOB and with PowerShell. Then we'll modify a default search topology in SharePoint 2013. The steps learned in the section on modifying topology can be used in 2016, 2013, or 2010.

© Stacy Simpkins 2017
S. Simpkins, *Troubleshooting SharePoint*, https://doi.org/10.1007/978-1-4842-3138-8_7

We'll work with the index, finding it, resetting it, and blowing it away. We'll stop search and start search. We'll do the same for the node controller. We'll look at the crawler history and show a really awesome PowerShell script. And, we will discuss installing cumulative updates on a SharePoint farm where search is deployed with a topology that uses high availability.

When it comes to PowerShell, there will be plenty of it in this chapter. And, as I mentioned earlier, we'll look at a default install of search and compare that with an install that used PowerShell in order contrast the differences and set a firm foundation of what should be in place in a good build in regards to the Search Services Application. A search chapter would not be complete if it didn't discuss best practices; so, we'll get into best practices too.

Installing search using the GUI results in databases with GUIDs appended to the end of their names. When it comes to SharePoint Foundation, this is the only way search can be installed, as it is not possible to install search in foundation using PowerShell in a supported fashion. There are hacks out there that are seriously gifted programmers, who have created PowerShell scripts to fool SharePoint foundation into allowing a PowerShell install of Search on Foundation, but that is very dangerous territory to get into, as it is not supported.

When SharePoint databases, search or otherwise have GUIDS in their names, this makes for larger logs. Overtime. Because, as that GUID has to get written numerous times, extra space is required. The fact that GUIDS are not necessarily human-friendly adds to the already complex task of deciphering log data, by giving the eye an ugly GUID to look through and around. Another by-product of installing search with the Graphical User Interface (GUI) is that there is no means to stratify the topology. That's to say, all of the search components are automatically spun up on the server running Central Administration.

When you want to check the performance level of your search service application, you need to use PowerShell because the performance level is not available via the Central Administration site. The same is true if when determining where the index is located on disk. There are still things that can be done via the GUI where you can set the file types that search crawls and create, edit, and modify:

- Server name mappings

- Crawler impact rules

- Authoritative pages (former best bets)

- Result sources

- Query Rules

- Query Client Types and their Throttling tiers

- Managed Properties, Crawled Properties, and Categories (Search Schema)

- Query Suggestions

If you open your search service application, after it has been freshly created with PowerShell, it will look similar to Figure 7-1.

Figure 7-1. *Search Service Application: Search Administration*

There are many things in Figure 7-1 worth talking about; but one noteworthy thing is the default content access account. At first glance, it appears that that identity of the account being used to crawl through all the data and send it to the content processor is different that the identity used to run the search service, just judging from the name. In looking at services.msc, we see that indeed, that is the case, the services run under an account that has the logon as a service right, CONTOSO\2013Searchsvc, as shown in Figure 7-2.

Name		Description	Status	Startup Type	Log On As
Server		Supports fil...	Running	Automatic	Local System
SharePoint Administration		Performs ad...	Running	Automatic	Local System
SharePoint Search Host Controller		Performs h...	Running	Automatic	CONTOSO\2013Searchsvc
SharePoint Server Search 15		Administers...	Running	Manual	CONTOSO\2013Searchsvc
SharePoint Timer Service		Sends notifi...	Running	Automatic	CONTOSO\2013Farm
SharePoint Tracing Service		Manages tr...	Running	Automatic	CONTOSO\2013svcapps
SharePoint User Code Host		Executes us...	Running	Automatic	CONTOSO\2013svcapps
SharePoint VSS Writer		SharePoint ...		Manual	Local System
Shell Hardware Detection		Provides no...	Running	Automatic	Local System
Simple Mail Transfer Protocol (SMTP)		Transports ...	Running	Automatic	Local System
Smart Card		Manages ac...		Disabled	Local Service

Services (Local). Select an item to view its description. Extended / Standard

Figure 7-2. *Search service is not run by the crawler account*

This is important for least privileged search results. If search uses the same identity to run the service as it uses to crawl the content, then the results will not come back least privileged and they will allow users who should not be able to read unpublished drafts, to read those items in search results. It's a best practice for search to use, at a minimum, two accounts this way, one to crawl and one to run the services. When it comes to the actual crawling, it is a best practice to use one crawl account, as much as possible, unless you need to crawl sources that require any of the following:

- Anonymous access is used by the site

- Form credentials are needed to access content

- A cookie for crawling is needed to read

- A different content access account is needed to access, a file share for example

- A client certificate is needed to crawl content

If your solution has any of the aforementioned bullets, you can use a crawl rule to make that happen and if you're troubleshooting issues with content not coming back in search results from certain sources, checking that the crawl account or the account used by the crawl rule has proper access is the first step in that situation. The next step would be to open a browser with the appropriate account (e.g., the account used to access the content during the crawl) and then navigate to the content. If the content does not display in either step 1 or 2, then that is what needs to change. It might be an ACL entry or possibly a certificate that needs adding, or renewal.

When the crawler finds a document, spreadsheet, picture, list item, or something else that it deems worthy of being included in the index it records an entry in the ULS with event ID DS86. And then the crawler puts that content in a file share (e.g., \\srv\gthrsvc\network share). This is all good and everything, but it will probably never happen if the hidden SharePoint service named SSP Job Control service is not running, in fact, you might not see any entries at all if the SSP Job Control Service is not online.

This hidden SharePoint service runs on all servers that have the SharePoint binaries installed. And, it does not display on the services on server page, because it's hidden. You can verify that it is online using the following one-liner of PowerShell code:

```
(Get-SPFarm).Servers["<servername>"].ServiceInstances | where {$_.typename -eq "SSP Job
Control Service"}
```

Figure 7-3 demonstrates this one-liner in action. The <servername> is replaced by the actual server name.

Figure 7-3. *Hidden service is online*

There are seven hidden SharePoint Service instances in SharePoint 2013 and they are as follows:

- Information Management Policy Configuration Service

- SharePoint Server Search

- Microsoft SharePoint Foundation Usage

- Microsoft SharePoint Foundation Tracing

- SSP Job Control Service

- Portal Service

- Security Token Service

And, as I mentioned earlier, you won't see them on the services on server page, but they need to be online, not disabled, or offline, or whatever. If any of them are erroneously stopped, you'll notice issues and you'll want to get them started, or provisioned.

If for some reason the service is disabled, you'll need to get it online by provisioning it. If it is stuck on provisioning, you'll want to disable it, and then freshly provision it. You already know what to do to find the method needed to provision it; just pipe that one-liner to the get-member cmdlet or its alias, as shown here:

```
(Get-SPFarm).Servers["<servername>"].ServiceInstances | where {$_.typename -eq "SSP Job
Control Service"} | gm
```

And, you can see, there is a method called *provision*. Now all you would need to do is instantiate the object that the one-liner returned, into a variable, and then call the provision method against that object. In other words, you would run these lines to instantiate the variable named $svc and then call the provision().

```
$svc = (Get-SPFarm).Servers["<servername>"].ServiceInstances | where {$_.typename -eq "SSP
Job Control Service"}
$svc.provision()
```

■ **Note** When you're running commands to provision services, you either need to be on the machine where the service will run or have a remote PowerShell session opened to that machine.

Now that we're certain that search is writing events to the ULS logs, we could crack open the logs and find some event ID DS86, if we had already turned up the logging level. Make sure to increase logging to VerboseEX when troubleshooting issues, so that you can get the full picture, and then turn it back down to normal levels with clear-SPLogLevel, after you've finished.

After the crawler finds something worthy of indexing and has retrieved it and put it in the file share (\\src\gthrsvc\network share) and recorded the event ID DC86, an event ID AF7YN is entered in ULS when the crawler tells the content processing component about the document and hands it off to the content processing component for processing. The crawler says, "Hey, content processor. There's information for you to process. It's in that network share, OK? I'm going to record that I told you that in the logs with this AF7YN event ID."

Then the content processor says, "Roger that. I'll copy that content over from the file share so that I can find out what is inside of it, and I'll log an event ID AI3EF to the ULS stating that I copied the content over and started processing the document." During this process, the content processing component will get all the key words and content out of the document in preparation to write them into the index. When the content processor writes the data into the index, the content processor writes an event ID AJPND into the ULS as the words are processed and written into the index by the content processor.

At this point, the index lets the content processor and the crawler know to the status of the indexing. The index tells the crawler what happened with the document and an event ID E5G1 is written to the ULS logs. This event tells the outcome of the indexing when the content processor and the crawler make note in the crawl store, as to how things indexed and where to find that information.

The correlation IDs that are generated for crawling portion of search are two-fold. That is, one correlation ID is generated for the Crawling and Gathering and one is generated for the Feeding and Processing. Event IDs DS86, AF7YN, and E5G1 fall under the Crawling and Gathering and event IDs AI3EF and AJPND fall under the feeding and processing. Together they comprise the Event IDs that you will want to filter on when troubleshooting Search.

There are key parts of troubleshooting this process of getting content into the search results that do not have correlation IDs. Those key parts can be located by identifying the document ID number. After you have the document ID number and the two correlations, you can sort your ULS output by those values, accordingly. The way you would do that is:

- Turn up logging level and perform a crawl

- Query your ULS for the 5 event IDs DS86, AF7YN, E5G1, AI3EF, and AJPND

- Identify the two correlation IDs

- Find a document ID

- Query your ULS for the two correlation IDs and the Document ID

The visual representation of the first part of the process is shown in Figure 7-4 where the logging level has already been turned up and a crawl has been performed. In Figure 7-4, we see the filter that is used in ULS Viewer for the search event IDs.

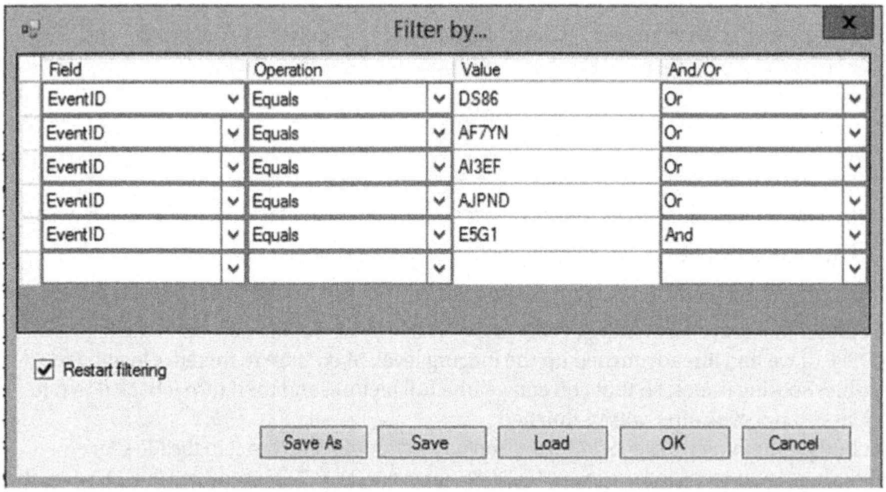

Figure 7-4. *Search event IDs in a ULS filter*

A good practice is to save this filter. We'll discuss how that is done in Chapter 9 when we go into more depth on using the ULS Viewer. After the results come back, you need to find the correlation ID for both sides of the process for a given document. You could read through the messages looking for a document ID, or you could run another query on your ULS log that was gathered while logging was capturing VerboseEX.

And, that query you would run would include the following two lines, assuming you were looking for a document with Document ID 221. You can find the document ID (number 221 in this example) inside of Central Admin, in the crawl log inside the search service application:

- strDocID = ssic://221

- Submitting document: id=221

The results will come back with two correlation IDs. At this point, look for event ID AJPND or AI3EF and note the correlation ID. Take note of the other correlation ID, as well. Now that you have the two correlation IDs and the document ID you can create your filter that will give you the play by play of the crawling and gathering, as well as the feeding and processing. Figure 7-5 shows an example of this filter.

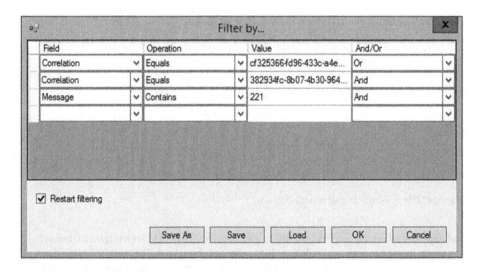

Figure 7-5. *Getting a document into the index*

Recall that after the index has completed processing the document, it will register the E5G1, which means the URL for the content has been written to the MSSCrawlURL table inside the CrawlStore DB. Here's an example of an E5G1 entry:

```
06/19/2017 13:17:53.52  mssearch.exe (0x0F00)   0x70D0   SharePoint Server
Search        Crawler:Gatherer Plugin e5g1   VerboseEx        CGatherer::CommitTransaction
succeeded CrawlID 857, DocID 221               [gatherobj.cxx:8832]  search\native\
gather\server\gatherobj.cxx      cf325366-fd96-433c-a4e7-c7683692e7bc
```

Looking at search this way will let you see things that you cannot see from the GUI, or from PowerShell. After you have the two correlation IDs that correspond to your document ID, you can trace the document or list item all the way from when it is first discovered until the indexer is finished processing it. This way you know it is in the index and should be available to users who have permission to view it.

When you look at the results of the correlation ID and doc ID filter, you'll notice that the analytics component is getting information pumped into it. If for some reason you don't see that, change the filter to use two "or's" and then the Message that contains the doc ID number, as shown in Figure 7-6. Depending on the doc ID, you might get some information related to other documents when sorting this way. Keep that in mind.

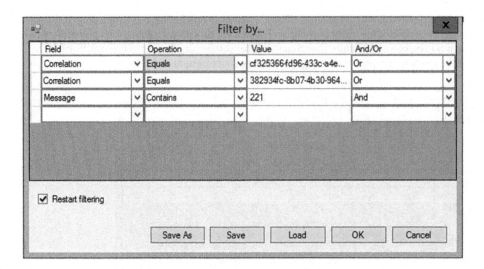

Figure 7-6. *Low document IDs generate bogus results this way*

Let's look at what happens when a user creates a query and submits it to the search engine. The user enters in some search terms in the browser and submits this to the web front end. The web front end doesn't have a clue on how to process a search query. But, the search service application knows how to process a query and the web server knows about the search service's endpoints and how to contact the search service application using a WCF send request. The web application has a service connection to the search service application. In Figure 7-7, you can see where this is configurable at the web application level. You can verify that the search service application proxy is connected to the web application by looking at the service connections on the manage web application page.

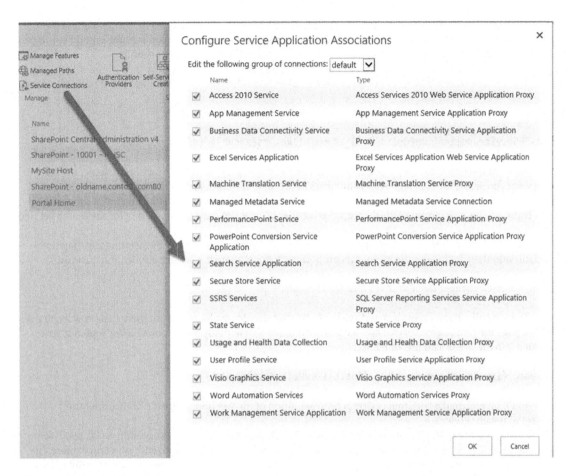

Figure 7-7. *Service Connections*

You could configure a custom group of service connections for any given web application at this page if you wanted. You can also configure service application association to web application's, by clicking Application Management, configure service application associations, and then clicking a web application and changing it from the default application proxy group to a custom group that you create. The main takeaway here is that these are the places in Central Administration to determine if you should see a service connection in IIS.

Once you know that the service application proxy exists, you can run the PowerShell to determine its GUID, and can trace it into the IIS application pool. You also know how to troubleshoot if the web service is accessible to SharePoint. We'll look at this as a refresher now and then we will continue talking about search. To track the search service application proxy to its search service application, you can run this:

```
Get-SPServiceApplicationProxy | ? {$_.typename -like "search*"} | ft name,
serviceendpointuri -wrap
```

And the output will show you the Service endpoint URI, which is traceable to the virtual path of the service application. If you expand the application pool that the service application is represented by, you can see this virtual path. The service application pool can be found by opening IIS or running

```
Get-SPServiceApplication | ? {$_.typename -like "search*"} | ft name, applicationPool -wrap
```

Knowing the application pool name, you can query PowerShell, as follows:

```
Get-SPServiceApplicationPool | ? {$_.name -like "*search*"} | ft name, id
```

After completing these steps, you have obtained the visual proof from the SharePoint object model, that what you see in IIS, is in fact what your farm's object model thinks, is the correct information. If you open application pools in IIS and find the search service application pool. Now that you know the number, you'll also see the two virtual paths that represent endpoints for the search service, one for the search service application and one for the search administrative controller.

You can double or triple check this against your search service application by instantiating that into a variable and then calling out the endpoints properties. To instantiate the service application, just run

```
$ssa = Get-SPEnterpriseSearchServiceApplication
```

Then to call out the endpoints and see the URI's that should resolve if you put them in a browser, to the WSDL page for your search service applications endpoints that actually are responsible for search queries making it to the index, run this one liner:

```
Foreach ($pt in $ssa.endpoints) {$pt.ListenUris.AbsoluteUri}
```

You'll be returned a URL that is virtual representation of the site housed inside of IIS under the SharePoint web services.

Finally, if you expand the SharePoint Web services IIS site, and as long as everything is OK, you'll see that the Search Service endpoints are represented. Right-click the search service endpoint and explore the file system to see that the SearchService.svc file date is what it should be, assuming it wasn't modified by a cumulative update.

So, now that we've identified that search is wired up in IIS and that this agrees with what is in the farm for search, we know about the plumbing that the web server uses when a query is input. The SharePoint web server sends the query in the form of a WCF send request to the SearchService.svc via the Search Query and Site Settings (SQSS) service. When this happens, you'll see the WCF Send Request listed in the ULS and it will be headed to SearchService.svc. In SharePoint 2010, the Search Query and Site Settings service was responsible for the security trimming and making the query; however, in SharePoint 2013 the SQSS is more less a middleman that routes the query to the Query Processing Component.

The SQSS takes the WCF send request and sends it to the Query Processing Components Net.TCP endpoint named IMSQueryInternal and calls this a Juno Send Request. In the ULS, you'll see this listed as JunoSendRequest. From here, the query processor will call up the index for the information requested and this call is called a Mars Lookup Operator. Again, in ULS it will be found using MarsLookupOperator. And, the best part about all of this is that there is a single correlation ID associated with all of this activity. This is why Merge-SPLogFile is your buddy when it comes to correlation ID received when trying to run a search. In other words, if you enter some query terms into search, and then when you submit the search, you get a "Sorry, something went wrong" grab that correlation and follow it through the process.

If there are breakdowns in this process, make sure that the ports for search are open. The various servers within the farm need to all be able to communicate with each other across the port used by Windows Communication Framework in order for the WCF send requests and for the requests that use Net.TCP to happen, and that port is port number 808. The other ports involved in search are ports 16500 through 16519 for the search indexer, and then the two ports used by SharePoint communication, 32843 and 32844. If any of these ports are closed, search will have issues.

If you are seeing really slow queries, you should check that TCP Chimney and Task Offload are disabled. To find the status of these two, you run the following commands from a command line:

```
Netsh int tcp show global  | findstr Chimney
Netsh int tcp show global  | findstr "Task Offload"
```

To set them both to disabled, just run:

```
Netsh int tcp set global chimney=disabled
```

"The TCP Chimney Offload is a networking technology that helps transfer the workload from the CPU to a network adapter during network data transfer." – TechNet

If you're having trouble with queries taking a long time, query your ULS for "ExecuteQuery timings" and it will return back metrics about each of the various steps involved with getting data out of the index. This will give you more insight into the problem. Maybe your index is corrupted or possibly the server it is running on does not have enough resources to run at the performance level that the search service application is set to run. Querying ULS for "EndPointFailure" will quickly show you information about problems with any components in your search topology that are having trouble.

When it comes to the SQSS service, you will find it on all your SharePoint servers' services on server page. It should only be running or started on servers that house the query processing component. And if you find it running on other servers that are not running the query processing component, you should unprovision it, as search handles starting this and it should not be started manually, unless troubleshooting the service on a server running the query processing component. This is a best practice.

When it comes to search getting messed up, I'd wager that the most common occurrence is when someone modifies an alternate access mapping incorrectly and/or when the start address for search is set to a zone other than the default zone. Another way to say that is, the Local SharePoint Sites content source, start address, is set to crawl a URL in either the intranet, Internet, custom, or extranet zone, and not set to crawl the URL for the default zone. What happens here is the crawler comes in and it indexes the non-default zone, which in this example we'll refer to as Stacy's Mom, and then it records everything it finds inside of and underneath the Stacy's mom URL. After the crawler finishes, it has found all sorts of URLs in the index that start with Stacy's mom; for example:

- Stacysmom.com/records

- Stacysmom.com/songs

- Stacysmom.com/favoritefoods

Let's also pretend that the default zone is called JT. And remember Stacy's mom is just an extended zone off the default zone JT. Another way to say that is Stacy's Mom is an extension of JT. The JT zone is not inside of Stacy's Mom, but Stacy's Mom and JT both lead users to the same data. The default zone, JT, is the zone that Stacy's Mom was extended off of when she was created. In this case it was to use forms based authentication.

Now let's assume Joe user navigates to one of the JT sites and issues a query for hot dogs, for example, which is one of Stacy's Mom's favorite foods. And, is one of JT's favorite foods, as well. The result equals nothing returned hot dogs. This isn't because JT doesn't like a hot dog every now and again, because he loves hot dogs. The same could be said for Stacy's Mom and there are hot dog sites galore under both URLS.

The user knows this, so he navigates to one of the sites inside stacysmom.com and searches and also turns up nothing. The reason for this is that the query processor takes the query submission, and even though it was issued from either site, it converts the non-default zone, Stacy's mom, portion of the URL to JT. It does this because the Query processor knows that JT is the default site and that there is (insert sarcasm) no way that the start address would not use a non-default zone to crawl. In other words, SharePoint expects the start address for search to be the default zone URL. SharePoint assumes that the default zone was used, so it knows that it needs to convert queries coming from non-default zones to find stuff in the index.

Since the index is full of Stacy's mom URL's nothing is found when it looks for URL's that start with JT, because remember the crawler didn't crawl JT, it crawled Stacy's mom. And, when the start address is other than the default zone, the crawler does not map the alternate access mappings when constructing the index.

The same thing is true when the user submits the query from the JT site, the index is searched for URLs starting with JT, the default zone in this example, but because the crawler started at Stacy's Mom, in won't find JT inside Stacy's Mom, because Stacy's Mom is not the default zone, JT is the default zone; but JT wasn't crawled, Stacy's Mom was crawled and the crawler didn't map the alternate access mappings because Stacy's mom is not the default zone. This is why you always crawl the default zone. The crawler when crawling the default zone is smart enough to know about the other zones that are extended off the default zone and when it creates the index, it will map the extended zones based on the alternate access mappings. The query processor also expects this behavior and that is why it converts the URL to the default zone before searching through the index, since it expects everything to spider off the default zone.

Avoid trying to band aid this situation using some server name mappings and map JT to Stacy's Mom. This will only make the matter worse. The correct method to get all search results to work correctly, and, the first place to look when troubleshooting search when results are not coming back in queries, is to determine what the default zone should be and then make sure that that is, indeed, the start address in the search service application content sources. If you're having trouble with Office web apps not giving document previews on hover panel, check that you are not a victim of server name mappings.

If you find that this has happened to you, get everything set the way you want it, such as the names of the default sites correct for the default zones. Validate that the search account can open them in the browser. Make sure the start addresses in the search service application are correctly using the default zones sites. Reset the index and then perform a full crawl.

There are other reasons to perform a full crawl besides doing one immediately after an index reset. You want to perform a full crawl for content sources that have never been crawled, when you've added crawl rules, or as previously mentioned, when repairing a corrupted index. If you change the default crawl account or if you're experiencing numerous incremental crawl failures, then you will want to perform full crawls, in both of these cases, as well. The system will automatically force a full crawl when any of the following happen:

- A search administrator stops a crawl

- A content database gets restored or is detached and reattached

- A full crawl of the site was never performed from this SSA

- The change log is empty for the addresses being crawled

Other reasons that you'll want to manually kick off full crawls include:

- Immediately after cumulative updates are installed

- After adding new managed properties and you want it to take effect immediately

- You're working with a WSS 3.0 or Moss 2007 SharePoint and want to reindex aspx pages

When your crawl appears to be taking an abnormally long time to complete, it might be stuck. When this happens, there is a SQL query that you can run to help you determine if the issue is related to the crawl component or if it is related to the crawl database. Now, remember what I said about reading directly from your SharePoint databases, and be good admins and make a backup of the search admin database that you can restore somewhere else to query against it.

Once you've found the Search Admin database to query against it, run the following query to find any crawls that are not failed, completed, or stopped.

```
SELECT
        hist.CrawlId, hist.CrawlType, hist.ContentSourceId, hist.StartTime, hist.Status,
        hist.SubStatus, hist.Request, ccState.ComponentID, ccState.Status as ccStatus,
        ccState.SuspendedCount
FROM [SEARCHDBNAME].[dbo][MSSCrawlHistory] AS hist WITH (nolock)
INNER JOIN
        [SEARCHDBNAME].[dbo].[MSSCrawlComponentsState] AS ccState
        ON hist.CrawlId = ccState.CrawlID
WHERE hist.Status Not In (5,11,12)
And hist.crawlId > 2
```

If you have a crawl currently underway, the results of running the preceding SQL query will result in something like that shown in Figure 7-8.

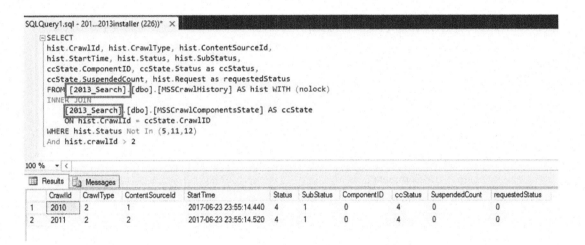

Figure 7-8. *What is crawl doing?*

This is something that you would do only in the most extreme troubleshooting situations and is not something that you would want to do on a regular basis as it could lead to an unsupported state. That is why I mentioned that a backup of the database would be better suited to run the query. That being said, I just ran it against my lab farm and the earth is still rotating around the sun. All is well.

The best part of these results is the substatus and what this means. Table 7-1 is a cheat sheet for translating what the status and substatus represent.

Table 7-1. *Crawler status matrix*

Status	Sub-Status	This combination means ...	Crawl Component	Database Issue
0	0	New crawl, requesting start		X
1	1	Starting, Add Start Address(es)		X
1	2	Starting, waiting on crawl components	X	
4	1	Crawling		
4	2	Crawling, Unvisited to Queue		
4	3	Crawling, Delete Unvisited		X
4	4	Crawling, Wait for All Databases		X
5	0	Failed to start (e.g., Another Crawl is already running)		
7		Resuming		
8	1	Pausing, Waiting on Crawl Components to Pause	X	
8	2	Pausing, Complete Pause		X
9		Paused		
11	0	Completed		
12		Stopped		
13	1	Stopping, Waiting on Crawl Component(s) to Stop	X	
13	2	Stopping, Complete Stop		X
14	1	Completing, Waiting on Crawl Components to Complete	X	
14	2	Completing		X
14	4	Completing, Get Deletes Pending		X

Table 7-1 is taken from a blog post by Brian Pendergrass at `https://blogs.msdn.microsoft.com/sharepoint_strategery/2014/03/06/cheat-sheet-finding-the-real-crawl-state/`.

▪ **Note** There is a good YouTube video about this at `https://www.youtube.com/watch?v=JxYMmCLhazY`.

Table 7-1 is very handy when a crawl is taking a much longer than the normal time to complete and the ULS logs do not show that it is still in the process of gathering data. In other words you're not seeing DS86 and AF7YN event IDs about new content and the Content processor is also fairly silent, that is you're not seeing AI3EF, AJPND, or E5G1 event IDs, yet the crawler is still showing crawling. This is why you should have a rough idea on the number of items that are in your corpus. Another way to say that is, know the size of your index and about how long your crawls normally require to complete. Knowing your environment will help you in troubleshooting.

■ **Note** When you start seeing issues that point to the database being the bottleneck, you should check for full transaction logs, non-contiguous white space, or maybe a lack of disk space for SQL.

This PowerShell will give you a very cool report in a power-grid that you can use to analyze your crawls. It allows you to sort based on type of crawl and duration, among other things. Just copy this code that Stephen Swinney shared with me, and I'm now sharing with you, into a PowerShell window and hit enter, or if you want to be extra fancy you could put it into a ps1 and call the file:

```
$numberOfResults = 1000
$contentSourceName = "Local SharePoint Sites"

[System.Reflection.Assembly]::LoadWithPartialName("Microsoft.Office.Server.Search.
Administration")

$searchServiceApplication = Get-SPEnterpriseSearchServiceApplication
$contentSources = Get-SPEnterpriseSearchCrawlContentSource -SearchApplication
$searchServiceApplication
$contentSource = $contentSources | ? { $_.Name -eq $contentSourceName }

$crawlLog = new-object Microsoft.Office.Server.Search.Administration.CrawlLog($searchService
Application)
$crawlHistory = $crawlLog.GetCrawlHistory($numberOfResults, $contentSource.Id)
$crawlHistory.Columns.Add("CrawlTypeName", [String]::Empty.GetType()) | Out-Null

# Label the crawl type
$labeledCrawlHistory = $crawlHistory | % {
$_.CrawlTypeName = [Microsoft.Office.Server.Search.Administration.
CrawlType]::Parse([Microsoft.Office.Server.Search.Administration.CrawlType], $_.CrawlType).
ToString()
return $_
}

$labeledCrawlHistory | Out-GridView
```

You can modify the $numberOfResults variable or the $ContentSourceName variable to your, SharePoint, heart's content. When reading the information, a Delete crawl has a crawl type number of 6, an incremental as a crawl type number of 2, and a full crawl has a crawl type number of 1 and you can see the type of crawl by scrolling to the right of the output to the crawl type names column is located. Figure 7-9 shows the ouput.

ContentSourceID	ContentSourceName	CrawlStartTime	CrawlEndTime	CrawlDuration	CrawlType	Successes	Warnings	Errors	TopLevelErrors	Deletes	NotModified	SecurityUpdates
1	Local SharePoint sites	6/23/2017 11:55:14 PM	6/24/2017 12:59:36 AM	01:04:22.3000000	2	16	0	1	0	0	0	0
1	Local SharePoint sites	6/23/2017 9:55:13 PM	6/23/2017 10:59:36 PM	01:04:22.1600000	2	17	0	1	0	0	0	0
1	Local SharePoint sites	6/23/2017 7:55:15 PM	6/23/2017 8:59:14 PM	01:03:59.7000000	2	16	0	1	0	0	0	0
1	Local SharePoint sites	6/23/2017 6:55:13 PM	6/23/2017 6:56:46 PM	00:01:32.3540000	2	17	0	1	0	0	0	0
1	Local SharePoint sites	6/23/2017 4:55:14 PM	6/23/2017 5:59:17 PM	01:04:03.2830000	2	16	0	1	0	0	0	0
1	Local SharePoint sites	6/23/2017 3:55:16 PM	6/23/2017 3:55:46 PM	00:00:30.2900000	2	16	0	1	0	0	0	0
1	Local SharePoint sites	6/23/2017 2:55:13 PM	6/23/2017 2:55:44 PM	00:00:30.3070000	2	16	0	1	0	0	0	0
1	Local SharePoint sites	6/23/2017 1:55:15 PM	6/23/2017 1:56:39 PM	00:01:24.4940000	2	17	0	1	0	0	0	0
1	Local SharePoint sites	6/23/2017 12:56:00 PM	6/23/2017 12:57:41 PM	00:01:40.3400000	2	17	0	1	0	0	0	0
1	Local SharePoint sites	6/23/2017 11:55:58 AM	6/23/2017 11:56:40 AM	00:00:42.3630000	2	16	0	1	0	0	0	0
1	Local SharePoint sites	6/23/2017 10:55:59 AM	6/23/2017 10:58:05 AM	00:02:06.5170000	2	17	0	1	0	0	0	0
1	Local SharePoint sites	6/23/2017 9:55:59 AM	6/23/2017 9:57:07 AM	00:01:08.4730000	2	16	0	1	0	0	0	0
1	Local SharePoint sites	6/23/2017 8:56:00 AM	6/23/2017 8:59:23 AM	00:03:22.7900000	2	15	0	2	1	0	0	0

Figure 7-9. A power grid output

This is useful when you want to quickly determine the normal time for your crawls. Also, there's no reason you couldn't pipe the content out to a file and then look at it in Excel. I'd recommend using export-csv and then opening it in Excel, if you don't find the power grid useful or if you want a historical report outside of SharePoint.

Now that you know if a crawl should be finished from looking at the crawl log history, you have a better idea on how to troubleshoot issues. It's also important to have a good understanding of what is happening inside the crawl and other settings that might be impacting your issue. You can determine this by looking at crawler impact rules, crawl rules, content sources, order of crawls, the search performance level, and the built in crawl health reports. There are also reports for the other side of search, aka query health reports and usage reports.

When designing your crawl, you'll make sure to include the start addresses for the default zones of your web applications in the local SharePoint sites content source. You'll also create a People content source that crawls the MySite host URL with http://MysiteHostURL or https://mysitehostURL, depending on how you've set up your sites. You'll include the sps3://mysitehostURL or sps3s://mysitehostURL as one of the start addresses for the People content source, as well. After you get the content source set and before you make your first crawl of the people source, make sure to set the permission on the User Profile service application so that the crawl account has "**Retrieve people data for search crawlers**" checked. Then, you'll schedule the crawls so that the people content source is crawled, and finishes **at least two hours before** the Local SharePoint Sites content source crawl starts. This ensures that result blocks for documents are accurate and inclusive.

If you crawl user profiles after or during the same time as the local SharePoint sites content source the search system will not be able to standardize user names, as well as it would have if you had crawled the people content first. In other words, if you crawl people first and wait a couple hours after the crawl finishes before crawling the local SharePoint sites, then documents in the local SharePoint sites that are authored by A. Finkelstein, Alfred Finkelstein, and AFinkel will all show up in the same result block and will not appear as authored by different people, because the people content source will have standardized AFinkel, A. Finkelstein, and Alfred Finkelstein.

If you have users that are complaining about not seeing the correct results in search and you've already verified that they have at least read permissions for the items, you should check to make sure that there is a start address for the web application that those items are located inside of and that the crawler can access the items. After or before that assuming you know the start addresses in your content sources and that they are all default zones, check that there isn't a crawl rule that is excluding the content and that the library or list is being indexed. If all of those things are true, find the document ID for the document in the crawl log and then crack open the ULS Viewer and perform a crawl while watching the logs for that document ID by looking at the five event IDs and the string for the document, as I mentioned earlier. Once you've found the two correlation IDs you'll be able to determine if the document is making it into the index. The crawl log history in Central Admin will also give you information that you can use to make this determination, unless there are issues.

Sometimes crawl rules accidentally exclude documents, so if you've already verified that, and you can see that the item is making it into the index, it might be that your users are just looking for crawls to happen more frequently. Maybe this content is suitable for a content source that uses the continuous crawl, or maybe you can get away with increasing the frequency of the incremental crawl for the start address that this content lay under. Keep in mind that content sources that use the continuous crawl cannot be given priority over incremental crawls and that by default continuous crawls occur every 15 minutes. Another point to keep in mind if you have continuous crawls going for the location where this content is stored is that continuous crawls do not process a retry on any items that have failed to make it into the index more than three times. And, every 4 hours there is an incremental crawl that automatically runs on content sources that have continuous crawl selected, to clean up and then recrawl any items that had returned errors. This is yet another reason to use the ULS Viewer in troubleshooting.

When it comes to changes to content and extra work for your crawler, one thing you can do is to use Active Directory security groups to provide access to SharePoint content vs. directly adding user accounts to SharePoint groups or SharePoint objects. The reason is that when you use Active Directory users directly to provide access, every time you remove a user, the crawler has to perform a "security only" crawl across all content. This can get really expensive from a resource point of view; whereas **if you use Active Directory groups, SharePoint doesn't see the changes to those groups as a reason to perform a security only crawl**. If you remove an Active Directory group from a SharePoint group or SharePoint Object, then a security only crawl will occur.

Using content sources and crawl schedules to increase crawler performance is definitely something to take into account when troubleshooting how well your crawl is performing. Consider things like the size of the data corpus being crawled; for example, the size of the site collection. Even though you can find the database size via (get-spcontentdatabase <name of database>).disksizerequired, that doesn't tell you how much space a particular site collection encompasses, unless only one site collection is stored inside of the database. So, here's a pretty cool couple of lines of PowerShell to tell you how much space a site collection encompasses. Run this from a SharePoint Management Shell:

```
$site = get-spsite <URL to site>
$site.usage.storage / 1MB
```

You'll also want to take into account the power of the server, or servers, handing the crawling, content processing, and indexing and if possible use dedicated servers for some of these roles. We'll talk more about topologies a little later on. If you find some content that changes frequently, you might want to break that content out into its own content source and crawl it continuously. Or, maybe you just want to use a content source with an incremental crawl that has a higher priority and frequency of no lower than 5 minutes. I also would not recommend changing the continuous crawl to lower than 5 minutes from its default of 15 minutes. Here is one line of code that you can use to set the interval to 5 minutes

```
(Get-SPEnterpriseSearchSrviceApplication).SetProperty("ContinuousCrawlInterval",<TimeInMinutes>)
```

In other words,

```
(Get-SPEnterpriseSearchSrviceApplication).SetProperty("ContinuousCrawlInterval",5)
```

The shorter you make the interval, the greater the resource demand, and then when considering this you'll also want to know the performance level of your search service. By default, the Search Service Application performance level is set to reduced. There are three settings for search performance:

- Reduced
- Partly Reduced
- Maximum

Table 7-2 lists out the three different levels and what they mean

Table 7-2. *Search Performance levels*

Level	Total number of threads
Reduced	same number of threads as there is processors (e.g., 4 processors, 4 threads)
Partly Reduced	4 times the number of processors (e.g., 4 processors, 16 threads)
Maximum	16 times the number of processors (e.g., 4 processors, 64 threads)

If your search starts having trouble, it may be that the amount of change happening in the environment and the performance level are not a good match, or maybe a crawler impact rule was created by a junior admin that selects a bunch of documents at a time from a site that has a high frequency of change. Sometimes, decreasing the performance has the desired affect and sometimes increasing the performance level is what you're after. You'll just have to monitor the resources on the servers in your search infrastructure. Here is how to change to check the performance level:

```
Get-SPEnterpriseSearchService
```

After you run this command, you'll be presented the output shown in Figure 7-10.

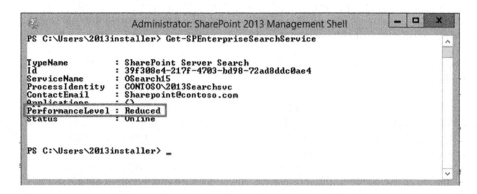

Figure 7-10. *Default level is Reduced*

Remember by increasing the performance level you will give search more threads on your processor when it runs and this may result in needing to increase the memory on your server, as the processor may need additional memory to run at the increased search performance level effectively.

Speaking of running effectively, do not crawl irrelevant content and complex URL's. What you'll find is that by not crawling complex URL's your index will be much cleaner. Whereas, if you crawl complex URLs (include "?") your crawl database will fill up with redundant links and in turn your index will be erroneously bloated. You can use crawl rules to exclude the irrelevant content.

Microsoft recommends that for indexes that are 10 million items or less that the drive size should be 500GB. This size will vary depending on the types of things being indexed.

In a TechNet post, Microsoft goes into detail about their size recommendations and topologies for various search farms, small, medium, and large (https://technet.microsoft.com/en-us/library/dn727116.aspx). You need to be prepared to grow your storage as users start to pump more data into your farm. And as you get more data in your farm, you'll want to increase the number of content processing components to shorten your crawl window. It is a balancing act and you'll need to modify the search topology as you go.

One way to minimize the impact that crawling has on user experience is to have the crawl server crawl itself or crawl a server or servers that are not used to serve user requests for pages. Another way to think of that is that the application server that runs the crawler, or other search roles, maybe all of the search roles, does not crawl the server that end users use when requesting a page; since it is an application server and not a web front end. It is not uncommon to see the index component and the query processing component on the web front-end server and the search administration, crawler, and content processing components on the application server, in a farm with one application server, one web front-end server, and one database server.

If you're having performance issues related to crawling where the response time is slow from the server then it's time to give that server more power. Increase the CPU, RAM, and give it faster disks. When your crawl is taking a long time to process the content, you can increase the performance level and provide more CPU's to the actual servers that are running the content processing components. If you only have one content processor, you can add more, but you will find that the balancing act comes into play here too, since the indexing component or components have to be beefy enough to handle all the content being processed and sent to them, while at the same time taking requests from the query processing components for user requests. In the case of slow processing by your index components, you should add I/O resources to these servers.

Before you make changes to your server's resources, you should consider adding more search components to existing servers, if possible. So to scale out your topology, you'll need to know the topology layout. And, if you're not sure of your search topology, you can find this in Central Administration in the search service application or you can run this PowerShell to find the topology:

```
$ssa = Get-SPServiceApplication –Name "Search Service Application" $active = Get-
SPEnterpriseSearchTopology -SearchApplication $ssa -Active
Get-SPEnterpriseSearchComponent -SearchTopology $active
```

This will give you the active search components in your SharePoint Object Model's search topology and it will give you each component's name, server name, and the associated GUIDs for each component. To see a neater view of this information, run the following PowerShell after you've instantiated the search service application into the $ssa variable:

```
get-spenterprisesearchstatus -SearchApplication $ssa -Detailed -Text
```

If you get an error, make sure that when you run this line, that you're using the correct name:

```
$ssa = Get-SPServiceApplication –Name "Search Service Application"
```

The name of your search service application is what you see when you look at manage service applications. And, if you're looking for the location of your index on disk, you can run this command:

```
(Get-SPEnterpriseSearchServiceInstance).components
```

Don't be alarmed if you see two locations. This means that when SharePoint was installed, the option to move some of the files off the operating system drive was chosen, and when it comes to the search index, some of the files remain no matter which option you chose. In my opinion this is one of those just because you can doesn't mean you necessarily have too things. SharePoint will run fine if you leave the default locations alone when installing the binaries; but, if you want the OS drive to have less writing, move the stuff you can to another drive.

Remember if the Application Server Administrative Service timer job is not working, all hope is lost. This job has to work for SharePoint to work and it fires every minute. So, if you look at services.msc and see that the SharePoint Timer is running, make sure that the service it depends heavily on is also running. Without the SSP Job Control Service online, all sorts of issues abound that do not necessarily indicate the SSP Job Control Service as the driver. Check the SSP job control service with this PowerShell, as explained earlier:

```
(Get-SPFarm).Servers["<servername>"].ServiceInstances | where {$_.typename -eq "SSP Job
Control Service"}
```

Normally, this service will never stop, but it is easy to accidentally stop it with some PowerShell script. And if that should happen, just instantiate it into a variable and provision it, or wrap all of that one line with parenthesis and call the provision method, like this:

```
((Get-SPFarm).Servers["<servername>"].ServiceInstances | where {$_.typename -eq "SSP Job
Control Service"}).Provision()
```

If you get some dorked message about can't call Provision with zero (0) arguments, as I've seen sometimes, you can run it like this:

```
((Get-SPFarm).Servers["<servername>"].ServiceInstances | where {$_.typename -eq "SSP Job
Control Service"}).Provision($true)
```

I've only seen that happen, where the PowerShell barks about the provision method not having arguments, when working with distributed cache, but thought I'd mention it here in any event and in case it was encountered in your farm.

The crawl health reports in Central Administration are very handy for identifying various components that might be contributing to poor search performance. You can get information about Crawl Rates, Latency, Freshness, CPU and Memory Load, Content processing Activity, Crawl queue, and continuous crawl. These reports can be instrumental in helping diagnose search related issues and often give you a good idea of which servers might need more resources.

From looking at these reports and from monitoring the search process you may decide to scale out the search topology. Make sure that no crawl is taking place when you get ready to change the topology of your farm. The high-level process of changing the search topology is different depending on whether you have items in your index. If your index is relatively small, or if you don't mind recrawling the data corpus, you may want to consider resetting the index before changing your search topology.

If you're working with a search topology with an empty index these are the high level steps to change a search topology:

- Make sure no crawls are underway

- Start the search service instance on every server that will be part of the new topology

- Create a new empty search topology

- Add the search components to the new search topology

- Activate the new topology

- Verify that the new topology is active

- Get rid of the inactive components (optional, but recommended)

Here's the PowerShell Scott Fawley uses to make this happen, assuming you've already verified that no crawls are occurring.

```
# Load SharePoint Admin Shell
Add-PSSnapin Microsoft.SharePoint.PowerShell -EA 0


 # Start the search service instance on every server that will be part of the new topology
$HOSTA = GET-SPENTERPRISESEARCHSERVICEINSTANCE -IDENTITY "sfawley-2013"
$HOSTB = GET-SPENTERPRISESEARCHSERVICEINSTANCE -IDENTITY "sfawley-2013-ap"
START-SPENTERPRISESEARCHSERVICEINSTANCE -IDENTITY $HOSTA
START-SPENTERPRISESEARCHSERVICEINSTANCE -IDENTITY $HOSTB


#Wait until all servers show that the service is online by running a
GET-SPENTERPRISESEARCHSERVICEINSTANCE -IDENTITY "<servername>"


$host1 = "sfawley-2013"
$host2 = "sfawley-2013-ap"


 # Create a new empty search topology
$SSA = GET-SPENTERPRISESEARCHSERVICEAPPLICATION
$Clone = NEW-SPENTERPRISESEARCHTOPOLOGY -SEARCHAPPLICATION $SSA


 # Add the new components
New-SPEnterpriseSearchAdminComponent –SearchTopology $clone -SearchServiceInstance $host1
New-SPEnterpriseSearchContentProcessingComponent –SearchTopology $clone
-SearchServiceInstance $host2
New-SPEnterpriseSearchAnalyticsProcessingComponent –SearchTopology $clone
-SearchServiceInstance $host2
New-SPEnterpriseSearchCrawlComponent –SearchTopology $clone -SearchServiceInstance $host2
New-SPEnterpriseSearchIndexComponent –SearchTopology $clone -SearchServiceInstance $host1
-RootDirectory "D:\SharePointIndex\Partition 0"
New-SPEnterpriseSearchIndexComponent –SearchTopology $clone -SearchServiceInstance $host2
-RootDirectory "D:\SharePointIndex\Partition 0"
New-SPEnterpriseSearchQueryProcessingComponent –SearchTopology $clone -SearchServiceInstance
$host1
New-SPEnterpriseSearchQueryProcessingComponent –SearchTopology $clone -SearchServiceInstance
$host2
```

```
#Activate the new topology

SET-SPENTERPRISESEARCHTOPOLOGY -IDENTITY $Clone

#Remove inactive components

$sa = Get-SPEnterpriseSearchServiceApplication
foreach($topo in (Get-SPEnterpriseSearchTopology -SearchApplication $sa |
?{$_.State -eq "Inactive"}))
{
Remove-SPEnterpriseSearchTopology -Identity $topo -Confirm:$false
}
```

■ **Note**   Make sure that the "D:\SharePointIndex\Partition 0" path exists before running the script and make sure it is empty. To modify the search topology, you have to make a clone of the topology, make your modifications, and then set the clone as the active topology.

If you're ever working with distributed cache, fighting it for some reason, and you decide that to get it provisioned you need to remove a server from the farm and add that server back, make sure that that server is not running any crawl components, or other search components, before you remove the server from the farm. If you fail to do this, there is a good chance that your search administrative component will have issues and will report back that it cannot contact the component such and such at such and such location. Here's an example of what I mean:

```
Administrative status: The search service is not able to connect to the machine that hosts
the administration component. Verify that the administration component '6fb84e80-2d1b-4f24-
a49f-d0b9132c370b' in search application 'Search Service Application' is in a good state and
try again.
```

In that case, the engineer had removed the server from the farm before modifying the topology and as a result, the search admin service was smoked. Smoked is a slang term for corrupted. The fix was rebuilding the search service application.

When it comes to adding a new index partition to a farm that already has data in its index, you have to make sure you have a good backup of the search service application, that the current active topology is healthy, and that you have enough disk space to make the new index partition. This TechNet article has decent guidance on making a backup (https://technet.microsoft.com/en-us/library/ee748635.aspx).

A good rule of thumb for how big to request your index disks for the new partition and replicas, or new replica, is to use the same size disks as the disks that hold the current index and to create equal room for growth on all disks, then make the new index. The amount of free space needed to make the new index is based on how many partitions the index currently has and how many are being added. For example, assuming the index currently has two partitions, and an additional partition was being added; then the formula to determine the needed free space would be $100\% \times 1 / (2 + 2*1)$, or 25% free space on all drives. To be safe, you should add a buffer to that number. The way that is calculated is 100% times the number of partitions being added divided by the product of 2 existing partitions plus 2 times the number of partitions being added. For example, if we were adding two partitions to an index that only had one partition, then the formula would be $100\% \times 2 / (1 + 2*2)$ or 200% / 5 or 40% free space.

After the backup of the search service application is created, and the disks are in place with enough free space, the following are the high-level steps to add a partition.

1. Start the search service instance on all the servers that you want to add the index replica for the new index partition.

2. Wait until the search service instances are running.

3. Clone the active search topology.

4. Add a new index partition in the correct number, if you have an index with replicas on hosts A and B; then when you create a new index partition, you'll create replicas on hosts C and D.

5. Determine if the index has fully replicated by checking that the search service application is running and do not continue until is running.

6. Once the index is fully replicated, activate the cloned topology and start the process of index repartitioning.

7. In a new management shell, monitor the progress of the index repartitioning process.

8. Find the primary index replica of each of the existing index partitions so you can monitor.

9. Monitor each primary index components repartitioning progress.

10. Monitor the distribution of the index to the new replicas.

11. Verify that the search topology activation has completed.

12. Restart the host node controller on the servers that originally hosted the index components before all this work started. Do this one at a time and check that at least one index component is showing running before restarting the next host node controller.

13. Resume the search service application.

Note that this process is different from taking an existing index and making a replica of it on another server in the farm. The two processes are similar up to a point and then they deviate, thus making them different. You create a replica of your index when you want to make your farm fault tolerant. You create a new Index partition when you need to index more than 10 million items. The official Microsoft guidance recommends a new index at every 10 million items in the data corpus.

The following are the high-level steps to create a replica of an existing index.

1. Make sure the current topology is healthy.

2. Start the search service instance on all the servers that you want to add the index replica to for the existing index partition.

3. Wait until the search service instances are running.

4. Clone the active search topology.

5. Add the new index component and associate it with a partition.

6. Activate the cloned topology.

7. Verify that the new cloned topology is healthy.

8. Monitor the distribution of the existing index and once its state changes from degrade to active.

9. Verify that the search topology activation has completed.

10. Restart the SharePoint Search Host Controller service on all the servers that hosted index components (representing a primary index replica or any other index replica) prior to the repartitioning.

11. Resume the search service application.

The additional replica is how you split the load between servers for indexing. When you have a medium to large data corpus, greater than 10 million items, you'll want to add an additional index partition or partitions, as opposed to just adding only replicas, so that all of your items can get into the index. And, as I mentioned earlier, if your existing index has two replicas in the partition then you should plan to have two replicas in your new partition, which would mean you need two servers. The process for adding a new partition differs from the process for adding a new replica in that you have to wait for the index to be fully replicated before activating the cloned topology.

Here's the PowerShell to add a new partition, along with some helpful notes:

```
# Make sure the current topology is healthy
Get-SPEnterpriseSearchStatus .


# Start the search service instance on all the servers that you want to add the index
replica for the new index partition

$<host n> = Get-SPEnterpriseSearchServiceInstance -Identity "<Server name>"
Start-SPEnterpriseSearchServiceInstance -Identity $<host n>

$hostC = Get-SPEnterpriseSearchServiceInstance -Identity "Server3"
Start-SPEnterpriseSearchServiceInstance -Identity $hostC
$hostD = Get-SPEnterpriseSearchServiceInstance -Identity "Server4"
Start-SPEnterpriseSearchServiceInstance -Identity $hostD

# Wait until the search service instances are running

Get-SPEnterpriseSearchServiceInstance -Identity $<host n>

Get-SPEnterpriseSearchServiceInstance -Identity $hostC
Get-SPEnterpriseSearchServiceInstance -Identity $hostD

# Clone the active search topology

$ssa = Get-SPEnterpriseSearchServiceApplication
$active = Get-SPEnterpriseSearchTopology -SearchApplication $ssa -Active
$clone = New-SPEnterpriseSearchTopology -SearchApplication $ssa -Clone -SearchTopology
$active
```

■ **Note** make a note of the clones GUID

```
# add a new index partition by adding one or more index components and associate them with
the new index partition. We recommend that you create the same number of index replicas
for the new index partition as you have for the existing partitions. For each new index
component, at the Windows PowerShell command prompt, type the following command(s):

# If you have an existing index partition 0 with index replicas on Host A and Host B, then
you'll want to add a new index partition with index replicas on Host C and Host D:

New-SPEnterpriseSearchIndexComponent -SearchTopology $clone -SearchServiceInstance $hostC
-IndexPartition 1
New-SPEnterpriseSearchIndexComponent -SearchTopology $clone -SearchServiceInstance $hostD
-IndexPartition 1

# Determine if the index has fully replicated by checking that search service application is
running, and do not continue until is running
# Verify that the Search service application is running. At the Windows PowerShell command
prompt, type the following command(s):

$ssa.IsPaused() -ne 0
```

■ **Note**   If this command returns False, the Search service application is running then it is OK to continue. However, If this command returns True, the Search service application is paused and you need to get it started before continuing, it might be paused for the repartitioning, just let it run its course. If the Search service application is paused, you need to wait for it to complete before you can continue with activating the clone. You can use the guidance found at https://technet.microsoft.com/en-us/library/dn745901.aspx to troubleshoot a paused index. Some of that post is also available in this chapter, a little later on.

```
# Once the index is fully replicated, activate the cloned topology and start the process of
index repartitioning
$ssa.PauseForIndexRepartitioning()
Set-SPEnterpriseSearchTopology -Identity $clone

# In a new Management shell, Monitor the progress of the index re-partitioning process
#Find the primary index replica of each of the existing index partitions so you can monitor

$ssa = Get-SPEnterpriseSearchServiceApplication
Get-SPEnterpriseSearchStatus -SearchApplication $ssa -Text
```

This command returns a list of index components and their properties. The primary index components have a property where Primary: True is displayed.

```
Name      : IndexComponent1
State     : Active
Primary   : False
Partition : 0
Host      : 2013appw2k12
Name      : Cell:IndexComponent1- SP65b7a6475e9bI.0.0
```

```
State      : Active
Primary    : False
Partition  : 0

Name       : IndexComponent2
State      : Active
Primary    : True
Partition  : 0
Host       : 2013app2
Name       : Cell:IndexComponent2-SP65b7a6475e9bI.1.0
State      : Active
Primary    : True
Partition  : 0
```

```
# Monitor each primary index components repartitioning progress

Get-SPEnterpriseSearchStatus -SearchApplication $ssa -Healthreport -Component <Index
component name> | ? { ($_.name -match "repart") -or ( $_.name -match "splitting") } |
ft -AutoSize Name, Message
```

<Index component name> is the name of the primary index component that you found in the previous step. In this case, that name is IndexComponent2.

Keep watching the output of the command for each primary index component. The output contains progress information about how the index is repartitioning. During the initial phase of the index repartitioning, you'll see something like this:

```
Name                                  Message
----                                  -------
repartition_component_state[SP...]    Pending
```

The main phase of the index repartitioning process splits the index partitions and you'll see something like this:

```
Name                                        Message
----                                        -------
index splitting: current fusion progress[SP...]   <Percentage value>
index splitting: splitting state [SP...]           Index splitter running fusion, building:
                                                    <Folder>
repartition_component_state [SP...]                Splitting
```

Thankfully, there is a percentage value in the output, which indicates the approximate progress of the repartitioning process.

Continue running this command for all primary index components until the command no longer returns any values. Once the command returns only a new line, the index repartitioning process is complete. The repartitioned index will start replicating and being distributed over the servers, which will more than likely consume several hours.

```
# Monitor the distribution of the index to the new replicas

# To do this, verify that your new topology is active, and that all search components are
healthy.
# At the Windows PowerShell command prompt of the second SharePoint 2013 Management Shell,
type the following command(s):

Get-SPEnterpriseSearchStatus -SearchApplication $ssa | ft -AutoSize Name, State, Details

# During the distribution of the index to the new index replicas, the added index replicas
will return the state Degraded. When all index components return the state Active in the
output, the distribution is finished. This could take several hours.

# While all this is happening, you'll see yellow triangles in your search service
application, because things are not fully online.  For example, the query processing
components were suspended when you have paused the Search service application for index
repartitioning. This is why you're seeing a state of Uknown in the output for the query
processing components.

# At this point, you have two SharePoint powershell sessions open.  Go back to the original
SharePoint management Shell, the first one where all this started, Verify that the search
topology activation has completed.  You should see a new empty powershell line.

# Restart the SharePoint Search Host Controller service on all the servers that hosted index
components (representing a primary index replica or any other index replica) prior to the
repartitioning.
# Perform this step to get a correct document count and free up memory after repartitioning
the search index. If you decide not to perform this step, it will take a few days and
some indexing iterations for the memory usage to be gradually reduced and the document
count (as returned by PowerShell cmdlets and in the Search Administration page in Central
Administration) to be correct.
```

■ **Note**   To avoid query outages, ensure that at least one index component returns the Running state for each index partition before you restart the SharePoint Search Host Controller service.

Do not use the Services on Server page on the SharePoint Central Administration website to restart this service.

- To stop the SharePoint Search Host Controller, type this command: **net stop spsearchhostcontroller**

- To restart the SharePoint Search Host Controller, type this command: **net start spsearchhostcontroller**

```
# Resume the Search service application.
$ssa.ResumeAfterIndexRepartitioning()
```

Whew, that's a lot of stuff to take into account!

■ **Note**   It's very important that the search service application is not paused when you run $ssa.IsPaused() -ne 0, and that you get it started before continuing if it is paused. It's also paramount that all of the search components return a state of active before you activate the new topology.

It really is a lot easier to work with an empty index, but sometimes it is hard to anticipate what the future holds when rolling out a new SharePoint. If you know how big the index is going to get and if you have the extra cash to build the farm the way it needs to be in its end state, then I recommend doing that from the get go, when the index is empty. Here's how you would create a replica inside your existing partition. I would say using PowerShell; but what's the point, that is the only way you can perform any of these search topology changes, within SharePoint 2013 or 2016.

Start the search service instance on all the servers that you want to add the index replica to for the existing index partition

```
$HostB = Get-SPEnterpriseSearchServiceInstance -Identity "Server2"
Start-SPEnterpriseSearchServiceInstance -Identity $HostB
```

Wait until the search service instances are running

```
Get-SPEnterpriseSearchServiceInstance -Identity $HostB
```

Clone the active search topology

```
$ssa = Get-SPEnterpriseSearchServiceApplication
$active = Get-SPEnterpriseSearchTopology -SearchApplication $ssa -Active
$clone = New-SPEnterpriseSearchTopology -SearchApplication $ssa -Clone -SearchTopology
$active
```

■ **Note**   Make a note of the clones GUID.

```
# Add the new index component and associate it with a partition
New-SPEnterpriseSearchIndexComponent -SearchTopology $clone -SearchServiceInstance $hostB
-IndexPartition 0
```

This is the syntax of this command, explained:

```
IndexComponent -SearchTopology $clone -SearchServiceInstance $<host n> -IndexPartition
<Index partition number>
```

$clone is the cloned topology that you are cloning to change the clone. That's alot of cloning around.

$<host n> is the PowerShell object reference to the running search service instance on the server that you want to add the index replica to. It is not the server that has the current index.

<Index partition number> is the number of the existing index partition that you are creating a replica of on the new server. In most cases, you're probably working with an install with only one index partition, in this case and you'll be choosing to create an index replica of index partition 0, and you will choose "0" as the parameter value.

You can use this PowerShell to determine the index partition number

```
$ssa = Get-SPEnterpriseSearchServiceApplication
Get-SPEnterpriseSearchStatus -SearchApplication $ssa -Text
```

Activate the cloned topology

```
Set-SPEnterpriseSearchTopology -Identity $clone
```

Verify that the new cloned topology is healthy

```
Get-SPEnterpriseSearchTopology -Active -SearchApplication $ssa
```

Monitor the distribution of the existing index to the new replica. The added index replica will have the state Degraded until the distribution is finished. At the Windows PowerShell command prompt, type the following command(s):

```
Get-SPEnterpriseSearchStatus -SearchApplication $ssa -Text
```

Repeat this command until all search components, including the new index component, output the state Active. For a large search index, this could take several hours.

Once the "Get-SPEnterpriseSearchStatus -SearchApplication $ssa –Text" returns Active for the index component the replication is complete and the index is indexing again. You can use this process to move an index from one server to another. Make sure that before you remove an existing index replica that you have another replica that is working. This is true for any component you're moving; make sure it exists and is activated on another server before you remove it.

To remove an existing component that is active, you need to create a clone of the search topology and then remove the component from the clone. After the component is removed, you can activate the clone. This is the command you'd use to remove a component:

```
Remove-SPEnterpriseSearchComponent -Identity <Search component id> -SearchTopology $clone
```

The process to move a search component was already discussed in the changing search topology, but here are the high-level steps again, as sometimes you need to clone more than once, depending on which component you're moving. And, this gives us a good wrap on working with search and troubleshooting issues with your topology that often require you to create new components:

- Create a clone
- Add the new component to the clone
- Activate the clone
- Make sure the new topology is healthy
- Clone the topology again
- Remove the unwanted component
- Activate the clone once more

■ **Note**   This process is very important when moving the query processing component. It is imperative that you have two query processing components before you remove the query processing component.

Creating a new component is not always the correct answer, when troubleshooting search issues. Using ULS is the first place you should go, along with the application and system log in the event viewer. Max Melcher, MCSE, MCPD, wrote a good blog post on an issue he encountered with a degraded, or fragmented index at https://melcher.it/2014/10/hes-dead-jim-sharepoint-2013-search-troubleshooting/. In that post, there are some good screen shots and an excerpt from the ULS logs where SharePoint was reporting the index fragmentation issue.

```
"SearchServiceApplication::Execute-Exception: Microsoft.SharePoint.SPException: Tried IMS
endpoints for operation Execute: Cannot plan query for index system SP2f28f6df0f54. Index
fragment '1' has no available cells. Cell statuses: [Cell I.0.1 on node IndexComponent3:
Cell status is set to 'not available' (cell out of sync or seeding)] at Microsoft.Office.
Server.Search.Query.Ims.LoadBalancer.RoundRobinLoadBalancerContext.NextEndpoint(String
operationName, String failMessage) at Microsoft.Office.Server.Search.Administration.
SearchServiceApplication._ImsQueryInternalType.DoSpLoadBalancedImsOp[T](ImsBackedOperation`1
imsCall, Int32 timeoutInMilliseconds, Int32 wcfTimeoutInMilliseconds, String operationName)
at Microsoft.Office.Server.Search.Administration.SearchServiceApplication.... fe0fc09c-8c99-
b017-25c9-d3feac78a369" - M. Melcher
```

A simple index reset was all it took in this case. When encountering issues with indexing you definitely want to try resetting, making sure the index is not paused beforehand, and before you take more drastic actions, like restoring your search service application. And as always, make sure search is not crawling before making any changes.

Make sure search is not paused before resetting the index. When you know the reason your search was paused it is OK to resume. However, when you're unsure why your search was paused, you should use the PowerShell in Table 7-3 to determine the reason and the action you should take. Failure to do so could result in loss of your index or index corruption, assuming it's not already corrupted.

Table 7-3. *Working with Paused Search*

Command	If the command returns True, the Search service application is paused for this reason	Action
($ssa.IsPaused() -band 0x01) -ne 0	A change in the number of crawl components or crawl databases is in progress.	Wait until the topology change completes.
($ssa.IsPaused() -band 0x02) -ne 0	A backup or restore procedure is in progress.	Wait until the backup or restore completes. After the procedure completes, run the command $ssa.ForceResume(0x02) to verify. For more information, see Restore Search service applications in SharePoint 2013. https://technet.microsoft.com/en-us/library/ee748654%28v=office.15%29.aspx
($ssa.IsPaused() -band 0x04) -ne 0	A backup of the Volume Shadow Copy Service (VSS) is in progress.	Wait until the backup completes. After the VSS backup completes, run the command $ssa.ForceResume(0x02) to verify.

(*continued*)

Table 7-3. (*continued*)

Command	If the command returns True, the Search service application is paused for this reason	Action
($ssa.IsPaused() -band 0x08) -ne 0	One or more servers in the search topology that host query components are offline.	Wait until the servers are available again.
($ssa.IsPaused() -band 0x20) -ne 0	One or more crawl databases in the search topology are being rebalanced.	Wait until the operation completes.
($ssa.IsPaused() -band 0x40) -ne 0	One or more link databases in the search topology are being rebalanced.	Wait until the operation completes.
($ssa.IsPaused() -band 0x80) -ne 0	An administrator has manually paused the Search service application.	If you know the reason, you can resume the Search service application. Run the command $ssa.resume() to resume the Search service application. If you don't know the reason, find out why someone has manually paused the Search service application.
($ssa.IsPaused() -band 0x100) -ne 0	The search index is being deleted.	Wait until the search index is deleted.
($ssa.IsPaused() -band 0x200) -ne 0	The search index is being repartitioned.	Wait until the operation completes.

If you come across a site that is not being indexed and you don't have a crawl rule set to exclude it, make sure that the site settings are allowing it to be indexed. Open Site Settings and look under the section titled "Search" for the "Search and Offline Availability". Make sure that the "Allow this site to appear in search results?" option is marked Yes. If you're working with an anonymous site that is not appearing in search results, changing the "Indexing ASPX Page Content" from the default of "Do not index Web Parts if this site contains fine-grained permissions" over to "Always index Web Parts on this site" has fixed issues for me in the past with regards to Anonymous sites showing content in search results. You can use the Reindex Site button on this page to force the entire site to be crawled during the next crawl. You can find a Reindex List or Reindex Library button on the advanced setting page of your lists and libraries. If you find a situation where the button is greyed out, that is because the "Allow items from this list to appear in search results" was changed to No, or set to No by default, in the case of system lists that are not indexed.

Sometimes you just want to find stuff out about your search service application and these lines of PowerShell shared earlier, is where you'll get that topology:

```
$ssa = Get-SPServiceApplication –Name "Search Service Application"
$active = Get-SPEnterpriseSearchTopology -SearchApplication $ssa -Active
Get-SPEnterpriseSearchComponent -SearchTopology $active
```

I share them here again, because it's easy for all this search stuff to become a veritable maze of confusing information in your head, and this little gem is worthy of two mentions. The only thing you have to do to make these lines work for your environment is replace the name of the search service application.

There might be a time when you want to reset the index but the search service application page is not opening. If that happens, or if you just want to be a PowerShell badass, run this command to reset the index from the SharePoint Management Shell:

```
$ssa = Get-SPEnterpriseSearchServiceApplication

$disableAlerts = $true

$ignoreUnreachableServer = $true

$ssa.reset($disableAlerts, $ignoreUnreachableServer)

if (-not $?) {

 Write-Error "Reset failed"

}
```

Kristopher Loranger has written an excellent blog post on fixing an index that seems to be stuck at his blog post, where the previous lines were gleaned from https://blogs.msdn.microsoft.com/kristopherloranger/2014/09/26/sharepoint-2013-on-prem-reset-index-stuck-resolution/. I highly recommend that you navigate to this post and copy it into your OneNote and favorite this awesome post!

"When you reset the search index, all content is immediately removed from the search index and users will not be able to retrieve search results. After you reset the search index, you must perform a full crawl of one or more content sources to create a new search index. Users will be able to retrieve search results again when the full crawl is finished and the new search index is created." – TechNet, Microsoft

If you ever come across a situation where search is running on a server, even though that server is not in the search topology, you can thank Scott Fawley for this nugget:

```
$svc = Get-SPEnterpriseSearchServiceInstance -Local
$svc
$svc.Unprovision()
```

By running the $svc by itself you can make sure you have the correct service instance before you disable it. These commands need to be run from the server that should not be in search.

When it comes to working with crawls via PowerShell here is a collection you'll want to add to your arsenal as Stephen Swinney, often says:

To stop a specific crawl:

```
$searchapp = Get-SPEnterpriseSearchServiceApplication "NameofSearchService application"
$contentsource = Get-SPEnterpriseSearchCrawlContentSource "NameofContentsource"
-SearchApplication $searchapp
$contentsource.StopCrawl()
```

Just modify the NameOfSearchService application and the NameOfContentSource to match your requirements and environment.

The following stops all crawls (make sure you have the correct search application name):

```
Get-SPEnterpriseSearchCrawlContentSource -SearchApplication "SharePoint Search Service" |
ForEach-Object {
    if ($_.CrawlStatus -ne "Idle")
    {
        Write-Host "Stopping currently running crawl for content source $($_.Name)..."
        $_.StopCrawl()

        do { Start-Sleep -Seconds 1 }
        while ($_.CrawlStatus -ne "Idle")
    }
}
```

Remember that if you're going to restart crawls, to crawl the people content source first, let it finish, and then wait two hours before crawling the local SharePoint sites and other content sources, so that user names can standardize. Also, always go to the logs and look for root causes before deciding to re-create the topology. Try less invasive tactics first.

When the Search node controller gets stuck on starting and the services on server just shows it as starting, you can run this PowerShell that Marco Wiedemeyer, a SharePoint Architect hailing from Hamburg, Germany wrote to get the node started:

```
$acl = Get-Acl HKLM:\System\CurrentControlSet\Control\ComputerName
    $person = [System.Security.Principal.NTAccount]"Users"
    $access = [System.Security.AccessControl.RegistryRights]::FullControl
    $inheritance = [System.Security.AccessControl.InheritanceFlags]"ContainerInherit,
    ObjectInherit"
    $propagation = [System.Security.AccessControl.PropagationFlags]::None
    $type = [System.Security.AccessControl.AccessControlType]::Allow
    $rule = New-Object System.Security.AccessControl.RegistryAccessRule($person, $access,
    $inheritance, $propagation, $type)
    $acl.AddAccessRule($rule)
    Set-Acl HKLM:\System\CurrentControlSet\Control\ComputerName $acl

    $sh = Get-SPServiceInstance | ? {$_.TypeName -eq "Search Host Controller Service"}
    $sh.Unprovision()
    $sh.Provision($true)
```

And if for some reason, the script times out, you should check your event viewer application log for event ID 1000 and 1026 as they relate to the following services not being started, so check that the Net.TCP port sharing service, Net.TCP listener adapter, Net.Pipe listener adapter, and remote registry are running. You'll also want to verify that your Distributed Cache is not having issues.

Then if you are still having this issue, you should check that you don't have a situation where installing the hotfix that resolved the ASP.NET race condition could fix (see http://support.microsoft.com/kb/2765317). This situation is very rare, but you never know what level a person's farm might be at, so I thought it worth mentioning. If you look at the application log and see NullReferenceException references or are seeing deadlock and references to PreSendRequestHeaders or PreSendRequestContent, then, and only then would I recommend applying the KB 2765317.

If you are encountering event ID 8193 when provisioning search, you should check that the following registry key is allowing access to the identity that is running your search application pool in IIS:

HKLM\System\CurrentControlSet\Services\VSS

When you get to the VSS key just right-click the folder and choose permissions, then add the identity that is running your search service application pool with full control. You then need to check that this is the same on all of your SharePoint VMs. I'd like credit Vlad Catrinescu with that little tidbit of noteworthy SharePoint troubleshooting gold. To read another synopsis of making this change, visit https://absolute-sharepoint.com/2014/10/event-id-8193-volume-shadow-copy-service-error-unexpected-error-calling-routine.html.

If this happens to you, you'll see something like this in your application log:

```
Log Name:      Application
Source:        VSS
Date:          10/2/2017 4:20:00 PM
Event ID:      8193
Task Category: None
Level:         Error
Keywords:      Classic
User:          N/A
Computer:      2013appw2k12.contso.com
Description:
Volume Shadow Copy Service error: Unexpected error calling routine RegOpenKeyExW
(-2147483646,SYSTEM\CurrentControlSet\Services\VSS\Diag,...).  hr = 0x80070005, Access
is denied.

Operation:
   Initializing Writer

Context:
   Writer Class Id: {0ff1ce15-0201-0000-0000-000000000000}
   Writer Name: OSearch15 VSS Writer
   Writer Instance Name: OSearch15 Replication Service
   Writer Instance ID: {e8f76bea-e787-486a-9627-3ef20d65cdb0}
```

When it comes to patching your farm, always test your crawl after the patching has occurred, as sometimes administrators will pause the search service application to decrease the patch application time. In that case, you would know why the search service application was paused and you'd be safe to resume, assuming that patching was completed. In fact, whenever you're applying a CU it is always faster to stop the following Windows services in this order:

- SharePoint Timer Service (SPTimerV4)

- SharePoint Server Search 15 (OSearch15)

- SharePoint Search Host Controller (SPSearchHostController)

This is one of the few times when it is OK to stop services with the services console or the net stop command, rather than using the Central Administration GUI. After the services have stopped, you apply the patch to that server and then start the services in the reverse order; for example, SPSearchHostController, OSearch15, and finally SPTimerV4. Kirk Stark wrote an excellent blog post on patching a search farm, where search components and high availability is happening, at https://blogs.technet.microsoft.com/tothesharepoint/2013/03/13/how-to-install-update-packages-on-a-sharepoint-farm-where-search-component-and-high-availability-search-topologies-are-enabled/. If you haven't read it yet, it's worth your time.

After search is started and everything is happening, you might want to monitor which search components are using up the most resources on your server. If you crack open process monitor in Windows Task Manager and look at the Details tab, you quickly see that it does not provide enough detail. While it shows you the mssearch.exe and mssdmn.exe are related to the crawler component, it doesn't distinguish between the various noderunner.exe processes. You can see the memory and CPU being used, but you have no way of determining which component the various noderunner.exe processes represent.

The easiest way to determine which search component that each noderunner process is representing is to use a tool from sysinternals named Process Explorer. Just download Process Explorer for free location at https://technet.microsoft.com/en-us/sysinternals/bb896653. After it is loaded, you can hover over the process name and you'll be able to see which search component is attributed to any given noderunner. exe. In my farm the content processing component was king resource sucker. Figure 7-11 demonstrates the difference between Task Manager Details tab and the sysinternals Process Explorer.

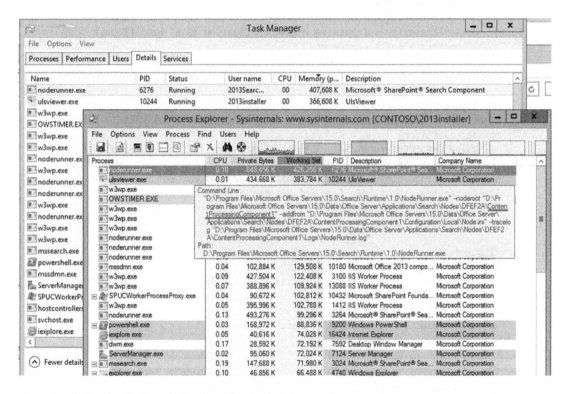

Figure 7-11. *Process Explorer to show which components are using up resources*

This information is good to know stuff when you're looking at changing the search topology to increase performance.

When you just want to know everything about your search service application, you can use this PowerShell:

```
<#
.SYNOPSIS
        The purpose of this SharePoint 2013 script is to present the status of the Search
        Service Application, with main focus on the state of the search topology.
.DESCRIPTION
        The script consolidates data from multiple cmdlets and sources:
        - Key topology status data from Get-SPEnterpriseSearchStatus
                Get-SPEnterpriseSearchStatus -SearchApplication $ssa
                Get-SPEnterpriseSearchStatus -SearchApplication $ssa -Primary
                -<Admin Component>
                Get-SPEnterpriseSearchStatus -SearchApplication $ssa -JobStatus
                Get-SPEnterpriseSearchStatus -SearchApplication $ssa -HealthReport
                -Component <Search Component>
                        Printing selected info relevant for degraded states
        - Crawl status (crawling/idle/paused)
                $ssa.Ispaused()
                $contentSource.CrawlState
        - Number of indexed documents including index size alert (currently 10 mill.
        items per partition)
                Using Get-SPEnterpriseSearchStatus -SearchApplication $ssa -HealthReport
                -Component <Search Component>
        - HA status for topology, indicating which roles that may not have high availability
                Aggregated status info from Get-SPEnterpriseSearchStatus
        - Host controller repository status (for search dictionaries)
                Get-SPEnterpriseSearchHostController

        Limitations:
        - The script only supports one SSA in the farm.
          If multiple SSAs found, the script prints status for the first SSA found.
.NOTES
  File Name : Get-SPSearchTopologyState.ps1
  Tags      : SharePoint 2013, Enterprise Search, SP2013ES

#>


# ===============================================================================================
# Get status for search topology
# ===============================================================================================


# -----------------------------------------------------------------------------
#  Writes error message to the user in red color and exits the script.
# -----------------------------------------------------------------------------
Function WriteErrorAndExit($errorText)
{
    Write-Host -BackgroundColor Red -ForegroundColor Black $errorText
    Write-Host -BackgroundColor Red -ForegroundColor Black "Aborting script"
    exit
}
```

```
# -------------------------------------------------------------------------
# GetSSA: Get SSA reference
# -------------------------------------------------------------------------
Function GetSSA
{
    $ssas = @(Get-SPEnterpriseSearchServiceApplication)
    if ($ssas.Count -ne 1)
    {
        WriteErrorAndExit("This script only supports a single SSA configuration")
    }

    $global:ssa = $ssas[0]
    if ($global:ssa.Status -ne "Online")
    {
        $ssaStat = $global:ssa.Status
        WriteErrorAndExit("Expected SSA to have status 'Online', found status: $ssaStat")
    }

    Write-Output "SSA: $($global:ssa.Name)"
    Write-Output ""
}


# ----------------------------------------------------------------------------
# GetCrawlStatus: Get crawl status
# ----------------------------------------------------------------------------
Function GetCrawlStatus
{
    if ($global:ssa.Ispaused())
    {
        switch ($global:ssa.Ispaused())
        {
            1     { $pauseReason = "ongoing search topology operation" }
            2     { $pauseReason = "backup/restore" }
            4     { $pauseReason = "backup/restore" }
            32    { $pauseReason = "crawl DB re-factoring" }
            64    { $pauseReason = "link DB re-factoring" }
            128   { $pauseReason = "external reason (user initiated)" }
            256   { $pauseReason = "index reset" }
            512   { $pauseReason = "index re-partitioning (query is also paused)" }
            default { $pauseReason = "multiple reasons ($($global:ssa.Ispaused()))" }
        }
        Write-Output "$($global:ssa.Name): Paused for $pauseReason"
    }
    else
    {
        $crawling = $false
        $contentSources = Get-SPEnterpriseSearchCrawlContentSource -SearchApplication
        $global:ssa
        if ($contentSources)
        {
            foreach ($source in $contentSources)
```

```
            {
                if ($source.CrawlState -ne "Idle")
                {
                    Write-Output "Crawling $($source.Name) : $($source.CrawlState)"
                    $crawling = $true
                }
            }
            if (! $crawling)
            {
                Write-Output "Crawler is idle"
            }
        }
        else
        {
            Write-Output "Crawler: No content sources found"
        }
    }
}


# --------------------------------------------------------------------------------
# GetTopologyInfo: Get basic topology info and component health status
# --------------------------------------------------------------------------------
Function GetTopologyInfo
{
    $at = Get-SPEnterpriseSearchTopology -SearchApplication $global:ssa -Active
    $global:topologyCompList = Get-SPEnterpriseSearchComponent -SearchTopology $at

    # Check if topology is prepared for HA
    $adminFound = $false
    foreach ($searchComp in ($global:topologyCompList))
    {
        if ($searchComp.Name -match "Admin")
        {
            if ($adminFound)
            {
                $global:haTopology = $true
            }
            else
            {
                $adminFound = $true
            }
        }
    }

    #
    # Get topology component state:
    #
    $global:componentStateList=Get-SPEnterpriseSearchStatus -SearchApplication $global:ssa

    # Find the primary admin component:
    foreach ($component in ($global:componentStateList))
```

```
    {
        if ( ($component.Name -match "Admin") -and ($component.State -ne "Unknown") )
        {
            if (Get-SPEnterpriseSearchStatus -SearchApplication $global:ssa -Primary
            -Component $($component.Name))
            {
                $global:primaryAdmin = $component.Name
            }
        }
    }
    if (! $global:primaryAdmin)
    {
        Write-Output ""
        Write-Output "-----------------------------------------------------------------------"
        Write-Output "Error: Not able to obtain health state information."
        Write-Output "Recommended action: Ensure that at least one admin component is
        operational."
        Write-Output "This state may also indicate that an admin component failover is in
        progress."
        Write-Output "-----------------------------------------------------------------------"
        Write-Output ""
        throw "Search component health state check failed"
    }
}


# -------------------------------------------------------------------------------------
# PopulateHostHaList: For each component, determine properties and update $global:hostArray /
$global:haArray
# -------------------------------------------------------------------------------------
Function PopulateHostHaList($searchComp)
{
        if ($searchComp.ServerName)
        {
            $hostName = $searchComp.ServerName
        }
        else
        {
            $hostName = "Unknown server"
        }
        $partition = $searchComp.IndexPartitionOrdinal
        $newHostFound = $true
        $newHaFound = $true
        $entity = $null

        foreach ($searchHost in ($global:hostArray))
        {
            if ($searchHost.hostName -eq $hostName)
            {
                $newHostFound = $false
            }
        }
```

```
    if ($newHostFound)
    {
        # Add the host to $global:hostArray
        $hostTemp = $global:hostTemplate | Select-Object *
        $hostTemp.hostName = $hostName
        $global:hostArray += $hostTemp
        $global:searchHosts += 1
    }

    # Fill in component specific data in $global:hostArray
    foreach ($searchHost in ($global:hostArray))
    {
        if ($searchHost.hostName -eq $hostName)
        {
            $partition = -1
            if ($searchComp.Name -match "Query")
            {
                $entity = "QueryProcessingComponent"
                $searchHost.qpc = "QueryProcessing "
                $searchHost.components += 1
            }
            elseif ($searchComp.Name -match "Content")
            {
                $entity = "ContentProcessingComponent"
                $searchHost.cpc = "ContentProcessing "
                $searchHost.components += 1
            }
            elseif ($searchComp.Name -match "Analytics")
            {
                $entity = "AnalyticsProcessingComponent"
                $searchHost.apc = "AnalyticsProcessing "
                $searchHost.components += 1
            }
            elseif ($searchComp.Name -match "Admin")
            {
                $entity = "AdminComponent"
                if ($searchComp.Name -eq $global:primaryAdmin)
                {
                    $searchHost.pAdmin = "Admin(Primary) "
                }
                else
                {
                    $searchHost.sAdmin = "Admin "
                }
                $searchHost.components += 1
            }
            elseif ($searchComp.Name -match "Crawl")
            {
                $entity = "CrawlComponent"
                $searchHost.crawler = "Crawler "
                $searchHost.components += 1
```

```
        }
        elseif ($searchComp.Name -match "Index")
        {
            $entity = "IndexComponent"
            $partition = $searchComp.IndexPartitionOrdinal
            $searchHost.index = "IndexPartition($partition) "
            $searchHost.components += 1
        }
    }
}

# Fill in component specific data in $global:haArray
foreach ($haEntity in ($global:haArray))
{
    if ($haEntity.entity -eq $entity)
    {
        if ($entity -eq "IndexComponent")
        {
            if ($haEntity.partition -eq $partition)
            {
                $newHaFound = $false
            }
        }
        else
        {
            $newHaFound = $false
        }
    }
}
if ($newHaFound)
{
    # Add the HA entities to $global:haArray
    $haTemp = $global:haTemplate | Select-Object *
    $haTemp.entity = $entity
    $haTemp.components = 1
    if ($partition -ne -1)
    {
        $haTemp.partition = $partition
    }
    $global:haArray += $haTemp
}
else
{
    foreach ($haEntity in ($global:haArray))
    {
        if ($haEntity.entity -eq $entity)
        {
            if (($entity -eq "IndexComponent") )
            {
                if ($haEntity.partition -eq $partition)
                {
```

301

```
                                $haEntity.components += 1
                    }
                }
                else
                {
                    $haEntity.components += 1
                    if (($haEntity.entity -eq "AdminComponent") -and ($searchComp.Name
                    -eq $global:primaryAdmin))
                    {
                        $haEntity.primary = $global:primaryAdmin
                    }
                }
            }
        }
    }
}


# -------------------------------------------------------------------------------
# AnalyticsStatus: Output status of analytics jobs
# -------------------------------------------------------------------------------
Function AnalyticsStatus
{
    Write-Output "Analytics Processing Job Status:"
    $analyticsStatus = Get-SPEnterpriseSearchStatus -SearchApplication $global:ssa -JobStatus

    foreach ($analyticsEntry in $analyticsStatus)
    {
        if ($analyticsEntry.Name -ne "Not available")
        {
            foreach ($de in ($analyticsEntry.Details))
            {
                if ($de.Key -eq "Status")
                {
                    $status = $de.Value
                }
            }
            Write-Output "    $($analyticsEntry.Name) : $status"
        }
        # Output additional diagnostics from the dictionary
        foreach ($de in ($analyticsEntry.Details))
        {
            # Skip entries that is listed as Not Available
            if ( ($de.Value -ne "Not available") -and ($de.Key -ne "Activity") -and ($de.Key
            -ne "Status") )
            {
                Write-Output "        $($de.Key): $($de.Value)"
                if ($de.Key -match "Last successful start time")
                {
                    $dLast = Get-Date $de.Value
                    $dNow = Get-Date
                    $daysSinceLastSuccess = $dNow.DayOfYear - $dLast.DayOfYear
```

```
                        if ($daysSinceLastSuccess -gt 3)
                        {
                            Write-Output "         Warning: More than three days since last
                            successful run"
                            $global:serviceDegraded = $true
                        }
                    }
                }
            }
        }
    }
    Write-Output ""
}


# --------------------------------------------------------------------------------------
# SearchComponentStatus: Analyze the component status for one component
# --------------------------------------------------------------------------------------
Function SearchComponentStatus($component)
{
    # Find host name
    foreach($searchComp in ($global:topologyCompList))
    {
        if ($searchComp.Name -eq $component.Name)
        {
            if ($searchComp.ServerName)
            {
                $hostName = $searchComp.ServerName
            }
            else
            {
                $hostName = "No server associated with this component. The server may have
                been removed from the farm."
            }
        }
    }
    if ($component.State -ne "Active")
    {
        # String with all components that is not active:
        if ($component.State -eq "Unknown")
        {
            $global:unknownComponents += "$($component.Name):$($component.State)"
        }
        elseif ($component.State -eq "Degraded")
        {
            $global:degradedComponents += "$($component.Name):$($component.State)"
        }
        else
        {
            $global:failedComponents += "$($component.Name):$($component.State)"
        }
        $global:serviceDegraded = $true
    }
```

```powershell
    # Skip unnecessary info about cells and partitions if everything is fine
    $outputEntry = $true

    # Indent the cell info, logically belongs to the component.
    if ($component.Name -match "Cell")
    {
        if ($component.State -eq "Active")
        {
            $outputEntry = $false
        }
        else
        {
            Write-Output "     $($component.Name)"
        }
    }
    elseif ($component.Name -match "Partition")
    {
        if ($component.State -eq "Active")
        {
            $outputEntry = $false
        }
        else
        {
            Write-Output "Index $($component.Name)"
        }
    }
    else
    {
        # State for search components
        $primaryString = ""
        if ($component.Name -match "Query") { $entity = "QueryProcessingComponent" }
        elseif ($component.Name -match "Content") { $entity = "ContentProcessingComponent" }
        elseif ($component.Name -match "Analytics") { $entity =
        "AnalyticsProcessingComponent" }
        elseif ($component.Name -match "Crawl") { $entity = "CrawlComponent" }
        elseif ($component.Name -match "Admin")
        {
            $entity = "AdminComponent"
            if ($global:haTopology)
            {
                if ($component.Name -eq $global:primaryAdmin)
                {
                    $primaryString = " (Primary)"
                }
            }
        }
        elseif ($component.Name -match "Index")
        {
            $entity = "IndexComponent"
            foreach ($searchComp in ($global:topologyCompList))
            {
```

```
            if ($searchComp.Name -eq $component.Name)
            {
                $partition = $searchComp.IndexPartitionOrdinal
            }
        }
        # find info about primary role
        foreach ($de in ($component.Details))
        {
            if ($de.Key -eq "Primary")
            {
                if ($de.Value -eq "True")
                {
                    $primaryString = " (Primary)"
                    foreach ($haEntity in ($global:haArray))
                    {
                        if (($haEntity.entity -eq $entity) -and ($haEntity.partition -eq
                        $partition))
                        {
                            $haEntity.primary = $component.Name

                        }
                    }
                }
            }
        }
    }
}
foreach ($haEntity in ($global:haArray))
{
    if ( ($haEntity.entity -eq $entity) -and ($component.State -eq "Active") )
    {
        if ($entity -eq "IndexComponent")
        {
            if ($haEntity.partition -eq $partition)
            {
                $haEntity.componentsOk += 1
            }
        }
        else
        {
            $haEntity.componentsOk += 1
        }
    }
}
# Add the component entities to $global:compArray for output formatting
$compTemp = $global:compTemplate | Select-Object *
$compTemp.Component = "$($component.Name)$primaryString"
$compTemp.Server = $hostName
$compTemp.State = $component.State
if ($partition -ne -1)
{
    $compTemp.Partition = $partition
```

```
        }
        $global:compArray += $compTemp

        if ($component.State -eq "Active")
        {
            $outputEntry = $false
        }
        else
        {
            Write-Output "$($component.Name)"
        }
    }
    if ($outputEntry)
    {
        if ($component.State)
        {
            Write-Output "    State: $($component.State)"
        }
        if ($hostName)
        {
            Write-Output "    Server: $hostName"
        }
        if ($component.Message)
        {
            Write-Output "    Details: $($component.Message)"
        }

        # Output additional diagnostics from the dictionary
        foreach ($de in ($component.Details))
        {
            if ($de.Key -ne "Host")
            {
                Write-Output "    $($de.Key): $($de.Value)"
            }
        }
        if ($global:haTopology)
        {
            if ($component.Name -eq $global:primaryAdmin)
            {
                Write-Output "    Primary: True"
            }
            elseif ($component.Name -match "Admin")
            {
                Write-Output "    Primary: False"
            }
        }
    }
}
```

```
# ------------------------------------------------------------------------------
# DetailedIndexerDiag: Output selected info from detailed component diag
# ------------------------------------------------------------------------------
Function DetailedIndexerDiag
{
    $indexerInfo = @()
    $generationInfo = @()
    $generation = 0

    foreach ($searchComp in ($global:componentStateList))
    {
        $component = $searchComp.Name
        if ( (($component -match "Index") -or ($component -match "Content") -or ($component
        -match "Admin")) -and ($component -notmatch "Cell") -and ($searchComp.State
        -notmatch "Unknown") -and ($searchComp.State -notmatch "Registering"))
        {
            $pl=Get-SPEnterpriseSearchStatus -SearchApplication $global:ssa -HealthReport
            -Component $component
            foreach ($entry in ($pl))
            {
                if ($entry.Name -match "plugin: number of documents")
                {
                    foreach ($haEntity in ($global:haArray))
                    {
                        if (($haEntity.entity -eq "IndexComponent") -and ($haEntity.primary
                        -eq $component))
                        {
                            # Count indexed documents from all index partitions:
                            $global:indexedDocs += $entry.Message
                            $haEntity.docs = $entry.Message
                        }
                    }
                }
                if ($entry.Name -match "repartition")
                    { $indexerInfo += "Index re-partitioning state: $($entry.Message)" }
                elseif (($entry.Name -match "splitting") -and ($entry.Name -match "fusion"))
                    { $indexerInfo += "$component : Splitting index partition (appr.
                    $($entry.Message) % finished)" }
                elseif (($entry.Name -match "master merge running") -and ($entry.Message
                -match "true"))
                {
                    $indexerInfo += "$component : Index Master Merge (de-fragment index
                    files) in progress"
                    $global:masterMerge = $true
                }
                elseif ($global:degradedComponents -and ($entry.Name -match "plugin: newest
                generation id"))
                {
                    # If at least one index component is left behind, we want to output the
                    generation number.
                    $generationInfo += "$component : Index generation: $($entry.Message)"
```

```
                    $gen = [int] $entry.Message
                    if ($generation -and ($generation -ne $gen))
                    {
                        # Verify if there are different generation IDs for the indexers
                        $global:generationDifference = $true
                    }
                    $generation = $gen
                }
            elseif (($entry.Level -eq "Error") -or ($entry.Level -eq "Warning"))
            {
                $global:serviceDegraded = $true
                if ($entry.Name -match "fastserver")
                    { $indexerInfo += "$component ($($entry.Level)) : Indexer plugin
                    error ($($entry.Name):$($entry.Message))" }
                elseif ($entry.Message -match "fragments")
                    { $indexerInfo += "$component ($($entry.Level)) : Missing index
                    partition" }
                elseif (($entry.Name -match "active") -and ($entry.Message -match "not
                active"))
                    { $indexerInfo += "$component ($($entry.Level)) : Indexer generation
                    controller is not running. Potential reason: All index partitions
                    are not available" }
                elseif ( ($entry.Name -match "in_sync") -or ($entry.Name -match "left_
                behind") )
                {
                    # Indicates replicas are out of sync, catching up. Redundant info in
                    this script
                    $global:indexLeftBehind = $true
                }
                elseif ($entry.Name -match "full_queue")
                    { $indexerInfo += "$component : Items queuing up in feeding
                    ($($entry.Message))" }
                elseif ($entry.Message -notmatch "No primary")
                {
                    $indexerInfo += "$component ($($entry.Level)) : $($entry.
                    Name):$($entry.Message)"
                }
            }
        }
    }
}

if ($indexerInfo)
{
    Write-Output ""
    Write-Output "Indexer related additional status information:"
    foreach ($indexerInfoEntry in ($indexerInfo))
    {
        Write-Output "    $indexerInfoEntry"
    }
    if ($global:indexLeftBehind -and $global:generationDifference)
    {
```

```
            # Output generation number for indexers in case any of them have been reported
            # as left behind, and reported generation IDs are different.
            foreach ($generationInfoEntry in ($generationInfo))
            {
                Write-Output "    $generationInfoEntry"
            }
        }
        Write-Output ""
    }
}


# ------------------------------------------------------------------------------------------
# VerifyHaLimits: Verify HA status for topology and index size limits
# ------------------------------------------------------------------------------------------
Function VerifyHaLimits
{
    $hacl = @()
    $haNotOk = $false
    $ixcwl = @()
    $ixcel = @()
    $docsExceeded = $false
    $docsHigh = $false
    foreach ($hac in $global:haArray)
    {
        if ([int] $hac.componentsOk -lt 2)
        {
            if ([int] $hac.componentsOk -eq 0)
            {
                # Service is down
                $global:serviceFailed = $true
                $haNotOk = $true
            }
            elseif ($global:haTopology)
            {
                # Only relevant to output if we have a HA topology in the first place
                $haNotOk = $true
            }

            if ($hac.partition -ne -1)
            {
                $hacl += "$($hac.componentsOk)($($hac.components)) : Index partition $($hac.
                partition)"
            }
            else
            {
                $hacl += "$($hac.componentsOk)($($hac.components)) : $($hac.entity)"
            }
        }
        if ([int] $hac.docs -gt 10000000)
        {
            $docsExceeded = $true
```

```
            $ixcel += "$($hac.entity) (partition $($hac.partition)): $($hac.docs)"
        }
        elseif ([int] $hac.docs -gt 9000000)
        {
            $docsHigh = $true
            $ixcwl += "$($hac.entity) (partition $($hac.partition)): $($hac.docs)"
        }
    }
    if ($haNotOk)
    {
        $hacl = $hacl | sort
        if ($global:serviceFailed)
        {
            Write-Output "Critical: Service down due to components not active:"
        }
        else
        {
            Write-Output "Warning: No High Availability for one or more components:"
        }
        foreach ($hc in $hacl)
        {
            Write-Output "    $hc"
        }
        Write-Output ""
    }
    if ($docsExceeded)
    {
        $global:serviceDegraded = $true
        Write-Output "Warning: One or more index component exceeds document limit:"
        foreach ($hc in $ixcel)
        {
            Write-Output "    $hc"
        }
        Write-Output ""
    }
    if ($docsHigh)
    {
        Write-Output "Warning: One or more index component is close to document limit:"
        foreach ($hc in $ixcwl)
        {
            Write-Output "    $hc"
        }
        Write-Output ""
    }
}

# -------------------------------------------------------------------------------------
# VerifyHostControllerRepository: Verify that Host Controller HA (for dictionary repository) is OK
# -------------------------------------------------------------------------------------
```

```
Function VerifyHostControllerRepository
{
    $highestRepVer = 0
    $hostControllers = 0
    $primaryRepVer = -1
    $hcStat = @()
    $hcs = Get-SPEnterpriseSearchHostController
    foreach ($hc in $hcs)
    {
        $hostControllers += 1
        $repVer = $hc.RepositoryVersion
        $serverName = $hc.Server.Name
        if ($repVer -gt $highestRepVer)
        {
            $highestRepVer = $repVer
        }
        if ($hc.PrimaryHostController)
        {
            $primaryHC = $serverName
            $primaryRepVer = $repVer
        }
        if ($repVer -ne -1)
        {
            $hcStat += "          $serverName : $repVer"
        }
    }
    if ($hostControllers -gt 1)
    {
        Write-Output "Primary search host controller (for dictionary repository):
        $primaryHC"
        if ($primaryRepVer -eq -1)
        {
            $global:serviceDegraded = $true
            Write-Output "Warning: Primary host controller is not available."
            Write-Output "    Recommended action: Restart server or set new primary host
            controller using Set-SPEnterpriseSearchPrimaryHostController."
            Write-Output "    Repository version for existing host controllers:"
            foreach ($hcs in $hcStat)
            {
                Write-Output $hcs
            }
        }
        elseif ($primaryRepVer -lt $highestRepVer)
        {
            $global:serviceDegraded = $true
            Write-Output "Warning: Primary host controller does not have the latest
            repository version."
            Write-Output "    Primary host controller repository version: $primaryRepVer"
            Write-Output "    Latest repository version: $highestRepVer"
            Write-Output "    Recommended action: Set new primary host controller using Set-
            SPEnterpriseSearchPrimaryHostController."
            Write-Output "    Repository version for existing host controllers:"
```

311

```
            foreach ($hcs in $hcStat)
            {
                Write-Output $hcs
            }
        }
        Write-Output ""
    }
}


#---added by bspender----------------------------------------------------------------
# VerifyApplicationServerSyncJobsEnabled: Verify that Application Server Admin Service Timer
  Jobs are running
# ---------------------------------------------------------------------------------------
function VerifyApplicationServerSyncJobsEnabled
{
$timeThresholdInMin = 5

$sspJob = $((Get-SPFarm).Services | where {$_.TypeName -like "SSP Job Control*"})
if ($sspJob.Status -ne "Online") {
Write-Warning ("SSP Job Control Service is " + $sspJob.Status)
$global:serviceDegraded = $true
}

$serverNames = $((Get-SPFarm).Servers | Where {$_.Role -eq "Application"}).Name
foreach ($server in $serverNames) {
$sspJobServiceInstance = $((Get-SPFarm).Servers[$server].ServiceInstances | where {$_.
TypeName -like "SSP Job Control*"})
if ($sspJobServiceInstance.Status -ne "Online") {
Write-Warning ("SSP Job Control Service Instance is " + $sspJobServiceInstance.Status + " on
" + $server)
$global:SSPJobInstancesOffline.Add($sspJobServiceInstance) | Out-Null
$global:serviceDegraded = $true
}
}

if ($serverNames.count -eq 1) {
$jobs = Get-SPTimerJob | where {$_.Name -like "job-application-*"}
} else {
$jobs = Get-SPTimerJob | where {$_.Name -eq "job-application-server-admin-service"}
}

foreach ($j in $jobs) {
Write-Host ($j.Name)
Write-Host ("-------------------------------------")
if (($j.Status -ne "Online") -or ($j.isDisabled)) {
if ($j.Status -ne "Online") { Write-Warning ($j.Name + " timer job is " + $j.Status) }
if ($j.isDisabled) { Write-Warning ($j.Name + " timer job is DISABLED") }
$global:ApplicationServerSyncTimerJobsOffline.Add($j) | Out-Null
$global:serviceDegraded = $true
} else {
```

```
$mostRecent = $j.HistoryEntries | select -first ($serverNames.count * $timeThresholdInMin)
foreach ($server in $serverNames) {
$displayShorthand = $server+": "+$($j.Name)
$mostRecentOnServer = $mostRecent | Where {$_.ServerName -ieq $server} | SELECT -First 1
if ($mostRecentOnServer -eq $null) {
Write-Warning ($displayShorthand + " timer job does not appear to be running")
#and add this server to the list
$global:ApplicationServerSyncNotRunning.Add($displayShorthand) | Out-Null
$global:serviceDegraded = $true
} else {
$spanSinceLastRun = [int]$(New-TimeSpan $mostRecentOnServer.EndTime $(Get-Date).
ToUniversalTime()).TotalSeconds
if ($spanSinceLastRun -lt ($timeThresholdInMin * 60)) {
Write-Host ($displayShorthand + " recently ran " + $spanSinceLastRun + " seconds ago")
} else {
Write-Warning ($displayShorthand + " last ran " + $spanSinceLastRun + " seconds ago")
$global:ApplicationServerSyncNotRunning.Add($displayShorthand) | Out-Null
}
#(For added verbosity, uncomment the following line to report the last successful run for
this server)
#$mostRecentOnServer
}
}
}
}
}


# -------------------------------------------------------------------------------------------
# Main
# -------------------------------------------------------------------------------------------

Write-Output ""
Write-Output "Search Topology health check"
Write-Output "============================="
Write-Output ""
Get-Date
# -------------------------------------------------------------------------------------------
# Global variables:
# -------------------------------------------------------------------------------------------

$global:serviceDegraded = $false
$global:serviceFailed = $false
$global:unknownComponents = @()
$global:degradedComponents = @()
$global:failedComponents = @()
$global:generationDifference = $false
$global:indexLeftBehind = $false
$global:searchHosts = 0
$global:ssa = $null
$global:componentStateList = $null
$global:topologyCompList = $null
```

```
$global:haTopology = $false
$global:primaryAdmin = $null
$global:indexedDocs = 0
$global:masterMerge = $false

#---added by bspender-----------------------
$global:SSPJobInstancesOffline = $(New-Object System.Collections.ArrayList)
$global:ApplicationServerSyncTimerJobsOffline = $(New-Object System.Collections.ArrayList)
$global:ApplicationServerSyncNotRunning = $(New-Object System.Collections.ArrayList)
#--------------------------------------------

# Template object for the host array:
$global:hostTemplate = New-Object psobject
$global:hostTemplate | Add-Member -MemberType NoteProperty -Name hostName -Value $null
$global:hostTemplate | Add-Member -MemberType NoteProperty -Name components -Value 0
$global:hostTemplate | Add-Member -MemberType NoteProperty -Name cpc -Value $null
$global:hostTemplate | Add-Member -MemberType NoteProperty -Name qpc -Value $null
$global:hostTemplate | Add-Member -MemberType NoteProperty -Name pAdmin -Value $null
$global:hostTemplate | Add-Member -MemberType NoteProperty -Name sAdmin -Value $null
$global:hostTemplate | Add-Member -MemberType NoteProperty -Name apc -Value $null
$global:hostTemplate | Add-Member -MemberType NoteProperty -Name crawler -Value $null
$global:hostTemplate | Add-Member -MemberType NoteProperty -Name index -Value $null

# Create the empty host array:
$global:hostArray = @()

# Template object for the HA group array:
$global:haTemplate = New-Object psobject
$global:haTemplate | Add-Member -MemberType NoteProperty -Name entity -Value $null
$global:haTemplate | Add-Member -MemberType NoteProperty -Name partition -Value -1
$global:haTemplate | Add-Member -MemberType NoteProperty -Name primary -Value $null
$global:haTemplate | Add-Member -MemberType NoteProperty -Name docs -Value 0
$global:haTemplate | Add-Member -MemberType NoteProperty -Name components -Value 0
$global:haTemplate | Add-Member -MemberType NoteProperty -Name componentsOk -Value 0

# Create the empty HA group array:
$global:haArray = @()

# Template object for the component/server table:
$global:compTemplate = New-Object psobject
$global:compTemplate | Add-Member -MemberType NoteProperty -Name Component -Value $null
$global:compTemplate | Add-Member -MemberType NoteProperty -Name Server -Value $null
$global:compTemplate | Add-Member -MemberType NoteProperty -Name Partition -Value $null
$global:compTemplate | Add-Member -MemberType NoteProperty -Name State -Value $null

# Create the empty component/server table:
$global:compArray = @()

# Get the SSA object and print SSA name:
GetSSA
```

```
VerifyApplicationServerSyncJobsEnabled

# Get basic topology info and component health status
GetTopologyInfo

# Traverse list of components, determine properties and update $global:hostArray /
$global:haArray
foreach ($searchComp in ($global:topologyCompList))
{
    PopulateHostHaList($searchComp)
}

# Analyze the component status:
foreach ($component in ($global:componentStateList))
{
    SearchComponentStatus($component)
}

# Look for selected info from detailed indexer diagnostics:
DetailedIndexerDiag

# Output list of components with state OK:
if ($global:compArray)
{
    $global:compArray | Sort-Object -Property Component | Format-Table -AutoSize
}
Write-Output ""

# Verify HA status for topology and index size limits:
VerifyHaLimits

# Verify that Host Controller HA (for dictionary repository) is OK:
VerifyHostControllerRepository

# Output components by server (for servers with multiple search components):
if ($global:haTopology -and ($global:searchHosts -gt 2))
{
    $componentsByServer = $false
    foreach ($hostInfo in $global:hostArray)
    {
        if ([int] $hostInfo.components -gt 1)
        {
            $componentsByServer = $true
        }
    }
    if ($componentsByServer)
    {
        Write-Output "Servers with multiple search components:"
        foreach ($hostInfo in $global:hostArray)
        {
            if ([int] $hostInfo.components -gt 1)
```

```
        {
            Write-Output "    $($hostInfo.hostName): $($hostInfo.pAdmin)$($hostInfo.
sAdmin)$($hostInfo.index)$($hostInfo.qpc)$($hostInfo.cpc)$($hostInfo.apc)$($hostInfo.crawler)"
        }
    }
    Write-Output ""
    }
}


# Analytics Processing Job Status:
AnalyticsStatus

if ($global:masterMerge)
{
    Write-Output "Index Master Merge (de-fragment index files) in progress on one or more
    index components."
}

if ($global:serviceFailed -eq $false)
{
    Write-Output "Searchable items: $global:indexedDocs"
}


GetCrawlStatus
Write-Output ""

if ($global:unknownComponents)
{
    Write-Output "The following components are not reachable:"
    foreach ($uc in ($global:unknownComponents))
    {
        Write-Output "    $uc"
    }
    Write-Output "Recommended action: Restart or replace the associated server(s)"
    Write-Output ""
}

if ($global:degradedComponents)
{
    Write-Output "The following components are degraded:"
    foreach ($dc in ($global:degradedComponents))
    {
        Write-Output "    $dc"
    }
    Write-Output "Recommended action for degraded components:"
    Write-Output "    Component registering or resolving:"
    Write-Output "        This is normally a transient state during component restart or re-
                     configuration. Re-run the script."
```

```
    if ($global:indexLeftBehind)
    {
        Write-Output "    Index component left behind:"
        if ($global:generationDifference)
        {
            Write-Output "        This is normal after adding an index component or index
            component/server recovery."
            Write-Output "        Indicates that the replica is being updated from the
            primary replica."
        }
        else
        {
            Write-Output "        Index replicas listed as degraded but index generation is OK."
            Write-Output "        Will get out of degraded state as soon as new/changed
            items are being idexed."
        }
    }
    Write-Output ""
}

if ($global:failedComponents)
{
    Write-Output "The following components are reported in error:"
    foreach ($fc in ($global:failedComponents))
    {
        Write-Output "    $fc"
    }
    Write-Output "Recommended action: Restart the associated server(s)"
    Write-Output ""
}

if ($global:serviceFailed)
{
    Write-Host -BackgroundColor Red -ForegroundColor Black "Search service overall state:
    Failed (no queries served)"
}
elseif ($global:serviceDegraded)
{
    Write-Host -BackgroundColor Yellow -ForegroundColor Black "Search service overall state:
    Degraded"
}
else
{
    Write-Host -BackgroundColor Green -ForegroundColor Black "Search service overall state: OK"
}
Write-Output ""
```

The script will give you all the important details about your search service application. The output of this awesome script is shown in Figure 7-12.

Figure 7-12. GetSearchTopology.ps1 output

Essentially, fixing issues with performance boils down to either increasing the number of search components, which is called *scaling out,* or increasing the resources on the servers with the components, which is called *scaling up.* In some cases, you may do both, Microsoft has an excellent TechNet post at `https://technet.microsoft.com/en-us/library/dn727118.aspx`, which is titled Redesign Enterprise Search Topology for Specific Performance Requirements in SharePoint 2013.

To increase the crawl rate and getting data ingested by the index, is a balancing act between the crawler, the content processing component, and the indexing component. Scaling up will always increase how fast one component can process and this is why it's a good thing to study the noderunner.exe and which processes are using the most memory or having a greater requirement to get their work done. Use Process Explorer to analyze Noderunner.exe. The crawl rate, management of crawling, and link discovery, are what really pull on the resources of the server hosting the craw component. And, usually when you add an additional crawl component, it is the panacea to the resource drain. Increasing the search service application performance level will put more strain on resources and may be the reason for a sudden increase in CPU and Memory utilization. Keep this in mind when using this option to increase performance.

Crawl databases are good for 20 million items per database, so in a search environment with 16 million items, you're cool with one crawl database, but if you wanted to scale out the topology, here's how you would add a crawl db.

```
$SSA = Get-SPEnterpriseSearchServiceApplication
$searchCrawlDBName = "SharePoint_Search_Service_CrawlDB2"
$searchCrawlDBServer = "SharePointSQL"
$crawlDatabase = New-SPEnterpriseSearchCrawlDatabase -SearchApplication $SSA -DatabaseName
$searchCrawlDBName -DatabaseServer $searchCrawlDBServer
$crawlStoresManager = new-Object Microsoft.Office.Server.Search.Administration.CrawlStorePa
rtitionManager($SSA)
$crawlStoresManager.BeginCrawlStoreRebalancing()
```

Change $searchCrawlDBName and $searchCrawlDBServer to match your environment. Then to check the status of adding the crawl database, you would run:

```
cls
$SSA = Get-SPEnterpriseSearchServiceApplication
$crawlStoresManager = new-Object Microsoft.Office.Server.Search.Administration.CrawlStorePa
rtitionManager($SSA)
Write-Host "CrawlStoresAreUnbalanced:" $crawlStoresManager.CrawlStoresAreUnbalanced()
Write-Host "CrawlStoreImbalanceThreshold:" $ssa.GetProperty("CrawlStoreImbalanceThreshold")
Write-Host "CrawlStoresAreUnbalanced:" $crawlStoresManager.CrawlStoresAreUnbalanced()
Write-Host "CrawlPartitionSplitThreshold:" $ssa.GetProperty("CrawlPartitionSplitThreshold")
$crawlLog = New-Object Microsoft.Office.Server.Search.Administration.CrawlLog $SSA
$dbInfo= $crawlLog.GetCrawlDatabaseInfo()
Write-Host "Number of Crawl Databases:"
$dbInfo.Count
$dbInfo.Values
```

Remember to look at the disk IOPS for the disks where the crawl databases are housed and the resources on the servers that house the crawl components and are performing the actual crawling. The crawl health reports in Central Administration will let you know if your freshness rate is to your liking. And, since crawling involves downloading content, an increase in the network speed between the content source and the server doing the crawling, will increase how fast the content is crawled and ingested into the index.

It is a balancing act for sure. When you add more crawlers, you may need to add an additional Content processor or throw more CPUs into the mix on the server that houses the content processing component. If you see the PID for the content processing component changing often then consider adding enough memory to give each CPU around 2GB of RAM, per CPU. So this means a 4CPU server would have 8GB of RAM by Microsoft's guidelines. In reality, 24GB for a SharePoint Application Server is the sweet spot.

Another way to increase ingestion into the index is through the use of an additional replica. Additional replica's server two functions, they allow search to spread the load of indexing content and they allow search to serve more queries in parallel and therefore decrease latency in queries. Adding additional CPU is sometimes needed when it comes to querying the index. The bigger the index gets, the more processing power you need to query it.

And, when it comes to the index, you should make more than one partition when you anticipate having more than 10 million items in your data corpus. If you want redundancy, you can use replicas or you can add partitions. Plan to add a partition for each 10 million items. For example if you have 16 million items in your corpus, you'll need to have two partitions. And if you want redundancy, you would have a total of four replicas, two per partition, which would mean you would need four servers to handle the index, one for each replica.

The Analytics Processing component stores information in the link database about searches and crawled documents, and this database has a supported limit of 60 million items. So, if the data corpus had 121 million items, you would need to have three link databases, according to the 60 million items per. There is another limit when it comes to link databases, which is four of them per service application. Microsoft has documented the search topology limits, item size limits, dictionary limits, Schema limits, crawl limits, query and result limits, ranking limits, and indexing limits at https://technet.microsoft.com/en-us/library/6a13cd9f-4b44-40d6-85aa-c70a8e5c34fe#Search. If you're looking to scale out the number of links databases in the topology, here's the only way to do it in SharePoint 2013 and 2016:

```
$SSA = Get-SPEnterpriseSearchServiceApplication
New-SPEnterpriseSearchLinksDatabase -DatabaseName LinksDB_2 -SearchApplication $SSA
```

Redesigning the search topology is nothing to take lightly. And, that is why there is so much written about the topic. Microsoft has a great post at https://technet.microsoft.com/en-us/library/dn727118.aspx, which is where the information you just read was gleaned. I'll bet you could Bing search any of that and find it reblogged, as well. Before we look at creating a search topology and re-creating a search topology, I'd just like to mention one more thing (from that TechNet post) and that is that the analytics processing component will need another database when you see the total processing time starting to take a lot longer than normal. You'll want to add a database when this happens and if the time starts to exceed 24 hours, you'll want to add more analytics components, or more resources to the VMs.

When it comes to creating a search service application vs. re-creating one, or migrating a search service application, there really is one primary difference and that is the PowerShell cmdlet either creates a new admin database or restores from an existing admin database. Depending on your troubleshooting situation you might be attempting to restore from an existing admin db or you might be creating a fresh $SSA.

If you're creating a fresh $SSA that will house its service endpoints in its own application pool within IIS, this is the PowerShell:

```
####Run with an account that is a farm admin, use the search service account for the app
pool user####

$ssaAppPoolName = "SharePoint Search Service Application Pool"
$SearchappPoolUserName = "Contoso\2013Search"

$ssaAppPool = Get-SPServiceApplicationPool -Identity $ssaAppPoolName -EA 0
if($ssaAppPool -eq $null)
{
Write-Host "Creating Search Service Application Pool..."

$SearchappPoolAccount = Get-SPManagedAccount -Identity $SearchappPoolUserName -EA 0
if($SearchappPoolAccount -eq $null)
{
Write-Host "Please supply the password for the Service Account..."
$ssappPoolCred = Get-Credential $SearchappPoolUserName
$SearchappPoolAccount = New-SPManagedAccount -Credential $ssappPoolCred -EA 0
}

$SearchappPoolAccount = Get-SPManagedAccount -Identity $SearchappPoolUserName -EA 0

if($SearchappPoolAccount -eq $null)
{
```

```
Write-Host "Cannot create or find the managed account $SearchappPoolUserName, please ensure
the account exists."
Exit -1
}

New-SPServiceApplicationPool -Name $ssaAppPoolName -Account $SearchappPoolAccount -EA 0 >
$null


}

## Search Specifics, we are single server farm ##

$searchServerName = (Get-ChildItem env:computername).value

$serviceAppName = "Enterprise Search Services"

$searchDBName = "Search"

## Grab the Application Pool for Service Application Endpoint ##

$ssaAppPool = Get-SPServiceApplicationPool $ssaAppPoolName

## Start Search Service Instances ##

Write-Host "Starting Search Service Instances..."

Start-SPEnterpriseSearchServiceInstance $searchServerName

Start-SPEnterpriseSearchQueryAndSiteSettingsServiceInstance $searchServerName

## Create the Search Service Application and Proxy ##

Write-Host "Creating Search Service Application and Proxy..."

$searchServiceApp = New-SPEnterpriseSearchServiceApplication -Name $serviceAppName
-ApplicationPool $ssaAppPoolName -DatabaseName $searchDBName

$searchProxy = New-SPEnterpriseSearchServiceApplicationProxy -Name "$serviceAppName Proxy"
-SearchApplication $searchServiceApp

## Clone the default Topology (which is empty) and create a new one and then activate it ##

Write-Host "Configuring Search Component Topology..."

$appserv = Get-SPEnterpriseSearchServiceInstance -Identity $searchServerName

Get-SPEnterpriseSearchServiceInstance -Identity $appserv

$ssa = Get-SPEnterpriseSearchServiceApplication

$newTopology = New-SPEnterpriseSearchTopology -SearchApplication $ssa
```

```
New-SPEnterpriseSearchAdminComponent -SearchTopology $newTopology -SearchServiceInstance
$appserv

New-SPEnterpriseSearchCrawlComponent -SearchTopology $newTopology -SearchServiceInstance
$appserv

New-SPEnterpriseSearchContentProcessingComponent -SearchTopology $newTopology
-SearchServiceInstance $appserv

New-SPEnterpriseSearchAnalyticsProcessingComponent -SearchTopology $newTopology
-SearchServiceInstance $appserv

New-SPEnterpriseSearchQueryProcessingComponent -SearchTopology $newTopology
-SearchServiceInstance $appserv

New-SPEnterpriseSearchIndexComponent -SearchTopology $newTopology -SearchServiceInstance
$appserv

Set-SPEnterpriseSearchTopology -Identity $newTopology

Write-Host "Search Service Application installation Complete!"

##END SEARCH
```

The only thing you'll want to change for your environment are definitely the value stored in $SearchappPoolUserName and possibly the name of the app pool that is stored in $ssaAppPoolName. And, as I mentioned earlier, the only real difference between creating a new search service application and restoring one from an existing topology, is the admin database.

If you notice in the previous script, we are issuing the New-SPEnterpriseSearchServiceApplication cmdlet and in the script that follows, we are issuing the Restore-SPEnterpriseSearchServiceApplication cmdlet and specifying the database name for the admin database, Prod_Search. This restore script assumes that the Prod_Search database and the SQL logins are already in place in the SQL server.

```
Add-PSSnapin "Microsoft.SharePoint.PowerShell"

$SPSearchPoolAccount = Get-SPManagedAccount "PROD-SP_SearchSvc"
New-SPServiceApplicationPool -Name "SharePoint Search Services" -Account
$SPSearchPoolAccount

$applicationPool = Get-SPServiceApplicationPool "SharePoint Search Services"

# Gets the Search service instance and sets a variable to use in the next command
$searchInst = Get-SPEnterpriseSearchServiceInstance -local

Restore-SPEnterpriseSearchServiceApplication -Name 'SharePoint Search Service'
-applicationpool $applicationPool -databasename 'Prod_Search' -databaseserver SharePointSQL
-AdminSearchServiceInstance $searchInst
```

```
$ssa = Get-SPEnterpriseSearchServiceApplication
New-SPEnterpriseSearchServiceApplicationProxy -Name "SharePoint Search Service Proxy"
-SearchApplication $ssa

$ssap = Get-SPEnterpriseSearchServiceApplicationProxy
Add-SPServiceApplicationProxyGroupMember -member $ssap -identity " "

$newTopology = New-SPEnterpriseSearchTopology -SearchApplication $ssa
$host1 = "Cicintapp2"
$searchServiceInstance = Get-SPEnterpriseSearchServiceInstance | Where {$_.Server.Address
-eq "$server"}
New-SPEnterpriseSearchAdminComponent –SearchTopology $newTopology -SearchServiceInstance
$host1
New-SPEnterpriseSearchContentProcessingComponent –SearchTopology $newTopology
-SearchServiceInstance $host1
New-SPEnterpriseSearchAnalyticsProcessingComponent –SearchTopology $newTopology
-SearchServiceInstance $host1
New-SPEnterpriseSearchCrawlComponent –SearchTopology $newTopology -SearchServiceInstance
$host1
New-SPEnterpriseSearchIndexComponent –SearchTopology $newTopology -SearchServiceInstance
$host1
New-SPEnterpriseSearchQueryProcessingComponent –SearchTopology $newTopology
-SearchServiceInstance $host1

Set-SPEnterpriseSearchTopology -Identity $newTopology

Write-Host "Search Done!"
```

And that's basically all you have to do to restore your search service application to the same version of SharePoint, since the admin database has all the information about the previous service application. If you had extended the number crawl databases or link databases, you'll want to do that again.

When it comes to removing a corrupted search service application and all of its databases, you can use the Central Administration GUI or you can use these two lines of PowerShell:

```
get-spserviceapplication | Where-Object {$_.typename -like "search service*"} |
Remove-spserviceapplication -RemoveData -confirm:$false
get-spserviceapplicationproxy | Where-Object {$_.typename -like "search service*"} |
Remove-spserviceapplicationproxy -RemoveData -confirm:$false
```

Before we end this chapter, let's do one exercise.

PREPARING FOR A PEOPLE CONTENT SOURCE

The purpose of this exercise is to prepare for crawling people content. The prerequisites for people search to work are as follows:

- Create a working Search Service Application

- Create a managed metadata service application and make sure managed metadata service is running

- User Profile Synchronization is configured and is synching

1. Open Central Administration, navigate to Application Management > Manage Service applications.

2. Click the row that contains your User Profile service application, making sure not to open the User Profile service application. This causes the ribbon to illuminate.

3. Click **Administrators** in the ribbon.

4. Type the user name for the default crawl account that will be used to retrieve people data in Domain\UserName format and click **Add**.

5. In the permissions list, select the **Retrieve People Data for Search Crawlers** check box.

6. Click **OK**.

To make sure that that account is used to crawl the profile store, you next need to create a crawl rule.

1. Navigate to the search service application.

2. Click **Crawl Rules**.

3. On the Manage Crawl Rules page, click **New Crawl Rule**.

4. If you used HTTP for the MySite host, type **sps3://<url to mysite host>** and if you used HTTPS for the MySite host, type **sps3s://<url to the mysite host>** in the path.

5. Select the **Use regular expression syntax for matching this rule** check box.

6. Select **Include all items in this path**.

7. Select **Specify a different content access account** and give the account that you gave the Retrieve People Data for Search Crawlers in the domain\username format, once more.

8. Enter the password and confirm it.

   If you are using SSL to encrypt website traffic, go ahead and clear the "Do not allow Basic Authentication" if you want. **If you are not using SSL, do not clear the** "Do not allow Basic Authentication" because if you do, you will be allowing credentials to go across the wire in plain text.

9. Click **OK**.

Now you are ready to create the People content source.

10. Make sure that the start address for the MySite host and its associated start address for the User Profile service are not inside of any existing content sources and if they are, remove the start addresses for the MySite host and User Profile service from the existing content source.

11. Click **New Content source** from the Content Sources page.

12. Name the content source **People**. Use **SharePoint sites** for the content source.

13. Add the MySite host URL and the User Profile service profile store to the start addresses.

14. Leave the **Crawl everything under the host name for each start address** check box selected and create some crawl schedules, making sure that they finish at least two hours before the other non-people content sources start.

15. Start a full crawl.

16. After the full crawl completes, and if you are synching user photos from Active Directory, run the following PowerShell.

```
Update-SPProfilePhotoStore -CreateThumbnailsForImportedPhotos 1
-MySiteHostLocation "<URL to mysites host>"
```

The URL of the MySites host is something like `https://mysites.domain.com`.

In this chapter, we skimmed a few proverbial snowflakes off the top of the iceberg that is search administration. There is certainly deeper water than what we went into here; however, that's not to discredit anything here because there was a lot of good information about troubleshooting the various parts of the search process. There was some really cool PowerShell and a lot of references to Microsoft TechNet and other blog posts that can help with diving deeper into the search ocean.

In the next chapter, we're going to bounce all over SharePoint with examples of various issues you might encounter as we discuss the fixes to those issues.

CHAPTER 8

Service Application Troubleshooting

In order to troubleshoot something, you have to know how it works. Consider a race car mechanic; she needs to know how the engine fits together and what makes it work, in order to troubleshoot why it is not working as desired. Also, race car mechanics do say, "As desired." Knowing how things fit together is why in the previous seven chapters, we've covered quite a bit of information, not in hopes of turning you into a female race car mechanic, but to better acquaint you with the underpinnings of SharePoint. In those chapters, we saw what changes SharePoint brings to a Windows server's file system, IIS, and registry. We talked about the back-end SQL server. I spoke at some length about search and modifying the search topology.

In this chapter, we'll talk about some issues you might encounter with service applications. And just a forewarning at times it might seem like we are bouncing, wildly, from topic to topic, much like you might have to do if you ever find yourself in a support role for SharePoint. There will be drastic "fly hitting the windshield" stops that are followed by completely different service applications. We'll talk a little bit about configuration of various services, but not nearly as much as the previous chapters, since we're assuming you've configured the service application with the AutoSPInstaller, or via PowerShell, or via the GUI. In some situations, I'll mention things that are not configured OOTB, where it's needed.

For example, when it comes to getting Excel Services to render spreadsheets, you might experience a message that is similar to "The workbook cannot be opened" like that shown in Figure 8-1.

Figure 8-1. *The workbook can't be opened.*

S. Simpkins, *Troubleshooting SharePoint*, https://doi.org/10.1007/978-1-4842-3138-8_8

Or, you might receive a message that reads "Unable to process request, check with your administrator." In either of these cases, you should take note of the web application that houses the files you're working with and trying to open in the browser using Excel Services. To get the web application, you could run get-SPWebApplication and then find the part of the URL that correlates to the URL for where you documents are located. Then once you have this web application, you'll want to instantiate it into a variable that you can call the GrantAccessToProcessIdentity method for the identity that Excel Services uses to connect to the endpoint within IIS. You already know how to determine that from earlier in the book, finding the app pool in IIS, then viewing the applications, similar to Figure 8-2.

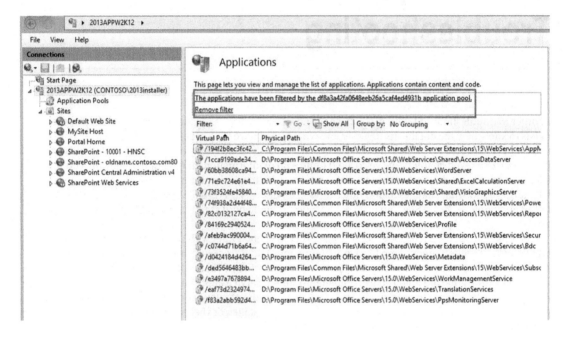

Figure 8-2. Endpoints inside of an application pool

We can see in Figure 8-2, that the application pool named df8a3a42fa0648eeb26a5caf4ed4931b
that runs under CONTOSO\2013svcapps has the endpoint for the Excel services application where it says
D:\Program Files\Microsoft Office Servers\15.0\WebServices\ExcelCalculationServer. It is the fourth line
down on the eyechart in Figure 8-2. Figure 8-3 shows the identity being used for the app pool with name of
df8a3a42fa0648eeb26a5caf4ed4931b in IIS.

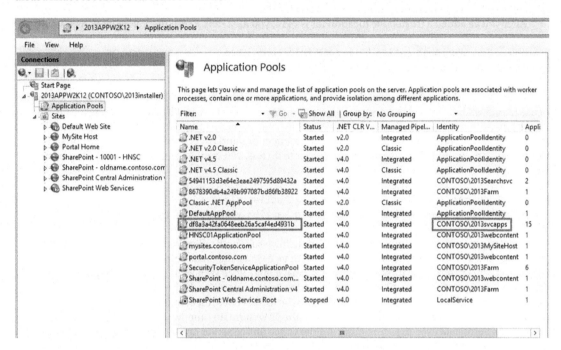

Figure 8-3. *The app pool named df8a3a42fa0648eeb26a5caf4ed4931b*

Another way that we could have found the identity that we need for the GrantAccessToProcessIdentity
method, is by opening Central Administration and looking at configure service accounts and looking at the
Excel services application, as shown in Figure 8-4.

Service Application Pool - SharePoint Hosted Services

Changing this account will impact the following components in this farm:

Access 2010 Service (Access Services 2010 Web Service Application)
App Management Service (App Management Service Application)
Business Data Connectivity Service (Business Data Connectivity Service Application)
Excel Services Application (Excel Services Application Web Service Application)
Machine Translation Service (Machine Translation Service)
Managed Metadata Service (Managed Metadata Service)

Select an account for this component

CONTOSO\2013svcapps

Register new managed account

Figure 8-4. *Excel Services is using Contoso\2013svcapps*

One more thing to take into account is whether the files live inside sites with URLs that begin https. If they do, you'll need to add a trusted file location for HTTPs. By default, a trusted file location for http will exist, but HTTPs will need to be added. You can do this from within the Excel services application. Before you add it, check if there are any user-defined functions assemblies registered by clicking User Defined Function Assemblies. If there are assemblies, then remember to check the box to allow user-defined function assemblies when you create the trusted file location for HTTPs.

After you've added a trusted file location for HTTPs, you are ready to run the following PowerShell:

```
$webApp = Get-SPWebApplication http://portal.contoso.com
$webApp.GrantAccessToProcessIdentity("CONTOSO\2013svcapps")
```

Now you should be able to open those Excel workbooks. If you have an Office Web Apps farm and want to use Excel workbooks that have external data connections configured, you'll want to change the OWA so that it does not try to view the Excel workbooks and instead uses Excel Services. This is because Office Web Apps does not support Excel workbooks with data connections and Excel Services happily supports these workbooks with external data connections. In order to do this, you want to suppress Office Web Apps from viewing .xls and .xlsx workbooks.

```
New-SPWOPISuppressionSetting -extension xlsx -action view
 New-SPWOPISuppressionSetting -extension xls -action view
```

Speaking of Office Web Apps, if you're experiencing issues with Office Web Apps, it might be that the farm is not able to resolve to the SharePoint server or vice versa, the SharePoint server cannot resolve to the OWA farm. Things that cause this are ports being closed, the Office Web Apps servers being patched while the Office Web Apps farm was still connected to SharePoint, or possibly the certificate used by Office Web Apps has expired or was renewed with a certificate whose SAN does not contain the FQDNs of the machine names for the OWA servers along with the name of the OWA farm. In other words, the subject alternative name of the certificate used to secure traffic for the Office online server only contains the name of the Host that is running the OWA farm, or only contains the name of the OWA farm (e.g., owa.contoso.com) and not the name of the host or hosts in the farm.

Office Online Server or Office Web Apps server requires port 80 for HTTP traffic, port 443 for https traffic, and port 809 if more than one host in the Office Web Apps farm. Connectivity to SharePoint from the Office Web apps farm can be tested by using telnet, ping, and by trying to resolve one of the SharePoint sites. The same connectivity can be performed from SharePoint to the Office Web Apps farm using telnet and ping. When testing connectivity to the Office Web Apps farm , just take the farm address (e.g., https://owa.contoso.com) and append /hosting/discovery to that URL to make https://owa.contoso.com/hosting/discovery. This should open to an XML file that shows the various connections to Office Web Apps.

When applying patches to an Office Web Apps farm, it's a good idea to remove the WOPI binding from SharePoint, remove the Office Web Apps farm, then patch the server, then create the Office Web Apps farm, and then re-create the binding. This is why if you have two Hosts in your Office Web Apps farm, or Office Online server farm, as it is called in the new 2016 era, you can avoid the end user experiencing down time. If this hasn't happened, and your Office Web Apps farm is down, you should run:

```
Remove-SPWopiBinding -All:$true
```

This will remove the connection to the Windows Open Platform Interface (WOPI) farm from SharePoint. Next, you can log in to the Office Web Apps farm, and if you only have one machine in the farm run:

```
Remove-OfficeWebAppsMachine
```

If you have more than one machine, run Remove-OfficeWebAppsMachine on all the machines, then after you have made sure that the certificate subject alternative name contains the name of the OWA farm (e.g., owa.contoso.com) and then names of any hosts that will be part of the farm (e.g., Server1.contoso.com) go ahead and run:

```
New-OfficeWebAppsFarm –InternalURL https://owa.contoso.com -ExternalUrl
https://owa.contoso.com -EditingEnabled -CertificateName owa
```

This command will create a new Office web app farm on the master server. If more servers are going to join the farm, you'll need to run:

```
New-OfficeWebAppsMachine -MachineToJoin server1.contoso.com
```

Where server1.contoso.com is the first server in the Web Apps farm and this command is being run on server2.contoso.com. Server2.contoso.com would also already have the cert with the friendly name of "owa" already installed.

So, in a nutshell, if you have a one-server OWA farm and it is accidentally patched while it is bound to SharePoint or while it is part of an Office Web Apps farm, you'll need to fix the host. The cleanest way is to re-create the Office Web Apps farm, in this case. Remove the WOPI binding (Remove-SPWopiBinding) from SharePoint, then Remove the Office Web Apps farm, by running Remove-OfficeWebAppsMachine. If you get trouble running Remove-OfficeWebAppsMachine and are in an Office Web Apps farm with more than one Web Apps host, go to another host and run Repair-OfficeWebAppsFarm. Repair-OffieWebAppsFarm will remove any servers marked as unhealthy from the Web Apps farm; so, be careful where you run it from, unless that is your intention.

When SharePoint is unable to reach SQL and sometimes when a configuration has been changed somewhere, you'll get to see the beautiful Server Error in / Application screen. Sometimes this screen is referred to as the YSOD, or Yellow Screen of Death. A sample of this screen is shown in Figure 8-5.

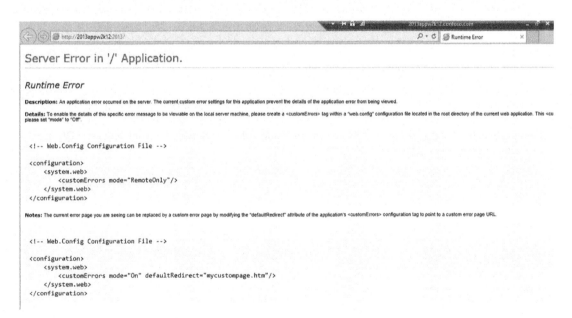

Figure 8-5. *Yellow screen of death*

The yellow screen of death advises how you can see more information. It says to change the custom Errors from its default of On to RemoteOnly. You can easily do this by opening IIS manager and exploring to the web.config for Central Administration. Whenever you work with web.configs, be sure to make a backup copy. After you take the backup, you can open the web.config with Notepad, search for customErrors and then change the mode to RemoteOnly, as shown here:

```
<httpHandlers />
    <customErrors mode="RemoteOnly" />
    <httpRuntime maxRequestLength="51200" requestValidationMode="2.0" />
```

Now that you've updated the web.config to show you more information, you will see something similar to Figure 8-6.

Figure 8-6. *Not joined to a farm, or can't reach SQL*

The screen tries to tell you what is going on, but you can't necessarily take it literally until you rule out connectivity to the SQL server and that the SQL server instance is online. If you connect to your SQL and see something like this image (see Figure 8-7), you can probably rule out the need to telnet between SQL and SharePoint, or perform ping tests.

Sql Server Configuration Manager					
Name	State	Start Mode	Log On As	Process ID	Service Type
SQL Full-text Filte...	Stopped	Manual	NT Service\MSSQL...	0	
SQL Server (MSS...	Stopped	Automatic	contoso\sqldba	0	SQL Server
SQL Server Browser	Stopped	Other (Boot, Syste...	NT AUTHORITY\LO...	0	
SQL Server Agent...	Stopped	Automatic	contoso\sqldba	0	SQL Agent

Figure 8-7. *SQL service started?*

Just start the SQL instance and SQL Agent and then refresh your Central Administration or SharePoint site. This will happen when SQL is not set to automatically restart after power outages, and so forth. If you get the YSOD, you should immediately check that the SQL instance is online. If you've determined that the instance is online, you next need to telnet between SharePoint and SQL on port 1433 or whichever port SQL is listening on. Ping should also be successful. If both of those are true, ask your DBA, or if you have the necessary access to run the sp_who stored procedure and provide the output, as it is possible that the server fell out of the farm. If for some stupid reason VMware snapshots, or hyperV snapshots were used on this SharePoint farm, you might be in a rebuild scenario if presented with the YSOD, and you know that you have not disjoined the VM from the farm.

If you're experiencing issues with page loads or want to get more logging about errors, you can turn on failed request tracing and set runtime error debugging to Off as opposed to Remote Only. This way you can run the request from your machine or from a server that is not involved with serving page requests, in order to get a cleaner and possibly clearer idea of what is causing the issue. In a future chapter, we will use ProcMon to track file system level issues that could also play into performance, or lack thereof.

To enable runtime error debugging, make a backup of the web.config for the web application where the trouble sites are under and then in the web.config set CustomErrors mode="Off". The default is CustomErrors="On" so make sure to turn it to off. Then run a search in the web.config for "compilation" and find the line that reads <compilation batch="false" debug="false"> and then set the debug to true, so that it reads, <compilation batch="false" debug="true">. Now reload the page and you'll get results that may better help you identify the issue at hand.

These are the various locations on the file system where web.configs are located.

- \\Inetpub\wwwroot\wss\VirtualDirectories\ Port_Number or site name. The web.config file that defines configuration settings for a SharePoint content Web application.

- \\Inetpub\wwwroot\wss\VirtualDirectories\ Port_Number_of_Central_ Administration. The web.config file that defines configuration settings for the SharePoint Central Administration application.

- %ProgramFiles%\Common Files\Microsoft Shared\web server extensions\15\ CONFIG. The web.config file and other .config files that together define configuration settings for extending other Web applications.

- %ProgramFiles%\Common Files\Microsoft Shared\web server extensions\15\ ISAPI. The web.config file that defines configuration settings for the /_vti_bin virtual directory.

- %ProgramFiles%\Common Files\Microsoft Shared\web server extensions\15\ TEMPLATE\LAYOUTS. The web.config file that defines configuration settings for the /_layouts virtual directory.

Normally, you only need to modify the web.config for the actual site itself, but these other locations may be helpful in some cases. Just make sure to make a copy of the web config and then rename the copy to web.config.bak before editing the actual web.config

Failed request tracing is enabled inside of IIS and then it stores information about failed requests in logs under the %SystemDrive%\inetpub\logs\FailedReqLogFiles directory. To enable failed request tracing you need to specify the types of content to trace. For example, if you know the name of the page that you're looking to trace you can specify just the name of the page, or you could leave Failed Request Tracing set for all content. If you're not sure just leave it set for all content, as shown in Figure 8-8.

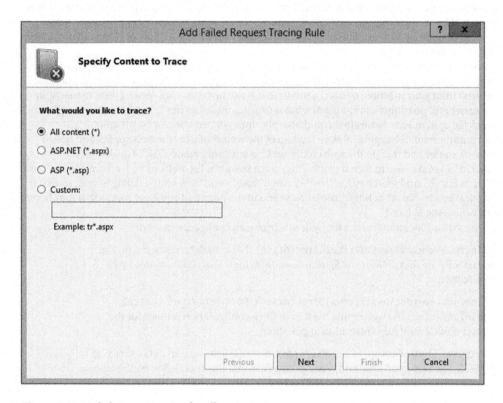

Figure 8-8. *Failed request tracing for all content*

After, clicking next, you'll need to know what event IDs you want to trace. If you're getting access denied, you might want to trace on event 401, or maybe you want 400-499. It's up to you. You can also trace based on Time taken, and event severity. Figure 8-9 demonstrates where this is set and you must make trace condition before you can enable tracing at the site level.

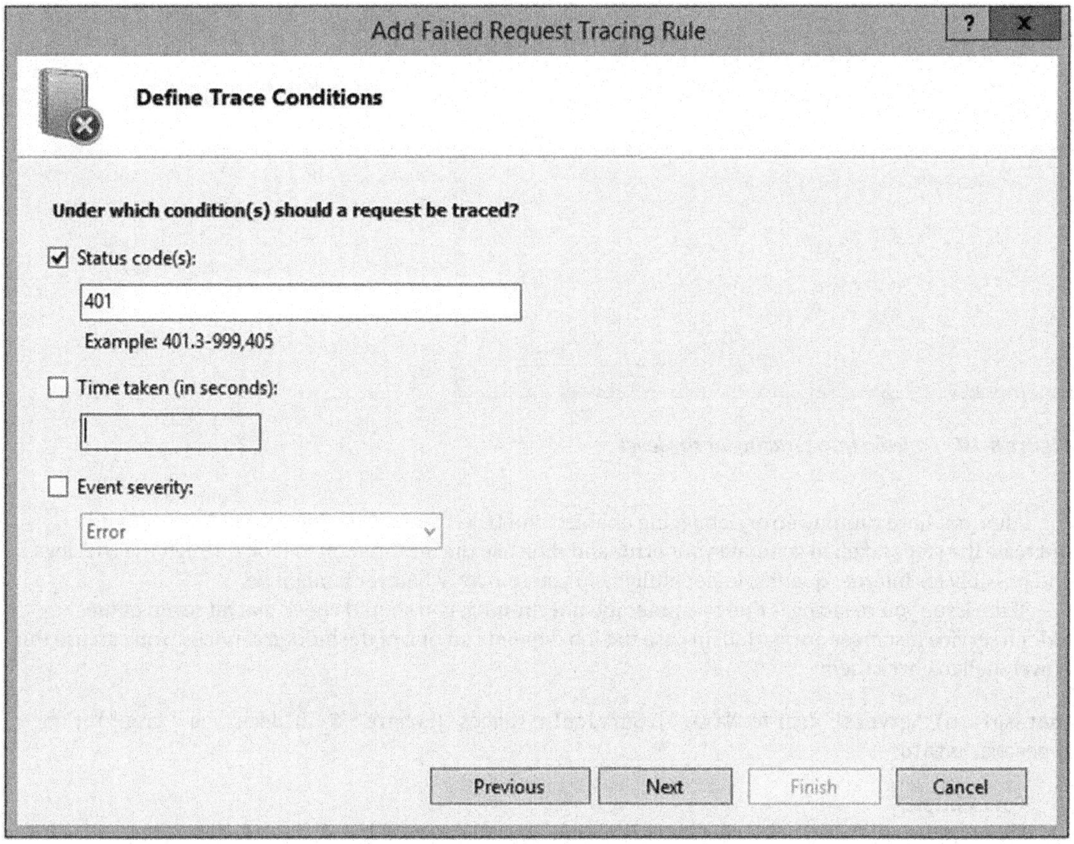

Figure 8-9. *Tracing on status code for event ID 401*

When it comes to the screen to select trace providers, just leave them all selected unless you know you do not care about one or more, then click finish. After you have selected the server node, clicked failed request tracing, clicked add... and then went through the steps we just discussed, you can go to the site level under sites, and enable failed request tracing. Figure 8-10 shows the checkbox to enable failed request tracing at the site level. You can also add more details and rules at the site level.

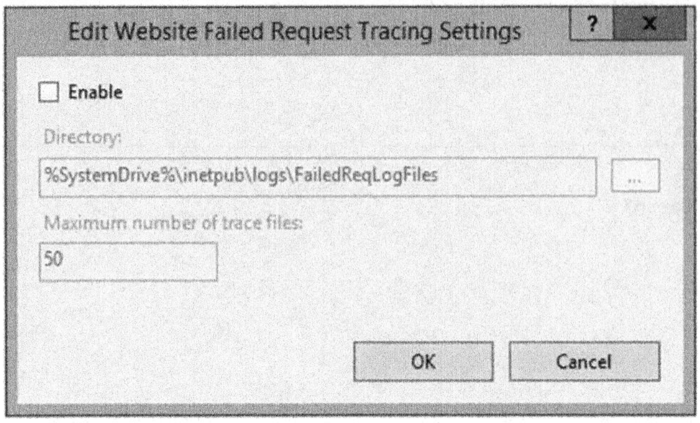

Figure 8-10. *Failed request tracing at site level*

After you have runtime error debugging enabled and failed request tracing enabled, you should re-create the steps taken to generate your error and then use the information to look through the ULS logs, and possibly for Internet queries, to hopefully help you resolve, whatever it might be.

If the issue you're facing is due to a timer job not running, you should check that all seven of the hidden service instances are started, in case the job depends on one of the hidden services. You can use this PowerShell to check them:

```
(get-spfarm).Servers["<serverName>"].ServiceInstances | where {$_.hidden -eq "true"} | ft
typename, status
```

For example,

```
(get-spfarm).Servers["2013appw2k12"].ServiceInstances | where {$_.hidden -eq "true"} | ft
typename, status
```

If any of them are disabled and not online, you'll need to provision them. Just instantiate whichever service instance is disabled to a variable and then call the provision method. After you've verified that all seven hidden service instances are online, you can look for any failing timer jobs that may be contributing to your issue using this powershell script written by Stephen Swinney.

```
##Find Failed Timer Job History Entries
        $Timers = Get-SPTimerJob | where { $_.HistoryEntries.Status -eq "Failed" }
            ForEach ($Timer in $Timers)
                {
                    Write-Host $Timer is processing -foregroundcolor Blue
                    $Output += $Timer.HistoryEntries | select -first 10000 -Property
JobDefinitionTitle, JobDefinitionId, Status,StartTime,EndTime,ErrorMessage,
WebApplicationName, WebApplicationId, ServiceId, ServerId
                }
$Output | Out-Gridview
```

The cool thing about this script is that it outputs to a power grid, where you can filter and sort it further.

Once you have the Job Definition ID (JobDefinitionID), you could use this next bit of PowerShell to find the last ten times the timer job ran, because the job may have succeeded on other servers in the farm. You can also change the number from 10 to find more—say 20 or 200. It's your call. You can pipe the output to a file if you'd like, using out-file <path to a file>.

```
Get-SPTimerJob -Identity "80074ddf-ef54-46d3-a186-feaec4e4d2f4").HistoryEntries | select -
first 10
```

If you wanted to get that into a format where you could output it to a power grid, you could include more items and then pipe it into a table:

```
Get-SPTimerJob -Identity "80074ddf-ef54-46d3-a186-feaec4e4d2f4").HistoryEntries | select
-first 200 | Format-Table -Property Status,StartTime,EndTime,ErrorMessage –AutoSize
```

Then you could output it to a power grid using out-gridview

```
Get-SPTimerJob -Identity "80074ddf-ef54-46d3-a186-feaec4e4d2f4").HistoryEntries | select -
first 200 | Format-Table -Property Status,StartTime,EndTime,ErrorMessage –AutoSize | Out-
GridView
```

There are numerous timer jobs in SharePoint and they are trying to control SharePoint; so, if your farm is having issues, make sure that it is not due to any failed timer job. If you're only concerned with what has recently failed, and you are not concerned with finding the last 10,000 jobs with failure messages, you could run this:

```
Get-SPTimerJob | where { $_.HistoryEntries.Status -eq "Failed" } | Format-List displayname,
ID, LastRuntime
```

PowerShell will output the timer jobs that have failed. Then you could take one of the IDs and run the following:

```
(Get-SPTimerJob -Identity <ID>).historyentries | ? {$_.status -eq "failed"} | select -first 1000
```

For example,

```
(Get-SPTimerJob -Identity 71d95ef9-7af9-41e9-9667-a3ff3b7d4e6b).historyentries | ? {$_.
status -eq "failed"} | select -first 1000
```

The result will tell you what jobs have failed, when they failed, and the error message that was received. This is all information that is not available to you in the GUI without numerous clicks. While it is possible to go to Central Administration ➤ Monitoring ➤ Timer Jobs ➤ Check Job Status ➤ Job History ➤ View: Failed Jobs and see all of the information about when the job failed; you're not able to get the error message from Central Administration. Figure 8-11 shows an example of one of the error messages.

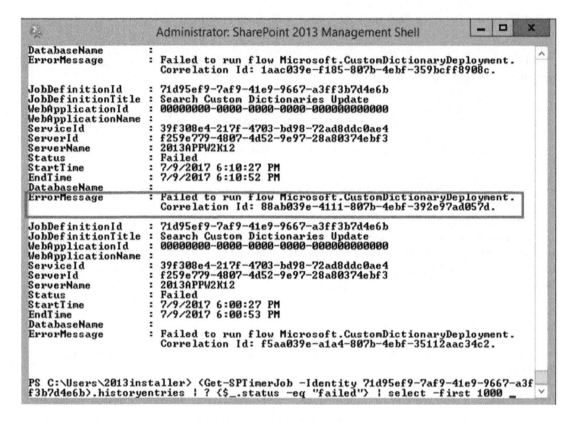

Figure 8-11. *Error message not available in Central Administration*

In this case, the issue was due to the default content access account not having read access to the managed metadata store. Finding this answer is much easier when you have the error message "Failed to run Microsoft.CustomDictionaryDeployment" to use for Bing queries. Figure 8-12 shows the change to the permissions for the managed metadata service application.

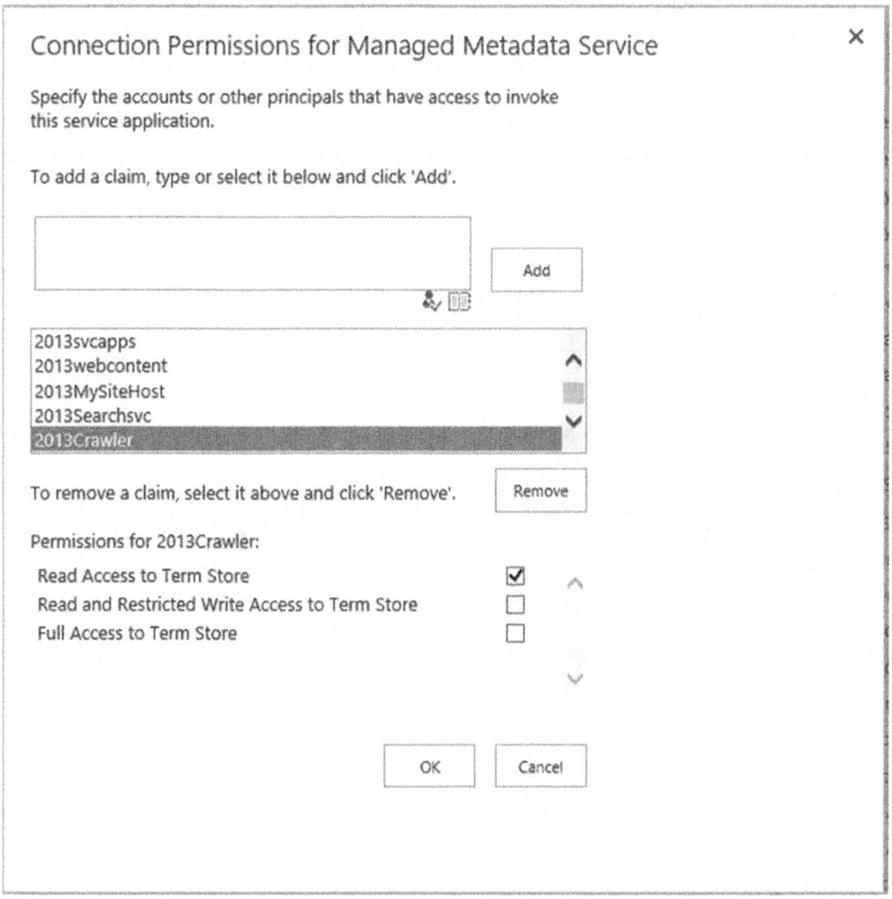

Figure 8-12. *Read permission for the default content access account to Managed Metadata*

The change to the permissions is open Managed Service Applications. Select the row for managed metadata without opening the term store, so as to illuminate the ribbon. Then click Permissions and add the content access account. If you installed your SharePoint using AutoSPInstaller, you'll see similar accounts as shown in Figure 8-12, but you might not see the default content access account and you might have the Search Custom Dictionaries Update timer job failing every ten minutes.

The managed metadata service is easily migrated from one farm to another by simply creating a new managed metadata service application and specifying the name of the migrated database. Or, creating a managed metadata service application and then changing the database using the Properties button on the ribbon in Managed Service Applications.

Sometimes the Managed Metadata service application gives the message "The Managed Metadata Service or Connection is currently not available. The Application Pool or Managed Metadata Web Service may not have been started. Please Contact your administrator." When this happens, make sure that Anonymous Authentication is enabled for the server and that it is set to IUSR, as shown in Figure 8-13.

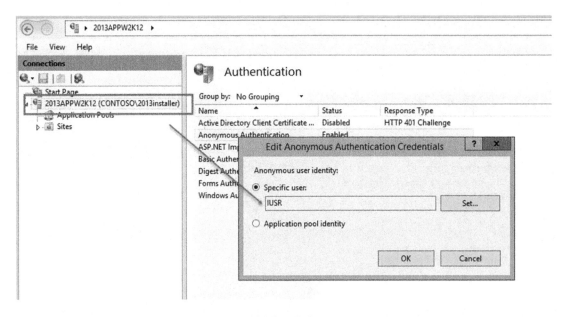

Figure 8-13. *Server-level Anonymous access–enabled and identity is IUSR*

Then after you've verified that Anonymous authentication is enabled for the server, go ahead and make sure that the account that the **identity used for the web application's application pool in IIS** has read access to the term store, by checking the permissions, the same way we did for the default content access account. Finally, make sure that the managed metadata service instance is provisioned and online and then make sure that the database server is not out of space.

Microsoft has a really decent TechNet post for timer jobs at https://technet.microsoft.com/en-us/library/cc678870.aspx that I then took that information and formatted it into a really nice table that is available at https://anothersharepointblog.com/timer-jobs-in-sharepoint.

If you ever want to stop all the timers in your farm, and then start them, this is the PowerShell you'll want to use:

```
# execute mode of Stop, Start, or Restart
$executeMode = "Start"
# comma separate server names
$servers = "Server-WFE,Server-WFE1,Server-WFE2,Server-APP,Server-APP1,Server-APP2"

foreach($s in $servers.Split(','))
  {
    Try
    {
        Write-Host "Getting Timer Service for " $s
        $service = Get-WmiObject -ComputerName $s Win32_Service -Filter "Name='SPTimerv4'"
        Write-Host "Got Service: " $service
        if($executeMode.ToLower() -ne "start")
        {
            #this is a stop or a restart, so stop the timer
            Write-Host "Attempting to Stop Timer on " $s
            $service.InvokeMethod("StopService",$null)
            Write-Host "Timer Stopped on " $s
        }
        if($executeMode.ToLower() -ne "stop")
        {
            #this is a start or a restart so start the timer
            Write-Host "Attempting to Start Timer on " $s
            $service.InvokeMethod("StartService",$null)
            Write-Host "Timer Started on  " $s
        }
    }
    Catch [System.exception]
    {
        "Exception occurred"
    }

  }
```

When troubleshooting any issue in SharePoint, it's a good idea to get a new log file, then turn up the logging level to verboseEX, once you've tried looking for the data without verboseEX levels set. Here are the PowerShell lines to get a new log file on a particular server and then turn up the logging level in the entire farm.

As a result, you might want to run the new-splogfile on all servers before you turn up the logging level

```
New-SPLogFile
Set-SPLoglevel -traceseverity VerboseEx
```

After you've finished re-creating the steps that led to the error, you can set the logging level back to the OOB defaults, and you'll want to in order to keep your log sizes low, by running this one-liner on one of the servers in your farm:

```
Clear-SPLogLevel
```

341

Getting outgoing email working on your SharePoint farm is a fairly straightforward process and incoming is a little bit more involved. To configure outgoing and incoming email you need to install the Simple Mail Transfer Protocol (SMTP) feature in Windows Server. You can do this with these two lines of PowerShell:

```
Import-Module ServerManager
Add-WindowsFeature SMTP-Server
```

Then you can either use the Windows services management console (services.msc) or run these PowerShell lines to set the service to automatic and started

```
Set-Service SMTPSVC -startuptype "Automatic"
Start-Service smtpsvc
```

Incoming mail is dependent on the DNS environment and/or exchange routing mail to your SharePoint. In order for the mail to get to your SharePoint servers there needs to be a Mail Exchanger (MX) record in your domain that routes mail to your SharePoint server. If you want your SharePoint server to send mail from SharePoint.Contoso.com as opposed to 2013Appw2k12.Contoso.com you'll need to point the MX record to an A record named SharePoint.Contoso.com that points to the primary IP of the 2013Appw2k12 server. Then you would need to modify the SMTP service so that it has a domain named, SharePoint.Contoso.com. To modify the default domain, just right-click it and rename it from Servername.contoso.com to the name of the A record that the MX record points traffic toward.

After the SMTP feature is installed and started, you'll want to open it and capture events about email. To do this just open Internet Information Services (IIS) Manager 6.0 (inetmgr6), drive down until you see the SMTP Virtual Server, right-click and choose properties, and enable logging. After logging is enabled, click the Properties button, and then click the Advanced tab. Select all the extended logging options, as shown in Figure 8-14.

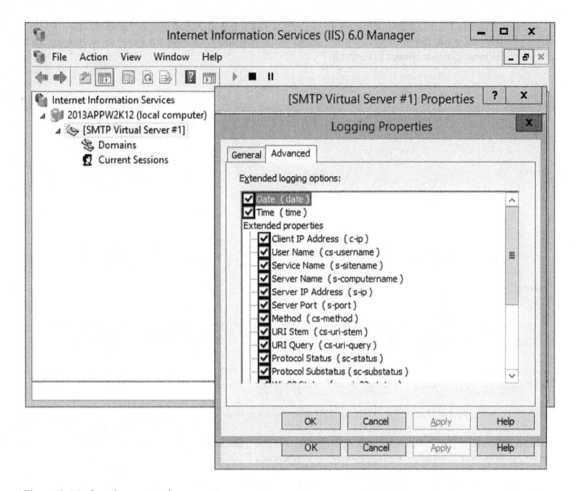

Figure 8-14. *Logging properties*

After you've selected all the logging properties and applied your changes, click the Access tab, and then click the Relay Restrictions button. Select the "Only the list below" radio button, and then add the following:

- Local host 127.0.0.1

- IP address of the server

- Network range that the server is part of (group of computers)

- IP address of any Exchange servers serving as Exchange Hubs, not in the network range

Next, click the Connection button and make sure that the "All except the list below" radio button is selected, and then click OK. After you click OK, open the Windows Services console (services.msc) and make sure that the Simple Mail Transport Protocol is set to restart on the Recovery tab. Make sure it starts. Finally, open the Drop folder security by navigating to C:\inetpub\mailroot\drop. Assuming that the Drop folder location has not been modified, and then once on the Drop folder, give WSS_WPG NTFS Read & Execute rights, List Folder Contents, and Read permissions. And, give WSS_ADMIN_WPG NTFS Full Control rights. You'll want to do this for each SharePoint Server handling Incoming Email.

Now, go back to Central Administration and open the Outgoing email settings and enter in the name of the server that you're on, an email Alias for the SharePoint farm (doesn't matter if it exists in Exchange), and a Reply-to address, like that shown in Figure 8-15.

Outgoing E-Mail Settings ⓘ

Mail Settings
Specify the SMTP mail server to use for Microsoft SharePoint Foundation e-mail-based notifications for alerts, invitations, and administrator notifications. Personalize the **From address** and **Reply-to address**.

Outbound SMTP server:

| 2013APPW2K12 |

From address:

| Sharepoint@contoso.com |

Reply-to address:

| No-reply@contoso.com |

Character set:

| 65001 (Unicode UTF-8) | ∨ |

Figure 8-15. Outgoing email

At this point, you can send mail from the SharePoint server. After you finish, you can test that email is working by using the following PowerShell:

```
Send-MailMessage -To "<enter an email address here>" -From "Sharepoint@contoso.com" -Subject
"Testing Smtp Mail" -Body "Message Body" -SmtpServer "<Enter Server Name here>"
```

An example of what this script would look like for the farm shown in Figure 8-15, would be as follows:

```
Send-MailMessage -To "zstacemeister@gmail.com" -From "Sharepoint@contoso.com" -Subject
"Testing Smtp Mail" -Body "Message Body" -SmtpServer "2013APPW2K12"
```

In order to receive mail, you have to make sure that exchange has a connector. This is the PowerShell that you could use, assuming the name of the MX record was SharePoint, and that you created an A record that was named SharePoint.contoso.com that pointed to your SharePoint server, if your server name was not SharePoint.Contoso.com. In other words, if your opted not to rename your default domain in the SMTP service on your server, the connector would use the server name where you see SMTP:sharepoint.contoso. com;1 beneath, for example, SMTP:2013APPw2k12;1.

```
New-SendConnector -Name 'SharePoint' -Usage 'Custom' -AddressSpaces
'SMTP:sharepoint.contoso.com;1' -IsScopedConnector $false -DNSRoutingEnabled $true
-UseExternalDNSServersEnabled $false -SourceTransportServers 'EXCHANGE'
```

The previous powershell is ran on the Exchange server, usually by the Exchane Admin. If you're not going to allow SharePoint to create distribution groups in Active Directory, you're only a few steps from having incoming mail configured. Just turn on Microsoft SharePoint Foundation Incoming E-Mail service on the services on server page for the servers in your farm that will have the SMTP feature installed. Servers that are not running SMTP do not need the Microsoft SharePoint Foundation Incoming E-Mail service enabled. After you have the incoming mail service instance started, navigate to incoming e-mail settings, select yes to enable sites to receive email, click the advanced settings mode, and enter in the location of your drop folder.

In order to use the advanced method that allows SharePoint to create distribution groups, you need to make sure that the account that runs the timer service has read write permissions on an OU in your Active Directory and this OU needs to specify in the incoming email settings. When you allow SharePoint to create distribution groups and contacts, you can make it so the SharePoint administrator has to approve the Distribution Groups before they are created. If you go this route, you'll need to manually approve the Distribution groups, but this will allow users to find email enabled lists in their Outlook address book.

Microsoft has an excellent TechNet article on configuring incoming mail at `https://technet.microsoft.com/en-us/library/cc262947.aspx`; however, the best article that I've seen, is written by Trevor Seward, and is located on the SharePointFarm.com at `https://thesharepointfarm.com/2013/02/a-practical-guide-to-implementing-incoming-email-using-the-sharepoint-directory-management-service/`.

When troubleshooting email, check connectivity using telnet and ping, check access lists in the SMTP service, check if alternate domain name is being used and that it is set in the SMTP service, verify DNS records, and exchange connectors are set. When you attempt to telnet, do so over port 25, the port that email uses. Also, check that the firewall is not blocking port 25 on your SharePoint Server. Chapter 6's Table 6-1 listed all the port that SharePoint needs open in order to operate effectively.

SQL Server Reporting Services is a really cool feature that SharePoint On-Premises supports that Office 365 does not support. If you ever find yourself in a position where you need to migrate the SSRS service application and all the SSRS reports from one SharePoint farm to another SharePoint farm, make sure the farms are at the same versions and then follow these steps:

1. Report server database names are fixed and cannot be renamed on new computer.

2. Report databases have not been copied or moved to SQL.

3. Pre-requisites: determine if there is an execution account; if yes, what are the credentials?

4. Get the login information for the SSRS databases.

To back up SSRS databases, service application, and proxy, follow these steps.

1. Log in to Source Farm and navigate to SSRS Manage Service Applications ➤ SSRS Services.

   The backup key to a password-protected file password is P@ssw0rd!. Click Manage Service Applications ➤ SSRS Services ➤ Key Management ➤ Backup Encryption Key.

2. Create a password and export the key to a directory.

3. Copy the key file to the target farm server and store in the backup\restore directory.

4. Backup the SSRS Service application using the SharePoint Backup and Restore. Click Backup and Restore ➤ Perform a Backup. Expand the Shared Service Applications. Select SSRS Services. Click Next and Select a backup location (make sure WSS_Admin_WPG and WSS_WPG have modify, read&execute, read on the backup location).

5. Backup the SSRS Service application proxy using the SharePoint Backup and Restore. Click Backup and Restore ➤ Perform a Backup. Expand Shared Service Proxies. Select SSRS Services . Click Next. Select a backup location.

6. Copy the backed up file to the destination server backup\restore directory.

To restore SSRS databases, service applications, and proxy, do the following.

1. Log in to the target\destination farm and run install-sprsservice and install-sprsserviceproxy.

2. Open Central Administration and navigate to Backup and Restore.

3. Click Restore from backup. Enter the backup\restore directory and click Refresh.

4. Select the service application backup from the top component and click Next.

5. Select the Reporting Services application and click Next.

6. When prompted for Login Names and Passwords, type the password for the login name that is displayed. The login name box should already be pre-populated with the login that was previously in use.

7. Click Start restore.

8. Repeat the process, but instead of restoring the service application, expand the Shared Services node and then expand the Shared Service Applications node.

9. Click Manage Service Applications ➤ SSRS Services ➤ Key Management ➤ Restore Encryption Key. Enter or browse to the path from step 3 of the backup steps, use the password from step 2 of the backup steps.

10. If there is an unattended execution account then enter that information.

11. Navigate to one of your lists that house reports and open a report.

If you ever get a weird issue related to access, when trying to run the report builder for SSRS, make sure to run this command that grants access to the account that is used by the application pool that houses the SSRS endpoint.

```
$webApp = Get-SPWebApplication "<web app url>"
$webApp.GrantAccessToProcessIdentity("<service app account>")
```

That little gem does wonders for Excel Services and other service applications whenever there is any oddball access denied or permission related issues.

If ever you're looking at Central Administration's upgrade and patch management, review database status and notice that some databases have the status 'Database is up to date, but some sites are not completely upgraded' you can identify the web application for the database by running

```
(Get-SPContentDatbase <databaseName>).webapplication
```

Where <databaseName> is replaced by the name of the database. Then you can run these lines of PowerShell to upgrade all of your content databases, if you only have one web application with a number of content databases.

```
$wa = Get-SPWebApplication -Identity "<WA URL>"
foreach($ContentDB in $wa.ContentDatabases)
{
    Upgrade-SPContentDatabase -id $ContentDB –confirm:$false
}
```

When you have numerous content databases to attach to one web application, you can use this PowerShell that Danny Pugh shared with us. You'll need to save it into a ps1 file and then call the ps1 file. You'll also need a txt file that contains, only the names of your databases and nothing more. Update the

$inputCSV variable to point to your text file that contains the database names. Update the $destinationpath variable to a location where you would like to log the outcome of the PowerShell script. And finally, update the $SPLogFileLoc variable to your SharePoint logging location. Use get-spdiagnosticconfig if you're not sure of the logging location.

Update any paths (e.g., E:\) to the valid paths in your environment and make sure the SQL Alias is correct per your cliconfg.exe.

```
add-pssnapin microsoft.sharepoint.powershell -ea 0

$OutputFile = "E:\upgrade_output_logs\MountResults.txt"
$timefile = "E:\upgrade_output_logs\times.txt"


function OutRedirect

{
## DEFAULT Values
$SQLInstance = "SharePointSQL"
$WebApp = "http://hnsc.OaklynOrion.local"
$InputCSV = "E:\MountData\InputDBs.txt"
$DestinationPath = "E:\upgrade_output_logs"
$SPLogFileLoc = "D:\Logs\SharePoint"

## Set DB SERVER INSTANCE ##

## Import CSV
$DBNameFile = Import-csv $inputCSV

## Mount each DB in InputCSV
ForEach ($item in $DBNameFile){
                $time = Measure-Command { Mount-SPContentDatabase –Name $item.ContentDB –
                WebApplication $WebApp -DatabaseServer $SQLInstance -Outvariable mountoutput
                -errorvariable mounterrors}

                write-output "$($item.ContentDB) took (Hours:Minutes::Seconds) $($time.
                Hours):$($time.Minutes)::$($time.Seconds) and $($time.Milliseconds)
                milliseconds","" |out-file $timefile -append -NoClobber
                write-output "$($item.ContentDB) took (Hours:Minutes::Seconds) $($time.
                Hours):$($time.Minutes)::$($time.Seconds) and $($time.Milliseconds)
                milliseconds",""
                write-output "The following output was produced by the mount command:",
                $mountoutput,""
                write-output "The following error data was provided:",$mounterrors

    ## Move Log from each mount/upgrade operation
                Set-Location $SPLogFileLoc

                $files = Get-ChildItem -Path $SPLogFileLoc "Upgrade*"

                ForEach ($file in $files) {
                                $oldname = $file.name
                                $newname = "$($item.ContentDB)-$($oldname)"
                                Copy-Item $file "$($destinationpath)/$($newname)"
```

347

```
                          Rename-Item $file $newname
                          write-output "`n$($item.ContentDB) has been attached,
                          the logs for the mount operation have been copied to
                          $($destinationpath) and begin with the name of the database"
                          }
            write-output "#######################################################`n"
            Set-Location $home


            }
}
OutRedirect|out-file $OutputFile
```

Another really important thing to remember about working with databases that are mounted to SharePoint, is to remember to use the Dismount-SPContentDatabase before you remove them from SQL. In fact, as an admin, you should make this a standard practice for any database move between farms, make sure to dismount from SharePoint before SQL. For example, don't detach a database from the SQL instance before you dismount it from the SharePoint web application. When this happens to a database, it becomes "dorked out" which is slang for it is an orphaned content database. You might be able to rectify the situation by re-attaching the database to SQL and then running dismount-spcontentdatabase, but that is a stretch and if it fails, you could try mount-spcontentdatabase back to the same web application that it was once mounted. If you are dealing with a truly orphaned content database, neither of these will work. You should detach the database once more from your SQL, and then you should run:

```
$wa = Get-SPWebApplication http://spwebApplicationUrl
$wa.ContentDatabase
```

The spwebApplicationURL equals the web application that it was previously attached. This is why you need to know about your farm. If the database is truly orphaned, this $wa.ContentDatabase will return a GUID that you can use to delete the orphaned entry with this command:

```
$wa.ContentDatabases.Delete("GUID_Value")
```

After you run this command, go ahead and refresh the sites in the configuration database by running this one-liner:

```
Get-spcontentdatabase -webapplication http://spwebapplicationURL | % {$_.
RefreshsitesInConfigurationDatabase()}
```

After this command completes, you should be able to remount the content database to your farm after re-attaching it to the SQL server. If you're still unable to mount the database, you're looking at an unattached restore and you'll want to make sure that the site collections that are in the database are not living somewhere else in your farm.

Sometimes really odd situations can be resolved by farm restarts, but before you perform a full shutdown and restart of the entire farm, you should attempt to clear the SharePoint Configuration cache. The manual method for clearing the config cache can sometimes be the only way to get a good clean clearing of the cache. These are the steps:

1. Stop the SharePoint Timer Service (SPTimerV4) on all servers in the farm.

2. Navigate to C:\ProgramData\Microsoft\SharePoint\Config.

3. Make a backup copy of the folder that has a current date stamp and save it somewhere else.

4. Open the GUID folder, not the backup, but the actual GUID folder.

5. Sort the contents by file type and delete all the XML files.

6. Edit the cache.ini file and change its value from whatever it is to 1.

7. After you've reset the value to 1, restart the SharePoint Timer Service.

There are cool scripts that you can use to reset the timer service. Here's a link to one that works like a champ: https://anothersharepointblog.com/clearing-the-config-cache-with-powershell. If you ever encounter a situation where some of the server's cache.ini files are not updating, you might be able to get them to start updating by stopping the SharePoint Administration (SPAdminV4) service and then running the stsadm –o execadmsvcjobs. Running this command will cause any hung solution deployments to finish. You should then be able to reset the config cache and have it properly increment.

I have seen times where the configuration database had become corrupted to the point where the config cache cannot be reset. This is often accompanied by very slow page load times on sites and some customization or in one case a manual entry to the config database. The fix for a corrupted config database is a farm rebuild, in most cases.

Another thing that will very rarely fix this sort of issue is running the post-setup configuration wizard (psconfiggui.exe). After you run the wizard, take a look at the log file it creates in the default logging location for any errors. You can find this from Central Administration by navigating to upgrade and migration, Check upgrade status. This page will give you the log file name and location.

I usually only run the PowerShell one-liner, when the GUI has failed. This is the command:

```
PSConfig.exe -cmd upgrade -inplace b2b -force -cmd applicationcontent -install -cmd
installfeatures
```

After that command succeeds, check the upgrade status page once more and review the logs. If the upgrade page says you had a successful run and the one-liner or the GUI based wizard says success, take that into account when reading the logs. Sometimes you might get bogus failures due to missing features in content database. When this happens, run

```
Upgrade-SPContentDatabase <DBName> -SkipIntegrityChecks
```

When applying SharePoint cumulative updates, you should always stay at least 90-180 days behind the most recent CU. The only reason to go to the new cumulative update is if it is advertised to fix an issue that your farm is having or if it has been three to six months since it was released, and it adds functionality that you could use in your farm. The November 2016 CU for SharePoint 2016 is a good example of this as it adds two additional minroles. The June 2017 CU is very stable on all versions since 2010.

When patching 2013 and lower versions of SharePoint, you need only be concerned with the version of SharePoint that you have (e.g., Foundation, Standard, or Enterprise), because the language packs are not separated CUs. This has all changed with the SharePoint 2016 Cumulative Updates. For 2016, there is a server cumulative update and a *multilingual user interface* (MUI) CU, beginning with the May 2016 updates. It is unknown if this will continue to be the case, but as this book was being written in mid-2017, the MUI patches only applied to the language pack and did not update the farm to the build level.

■ **Note** SharePoint updates are available at https://technet.microsoft.com/en-us/library/ mt715807(v=office.16).aspx.

Get-SPProduct –local is one command that you'll find handy if you ever get a situation where you're pretty much certain that your servers all have the same patches and binaries installed, but when you run the psconfig wizard it starts barking about missing this or that KB. This is due to a timer job named Product

Version Job timer job that will trigger if the registry key at HKLM\Software\Microsoft\Shared Tools\Web Server Extensions\15.0\WSS named CreateProductVersionJob equals 1. The CreateProductVersionJob registry key is set to 1 after the psconfig wizard runs. Then when the timer is restarted after the psconfig wizard finishes, the timer will check this registry value and if it is 1 it will create the Product Version timer job, which will update the configuration database with the KBs that are present on the server. Then the timer sets the CreateProductVersionJob registry key back to 0.

Get-SPProduct –local does essentially the same thing as the product version timer job does and as a result the config database is updated with the KBs that you thought and knew were on the server, but the config db didn't know. Pretty weird that a command that starts with Get would actually Set something, right? The SharePoint 2016 August 2016 CU updated the psconfig wizard so that it performs the same function as the product version job and the get-spproduct –local.

When it comes to updates in 2016 SharePoint, and in SharePoint 2013 for the most part, you can no longer rely on the (get-spfarm).buildversion to determine the build version of a farm. The same is true for the Servers in Farm page, you cannot use it as a definitive source. You also cannot rely on the registry location: HKLM\software\microsoft\office servers\16 buildversion key. Instead, look at the "Check product and patch installation status" page in Central Administration. And, check the file list from the File Information section of the CU page on support.microsoft.com to verify product versions of key files that reside in the C:\Program Files\Common Files\Microsoft Shared\Web Server Extensions\<Hive Number>\ ISAPI folder and in the C:\Program Files\Microsoft Office Servers folder.

In Chapter 2, we talked about setting the publishing super user and reader accounts in the object model, but we left out the user policy setting that is the other half of making publishing work. This is the repeat from Chapter 2:

```
$wa = Get-SPWebApplication -Identity "<WebApplication>"
$wa.Properties["portalsuperuseraccount"] = "<SuperUser>"
$wa.Properties["portalsuperreaderaccount"] = "<SuperReader>"
$wa.Update()
```

And after that runs, the user policy is needed to be set. You need to be careful to set the user policy on all zones using this code:

```
$wa = Get-SPWebApplication https://www.stacylab.com
$policy = $wa.Policies.Add("i:0#.w|STACYLAB\SP_CacheUser", "Portal Super User")
$policyRole = $wa.PolicyRoles.GetSpecialRole("FullControl")
$policy.PolicyRoleBindings.Add($policyRole)
$policy = $wa.Policies.Add("i:0#.w|STACYLAB\SP_CacheRead", "Portal Super Reader")
$policyRole = $wa.PolicyRoles.GetSpecialRole("FullRead")
$policy.PolicyRoleBindings.Add($policyRole)
$wa.Update()
```

If you take care to set the infrastructure on all zones, you will not encounter weird lock out situations in future extended zones when enabling publishing. For example, if you use this code to set the user policy:

```
$wa = Get-SPWebApplication https://www.stacylab.com
 $zp = $wa.ZonePolicies("Default")
 $policy = $zp.Add("i:0#.w|STACYLAB\SP_CacheUser", "Portal Super User")
 $policyRole = $wa.PolicyRoles.GetSpecialRole("FullControl")
 $policy.PolicyRoleBindings.Add($policyRole)
 $policy = $zp.Add("i:0#.w|STACYLAB\SP_CacheRead", "Portal Super Reader")
 $policyRole = $wa.PolicyRoles.GetSpecialRole("FullRead")
 $policy.PolicyRoleBindings.Add($policyRole)
 $wa.Update()
```

It will only set the user policy on the **default zone** and then if you later extend the web application to the intranet zone, things will be OK until you enable publishing, at which point you'll be locked out. You could of course add the user policy to the intranet zone via Central Administration and be back in business; but it might not be that clearly evident. Another way to think of this is that if you are locked out of a site after enabling publishing the reason might be that the identity used by publishing has not been given the user policy at the web application level to the zone you're locked out of and you need to change that.

When it comes to publishing, if you ever need to disable it on a site collection with numerous subsites and then re-enable it, maybe for testing the speed that it brings vs. the minimal download strategy, this is the PowerShell to disable the publishing infrastructure:

#Step 1: Then Disable the SharePoint Server Publishing feature to all webs in Site collection.

```
$siteUrl = "http://sharepoint/sites/projects"
$siteCollection = Get-SPSite $siteUrl #Into Site Collection level
$siteCollection | Get-SPWeb -limit all | ForEach-Object{
write-host "De-Activating the PublishingWeb feature on " $_.Url
Disable-SPFeature -Identity "PublishingWeb" -Url $_.Url -confirm:$false #where the
PublishingWeb is the internal name of the SharePoint Server Publishing feature
write-host "De-Activating the PublishingWeb feature on " $_.Url
}
$siteCollection.Dispose()
```

#Step 2: The SharePoint Server Publishing Infrastructure Feature needs to be Disabled in site collection level

```
$PublishingSitefeature = Get-SPFeature PublishingSite #where the PublishingSite is the
inernal name of the SharePoint Server Publishing Infrastructure Feature
write-host "The feature name is " $PublishingSitefeature.DisplayName
$siteUrl = "http://sharePoint/sites/projects"
$siteCollection = Get-SPSite $siteUrl #Into Site Collection level
write-host "De-Activating " $PublishingSitefeature.DisplayName " on " $siteCollection.Url
Disable-SPFeature $PublishingSitefeature -Url $siteCollection.Url -confirm:$false #Enable
the feature to the site collection
write-host "Activated " $PublishingSitefeature.DisplayName " on " $siteCollection.Url
$siteCollection.Dispose()
```

All you need to do is set the **$siteUrl** in both of the steps to replace the site collection URL http:// sharepoint/sites/projects with your site collection URL. Then when you are ready to enable Publishing, you can run this PowerShell:

#Step 1: The SharePoint Server Publishing Infrastructure Feature needs to be enabled in site collection level

```
$PublishingSitefeature = Get-SPFeature PublishingSite #where the PublishingSite is the
inernal name of the SharePoint Server Publishing Infrastructure Feature
write-host "The feature name is " $PublishingSitefeature.DisplayName
$siteUrl = "http://sharePoint/sites/projects"
$siteCollection = Get-SPSite $siteUrl #Into Site Collection level
write-host "Activating " $PublishingSitefeature.DisplayName " on " $siteCollection.Url
Enable-SPFeature $PublishingSitefeature -Url $siteCollection.Url -confirm:$false #Enable the
feature to the site collection
write-host "Activated " $PublishingSitefeature.DisplayName " on " $siteCollection.Url
$siteCollection.Dispose()
```

351

#Step 2: Then enable the SharePoint Server Publishing feature to all webs in Site collection.

```
$siteUrl = "http://sharepoint/sites/projects"
$siteCollection = Get-SPSite $siteUrl #Into Site Collection level
$siteCollection | Get-SPWeb -limit all | ForEach-Object{
write-host "Activating the PublishingWeb feature on " $_.Url
Enable-SPFeature -Identity "PublishingWeb" -Url $_.Url -confirm:$false #where the
PublishingWeb is the internal name of the SharePoint Server Publishing feature
write-host "Activated the PublishingWeb feature on " $_.Url
}
$siteCollection.Dispose()
```

This will enable publishing on all of your sites below the site collection. Again, you'll need to replace the $siteURL = "http://sharepoint/sites/projects" with whichever one of your site collection URLs you are looking to affect with this PowerShell. After the code has run to enable the publishing, you should open Site Settings ➤ Site Collection Administration ➤ Site Collection Output Cache, and enable the output cache. Then after you've enabled the site collection output cache, click Site Output Cache under Site Administration, and then click, "Apply these settings to all subsites". When you do this, you allow the site collection to take advantage of the RAM that is installed on your server by allowing the site to cache in memory and cause end user requests to experience a much faster page load due to the site is living in memory on the web front end. It is not necessary to call to the back-end database, necessarily.

Don't worry, memory is not going to fill up and crash. The default settings allow the cache to flush every 180 seconds for the intranet cache profile. And, the profile is cognizant of the type of browser being used to access the site, as well. If you run into issues with some users not being able to see content, check to see if someone with site collection admin privileges has erroneously removed the "Vary by User Rights." Select the box, reset IIS, and have the user flush their browser cache. Then try to access the site again.

Another way to speed up page loads is to use the blob cache. Sometimes, this is incorrectly referred to as *remote blob storage*, since content is actually stored in the database, with pointers to the data pointers that get stored in the web front end blob cache location on disk. These pointers point to the database content and allow for quicker page loads. Remote Blob Storage actually moves the content out of the content database into cheaper storage and is always accompanied by a Third-party solution. To configure the blob cache, you need to edit the web.config. When setting the BLOB cache you need to have a good idea of how much data you'll store there. Microsoft recommends not setting the maxSize of the cache lower than 10GB and they also recommend giving at least a 20% buffer. In other words, if you think you're going to have 8GB of data then set the maxSize at 10GB, but if you think you're going to have 10GB of data in the cache, then set the maxSize at 12GB.

The blob cache should be housed on a drive that does not house the operating system, but that is not mandatory, it's just for best performance. You'll also want to take into account how many megapixels you want to use when rendering images. By default, the images will render at 40 megapixels. This web.config line will allow you to render images at 100 megapixels.

```
<BlobCache location="D:\BlobCache\15" path="\.(gif|jpg|jpeg|jpe|jfif|bmp|dib|tif|ti
ff|themedbmp|themedcss|themedgif|themedjpg|themedpng|ico|png|wdp|hdp|css|js|asf|avi
|flv|m4v|mov|mp3|mp4|mpeg|mpg|rm|rmvb|wma|wmv|ogg|ogv|oga|webm|xap)$" maxSize="10"
imageRenditionMaxSourcePixels="100000000" enabled="true" />
```

Before you could set this in the web.config, you need to make sure that the location D:\BlobCache\15 exists on all servers that will have the Microsoft SharePoint Foundation Web Service running. Notice, how the maxSize is set at 10GB, this means that the admin has decided that she's only going to have about 8GB or less of data caching into the blob cache. The BLOB cache should not be confused with Remote Blob Storage. And, don't confuse it with the output cache and object cache that the Publishing Infrastructure utilizes, either.

In a perfect world, the BLOB cache always functions without any issues after you set the enabled value to true. Sometimes, the world is not perfect though and you need to flush the BLOB cache. For example, and it might seem like I'm skipping gears here a little bit; but you'll see what I mean in a few sentences. Sometimes, publishing infrastructure gets enabled on a site before the minimal download strategy is deactivated. When this happens, there will sometime be issues with host named site collections that use NTLM and they will return "401 Unauthorized" to users. You can easily rectify this by disabling publishing, deactivating Minimal download strategy, and then re-enabling publishing.

You can tell if minimal download strategy (MDS) is enabled because the URL's to pages will include start.aspx#, as shown in Figure 8-16.

Figure 8-16. *MDS start.aspx#*

If you ever find this to be the case, and you know that you're going to be using publishing and the blob cache to store your video, images, and theme type files, then you should deactivate publishing and remove the MDS from the sites. You can do that manually, or you can use PowerShell. Here's a pretty cool PowerShell script to disable MDS in all the subsites of a site collection:

```
$siteCollection = Get-SPSite http://getinto.contoso.com
foreach ($site in $siteCollection)
{
$webs = $site | Get-SPweb -limit all
foreach ($web in $webs)
    {
    $url = $web.URL
    write-host "Web URL = " $url -foregroundcolor "blue"
    Disable-SPFeature -Identity  "87294c72-f260-42f3-a41b-981a2ffce37a" -url $url
-Confirm:$False
    }
}
```

If you've come across this 401 unauthorized, when you look at site features, you will not see the MDS activated, but when you deactivate publishing at the web level, you'll notice that MDS is strangely activated. This odd behavior occurs when MDS is not deactivated prior to activating publishing. You should flush the BLOB cache after you have repaired this situation, if you come across it.

To flush the blob cache on your servers, you can run this code from within PowerShell:

```
Write-Host -ForegroundColor White " - Enabling SP PowerShell cmdlets..."
 If ((Get-PsSnapin |?{$_.Name -eq "Microsoft.SharePoint.PowerShell"})-eq $null)
{
$PSSnapin = Add-PsSnapin Microsoft.SharePoint.PowerShell -ErrorAction SilentlyContinue |
Out-Null
}
```

```
$webAppall = Get-SPWebApplication
    foreach ($URL in $webAppall)
        {
        $webApp = Get-SPWebApplication $URL
        [Microsoft.SharePoint.Publishing.PublishingCache]::FlushBlobCache($webApp)
        Write-Host "Flushed the BLOB cache for:" $webApp
        }
```

Just save that code to a file and save that text file with a .ps1 extension and then run it from an administrative PowerShell session on each server that serves pages. You'll want to flush the blob cache if you have recently restored the content database. The blob cache should be the same across front-end servers that serve content and if there is a difference, than something has possibly corrupted a web.config file. Sometimes the best fix for this is to determine which server is serving the page the way you'd expect and then disjoin the other server from the farm and rejoin it. The only downside is that if the issue has corrupted the config database, the server might not join back in. This is why it's better to try flushing the blob cache first.

If you think you have a difference in the web.config files in your SharePoint farm, you can run the following PowerShell to find the modifications that have been made to your web.config since SharePoint has been installed.

```
$wa = Get-SPWebApplication -Identity http://yourWebAppURL
$wa.webConfigModifications
```

The results will spit out modifications that were made on the current server's web.config. You can run these two lines on additional servers. The results are not all errors, some of them are due to solutions that have been deployed, and then again some of them are errors. Maybe a solution has been retracted and removed from SharePoint, but it left "virtual turds," slang for corrupt entries in the web.configs. Or maybe the web.configs are not contiguous between servers. This is a quick way to find out.

If all of the modifications are corruptions, you can clear them all out using this powerful and very dangerous command, if in the wrong hands:

```
$wa.WebConfigModifications.Clear()
$wa.Update()
```

If you know that a particular modification is not needed and needs to be removed, you could use these two lines to remove the modification:

```
$wcm = $wa.WebConfigModifications | Where { $_.Name -eq "<name of entry to remove>" }
$wa.WebConfigModifications.Clear($wcm)
```

In Figure 8-17, we see a modification named as follows:

```
SafeControl[@Assembly='Microsoft.Office.DocMarketplace, Version=15.0.0.0, Culture=neutral,
PublicKeyToken=71e9bce111e9429c'][@Namespace='Microsoft.Office.DocMarketplace'][@TypeName=' ']
[@Safe='True'][@AllowRemoteDesigner='True'][@SafeAgainstScript='True']
```

Figure 8-17. *See the modification*

The modification in Figure is not a corrupt modification. Let's pretend that its name was displayed like this:

```
Name             : add[@key='SomeCrazyServiceURL']
```

If it was displayed like the preceding example, we could remove it with this PowerShell.

```
$wcm = $w.WebConfigModifications | Where { $_.Name -eq "add[@key='SomeCrazyServiceURL']" }
$wa.WebConfigModifications.Clear($wcm)
$wa.Update()
```

And then after we run that, we would need to go to manage web applications in Central Administration and deactivate the web application feature, by selecting the web application, clicking manage features in the ribbon, and then deactivating said feature.

If you ever find that SharePoint 2010 web applications are not replicating, it might be that the default time allotment is not giving enough time for your web application. This could be due to customizations. Whatever the cause is, when it happens you'll see this lovely message: "SharePoint 2010: While creating a new web application, a 404 'Page not found' error is displayed and the web application is only provisioned on the local server" This message will appear in place of the message that tells you that the web application had been created. This can happen in other versions of SharePoint, as well, and the resolution is still the same – increase the application pool's Shutdown Time Limit from 90 seconds to some greater value. These are the steps: "On the server(s) hosting Central Admin, open IIS manager. In the tree view, expand the server name and click on Application Pools. Locate the SharePoint Central Administration v4 application pool. Right click on it and choose Advanced Settings. In the Process Model section, set the Shutdown Time Limit to a greater value. As an example, 300. Restart IIS." (Microsoft TechNet, http://support.microsoft.com/kb/2543306/en-us).

After making the change to the amount of time that the web application can use to process the creation of the web application, you might still have the issue. When this sort of thing happens, it's usually due to some dorked-up, custom code, already present in the farm or the server not having enough RAM. Use the get-spsolution sorted by last operation end time to find a list of the recent changes to the farm from a solution deployment standpoint:

```
Get-SPSolution | sort lastoperationendtime | ft Displayname, LastOperationEndTime
```

This is one of those places in this chapter where I feel like we're about to bounce around (as if we haven't already); so brace yourself. I was working at a company, can't remember which one, but the environment was, and I'm using air quotes here (that's where you use your hands to make quotes as you say something sarcastically), "locked down." Too much, "lock down" is counterproductive, in my opinion, and is a waste of everyone's time, since you can get around anything. Anyways, before I go off on a total rant, if you find that you are unable to open SharePoint Designer for a SharePoint site, check that SharePoint Designer is an allowed feature at the web application level, and that the "add and customize pages" user permission for the web application is indeed checked. You may still find that you're not able to open sites with Designer, however.

If you still cannot open Designer and you've verified that along with "add and customize pages" that the Browse Directories and "Use client integration features" permissions are also available at the web application, check that nothing has been modified at the site level from a permission standpoint for the Designer permission level or higher.

If you find a permissions-related issue, make sure that you don't over-permission any permission when correcting the issue. This is why it's a best practice to never modify the base permissions in SharePoint and why it's a good idea to make a copy of a permission level before modifying. The permissions that are usually removed in order to lock out Designer are the three that I mentioned, plus the ability to manage web site, manage lists and libraries, use remote interfaces, and enumerate permissions. The "use remote interfaces" is where the novice site collection admin gets into trouble, because unselecting this also makes it so documents, spreadsheets, and other SharePoint artifacts no longer open in the client application. The reason is "use remote interfaces" is the parent to "use client integration." In fact, you never want to uncheck either of these if you want SharePoint to work with Office applications like Word, Excel, PowerPoint, and the like.

Then after you have checked permissions, you'll need to check the site's Onet.xml file. Every site definition has a Onet.xml file. The files are located in the hive on each server inside of the site definition folder and then inside the XML folder. This is the exact location on a 2013 SharePoint farm.

C:\Program Files\Common Files\microsoft shared\Web Server Extensions\15\TEMPLATE\ SiteTemplates

One way you'll know that this sort of tomfoolery has taken place is if your verified permissions have not been jacked with and you can open a publishing site in SharePoint Designer, but you cannot open a team site, or vice versa. In either case, you need to know the template ID. For the publishing sites, you might be tempted to open the Publishing folder and that would be true if you're unable to open publishing sites that were created by the variations feature, but if you're working with a regular publishing site, you'll probably want to open the BlankInternet folder's XML folder.

You can identify the type of site you're working with by inspecting the source code for the wsaSiteTemplateID. The site in Figure 8-18 uses STS#0 which means we would need to check the Onet.xml file in the STS folder.

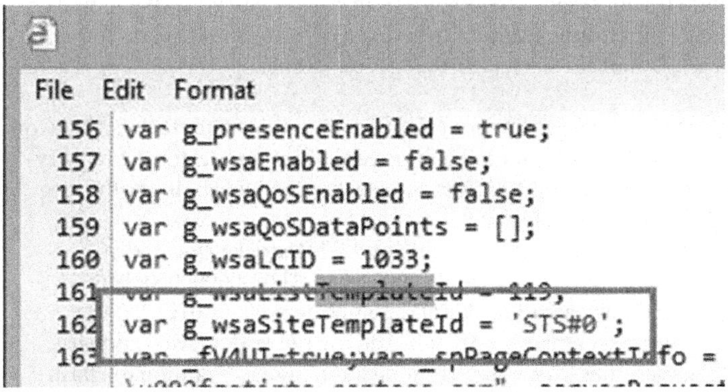

```
File   Edit   Format
156  var g_presenceEnabled = true;
157  var g_wsaEnabled = false;
158  var g_wsaQoSEnabled = false;
159  var g_wsaQoSDataPoints = [];
160  var g_wsaLCID = 1033;
161  var g_wsaListTemplateId = 119;
162  var g_wsaSiteTemplateId = 'STS#0';
163  var _fV4UI=true;var _spPageContextInfo =
```

Figure 8-18. *View source*

Once you've found the Onet.xml, open it with Notepad and find the <Project > tab. Look for a line that reads DisableWebDesignFeatures=wdfopensite and remove that junk. Leave the <Project > tag but remove the DisableWebDesignFeatures=wdfopensite line. This is what an OOB team site Onet.xml <Project tag> looks like this:

```
<Project Title="$Resources:onet_TeamWebSite;" Revision="3" ListDir="$Resources:core,lists_
Folder;" xmlns:ows="Microsoft SharePoint" UIVersion="15" HideSiteContentsLink="true">
```

For you folks that are looking to use this to "lock down" the environment, remember that this change would need to be made on all servers in the farm and you would need to do it for every site definition if you didn't want any sites to be editable in SharePoint Designer. If you're working with a 2007 SharePoint, here's the official Microsoft link: https://support.microsoft.com/en-us/help/940958/how-to-prevent-sharepoint-designer-2007-users-from-changing-a-windows. And, please don't get me wrong, I like security as much as the next guy, but I don't like to reduce productivity, needlessly. SharePoint permissions can control who can and cannot use Designer and making manual changes at the server file system level, even though in this case, won't hurt, should normally be avoided. Finally, after making the change to all of the onet.xml files, go ahead and restart IIS. Then you should create a new web application and then create a new site collection to make sure things are still working. It also wouldn't hurt to take a backup of the entire site templates folder before starting to hack up the onet.xml files. And, don't blame me if your SharePoint doesn't like manual changes to its file system.

Another thing that sometimes happens, that is even more destructive than any manual file system change, is the use of snapshots with SharePoint. And by snapshots, we're not talking about SQL snapshots; but rather vmware\hyperV or storage snapshots. The only semi-safe way to ever work with snapshots (which, by the way, is still not supported) is to make the snapshots when SharePoint and SQL are in a powered-off state.

I'm not a fan of snapshots. I would rather rebuild a farm than risk the things that can come from using snapshots. Any snapshots taken when machines are powered on, even if taken at the storage area network level, will eventually lead to a very dark and unforgiveable, SharePoint Hell-scape. If you would like to read a really awesome blog post about this, check out this post by Chris Mullendore at https://blogs.msdn.microsoft.com/mossbiz/2013/01/14/sharepoint-vs-snapshots/. Chris uses an analogy of SharePoint being a juggler and all the timer jobs and services that are part of a SharePoint farm being the balls. Read the post to see how snapshots can cause SharePoint to drop its balls. And what good is a juggler without his balls?

A common error that is easily correctable is the error message, "An update conflict has occurred, and you must retry this action." This error manifests itself in the server's application logs and in ULS with event ID 6398. This error will fire when the contents of the file system cache are newer than the contents of the configuration database. This can happen when restoring a content database from backup, for example.

When you have the event ID 6398, with the message "An update conflict has occurred, and you must retry this action" you should clear the SharePoint Configuration Cache in all of the farm's servers. You can do this manually or with the script at `https://anothersharepointblog.com/clearing-the-config-cache-with-powershell`, or one like it.

event ID 10016 happens when the accounts that run the service application pools and the local Network service does not have local launch permission on the distributed component object model for the registry key 000C101C-0000-0000-C000-000000000046. This event ID is just a noise. In other words, it's nothing to worry about. But, if you're like me, you like to have clean logs.

Here's the process to clean up the event ID 10016. Take ownership of the registry key located at HKEY_LOCAL_MACHINE\SOFTWARE\Classes\AppID\{000C101C-0000-0000-C000-000000000046, then open the component Services console and navigate to the DCOM component 000C101C-0000-0000-C000-000000000046 and right-click it and select the Security tab. Add the network service and give it local activation and local launch. Add the identities that run your application pools, including the farm account and give them local activation and local launch. You could just as well add the WSS_Admin_WPG and the WSS_WPG local groups with local launch and local activation instead of manually adding the application pool identities. If you took this approach, you wouldn't have to worry about a new application pool's identity not having local activation and launch, since the wss_wpg would automatically have that identity, if SharePoint were used to create the app pool.

If your logs have event ID 5586, there is an issue with a database, or possibly databases. Event ID 5586 occurs when one or more of the following events transpire:

- Someone changes a login in SQL and causes an account that SharePoint is using to receive insufficient privileges

- The SQL Server collation is wrong

- The SQL DB is set to Read-Only

- The SQL DB runs out of room

- The database becomes corrupted

An easy way to remember that event ID 5586 is a problem related to SQL Server is that 55 looks like SS, which could stand for SQL Server, and 86 is a nautical slang term for something that has been junked.

In Chapter 5, we went over a PowerShell that you can use to find out when logins were changed. event ID 5586 will tell you which database is affected, so that will help on troubleshooting, login changes. This is also where a pristine lab environment will come in handy, provided it is a least-privileged untarnished place. The collation that SharePoint uses for its databases is Latin1_General_CI_AS_KS_WS. Every database that SharePoint creates will use that collation. If someone changes a collation you may be able to change it back without issue, or the initial act of changing it might have corrupted things. And, as each issue is somewhat unique, you'll have to address each situation separately.

In regards to the database being set to Read-Only, if it is a content database you should set it back to read-write through the GUI or via the SharePoint Object model. Try to avoid having to use the SQL Server Management studio for these types of changes, either to set a database to read only or to set it back to read-write. Make sure SharePoint knows about changes, by using PowerShell cmdlets with nouns that begin with SP, or by using Central Administration.

If the SQL DB has run out of room, as is sometimes the case with the usage logging database that is used to track user analytics (I know this is sort of review; but, you'll be happy to have it here too, hopefully), you can use the following PowerShell to set the Usage definition so that it will generate a larger database, which hopefully is big enough to capture all of the events:

```
$pages=Get-SPUsageDefinition -Identity "page requests"
$pages.MaxTotalSizeInBytes=12400000000
$pages.update()
```

Then immediately after you have set the maximum total size that the database can use, you need to create a new database. This is due to the size of the partition is based on how many days retention you have set for logging and that the size that each partition can encompass, can only be set when the database is created, based on the MaxTotalSizeInBytes. This is the one-liner that you would run to create the new usage service application:

```
Get-spusageapplication | Set-SPUsageApplication –DatabaseServer <dbServer> –DatabaseName
<newDBname>
```

Sometimes when the usage database gets too big, simply lowering the retention period is enough to decrease it to a point where Event 5586 stops firing. However, if the partition size is too small to hold one full days' worth of tracking event 5586 will still fire, since the database is full. The partition size is calculated by taking the maxtotalsizeInBytes and dividing that by the number of days retention. The default days retention is 14 days. To change the retention period you can do this via the GUI or via PowerShell. Here's the PowerShell to change all the usage definition categories to a set period:

```
Get-SPUsageDefinition | ForEach-Object {Set-SPUsageDefinition -Identity $_.name
-DaysRetained <# of days>}
```

It's always best to run Get-SPUsageDefinition first to see if the farm you're working with has different periods for different categories. And, after you've modified the database, you should go into SQL and shrink it if you've only changed the retention period. If you created a new usage logging db, you can delete your old logging database using SSMS. You can use (Get-spusageapplication).usagedatabase to make sure you're not deleting the wrong database, as this cmdlet will tell you which database is being used by your farm for the usage service application.

When it comes to usage logs (and, here's the part that is not review, thus the sorta comment), if you find that you're not getting new logs or are showing zeros in your usage reports, you should first make a backup of the current logs that you do have, and their importprogress.ini files. Then after you've backed up the usage log folders and the logs, you should check the inportprogress.ini files for errors. Figure 8-19 shows the usage logs folders.

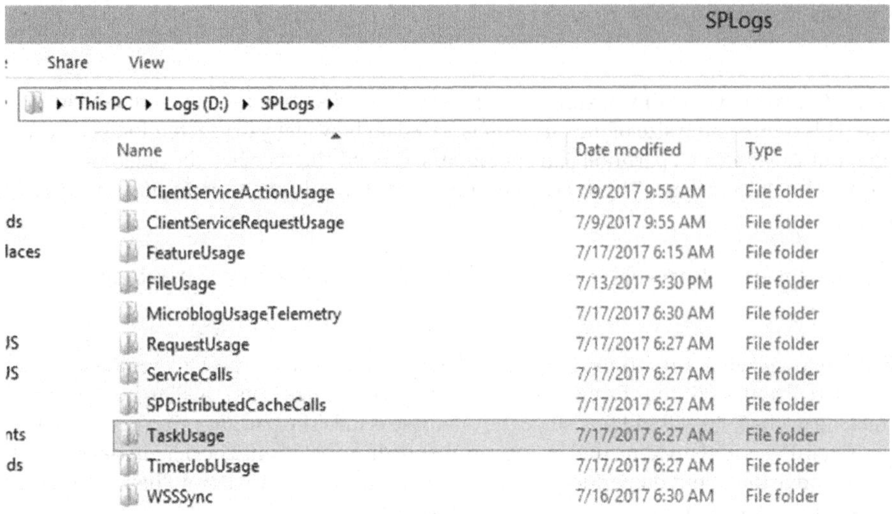

Figure 8-19. Usage logs folders in the hive

You can determine where your usage logs are stored using Central Administration or using PowerShell. To determine where the logs are located using PowerShell, just run the following:

```
(Get-SPUsageService).UsageLogDir
```

Once you've found the usage logs, you'll notice that each type has an importprogress.ini file. If you're imports are failing or you have zeros in usage reporting, look at each .ini file and what you should see is the name of a file and then -1. If you see anything else, for example a file name and then some other number, this log is possibly corrupted and needs to be deleted.

Always make a backup that you can remove after a few days of successful imports, make a note of the most recent log file in the folder, noting its file name. After you've noted the file name, which should be for a date and time earlier than the current date and time, go ahead and delete the log files from the actual folder, leaving only the importprogress.ini file. Now, edit the importprogress.ini file so that line one is the name of the usage file and line two is –1. Figure 8-20 shows an example of an .ini file after it's edited.

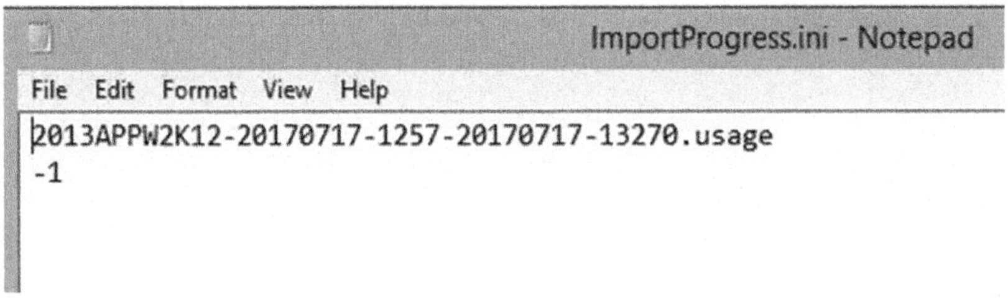

Figure 8-20. importprogress.ini insides

Now go ahead and stop and start the timer service recycle job. The best way to handle this is either through Central Administration of via PowerShell, since SharePoint knows about it, rather than stopping the timer via the Services console or via the cli SC command. The PowerShell cmdlet is Start-SPTimerJob. To start the Timer service Recycle job run this:

```
Get-SPTimerJob job-timer-recycle | Start-SPTimerJob
```

To start it via Central Administration, you drive into Monitoring, and then find the job named Timer Service Recycle. Open it and then click Run Now. Depending on how many servers are in your farm and on how many custom timer jobs you've created, **this job might be a few pages deep, which is why PowerShell is faster**.

Sometimes this issue is not with the Usage database getting the data and is related to the search analytics database getting the data. So, instead of modifying files, there is a script written by Brian T. Jackett that will link this back up for us. What Brian found was that there were no receivers enabled for whatever reason. This is the PowerShell that he used to determine the receivers were disabled:

```
$aud = Get-SPUsageDefinition | where {$_.Name -like "Analytics*"}
$aud | fl

$prud = Get-SPUsageDefinition | where {$_.Name -like "Page Requests"}
$prud | fl
```

After identifying that, he wrote this script to enable them and then he restarted the SharePoint timer by recycling the timer.

```
if((Get-PSSnapin -Name Microsoft.SharePoint.PowerShell) -eq $null)
{
    Add-PSSnapin Microsoft.SharePoint.PowerShell
}
$aud = Get-SPUsageDefinition | where {$_.Name -like "Analytics*"}
# if analytics usage definition receivers is empty then manually add back receiver
if($aud.Receivers.Count -eq 0)
{
    $aud.Receivers.Add("Microsoft.Office.Server.Search.Applications, Version=15.0.0.0,
Culture=neutral, PublicKeyToken=71e9bce111e9429c", "Microsoft.Office.Server.Search.
Analytics.Internal.AnalyticsCustomRequestUsageReceiver")
}
# if analytics usage definition receiver is not enabled then enable it
if($aud.EnableReceivers -eq $false)
{
    $aud.EnableReceivers = $true
    $aud.Update()
}
$aud | fl

$prud = Get-SPUsageDefinition | where {$_.Name -like "Page Requests"}
# if page requests usage definition receivers is empty then manually add back receiver
if($prud.Receivers.Count -eq 0)
{
```

```
    $prud.Receivers.Add("Microsoft.Office.Server.Search.Applications, Version=15.0.0.0,
    Culture=neutral, PublicKeyToken=71e9bce111e9429c", "Microsoft.Office.Server.Search.
    Analytics.Internal.ViewRequestUsageReceiver")
}
# if page requests usage definition receiver is not enabled then enable it
if($prud.EnableReceivers -eq $false)
{
    $prud.EnableReceivers = $true
    $prud.Update()
}
$prud | fl
```

To read the full blog post where this code was first shared, you should check out his blog post at https://briantjackett.com/2013/08/26/powershell-script-to-workaround-no-data-in-sharepoint-2013-usage-reports/, and then remember to recycle the timer, as follows:

```
Get-SPTimerJob job-timer-recycle | Start-SPTimerJob
```

After resetting the timer job, just wait 24 hours for the usage reports to again show data and stop showing zeros. And, finally, I'd like to end this discussion with a quote from another excellent post on usage logging from Daniel Kloyber: "The whole platform behind the usage analytics reports is expandable. The out-of-the-box code is not meant to cover all usage reporting scenarios. For more special reporting needs, I recommend developing a custom solution that includes SPUsageReceivers and event custom usage definitions. Also, I would like to extend again the warning, that changing settings of the different analyses will cause the engine to fail. Do not change settings you don't understand."

You can read the full post that goes into more detail than we have in this chapter, at https://blogs.msdn.microsoft.com/spblog/2014/04/03/sharepoint-2013-usage-analytics-the-story/.

Switching gears again, if you ever encounter event ID 7043 in your application logs, it will look something like this:

```
Event Type: Error
Event Source: SharePoint Foundation
Event Category: None
Event ID: 7043
Computer: SERVERNAME
Description: Load control template file /_controltemplates/TaxonomyPicker.ascx failed:
Could not load type 'Microsoft.SharePoint.Portal.WebControls.TaxonomyPicker' from assembly
'Microsoft.SharePoint.Portal, Version=14.0.0.0, Culture=neutral, PublicKeyToken=71e9bce111e
9429c'.
```

The cause for this error is a stale control template in the control templates folder. To fix this error perform the following steps, according to Microsoft:

- Navigate to /14/TEMPLATE/ControlTemplates/TaxonomyPicker.ascx user control

- Open the user control in a text editor and locate the first line

- Find the character string , and replace with a comma ',' (without quotes).

- Save the user control

That's a pretty simple fix, right? Just replace this ',' with this ',' (not including the quotes). Very cool! The full TechNet reference is at https://support.microsoft.com/kb/2481844/.

Event ID 17806, SSPI handshake failed with error code 0x80090311, will happen when disableLoopbackcheck is not set disabled on the SQL server. Just open registry and set the value of the disableLoopbackcheck to 1. You can use PowerShell, again, to see if it is enabled:

```
Get-Item -Path Registry::HKEY_LOCAL_MACHINE\SYSTEM\CurrentControlSet\Control\Lsa | Get-
ItemProperty -name DisableLoopbackCheck
```

If the command pukes, just create a DWORD (32-bit) Value at HKLM\SYSTEM\CurrentControlSet\Control\Lsa and name it DisableLoopbackCheck and that should take care of your issue.

Event IDs 22 and 234 are related and they relate to User Profile service creating certificates on a daily basis. The situation faced with the higher of these two event IDs is that the User Profile service works OK, but it is trying to create certs on the server in the cert store daily. This results in the logs recording things like this, telling us that the cert could not be created and that there was errors.

```
ILM Certificate could not be created: netsh http error:netsh http add urlacl url=http://+:5725/
user=Domain\spfarm sddl=D:(A;;GA;;;S-1-5-21-2972807998-902629894-2323022004-1104)
```

Then along comes event ID 22, and it is complaining that the Forefront Identity Management service cannot connect to the SQL DB Server. This is a little bit alarming and can be a bit confusing, especially since the connection is fine. The cause of both of these errors is from performing a SharePoint backup that includes the User Profile service application. These errors can be resolved by deleting the new certs from the certificate store.

■ **Note**   It is very important that you delete the correct certs, though. Make sure that you inspect all the certs and look at the "valid from" on the Details tab to make sure you leave the oldest certificate in place.

After deleting the new certs, you should run a full user profile import. And, if you have MySites set up, you should navigate to a MySite. One of the misunderstood things about User Profile service is to think that it needs a MySite web application, which is absolutely not the case. One thing that can happen though, when using the AutoSPInstaller to create your SharePoint is that the URL for the MySite web application is sort of orphaned in the User Profile service, if you allow the AutoSPInstaller to create the MySite web application and then after the web application is created, you delete it.

When you're in a situation where you've removed the MySite web application, maybe because you don't want MySites, but you want user profile metadata, you can't remove this entry from the User Profile service using the Central Administration website. However, you can remove it with PowerShell.

Here is the PowerShell to remove the orphaned MySite Host URL from the user profile MySite settings. This one comes courtesy of a fellow Racker, Ryan Holderread:

```
$site = get-spsite <Central Administration URL:Port>
$context = Get-SpServiceContext $site
$profileManager = New-Object Microsoft.Office.Server.UserProfiles.UserProfileManager($context)
$profileManager.MySiteHostUrl = ""
```

After you run that PowerShell, you should make sure the sync is still running and possibly restart the sync. We covered starting the user profile sync in Chapter 2, so there's no need to kick that horse, so to speak. There's a lot to User Profile service that I didn't cover, and I won't cover everything here in one chapter, but there are few more things about the User Profile service that we should talk about.

First off, let's talk about a user's display name being incorrect on a site collection. When this happens, the user account has been updated in Active Directory and is even showing correctly in the User Profile service application, but at the site collection level, it is still showing the old name. Hopefully, the name change that occurred in Active Directory, did not involve creating an entirely new account. We can deal with a new account, but it is far easier to deal with just a rename in the existing account.

Back in 2007, SharePoint allowed you to access the All People group right off of the settings of the site. But, with the advent of SharePoint 2010 and all versions that followed, that group is hidden. The primary reason for hiding that group is that removing a user from that group effectively removes them from all SharePoint Groups, lists, and Libraries within the site. Accidentally doing this could be a semi-traumatic experience. This is why before removing a user account from the all people group, you need to enumerate all the places that they have access, so that you can put their user account back, where needed. Table 8-1 shows how to access the hidden lists.

Table 8-1. *Accessing Hidden User Lists*

SharePoint Version	How to Access Hidden User List Append to Site Collection URL
2010	/_layouts/people.aspx?MembershipGroupId=0&FilterField1=ContentType&FilterValue1=Person
2013	/_layouts/15/people.aspx?MembershipGroupId=0
2016	/_layouts/16/people.aspx?MembershipGroupId=0

You might be able to fix the issue without deleting the user from all users by attempting to try to force SharePoint to update the information in the users table, using PowerShell. These are the lines to use and they only update the Name, Display Name, and email fields. They don't affect the title, department, or any other fields that you might have changed:

```
$login= "i:0#.w|contoso\TestUser1"
$site= "http://intranet.contoso.com/sites/abcsite"
Set-SPUser -Identity $login -web $site -SyncFromAD
```

If a user account that was deleted from Active Directory and then re-created, this will usually cause what is affectionately known as a SID Mismatch. The fix for this can be as simple as running this PowerShell:

```
$user = Get-SPUser -Web "http://mysite.domain.com/personal/username" -Identity
"i:0#.w|domain\username"
 Move-SPUser -Identity $user -NewAlias "i:0#.w|domain\username" -IgnoreSID
```

And then running that command for every site the user had access into. If the person who erroneously deleted the user from Active Directory and then re-created the user in Active Directory, unbeknownst to SharePoint, and then that same administrator got even more crazy and tried to sync the User Profile service with Active Directory, it is time for a user profile version of a "frontal lobotomy." The User Profile account and all the users' permissions will need to be removed at this point.

To fix this situation, completely remove the user from SharePoint by removing the user from the hidden lists from all site collections and then remove the user profile from the User Profile service application. After the user does not exist in SharePoint, go ahead and run a full user profile sync. Don't run the sync before the user's account is fully removed though. The reason for the full profile sync is that SharePoint lists and libraries that utilize Active Directory security groups for permissions, get this group information from User profile service. This saves on chattiness to Active Directory.

The reason that this order of operation is important is that "If a user profile and the relevant group memberships for the user are not synchronized, SharePoint Server 2013 may incorrectly deny access to a given resource." Here's the TechNet reference: https://technet.microsoft.com/en-us/library/jj729797.aspx. This does not apply to 2010, as 2010 SharePoint still checks Active Directory for ad group memberships; whereas, in 2013 and 2016 SharePoint Active Directory is not checked after synchronization has taken place.

When you get a sid mismatch in 2010 and earlier versions, you can usually get by without the user profile sync, but I would still do it, just in case anything else has changed. User profile service stores a lot of metadata about your users, and it can even write this out to Active Directory depending on how you have configured the account that pulls the data, or in the case of writing, pushes data to Active Directory.

Multi-string values store their data in the managed metadata service in your farm. If the managed metadata service is not configured correctly, you will more than likely see odd behavior where user profiles do not seem to keep the updates to multistring fields. The fix for this is to configure the managed metadata term sets for the multistring values and configure the service connection on the managed metadata service application proxy so that it has "This service application is the default storage location for column specific term sets" selected. And, as a side note, and not related to User Profile service, if your environment has a content type hub configured, you will also want to check the box for "Push-down Content Type Publishing Updates from the Content Type Gallery to subsites and lists" in order for changes to replicate. Click the Managed Metadata Proxy on the Manage service Applications page.

Normally, you shouldn't have to even worry about the managed metadata service application being the default storage location, since the User Profile service application sees the managed metadata service application when the UPA is created, and selects it. Although, in a situation where the Managed Metadata service application is re-created or migrated, you may need to make the changes I just mentioned.

Another thing to remember about User profile service applications that sync user pictures from Active Directory is the need to generate the thumbnails after a user import. PowerShell is the savior again. Run this PowerShell after performing a full user profile sync in order to create the user photos immediately.

```
Update-SPProfilePhotoStore -CreateThumbnailsForImportedPhotos 1 -MySiteHostLocation <enter mysite name here>
```

If your users are reporting that MySites are not creating, you should check that the timer job "MySite Instantiation Interactive Request Queue" is being queued up for the web application where the MySite host has been established. When you're troubleshooting this process, you find the information about timer job in the ULS category named Personal Site Instantiation. By searching ULS for that category during site creation, you'll find information that will help you in troubleshooting the creation of MySites for your web application. It might be a login changed erroneously. Basically, whenever something that worked previously, stops working, you need to ask the questions "What has changed?" and, "What is happening?"

Tip: if you would like to take a deeper dive on this, check out this post from Wictor Wilen at www.wictorwilen.se/sharepoint-2013-personal-site-instantiation-queues-and-bad-throughput.

If you are receiving an ugly "Sorry, Something went wrong – Unable to process put message" error like the one in Figure 8-21, there are a couple of things that have been known to help.

Figure 8-21. *Unable to process put message*

The first thing you can do is to troubleshoot if the account being used in the connection to Active Directory has "Directory replicating Changes" for SharePoint 2013, and "Directory replicating Changes" and "Directory replicating Changes All" for SharePoint 2010 on servers with the Windows 2008 R2 Operating System. Once you've verified that those permissions are in place, you might try deleting the sync connection and re-creating the connection. If the issue persists, make the account that is used in the sync connection a member of these local groups on the server that runs sync:

- FIMSyncBrowse

- FIMSyncJoiners

- FIMSyncOperators

- FIMSyncPasswordSet

And, finally, make sure that the component services "My computer" object has Local Launch, remote launch and remote activation under the ACL for Launch and Activation permissions of the COM security. You can set that by opening the Component Services (comexp.exe), click Component Services ➤ Computers ➤ My Computer ➤ COM Security ➤ Launch and Activation Permissions, and then add the account that runs the SPTimerV4 service with those permissions.

If you are seeing event ID 1001, 1004, or 1015 and the description of the problem mentions 'PeopleILM', {90150000-104C-0000-1000-0000000FF1CE}, or mentions Microsoft.ResourceManagement.Service.exe, you should add the Network Service to the local WSS_WPG group. After you've added the Network Service to the WSS_WPG group, test that the issue is resolved by running a user profile synch.

Let's do a few exercises before we end this chapter.

DETERMINE IF A SOLUTION WAS RECENTLY DEPLOYED

The purpose of this exercise is to determine if a solution was recently deployed. What's changed?

1. Open a SharePoint Management Shell.

2. Type **Get-SPSolution | sort LastOperationEndTime | ft displayname, lastoperationendtime**.

USE POWERSHELL TO BECOME FAMILIAR WITH SERVICE INSTANCES

The purpose of this exercise is to become familiar services using PowerShell.

Sometimes when a service will not stop or is stuck on starting, and you need to either stop or start the service, PowerShell is your best bet.

1. Open a SharePoint Management Shell.

2. Type **get-spserviceinstance** and press **Enter**.

3. After the screen finishes scrolling, type **get-spserviceinstance | ft typename, ID**.

4. Now type **get-spserviceinstance | ft name, ID**.

5. Look at some of the output from step 2 and notice how most of the name fields are null. This is why we use the typename.

INSTANTIATE THE DISTRIBUTED CACHE SERVICE INTO A VARIABLE

The purpose of this exercise is to stop and start the Distributed Cache service instance.

■ **Note** This should be performed in a development or lab environment.

---

1. Open a SharePoint Management Shell administratively.

2. Type **get-spserviceinstance | ft typename, ID**.

3. Type **get-spserviceinstance | ? {$_.typename –eq "Distributed Cache"} | ft typename, ID, status –auto**.

4. Take note of the ID from step 3.

5. Type **$var = get-spserviceinstance –id <ID from step 3>**.

For example, assuming the ID from step 3 was c54d7c45-af66-43af-8c31-9a65d5db424f, you would type

$var = get-spserviceinstance –id c54d7c45-af66-43af-8c31-9a65d5db424f

Now that you have the Distributed Cache service instantiate into $var, you could call the Unprovision method against it with this line: $var.Unprovision().

If you choose to do that, check out the status of the service instance from services on server, or by running $var and pressing enter

Now you can provision the service by typing **$var.Provision()**

If you get an error that reads

```
Exception calling "Provision" with "0" argument(s): "A failure occurred
SPDistributedCacheServiceInstance::Provision() Available memory is '93' MB,
needed memory'202' MB"
At line:1 char:1
+ $var.Provision()
+ ~~~~~~~~~~~~~~~~~
    + CategoryInfo      : NotSpecified: (:) [], MethodInvocationException
    + FullyQualifiedErrorId : InvalidOperationException
```

Try typing **$var.Provision($true)**.

And if you get an error that reads

```
Exception calling "Provision" with "1" argument(s): "Cannot start service
AppFabricCachingService on computer '.'."
At line:1 char:1
+ $var.Provision($true)
+ ~~~~~~~~~~~~~~~~~~~~~~
    + CategoryInfo      : NotSpecified: (:) [], MethodInvocationException
    + FullyQualifiedErrorId : InvalidOperationException
```

6. Type **$var.server** and see if the name returned equals the name of the host that you're currently on, if you received the error that the server name returned by $var. server probably does not equal the hostname.

7. Log in to the server that was returned by $var.server and instantiate the service to a variable by running the following.

```
$var = get-spserviceinstance -id <ID from step 3>
```

8. And then provision the service, it should provision immediately after you run

```
$var.provision()
```

In this chapter, we looked at troubleshooting User Profile Synchronization Connections, Excel Services, Office Web Apps Connections, and Patching Office Web Apps. We looked at managed metadata term stores and discussed the connection to User Profile service. We discussed web.config modifications and used PowerShell to determine if the web.config is modified. Along with looking at web.config, we used PowerShell to interrogate timer jobs, log levels, and databases. Finally, PowerShell was used to unprovision and provision services.

In the next chapter, we'll crack open the ULS viewer program and look at its features.

And, like a bug's life hitting a windshield, this chapter is over.

CHAPTER 9

■ ■ ■

ULS Viewer

At this point, we've reviewed the base build, least privileging, file system changes, IIS modifications, SQL Server, Search, command-line shortcuts, numerous PowerShell troubleshooting cmdlets, T-SQL queries, unsupported vs. supported actions, service applications, various event IDs of errors, and I've mentioned the ULS Viewer. But, we haven't talked about ULS Viewer as much as we're going to now!

In this chapter, we're going to discuss what could easily be argued as one of the best, if not the best, troubleshooting tools for SharePoint. On the GitHub for this book, I've saved two versions of the ULS Viewer. One of the versions works awesome with Windows Server 2008 (version 2.0.3530.27850) and earlier operating systems, and the other (version 16.0.3129.1000) is awesome with Windows Server 2012 and later operating systems.

The SharePoint Unified Logging System (ULS) records information about the servers in the farm in ULS logs on all the SharePoint servers and these logs are the go-to source for diagnosing issues. The ULS logs will capture information about event IDs that occur in the Windows Server System and Application log. Entries that make it into both the Windows logs and the ULS logs are usually listed with the ULS critical level. Critical events demand attention from the administrator and should be given enough attention to either solve the underlying cause or attribute what might have caused it and rule out that it would occur again.

When searching through the ULS, you can watch the livestream or you can look at a file that covers the time frame of whenever the issue happened. Sometimes, you only know what the user did to make the error happen and you can run your own capture. When you do this, it's best practice to get a new log file on every server in the farm, turn up the verbosity of the logging, create the issue, then turn down the logging and create a new log files, so that you have the issue trapped inside the first set of log files that you created in this process.

If you don't have custom logging levels set for any of the logging categories and you're using the default out of the box logging levels, I highly recommend that you take advantage the script that Russ Maxwell created. This script will do all the steps that I just mentioned, plus copy the log files into a directory that you can then use ULS Viewer to merge them into view. I reblogged the script at `http://anothersharepointblog.com/troubleshooting-an-issue`. In the reblogged post, I noted that you would want to make a note of any custom trace severity levels you may have set as the script sets all area's back to the OOB trace severity, which is medium.

It's a best practice to get a new log file on every server before reproducing an issue. This gives you a clean starting point and a definitive, doubt-free, understanding of which log files will have any of the information about the issue that you're troubleshooting. Using Russ's script is makes this even that much simpler, especially if you have a few servers in your farm. In short, if you learn to love the ULS logging system and the information that it provides, you'll be able to resolve issues much faster.

Here's another way to speed up the process. If you train your users to provide you with the exact steps they took to get the error to occur; and better yet, to also provide you with the time the error occurred; and most importantly, the correlation ID, you'll be well on your way to using Brian Pendergrass's script, which not only merges the log files for that correlation ID, but also opens the ULS Viewer once the logs are merged.

371

S. Simpkins, *Troubleshooting SharePoint*, https://doi.org/10.1007/978-1-4842-3138-8_9

This is the way it works: You give the script the location of your ULS Viewer executable in the variable named $pathToULSViewer and then you call the script, as follows:

```
.\mergeULSBasedOnCorrID.ps1 "406da94e-7e50-4025-8e98-21ea3e45847f"
```

Brian first shared this script with the world at the 2014 SharePoint Conference in session 375, Troubleshooting Search. You can read more about the script at https://blogs.msdn.microsoft.com/ sharepoint_strategery/2014/03/05/from-spc14-troubleshoot-search-session-spc375/ and here's the script for posterity:

```
$pathToULSViewer = "D:\Toolbox\UlsViewer.exe"
if ($args[0] -ne $null) {
    if ($args[1] -ne $null) {
        $outputPath = $args[1]
    } else {
        $outputPath = Join-Path $Pwd.Path $("byCorrelation_" + $args[0] + ".log")
    }
    Merge-SPLogFile -Path $outputPath -overwrite -Correlation $args[0] | Out-Null
    if (Test-Path $outputPath) { Invoke-Expression "$pathToULSViewer $outputPath" }
    else { Write-Warning ("=== Found No Matching Events for this Correlation ===") }
} else { Write-Warning ("=== No CorrelationId Provided ===") }
```

The ULS Viewer is available for download from Microsoft at https://www.microsoft.com/en-us/ download/details.aspx?id=44020. This version at the download works great with Server 2012 and higher. And, for the most part, it works great with earlier versions of Windows Server. In those situations where the current version gives an error on opening, I also have a version that works great with Server 2008. You can download the version that is compatible with all flavors of Windows Server 2008 and earlier from the book's GitHub. You should download a copy and add it to your toolbox. I keep all of my tools in OneNote and then load them onto the servers in the farm into a toolbox folder.

The Windows Event Viewer logs and the Unified Logging System logs are related in that most critical events that surface in the Windows logs are able to be traced into the ULS logs either by their event ID and, or by their correlation activity ID that will be present in the Windows Log event's XML data. Not all Windows event IDs have correlation activity IDs. Critical event IDs in the Application and System logs have correlation activity ID that when queried in the ULS logs will bring back the information that pertains to the critical event. You can get the correlation activity ID, by right-clicking the Windows event ID and then choosing Copy and "Copy Details as text", at which point you can paste them into Notepad.

Consider this example, shown here for this critical event ID 6398. Also recall that 6398 can often be cleared out by clearing the SharePoint Configuration Cache. And, notice how the description only gives the ID of the timer job, ID 77d31f86-ae62-44a0-ba76-6125171966ff, which encountered the lock and lost. You can see that the XML data gives the correlation activity ID, 67CF079E-913A-807B-4EBF-31FF53646F94. The correlation activity ID is the ID that you'd query in the ULS logs. This would bring back more records than just the one record that registered the application log event, or system log event.

```
Log Name:      Application
Source:        Microsoft-SharePoint Products-SharePoint Foundation
Date:          7/22/2017 7:53:15 AM
Event ID:      6398
Task Category: Timer
Level:         Critical
Keywords:
User:          CONTOSO\2013farm
```

```
Computer:        2013appw2k12.contoso.com
Description:
The Execute method of job definition Microsoft.SharePoint.Administration.
SPAppStateQueryJobDefinition (ID 77d31f86-ae62-44a0-ba76-6125171966ff) threw an exception.
More information is included below.

Sorry, we can't seem to connect to the SharePoint Store. Try again in a bit.
Event Xml:
<Event xmlns="http://schemas.microsoft.com/win/2004/08/events/event">
  <System>
    <Provider Name="Microsoft-SharePoint Products-SharePoint Foundation" Guid="{6FB7E0CD-
52E7-47DD-997A-241563931FC2}" />
    <EventID>6398</EventID>
    <Version>15</Version>
    <Level>1</Level>
    <Task>12</Task>
    <Opcode>0</Opcode>
    <Keywords>0x4000000000000000</Keywords>
    <TimeCreated SystemTime="2017-07-22T14:53:15.2546872002" />
    <EventRecordID>58981</EventRecordID>
    <Correlation ActivityID="{67CF079E-913A-807B-4EBF-31FF53646F94}" />
    <Execution ProcessID="10900" ThreadID="12588" />
    <Channel>Application</Channel>
    <Computer>2013appw2k12.contoso.com</Computer>
    <Security UserID="S-1-5-21-3668628078-3563022244-1227891794-1112" />
  </System>
  <EventData>
    <Data Name="string0">Microsoft.SharePoint.Administration.SPAppStateQueryJobDefinition</Data>
    <Data Name="string1">77d31f86-ae62-44a0-ba76-6125171966ff</Data>
    <Data Name="string2">Sorry, we can't seem to connect to the SharePoint Store. Try again
    in a bit.</Data>
  </EventData>
</Event>
```

Warnings and errors in the Windows application and system logs, will more than likely, not have Correlation Activity IDs but Critical Events, in both of these event logs, will have these hidden gems in their XML that you can use when searching ULS. That is, you can take that Correlation Activity ID and quickly find the related events that led up to the unexpected condition by querying the ULS files around the time of the error. Or if you want, you could run a merge-splogfile and include a start and end time parameter. And, depending on how soon the event occurred, you may not even need to use the start and end time parameters with your merge log file. The benefit of merging log files is you would find any events from other servers in the farm that are somehow related, if any.

Let's crack open the ULS Viewer and look at its various features while discussing an event ID that does not have a correlation activity ID, event ID 6801. When you first open the ULS Viewer, it looks a lot like a foreign landscape or some weird control panel, or something. We're going to discuss a few basic ways to view ULS logs, or merged logs, using ULS, and then we'll venture into the other features of the ULS Viewer. To open the ULS Viewer, you can create a shortcut to its executable and then run it by double-clicking the shortcut, or you could just run it straight from the .exe file, by double-clicking the file you downloaded. Figure 9-1 shows the default view of the ULS Viewer.

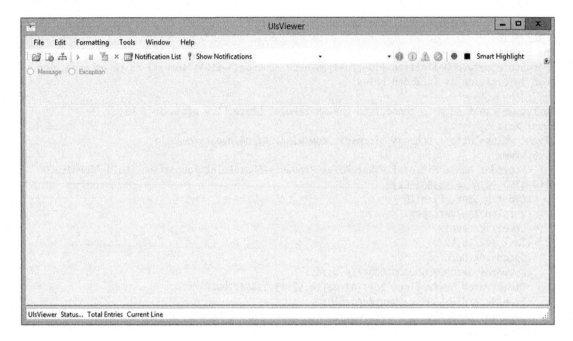

Figure 9-1. *ULS Viewer without any files open*

The first thing to do if you have never used the ULS Viewer is to make yourself familiar with the menu bars. The File menu allows you to open the ULS logs from the live stream, also known as the *real- time feed*, in other words as the logs are actively being written. The menu option that allows you to open the logs as they are "live streaming" is called "Open from ULS" or "Append from ULS". I haven't been able to discern the difference between Open from ULS and Append from ULS, when first looking at the live stream, as the end result is that you will start seeing the ULS events scrolling in the ULS Viewer. The difference between Open from ULS, and Append from ULS, is that "Append from ULS" allows you to take a ULS log that you had used the "Open from File" or "Append from File" and then start the live stream.

For example, if you look at Figure 9-2, you see a few things immediately:

- There is a break in the time stamps from 06:58 AM to 08:06 AM

- The logging is paused, and if you unpause, it does not say, "done processing"

- The logs are located in a custom location

- The ULS Viewer opened a ULS log to begin with

The fact that the log is paused is our clue that this is a live stream, because using the pause icon has no effect on a ULS log that was opened from file or appended from file.

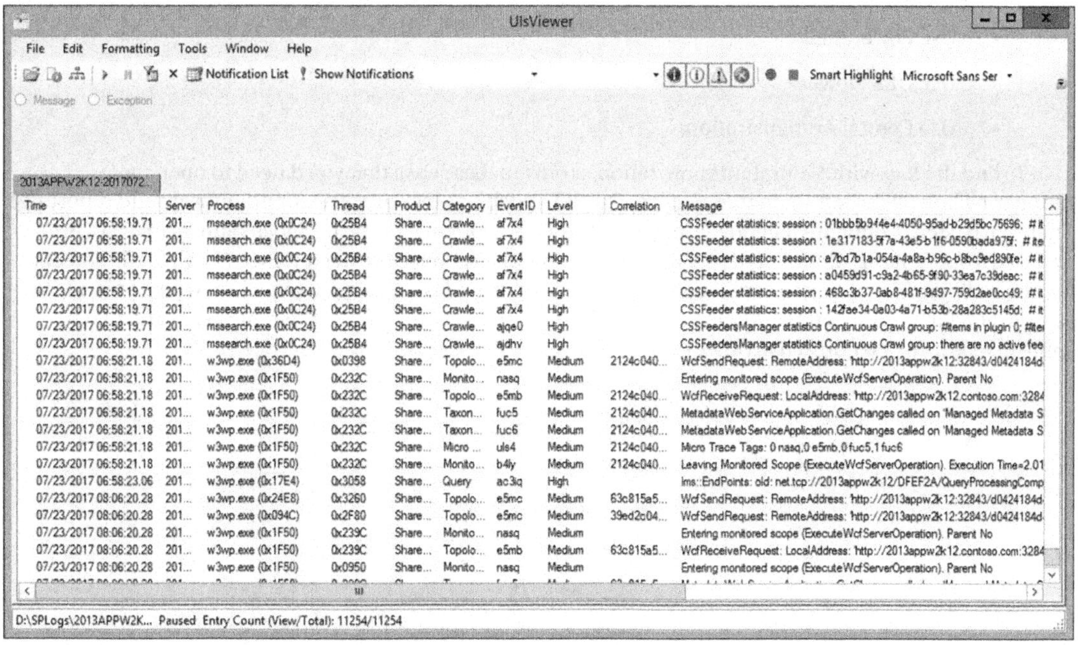

Figure 9-2. *Open from File then append from ULS*

There might be times when you're troubleshooting an issue, have opened a ULS log, based on the time that the event occurred in the Windows application event log, and then need to get the live stream without losing your place or the ability to filter on the log that you currently have open.

ULS logs are named in the ServerName-YYYYMMDD-HHMM.log format. So if you were looking for an event that occurred at 7:18 AM, and you opened your logging directory and saw the logs, as shown in Figure 9-3, you would open that began logging at 06:58 AM, 2013APPW2K12-20170723-0658.log.

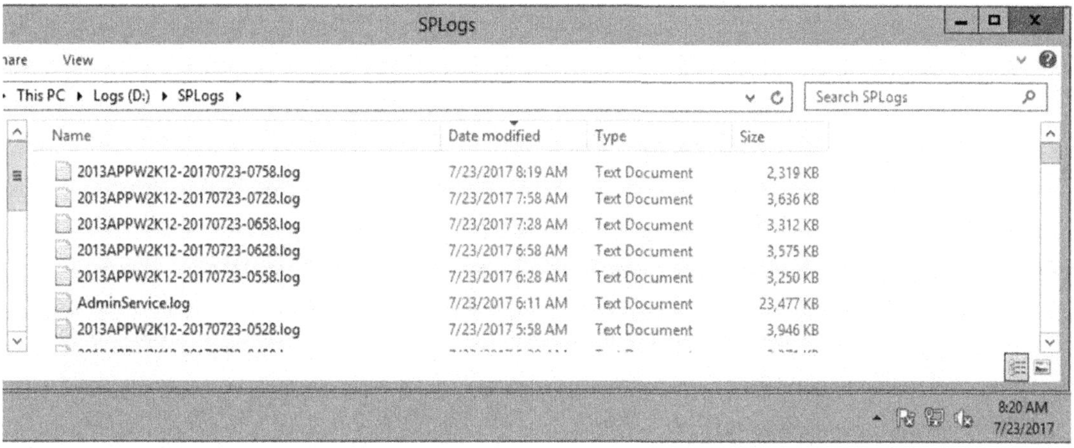

Figure 9-3. *Opening from file*

By default the logs are stored the logging directory inside the hive and the log interval for new logs is a new log every 30 minutes. If the logging directory has been moved off the C:\ drive and moved onto a drive that does not house the operating system there are a few ways to find out where the logs are located:

- Use PowerShell

- Use ULS Viewer

- Use Central Administration

To find the logs with Central Administration, it only makes sense that you'd need to open the Monitoring link off the left-hand menu (a.k.a. Quick Launch), as logs are used for monitoring and reporting. Then you'd click "Configure diagnostic logging" if you were looking for the ULS logs settings that can be changed from Central Administration. Figure 9-4 shows that we have the default Event Log Flood Protection feature enabled. The option to turn it off might be used in troubleshooting, in a situation where you wanted to turn it off for a few seconds and then turn it right back on to capture a few different events and maybe some different correlation activity IDs.

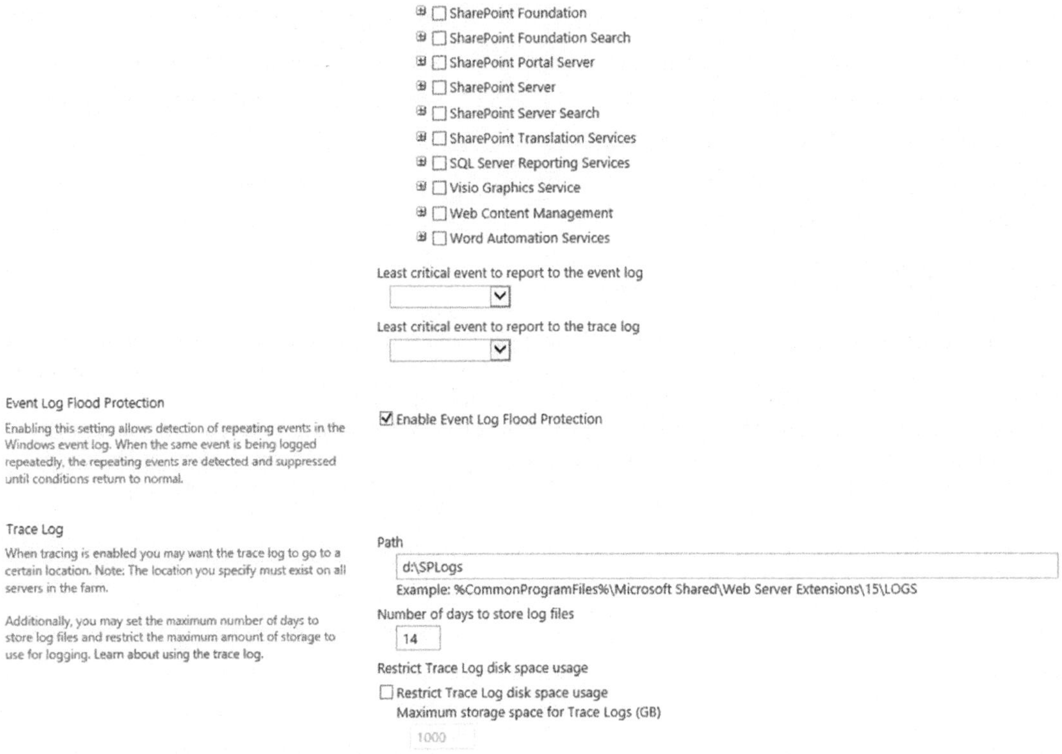

Figure 9-4. *Keep your flood protection enabled*

In looking at Figure 9-4, we can see a few of the categories:

- SharePoint Foundation Search

- SharePoint Portal Server

- SharePoint Server

- SharePoint Server Search

- SharePoint Translation Services

- SQL Server Reporting Services

- Visio Graphics Service

- Web Content Management

- Word Automation Services

One noticeable thing that the trained eye sees right off the bat is that all of these categories are at their default settings of "Information" being the lowest level of event to log in the Windows event log and Medium being the lowest level of event to log in the ULS, or trace log. Had one of the categories been modified, it would have been displayed with bold font, like the Visio Graphics Service category in Figure 9-5.

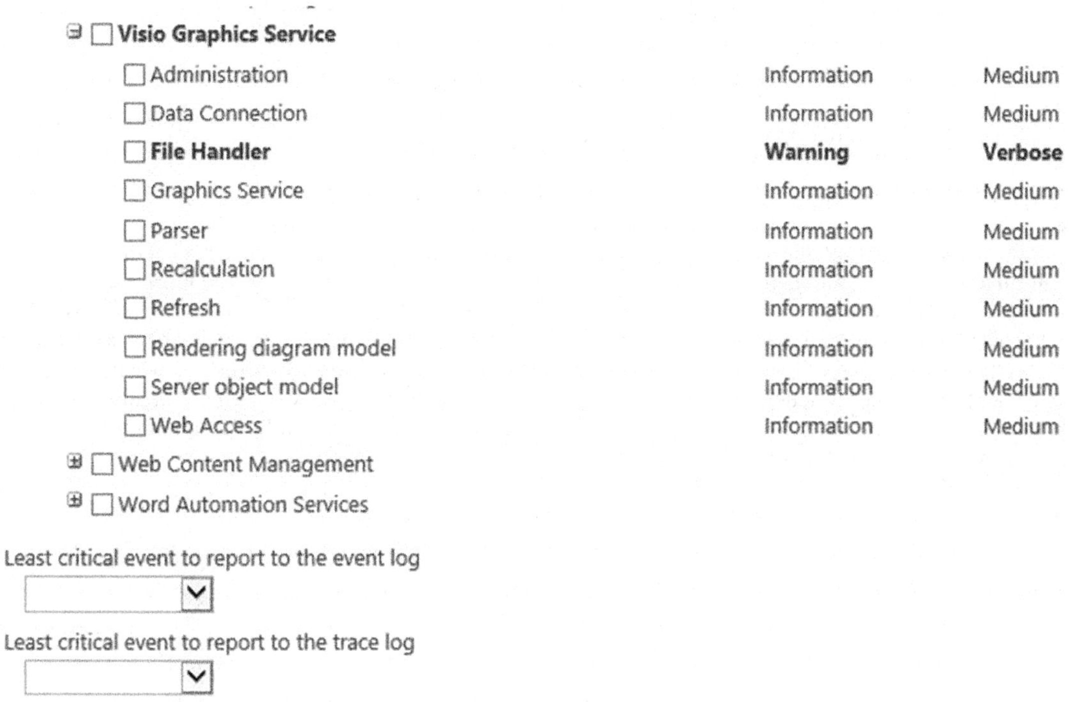

Visio Graphics Service		
Administration	Information	Medium
Data Connection	Information	Medium
File Handler	**Warning**	**Verbose**
Graphics Service	Information	Medium
Parser	Information	Medium
Recalculation	Information	Medium
Refresh	Information	Medium
Rendering diagram model	Information	Medium
Server object model	Information	Medium
Web Access	Information	Medium
Web Content Management		
Word Automation Services		

Least critical event to report to the event log

[⌄]

Least critical event to report to the trace log

[⌄]

Figure 9-5. If your event logs are filling, you may only want warnings

When you run Clear-SPLogLevel from an administrative SharePoint Management Shell session, it essentially the same as selecting the "Reset to default" options from both of the drop-down menus and setting everything back to the default levels. The drop-down menu that affects the lowest level of Windows event logs is named, "Least critical event to report to the event log". The other menu is for the ULS or trace log. Since we started looking at this page to find the path to the ULS logs, it only makes sense to mention that the Path text box shows where the logs will be stored as long as the following are true:

- The logging directory location exists on all servers in the farm

- The local groups created by SharePoint have read and write permissions to this file system path

- The account used by the SharePoint Tracing Service is a member of WSS_WPG, Performance Log Users, and Performance Monitor Users

- The SharePoint Tracing Service is started

- The account used by the SharePoint Tracing Service is the same on all farm servers

The "Configure diagnostic logging" feature allows you to change the number of days logging and to restrict the total amount of space on disk to be used for logging. By default, SharePoint will attempt to track 14 days' worth of trace logs, provided the disk space allows. And, the default disks space is set so that SharePoint will fill up the C drive, which would be a bad thing, and yet another reason to move that logging off the operating system drive. We already covered using PowerShell in determining where the diagnostic logs located in Chapter 2; but we didn't discuss using PowerShell to check the settings that we just looked at in the GUI.

To get information about the ULS logs, you use the Get-SPDiagnosticConfig cmdlet, so it only makes sense that to set the ULS logging location with PowerShell, that you'd use the Set-SPDiagnosticConfig cmdlet. The actual command is as follows:

```
Set-SPDiagnosticConfig -LogLocation "E:\Path to Logging Location"
```

Or, preferably without spaces in the folder name

```
Set-SPDiagnosticConfig -LogLocation E:\PathtoLoggingLocation
```

Between the Get-SPLogLevel and the Get-SPDiagnosticConfig cmdlets, you can get all of the information that the _admin/metrics.aspx page in Central Administration provides, and more. For example, the Get-SPDiagnosticConfig cmdlet will give you the logging interval in minutes, which is sort of what led to us talking about troubleshooting how logging is configured, permissioned, and turned on. The Get-SPLogLevel cmdlet will spew out all of the logging levels in an alphabetical list and you will not have to expand each category to determine which subcategory is modified, if any. We can see in Figure 9-6, the trailing end of having ran the Get-SPLogLevel and that the Get-SPDiagnosticConfig lists out information, once again, that is not available in the GUI.

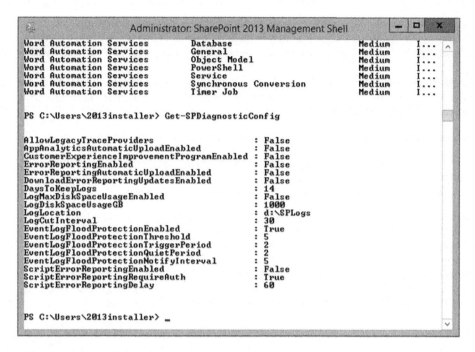

Figure 9-6. *Get-SPLogLevel and Get-SPDiagnosticConfig*

When an event ID is a warning or error, it more than likely does not have the correlation activity ID. If you look in Windows Event Log – Application Log to see event ID 6801, the short answer is you may need to delete and then re-create the proxy for the User Profile service application. The description and XML from the event will give you text to this affect.

"System.Reflection.TargetInvocationException: Exception has been thrown by the target of an invocation. ---> Microsoft.Office.Server.UserProfiles. UserProfileApplicationNotAvailableException: No User Profile Application available to service the request...."

You can search your ULS logs and see that there are all sorts of entries that pertain to the User Profiles category. Microsoft has released guidance at https://support.microsoft.com/en-us/help/2520394. The steps to re-create the User Profile service application proxy, are straightforward. First, you remove the corrupted proxy and then you create a new proxy. Finally, you associate the newly created proxy with any existing web applications.

Here's the PowerShell to remove the User Profile service application proxy:

```
$proxy = Get-SPServiceApplicationProxy | where {$_.typename -eq "User Profile Service
Application Proxy"}
Remove-SPServiceApplicationProxy -Identity $proxy -confirm:$false
```

And here is the PowerShell to create the User Profile service application proxy:

```
$upa = Get-SPServiceApplication | where {$_.name -eq "<name here>"}
New-SPProfileServiceApplicationProxy -Name <proxyName> -Uri $upa.uri.absoluteURI
```

If you look at the manage service application page an do not see the User Profile service application proxy you should still run a get-spserviceapplicationproxy to make sure you do not have an orphan hanging out in the object model. Neither ULS Viewer nor the GUI will tell you if this is the case, but PowerShell will let you know.

OK, let's get back to looking at the ULS Viewer. ULS Viewer is the third way to find out where the logs are located. If you choose File, Open from ULS, or Append from ULS, the ULS Viewer will sense where the logs are located as long as logging is currently enabled.

■ **Note**   When troubleshooting, you need to answer a bunch of questions, including "When did this happen?" and "Was there a correlation ID?".

Once we've determined the file that encompasses the time that the error occurred, we can open it in ULS Viewer and filter based on the correlation activity ID, if we have one, or based on the correlation ID provided by a user screenshot. This is why it's a good idea to train your users to send the "Sorry, something went wrong" screenshot with the technical details expanded. When you are working with the application event log or system event log, you'll be able to get a correlation ID from the XML data of the critical event.

Once you have the correlation, you can filter the log by using the filter icon, or by pressing Ctrl+M, as shown in Figure 9-7.

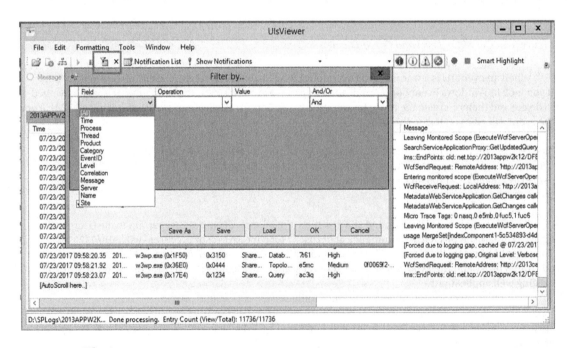

Figure 9-7. *Filter icon*

Some prefer to filter on a specific field in the logs for the correlation ID, namely the correlation field. I used to be one of those folks, until I learned that sometimes the correlation field is empty and the correlation that I'm after could also reside in the message field, or another field. So, for that reason alone, I filter on all fields, with the operation of contains and the value of the correlation; while making sure that the correlation that is pasted into the Value field does not include any leading or trailing spaces. Often when copying a correlation from the "Sorry, Something went wrong" message it is easy to get a trailing space. So, watch out of that trailing space. Figure 9-8 shows an admin about to try and filter the diagnostic log for a correlation **with a trailing space**. This could potentially yield zero results.

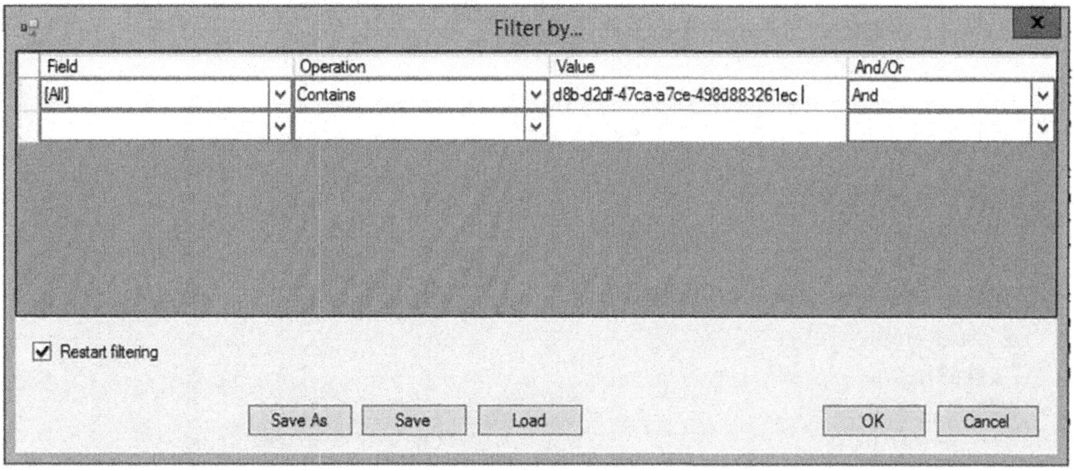

Figure 9-8. *Trailing space yields zero results*

The quickest way to clear the filters is to press Ctrl+E, or choose Edit ➤ Clear Filters. You can also clear them manually by clicking around in the filter window, if you only need to remove one line for example.

Knowing a few ULS keyboard shortcuts helps with getting around in the ULS logs, which is much quicker than scrolling. For example, after you have filtered, or even before you have filtered, you can use Ctrl+G to go to the closest time to the time you enter in the Goto Time window. So, in a case where you know the time that something happened, maybe from a screenshot, you can open the correct ULS log and use Ctrl+G to get the closest to that time and date. Figure 9-9 demonstrates how you could look for the 9:58 AM location in this log.

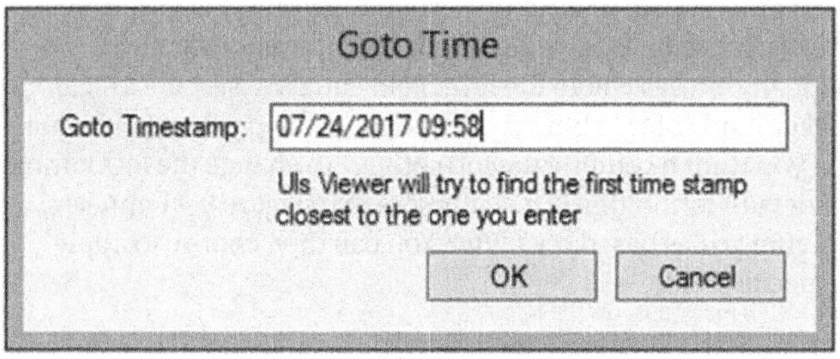

Figure 9-9. *Jump to a time*

It's easy to discount that Goto Time feature with the logic of something along the lines of, "Or, I could just scroll to it." And that is true: you could just scroll to it. But I guarantee you that learning to use the Ctrl+G will quickly become, and pardon the pun, your go-to method for finding an entry in a log. Then after you've located the time, you may or may not have found the correlation and once you find the entry with the same correlation that you're looking for, you can jump to the next entry with that same correlation using the keys Ctrl+I. If once you get to this next occurrence you decide you want to look at the entry you were previously on, then you can move back to the previous correlation by using Ctrl+Shift+I.

When you're troubleshooting a process, you can start at the top of your log, filtered or not, and then find the first occurrence of your process by using the search feature. You already know how to search because ULS Viewer uses the international key combination to find stuff, the same combination is used in Notepad, Excel, numerous browsers, and without further ado, Ctrl+F will allow you to find whatever you're looking for in the log. Sometimes, this is more fun that running a filter. When you use Ctrl+F to find text, make sure to take it to search all field, as shown in Figure 9-10.

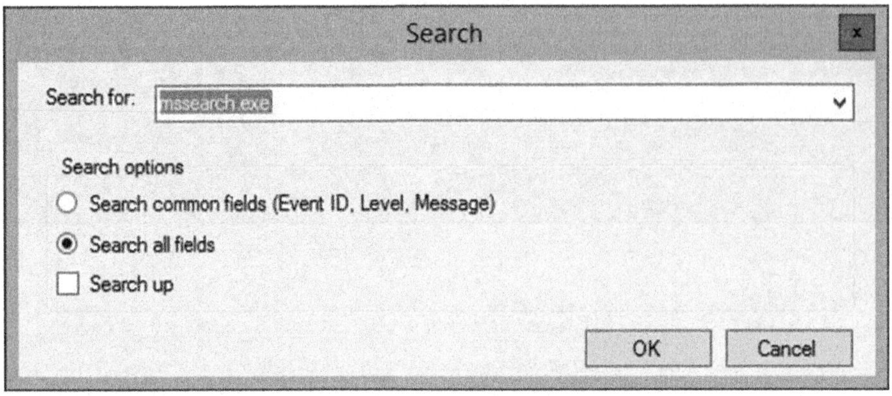

Figure 9-10. *Ctrl+F all fields*

After you find what you're looking for, you can use F3 (just like you can in registry) to find the next occurrence. And, you can use Shift+F3 to move back to the previously found instance of whatever it was you were searching. As you're reading through the logs and you come across an entry that you think might be worth coming back to, or possibly including in a report to the business or to another admin, you should bookmark that entry by pressing Ctrl+ F2. Then you can use F2 to jump between all your bookmarked entries and F3 to clear the bookmarks, after you've finished with the log.

When you use bookmarks, the ULS Viewer places a bookmark icon to the leftmost position of the bookmarked entries and this provides a visual queue to your eye when scrolling through or moving through the logs with the mouse or keyboard shortcuts. Another way to make entries standout visually is to specify custom formatting for these entries that meet certain criteria. By default, the ULS Viewer has custom formatting that sets the background to salmon for any entries where the level field equals Assert or Critical. There is also default formatting that sets the background color to blue for items where the product field equals ULS Viewer. You can create whatever formatting you want by editing the formatting. To change the formatting, click the Formatting menu, and then click "Edit default formatting". Once the screen in Figure 9-11 appears, you can click to add more columns and set formatting rules based on a filter. You can then choose to apply background color to the entire row, or just to a specific field.

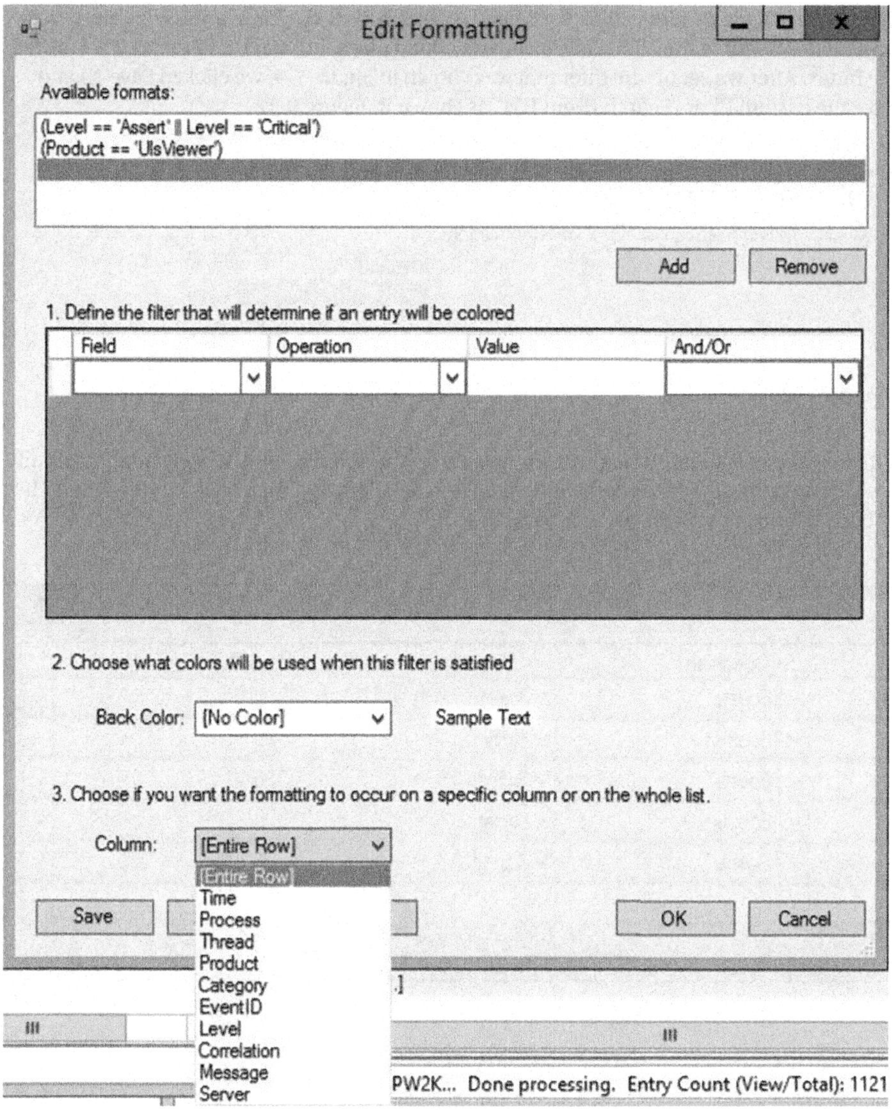

Figure 9-11. *Custom formatting and filter*

When you clear formatting off the Formatting menu, this also clears the default formatting, which to me seems counterintuitive, but hey it does say clear formatting and that is exactly what it does, including the default formatting. You can get the default formatting back by closing the ULS Viewer and reopening it, or by manually re-creating it, though.

By default, the ULS Viewer creates a notification list that allows you to create links to these events that have a level of Critical or Assert level. All you have to do is open the Notification list and the click the Bookmark and Clear button. This will set bookmarks on all of these entries. Now all you need to do is press F2 to get to the first bookmark and then press F2 to go to the next. You can modify the Notification filter off the Tools menu, by adding additional filters, or changing or removing the default notification filters.

If you recall from Chapter 7, we created a filter for search, with the five key ULS event ID that pertain to search to track down search activity in the ULS while a crawl is taking place and track an item as it is crawled and then put into the index. After we set up the filter that was shown in Figure 7-4, we clicked Save As and this allowed us to have the custom filter "Search Event IDs" as shown in Figure 9-12.

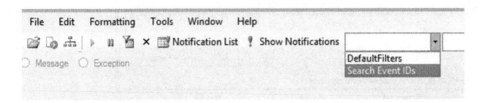

Figure 9-12. Custom event IDs

After selecting the custom event IDs our log will filter based on the settings. And, if we wanted to modify the custom event IDs we could hit Ctrl+M, click the filter icon, or click Edit, and then click Modify Filter. The filter changes to our custom filter, as we can see in Figure 9-13.

Field		Operation		Value		And/Or	
EventID	∨	Equals	∨	ds86		Or	∨
EventID	∨	Equals	∨	af7yn		Or	∨
EventID	∨	Equals	∨	e5g1		Or	∨
EventID	∨	Equals	∨	ai3ef		Or	∨
EventID	∨	Equals	∨	ajpnd		And	∨
	∨		∨				∨

Filter by... ✕

☑ Restart filtering

[Save As] [Save] [Load] [OK] [Cancel]

Figure 9-13. Search event IDs filter

Event ID 1148 is a critical event ID that fires if the Secure Store service key was not generated or was improperly refreshed after the Secure Store service was provisioned. When this happens, the Performance Point service application fails to save the unattended account, and when you try to enter the account and save the service application, event ID 1148 is generated in the application log and SharePoint logs events in the ULS.

This is what you'll see in the ULS log:

```
01/04/2017 17:05:41.07 w3wp.exe (0x1E0C)     0x1AD0 PerformancePoint Service
PerformancePoint Services    1148    Critical    The Unattended Service Account
cannot be set for the service application. The Secure Store Service key might not have
been generated or properly refreshed after the service was provisioned. Error Details:
Microsoft.Office.SecureStoreService.Server.SecureStoreServiceException: Application
Server does not have the latest key.    at Microsoft.Office.SecureStoreService.Server.
SecureStoreServiceApplicationProxy.Execute[T](String operationName, Boolean validateCanary,
ExecuteDelegate`1 operation)    at Microsoft.Office.SecureStoreService.Server.
SecureStoreServiceApplicationProxy.CreateApplication(Guid rawPartitionId, TargetApplication
application, IList`1 applicationFields, TargetApplicationClaims applicationClaims)    at
Microsoft.Office.SecureStoreService.Server.SecureStore.CreateApplication(TargetApplication
application, IList`1 applicationFields, TargetApplicationClaims applicationClaims)    at
Microsoft.PerformancePoint.Scorecards.Server.ManagedSharedIdentityTargetApplication.
CreateTargetApp(ISecureStore sss, String friendlyName, String email, List`1 targetAppFields,
TargetApplicationClaims claims)    at Microsoft.PerformancePoint.Scorecards.Server.
ManagedSharedIdentityTargetApplication.CreateNewTargetApplication
(String displayName, ISecureStore sss, List`1 targetAppFields, String appPoolId)    at
Microsoft.PerformancePoint.Scorecards.Server.ManagedSharedIdentityTargetApplication.
Provision(ISecureStore sss, String displayName, List`1 targetAppFields, Boolean
preserveExistingCredentials, List`1 newCredentials, String appPoolId)    e5c9c79d-0791-
d094-dbd7-65a59bfa0ec7
```

Figure 9-14 displays what you'll see in the Sorry, something went wrong message.

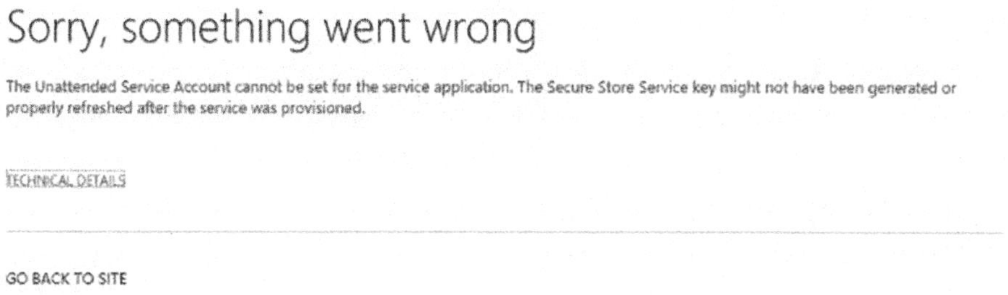

Sorry, something went wrong

The Unattended Service Account cannot be set for the service application. The Secure Store Service key might not have been generated or properly refreshed after the service was provisioned.

TECHNICAL DETAILS

GO BACK TO SITE

Figure 9-14. *Sorry, something went wrong*

When we copied the full message out of the browser, after expanding the technical details, we were able to see that correlation ID, and date and time, as shown here:

```
Sorry, something went wrong
```

The Unattended service account cannot be set for the service application. The Secure Store service key might not have been generated or properly refreshed after the service was provisioned.

```
Technical Details

Troubleshoot issues with Microsoft SharePoint Foundation.

Correlation ID: e5c9c79d-0791-d094-dbd7-65a59bfa0ec7
```

Date and Time: 1/4/2017 5:05:41 PM

Go back to site

If you query the Internet for the text shown in the "Sorry, something went wrong" message, you will find this: "The Unattended service account cannot be set for the service application. The Secure Store service key might not have been generated or properly refreshed after the service was provisioned." You'll find a lot of posts that advise creating the Secure Store key. And, unfortunately, in this case that had already been completed. The Secure Store service application was provisioned and the key had been generated.

The fix in this case was to generate a new master key after stopping the Security Token Service application pool. These are the actual steps.

1. Take inventory of all the target application IDs so they could be manually re-created if needed.

2. Stop Secure Store service instance on servers that run the Secure Store service.

3. Stop the security token service application pool on servers that run the Secure Store service.

4. Start the security token service application pool on servers that run the Secure Store service.

5. Start the Secure Store instance on servers that run the Secure Store service.

6. Generate master key and refresh key.

7. Manually re-create the target application IDs using information stored in the GUI, as needed.

Earlier we were talking about those W questions and one of them being when something happened. If ever you go to merge a log file and are not returned any results try using the startTime and endTime parameters, as follows:

```
Merge-SPLogFile –Path <pathToOutputFile> -Correlation <CorrelationID> -startTime "mm/dd/yyyy 24HR:MM" –endTime "mm/dd/yyyy 24HR:MM"
```

For example,

```
Merge-SPLogFile -Path d:\troubleshooting\perfpoint.txt  -Correlation e5c9c79d-0791-d094-dbd7-65a59bfa0ec7 -startTime "01/04/2017 17:00" –endTime "01/04/2017 17:15"
```

The sooner you can start troubleshooting the better, especially if you're going to merge log files. The ULS logs by default, and if there is enough disk space allocated to the logs, should have history back 14 days. This is probably a lot more time than is available in the Windows logs, since the Windows logs usually are not set to maintain that much history.

When it comes to the PowerShell involved with ULS logs, Table 9-1 lists the names of the cmdlets, a description of each cmdlet and the purpose that each cmdlet serves.

Table 9-1. *ULS PowerShell cmdlets and Official Microsoft Descriptions and Purposes*

cmdlet Description	Description	Purpose
Get-SPDiagnosticConfig	Retrieves Diagnostic Configuration values.	Diagnostic configuration
Set-SPDiagnosticConfig	Allows setting Diagnostic Configuration values.	Diagnostic configuration
Get-SPLogLevel	Returns IDiagnosticsLevel2 objects or displays a list of diagnostics levels.	Trace log and event log throttling
Set-SPLogLevel	Allows the user to set the trace and event level for a set of categories.	Trace log and event log throttling
Clear-SPLogLevel	Resets the trace and event levels back to their default values.	Trace log and event log throttling
New-SPLogFile	Ends the current log file and starts a new one.	Log file control
Get-SPLogEvent	Reads/queries ULS trace logs.	Trace log querying and filtering
Merge-SPLogFile	Combines trace log files from all farm servers into a single file.	Trace log merging

The Get-SPLogEvent can be used to filter through the ULS logs in many different ways. If you would like to find all the unexpected events in your farm's ULS logs, for the last hour, and assuming the current time and date was 5:09 PM on July 23, 2017, you could run this:

```
Get-SPLogEvent -StartTime "07/23/2017 16:09" -EndTime "07/23/2017 17:09" | ? {$_.Level -Eq
"Unexpected"}
```

The dates and times are in the 24-hour clock format and are localized to the United States of America, so MM/DD/YYYY for the date portion. The result of that command in my lab returned seven entries that need looking into. The entries are shown in Figure 9-15.

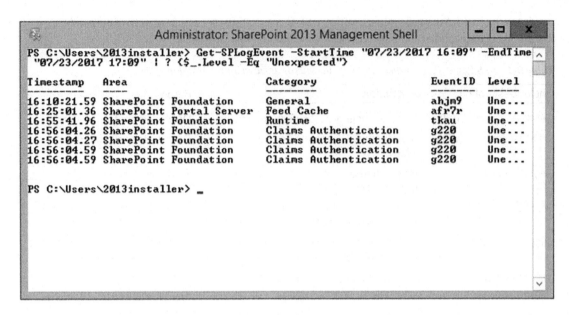

Figure 9-15. PowerShell to find unexpected conditions

At this point, I could open ULS Viewer and determine which log files to open and then using Ctrl+G, I could get directly on the various entries to begin troubleshooting. This knowing when the unexpected conditions occurred can also help me understand where to look in the application and systems event logs, too.

Now that we've demonstrated a couple of the basic ways to use the ULS Viewer tool, let's talk about some of its other features. We've already covered moving around inside the tool using keyboard shortcuts and the menu. We also went over most of the formatting options, including the editing the default formatting. I should've mentioned the Smart Highlight feature on the toolbar, which when enabled, quickly shows similar entries in the Message category. This is most helpful when looking for trends and it is similar to Ctrl+I (next same correlation ID), Ctrl+T (next same thread), and Ctrl+P (next same process), the only difference being you can't use it to skip to the same message. That is, you can only use the smart highlighter to highlight messages that are the same, as shown in Figure 9-16.

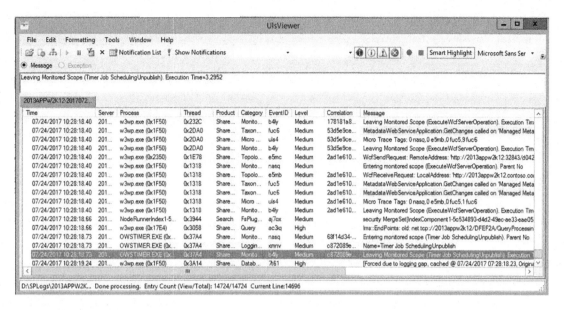

Figure 9-16. *Smart highlight*

Another feature of the ULS Viewer is the ability to save a workspace. Saving a workspace will save a small file with a .ulsworkspace extension to the directory of your choosing. Then when you open the workspace, it will reopen whichever files you had opened. The workspace does not save any bookmarks you may have set in those files; it only keeps the references to the various log files that were last opened. I find this feature useful if I need to save my work at the end of a workday and be able to return to the log files at the start of my next shift, or hand this off to another SharePoint engineer.

You can see the save a workspace feature and then load a workspace feature in Figure 9-17. Figure 9-17 also demonstrates the recent files list, which is arguably just about as useful. The only benefit of using the saved workspace rather than the recent files list is that the workspace is not overwritten and the recent files list cycles. And, after a certain period of time, the workspace may become an empty window, if the logs have truncated, as the workspace does not save copies of the logs, just pointers to the files themselves. So, when the logs truncate from the logging directory, they also drop out of the workspace.

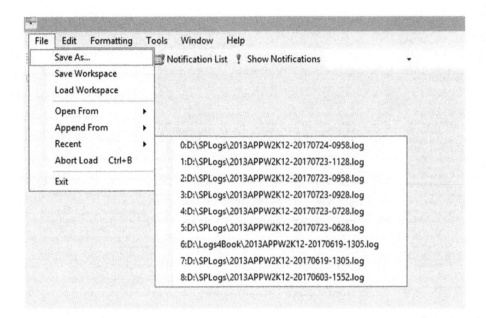

Figure 9-17. *File menu*

After you update the farm information by clicking the farm icon, and entering in the UNC path to your logging location, as shown in Figure 9-18 and 9-19, you can then use the Open From or Append From options on the File menu.

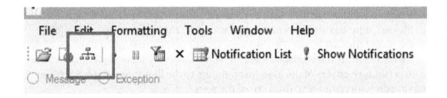

Figure 9-18. *Farm icon*

Figure 9-19 shows the farm information being entered. In this example farm, the ULS logs are stored on the D:\ drive of the servers in the SPLogs directory. Your farm may have the logs in the default location under the C:\Program Files\Common Files\Microsoft Shared\Web Server Extensions\15\Logs. If that is the case you would just replace the d$\splogs in Figure 9-19 with the path to your logging directory. The server names are all that is needed. You do not need to enter in the FQDN. Just enter the server's NetBIOS name and click Add. After all the servers in your farm are entered, you're ready to try out the logging for the entire farm.

Figure 9-19. Log location

Whenever you are viewing from ULS, this is work is happening in memory. The default setting for ULS Viewer is 120 minutes, after that time the program will stop logging. You can modify this setting by clicking the Tools menu and then clicking Options and modifying the "Real time feed duration". You can also change the smart highlight so that it will highlight the entire row, rather than the default setting of highlighting only the field. Along with changing the smart highlighting, you can change the tool so that the correlation tree is viewable in the default view without having to click the icon to toggle the correlation tree, as shown in Figure 9-20.

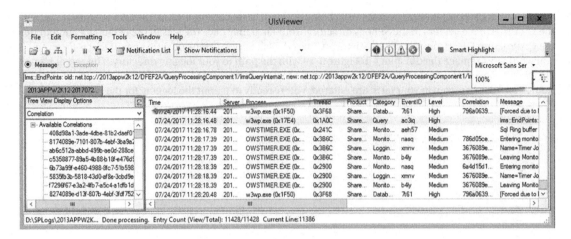

Figure 9-20. Correlation tree in action

The correlation tree is a nice way to quickly filter on a correlation. For example, assuming you used the search keyboard shortcut to find something (Ctrl+F), you could then open the correlation tree and find the correlation, click the correlation, to quickly toggle the view to that correlation. The tree view display also has a name option where you can choose records based on the name field. This can be helpful when troubleshooting a particular page or timer job, but keep in mind the filter that this applies is still based on the correlation associated with whichever instance of the timer job name you had chosen.

If you're still looking for a more robust way to query the log file, the "Filter by this Item" feature is what you need to check out. It allows you to quickly get granular. You can restrict your query based on any of the fields that you have in the current ULS Viewer. To get to the point shown in Figure 9-21, you just need to right click an entry and then choose "Filter by this Item".

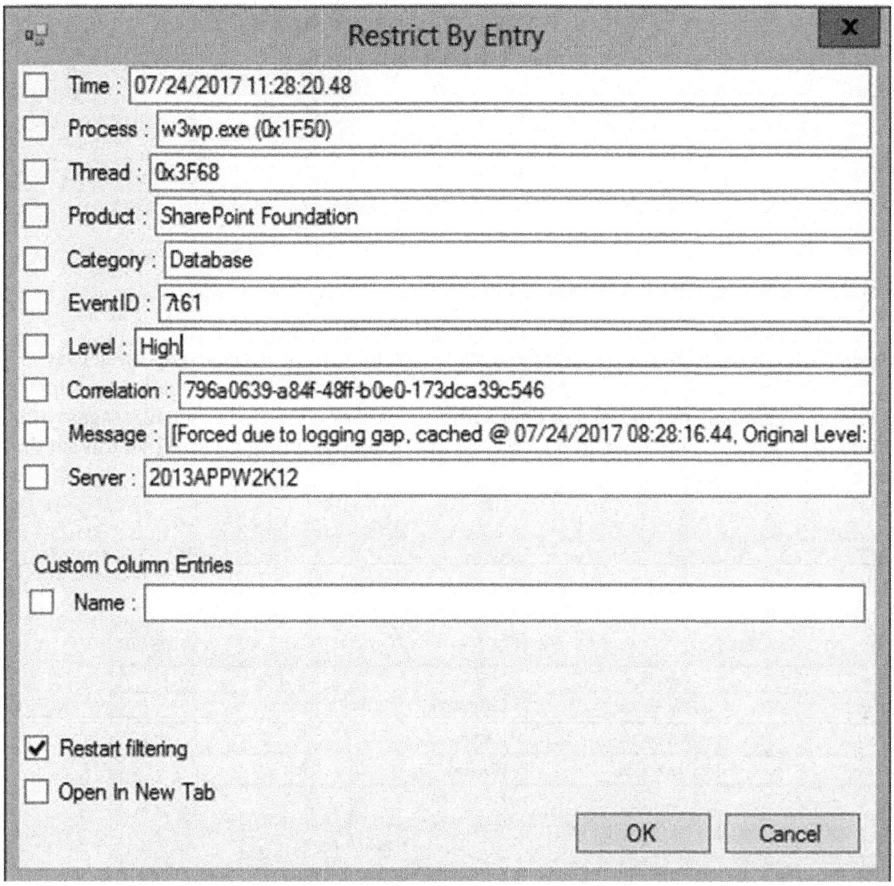

Figure 9-21. *You can even change the categories*

Using the filter by this item is a really quick way to filter the current log based on a single category and then open that in a new window, as you can see in Figure 9-21, there is an open in a new window option. When you use the "Filter by Item" and "Restrict by Entry" features to open the ULS log in a new window, you can always press Ctrl+E to remove the filter and then you're right back to the complete log once more; since the "Restrict by Entry" is just a filter.

The Window menu allows you to work with the various log files that you've opened. If you're prone to keyboard shortcuts, the Window menu will let you know what they all are, or you can just click the menu. My favorite is the Ctrl+F4 to close the current page. Figure 9-22 shows the Window menu and the various keyboard shortcuts.

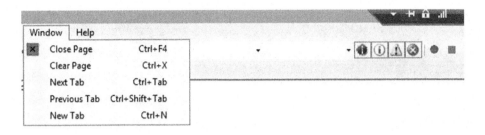

Figure 9-22. *Window menu and toggle buttons*

Figure 9-22 also shows the four toggle buttons that allow you to filter out entries based on level. I say 'Filter out' because as you click each toggle button the ULS Viewer creates a filter line that reads Level not equals whichever level you toggled off, or filtered out. For example, if you only wanted to see messages with a level of high, you could set the toggle as shown in Figure 9-23. You'll also see in Figure 9-23 that this set the filter so that it 'Filters out' the other levels.

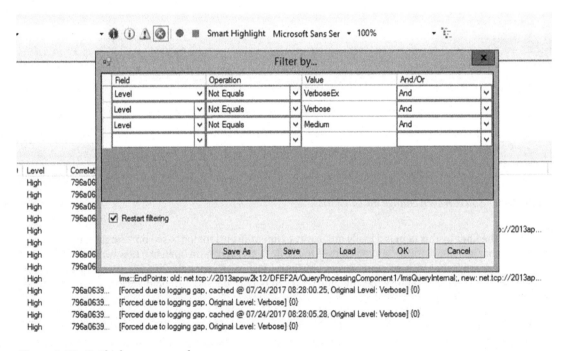

Figure 9-23. *Get high messages only*

At this point, we have given the ULS Viewer a pretty good look. The only parts that we haven't discussed yet are the self-explanatory font menu and size menu, the ability to save logs to CSV files, and how to delete individual rows in a custom filter. Consider the filter created by removing the VerboseEX, Verbose, and Medium log entries. Assume that you didn't have the ability to just click to show Medium, or that you wanted to delete a row from a filter. The steps to do this are shown in Figure 9-24.

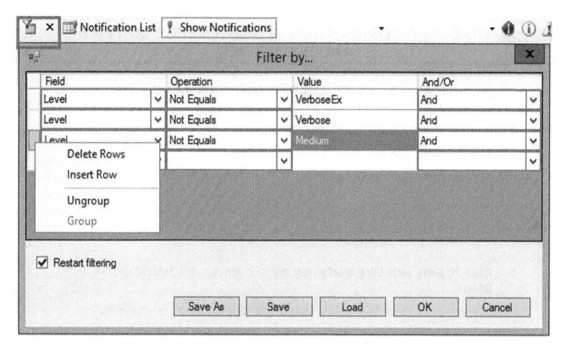

Figure 9-24. *Modify a filter*

From the filter icon, you can modify the filter by highlighting the row, right clicking, and then choosing Delete Rows or insert rows. If you're looking to get rid of the filter, just remove all the rows at once by using the keyboard shortcut of Ctrl+E.

The ULS logs provide us with search terms that we can use in Bing or Google, to hopefully find resolutions to the issue. The event logs also give us search terms that we can use in the ULS logs, Bing, and Google. Sometimes when searching, less is more, so if you exclude the time stamp, server name and only include the process, thread, product, category, event ID, level, and message, you might get better results. Some other things to try are to prune that even further, maybe only search on event ID, level, and message.

As we near the end of this chapter, the main takeaway is to understand that there is a connection between critical events in the Windows event logs and the ULS logs. The Windows events have a correlation activity ID, and that that correlation ID can usually be traced into the ULS diagnostic logs. It's important to know how to change the log verbosity using PowerShell to verboseEx by running

```
Set-SPLogLevel –TraceSeverity VerboseEx
```

And, it's important to know how to create a clean starting place to start troubleshooting from are all very important.

TRACING A CORRELATION ID USING MERGE LOG FILE AND ULS VIEWER

The purpose of this exercise is to see how to use the concepts in the chapter without harming your SharePoint environment.

1. Open the **All site content** page on your SharePoint site.

2. Change viewlsts.aspx to viewlists.aspx and press **Enter**.

The following screenshot demonstrates step 2.

3. When the **Sorry, something went wrong** message appears, click **Technical Details**.

The following screenshot shows the message in its default state without the correlation ID.

Sorry, something went wrong

An unexpected error has occurred.

TECHNICAL DETAILS

___

GO BACK TO SITE

The following screenshot displays the message with the technical details displaying. We can use that correlation ID in the next step.

Sorry, something went wrong

An unexpected error has occurred.

TECHNICAL DETAILS

Troubleshoot issues with Microsoft SharePoint Foundation.

Correlation ID: 0d7a089e-319b-807b-4ebf-30c630449114

Date and Time: 7/24/2017 12:35:23 PM

GO BACK TO SITE

4. Open the SharePoint Management Shell and run the following command, substituting the correlation ID with the one that your browser is displaying. Use a path for the output file of your choosing.

    ```
    Merge-SPLogFile –Correlation 0d7a089e-319b-807b-4ebf-30c630449114 –Path
    d:\PathToSaveFile\troubleshootingSharepoint.txt
    ```

After you enter the command, the merge-splogfile process will start. You'll just need to wait for the timer job to run. The image shown in the following screenshot will appear. After it finishes, the PowerShell will return a new line.

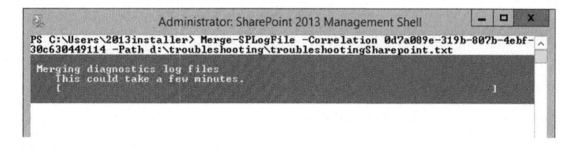

5. Now that the log file has been generated, open **ULS Viewer**.

6. Choose **File ➤ Open from file**. Navigate to the directory that you used in step 4 and open the file.

Notice how the entry with medium level, right above the entry with the unexpected level, says that the page does not exist. The unexpected level entry says another version of the medium line. Actually, this is what I call SharePoint robot-speak: "Application error when access /_layouts/15/viewlists.

aspx, Error=The file '/_layouts/15/viewlists.aspx' does not exist." I mean who talks that way? No one does because that is robot-speak! And that is what you want to look for when you are troubleshooting SharePoint. You want to learn to understand what the robot, SharePoint, is trying to say. The following screenshot shows the row I'm referring to.

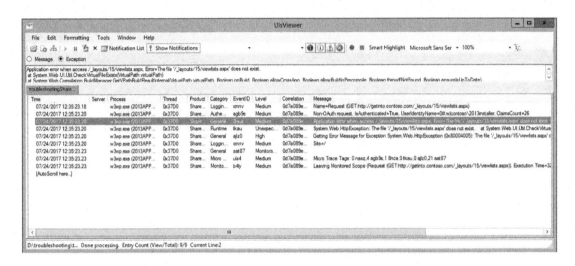

Now, let's see what happens if we filter on the correlation ID by copying it out of the browser

7. Highlight your correlation ID the way that I have done in the following screenshot, and paste it into the ULS Viewer.

Sorry, something went wrong

An unexpected error has occurred.

TECHNICAL DETAILS

Troubleshoot issues with Microsoft SharePoint Foundation.

Correlation ID: 0d7a089e-319b-807b-4ebf-30c630449114

Date and Time: 7/24/2017 12:35:23 PM

GO BACK TO SITE

8. Open the filter by entering **Ctrl+M**. Choose all fields, double-click the value field, and paste the correlation ID. Then, just to see what would happen if you didn't remove the trailing space, click **OK**.

The following screenshot demonstrates the correlation ID with the trailing space that is very easy to copy to the ULS Viewer if not careful.

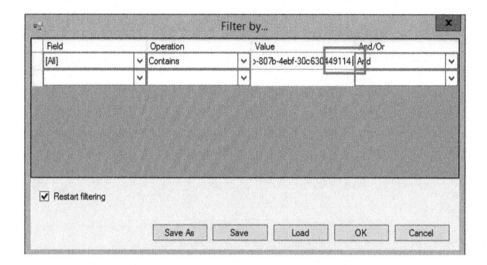

If you had a trailing space, you'll see that all the results are gone from the ULS Viewer. This is because all of the results in a merged log file have the correlation ID.

9. Now press **Ctrl+M**, edit the trailing space, and click **OK**. All the results return.

Hopefully, this chapter might have given you some new tricks to add to your ULS Viewer skill set. The connection between the Windows event log and the ULS log in regards to critical, error, and warning events is something to take away from this chapter. The correlation activity ID in the critical event IDs will become a quick go to when troubleshooting, but hopefully you won't need to use that advice.

The next chapter we will look at some tools to inspect web traffic, file system access issues, page load times, and IIS logs.

CHAPTER 10

■ ■ ■

Tools: Network Packet Tools and Page Performance

In Chapter 5, I spoke about the use of telnet to check that a port is open between the soon-to-be SharePoint servers and the SQL server(s), but we didn't go any further than looking at how to add and remove telnet. Chapter 6 featured the ports used by SharePoint in Table 6-1. I mentioned that telnet can be used to test communication on all ports and that you can check that the servers can find each other by pinging the various servers in your farm with ping.

In Chapter 7, we briefly looked at the Process Explorer tool by Mark Russinovich on Microsoft's sysinternals site. We used Process Explorer to get a deeper understanding of the node controller processes that SharePoint Search spins up. In this chapter, we'll look at Process Explorer and its good friend the Process Monitor as we talk about how both of these awesome tools can be used in troubleshooting. Before we get into those two tools, let's look at a few tools used in troubleshooting network communication and page performance.

As we look at various tools in this chapter, we'll shed light on these tools' application in troubleshooting. We will look at key parts of the various tools. We won't cover every single menu item of every tool, but by the end of the chapter, you'll see ways that you can use each tool to troubleshoot issues.

Outside of validating that two machines can talk to each other, we haven't really talked too much about how to troubleshoot network communication. In this chapter, we're going to look at a few tools that can be used to troubleshoot communication. We'll see how to inspect packets, troubleshoot page performance, and analyze IIS logs. And the best part, all of these tools are free to download and deploy!

Wireshark

Navigate to `https://www.wireshark.org/download.html` to download the version of Wireshark that matches your operating system. When troubleshooting SharePoint with Wireshark, I prefer to put Wireshark on one of the servers in the farm. Before you download Wireshark to your farm, make sure that you aren't immediately thrown in jail, by reading `https://www.wireshark.org/export.html`. Apparently, there existed, or might still exist, some countries where you cannot use this awesome tool. If you're not sure if you can use it in your country, then you should use caution, and just read about it. In other words, no special exclusions are conferred here in any way.

After you download the executable of your choice, double-click it and next through to victory. If you would like to be able to capture traffic to USB keys, make sure to select the option for USBPcap during the install. Once, the install is completed and you've opened Wireshark, you're presented with something like Figure 10-1 (Please Note: this is from a laptop with a home-lab spun up, thus all the odd connections that you will not see on your SharePoint server, I hope).

© Stacy Simpkins 2017
S. Simpkins, *Troubleshooting SharePoint*, https://doi.org/10.1007/978-1-4842-3138-8_10

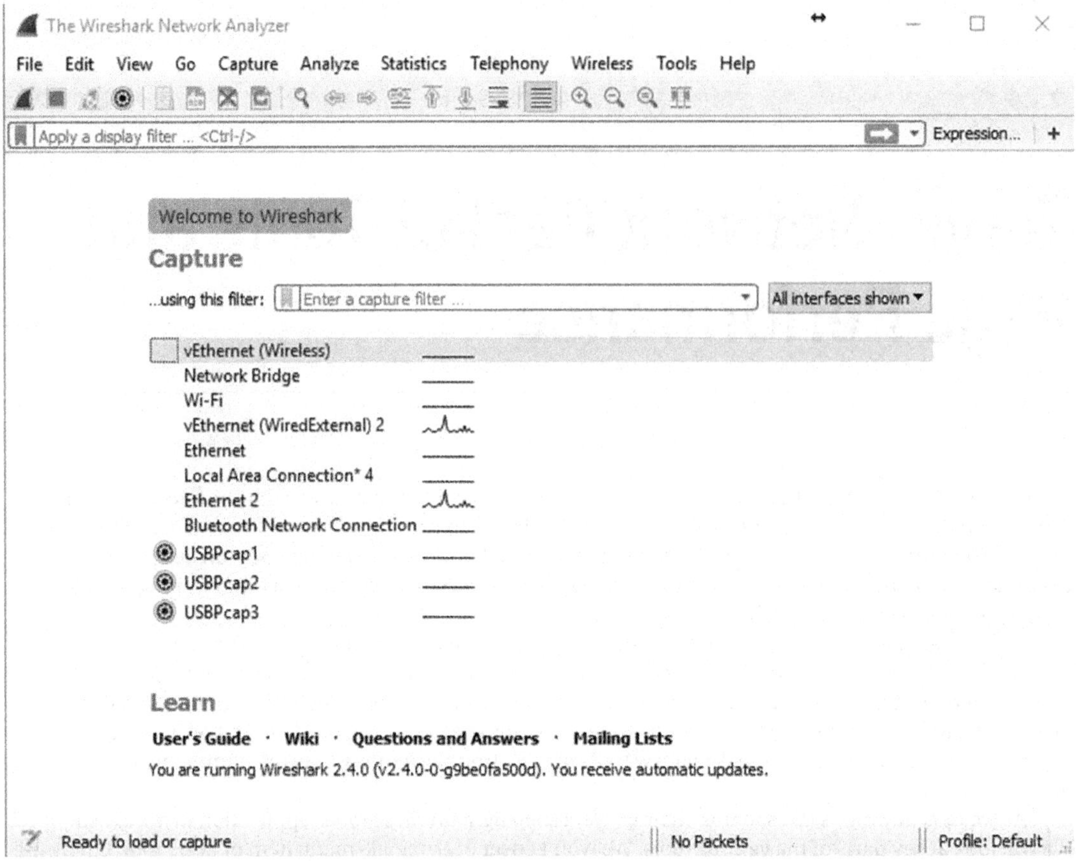

Figure 10-1. *Ready to load or capture*

Figure 10-1 shows that Wireshark is ready to load a .pcap file or begin a new capture. If you've ever used Wireshark, then you already know that the blue shark fin means that a capture is not underway. When a capture is underway, the blue shark fin turns gray, and the gray shark fin is illuminated green, and the stop square is illuminated red. As you can see in Figure 10-2, once the capture has started you cannot modify the capture filter. Unlike the capture filter, you can apply and modify a display filter during a capture.

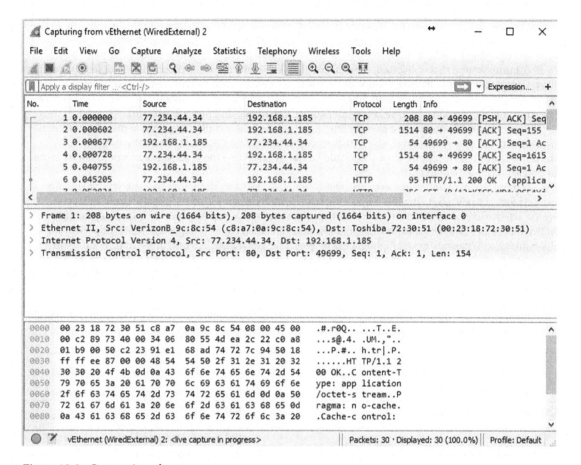

Figure 10-2. *Capture is underway*

After the capturing has been stopped, you can save the capture file. If you choose to start another capture before saving the current capture file, Wireshark will prompt you to save the capture file or start fresh and the choice is yours. Other than needing to ask someone else to review the capture, or possibly wanting to look at the capture after a while, I really can't think of a reason to save it. After you've saved it, you can reopen it with the Open Recent menu on the File menu. Once you have the file open, you can apply a filter to look at traffic that originated from a source IP by typing ip.src==77.234.44.34, where 77.234.44.34 is the actual IP address of the server, and then clicking the Apply button. This button looks like an arrow pointing to the right. It is shown with the display filter bar in Figure 10-3.

Figure 10-3. *Display filter*

When using Wireshark to troubleshoot communication, you'll want to remove the noise. In other words, Wireshark will capture all the communication that is currently underway on your network and you'll want to look at the pertinent packets and weed-out the non-pertinent packets. It's always nice to be able to get back to all communication that transpired, though, and that is the only reason to recommend not using a capture filter. Capture filters are nice when you know the type of traffic you want to capture, or in other words, you know what traffic you want to exclude. You definitely want to use a capture filter if you're going to keep the trace running for very long, so as to keep your capture file smaller and provide less work.

When you decide not to use a capture filter, you can use a display filter to get rid of the non-pertinent packets with the option to change which packets you consider non-pertinent, after the capture has transpired. If you use a capture filter, you would've already excluded those packets and would not have the option to consider them as pertinent.

As there is a lot of traffic on a network where an Active Directory domain is present, you can quickly exclude this from view by using this display filter: !(arp or dns or icmp). You might also decide that you would just like to look at TCP or UDP, in which case you could type **tcp** or **udp**. If you do this, you might notice that you're also seeing some dhcpv6 traffic and you could type "!(dhcpv6)&& tcp or udp" without the quotes and Wireshark would highlight the display filter bar yellow, because this syntax might return unexpected results and if you notice the bottom tool tip will recommend that it would be better if you typed it like this to include parenthesis: !(dhcpv6) && (tcp or udp). As soon as you type the display filter this way, you'll notice that you're dealing with a green light on the display filter toolbar, as well, indicating that you have a good filter.

Knowing which ports SharePoint is communicating over for whatever it is that you're troubleshooting is very helpful. Table 6-1 in Chapter 6 has a list of the ports used by SharePoint. Table 10-1 lists some ways to filter.

Table 10-1. *Display Filters*

Desired outcome	Filter
Filter by a source IP	ip.src == xxx.xxx.xxx.xxx
Filter by a destination IP	ip.dst == xxx.xxx.xxx.xxx
Filter by a TCP port	tcp.port == 443
Filter by a UDP port	ucp.port == 53
Looking for applications looking for websites	http.requests
Looking for HTTP response code 404	http.response==404
Looking for HTTP response codes 404 or 401	http.response==404||http.response==401
Exclude this protocol and include this or that port	!(Protocol Name) && (tcp.port == 443 || tcp.port == 1443)
All traffic except traffic coming from or going to this IP	!(ip.addr == xxx.xxx.xxx.xxx)
Look for packet loss	tcp.analysis.flags

Table 10-1 is not all encompassing of what you can do with display filters. The Wireshark blog at `https://wiki.wireshark.org/DisplayFilters` has many more examples. Table 10-2 displays the various operators that can be used in both capture and display filters.

Table 10-2. *Filter Operators*

Desired outcome	Operator
And	&&
Equals	==
Or	||
And	And
Equals	Eq
Or	Or
Not Equals	!=
Greater than	>
Greater than or equal to	>=
Less than	<
Less than or equal to	<=

When you're having trouble with SharePoint loading or throwing some error, Wireshark can shed light on the issue and you'll need to know how to filter. This Wireshark blog post goes into even more detail on comparison operators (`https://www.wireshark.org/docs/man-pages/wireshark-filter.html`). When applying a capture filter, make sure that you know which types of traffic you want to exclude.

After you've captured some traces and before or after you apply display filters, you should check that the machines are all present in your capture. Click the Statistics menu ➤ Endpoints. You see the endpoints by their *media access control* (MAC) addresses, as displayed in Figure 10-4.

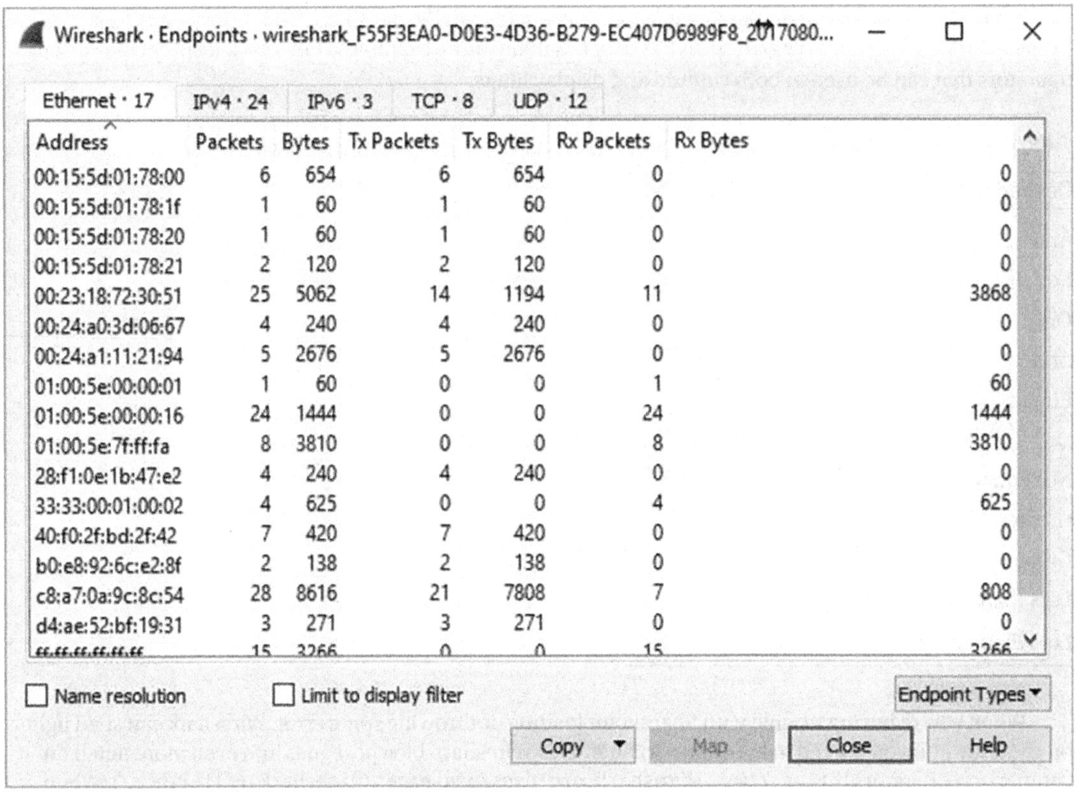

Address	Packets	Bytes	Tx Packets	Tx Bytes	Rx Packets	Rx Bytes
00:15:5d:01:78:00	6	654	6	654	0	0
00:15:5d:01:78:1f	1	60	1	60	0	0
00:15:5d:01:78:20	1	60	1	60	0	0
00:15:5d:01:78:21	2	120	2	120	0	0
00:23:18:72:30:51	25	5062	14	1194	11	3868
00:24:a0:3d:06:67	4	240	4	240	0	0
00:24:a1:11:21:94	5	2676	5	2676	0	0
01:00:5e:00:00:01	1	60	0	0	1	60
01:00:5e:00:00:16	24	1444	0	0	24	1444
01:00:5e:7f:ff:fa	8	3810	0	0	8	3810
28:f1:0e:1b:47:e2	4	240	4	240	0	0
33:33:00:01:00:02	4	625	0	0	4	625
40:f0:2f:bd:2f:42	7	420	7	420	0	0
b0:e8:92:6c:e2:8f	2	138	2	138	0	0
c8:a7:0a:9c:8c:54	28	8616	21	7808	7	808
d4:ae:52:bf:19:31	3	271	3	271	0	0
ff:ff:ff:ff:ff:ff	15	3266	0	0	15	3266

Figure 10-4. MAC addresses

If you click the Name Resolution check box, shown in Figure 10-4, Wireshark will automatically convert the first six digits to the manufacturer name of the endpoint device, which can help with troubleshooting. If you click the IPv4 tab, you'll see all the devices in your capture listed out by their IP addresses which lets you know that you're seeing all the servers in your farm, provided you know the IP addresses of the servers in the farm. The Copy button allows you to copy all of the endpoints from any given tab to CSV or YAML. The Endpoints drop-down a browser to display any devices in your network that can be mapped. The Close button shuts down your computer and the Help button causes your mouse to magically turn into a cat. No, just kidding, and now you know why I am not a comedian. The Close button does what it says, and closes the Endpoints window and the Help button opens the Wireshark blog to the Endpoints page at `https://www.wireshark.org/docs/wsug_html_chunked/ChStatEndpoints.html`.

If you look at the Conversations menu off the Statistics menu, a window will open that will show you all the machines that were talking to each other. This is a quick way to prune out just the TCP or TCP and UDP traffic in a SharePoint environment. Once the window opens, click the Conversation Types button and then change the selection so that only TCP, or TCP and UDP, are selected. This will show you the communication on the TCP and UDP ports, which is essentially the same as a display filter that reads TCP or UDP, the only difference is in the display. When you're looking for the SharePoint communication is happening, this is a great way to find it.

■ **Note** The Wireshark blog `https://wiki.wireshark.org/FrontPage` has loads and loads of additional information.

Fiddler

Another tool that you'll want to become familiar with is Fiddler. Fiddler uses a man-in-the-middle approach to looking at packets traversing your network. Fiddler is just as easy as Wireshark to install, and the process is similar, download executable and next through to victory. Then open Fiddler. Here's a link to the download page at `www.telerik.com/fiddler`. The same rules regarding Wireshark's use, also apply to Fiddler, when it comes to your company and, possibly, your country. Make sure you're approved to use it; no special rights are implied here.

Similar to Wireshark, Fiddler captures all the traffic that is coming from and to your PC or Server. Unlike Wireshark, Fiddler will begin capturing that traffic immediately. Figure 10-5 shows that Fiddler is capturing immediately. You can quickly stop capturing, and then click Edit ➤ Remove ➤ All Sessions to clear the screen. Figure 10-5 shows where to stop capturing, just click the Capturing button.

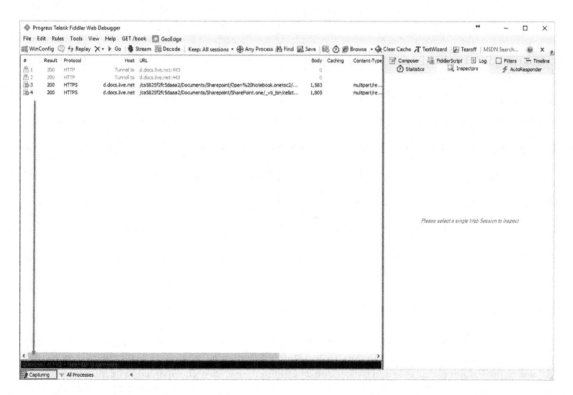

Figure 10-5. *Capturing*

When troubleshooting SharePoint page resolution between your machine and the server, Fiddler works best when you install it on your workstation and not on one of the SharePoint Servers, because sometimes the man-in-the-middle approach that Fiddler uses to inspect traffic can be bothersome to SharePoint. Fiddler also works best in troubleshooting SharePoint when using the IE browser and not Firefox or Chrome. The same could be said for basically any SharePoint functionality, that is, always try it in Microsoft's Internet Explorer before trying the process Google Chrome or Mozilla Firefox.

It is possible to use Fiddler to inspect search crawl related traffic by configuring Fiddler as a proxy server for SharePoint search. To do this, you would install Fiddler on your server that runs the crawl component and then when you open Fiddler, you would need to run Fiddler using the same identity used to crawl content. By default, Fiddler listens on port 8888 and you can verify this by looking at the Tools menu and then at the Connections tab on the Options menu, as shown in Figure 10-6.

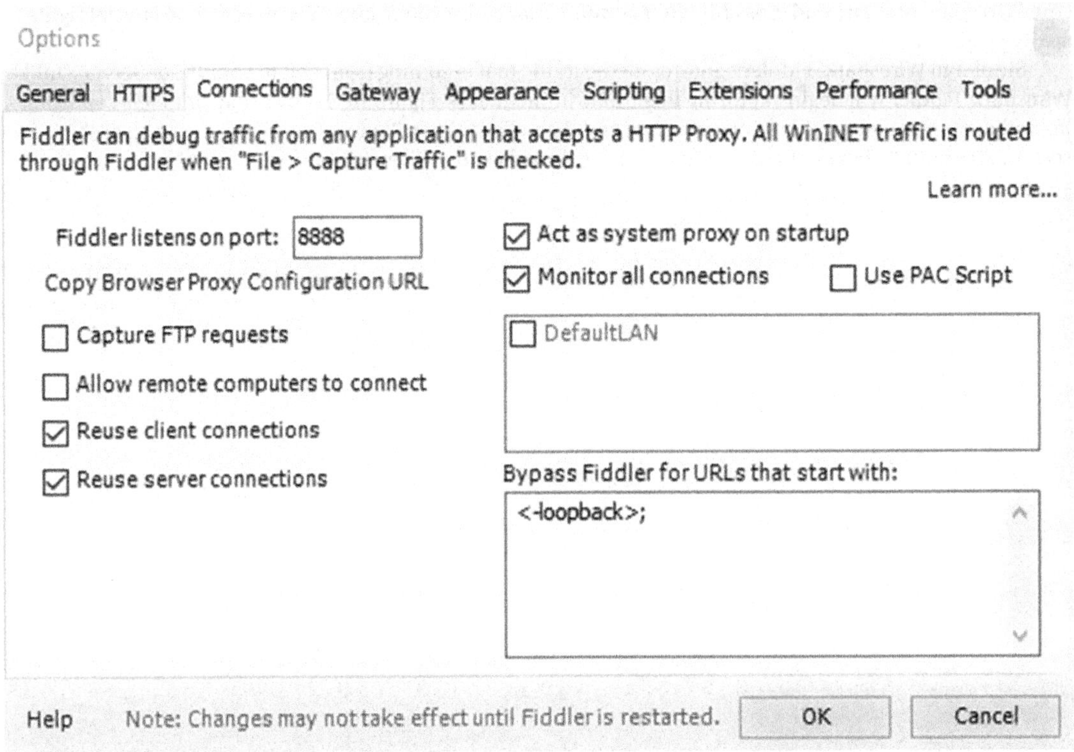

Figure 10-6. *Tools, Options, Connections*

After you verified that Fiddler is not going to listen on any SharePoint port, you're ready to run Fiddler with the crawl identity. Just hold down the Ctrl and Shift keys and then right-click the Fiddler executable or the link to the Fiddler executable and choose run as a different user. Search will need to be modified to use a specific proxy server and port. That proxy server will be the local host; since you've installed Fiddler on the server that is running the crawl component, and the port will be the port that Fiddler is listening on as shown in Figure 10-6. Figure 10-7 shows the Search Proxy configuration screen with the configuration set to use port 8888 on the localhost and since Fiddler is listening on port 8888, you're ready to run a full crawl and then inspect the traffic with Fiddler.

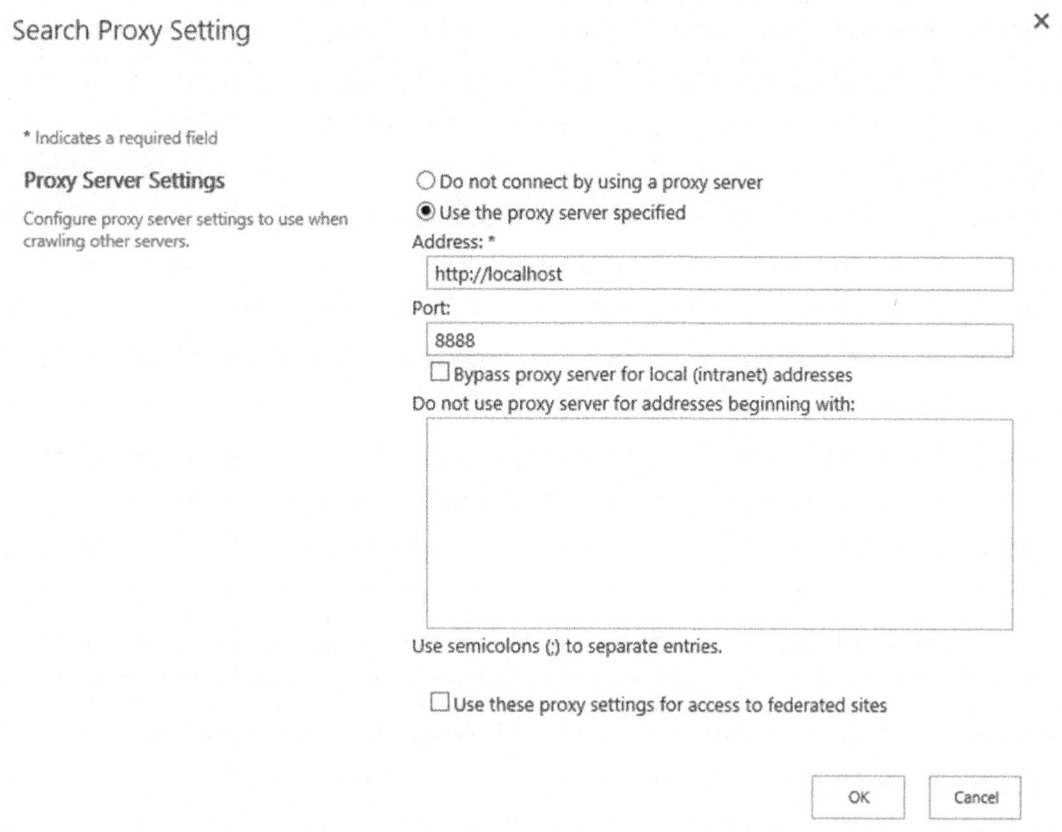

Search Proxy Setting   ✕

* Indicates a required field

Proxy Server Settings

Configure proxy server settings to use when crawling other servers.

○ Do not connect by using a proxy server
◉ Use the proxy server specified
Address: *

```
http://localhost
```

Port:

```
8888
```

☐ Bypass proxy server for local (intranet) addresses
Do not use proxy server for addresses beginning with:

Use semicolons (;) to separate entries.

☐ Use these proxy settings for access to federated sites

| OK | Cancel |

Figure 10-7. *Search Proxy set for Fiddler*

After you finish troubleshooting the crawl with Fiddler, it won't hurt anything to leave Fiddler installed, but you'll want to change the Search Proxy settings back to none.

Another cool thing about Fiddler is that Fiddler doesn't require you to know the capture and display filters syntax the way Wireshark requires. But, that is not to say that Fiddler does not have its own learning curve for filtering. You can do some insane things with Fiddlerscript! Unfortunately, I don't know Fiddlerscript and can't speak to it, yet, but there is a book written by the developer of Fiddler at `http://fiddlerbook.com/book/`. The URL is also available in the app itself from the GET\book menu.

As far as filters go, you can click the Filters menu with all sorts of options for filtering captures, real-time. These are very much like Wireshark Capture filters in that you need to know what you want to filter out. Figure 10-8 shows where the Filters tab is located.

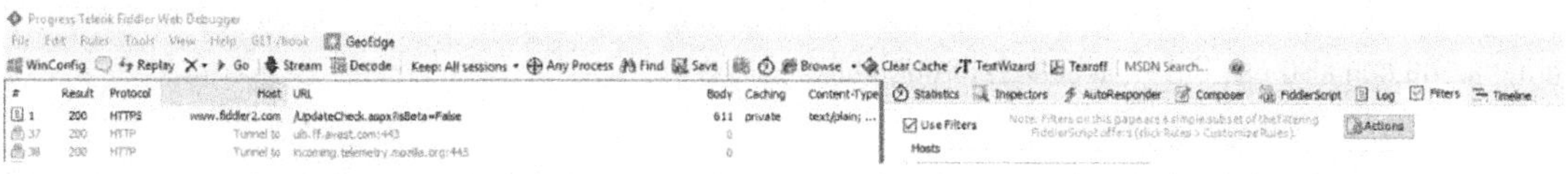

Figure 10-8. *Use Filters*

Another cool way to filter in Fiddler is through the use of the Alt key and a mouse click. Once you have a capture, or during a capture, you can use the Alt key mouse left-click combo. Then if you would like to see all the images in your capture, place your mouse over one of the packets, in the content-type column, hold down the Alt key and then click the content type for "image-jpeg", as shown in Figure 10-9.

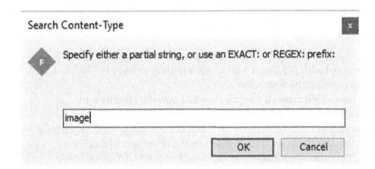

Figure 10-9. *Selecting images*

To filter on more than just one content-type, hold down the Alt key and click the left mouse on the image/jpeg. While still holding down the Alt key, hold down the Ctrl key, and click the left mouse on a few more content types. Another way to get all the images, and arguably easier, is to use the column filter on the content-type column. Just right-click the column, then click "Search this column" and when the Search Content-Type window pops up, enter **image** and click OK. Figure 10-10 shows the Search Content-Type window.

Search Content-Type

Specify either a partial string, or use an EXACT: or REGEX: prefix:

```
image|
```

OK   Cancel

Figure 10-10. *Search a column*

■ **Note**   The search feature is available on all columns, just right-click the column and enter in your search criteria. You can also use Ctrl+F to search through all sessions.

Now, back to your example of inspecting web traffic images, you could remove all of the remaining sessions, by using the Shift key and the Delete key (Shift+Del), or you could remove all the image files by using the Delete key. After which you could restore the deleted sessions using the Edit menu and then clicking Undelete, in case you meant to only look at the sessions related to images. After you've filtered out the results to just images, you can start looking at sizes and metadata in the images, which may be adding to the overall page load times.

If a page is failing to load, using Fiddler, you'll see where it is failing because fiddler will track the process up until the point of failure and it might give you some insight. You could then use the data provided to search through ULS, IIS, or possibly for some sort of filter in Wireshark.

Fiddler was created by Eric Lawrence and then later acquired by Telerik, so if you're going to look for some videos on fiddler, make sure to include those names in your search.

NetMon and Message Analyzer

Microsoft's NetMon is now deprecated, but you can still use it to troubleshoot network traffic. It uses the same filtering syntax that Wireshark uses. NetMon has been superseded by the feature-rich Message analyzer. Table 10-3 lists the download locations for NetMon and Message Analyzer.

Table 10-3. *Microsoft Network Tools*

Tool Name	Download URL
NetMon 3.4	https://www.microsoft.com/en-us/download/details.aspx?id=4865
Message Analyzer	https://www.microsoft.com/en-us/download/details.aspx?id=44226

▨ **Note**   Make sure to install the correct flavor for your operating system, which is more than likely x64, unless you have an Itanium processor or a 32-bit (x86) system. Message Analyzer has x64 and x86 versions. NetMon has all three.

When you install Message Analyzer, it will ask if you want it to be optimized; go ahead and answer yes. It's up to you on whether to allow message analyzer to auto update. I went ahead and selected Update items, knowing that I could turn that off later by going to Tools, Asset Manager, and clicking the Offline button. After you install Message Analyzer, you can choose to run it; one thing you'll immediately notice is that it is maximized on your screen.

If you're already familiar with Wireshark filtering, Message Analyzer uses the same syntax for capture and display. The same is true for NetMon 3.4 in regards to display filter syntax. When starting a new session in Message Analyzer, you can name your session something other than Session 2 enter in a capture filter in the block shown in Figure 10-11.

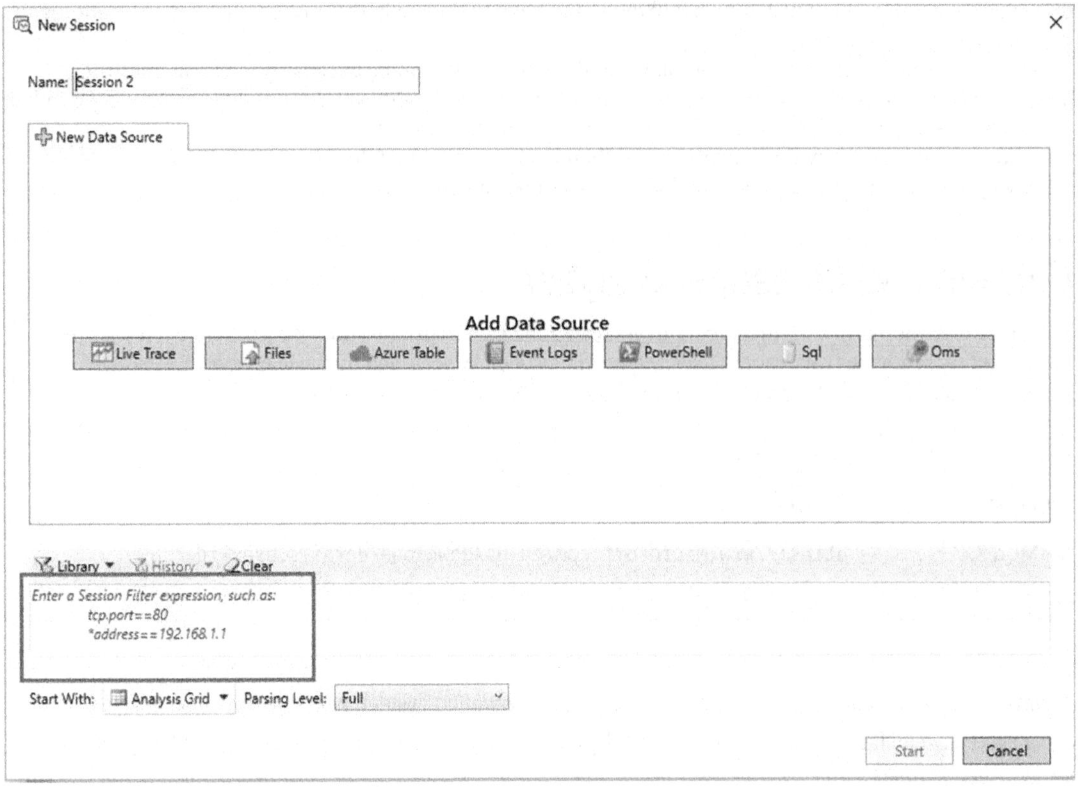

Figure 10-11. Name your session and capture filter

After you install Network Monitor 3.4 and start it up, you'll notice that it seems familiar if you are already used to Wireshark. In fact it sort of looks a little like a cousin of one of the earlier Wireshark's as you can see in Figure 10-12, which shows that you could create a capture filter; it is very intuitive.

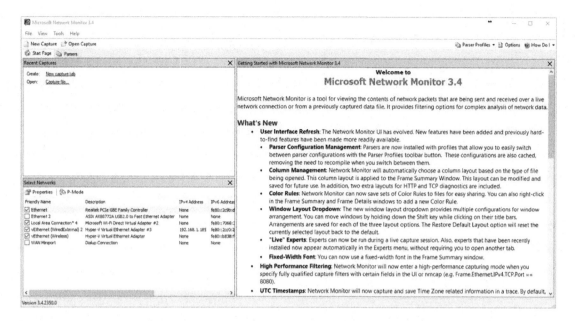

Figure 10-12. *Capture filter in default NetMon*

When comparing NetMon in Figure 10-12 to Message Analyzer in Figure 10-11, they seem worlds apart, but really they're not that far apart. If you're using message analyzer and you don't wish to use a capture filter, then leave the filter empty to capture all packets. You'll notice that you can use Message analyzer to look at event logs as well, and even at SQL, among other options. When you're using the New Session, you'll need to select a scenario to get the session started. The scenario gives you various options, as shown in Figure 10-13.

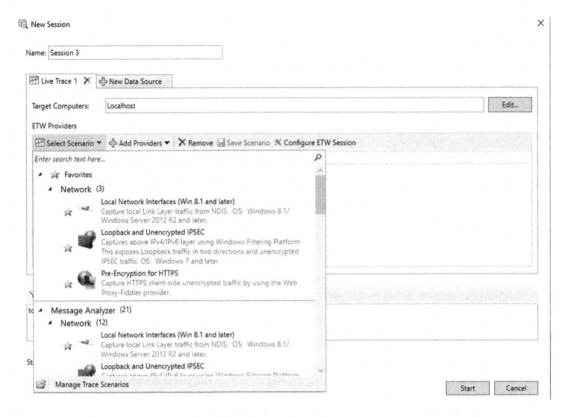

Figure 10-13. *Choose your LAN*

After you pick the LAN and click start, the new session will begin. If you look at NetMon in Figure 10-12, you can see that you click New Capture and then click Start. After the capture is started, the two tools use display filter syntax, just like Wireshark. A quick way to start a trace using Message Analyzer is to just click Start Local trace.

■ **Note**   Paul E. Long from Microsoft wrote an excellent blog post at `https://blogs.technet.microsoft.com/messageanalyzer/2015/07/21/message-analyzer-v1-3-vs-network-monitor-v3-4/` that discusses all the new features with Message Analyzer and he compares them to NetMon 3.4.

Developer Dashboard

SharePoint 2010 and 2013 have a built in utility that an administrator can enable for Site Collection Admins that allows the Site collection admin to view page performance and possibly identify slow loading components of pages. The Developer Dashboard is a farm-wide setting that can be enabled using the command-line interface using the stsadm command. You can also enable the dashboard using PowerShell.

The command-line options are as follows:

- stsadm -o setproperty -pn developer-dashboard -pv on

- stsadm -o setproperty -pn developer-dashboard -pv onDemand

- stsadm -o setproperty -pn developer-dashboard -pv off

The first option turns the dashboard on for site collection admins and the third option turn it off. The second option—my favorite and the recommended way—is to make it available on demand. When you enable the developer dashboard in On Demand mode an icon appears to the right of the user name, as shown in Figure 10-14.

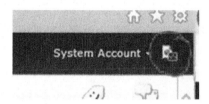

Figure 10-14. On Demand mode in SharePoint 2010

To enable the Developer Dashboard using PowerShell, these are the lines of code that you need to run from an administrative SharePoint Management Shell. Figure 10-15 displays how the code looks in action.

```
$service=[Microsoft.SharePoint.Administration.SPWebService]::ContentService
$devdashsetting=$service.DeveloperDashboardSettings
$devdashsetting.DisplayLevel=[Microsoft.SharePoint.Administration.SPDeveloperDashboardLevel
]::OnDemand
$devdashsetting.Update()
```

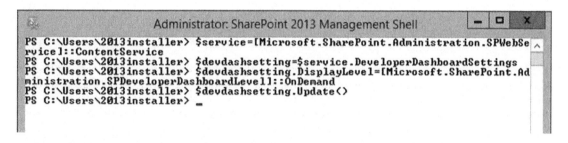

Figure 10-15. Typical PowerShell, super powerful, not dramatic

The developer dashboard is a really great troubleshooting tool for SharePoint! Since it is integrated, it has hooks that look into ULS, IIS, SQL, and service endpoints, just to name a few. After you enable it, activate the dashboard. Then navigate to a few pages. You'll see their URLs in the Requests tab. You won't see any data until you select one of the requests that you made. When you select one of the requests, as shown in Figure 10-16, you can then look at the various tabs.

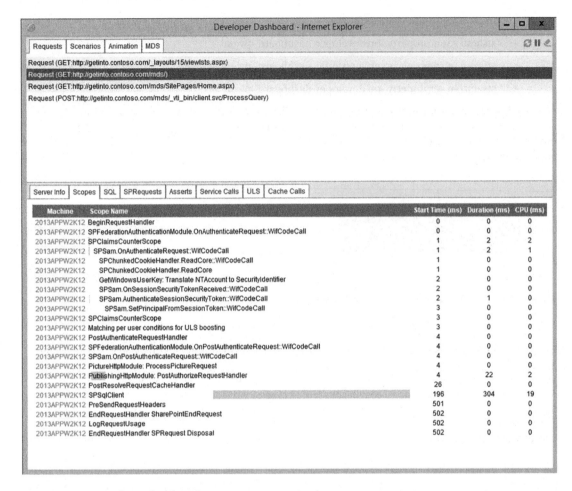

Figure 10-16. *Developer dashboard scopes*

In the Scopes tab, you can see which components of a page load are adding time to the load, or possibly contributing to a timeout. The ULS tab peers into Verbose and VerboseEx log entries, even if logging is not set to Verbose or VerboseEX. This can be handy in troubleshooting, as well, since you can quickly turn on dev dashboard, especially if you have it available on demand, and see the verbose and VerboseEX entries. Then if needed you could always turn the logging all the way up, assuming that you need to look at all the traffic in ULS. Figure 10-17 shows that the ULS tab displays Verbose and VerboseEX for various categories.

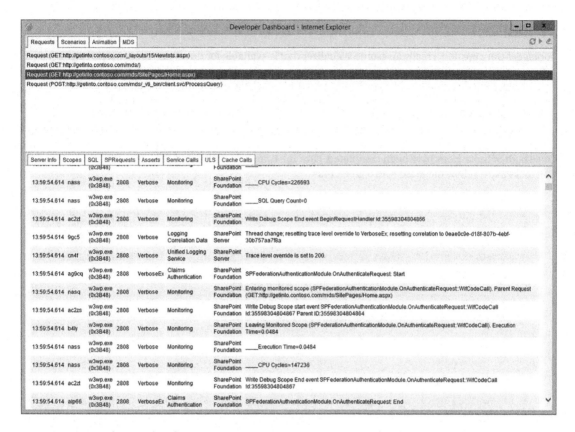

Figure 10-17. *Verbose and VerboseEX*

If a page load is dependent on or uses service requests, the Service Calls tab displays information about the service or if no service calls were needed for that request it will say, "No service calls happened during this request." If you'd like to see the call stack that is related to a particular page, click the SPRequests tab, and then click one of the links shown.

Finally, when using the Developer Dashboard, it will start to fill up with the requests that you've made and you can just click the clear icon, shown in Figure 10-18.

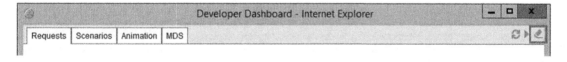

Figure 10-18. *Clear icon*

Webalizer

Tobias Schwarz created a really awesome Webalizer that is available for download from www.tobias-schwarz.net/programmierung/webalizer_guie.html. You should download the Webalizer GUI + Executable. After downloading just go ahead and double-click the executable to install the Webalizer Graphical User Interface and then open the Webalizer using the shortcut to C:\Program Files (x86)\Webalizer\WebalizerGUI.exe or by clicking the executable that is installed at this location.

Once the program comes open, modify the target directory, as shown in Figure 10-19. Then navigate to the Settings tab and select English as the language. Then click the LogFile tab and select IIS as the type of file. Once both of those steps have been completed, click the Choose Files tab and then click the add files icon that looks like a yellow database with a green plus.

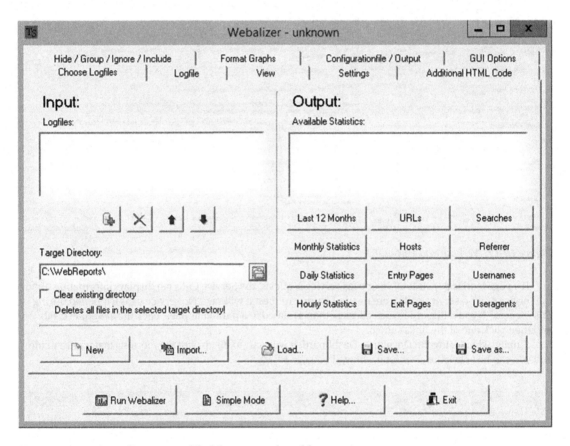

Figure 10-19. *Target directory modified, language selected from settings*

After clicking the open files icon, navigate to IIS logs location for whichever site you're looking to use Webalizer to analyze and select the log files for the previous days; make sure that you don't select the current file that is being written into. That's really the only downside to this tool. Figure 10-20 shows the admin about to select a bunch of logs. Make sure that when you select your logs that the files are sorted so that the earliest date is analyzed first. In other words, do not sort the files (as shown in Figure 10-20), since this would cause the logs to be analyzed from the oldest date first and the Webalizer may only look at the current month.

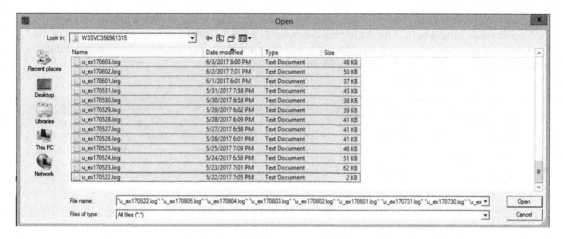

Figure 10-20. *IIS logs selected for site W3SVC356961315*

As you recall the site ID is used in the folder name, and this ID is found in IIS manager, by selecting the sites node, as shown in Figure 10-21.

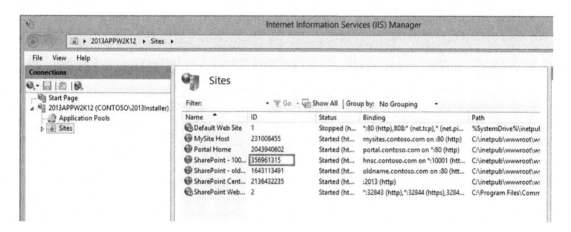

Figure 10-21. *Site ID*

After the files are loaded into the Webalizer, the default language changes from German to English, the LogFile type changes to IIS, and the log file directory changes to somewhere other than the root of the C:\. Go ahead and click Run Webalizer. This will cause the Webalizer to analyze the files and create the report. Figure 10-22 shows the Webalizer analyzing a bunch of IIS logs.

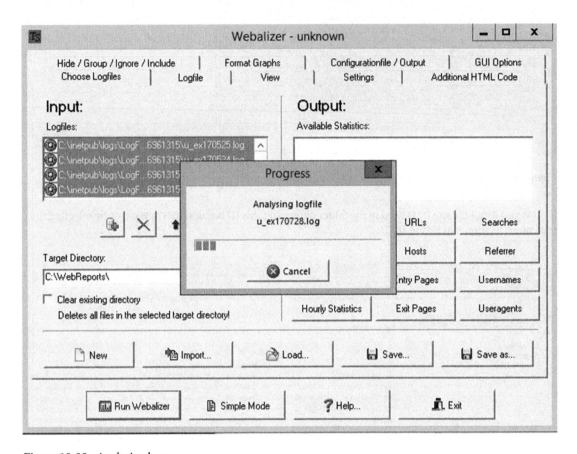

Figure 10-22. *Analyzing logs*

If you sorted the files in ascending order by date before pulling them into the Webalizer, the output available statistics will show all months, as shown in Figure 10-23.

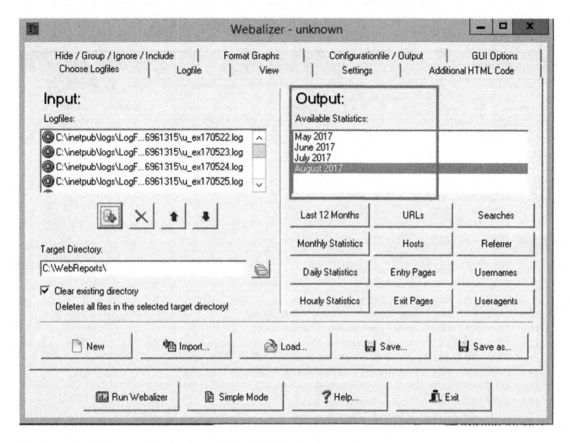

Figure 10-23. *Pick a month to review or look at last 12 months*

After you open one of the reports, you can easily look at the other reports. If you notice that some months are in German or some other language, you should make sure you have selected "Clear existing history" and all the other selections that were mentioned earlier, and then rerun the reports. The errors report shown in Figure 10-24 is probably the most helpful when it comes to troubleshooting.

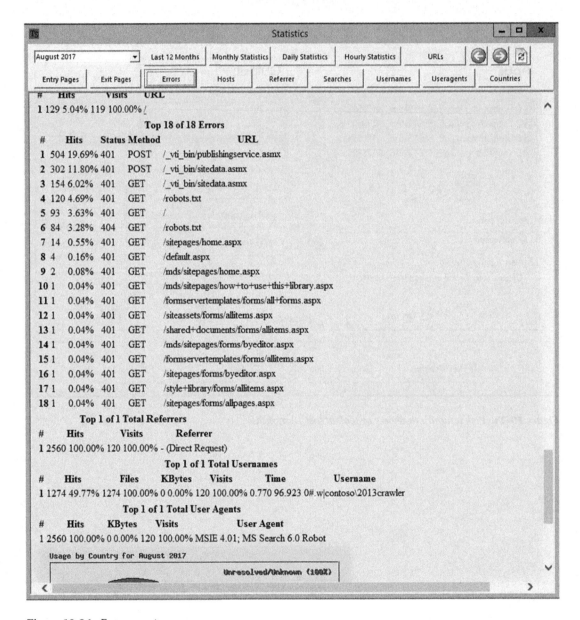

Figure 10-24. Error report

Indihiang

Like all tools on CodePlex, this one will be available in the archive after CodePlex is made read only in December. The details about this scary event are located at `https://blogs.msdn.microsoft.com/bharry/2017/03/31/shutting-down-codeplex/`.

I downloaded the 32-bit and 64-bit version of Indihiang and put it on the GitHub for this book. Make sure you install the correct version for your server's operating system. The install is a next-through-to-victory type of installation.

The Indihiang tool requires less configuration than the Webalizer that we just learned about. Sometimes you have to kick the tires on Indihiang by only loading a few log files into it, then removing that compilation and then loading more. In Figure 10-25, you can see Indihiang processing a few months' worth of log files. This is after asking it to process one month of files.

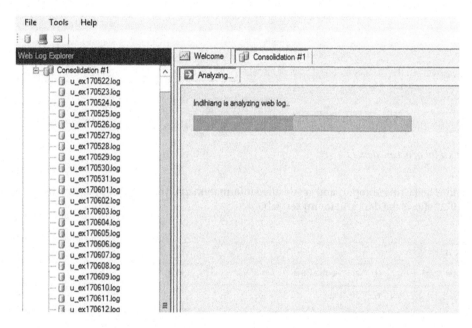

Figure 10-25. *Indihaing is crunching data*

After the files are loaded into the tool, you can click a tab, select the year, and then generate the report. Take a look at Figure 10-26. This lab server is reporting that 17.59% of the HTTP status codes inside its logs are 401s.

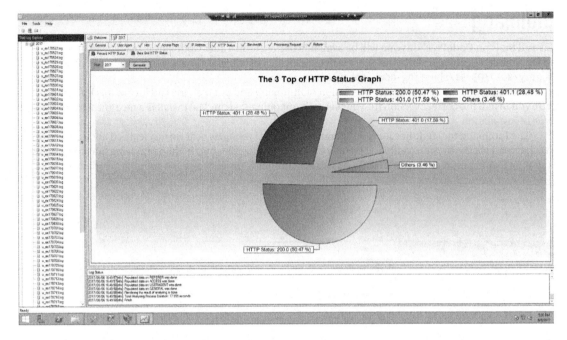

Figure 10-26. *That's a lot of access denied*

You can select the Data Grid subreport and get detailed information that you could copy and analyze with Excel. Figure 10-27 shows the data grid for my test lab.

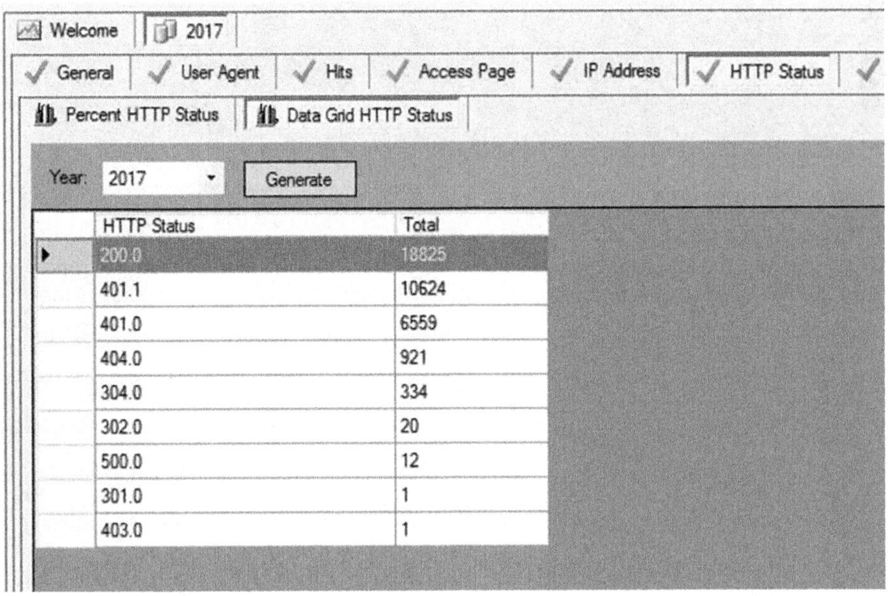

HTTP Status	Total
200.0	18825
401.1	10624
401.0	6559
404.0	921
304.0	334
302.0	20
500.0	12
301.0	1
403.0	1

Figure 10-27. *Status codes*

Backing up just a bit, to load the files in, click the icon that sort of looks like the universal symbol for a SQL database or you can right-click the Web Log files folder and select Open Log file(s) and then navigate to the log directory. Figure 10-28 shows the option to load files.

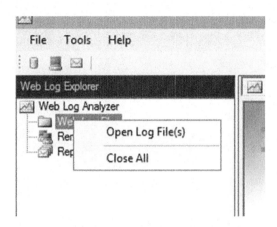

Figure 10-28. *Loading the files is easy*

The Webalizer and Indihiang are more monitoring tools than they are troubleshooting tools, but they can give you a quick overview of the environment and provide a starting point when looking for any issues that might exist.

SPS Farm Report utility

The SPS Farm Report utility runs either as an executable or as a PowerShell script. It generates an XML file that can be viewed in any browser using a stylesheet that comes with the product. It helps in troubleshooting a farm by giving you a detailed overview of the farm and all of the settings in the farm. You can download the utility from the CodePlex archive by searching for SPSFarmReport.zip, or you might be able to find it on GitHub. I put a copy that was available on CodePlex during the making of this text on the GitHub for this book as well. To install it, just unzip the files and place them on your SharePoint. Then, to run the utility drive into the appropriate folder and either execute the executable or if using the utility on SharePoint 2013, run the PowerShell. Figure 10-29 displays the 2013 version being executed.

Figure 10-29. *Where is the report stored?*

The only issue with this utility is knowing where the report is stored. The readme text explains that to find that out, you need to run [Environment]::CurrentDirectory, as shown in Figure 10-29. Once you've found the report you need to make sure that you copy it, or the .xslt file to the same directory, and then double-click the XML file.

After the report opens, there is a lot of information about your farm that you can drive into. For example, you can quickly find out the schedule of all the timer jobs on the farm, by scrolling to the bottom of the report and then expanding or unhiding the timer jobs section. Figure 10-30 gives an example of the report with one area fully expanded and another are only partially expanded.

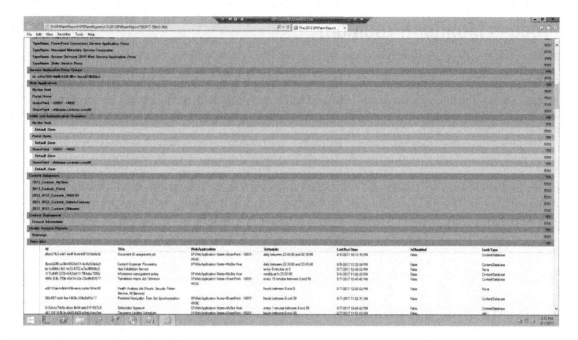

Figure 10-30. *Timer jobs, when do they run?*

The unexpanded report is shown in Figure 10-31. As you can see, the report obtains a lot of information in a relatively short time frame.

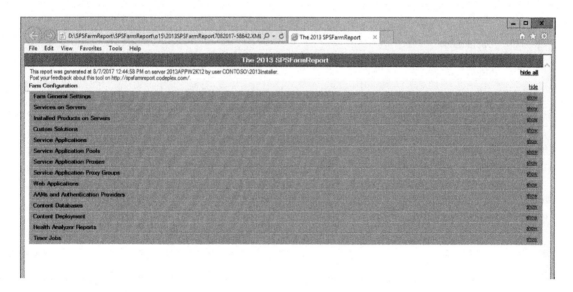

Figure 10-31. *Unexpanded report*

Process Monitor (ProcMon)

ProcMon is a file system, registry, process and thread, real-time monitoring tool that you can use to troubleshoot what is taking place on your server at the file system and registry level. Like Process Explorer, Process Monitor (or as it's commonly referred to, ProcMon) was created by Mark Russinovich. Process Monitor can see into the call stack of processes and find out all sorts of information about files, registry keys, and their respective settings. The uses for ProcMon in troubleshooting are vast, and the tool is a must-have in your SharePoint troubleshooting arsenal.

To install the tool, go to https://docs.microsoft.com/en-us/sysinternals/downloads/procmon and either run it directly from the link to the sysinternals live site, or download the executable to the server. The choice is yours. It depends on the issue that you're troubleshooting: you might not have Internet connectivity in your farm or the issue is related to the network in some way; in either case, you'll want to download. If you download, you don't have to "next through" to victory to start using the tool. Just double-click the .exe file and click Agree, as shown in Figure 10-32.

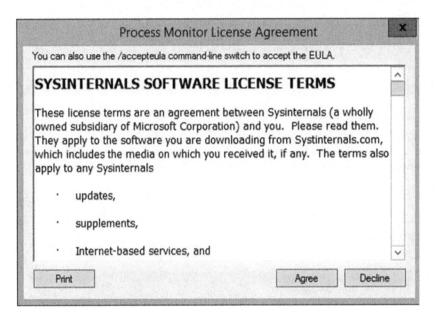

Figure 10-32. Agree

After you click Agree, ProcMon will open and immediately begin capturing file system, registry, and process thread transactions that are taking place on your server. You can turn off the capture by clicking the magnifying glass icon, shown in Figure 10-33.

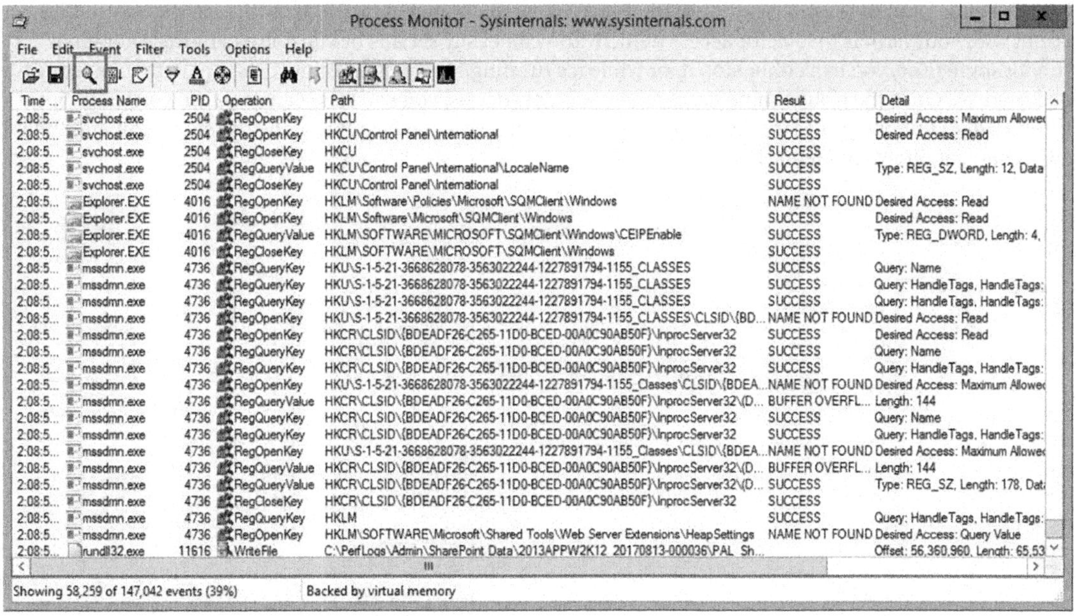

Figure 10-33. *Capture toggle on or off*

You can press Ctrl+E to stop and start the capture. And, then if you wanted too, you could press Ctrl+X to clear the capture. This gives you a clean slate in which to run a capture. The icon to clear the capture (Ctrl+X) looks like a piece of paper with an eraser part way up the page. It is located to the right of the Auto Scroll icon, which is directly to the right of the magnifying glass. You could click it to clear the display and then start the capture by clicking the magnifying glass icon or pressing Ctrl+E. After which time, you would immediately run the steps that are causing the issue, or in other words repeat the process or thing that you are troubleshooting.

Another way to think of it, is after clicking ProcMon.exe, just perform the steps that are causing the issue and then press Ctrl+E, or click the magnifying glass icon, when you're ready to stop capturing. You can always press Ctrl+E to start capturing again, without losing any of your previously captured data. In Figure 10-34, I've turned off the autoscroll by clicking its icon, or by pressing Ctrl+A, and I've also turned off the capture. Now all I have to do to start watching the processes in a live capture, is to unclick the Capture button, and the Autoscroll button, if I want to watch the processes fly by.

Figure 10-34. *Ctrl+E and Ctrl+A*

Once the process is underway, or before, you'll want to create filters. Probably the easiest way to find issues with your farm is to look for access denied. You can easily set this by starting a capture. After it has run for some time, you can either stop it, or while it's running, you can click the Tools menu, then on count occurrences. Once the Count Value occurrences window opens, you can select any column you want, but if you want to find the things that resulted in access denied, you need to choose the result column and then click count, as shown in Figure 10-35.

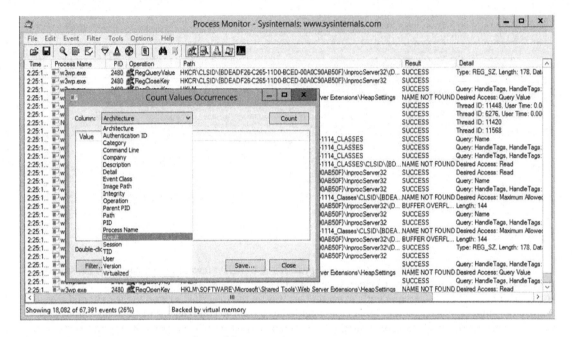

Figure 10-35. *Count occurrences of something*

After you click Count, the window will give you a drillable list. You can then double-click one of the values in the Count Value Occurrences window. Figure 10-36 shows that I've selected, Access Denied, but haven't double clicked it.

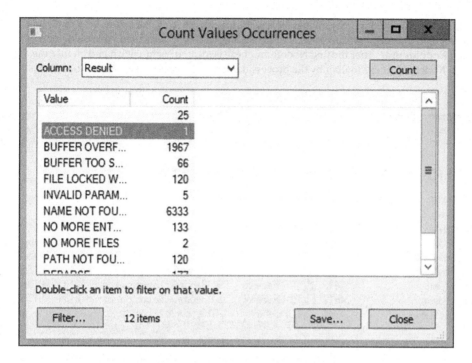

Figure 10-36. Access Denied

Now, if I double-click Access Denied, ProcMon will automatically apply the filter and display the single access denied entry. Next, as I right-click the entry in the capture window, I could jump directly to it in the file system, or in registry. As you can see in Figure 10-37, Ctrl+J would allow me to jump to the entry, as well.

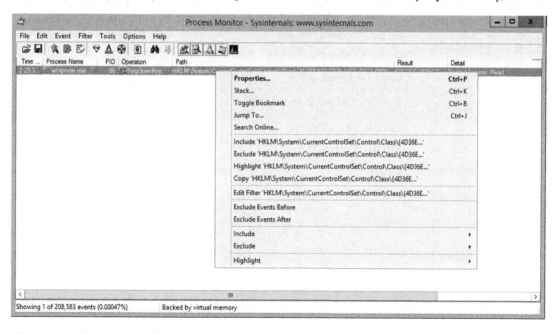

Figure 10-37. Jump to = Ctrl+J

Ctrl+F works the same as any other program and lets you find a string of text. For example, if you were looking to troubleshoot NodeRunner.exe process you could use the Edit ➤ Find menu or you could press Ctrl+F and then enter **NodeRunner**. After the first NodeRunner.exe is located, right-click it and choose the menu option, Include NodeRunner.exe to filter by the process named NodeRunner.exe. Figure 10-38 shows this action.

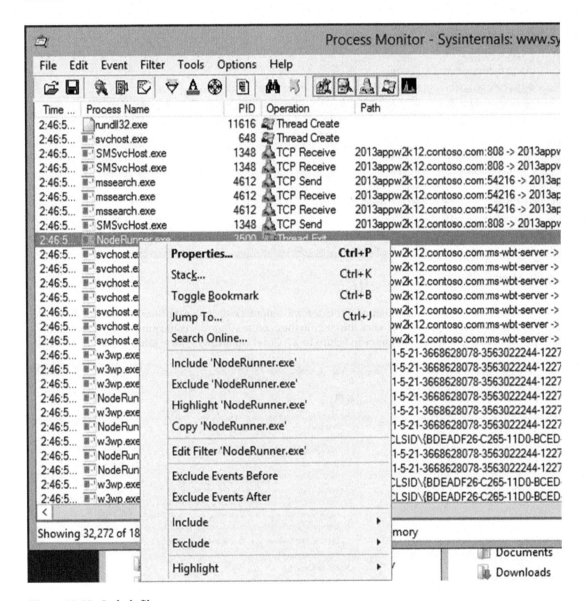

Figure 10-38. *Include filter*

CHAPTER 10 ■ TOOLS: NETWORK PACKET TOOLS AND PAGE PERFORMANCE

You could then filter by the result of Name Not Found, by using the same steps, only starting from the Result column. Or, you could modify the filter from the Filter menu by adding an entry for Result: Name Not Found. Figure 10-39 shows the second option, but notice how it does not show Name Not Found. If you select Unknown, you'll not get the expected results, which is why your best bet is to right-click and select Include: Name Not Found.

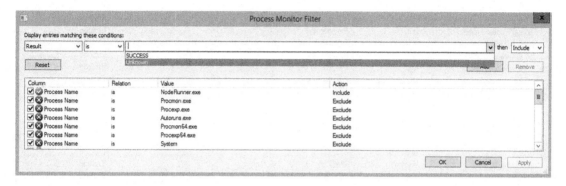

Figure 10-39. *Unknown not the same as NAME NOT FOUND*

If at any point, you'd like to reset the filter back to default, you can use the Ctrl+R keyboard shortcut, or use the Filter menu and select Reset Filter. This will remove the custom filters that you've added to the base filters. By default, Process Monitor filters out its system noise. To see this, take a look at the base filters. Figure 10-40 displays the processes and paths related to ProcMon and other sysinternals tools. Notice how they are excluded.

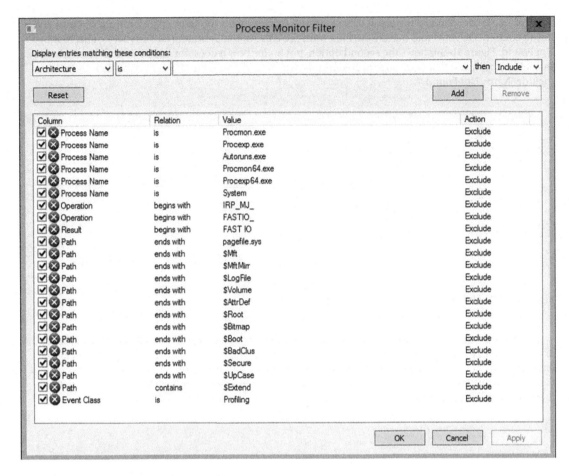

Figure 10-40. *Base filter*

Some additional awesome things that you can do with ProcMon include the ability to see the parts of registry that are being accessed. Just click the Tools menu's Registry Summary option. After it opens, select the line item you're interested in looking at and then double-click to filter. For example, if you were interested in calls made to HKLM\Software\Microsoft\Office Server\15.0\Search\Applications, you could double-click the record show in Figure 10-41.

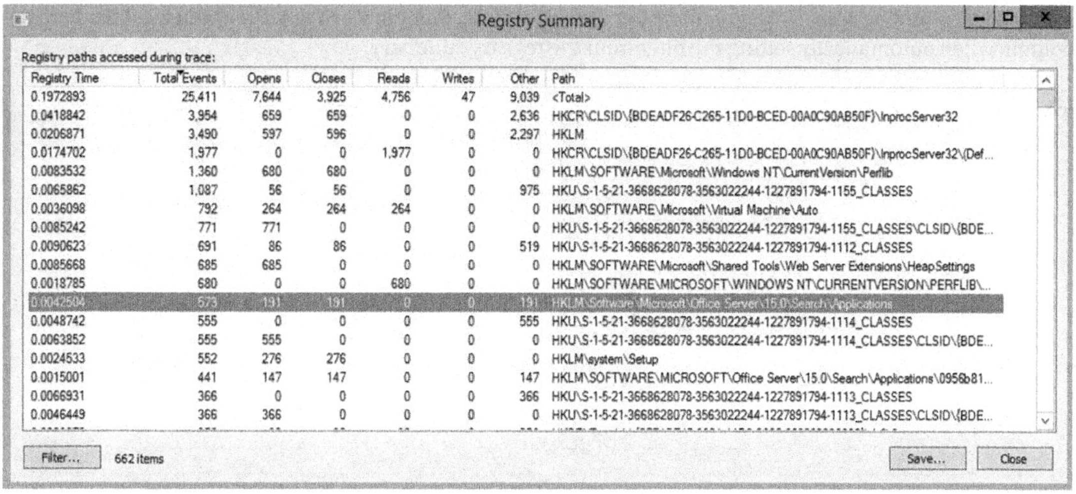

Figure 10-41. *Search Application*

After double clicking, ProcMon will automatically apply the filter to your capture, as shown in Figure 10-42. Notice how the count is now the same as the Total Events for this registry path. Also noteworthy, is that this capture was stopped.

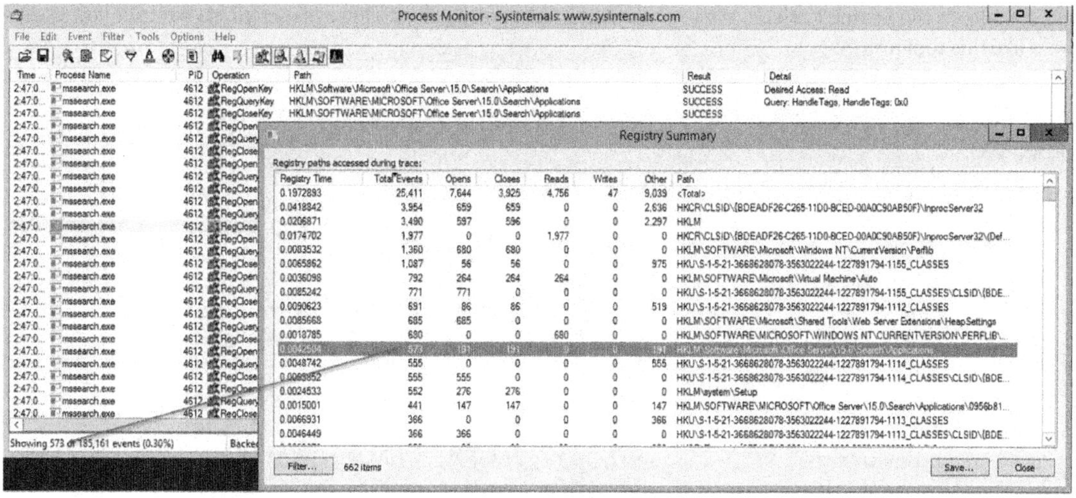

Figure 10-42. *Auto Filter*

435

In Figure 10-43, we've clicked on the Filter menu and then Filter to learn that ProcMon used the Path column when automatically setting the filter from the registry summary.

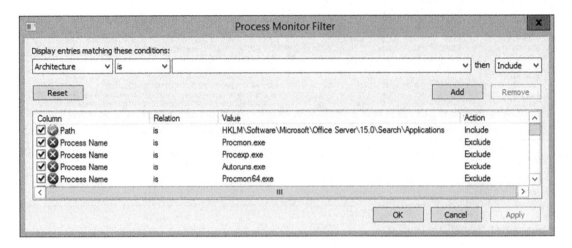

Figure 10-43. *Filtering*

If we're not sure what a particular process name represents, we can hover the process and ProcMon will display information it has found inside the process. As displayed in Figure 10-44, the mssearch.exe is the executable for the Search Crawler. We learned that in Chapter 7, but it's always nice to have reminders and help like this tool brings!

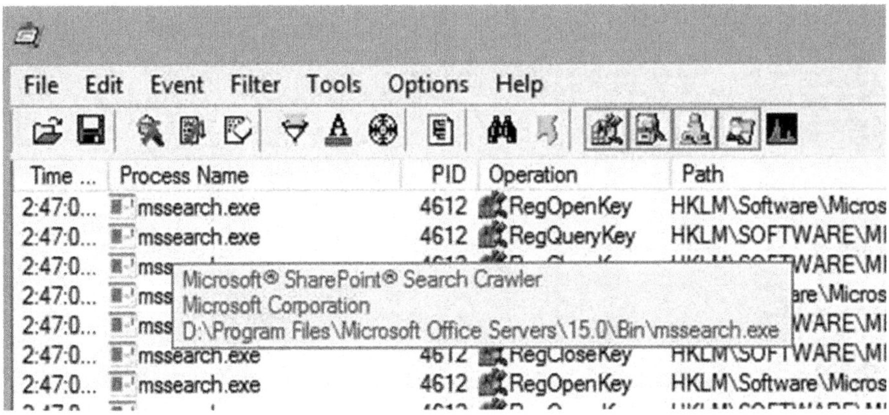

Figure 10-44. *What is this process?*

And before we finish our talk about ProcMon, if you wanted to filter on all the changes to the system during the capture, you would set a filter that chooses the column category where the value is Write. If you run this filter on a SharePoint Server, it will surely show you changes being made by the SharePoint timer to the SharePoint Config cache, unless there's an issue with the cache. In my farm, the server is updating the cache.ini, as shown in Figure 10-45.

436

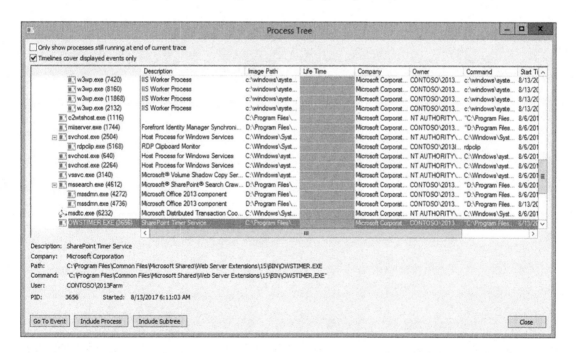

Figure 10-45. *Lots of stuff happening in the SharePoint config cache*

By selecting a process thread, and then clicking Ctrl+T, or clicking the Tools menu's Process Tree option, we can open the process tree. Notice how the process, displays the processes that let up to the file write to the cache.ini, including their process IDs. Figure 10-46 displays the process tree.

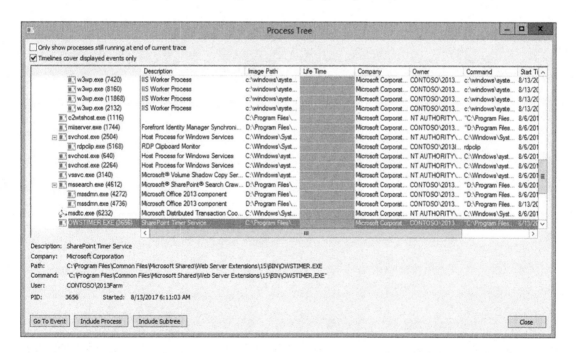

Figure 10-46. *Process tree*

ProcMon has the ability to drop filtered events. This allows you to run a capture over time and only capture the filtered includes. If you're going to run a trace over any length of time, make sure to enable this by going to the Filter menu ➤ Drop Filtered Events.

There is a lot more to ProcMon that we didn't cover. I hope this has shed some light on how to filter your captures; like anything, the more you do it, the better you become.

In this chapter, we talked about Wireshark, Fiddler, Microsoft Network Monitor, Microsoft Message Analyzer, the Developer Dashboard, Webalizer, Indihiang, the SPSFarm Report, and Process Monitor. As a result, we touched on most of the main parts of each tool. In Chapter 11, we'll look at some additional troubleshooting tools, including the built-In SharePoint Health Analyzer, and then we'll provide a summary discussion.

## CHAPTER 11

Tools: SharePoint Health Analyzer Demystified

If you have an issue with SharePoint, or even with Windows Server, or your network for that matter, the tools that we've looked and discussed up until this point will give you greater depth of vision into the situation. For example, the ULS Viewer that we looked at in Chapter 9, allows you to slice and dice the logs from SharePoint, and lets you find the issues or entries related to the issue that you can use as queries in your favorite search engine. The sysinternals tools discussed in the previous two chapters, Process Explorer and Process Monitor, are the best tools to peer into a Windows Server and help you identify troublesome things that might be otherwise unexplained. And finally, the various tools discussed in Chapter 10 will give you a deeper look at IIS logging and transactions, as well as your network.

In this final chapter, as we wrap up of the chapters on troubleshooting and the book, we will look at the built in SharePoint Health Analyzer tool, the Performance Analysis of Logs (PAL) tool, the SharePoint Admin Feature tool, and the SharePoint Manager Tool. The PAL tool, while not nearly as robust as ProcMon or Process Explorer, is another tool that could be used to look at more than just SharePoint, as you'll see when it is discussed. Let's talk about the SharePoint Health Analyzer tool.

SharePoint Health Analyzer Tool

The SharePoint Health Analyzer Tool is built into SharePoint and it relies on about 24 timer jobs that try to analyze various parts of the SharePoint farm and its health. In a default installation of SharePoint, there are 76 health analyzer rules, which are broken down into the following categories:

- Security: 5 rules

- Performance: 14 rules

- Configuration: 39 rules

- Availability: 17 rules

- System: 1 rule

All of the rules are enabled, by default. So if you have a SharePoint 2010 that is patched at February 2011 or higher and you run:

```
Get-SPHealthAnalysisRule | Sort Category | Format-Table Name, Category, Enabled
```

You'll get a list of all 76 jobs. All of the jobs should be enabled and have a value of true. If you see one or more that have a value of disabled, this is cause for investigation as to why the job is disabled.

The System category rule is not visible via the GUI of Central Administration. Most of the health analyzer rules rely on timer jobs that run on preset schedules, which normally should not need to be adjusted. And, it's possible for third-party application developers to create Healthy Analyzer rules. If you would like to take a count, you could run

```
(Get-SPHealthAnalysisRule).count
```

One of the most common configuration health analyzer rules that you'll come into contact with is the Missing Server Side Dependencies. The most common causes for this are:

- Content databases being migrated to a target farm that does not have the same solutions deployed as that of the source farm

- Solutions retracted from the farm before they've been deactivated in all of the lists, libraries, and sites

The best way to address this is to redeploy the solution, deactivate the features from within the lists and libraries, and then retract the solution. Things can get out of hand when tools like SharePoint Admin and clean up tool are used to attempt to resolve this rules findings. We'll talk about its use a little later in this chapter.

All of the jobs could be set to attempt to repair automatically, but this is not a good idea. It's a case of just because you can does not mean that you should. Table 11-1 lists the jobs that are set to attempt to repair automatically, by default by name and category.

Table 11-1. *Rules Where Automatic Repair Is Enabled by Default*

Rule Name	Category
Databases used by SharePoint have fragmented indices	Performance
Databases used by SharePoint have outdated index statistics	Performance
Search - One or more crawl databases may have fragmented indices	Performance
Firewall client settings on the cache host are incorrect.	Configuration
Web.config files are not identical on all machines in the farm	Configuration
One or more services have started or stopped unexpectedly	Availability
One of the cache hosts in the cluster is down	Availability

Another case of the just because you can does not mean you should, is with listening to the SharePoint Health Analyzer remedies. One case in point is the remedy for the security category rule named "Accounts used by application pools or service identities are in the local machine Administrators group.", advises the admin to browse to Central Administration, Security, Configure Service accounts and start modifying the accounts used by the services listed. Figure 11-1 displays the SharePoint Health Analyzer recommending that the admin change the farm account. Bad Idea.

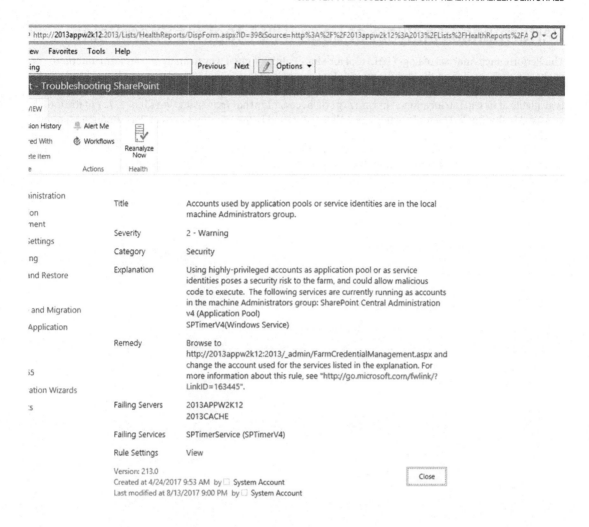

Figure 11-1. *Don't believe everything you read in SharePoint*

A better approach in this situation would be to remove the farm account from the local administrators on the two servers, 2013APPW2K12 and 2013CACHE, since the account only needs to be a member of local admins during the installation of SharePoint, and the configuration of Distributed Cache and the User Profile Synchronization service.

The key takeaway from this section is to know your farm and to know what is best for SharePoint, because it clearly does not always know what is best and will sometimes behave like a drunken sailor, making haphazard decisions (e.g., Argh, just change the farm account!). Let's look at another tool that is very handy when it comes to analyzing SharePoint and its performance, the Performance Analysis Logs tool.

Performance Analysis of Logs (PAL) Tool for SharePoint

The Performance Analysis of Logs (PAL) tool for SharePoint is a great way to analyze your farm and then get back helpful advice on the various metrics that are tracked by the tool. A Racker named Brad Slagle first turned me onto this tool. The tool is downloadable from the CodePlex archive by searching for "PAL" and it is available at its GitHub location at `https://github.com/clinthuffman/PAL`. Version 2.7.7 of the tool was used in this book. The tool creates a template to be used in the Windows System Performance Monitor (perfmon.msc).

You install the PAL tool on your workstation, and not on the SharePoint server itself, as you can see in Figure 11-2 we are installing the tool so that everyone using the computer can use the PAL.

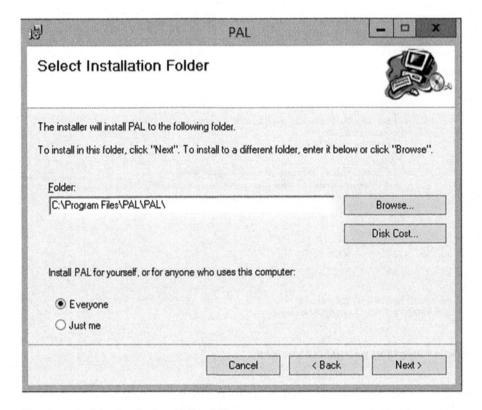

Figure 11-2. Selecting the installation folder

After you've installed PAL, you can open it by clicking the PAL Wizard executable (PALWizard.exe). You'll be presented with Figure 11-3 after you open the program.

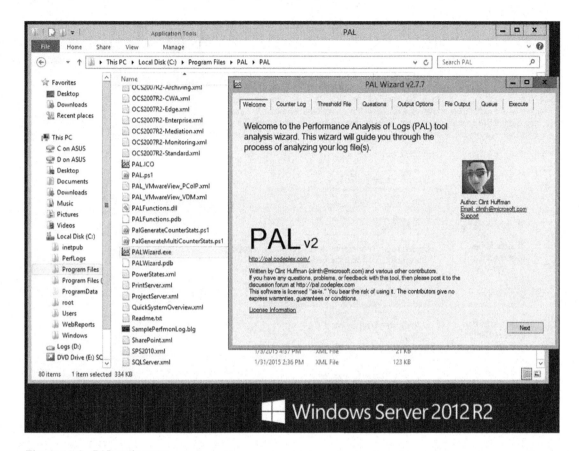

Figure 11-3. PAL main page

The next step in gathering the statistics about your farm is to generate the XML file that you'll use over on your SharePoint farm. Click the Threshold tab, and then click "Export to Perfmon template file...", as shown in Figure 11-4.

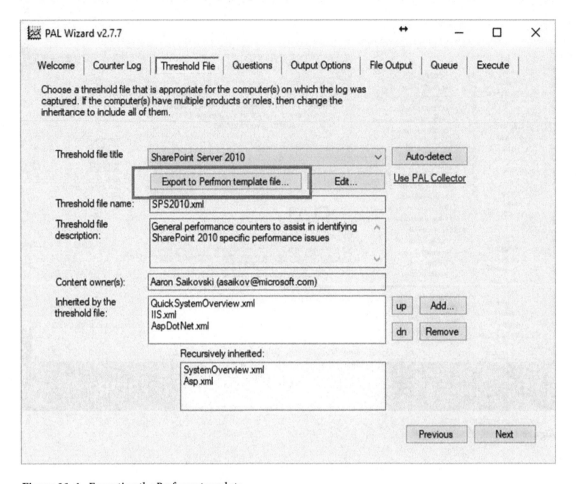

Figure 11-4. *Exporting the Perfmon template*

Remember where you save the XML file, and then navigate to that location and grab a copy of the XML file. In this example, we named the exported XML file, SharePoint.xml as you can see in Figure 11-5.

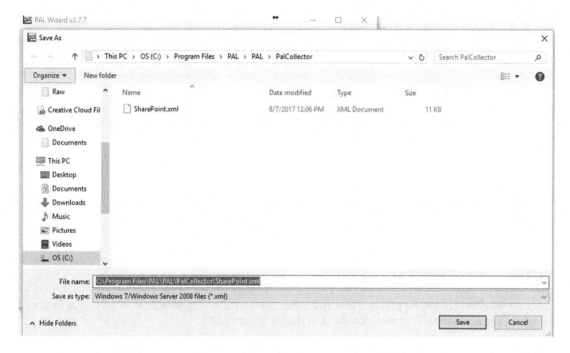

Figure 11-5. *XML file saved in Pal Collector directory*

After you have the XML file, copy it to your SharePoint server. Open the Performance Monitor by typing perfmon.msc on the run bar and clicking OK. Once the Performance Monitor comes open, expand Data Collector Sets, and right-click User Defined. Click New, Data Collector set, as shown in Figure 11-6.

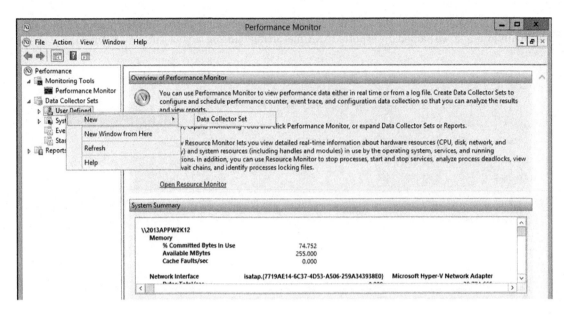

Figure 11-6. *New data collector set*

Give the data collector set a fancy name, like "SharePoint Data" and make sure to select Create from a template (Recommended), and then click Next, as shown in Figure 11-7.

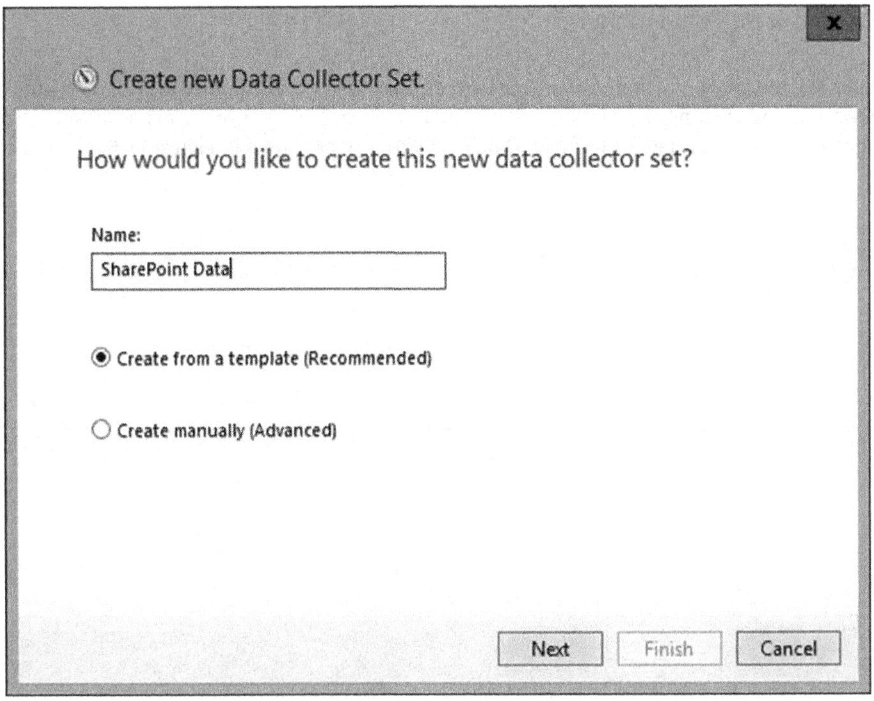

Figure 11-7. *Create new Data Collector Set from template*

When you're facing the "Which template would you like to use?" question, click the Browse button, as displayed in Figure 11-8.

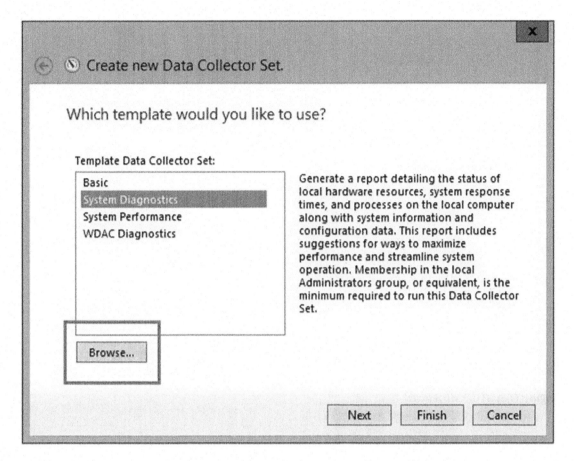

Figure 11-8. *Browse to the template you created with PAL*

Select the template that you created with the PAL tool after you browse to wherever you copied the XML file on your SharePoint server, as shown in Figure 11-9.

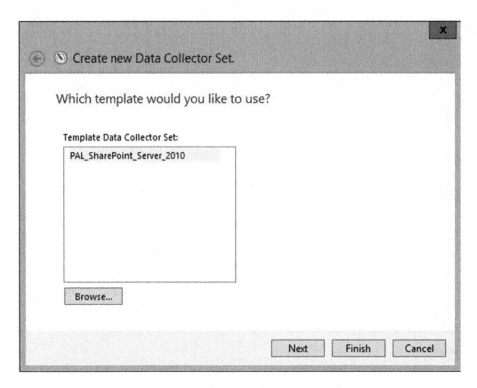

Figure 11-9. *PAL XML selected*

Click Next, and make a mental note of where the data is going to be saved. You can opt for a different location, at this point if you need to log to a separate drive, for storage reasons, for example. Figure 11-10 shows the option to browse to an alternative storage location for the logs.

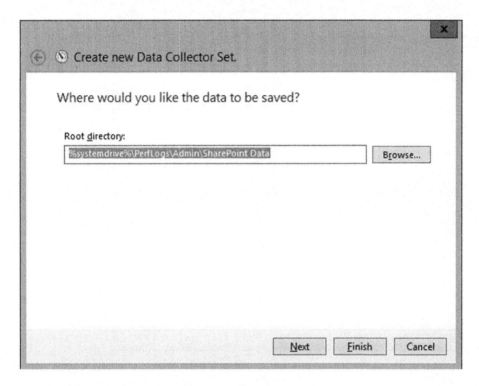

Figure 11-10. *Where would you like to save the data?*

On the Create the Data Collector Set screen, click the "Open properties for this data collector set", and then click Finish, as shown in Figure 11-11.

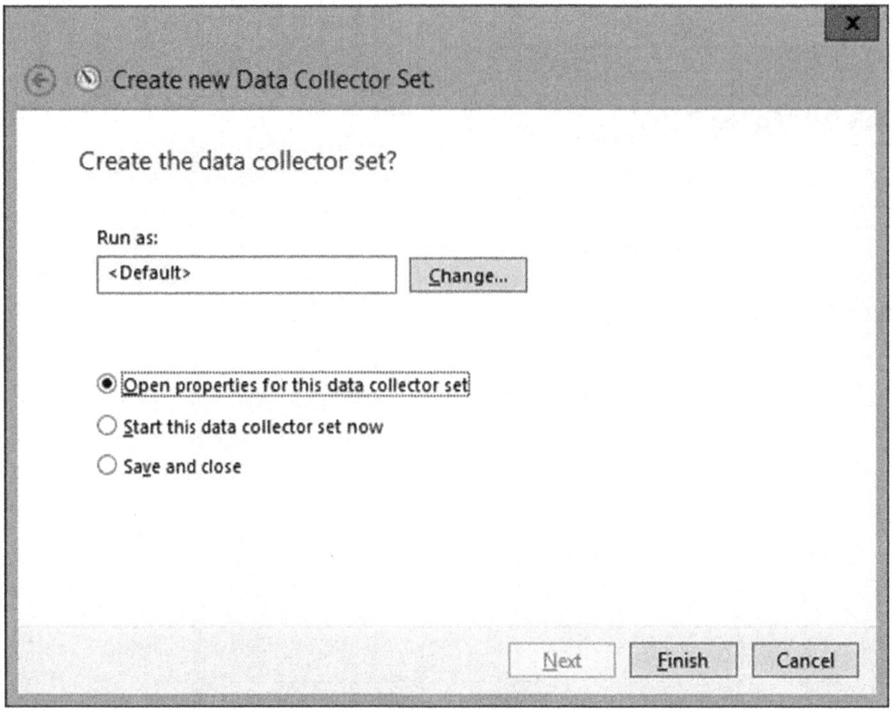

Figure 11-11. *Click finish*

If you chose the "Open properties for this data collector set" option, the SharePoint Data Collector Set properties window will open. You can now schedule the time that you'd like the collector to run and collect data about your farm, as shown in Figure 11-12.

Figure 11-12. *Scheduling the collection period*

You can always come back to the properties, by double clicking the collector set. The Stop Condition tab is used to tell the collector when to stop. If you want to, you could set the collector to restart every 24 hours, as shown in Figure 11-13.

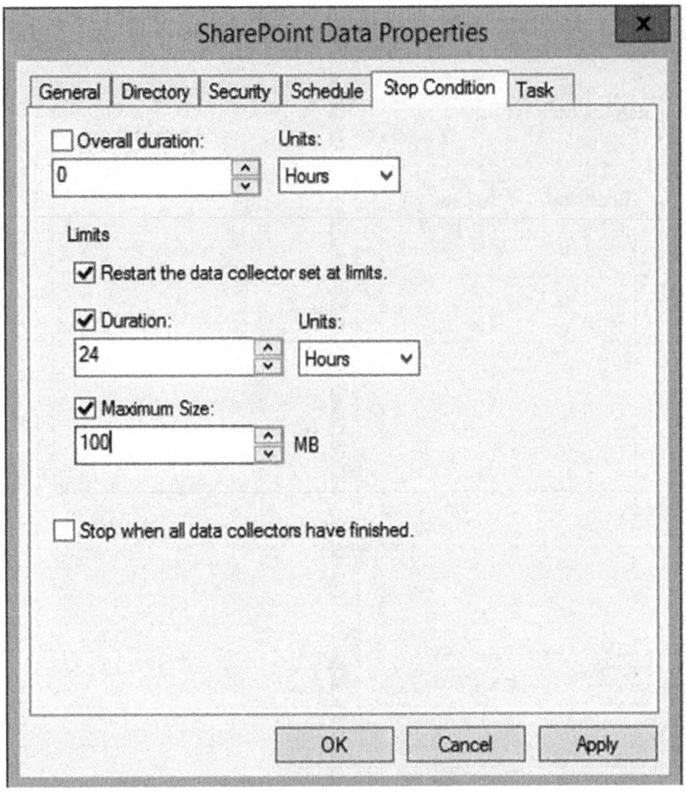

Figure 11-13. *Restart every 24 hours*

After the collector starts and when it is running, you'll see the status of running, as shown in Figure 11-14.

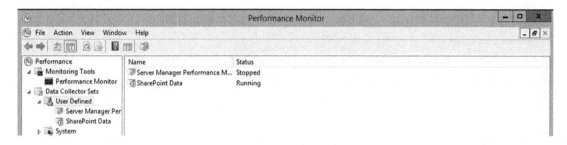

Figure 11-14. *Running*

After the data has been collected on your SharePoint server, you'll want to copy those files to the machine where PAL is installed. This machine is separate from your SharePoint farm because PAL is resource intensive when it runs to analyze the data. Up until this point, all we've done is gather the data, and now we're going to use PAL to analyze the data.

Now that you've copied the .blg file from your SharePoint server to the machine that you've installed PAL, open PAL by running the PALWizard.exe and then open the Counter Log tab. Once the Counter Log tab is open, click the ellipsis button and select one of your capture files, as shown in Figure 11-15.

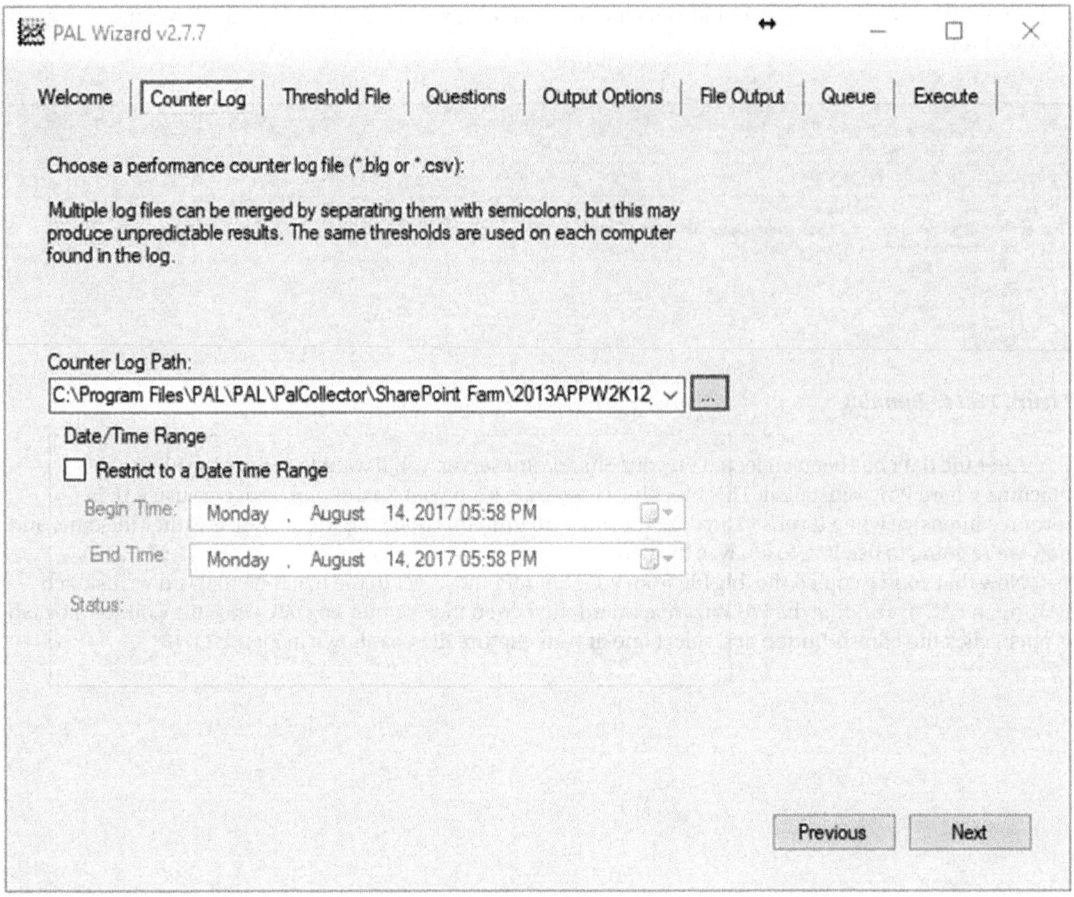

Figure 11-15. *Counter Log file selection*

Next, click next and then on the Threshold file, click the Auto Detect button, and then click Next, as shown in Figure 11-16.

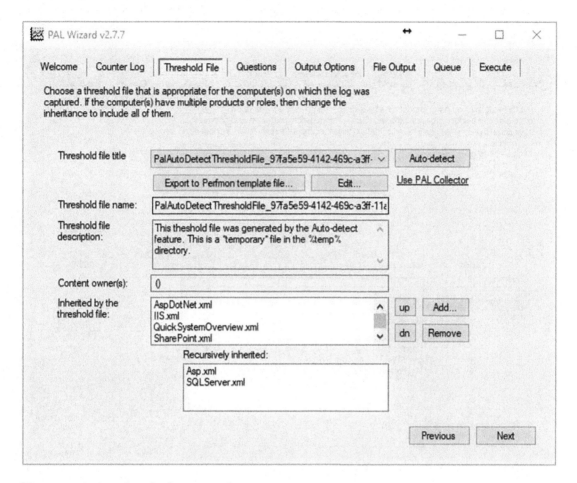

Figure 11-16. *Auto detection has occurred*

After you've used Auto detection, click Next. When you get to the Questions tab, answer any of the questions that may be different from your system. For example, if your VM has 16GB of RAM, then click Physical Memory and change the default value of 4GB to 16GB. Figure 11-17 shows the default value.

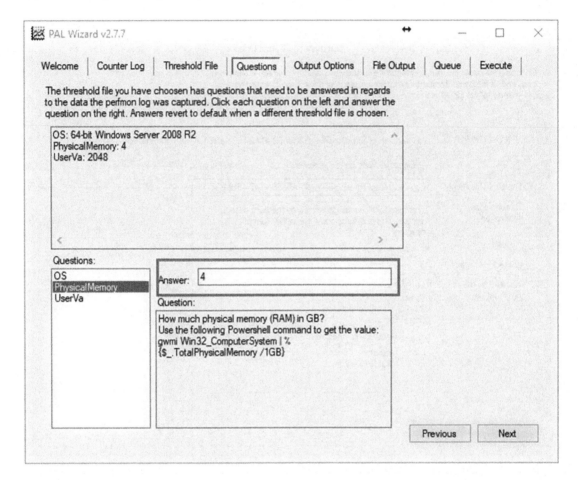

Figure 11-17. *Default may not be what you need*

Click Next. Then on the Output Options, you can go ahead and leave PAL on the default of every 30 seconds worth of data. Select the "Process all of the counters in the counter log(s)" check box and click Next. This brings you to the File Output. You can leave everything as it is here. What it is telling you is that it will create the PAL Reports directory under you My Documents director of the user that is logged in. Click Next and you are on the Queue tab, go ahead and click Next after you review the Queue tab. The Queue tab is just showing that you can modify the output of the bat file that the ps1 will use to analyze your logs.

Click Next. This brings you to the Execute tab, as shown in Figure 11-18.

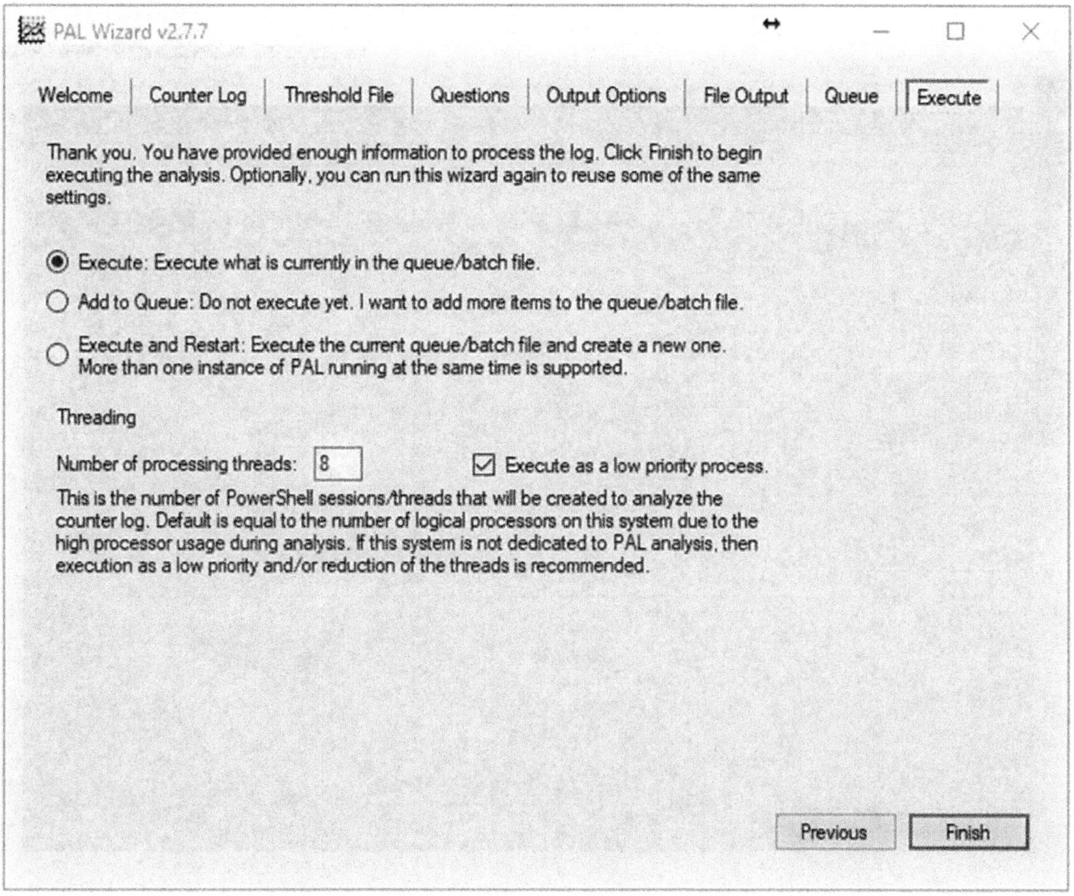

Figure 11-18. *Click Finish to execute*

After you click Finish, your computer will immediately execute the ps1 and the log analysis will begin. You'll be presented with an image similar to Figure 11-19.

Figure 11-19. *Analysis beginning*

As the analysis continues, the screen will change as shown in Figure 11-20.

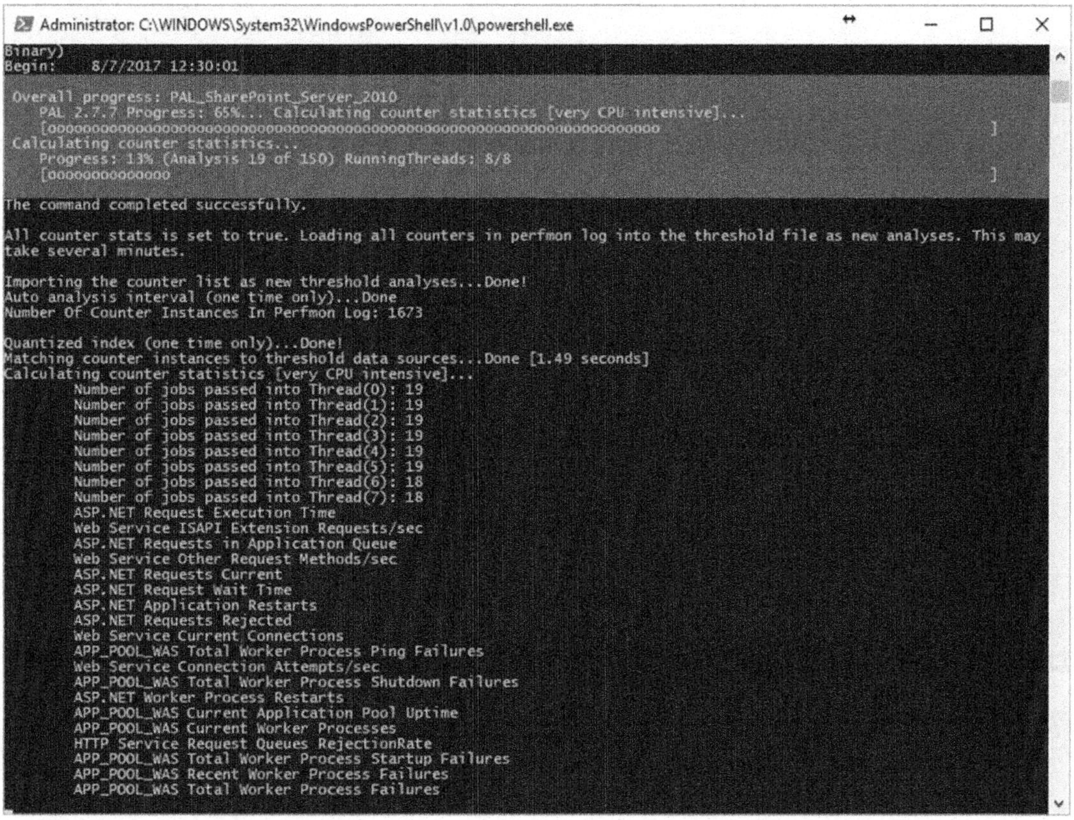

Figure 11-20. *Analysis continuing*

After the analysis of the log completed, the report will open in your default browser, as shown in Figure 11-21.

Figure 11-21. *report*

Sections that have data that exceeded a threshold are listed in chronological order and then within each section. So, as you scroll down the top section of the report there are links to each section. For example, in the capture for a SharePoint server there is a section with a bunch of SharePoint links, as shown in Figure 11-22.

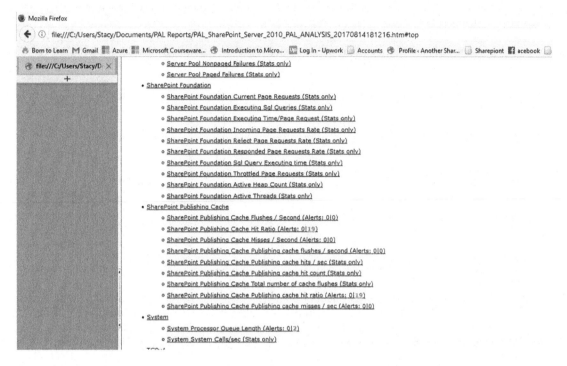

Figure 11-22. to SharePoint metrics

We're sorry if these last few figures were "eye charts," or in other words, hard to read. They do display that each metric has a link that will take you to a section on the report that lists any alerts that may be present. Figure 11-23 displays what you'll see if you click SharePoint Publishing Cache.

Figure 11-23. SharePoint Publishing Cache

461

Figure 11-23 says, "SharePoint is reliant on cache for high performance. A high amount of cache flushes per second could indicate an approaching problem with lack of memory, a worker process, or poor cache hits." Any sections that are listed with a white background are sections where no alerts were present, or are the default values for a metric. Sections that are listed with Green OK are good to go. Any alerts with yellow are things to look at, and anything with Red need to be addressed and the root cause investigated. And, this is where the PAL tool shines.

For example, in the data collected, we experienced an alert at 16:20 on 8/7/2017, and in clicking on that alert, the report jumped us to that summary section in the Alerts by Chronological order section. Here we found a display, shown in Figure 11-24.

2017.08.07-16:20:16 - 2017.08.07-16:28:12	Condition	Counter	Min	Avg	Max	Hourly Trend
	ASP.NET execution times are greater than 5 seconds	\\2013APPW2K12\ASP.NET Applications(_LM_W3SVC_2043940602_ROOT)\Request Execution Time	5,843	5,843	5,843	746
	More than 100 data IO operations (network, disk, or device IO) per second	\\2013APPW2K12\Process(w3wp#6)\IO Data Operations/sec	119	121	122	0
	More than 100 data IO operations (network, disk, or device IO) per second	\\2013APPW2K12\Process(w3wp#5)\IO Data Operations/sec	119	121	122	0
	More than 100 data IO operations (network, disk, or device IO) per second	\\2013APPW2K12\Process(w3wp#4)\IO Data Operations/sec	118	121	122	0
	More than 100 data IO operations (network, disk, or device IO) per second	\\2013APPW2K12\Process(w3wp#3)\IO Data Operations/sec	117	122	123	0
	More than 100 data IO operations (network, disk, or device IO) per second	\\2013APPW2K12\Process(OWSTIMER)\IO Data Operations/sec	120	141	190	0
	Less than 10 percent of RAM is available	\\2013APPW2K12\Memory\Available MBytes	329	334	343	25
	Greater than 15 ms physical disk WRITE response times	\\2013APPW2K12\PhysicalDisk(0 C:)\Avg. Disk sec/Write	0	.002	.024	0
	Greater than 15 ms logical disk WRITE response times	\\2013APPW2K12\LogicalDisk(C:)\Avg. Disk sec/Write	0	.002	.024	0
	Less than 1 Gbps connection	\\2013APPW2K12\Network Interface(isatap.{7719AB14-6C37-4D53-A506-239A343938E0})\Current Bandwidth	100,000	100,000	100,000	0
	Standby page life expectancy is less than 5000 seconds	\\2013APPW2K12\Memory\Long-Term Average Standby Cache Lifetime (s)				-2,499
	Greater than 15 ms logical disk response times	\\2013APPW2K12\LogicalDisk(C:)\Avg. Disk sec/Transfer	0	.003	.021	0

Figure 11-24. *Alerts at 4:20*

The only red alert listed was "Standby page life expectancy is less than 5000 seconds" and when we click it, the PAL tells us all about it. In this case, the PAL says the following:

Memory Long-Term Average Standby Cache Lifetime (s)

Description: A low Long-Term Standby cache lifetime might indicate a low physical memory condition when correlated with other memory related performance counters such as \Memory\Available MBytes, \Memory\Page Writes/sec, and disk related performance counters such as \LogicalDisk(*)\Avg. Disk sec/Transfer.

The \Memory\Long-Term Average Standby Cache Lifetime (s) performance counter measures the average lifetime in seconds of pages in the standby list cache over a long period of time. A low life expectancy could indicate that the pages on the standby list are frequently used i.e. the system has to replenish the standby list with pages from the modified list (pages that must be written to disk first) and the modified list is replenished by the working sets of processes.

The Standby page list is a list of physical pages that are no longer in use (they are available to be reused), but contain data that already exists on disk. If the data is needed again, then it can be served from the Standby list in physical memory instead of going to disk to get it. Therefore, it is part of the system available memory and it acts as disk cache—the larger the disk cache, the less demand on the disk.

This is trying to tell us that we don't have enough memory, or maybe some slow disks. Then, when we look back at Figure 11-24, we notice a condition named "greater than 15ms physical disk Write response times." When we click this link, it takes us to the PhysicalDisk Write Latency Analysis, as shown in Figure 11-25.

PhysicalDisk Write Latency Analysis

Description: Avg. Disk sec/Write is the average time, in seconds, of a write of data to the disk. This analysis determines if any of the physical disks are responding slowly.

If the response times are greater than **0.015 (15 milliseconds)**, then the disk subsystem is keeping up with demand.

If the response times are greater than **0.025 (25 milliseconds)**, then the disk subsystem is likely overwhelmed.

Reference:
Ruling Out Disk-Bound Problems
http://technet.microsoft.com/en-us/library/5bcdd349-dcc6-43eb-9dc3-54175f7061ad.aspx

\PhysicalDisk(*)\Avg. Disk sec/Write

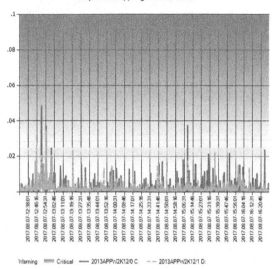

Figure 11-25. Where it shines

■ **Note**   All the underlined text in the report are hyperlinks.

In Figure 11-25, we see an example of where PAL shines, in my opinion. That link to TechNet takes you to https://technet.microsoft.com/en-us/library/5bcdd349-dcc6-43eb-9dc3-54175f7061ad.aspx, which is to a page entitled "Ruling out Disk-Bound Problems." And even though this particular link appears to be somewhat related to Exchange, the rules of disk access and programs with distinct I/O utilization patterns applies to SharePoint, as well, from time to time.

SharePoint Feature Administration and Cleanup Tool

This tool allows you to find orphaned features in SharePoint Lists and Libraries and take action to clean them up. **Use this tool with extreme caution**. Remember, the best approach to remove features is still to redeploy the solution, deactivate the feature in the site, and then retract the solution from the farm. To download the tool, navigate to its new location on GitHub at https://github.com/achimismaili/featureadmin/tree/master/Releases. Once, there you can find the current release for your version of SharePoint. At the time of this book writing, there were versions for SharePoint 2013, 2010, and 2007. To download this bad-boy, just click one of the versions, and then download the .exe and place it on your SharePoint server.

Make sure to execute the file using the farm account, or an account that has been given access to all of your various web applications and site collections. As you can see in Figure 11-26, the account that I used to install SharePoint does not have full access into everything and it is getting an access denied.

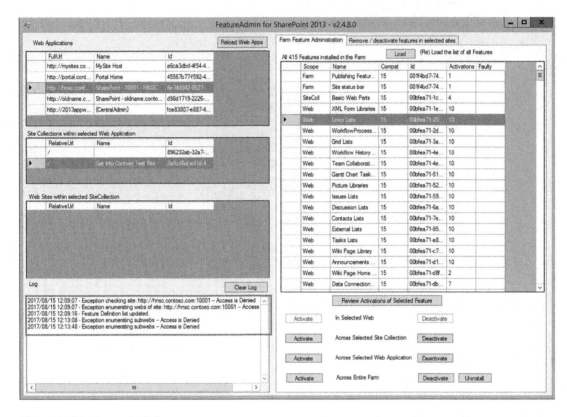

Figure 11-26. *Access denied*

If you Shift + right-click the .exe, you'll be able to run it using the farm account credentials and that will give it the access it needs to do its deeds. This tool should really be used as a last resort, when you don't have the ability to redeploy the solution, deactivate the features, and then retract. In Figure 11-27, we have opened the tool with the farm account, all of the sites are enumerated, there are no access denied messages, and all of the features are looking good!

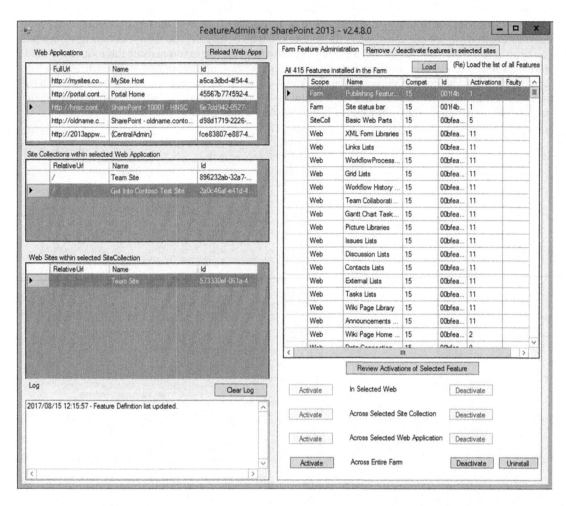

Figure 11-27. *No faulty features*

You could use this tool to remove standard OOB features, but I don't recommend that practice. If you don't want something deployed, limit the access to who can deploy features. Don't try to limit SharePoint's native features, as that will almost surely bite you in the hind region at a later date.

■ **Note** If you take a look at Figure 11-27, notice that it displays the Farm Feature tab and that none of the features show as faulty. There really isn't a reason to remove a non-faulty feature.

When you're looking to remove an orphaned feature, you will have usually already found out it's feature ID from reading a psconfig error log, or possibly from a "Sorry, something went wrong" message. The SharePoint Feature Admin and Cleanup tool allows you to remove a faulty or non-faulty features. Again, I advise against removing non-faulty features. I've already mentioned that at this point, we don't have access to the .wsp that installed the feature.

To remove a feature from a web, site collection, web application, or from the farm, click the "Remove/deactivate features in selected sites", select the feature you wish to remove, and then select the level on which you to no longer wish have references to. If it has come to the point where you're using this tool, you should start at the lowest level when removing the feature and then work your way back up to the farm. So, you would remove the feature from the web, then check to see if it is in the site collection, and remove it, and so on and so forth, until you reach the farm level. Figure 11-28 demonstrates how after a feature is selected, the various buttons to remove the feature from whichever scope is illuminated.

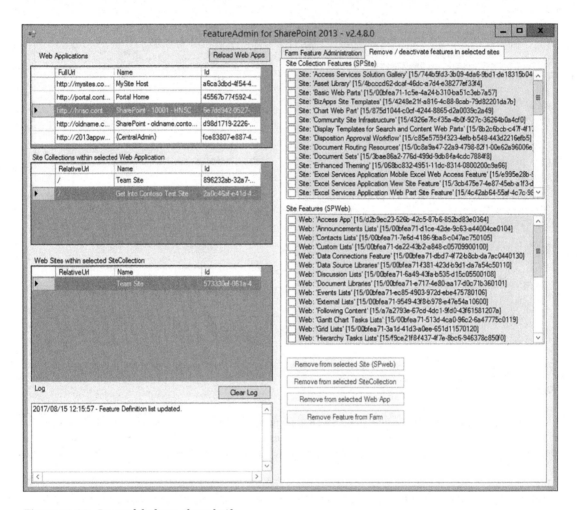

Figure 11-28. Be careful, sharp, sharp knife

After you've removed a feature from a particular scope (e.g., web, site, web app, or farm) then you should click the Reload Web App button, which is seen in all of the previous figures.

The SharePoint Feature Admin and clean up tool, can be used for more than clean up. You can use the tool to deploy features across the entire farm. This is much cooler than having to use PowerShell, but I still prefer to use PowerShell, since I feel more in control that way. To use the tool to deploy a feature, just select the feature you're looking to deploy, from the Farm Feature Administration tab, and then take the available action, as shown in Figure 11-29.

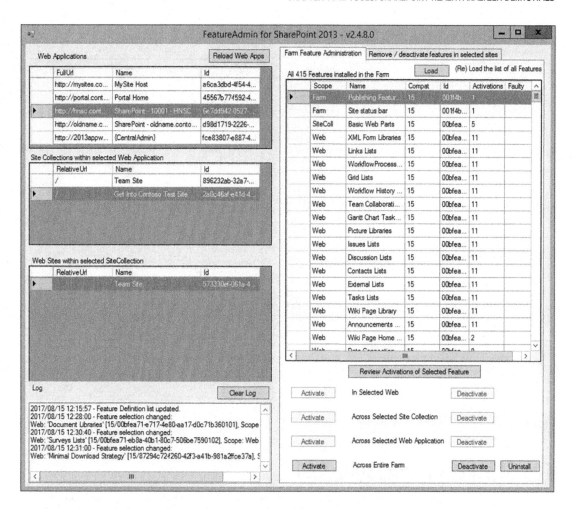

Figure 11-29. *More than just removal, you can administrate too!*

You can see how many features are installed in your farm using the feature. If a feature has both the Activate and Deactivate buttons illuminated, then that feature is activated somewhere in the farm. You can click the Review Activations of Selected Feature to troubleshoot where a feature is activated, and the location form will open, as shown in Figure 11-30.

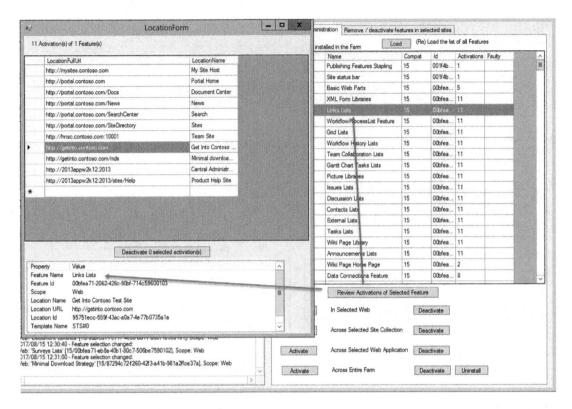

Figure 11-30. *Links list feature activated*

The SharePoint Manager Tool

Another Sharp knife that you can put in your troubleshooting arsenal is the SharePoint Manager tool. It currently is not on GitHub and is available on CodePlex at `https://spm.codeplex.com`. After you download the app, just extract the entire folder out of the zip file and store it somewhere on your SharePoint server. Then double click the executable named SharePoint Manager 2013.exe, if you're using the 2013 version, and you'll see the image shown in Figure 11-31.

Figure 11-31. *Preflight checks*

After the program scans your farm, it will open and the image shown in Figure 11-31 will disappear. This program is awesomely powerful! And like all sharp knives and powerful tools, it should be used with an ounce of caution. You can very easily change properties within your farm using this tool. It offers a deep view into the object model with drill down capability. The default Object Model View is set to medium for loading.

I would venture to guess this is for app performance reasons related to how fast it loads. You can modify the Object model from medium to full from the View menu.

Any properties that appear in bold font can be modified. When you select a node in the left hand pane, the type of object that you have selected is displayed in the bottom information bar. For example, in Figure 11-32, I've selected the MySite Host Web application and the information bar says, SPWebApplication.

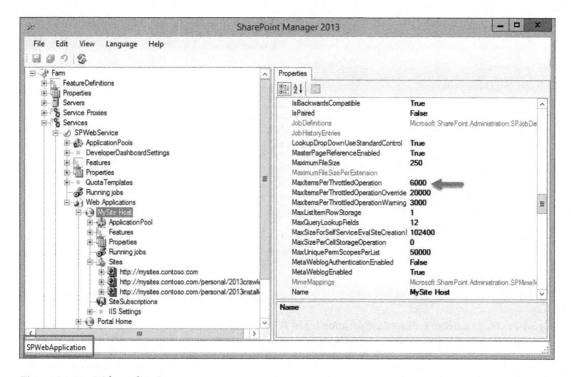

Figure 11-32. Web application

From the web application properties, there are all sorts of settings that I could manage all at the same time. In Figure 11-32, you can see that I had already adjusted the List View Threshold from the default of 5000 items, up to 6000 items. We can also see that nothing has been changed in Figure 11-32 because the ability to save changes is not illuminated. After a change has been made, the ability to save the change, save all changes, or remove all changes become highlighted, as shown in Figure 11-33.

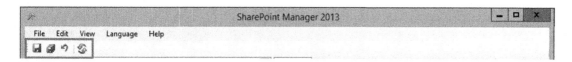

Figure 11-33. Save changes

After the changes are saved, the screen updates and the information bar displays Changes is Saved, which means the changes are saved. Figure 11-34 shows that the List View Threshold has been changed back to 5000.

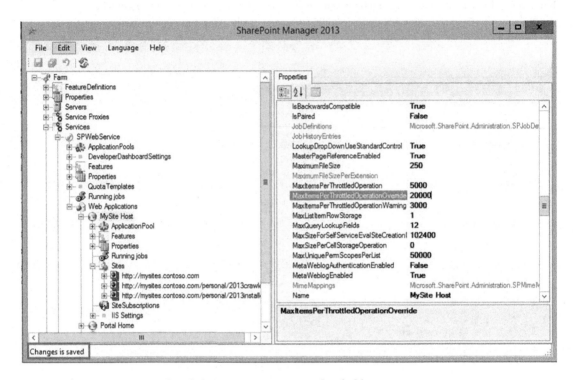

Figure 11-34. MaxItemsPerThrottledOperation is List View Threshold

The SharePoint Manager tool is easy to navigate if you follow your understanding for how SharePoint is logically organized. For example, you know that web applications store site collections and that the object model refers to site collections as sites. You also know that the object model refers to subsites as webs; so, it would make sense that to find a subsite, or web as it's referred to in the object model, that you would need to drill down into the web applications, then the site collections, and finally into the web object. As you can see in Figure 11-35, it would appear that the top site for the Get Into Contoso site collection is an SPWeb object named Get Into Contoso Test Site.

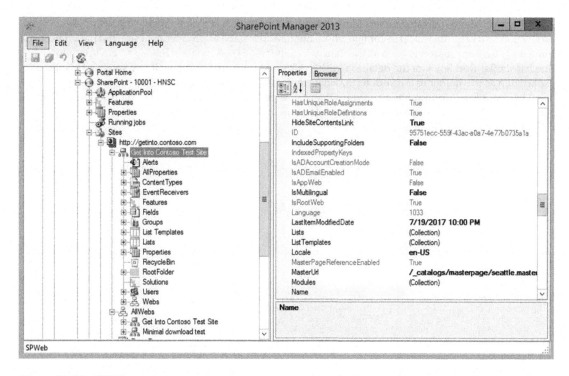

Figure 11-35. *SPWeb*

Be careful when using this tool to modify because even though a lot of the properties that you shouldn't modify are grayed out, there are still properties that may not take so kindly to being modified.

Wrap Up

Like a bug's life when hitting the windshield of a moving car, the discussion of troubleshooting has ended. I hope you've gained some useable info from these last three chapters that you can use to troubleshoot issues within your farm. Not every problem can be solved. Sometimes the server and/or the farm is damaged to a point of no return, other than a full rebuild. And, sometimes the data within the content databases tables has been modified in such a way that the very act of mounting the database to a new farm can corrupt said new farm. The remedy in that case is usually a site collection by site collection backup and restore.

There fortunately, and unfortunately, isn't a one size fits all for every SharePoint issue. I say fortunately because this keeps people like you and I employed and I say "unfortunately" because it sure would make our lives easier if there was such a thing. My friends Mike Ross and Mike Clarke, fellow Rackspace SharePoint engineers would say, "It's built in Job Security" and they're right! And, sometimes it's quicker and a much more solid remedy to rebuild, patch to the correct level, and attach databases or restore site backups, than it is to try and hack an issue out of a farm. If you find where someone else had the exact same error that you're experiencing, with the only difference being the GUID, it's a safe bet to follow the steps. And, anytime you can re-create the issue in a non-prod environment, before attempting the fix in production, you should take that route.

It's a good idea to refresh your test farm with the databases that are experiencing the issues in production and keep the test farm configuration, not data, the same as production. I say "not data" because there really isn't any reason to keep all the data twice; after all, SQL is not free. Having an environment that has similar workflows, or the database freshly refreshed from production, will give you a fairly solid expectation as to whether or not your fix for whatever issue will be successful.

I hope reading this book has given you a deeper insight into the labyrinth that is Microsoft SharePoint. May the SharePoint gods shine down on you and best of luck to you in all you do!

Index

© Stacy Simpkins 2017
S. Simpkins, *Troubleshooting SharePoint*, https://doi.org/10.1007/978-1-4842-3138-8

Get the eBook for only $5!

Why limit yourself?

With most of our titles available in both PDF and ePUB format, you can access your content wherever and however you wish—on your PC, phone, tablet, or reader.

Since you've purchased this print book, we are happy to offer you the eBook for just $5.

To learn more, go to http://www.apress.com/companion or contact support@apress.com.

Apress®

CPSIA information can be obtained
at www.ICGtesting.com
Printed in the USA
LVOW04s2139030118
561663LV00006B/230/P

9 781484 231371